Problems in the Behavioural Sciences
GENERAL EDITOR: Jeffrey Gray
EDITORIAL BOARD: Michael Gelder, Richard Gregory, Robert Hinde, Christopher Longuet-Higgins

Psychobiology of personality

Problems in the Behavioural Sciences

Psychobiology
of personality

Marvin Zuckerman
University of Delaware

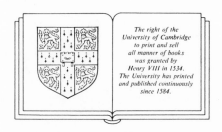

*The right of the
University of Cambridge
to print and sell
all manner of books
was granted by
Henry VIII in 1534.
The University has printed
and published continuously
since 1584.*

CAMBRIDGE UNIVERSITY PRESS

Cambridge
New York   Port Chester   Melbourne   Sydney

Published by the Press Syndicate of the University of Cambridge
The Pitt Building, Trumpington Street, Cambridge CB2 1RP
40 West 20th Street, New York, NY 10011, USA
10 Stamford Road, Oakleigh, Melbourne 3166, Australia

© Cambridge University Press 1991

First published 1991

Printed in the United States of America

Library of Congress Cataloging-in-Publication Data
Zuckerman, Marvin.
Psychobiology of personality / Marvin Zuckerman.
p.   cm. – (Problems in the behavioural sciences)
Includes bibliographical references and index.
ISBN 0-521-35095-6.   ISBN 0-521-35942-2 (pbk.)
1. Personality.   2. Psychobiology.   I. Title.   II. Series.
BF698.Z825   1991
155.2 – dc20   90-45367

British Library Cataloguing in Publication data applied for.

ISBN 0-521-35095-6 hardback
ISBN 0-521-35942-2 paperback

Dedicated to family
A construct that includes more than shared genes or shared environment
With love to
Sophia
Mary

April and David   Steven and Paula   Frances and Barney
Genevieve and Veronica   Ariel   Georgia

And those yet to come

Contents

Preface

It is not by a natural intellectual progression that one begins as a clinical psychologist in the 1950s, during the era of psychoanalytic and social-environmental theory, and ends by writing a book 40 years later on the "Psychobiology of Personality." The first stage of evolution was an increasing skepticism of dynamic post hoc explanations of personality during my early career as a full-time clinical psychologist. Not only the study of patients, but observations of my own developing children raised questions about the adequacy of environmental explanation alone. What father can remain an adamant environmentalist after he has his second child? I turned to a research career and had the good fortune to find a job at an interdisciplinary center, the Institute of Psychiatric Research in the Indiana University Medical Center. This early exposure to biological ideas in psychiatry, endocrinology, and the new science of psychopharmacology between 1956 and 1960 certainly played a role in a shift toward a biological orientation. In subsequent work on sensory deprivation, I started to use psychophysiological methods and discovered the great and seductive optimal-level-of-arousal construct formulated by Hebb. Because my interest had always been in personality, I decided that this construct might explain individual differences in reaction to sensory deprivation experiments and devised the first version of the *sensation seeking* scale to predict responses to an unstimulating and de-arousing environment. It was only several years after developing the idea of basing a *sensation seeking* trait on the optimal level of arousal, that I discovered that Hans Eysenck was applying the same construct as the biological basis of extraversion!

Collaboration with Harold Persky, an endocrinological colleague at The Albert Einstein Research Laboratory in Philadelphia, led to the study of adrenocortical arousal in sensory deprivation and sensory overstimulation. In the late 1960s a group of sensory deprivation investigators including Thomas Myers, Peter Suedfeld, and myself flew up to Manitoba on a cold winter day to plan a volume on sensory deprivation under the editorship of John Zubek. I was assigned two chapters on research and one on theory. It was the latter chapter that turned me down the path leading to this book. I attempted to explain the range of emotional and physiological reactions to sensory deprivation in terms of individual differences in arousal and/or arousability.

When the funding for my sensory deprivation research evaporated in the late 1960s, I moved to the University of Delaware and turned my full attention to less expensive research, which centered around the trait of *sensation seeking*. The trait was found to be related to many kinds of phenomena such as sex and drug experience, volunteering for unusual experiments, and sports preferences. Research on the biological basis of the trait began with psychophysiological studies of the orienting reflex and then moved on to study of evoked potentials using the paradigm developed by Buchsbaum. In 1974, findings at the laboratories of the National Institute of Mental Health on the relation of the enzyme monoamine oxidase to *sensation seeking* instigated a self-education course in psychopharmacology and the comparative neuropsychological literature that continues today. A sabbatical spent with Hans Eysenck in 1976 stimulated my interest in the area of behavior genetics and a study on the genetics of *sensation seeking*, in collaboration with David Fulker and Sybil Eysenck. Subsequent contacts with Larry Stein and a sabbatical with Jeffrey Gray in 1983 reinforced my fascination with psychopharmacology and its role in psychopathology and personality.

My 1979 book on *sensation seeking* ended with chapters on biological correlates of the trait and a biological model. The model was modified and broadened in my 1984 paper in *Behavioral and Brain Sciences* and a chapter in the *International Review of Neurobiology*. These last two theoretical works extended my interest from *sensation seeking* to other personality traits. In 1983, I edited a book on the *Biological Bases of Sensation Seeking, Impulsivity and Anxiety*. It is difficult to consider personality traits in isolation when analyzing their psychobiology. The brain is not divided like a phrenological map into areas that correspond to discrete traits. Behavioral models of human personality traits are not easily classifiable in terms of single human traits. The open-field test for rodents, for instance, is said to measure "emotionality" (*neuroticism?*) and "activity" (*extraversion?*) or "explorativeness" (*sensation seeking?*). Popular models for the measurement of anxiety through its response-suppressive properties also assess behavioral inhibition or disinhibition, the latter suggestive of the human traits of *impulsivity* and *sensation seeking*. Inevitably one must look at the psychobiology of all of personality to understand the basis for any trait.

Previous books and other theoretical works of such breadth have been written by Hans Eysenck and Jeffrey Gray. Eysenck's 1967 book *The Biological Basis of Personality* and his more recent book (1985) with his son Michael Eysenck, *Personality and Individual Differences*, attempted to establish a paradigm for workers in the field. The psychobiological areas dealt with in these books include mainly human behavior genetics, psychophysiology, and conditioning. Gray's book, *The Neuropsychology of Anxiety* deals primarily with this single trait, but in this and previous and subsequent chapters and papers he has outlined a model describing the neuropsychology of three major personality traits: *anxiety, impulsivity,* and *aggressivity*. Although he claims that these three traits are more directly aligned with three basic biological systems, he has taken pains to identify their locus within the coordinates established by Eysenck's supertraits of *extraversion, neuroticism,* and *psychoticism.* Gray's research and writing deals primarily with comparative studies, mostly using rats, attempting to define the neuropsychological, psychopharmacological, and conditioning basis for behavioral phenomena that could serve as models for human personality traits.

This book combines the top down approach of Eysenck and the bottom up approach of Gray. All levels of psychobiology including behavior genetics, neuropsychology, psychopharmacology, psychophysiology, and conditioning are dealt with in separate chapters. The comparative literature is discussed most in the areas of neuropsychology and psychopharmacology in which experiments on nonhuman species are vital for an understanding of the brain mechanisms involved in motivation and personality.

I have noticed that many personality psychologists know little about the biological bases of personality. This is quite understandable because most works on the topic assume a knowledge of basic concepts and definitions in the biological areas they deal with. It is not easy to acquire this knowledge if one has not been trained or widely read in the particular areas of biological science. Without this basic knowledge, reading about an area like psychopharmacology is like perusing a work in ancient Greek. A goal of this book is to present the reader with at least the basic concepts and definitions in each area of psychobiology, from behavior genetics to conditioning, before entering into a discussion of relationships to personality. Readers who are already well instructed in these concepts can skip these sections of the chapters and proceed to the personality relevant portions. I hope this effort will make the book more accessible to both students and researchers who need to understand the methods and definitions before they can fully comprehend the research.

The fact that people differ in behavior in many situations is axiomatic. The question of whether such differences are correlated across situations and can be organized and described in terms of broader trait dimensions is more arguable. This book uses a structural trait approach to organize the psychobiological data. Chapter 1 describes various approaches to the structural analysis of personality. Recently, a fair amount of agreement has emerged among those who subscribe to trait approaches that three to five broad traits can describe personality, although, for many purposes, narrower traits may be more useful. I believe that the hierarchal model of traits postulated by Eysenck is best because it can encompass both broad and narrow traits. The alternate model of a circumplex is less useful because it is generally limited to a two-dimensional model. Chapter 2 addresses the issues of consistency of behavior and the relative influences of situation, personality, and their interaction. I advocate an interactionist position, which is like advocating motherhood, God, and country among nationalists.

One is hard-pressed to find radical situationists or personologists these days. I also believe that the principle of aggregation has largely answered the question of behavioral and mood state consistency, particularly when researchers aggregate prototypical situations and behavior. Aggregation is not unique to psychology; even in physics one must sometimes aggregate observations of elementary particles to see lawful relationships.

Chapter 3 describes the area of behavior genetics and its contributions to personality study. During the writing of this book, the results from the largest twin studies done on personality and two major adoption studies of identical twins raised in different environments (a model for pure genetic effects) have been published. The questions of the proportions of contribution from heredity and environment have been succeeded by more specific questions on the types of heredity and environment involved in personality and biological traits. The reader will find that it is no longer possible to consider personality as purely the product of family and social environments. In addition, a surprising finding on the importance of non-shared environment in contrast to shared family environment seems to confound most social-dynamic theories of personality. New concepts of continually interacting influences of genotype and environment are emerging from this research.

What is inherited? It is certainly not personality traits or behavior, except for some limited reflexes. What we inherit are differences in nervous system structure and function that constitute part of the basis for differences in basic personality. Chapter 4 describes some of the neuropsychological structures that have been theorized to mediate the motivational, emotional, and reactive-style traits that form personality. The modern conception of structure is different from the old phrenology that assigned each trait to a particular locus in the brain. Modern neuropsychologists have attempted to define neural pathways involved in particular functions. However, there is still a persisting type of phrenology that would insist that each structure, such as the amygdala or the frontal lobes of the cortex, must underlie only one discrete personality trait. A more complicated picture emerges from the analyses of neuropsychology.

Because neural pathways are often identified by particular chemical neurotransmitters and regulating enzymes, the science of psychopharmacology, discussed in chapter 5, is inextricably wedded to concepts of neuropsychological structure. Keeping abreast of the relevant literature in psychopharmacology is not easy. While I was writing this book, some theories of the behavioral functions of particular neurotransmitters have been definitively rejected, and others have been turned around 180 degrees. The useful life of a psychopharmacological theory is exceedingly short. However, one cannot indefinitely postpone the writing of a book. This writer does not anticipate that much productive time is left to him, and scientific "truth," like the holy grail, is forever receding in the distance.

What is described as we enter the last decade of the twentieth century is bound to be inaccurate in terms of the science of future years. I would ask readers of the future to judge this work mercifully in the context of the time it was written.

Psychophysiology (chapter 6) provides an assessment of physiological function from electrodes attached to the exterior of the body, and therefore is less intrusive and more amenable to psychological experiments with humans. These methods have been applied to the study of emotions, motivations, information processing, conditioning, and individual differences. The constructs of generalized arousal and arousability have played an important role in several theories of personality, and psychophysiological methods have provided a means of testing these theories.

Conditioning is on the border between physiology and behavior because it describes how reflexive patterns of response can be transferred to new stimuli. Pavlov defined hypothetical brain states as the bases of conditioning phenomena, but he also suggested that individual differences in temperament among dogs could be explained by trait differences in brain physiology. American textbooks of introductory psychology almost always discuss Pavlov's general conditioning theory, but few of them devote any text to his psychobiological theory of temperament. Pavlov's theories, and modifications by later Soviet investigators, have continued to hold the interest of investigators in Eastern Europe, such as Strelau and his coworkers in Poland, and have certainly influenced the earlier ideas of Eysenck. Gray has developed a learning theory and a model for personality focused on instrumental conditioning and the learned and inherited responsivity to signals of reward and punishment. Research on human learning that is relevant to these theories is not as frequent as animal studies, but chapter 7 summarizes most of it.

Biological psychiatry furnishes a major source of psychobiological information from direct work with humans. The funds for research are more readily available to those who deal with abnormality rather than normality. The use of drugs in the treatment of anxiety, mood, and thinking disorders has stimulated research into the actions of these drugs in the central nervous system. Most of what we know about the psychopharmacology of the brain has emerged from such studies. I have selected two groups of disorders as representative of two extremes of major personality dimensions: anxiety disorders (chapter 8) for the *neuroticism-anxiety* dimension, and antisocial personality and other disinhibitory disorders (chapter 9) for the P-ImpUSS dimension, and have discussed these disorders in terms of their genetic, neuropsychological, psychopharmacological, psychophysiological, and learning aspects.

The final chapter (10) endeavors to summarize what has been learned and to attempt a preliminary psychobiological model for the major broad dimensions of personality. A book covering so many areas runs the risk of getting lost in specifics and never coming away from the trees to look at the forest. The other extreme is to deal only with generalities from some distant mountain top and never enter the forest at all. I have attempted to do some of both, discussing broad theories of psychobiology and reviewing the specific studies relevant to personality. This book should provide a useful primer to advanced students of personality and personality researchers. I hope that readers will be intrigued enough to pursue particular areas of interest by reading more specialized books and articles in particular areas.

Acknowledgments

The University of Delaware supported me in this project by giving me freedom from teaching duties in the form of a fellowship at the Delaware Institute for Advanced Studies during the academic year 1987–88 and a grant in 1990 for the final expenses on the book. The final stages of work on the manuscript, copyediting and proofreading, were done at the Netherlands Institute For Advanced Study in the Humanities and Social Sciences, where I was a Fellow during the academic year 1990–1991. Without their support this stage of the book's production would have taken much longer than it did.

I am grateful to Thomas Scott, the chairman of my department, for his support over the years in this effort. Various colleagues at my university and others have read chapters, answered questions, and given me the benefit of their constructive criticism; these include Jerome Siegel, Steven Grant, and Robert Simons from the University of Delaware, Hans J. Eysenck and Irene Martin from the University of London and the Institute for Psychiatry, and Robert Plomin from Pennsylvania State University. Robert Koback, a colleague at the University of Delaware, gave me special help in producing the manuscript by guiding me on the intricacies of the MacIntosh and giving me the use of his magnificent laser printer. A very great debt is owed to Jeffrey Gray, whose encouragement originally led me to explore the area of comparative neuropsychology and eventually write about it. As the editor of this book, he has had to suffer through the initial tedious draft and point out where I went wrong. I hope I have not disappointed him in this final version.

But my greatest debt is to Mary Hazard, without whose nurturance and love I could not have finished this work. Her dedication to her own work has set me an example during the many evenings and weekends we hunched over our word processors. Who else would have stood for this neglect of relaxation, recreation, and even household responsibilities? Perhaps some Sunday we will sit down and read the entire *New York Times* and work the crossword puzzle together as we used to. "Liebe, arbeite, *und* spiele, bitte."

1   Basic dimensions of personality

Overview

Sciences need systems for classifying their phenomena whether these are astronomical objects, units of matter, or species of animals. A science of astronomy that made no distinctions among planets, stars, and galaxies, a geology that regarded every rock as a unique structure, or a biology that could only distinguish two-legged from four-legged creatures, would not progress very far in understanding or prediction. Without a classification of species there could have been no *On the origin of Species* (Darwin 1859). However, many psychologists observe and experiment without concern for the classification of behavior and without knowing whether the behavior they are studying belongs to a larger class of adaptive behaviors. Disregard of species-specific behaviors has led some workers to erroneous conclusions in the study of rodent behavior (Bolles, 1970).

Disinterest in the classification of personality traits (if not total denial of the existence of behavioral consistencies) has led to faddish areas of study and endless generalizations about "personality," per se, rather than study of actual phenomena. Personality psychology has been more involved in the search for a paradigm than in the development of a paradigm, the exception being the work of Eysenck (1967, 1981) and Gray (1973, in press). One might say we are in an era of "paradigm conflict" (Kuhn, 1970) except that so few paradigms have evolved to any systematic level. Psychologists do not simply study behavior or personality any more than physicists simply study matter and energy or biologists simply study organic matter. Psychologists tend to make conceptual generalizations about the behaviors they study without empirical justification. Thus, a particular avoidance response becomes "defensive behavior" and a refusal of a small reward now in favor of a larger reward promised later becomes "tolerance of frustration."

Confusion arises when similar phenomena are given different labels or different phenomena are given the same label. Consider the range of labels given to one of the factors found consistently in all analyses of broad personality measures (Hogan, 1982): ego resiliency, emotionality, adjustment, general adjustment, neuroticism, emotional stability, objectivity, and anxiety. The only way we can find out that these labels describe similar phenomena is by looking at the questionnaires or rating scales that comprise the factors. In other types of theory, such as psychoanalytic theory, in

1

which there are no describable operations, we have no way of knowing which of the higher-order constructs are alike and which are different. One goal of this chapter is to bring some conceptual clarity into the classifications of trait dimensions.

Responses, habits, traits, and types

Eysenck's (1947) hierarchal model suggests a progression from single units of concrete responses to the highly abstract notion of types. Although the response is the basic unit in all areas of psychology, it is itself a kind of generalization designating a range of responses in a given situation under given conditions. A bar-press response of a rat consists of any reaction that depresses the lever, whether it uses its paw, its nose, or its rump. The animal may make many other responses that go unrecorded because the worker's interest is focused on the response linked to the automatically controlled contingencies. A human sociable response may consist of any kind of positive interaction with other humans, whether talking or playing. Other interactions, such as aggression, are not usually regarded as sociable responses.

The responses of most persons tend to be situationally constrained. We are social in a relaxed situation with friends, but our behavior is less predictable in a group of strangers. Aggressive behavior in most people occurs only in the context of frustrating or hostile situations and not, as in some psychotics and criminals, in other kinds of situations.

Although a single situationally specific response may be of some interest, personality psychologists are usually concerned with consistent behaviors, or *habits*. The concept of personality implies some degree of consistency of behavior over time. Because no two situations are precisely the same, personality also suggests some degree of consistency of response across situations. In a narrow behavioral sense, the term *habit* is applied only to observable responses. However, if we regard thoughts and images as internal behaviors that must be inferred from directly observable responses such as speech content, then we can think in terms of habitual cognitive responses. Many human interactions are not directly observable because we suppress verbal responses that would disrupt social relationships. Stereotypes are examples of automatic responses that are often kept at the preverbal level.

Trait is the term used to describe correlated habits of reaction. Traits subsume many types of habitual behavior and are not specific to a particular type of response behavior: Washing one's hands is a habit, cleanliness is a trait. Some research has been done on the types of acts that, if repeated habitually, are commonly assumed to comprise a trait (Buss & Craik, 1985). Buss and Craik go further to suggest that this kind of concrete "act frequency" (self-reported rather than directly observed acts) appraisal is a new and promising type of personality assessment. Block (1989) criticized this approach as being simply another kind of self-report measure that has no advantage over the usual type of personality trait questionnaire and has many disadvantages, such as ignoring the subject's cognitive and affective reactions and being so situationally specific that the occurrence of the habit may be rare.

Some information about the habit structure of a trait can be found in the content of the items in a trait test. If the worker has included a sufficient sampling of the conceptual aspects of the trait in the initial item pool (content validity), then factor analysis can clarify the structure of the trait in terms of its constituent factors, or in terms of the items that are more central to the trait. Cross-situational consistency is more likely to be assumed for traits than for habits. Some workers have questioned the existence of traits on the basis of low cross-situational correlations of reactions (Mischel, 1968). This issue is discussed in chapter 2.

Traits can be defined from rational and theoretical assumptions of correlated habits or from empirical factor analyses. However, there is always a pre-empirical phase of devising trait measures, during which the concepts and theories of the investigator determine the types of items that are written into the experimental version of the test. Factor analysis cannot supply the factors needed to begin with; it can only clarify the relationships among the variables supplied by the investigation. If the initial sampling of items is not representative of the traits to be measured, then the results will not be valid, no matter how reliable they may be.

The traits measured can vary from very specific to very broad. We can develop reliable scales that measure fear of snakes, fear of darkness, or fear of heights (Mellstrom, Cicala, & Zuckerman, 1976), or we can use a broader "phobic anxiety" scale, or an even broader "anxiety" scale. Analyses of the items of the Wolpe and Lang (1964) Fear Survey Schedule have revealed four classes of phobias: (1) social fears; (2) agoraphobic fears; (3) fears of bodily injury, death, and illness; (4) and fears of harmless animals (Arrindel, & van der Ende, 1986). These factors represent an intermediate breadth of trait definition. Narrow trait scales that are restricted to the range of phenomena to be predicted usually predict behavior in the relevant situation better than broader scales (Zuckerman, 1979a), but this is not always so. A broad anxiety scale may predict social fear responses, like those during examinations or performances, as well as narrow tests of examination anxiety or performance anxiety (Zuckerman, 1977). If there is no advantage to using narrowly defined trait scales, it is preferable to use the more broadly defined scales because they can predict across a greater variety of situations.

Types, the oldest units of personality classification, go back to the sanguine, choleric, melancholic, and phlegmatic type classification of the ancient Greeks. More recently, psychoanalytic theorists have proposed character typologies. Freud (1905) suggested a system, based on his theory of psychosexual development, consisting of oral (passive or sadistic), anal (sadistic or retentive), phallic, and genital types. Other observations also furnished a basis for character types such as narcissistic and passive-aggressive. Horney (1939) used a tripartite system to describe neurotic types as "moving towards" (dependency), "moving against (aggressive-competitive), and "moving away from" (isolation) other persons. As in the Greek theory of temperaments, Horney considered a neurotic as a person who behaves rigidly in one of these three fashions rather than having balanced and situationally appropriate reactions. The trait-dimension of introversion-extraversion, which has been consistently found in empirical trait studies, was described as two dichotomous types by Jung (1933).

What distinguishes these early type constructs from later ones developed by psychologists working with psychometric methods is the idea of *dimension*. The ancient Greeks and the psychoanalysts conceived of types as unique constellations of traits with no gradations between them; a person is either an introvert or an extravert, for instance. Psychologists who measured traits found that they are distributed in a normal bell-shaped curve, like most variations of within-species characteristics, with most persons falling close to the mean and fewer persons near the extremes of the distribution. Moreover, the distribution is continuous, rather than bimodal as expected from older type descriptions. Most persons are ambiverts, rather than introverts or extraverts, in the sense that their measured tendencies fall near the mean rather than at the two extremes. Of course, because the distribution is continuous, one could describe people on one side of the mean as extraverts and people on the other side of the mean as introverts, but the social behavior of people in the middle range would be expected to be less predictable than those scoring in the upper and lower thirds, or quartiles. People at the extremes of any very general trait can be regarded as types with one proviso: The trait must be a basic dimension of personality, covering a broad range of narrower correlated traits. Another way to define a type would be to examine the pattern of scores on several measures of a narrower trait and to group those persons who have similar profiles of scores as types. But it may be more accurate to speak simply of "basic dimensions" of personality.

What is a *basic dimension* of personality? A number of criteria must be applied, including (a) reliable identification of dimension factor structures across methods, genders, ages, and cultures and (b) stability of measured dimensions in the same invidividuals over time. From a psychobiological view there are four other crucial criteria: (1) identification of similar kinds of behavioral traits marking the factor in other species of animals, particularly mammals that live in social groups; (2) at least moderate heritability for the dimension; (3) the identification of the dimension with some significant biological markers; and (4) the ultimate identification of the biological systems comprising the neural substrate for the dimension. A more socially oriented personality theorist would not see the necessity for the last group of criteria. Psychobiological theorists (Eysenck & Eysenck, 1985; Gray, 1982; Zuckerman, 1984a) believe that basic personality traits of humans have evolved and are therefore based to some significant degree on inherited variations in crucial biological structures. Although the dimensions discovered through factor analyses of items, scales, and ratings may not show a one-to-one correspondence with biological factors (systems), they give us an important starting point for correlational investigations in humans.

For work with animals, in which biological experimentation is easier, we need models for comparison with traits found in humans. For some of the major dimensions this is not difficult. Sociability, emotionality, and antisocial tendencies (intraspecies aggression) can be identified in most mammalian colony dwellers. On the other hand, traits such as "culture" (Norman, 1963); "intellectance" (Hogan, 1982) or "openness to experience" (Costa, McCrae, & Arenberg, 1980) are not easily identifiable in other species, even though they might be universal in our own.

Is there a distinction between basic dimensions of personality and temperaments?

Strelau (1983) has defined temperament as "the relatively stable features of the organism, primarily biologically determined, as revealed in the formal traits of reactions which form the energy level and temporal characteristics of behavior" (p. 171). He (Strelau, 1983) differentiated temperament and personality along five dimensions: (1) biological factors are assumed to play a *relatively* stronger role in temperament whereas social determinants are more prominent in personality; (2) temperament is manifested in early childhood whereas personality is more likely to become apparent in adults after learning and socialization have made their impact; (3) temperament can be seen in other species of animals whereas personality describes the phenomena that are specific to humans such as "ego" and "self" or cognitive constructs such as "efficacy expectancy" and "locus of control"; (4) temperament describes the energetic, temporal, and stylistic characteristics of behavior (for example, activity or reactivity) whereas personality traits refer to the content or purposive direction of behavior such as "need for achievement" or "dominance"; (5) personality is more modifiable than temperament because it expresses the regulating function over temperamental traits such as activity, in which it would determine the direction a person's activity level might take. Other theorists (Allport, 1961; Buss & Plomin, 1975) have made similar distinctions between temperament and personality.

Strelau (1987) illustrates his distinction with the construct of "emotionality" as a general trait referring to the expression of all emotions in contrast to the specific directional effects implied by "anxiety." Strelau's distinction has some validity if the definition of emotions is limited to physiological arousal. But analyses of emotions at the level of affect traits consistently show two relatively independent dimensions of positive and negative affect (Meyer & Shack, 1989; Watson & Tellegen, 1985). Diener, Larsen, Levine, and Emmons (1985) have proposed an intensity dimension, orthogonal to a bipolar hedonic dimension, that would be compatible with Strelau's view of emotionality; but Meyer and Shack have shown that the intensity dimension describes the diagonal of the stronger positive and negative affect dimensions and that there are few adjectives that describe its extreme poles (astonished vs. quiet). Furthermore, positive and negative affect dimensions converge nicely with the trait dimensions of extraversion (positive affect) and neuroticism (negative affect) (Meyer & Shack, 1989). Evidence for the existence of distinctive biological systems involved in specific emotions, such as anxiety (Gray, 1982) and pleasure (brain reward systems, Stellar & Stellar, 1985), suggests that concepts like general arousal or emotionality are too imprecise to be of use in psychobiological approaches (Zuckerman, 1987a).

The distinction between style and content of behavior is not a clear one. Impulsivity and general emotionality seem to fit a stylistic category, but anxiety, which is at the core of most emotionality factors, is a specific emotion often associated with a particular kind of cognitive content (Beck, 1985). Sociability, which seems to qualify as a basic trait in almost every analysis, also has a specific content – namely, other people and the need to associate with them. A third basic dimension (Zuckerman, 1989), socialization versus antisocial tendencies, has both a strong genetic basis and a direction of response, specifically for or against other people and society in general. Almost all temperaments involve both intensity of response and a broad situational element. Activity varies with the motivation and goals of a person in particular situations. Even impulsivity is usually a trait that is shown in certain situations (performance or conflict) and therefore has an associated content.

The only way to evaluate the relative influence on personality of biology and social learning is through genetic analyses. Behavior genetics research (chapter 3) has shown that both influences play nearly equal roles in all broad personality traits. Furthermore, not all traits regarded as temperamental show a strong genetic component.

Some personality traits, such as sociability, are hard to discern in infants because their manifestation depends on maturation and social experience. Not all genetically influenced traits are present at birth. Genital sexuality, for instance, depends on maturation of the gonads and cannot be reliably assessed until early adolescence. On the other hand, some traits that appear early have little significance or predictive value for later-appearing basic personality traits. Crying in infants, for instance, does not predict adult emotionality, probably because much of it is caused by the discomforts of temporary internal disorders (e.g., colic) rather than intrinsic expressivity mechanisms.

Basic directional personality traits identified in humans, such as sociability, can be identified in other species if we use an appropriate species and translate our human concepts into behaviors that are species-specific. Obviously, cognitively defined personality traits cannot be studied in other species. Issues concerning animal models are discussed later in this chapter. The idea that personality is easily modifiable, in contrast to temperament, is also not entirely tenable. An antisocial personality is not easily modifiable, nor would it be easy to transform an introvert into an extravert or vice versa. On the other hand, studies by Thomas and Chess (1977), described in chapter 2, show that the adult outcome of a "difficult temperament" in an infant or child depends on how the parents react to the temperamental behavior of the child.

Although the distinction between temperament and personality seems at first glance to be clear, closer inspection reveals fuzziness in the distinctions that have been made. One can certainly distinguish methods that incorporate more expressive than directional characteristics, but there is no guarantee that these methods are measuring basic dimensions of temperament unless one can demonstrate their reliability over long periods of lives and their relationship to the later developing personality phenotype. This author does not feel that the distinctions between temperament and basic personality traits are vital, therefore the latter term is used in this book except where quoted authors refer to their dimensions as those of temperament.

Identifying basic dimensions of personality

Early expression of basic personality traits

Investigators who are interested in temperament believe that it is expressed early in life, even before significant interactions with the familial environment. One of the most important longitudinal investigations that began in infancy was the study conducted by Thomas and Chess (1977; Chess & Thomas, 1984). The study began in 1956, and the first group of 141 infants was evaluated in the six subsequent years. Contact was maintained with almost all of the subjects into adult life. The main purpose of the study was to determine if adult adjustment could be predicted from behavioral traits seen in infancy and parental reactions. The initial data were largely based on interviews with the parents when the children were 2–3 months of age. Pilot studies had determined that behavior prior to this age varied too much over short periods of time to be of value. Measures of Temperament must have some reliability over time.

The investigators intially established nine categories of behavior by "an inductive content analysis" of the parent interview protocols. These are described in the following list. The figures in parentheses are the rater reliabilities, which are very low for some of the categories, limiting their usefulness as measures of temperament.

1. *Activity level:* activity during bathing, eating, playing, dressing, and handling, including reaching, crawling, and walking (.71)
2. *Rhythmicity (regularity):* regularity in time of functions such as feeding, elimination, and sleep (.62)
3. *Approach or withdrawal:* reactions to novel stimuli such as new foods, toys, and persons (.84)
4. *Adaptability:* long-term responses to new or altered situations; modifiability of behavior (.58)
5. *Threshold of responsiveness:* the intensity level of stimulation in any sensory modality that is necessary to evoke a response (.15)
6. *Intensity of reaction:* the energy level of responses regardless of their quality or direction (.00)
7. *Quality of mood:* the amount of pleasant, joyful, and friendly behavior contrasted with the amount of unpleasant, crying, and unfriendly behavior (.37)
8. *Distractibility:* the ease of changing the direction of attention from one stimulus or activity to another (.61)
9. *Attention span and persistence:* the length of time a particular activity is pursued and the continuation in an activity in spite of attempts at interference (.43)

The investigators found very good reliabilities for *approach/withdrawal* and *activity* ratings; fair reliability for *rhythmicity, adaptability,* and *distractibility;* poor reliability for *quality of mood* and *persistence;* and practically zero reliability for *threshold* and *intensity* ratings. Part of the reason for the unreliability of some of the scales may be the general difficulty in getting reliable data from interviews, which compound the unreliability of the interviewee, the interviewer, and the rater, who must make scale judgments from transcribed interviews. However, another problem may reside in the lack of internal consistency in the areas that make up the scales. Only a factor analysis of the items can answer the question of the adequacy of the conceptualizations of these scales.

Rowe and Plomin (1977) constructed rating scales based on the interview protocols and gave the scales to mothers to directly rate their 2–6-year-old children. A factor analysis of these scales yielded seven rotated factors, only two of which replicated the Thomas and Chess dimensions. The contents of the remaining Thomas and Chess dimensions are distributed over the various Rowe and Plomin dimensions, which include *attention-span/persistence, soothability* (like Thomas and Chess' *distractibility*), *sociability, emotional-*

ity, stubbornness, sleep rhythmicity, and *reactions to foods.* The results illustrate that factor analysis should be used in the initial construction of an assessment device to provide content validity for the scales.

On the basis of factor analysis and qualitative analyses of the ratings, Thomas, Chess, and Birch (1968) grouped their scales into a dimension of adjustment. At one end of the dimension (*easy child*) are regularity, positive approach to new stimuli, adaptability to change, and primarily positive mood of mild and moderate degree. At the other end of the dimension (*difficult child*) are those children who show irregularity of biological function, negative withdrawal responses to new stimuli, nonadaptability or slow adaptability to change and intense expressions of negative moods. A second constellation (*slow-to-warm-up*) consisted of mild negative reactions and slow adaptation to new stimuli, but only mild intensity of emotional reactions and no irregularity. Forty percent of the children in the study were rated as *easy,* 10% as *difficult,* and 15% as *slow-to-warm-up;* the remaining third of the group could not be clearly classified into these categories.

This analysis represents typing by persons rather than by dimensions. Although the main interest of Thomas and Chess has been the prediction of adjustment and the scales constructed with this in mind, one can see the possibility of a temperamental prototype for some of the adult dimensions of personality, to be discussed next. Activity, for instance, seems to be a part of extraversion, though social response to people is notably absent in their ratings, except as a component of broader categories such as *approach-withdrawal.* *Approach-withdrawal* in the broad sense looks like a prototype for sensation seeking (Zuckerman, 1979b). *Quality of mood* and *adaptability* may represent an early manifestation of the dimension of *neuroticism–emotionality.* *Threshold* and *intensity* sound very much like the bases for the trait of *reactivity,* as described by Strelau (1983). However, without data that relate these dimensions to the adult personality dimensions in the same persons, we cannot be sure of the comparability of child and adult dimensions. The relation of the childhood ratings to adult adjustment (*neuroticism*) has been reported by Chess and Thomas (1984) and their findings are discussed in the later section on consistency.

Buss and Plomin (1975) developed scales of temperament for use of parents in rating their children and a self-report test for adults. Unlike the Chess and Thomas scales, the Buss–Plomin categories of temperament are similar for children and adults. The four temperaments in the rating scales for use by parents in rating children are the following.

1. *Emotionality:* gets upset and cries easily, is easily frightened and/or has a quick temper, and is not easy going
2. *Activity:* always on the go from the time of waking, cannot sit still for long, fidgets at meals and similar occasions, prefers active games to quiet ones

3. *Sociability:* likes to be with others, makes friends easily, prefers to play with others rather than alone, is not shy
4. *Impulsivity:* difficulty in learning self-control and resistance to temptation, gets bored easily, goes from toy to toy quickly

Factor analyses of these scales showed fairly good factorial validity in the sense that most of the rating items loaded on the factors they were supposed to. However, correlations among the a priori scales indicated a good deal of overlap between the impulsivity dimension and the emotionality and activity dimensions, particularly the latter.

Buss and Plomin (1975) also developed a self-report questionnaire for older children and adults (EASI III) containing scales for each of the four temperaments. Each of the major scales contains subscales:

1. *Emotionality:* general, fear, anger
2. *Activity:* tempo (fast), vigor (energy, forcefulness)
3. *Sociability*
4. *Impulsivity:* inhibitory control (lack of), decision time (quick), sensation seeking, persistence (lack of)

Factor analyses of the EASI II showed fairly good assignment of items to scales. Correlations of the four scales yielded some low but significant correlations between *emotionality* and *impulsivity,* and between *activity* and *sociability* for the women. Subscale correlations were moderate within the *activity* and *emotionality* scales but low within the *impulsivity* scale.

Questions about the factorial unity of the *impulsivity* scale and its heritability led the authors to drop *impulsivity* as one of their basic temperaments, leaving *emotionality, activity,* and *sociability* as their basic three temperaments (Buss & Plomin, 1975, 1984). Because *activity* becomes incorporated in other dimensions in higher order factor analysis, this would leave only two dimensions. The investigators seem to be ignoring at least one other important dimension of basic personality: *antisocial* versus *socialized tendency,* including autonomy, sensation seeking, impulsivity, and aggressiveness (Zuckerman, Kuhlman, & Camac, 1988). Buss and Plomin (1984) report a factor analysis of mothers' ratings of their children on an abbreviated version of the Behavioral Style Questionnaire. One of the stronger factors to emerge from this analysis was called *reaction to discipline.* This factor would seem to reflect the construct of socialization or acceptance versus resistance.

Factor dimensions found in older children and adults

Eysenck's three-factor model

Eysenck (1947) defined the three basic dimensions that constitute his concept of the structure of personality: *introversion-extraversion* (E), *neuroticism* (N) (or emotional instability), and *psychoticism* (P) (or tough-minded, antisocial tendencies vs. socialized humaneness). Two of the three dimensions (N and P) are considered to be dispositions that underlie clinical disorders, including the neurotic, psychopathic, and psychotic ones. Early studies of the P dimension were limited to criterion analysis methods applied to ratings of symptoms in patients (Eysenck, 1955) and some studies of objective tests in normals (Eysenck, 1952; S. B. G. Eysenck, 1956). The N dimension was the first to be measured by a questionnaire, the Maudsley Medical Questionnaire (Eysenck, 1959); however, this scale was deemed more appropriate for clinical disorders than for persons in the normal range. When Eysenck revised the N scale for normals, he also developed a scale for E, using items from scales developed by Guilford. The resultant scale, called the Maudsley Personality Inventory (MPI, Eysenck, 1959) contained E and N scales and a *lie* (L) scale to measure response distortion from a social desirability response set. According to the model, E and N dimensions should have been orthogonal, but the MPI showed persistent negative correlations between the two scales. To eliminate this anomaly, Eysenck and Eysenck (1964) did factor analytic studies to improve the factor structure of the test and developed the Eysenck Personality Inventory (EPI). They succeeded in removing the correlation between E and N scales; however, as we will see, the correlation keeps cropping up in subsequent studies. This illustrates an interesting point about the use of factor analysis to develop questionnaires. The actual relationships found among dimensions, as well as the nature of the dimensions themselves, depend on the initial items used. By eliminating items that fall between the principal axes and using only items that have high loadings on one factor and negligible loadings on the other, one can eliminate the correlation between the resultant scales. But is there an intrinsic relationship between the processes and genotypes underlying the dimensions? This is a question that cannot be answered by factor analyses of psychological tests or ratings but only by more fundamental research aimed at elucidating the nature of the dimensions. In this respect, Eysenck can rightly claim that his system rests on a body of psychobiological research not even approached by advocates of other dimensional models.

The P dimension was not included in the EPI, and a questionnaire measure of this dimension was not developed until much later (Eysenck & Eysenck, 1975), when it was included with E, N, and L scales in the Eysenck Personality Questionnaire (EPQ). In the intervening years a substantial theory and much research had centered around a two-factor system (Eysenck 1947, 1952, 1953, 1957, 1963, 1967), and the construct validity of the basic two scales was developed from these studies.

The E scale in the earlier EPI contained two main types of items: *sociability* (Sy) and *impulsivity* (Imp) items. Carrigan (1960) suggested that these two dimensions were orthogonal and did not belong in the same scale. In a later paper, Guilford (1975) suggested that Eysenck's E dimension represented a "shot-gun" wedding of Guilford's *rhathymia* (impulsivity) and *sociability* factors. S. B. G. Eysenck and H. J. Eysenck (1963) defended "the dual nature of extraversion" in an empirical study involving a factor analysis of the MPI. They claimed that Sy items are the main component of stable (low N) extraversion, and Imp items are related to N as well as E. According to their analysis, Sy and Imp correlate about .50. A closer perusal of their table of factor loadings shows that items loading highly on E with loadings of close to zero on N were almost all Sy items, and items loading above .3 and about equally on E and N were all Imp items. In other words, it appears that even then *sociability* was closer to the core of the E factor than *impulsivity*.

The argument over the nature of E was not an idle exercise in psychometrics because studies of conditioning (Eysenck & Levey, 1972) showed that the Imp dimension supported the theoretical predictions about E whereas the Sy dimension did not. But with the construction of the EPQ the issue about the dual nature of E has faded because of an empirical fait accompli. In the attempt to maintain orthogonality between the current three dimensions, items that loaded equally on E and P, or E and N, or P and N were discarded, and other items were reassigned according to their primary loadings or eliminated. As pointed out by Rocklin and Revelle (1981) and Gray (1981), the result has been that the new E scale is almost entirely composed of Sy type items. The Imp items have either gravitated to the new P scale or been dropped. Much of the previous theory describing antisocial tendencies as a combination of E and N may have to be modified because the new P dimension may in itself be a measure of antisocial tendencies (Block, 1977a, b). With this change in the nature of E, as defined by the questionnaire, many studies would have to be redone, and the conclusions about the construct of E may require change.

The theory of what was measured by the P scale (Eysenck & Eysenck, 1976) and the psychometric adequacy of the scale itself were challenged almost immediately (Bishop, 1977; Block, 1977a, b; Davis, 1974). The items in the scale are a mixture of impulsivity; sadism or lack of empathy; aggressiveness; sensation seeking; lack of concern about finances, work, or punctuality; uncommon social attitudes (e.g., marriage is old-fashioned and should be done away with); and a few, mild paranoid-type items. The earlier experimental scale (PEN) had contained more items suggesting psychotic delusional thinking, but these were mostly dropped in the EPQ version because they were so infrequently endorsed that they skewed the distribution of scores toward zero. A second revised version of the P scale (Eysenck & Eysenck, 1985) has carried the normalization trend further. The only way to modify the distribution of the P-scale scores was to add more items that were not so deviant that they would be rarely endorsed by normals. The actual content of the scale, as well as the scores of various groups (criminals and successful artists score higher than psychotics), have raised questions about the theory of the dimension and the name given to the scale (Zuckerman, 1989).

As mentioned previously, Eysenck's hierarchal model conceives of E, N, and P as broad "supertraits", which are composed of narrower traits. The traits recently subsumed under E, N, and P (Eysenck & Eysenck, 1985) are as follows:

E: sociable, lively, active, assertive, sensation seeking, carefree, dominant, surgent, venturesome
N: anxious, depressed, guilt feelings, low self-esteem, tense, irrational,
   shy, moody, emotional
P: aggressive, cold, egocentric, impersonal, impulsive, antisocial, unem-
   phatic, creative, tough-minded

Note that impulsivity is listed under P and sensation seeking is listed under E. What Eysenck and Eysenck (1985) point out is that some of the subscales of broader impulsivity and sensation-seeking scales are more correlated with E whereas others are more correlated with P. The placement of the broad impulsivity or sensation-seeking traits under E or P is therefore somewhat arbitrary. Evidence to be presented later in this chapter suggests that most types of impulsivity and sensation seeking should be listed under P and that hardly any have their major factor loadings on E.

At the time that the MPI was constructed, the two main models based on factor analyses of personality were those of Guilford and Zimmerman (1956) with 14 major dimensions of personality and of Cattell (1957) with 16 dimensions. How could Eysenck reconcile his two-factor system with the large number of dimensions in the other two models? Eysenck (Souief, Eysenck, & White, 1969) undertook a joint factorial study of the Guilford, Cattell, and Eysenck (EPI) scales in the same subjects. Essentially this consists of a second-order factor analysis because the subscales of the three tests were supposed to be based on primary factors. Actually, factor analyses of the items of the Guilford and Cattell scales yielded poor replication of their factors. The results of the factor analyses of the standard scales for all three tests showed two major factors in males and females: extraversion and neuroticism. A closer look at the factor plots for these analyses would indicate that what was regarded as the N dimension actually contains important elements of what is now called P. The highest positively loading scales for both sexes were *impulsivity, irritability,* and *mood swing* items from the EPI and *cycloid* tendencies from the Guilford test. *Agreeableness* and *superego strength* scales define the negative pole of the dimension. *Aggressiveness, impulsivity,* and *psychopathy* (weak superego) are now considered subtraits of P. The N type scales (*guilt proneness, depression, tension, inferiority*) actually fell in the N-introversion quadrant. As Eysenck and Eysenck (1985) remark, it would be interesting to repeat this analysis including the P scale as a marker for the third dimension.

There is no basic conflict between analyzing personality at narrow or broad trait levels. Cattell's higher order factor analysis (essentially a factoring of narrower factors) revealed two factors that closely resemble Eysenck's E and N. An argument against the use of narrow factors has been their lack of replicability. Eysenck, White, and Souief (1969) could not replicate Cattell's factors across sex, and Peterson (1965) could not replicate them across age (child vs. adult forms of the 16PF test). In contrast, the broad factors (E and N) derived from the 16PF did replicate across gender and age. Neither could Peterson find correlations between parent or peer ratings of subjects and subjects' scores on the 16 factors that were any higher than those for scores on different factors. Similarly, Becker (1960) could find no evidence for the matching of behavior rating and questionnaire factors. In other words, the scales show deficits in discriminant as well as convergent validity (Campbell & Fiske, 1959). In contrast, the scores on the broader factors showed some stronger convergent and good discriminant cross-method validities. Eysenck and Eysenck (1985, pp. 122–129) have summarized the long history of failure to replicate Cattell's factors in the 16PF: "The fact remains that the great majority of authors have failed to find any convincing degree of confirmation of the Cattell primaries and that even those who have succeeded to some extent still fail consistently to replicate all the scales; even Cattell himself . . . did not succeed very well in doing so." (pp. 125–127)

The five-factor model

Whereas the evidence suggests that 14 or 16 dimensions are too many (and 2 may be too few), a 5 or 6-factor model has been winning increasing support and claims for convergent and discriminant validity and replicability of the factors (Digman, 1990; Digman & Inouye, 1986; Digman & Takemoto-Chock, 1981; Fiske, 1949; Hogan, 1982; McCrae & Costa, 1985a; Norman, 1963; Tupes & Christal, 1961). The pioneering study was done by Fiske (1949) as part of the Research Project on the Selection of Clinical Psychologists (trainees in the Veteran's Administration) just after World War II. The subjects were veterans evaluated and rated by psychologists after a series of interviews and participation in situational tests. They were also rated by the other applicants (peers), and they rated themselves on the same set of personality scales. The rating scales were some of those devised by Cattell and based on his constructs. Staff, peer, and self-ratings were factor analyzed, and factor-score comparisons were made across the three methods. Five factors were rotated for each method. These are listed with the scales loading on them in all or in at least two of the three methods:

Table 1.1. *Correlations between loadings on primary factors from three sources of data: Self, staff, and peer ratings*

	Staff vs. team	Self vs. staff	Self vs. team
Social adaptability	.62	.60	.40
Emotional control	.86	.90	.92
Conformity	.36	.73	.31
Inquiring intellect	.61	.57	.77
Confident self-expression	.21	− .26	.38

Source: Fiske (1949), table 2, p. 339. Copyright 1949 by American Psychological Association. Adapted by author's permission.

1. *Social adaptability:* cheerful, talkative, adventurous, adaptable, placid
2. *Emotional control:* unshakable, self-sufficient, placid, limited overt emotional expression versus easily upset, worrying, anxious, dependent
3. *Conformity:* serious, conscientious, cooperative, trustful, good-natured, easy-going, predictable, cautious
4. *Inquiring intellect:* broad interests, independent-minded, imaginative
5. *Confident self-expression:* assertive, talkative, marked interest in women, frank, expressive, cheerful, adventurous

The first three factors seem a fair match for Eysenck's basic three: *social adaptability* with E, *emotional control* with N (reversed), and *conformity* with P (reversed). The similarities of the factors are shown in Table 1.1 in terms of the correlations among loadings on primary factors derived from the three sources. The *emotional control* factor was similar in all three analyses; the *social adaptability* and *inquiring intellect* showed fairly good cross-method similarity; but *conformity* showed similarity only in self and staff data sources, and *confident self-expression* evidenced little correspondence across methods.

The next landmark study, conducted by Norman (1963), was based on preliminary work done by Tupes and Christal (1961). These studies used rating scales that employed the trait-descriptive terms extracted by Cattell (1957) from the longer list of personality relevant terms compiled by Allport and Odbert (1936). Cattell (1957) had used these bipolar rating scales to identify primary personality factors and reported 12 very stable factors and 2 or 3 less definite factors. Tupes and Christal (1961) analyzed rating data from eight separate samples, including reanalyses of two of Cattell's samples. They found evidence for only "five relatively strong and recurrent factors and nothing more of any consequence" (p. 14). Using these scales, Norman obtained peer nominations from four groups of college students. His results showed remarkable confirmation of the hypothesized factors across samples; in almost every case the scales had their highest loadings on the factors to which they had been previously assigned. The five factors are as follows:

1. *Extraversion or surgency:* talkative-silent; frank, open-secretive; adventurous-cautious; sociable-reclusive
2. *Agreeableness:* goodnatured-irritable; not jealous–jealous; mild, gentle–headstrong; cooperative-negativistic
3. *Conscientiousness:* fussy, tidy-careless; responsible-undependable; scrupulous-unscrupulous; persevering-quitting, fickle
4. *Emotional stability:* poised-nervous, tense; calm-anxious; composed-excitable; not hypochondriacal–hypochondriacal
5. *Culture:* artistically sensitive–artistically insensitive; intellectual–unreflective, narrow; polished, refined-crude, boorish; imaginative–simple, direct

Although the factors showed high degrees of factor similarity, there was still substantial correlation between some of the factors based on correlations of factor scores. Table 1.2 shows the correlations between factor scores in two of the samples. Factors 2 and 4 were highly related, and factor 2 also correlated with factors 3 and 5. Although showing clear evidence for the separation of the five dimensions, the correlations among the dimensions suggest that a second-order factor analysis would have yielded a smaller number of factors, possibly two or three. Digman & Inouye (1986) reported such an analysis of the five factors, yielding extraversion and socialization superfactors. Emotionality loaded equally on these two higher order factors.

The Norman 5-factor model has been adopted by a number of investigators. Hogan (1982) actually developed a 6-factor model, splitting the extraversion factor into *surgency* (a more dominant, assertive type of social interaction) and *sociability*. Hogan developed a questionnaire measuring his six factors: *surgency, sociability, likability, conformity, adjustment,* and *intellectance*. Experience-seeking and thrill-seeking types of sensation-seeking items loaded negatively on the *conformity* factor. Norman, Eysenck, and McCrae and Costa all place sensation seeking (adventurous) in the extraversion dimension. Conformity is the opposite end of the P dimension, suggesting that sensation seeking should be placed in the P dimension because nonconforming behavior is a salient part of sensation seeking. Digman and Inouye (1986) applied the Norman scales to the rating of personality in school children with results showing replicability of the five factors found in the Fiske, Tupes, and Norman studies (Digman & Takemoto-Chock, 1981). Digman and Inouye (1986), pointing out the replication of two of Eysenck's factors, E and N, in all of these studies, asked what corresponds to Eysenck's P factor in the 5-factor model. He points to the *hostile-noncompliance* pole of the *friendly-compliance (agree-*

Table 1.2. *"Factor score" intercorrelations based on peer nomination data in two samples*

	Factor				
	1	2	3	4	5
Sample C: Fraternity groups (n = 215)					
1. Extraversion					
2. Agreeableness	.08				
3. Conscientiousness	−.27	.48			
4. Emotional stability	.20	.55	.10		
5. Culture	.02	.37	.63	.18	
Sample D: Residence hall groups (n = 241)					
1. Extraversion					
2. Agreeableness	−.02				
3. Conscientiousness	−.49	.49			
4. Emotional stability	.22	.44	.05		
5. Culture	−.02	.31	.59	.19	

Source: Norman (1963), table 4, p. 580. Copyright 1963 by American Psychological Association. Reprinted by author's permission.

ableness in Norman's terms) factor. However, a lack of conscientiousness is also obvious in many of the items in the P scale, and this factor in the model may also be part of P.

Costa, McCrae and Arenberg (1980) began with a three-dimensional model that included two of Eysenck's dimensions (E and N) and a dimension that differs somewhat from the P dimension: *openness to experience*. More recently, McCrae and Costa (1985a) have expanded their model to include the five Norman factors, equating *openness* with Norman's *culture* factor. Interestingly they found that *openness* correlates low ($r = .32$) but significantly with the WAIS vocabulary test. McCrae and Costa (1985b) examined the relationships between Eysenck's E, N, and P scales and their new 5-factor scales. E and N factors in both tests correlate substantially; *agreeableness* and *conscientiousness* did correlate negatively and significantly with P, but the correlations are not as high as those between E and N scales in the two inventories. A factor analysis of all of the scales showed the P scale loading (negatively) primarily on the *agreeableness* factor and secondarily on the *conscientiousness* factor.

The recent surge of interest in the 5-factor model might be called the "Norman conquest," though it is long delayed, occurring 20 years after the original Norman article and more than 30 years after the seminal Fiske article. The rallying around the "five robust factors", or the "big five" as their supporters call them, probably reflects disillusion with the complicated and unreliable Cattell multifactor system and the feeling that Eysenck's big three are not enough dimensions to account for the complexity of personality. However, the difference between the 3- and 5-factor models is much less than that which existed between the 3- and 16-factor models. In fact, two of Eysenck's primary dimensions (E and N) have been found in every analysis, and there is a strong possibility that two of the other five factors (*agreeableness* and *conscientiousness*) may represent the opposite pole of the P dimension. The *intellectance, culture,* and *openness to experience* factors represent the qualities of intellectual curiosity that are correlated with, but not totally a function of, intellectual ability. Most of the studies have involved ratings of personality in academic contexts, for which these intellectual qualities are particularly salient, but the idea of "smart," "wise," "learned," or "creative" is probably not limited to those settings. The question is whether intellectual quality constitutes a major dimension of personality that is independent of the ability realm.

Three-, 5- or even 16-factor models are not mutually incompatible in the hierarchal scheme of personality. Eysenck conceives of his three supertraits as encompassing narrower traits. Traits can be analyzed at any level along a dimension of specificity versus breadth. The *sensation-seeking* dimension has been found to yield four subfactors reliably: *thrill* and *adventure seeking, experience seeking, disinhibition,* and *boredom susceptibility* (Ball, Farnhill, & Wangeman, 1983; Birenbaum, 1986; Rowland & Franken, 1986; Zuckerman, 1971b; Zuckerman, Eysenck, & Eysenck, 1978). Factor analyses of fear survey schedules have revealed that the gross construct of anxiety can be subdivided into social anxiety; fear of tissue damage or mutilation; fear of travel, crowds, or strangers; and fear of small animals or insects (Kartsounis, Mervyn-Smith, & Pickersgill, 1983; Torgerson, 1979). These in turn could be subdivided into even narrower traits: Fear of small animals could be divided into specific animal fears such as snake fear or rat fear, and social anxiety could be subdivided into fear of failure and fear of being observed. Personality assessment is a trade-off between the need for general measures, useful in theory development and in a wide range of prediction problems, and the need for accuracy in prediction, which is often but not always achieved by narrower trait measures. Narrower, more specific measures have been developed mostly for assessment in behavioral therapies because they provide the more specific information that clinicians require to do therapy.

A neo-Pavlovian model: Strelau

Strelau's (1983) dimensions of personality contrast markedly with those discussed to this point. These dimensions, developed from the Pavlovian theory of temperament and based on largely hypothetical characteristics of central nervous system functioning, were initially defined by individual differences in laboratory phenomena such as conditioning, psychophysical, and psychophysiological processes. Until recently, the differences in approach to temperament in the East and the West resulted in little agreement or comparisons of dimensions. Since Strelau translated three of the Pavlovian dimensions into scales in a questionnaire, the Strelau Temperament Inventory (STI, Strelau, 1983), comparisons with the dimensions measured in Western questionnaires have been made. However, the omission of a crucial step in evolving a multidimensional psychometric instrument has led to a major problem with the STI that brings into question any validity studies done with the original scales.

The three dimensions of nervous system function that Strelau has attempted to bring out of the laboratory are as follows.

1. *Strength of excitation.* In early Pavlovian theory the concept of *strength of the nervous system* was equated with strength of both inhibitory and excitatory brain processes, but in later theory it came to be identified solely with the excitatory process. The strong nervous system is also resistant to inhibition, therefore *strength of excitation* as a personality trait is linked to the ability to continue working under intense, distracting, or disturbing conditions. Strelau calls persons with strong nervous systems "low reactives" and persons with weak nervous systems "high reactives."

2. *Strength of inhibition.* Inhibition is conceived of as conditioned inhibition produced by an association of a stimulus with the stimulus that has acquired inhibitory potential. In human behavioral terms, Strelau translates this trait into the ability to exercise behavioral restraint and to remain calm under provocation.

3. *Mobility of nervous processes.* This is the ease with which an organism can shift from excitation to inhibition or from inhibition to excitation. Strelau relates this to the quickness of starting work or other activities, the rapidity of relaxing or falling asleep (sleep efficiency), or the general ability to shift from one activity to another. Persons who are slow to change from one state or activity to another are regarded as having weak mobility.

Strelau based the items for his scales on his understanding of how the laboratory-defined processes would translate into behavioral phenotypes. One interesting sidelight, perhaps related to socialist values and goals, is the emphasis on how temperament is expressed in work activities. Until recently there was little psychometric development of the scales beyond the rational item selection. The results of subsequent factor analyses of the items have indicated that the purely rational method of item selection was a mistake. Laboratory concepts such as strength of excitatory and inhibitory processes do not easily translate into natural behavioral terms.

Carlier (1985) factor analyzed the STI given to French students, and Stelmack, Kruidenier, and Anthony (1985) did a factor analysis of the STI using Canadian students. The factors found in both studies were similar but did not correspond to the scales as defined by Strelau. Their factors were called *flexibility, work effort, restraint, emotional control,* and *social adaptability*. The last three factors showed substantial correlations with the Eysenck's personality scales: *social adaptability* with E, *emotional control* with N (negative *r*), and *restraint* with P (negative *r*). The content of the items empirically defined factors are mixtures of items from the three original scales.

What do the STI scales measure and what is their construct validity for the Pavlovian constructs embodied in the scales? From a content point of view, factor analyses show that the Western constructs provide a better description of how the subjects actually respond to the items of the test. Only one factor, *work effort,* is unique to the STI. Perhaps this factor would provide a good definition of *strength of excitation* in terms of resistance to inhibition or fatigue. However, Strelau has defined his much researched dimension of *reactivity* in terms of the STI *strength of excitation* scale and has shown some evidence for construct validity in terms of prediction of behavior.

A soviet model: Rusalov

Rusalov (1989) has based a concept of temperament on Anokhin's theory (not translated into English), which analyzes each behavioral act into four stages: afferent synthesis, programming (decision making), execution, and feedback. Rusalov uses each of these stages as the basis for a temperament trait on the assumption that each is represented by an underlying and distinct neural system that forms the basis for a separate temperament trait.

Translating the stages of acts into general behavioral terms, he interprets the first stage as *ergonicity,* or the degree of motivational-need strength in interaction with the environment. The concept closely resembles Strelau's (1983) interpretation of *strength of the nervous system* in behavioral terms. The second stage is translated as *plasticity,* or the ease or difficulty in switching from one process to another. *Plasticity* resembles Strelau's concept of the Pavlovian *mobility of the nervous system.* The third stage is called *tempo,* or the speed of execution of behavior. It bears some resemblance to the *strength of inhibition* dimension of Pavlov as interpreted by Strelau. The fourth stage, based on the discrepancy between the intention of action and its results (punishment or nonreward?), is interpreted as *emotionality. Emotionality* is not treated as a separate dimension of temperament in the Strelau model but is conceptualized as emotional restraint and combined with behavioral restraint in the *strength of inhibition* construct.

All four of these dimensions are interpreted in two aspects: reactions to the object world (work or tasks) and reactions to the social-communicative world. Rusalov makes the interesting observation that Eysenck's scales largely evaluate the social-communicative aspects of behavior whereas Strelau's inventory assesses mostly the object-related characteristics of behavior. Rusalov's scales attempt to cover both areas of life systematically. For each of the four dimensions, one subscale relates primarily to work activities and the other to social-communicative activities. The result is eight scales in the Structure of Human Temperament Questionnaire (STQ):

1. *Ergonicity* (Er): need for activity, work efficiency, and a liking for difficult and challenging jobs
2. *Social ergonicity* (SEr): classical sociability type items reflecting a strong motivation to be with and talk to other people and a liking of parties
3. *Plasticity* (P): flexibility and creativity in work and problem solving
4. *Social plasticity* (SP): impulsivity in social communication
5. *Tempo* (T): liking to do things quickly in general activity, games, and work
6. *Social tempo* (ST): speed in social communication
7. *Emotionality* (Em): anxiety, upset, or annoyance due to difficulties in work
8. *Social emotionality* (SEm): sensitivity and emotional upset in response to people or failures of communication and misunderstandings

Like Strelau, Rusalov avoided atheoretical factor analyses of items. Instead he used the method of latent structure analysis that tests the fit of items to categories determined by the theoretical model. The result is a redundancy of items within scales, with many items showing similar types of content. Undoubtedly, a standard factor analysis would have revealed the familiar extraversion and neuroticism factors found in all Western factor analyses of personality test items. In fact, when the eight scales are factor analyzed, the two emotionality scales (Em and SEm) form one factor [neuroticism?] and strongly correlate, indicating that the distinction between work and social sources of negative emotional response are less important than the overall trait. The remaining three social scales (SEr, SP, and ST) form a second factor, obviously extraversion. The remaining factor consisting of Er, P, T, and a *lie* scale seem to express an energetic, fast, and ambitious attitude toward work that is also associated with social desirability.

Correlations with scales from the EPI confirm the nature of the factors. The two emotionality scales correlated highly with Neuroticism, and the three social-communicative scales correlated highly with Extraversion. Object-related ergonicity (Er) and plasticity (P) did not correlate with either Extraversion or Neuroticism. Like the *work efficiency* factor found in the STI, these scales seem to measure a positive attitude toward work; measures of attitudes toward work are not found in most Western personality scales. Western definitions of personality seem to be based on an interpersonal definition whereas eastern European definitions give at least equal stress to the area of behavior in relation to objects or work. Neither the

STI nor the STQ contain a representation for the P dimension of personality or antisocial, sensation-seeking types of items. Although the items are somewhat different, the overlap in factorial dimensions is impressive. This does not mean that the constructs on which the eastern European scales are based are more or less valid. Laboratory and applied work could reveal that they have greater construct validity in certain areas. Work-efficiency scales, for instance, could be more predictive of performance in overload work situations in the laboratory or real work situations.

A study of personality dimensions

This study was designed by Zuckerman et al. (1988) to investigate the dimensions that underlie some of the personality traits measured by questionnaires, some of which have been used in research on the biological bases of personality. Forty-six scales were selected to provide markers for seven hypothesized dimensions: *activity, sociability, impulsivity, socialization, sensation seeking, emotionality* (subdivided into general, anxiety, and hostility), and *social desirability*. Ten factors had eigen values of over 1, but a scree test suggested a 5-factor solution. Because seven factors had been originally hypothesized, we started with a 7-factor, then a 5-factor, and finally a 3-factor rotation.

Five of the seven hypothesized factors were found in the initial 7-factor solution: *sociability, activity, impulsivity, socialization* (autonomy vs. conformity), and *emotionality* (separated into *anxiety* and *hostility* factors). Factor score correlations across subjects were used to track the factors moving from the 7- to the 5- to the 3-factor solutions. Figure 1.1 shows the way factors combine as we go from narrower to broader factors, using the factor score correlations to track the factors.

At the 5-factor level we find *sociability,* with Eysenck's E scale as a prominent marker (E-Sy), *activity* (Act), and a factor containing *aggression, sensation seeking* (*boredom susceptibility* and *disinhibition*) at the positive pole, and *responsibility, social desirability,* and *inhibition of aggression* at the negative pole (AggSS). These factors remained very much as they were at the 7-factor level. At the 5-factor level, *hostility* (anger) and *anxiety* combined to form a general emotionality factor with Eysenck's N scale as the highest marker (N-Emot). *Socialization* (*autonomy* vs. *conformity* and *socialization*) and *impulsivity* combined with a number of sensation-seeking scales (*monotony avoidance, risk taking, experience seeking*) and Eysenck's P scale to produce a factor called *impulsive unsocialized sensation seeking* (P-ImpUSS).

At the 3-factor level, *activity* (Act) and *sociability* (E-Sy) combined to form the familiar *extraversion* (without *impulsivity*), though *activity* also showed some negative correlation with the *emotionality* factor. The *emotionality* (N-Emot) factor, combining anxiety and hostility, remained un-

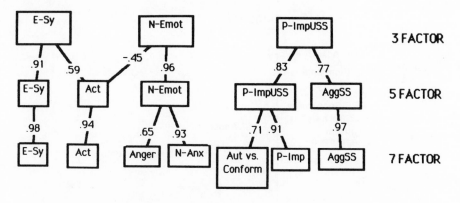

FACTOR SCORE CORRELATIONS ACROSS LEVELS

Figure 1.1. Factor score correlations between the 3-, 5-, and 7-factor analyses. (From "What lies beyond E and N? Factor analyses of scales believed to measure basic dimensions of personality" by M. Zuckerman, D. M. Kuhlman, and C. Camac, 1988, *Journal of Personality and Social Psychology*, *54*, p. 103. Copyright 1988 by the American Psychological Association.)

changed. The P-ImpUSS factor combined with the *aggressive sensation seeking* factor, containing the remaining sensation-seeking scales. Eysenck's scales E and N provided the best markers (highest loadings) for the *sociability* and *emotionality* factors, respectively, and the P scale was among the three best markers for the ImpUSS factor.

The three major factors can be better conceptualized from factor-loading plots because some of the variables load on more than one factor and therefore fall in the quadrants of 2-factor dimensional space. Figure 1.2 shows the plot of the E and N dimensions. The E dimension is defined primarily by sociability scales and the N dimension by anxiety and hostility scales. Although the *general emotionality* scale falls very close to the factor axis, the Eysenck N scale and most of the anxiety scales fall into the Introverted N quadrant; similarly, most of the *sociability* scales defining the E-*sociability* dimension fall in the stable (low N) *extraversion* dimension. No variables with loadings of any magnitude are in the other two quadrants. If we rotated the E scale 12 degrees to the E axis, the N scale, *psychasthenia* scale, and one of the *anxiety* scales would be moved to about 45 degrees from the axis, or midway between the two axes. What this indicates is that, despite Eysenck's attempt to maintain orthogonality between E and N, a negative correlation persists between these dimensions so that *neuroticism* and *anxiety* are associated more with *introversion* than with *extraversion*. The next plot also shows this correlation.

Figure 1.3 shows the relationship between the P-ImpUSS and E-Sy di-

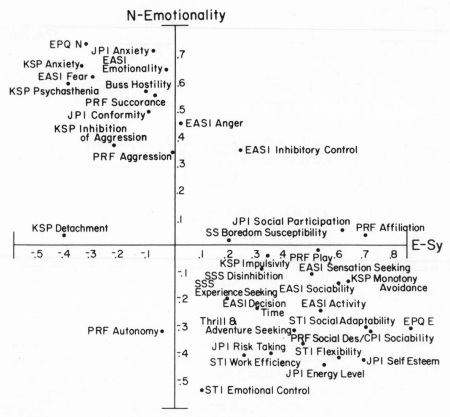

Figure 1.2. Loadings of personality scales plotted on the *extraversion-sociability* (E-Sy) and *neuroticism* (N)-*emotionality* factor dimensions.

mensions. In this plot, *extraversion* and *sociability* variables are closer to the E axis and, as in the previous plot, the negative pole of the dimension is defined by a *detachment* scale. However, in this plot we can see that the negative pole of *sociability* also has some secondary loadings from the *neuroticism* scale and *psychasthenia* and *anxiety* scales.

The *psychoticism* scale formed an excellent marker for the dimension it helps define, falling right on the axis along with an *autonomy* scale from the Jackson PRF test. The *sensation-seeking* scales form an important part of the P factor. The highest loading scale on the factor dimension was the *boredom susceptibility* scale from the SSS, and all of the sensation-seeking scales except the KSP *monotony avoidance* and the PRF *play* scale had their highest loading on the P factor, although some also had secondary loadings on the E factor. SSS *thrill and adventure seeking* loaded equally on both dimensions. *Aggression* and *impulsivity* also defined the dimension.

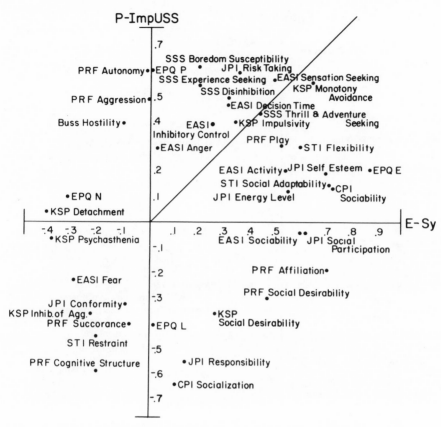

Figure 1.3. Loadings of personality scales plotted on the *psychopathy-impulsive unsocialized sensation seeking* dimension (P-ImpUSS) and *extraversion-sociability* (E-Sy) factor dimensions. (From "Personality in the third dimension: A psychobiological approach" by M. Zuckerman, 1989, *Personality and Individual Differences, 10*, p. 396. Copyright 1989 by Pergamon Press plc. Reprinted by permission.)

Socialization, responsibility, restraint, and *need for cognitive structure* (low tolerance for ambiguity) defined the low end of the P dimension.

Figure 1.4 shows the plot of variables on the N and P dimensions. The upper quadrants provide some interesting information. A cluster in the high-N–high-P quadrant included *hostility, anger, aggression,* and *lack of inhibition.* Although *aggression* and *anger-hostility* are split by a strictly hierarchal assignment, with the former placed in the P dimension and the latter in the N dimension, the factor plot shows that they are close in factorial space and that *anger-hostility* and *aggression* actually form a cluster intermediate between N and P. Another interesting cluster is found in the high-N–low-P quadrant and consists of *succorance, conformity,* and *inhi-*

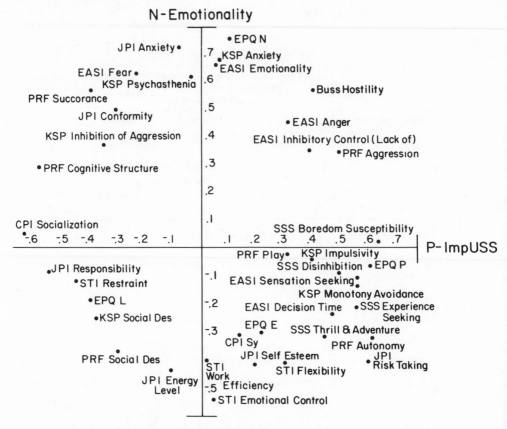

Figure 1.4. Loadings of personality scales plotted on the *neuroticism* (N)-*emotionality*, and *psychopathy-unsocialized-sensation-seeking* (P-ImpUSS) dimensions. (From "Personality in the third dimension: A psychobiological approach" by M. Zuckerman, 1989, *Personality and Individual Differences, 10,* p. 397. Copyright 1989 by Pergamon Press plc. Reprinted by permission.)

bition of aggression. Hostility-aggression and *conformity-inhibition* seem to represent opposite ways of reacting to neurotic anxiety. In contrast, *socialization, responsibility,* and *restraint* are nonneurotic, low-P traits.

One way to compare factors across samples is to calculate two sets of factor scores for each subject, one based on the factor score coefficient matrices from the subject's own sample and the other based on the matrices of the other sample. These two sets of factor scores can then be correlated within each sample of subjects yielding (1) the extent of similarity of factors thought to be alike and (2) the extent of similarity of factors to nonrelevant factors. This method was applied to the male and female samples in this study. The results for the 3-factor solution are shown in Table 1.3. In both

Table 1.3. *Correlations of male and female factor scores from three-factor analysis in males and females*

	Males Male factors				Females Male factors		
	E-Sy	P-ImpUSS	N-Emot		E-Sy	P-ImpUSS	N-Emot
Female factors				*Female factors*			
E-Sy	.98	.10	−.09	E-Sy	.78	.18	−.09
P-ImpUSS	.13	.98	.20	P-ImpUSS	.26	.91	−.02
N-Emot	−.25	.08	.97	N-Emot	−.22	−.08	.83

Source: Zuckerman, Kuhlman, & Camac (1988), table 7, p. 104. Copyright 1988 by American Psychological Association.

males and females, male- and female-derived factors are similar, approaching total identity in the males (*r*'s .97–.98) and showing strong similarity in the females (*r*'s .78–.91). In contrast, the correlations among the heterogeneous factors are low, none exceeding .3. Similar analyses of the 5- and 7-factor solutions showed fair identity for some of the factors, no identity for a few, and considerably more overlap among heterogeneous factors. The results bear out an argument of Eysenck's concerning his choice of broad factors rather than narrow ones: The broad factors are more replicable across populations, an important consideration in the search for universal factors.

Although the three superfactors were similar in structure for males and females, there were significant differences in levels. Males and females were compared on the factor scores derived from the factor analysis of the combined group. Males scored significantly (*p* < .001) higher than females on the *impulsive unsocialized sensation seeking* (P-ImpUSS) factor, and females scored significantly (*p* < .004) higher on the N-*emotionality* factor. There was no significant difference in the *sociability* factor.

Comparison of results with earlier factor-defined dimensions

The data from this study provide striking confirmation of the validity of the three broad factors suggested by Eysenck. Two of them, E-sociability and N-emotionality, were also found in the 5-factor models. The E factor consists primarily of *sociability* and secondarily of *activity*. *Impulsivity* is entirely subsumed by the P factor, but it appears that Eysenck himself has abandoned the 2-factor (*sociability* and *impulsivity*) theory of extraversion, though he maintains that the *liveliness* subscale of *impulsivity* is primarily related to E, and *risk-taking* correlates equally with E and P (Eysenck and Eysenck, 1977). A new *impulsivity* scale contains subscales of *narrow im-*

pulsivity (acting quickly) and *venturesomeness* (like *thrill and adventure seeking*). The former correlated primarily with P and the latter with E (Eysenck & McGurk, 1980). In the present study, a fast *decision time impulsivity* scale loaded primarily on the P factor, and the *thrill and adventure seeking* scale loaded equally on the E and P factors; however, all of the other sensation-seeking scales except *monotony avoidance* loaded primarily on the P factor. Although some of these scales have some secondary loadings on E, in a hierarchal model *sensation seeking* must be subsumed by the P dimension. In fact, it constitutes a major part of the definition of this dimension.

The N-emotionality dimension was defined by negative affect (anxiety, hostility or anger) and inability to modulate such negative emotions. It is also defined by general neurotic traits such as dependency, anxious conformity, and neurotic symptoms (psychasthenia), but it is primarily defined as general emotionality and lack of emotional control, which is orthogonal to *sociability*. *Anxiety* and *neuroticism* in general seem to show a negative correlation with sociability. Although *aggression,* as a behavioral expression, seems to fall into the P dimension whereas correlated attitudes and affects (*hostility* and *anger*) fall primarily in the N-emotionality dimension, all of these traits do form a coherent cluster in the N-P quadrant.

The P dimension proved to be the most complex of the three. In a broad sense it separates those persons who are highly socialized from those who have little regard for the conventions or rules of society. In a clinical sense, the label *psychopathy* would seem to be more appropriate and require fewer assumptions than *psychoticism*. At the antisocial pole, the P dimension is defined by sensation seeking, particularly susceptibility to boredom, the search for novel experiences, the enjoyment of disinhibition, independence from social demands and rules (autonomy), aggression, and impulsivity, particularly risk taking and precipitous decision making. In considering the N-P quadrants, it may be useful to make some distinctions between normal low-P tendencies, such as responsibility and restraint and neurotic low-P traits such as succorance, conformity, and the inhibition of aggression even to the extent of inhibiting normal self-assertiveness. The latter traits are what Block (1971) would call "overcontrol."

Despite these minor modifications of Eysenck's most recent conceptualizations of the three dimensions (Eysenck & Eysenck, 1985), the results of this study supported the major aspects of his model, and the EPQ scales provided good markers for each of the three dimensions. Still, there may be good reason to desire more specificity, particularly for the complex P dimension. Let us examine the 5-factor model.

Our study did not include possible markers for the intellectance or culture factor that is included in the 5-factor models. The nature of this factor is the most debatable of the big 5. Included in our primary five is the *activity* factor. Although Buss and Plomin (1984) regard this factor as one of their big 3, in our analysis it joins *sociability* to become part of the E factor at the broader level of analysis. Fiske (1949) and Norman (1963) did not even include a rating for *activity* in their analyses. Why has this factor been missed or submerged in other factors in the 5-factor studies? Probably because the theorists did not see it as important enough to warrant providing a number of markers. Those working with children may see *activity* as more salient than investigators working with adults, who are more concerned with the direction of activity than with the general energetic trait. The P-ImpUSS factor may correspond to what the 5-factor theorists have called *conscientiousness. Responsibility, scrupulousness,* and *persevering-ness,* which constitute part of this trait, would seem to be the other pole of *lack of socialization* and *impulsivity.* The cluster of *hostility* and *aggressiveness* found in the high N-P quadrant would correspond to the *agreeableness versus hostile* factor in the 5-factor model. *Extraversion* and *emotional stability* factors were found at both the 5- and 3-factor levels.

At the 7-factor level we find narrower factors, which may be useful for separately measuring *sociability, activity, anger, anxiety, autonomy* versus *conformity, impulsivity,* and a narrow kind of aggressive *sensation seeking.* The choice between narrow and broad factors depends on the purposes of assessment. Narrow factors are usually better for prediction (Zuckerman, 1979a), but broader factors are more useful for theoretical conceptualizations because of their greater generality and reliability. Because narrower factors are usually more translatable into behavioral terms, they can make cross-species comparisons easier. *Sociability* and *activity* can be observed in animals, *extraversion* cannot. Animals can be characterized as fearful or anxious but not as neurotic in the usual use of that term. Other species can be assessed for intraspecies aggressiveness but not for psychoticism or psychopathy.

Animal models

Animal models of human psychopathology are increasingly used by biological psychiatrists and psychopharmacologists who are trying to identify the brain systems involved in abnormal behavior and develop drugs to treat such disorders (Hanni & Usdin, 1977). Psychosocial theorists, who attribute disorders to the conflicts unique to the human family system or society, would not be interested in such models. Similarly, those workers who have beliefs that exclude biological considerations from the study of personality would not see the sense in studying consistent individual differences in behavior of species other than human. However, for those who believe that genetic variation and its biological consequences are important sources

A Model for Comparative Study of a Trait

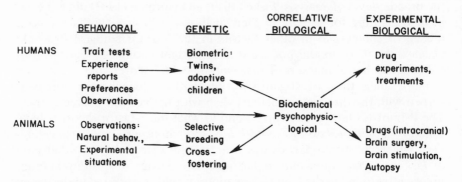

Figure 1.5. A model for a comparative study of a trait in humans and animals using the methods possible for each. (From "Sensation seeking: A comparative approach to a human trait" by M. Zuckerman, 1984, *Behavioral and Brain Sciences*, 7, p. 414. Copyright 1984 by Cambridge University Press.)

of human individual differences, it is essential to have animal models of the dimensions of personality identified in humans.

In a biological approach to personality the independent variables are biological and the dependent variables are behavioral. This means that relevant experimentation must involve alteration of neurological or biochemical systems so that the effects on behavior can be observed. Because this is practically and ethically difficult, most of the research at the human level is essentially correlational. Figure 1.5 shows the parallel methods that can be employed at the human and animal levels.

At the human level, behavior can be directly studied in experimental situations, but when an investigator wants information about behavior across a variety of situations and extensively in time, one must usually rely on self or other ratings, questionnaires, and reports of experience or preferences. In human experiments in which behavior is directly observed, the reactions of subjects can vary with the way the situation is construed rather than with the variables that are manipulated. Instructions and explanations to the subjects are crucial in limiting the range of hypotheses entertained by the subjects. In ambiguous experimental situations such as sensory deprivation, even physiological arousal can be influenced by the expectations created by the instructions and experimental milieu (Zuckerman, Persky, & Link, 1969).

With other animals, one does not have to worry about the effects of verbal instructions. Rats may have expectations, but they are strict behaviorists in that they expect what has happened before to happen again. Human motivations in an experiment are varied and problematical; rats take us more seriously because of the things that we can do to them, like making them extremely hungry or thirsty or administering painful levels of shock. Human motivations and emotional reactions in the usual experimental situation tend to be rather weak. When the experiment does not engage their interest, or if there is insufficient stimulation, they may rapidly lose motivation. On exposure to a novel situation or one that contains appropriate incentives, rats may be fearful or interested, but they are rarely bored.

Experimental genetics, possible only with animals, is the most direct and precise way to determine the extent of genetic control of a biological or behavioral trait. Biometric methods used with humans rely on natural variations of behavior and correlational methods of analysis (chapter 3). The comparison of identical and fraternal twins who are raised together is an attempt to hold the common environment constant while assessing the variation in genetic communality. Studies of separated identical twins provide a straight estimate of heritability. Studies of adopted children are analogous to the cross-fostering methods used with animals. The extent of correlation of traits of adopted children with their biological and adoptive relatives provides a comparison of genetic and environmental influences.

Experimental biological approaches in humans are limited. Although we can sometimes manipulate brain arousal in a gross way by legal drugs such as caffeine, some controlled drugs in medical settings, and manipulation of the experimental situation, these interventions are nonspecific in the systems affected, and the effects are of short duration. If we want to know which brain systems are involved in a behavioral trait, we must use the methods that are possible only with animals: drugs (administered to specific areas intracranially), brain surgery, electrolytic or chemical lesioning, brain stimulation, and autopsy to verify the structures and neurochemical systems affected by the manipulations.

Given the different approaches at the human and animal levels, how can we link data from the two kinds of observations and how do we know that a behavioral trait in humans can be equated with an apparently similar behavior in other species? Every species has behavioral expressions that are like those seen in humans. Primates interact socially by grooming, and who gets groomed is an index of social status. Although human adolescents are sometimes observed combing each others' hair, grooming is not as common a form of human socialization as conversation. The "smile" in other primates is not an expression of positive emotional arousal but of fear. Many mammals indicate territorial claims and defiance of a rival by urinating. Dominance is asserted or aggression expressed by mounting without apparent sexual motive. Ethologists tell us much about the behavioral expressions of a species and the functions they serve. Psychologists sometimes employ responses that are not characteristic of a species and therefore end with an inferior assessment of a class of responses, such as those involved in fear (Bolles, 1970). The defensive reactions of rodents are primarily freezing, fleeing, or fighting, not pressing bars.

As long as our understanding of the links between human and other animal behaviors depends solely on observed similarities of behaviors or their functions, we risk anthropomorphism if we extrapolate from humans to animals and zoomorphism if we generalize from animals to humans. Figure 1.5 suggests another criteria for establishing animal models. If we find that behaviors having the same *functional significance* in humans and animals also have common biological correlates, we are on safer ground for hypothesizing equivalencies. True, the biological bases of behavior have changed during the evolution of complexity. The limbic brain, which largely serves an olfactory function in less complex mammals, is an appetitive-emotional center in humans with input from many sensory systems and higher cortical centers. However, because evolutionary changes are slow and not necessarily comprehensive, it is reasonable to assume that the biological bases of the more basic human traits and emotional expressions have something in common with those of our mammalian cousins, particularly those in our nearest relatives, the primates.

Comparative models are hardly new in psychology. Until about 25 years ago, the theories of learning in academic psychology were based primarily on animal models. With the advent of cognitive psychology, the comparative approach has been used in psychobiology; and questions of perception, learning, and memory (information processing) are approached mostly through human paradigms. Because strong motivation is difficult to create in the laboratory, a great deal of motivational research must still be done using animal models, but few of these models have been addressed to questions of human personality, in which motivational traits play such a large role. Dollard and Miller (1950) applied models of learning, motivation, conflict, and fear developed from animal studies to human personality, with little attention paid to individual differences. The model of fear as a conditioned response, which served as the basic explanation for this important drive, must be questioned for reasons that are given later.

The Pavlovian theory provided the first animal model incorporating individual differences. Although it was initially based on the study of individual dogs, the theory eventually provided a model for human temperament that was based on hypothetical characteristics of the mammalian nervous system (Strelau, 1983). These characteristics were evaluated by conditioning and extinction methods in which the strength of the conditioned stimulus was varied, and conditioned inhibitory stimuli and others were presented to determine the strength of the *excitatory* process, strength of the *inhibitory* process, the *balance* between the characteristic strengths of excitatory and inhibitory processes and the *mobility* of the shift between excitatory and inhibitory processes. Various combinations of these nervous system characteristics produced types. There has been endless debate among Pavlov's followers about the number or types and the characteristics associated with each type (not unlike the debate among Western trait theorists).

Pavlov described four basic types, labeling them with terms originating in the medical classifications of ancient Greece (Strelau, 1983).

1. *Sanguine:* strong and balanced excitatory and inhibitory processes that are mobile (e.g., highly conditionable when adequately stimulated), tends toward drowsiness and sleep when not stimulated or when there is little variation in stimulation. This type resembles Eysenck's stable extravert.
2. *Phlegmatic:* strong and balanced excitatory and inhibitory processes that are not mobile (e.g., positive and negative conditioned reflexes are easily developed and once formed remain stable; they have difficulty in adjusting to changing conditions. The description is like that of the stable introvert in Eysenck's model.
3. *Choleric:* strong excitation, weak inhibition (unbalanced), slow mobility (e.g., forms positive conditioned reflexes easily but develops inhibitory reflexes with difficulty and slowly), may be either aggressive and emotionally undercontrolled or depressive. There is some correspondence to the neurotic extravert or the high-P personality in Eysenck's typology.
4. *Melancholic:* weak excitation and inhibition, conditioned responses develop with difficulty and easily disturbed by distracting or intense stimuli, tend to be maladapted and vulnerable to breakdown under stressful conditions. They clearly correspond to the introverted neurotic type in Eysenck's system.

Although Pavlov and his followers depended largely on conditioning experiments to classify their dogs, they also noted their responses in nonexperimental environments and their reactions to humans. These social reactions were often in marked contrast to the behavior in the conditioning apparatus. The sanguine dogs seemed "bored" by repetitious conditioned stimuli and would go to sleep in the harness, but outside of the laboratory they were active, curious, playful, and friendly in response to humans. The melancholic types, however, were hyperalert and attentive in the experimental chamber but restrained in activity and fearful of humans outside of the laboratory.

The dogs could have been more easily classified by their natural behavior and possibly with greater agreement than by use of the cumbersome and often inconclusive conditioning methods. Pavlovians would engage in debates about the proper classification of individual dogs based on the experimental results as described in the literature. Scott and Fuller (1967) used more natural methods with dogs, assessing behavioral traits such as playful aggressiveness, avoidance, and vocalization in response to handling tests, barking in a dominance situation in which two dogs were allowed to compete for a bone, sexual behavior, and quietness in a weighing situation. Ratings of behavior in these situations showed significant differences between standard breeds of dogs and predictable changes in cross-breeding experiments. Pavlov did not do genetic experiments that could establish the temperamental nature of the experimentally based traits.

Methods of studying animal behavior range from the purely ethological techniques of studying uncontrolled behavior in the natural environment to restricted experimental paradigms such as bar-pressing in an experimental chamber. Between these extremes are methods of studying animals in colonies maintained in the laboratory with more freedom for the animals and the possibility of studying natural social interaction in semicontrolled conditions.

An example of ethological technique is the longitudinal study by Goodall (1986) of chimpanzees in their natural African habitat. Although largely anecdotal, Goodall's careful observations over extended periods of time and in a variety of circumstances clearly show personality differences among the members of the group. She also observed phenomena such as murder, carnivorous behavior, invention of games, and the use of improvised tools. Such behaviors would probably not be observed or even appear in a restricted laboratory environment where observations are made only for brief periods of time in special experimental situations. However, because ethologists avoid intervening in animal interactions, experiments, which might add to our understanding of which variables control behavior, are precluded.

Correlational studies can be performed with minimal intervention in colonies maintained by research groups. In a study to be described in a later chapter, Redmond, Murphy, and Baulu (1979) studied the relationship between the enzyme monoamine oxidase (MAO), obtained from blood platelets, and observed social, dominance, aggressive, and sexual behaviors in monkeys maintained by the National Institute of Mental Health on an island in the Caribbean. Laboratory-maintained colonies can, of course, be used to study the experimental effects of biological interventions. Ellison (1977) constructed a room-sized rat colony that includes burrows for individual rats, a behavioral commons where animals can interact, and a separate feeding area with access limited by a narrow tube that allows only one animal at a time, to study dominance. The room also contains activity wheels, toys, ramps leading to a water tower, climbing structures, and numerous ledges. Although not a natural environment, this laboratory environment provides full opportunities for social interactions and other activities natural to the species. Ellison has used the colony to study the effects of chemical lesioning of neurotransmitter systems (Ellison, 1977) and prolonged infusion of amphetamine on social behavior. Because so much of human personality involves social interactions, it would seem obviously important to incorporate this characteristic in animal models.

Ellison's set-up seems to provide the optimal balance between the need for controlled observation of social behavior and the creation of a semi-natural environment.

Animals that are reared in the restricted cages of the typical laboratory may not exhibit behavior that is at all characteristic of their species, just as the behavior of caged zoo animals is abnormal. Suomi and Harlow (1976) have shown that monkeys reared in total or partial social isolation are abnormally fearful and timid as adults. Sackett (1972) found that monkeys reared in conditions of social and sensory deprivation have an exaggerated fear of novel and complex stimuli, which is not characteristic of feral monkeys or those reared in more stimulating laboratory environments. Rosenzweig, Bennett, Herbert, and Morimoto (1978) demonstrated that enriched laboratory environments, in contrast to impoverished cage habitats, cause differences in brain weight, RNA and DNA content of brain cells, and acetylcholinesterase activities of brain regions. These effects of a restricted inanimate environment were independent of social deprivation. Animal models that use rats reared in unnatural and restricted conditions may be generalizing from atypical members of the species. The equivalent for humans might be using autistic children or schizophrenic adults in personality studies.

A study of factors derived from behavioral observations of rhesus monkeys illustrates the problem of deriving valid traits of behavior from situational tests. Chamove, Eysenck, and Harlow (1972) obtained observations of four monkeys in a cage (group condition). Behavior was observed during at least thirty 60-minute sessions. The monkeys were all familiar with each other and had formed stable relationships. In the stimulus-testing situation the monkeys were suddenly exposed in sequence to an infant monkey, a juvenile male, or an adult male. In one condition the monkeys were exposed to the stranger alone, and in another condition they were in the company of a familiar monkey peer. Three fairly clear factors emerged from the simple group observation over time.

1. A *play* factor consisting of both social and nonsocial play and positive physical contact
2. A *fear* factor consisting of social exploration (watching other monkeys), nonsocial fear or withdrawal, appropriate withdrawal in the face of hostility or inappropriate withdrawal from another animal showing fear, playfulness, or exploratory behavior
3. An *aggression-hostility* factor consisting of hostile contact, such as biting, and noncontact hostility, presumably threat behavior

Eysenck quite naturally relates these three dimensions of monkey behavior to his basic three dimension of personality: *play* = E, *fear* = N, and *aggression* = P. The factors derived from the more complex experimental situations did not show much consistency across the situations.

Apparently, the stable individual differences in the familiar situation could not emerge in response to different stimulus objects, each eliciting a different kind of behavior.

Exposure to a novel situation can elicit fear or investigation, depending on many things including the characteristics of the situation, how the stimulus is presented, and the age and rearing history of the animal. Suomi and Harlow (1976) used mechanical toys, suddenly presented, to elicit strong fear reactions in young monkeys. Novel inanimate and quiet objects rarely caused fearful reactions.

The open-field (OF) test has been widely used as a test of *fearfulness* or *exploratory* tendencies in rodents. It consists of a large circular, square, or rectangular open enclosure. Devices for measuring activity are used, or the number of grids entered, or the degree of penetration to the center of the field are observed. In the evolution of small mammals, open fields have usually been dangerous places where predators from the air or ground can easily spot them. A certain amount of agoraphobia would therefore be likely to be part of the evolved biological makeup of such creatures. However, the need to forage for food requires some adventurousness in investigating new open situations. The typical mouse or rat enters the laboratory OF with some degree of emotional arousal, as commonly indicated by defecation, a sign of autonomic arousal. Activity may at first be limited to the periphery of the arena. With repeated trials there is typically some habituation of emotionality and increase in activity.

Factor analyses of rodent behavior in the OF have consistently yielded three factors (Royce, 1977): (1) activity (movement, latency to move, penetration to the center of the fields); (2) emotional reactivity or fearfulness (defecation); and (3) territorial marking (urination), interpreted by Royce as a measure of aggressiveness or social domination. The activity in the OF does not correlate with measures of general activity in the home cage and for this reason has been regarded as a measure of explorativeness rather than general activity. Activity in the OF has been considered as a possible model for sensation seeking (Zuckerman, 1984a) but was rejected because of the negative correlation usually found between activity and defecation at both the phenotypical and genotypical levels. As discussed in chapter 3, breeding mice for either activity or emotionality usually results in a correlated difference in the other trait. However, Garcia-Sevilla (1984) created a "low frightening" OF by reducing the white noise level (78 dB) of the Broadhurst (1957) OF to the level provided by the hum of an air-conditioner and thus eliminated the negative correlation usually found between activity and defecation. Goma and Tobeña (1985) showed that defecation was less in the open field at this background noise intensity than at the original 78-dB level. Garcia-Sevilla has offered this OF as an animal model for the human trait of extraversion. He has supported this claim with verified predictions from Eysenck's earlier theories relating E to strong inhibitory tendencies and therefore more rapid extinction of conditioned responses when trials are massed. Despite the amassing of data from a variety of techniques, the primary correlates of OF ambulation consist of ambulation in other situations such as the Planche a trous and Y-maze, alternation behavior in a light–dark shuttle box, and an aversive threshold test. These measures actually defined an E factor better than the OF ambulation measures.

Simmel (1984) and Simmel and Bagwell (1983) have argued that activity in the OF is not a measure of response to novelty or sensation seeking. They developed an apparatus that separates response to novelty from activity. The arena is divided into two parts: The walls in one half have black and white striped and checkerboard patterns, and the other half has homogeneous walls. One response factor consists of latency of the first cross to the novel side and time spent on that side of the arena. The other factor consists of number of shuttle box crossings and gross locomotor activity. Strains of mice that are high on *activity* are low on *novelty seeking* and vice versa. However, crossings from the plain to the novel side, a measure of alternation behavior, correlated with both factors. Perhaps changeability rather than preference for a novel situation is most characteristic of OF active rodents. Restlessness and need for change represent one type of sensation seeking (*boredom susceptibility*), which had the highest loading on the P factor in the Zuckerman et al. (1988) study described earlier in the chapter. Could it be that OF ambulation is more related to the Eysenck P factor than the E factor? The C57BL strain of mouse, which is the most active one in the OF test, is also the most aggressive (Ginsburg and Allee, 1942), and aggression is a likely candidate for the expression of P at the animal level. The core of the E factor is *sociability,* even though *activity* has a secondary loading on the supertrait. Unfortunately, none of the Garcia-Sevilla studies have related OF activity to *sociability* as might be judged in a controlled colony environment.

Ellison (1977) lesioned two different monoamine systems in rats and observed behaviors in the familiar colony environment and in the novel OF environment. The behaviors of the two groups were both diametrically opposite in the two situations: The group that was active and sociable in the colony environment was fearful and immobile in the OF; the group that was unsociable in the colony was fearless and active in the OF. Although these results may be peculiar to the operations performed on the rats, they do suggest that there is no necessary relationship between activity in the OF and *sociability;* if this is true of nonlesioned rats, then OF activity may not be a good model for E because *sociability* is central to the E factor in humans.

What about defecation in the OF as a measure of emotionality or, more precisely, fearfulness? Royce (1977) has found that this measure loads highly on a factor that includes measures of behavioral inhibition. In the

Garcia-Sevilla (1984) studies, the defecation in the OF had a low positive loading on a factor defined primarily by pain threshold and tolerance and some of the ambulation measures that loaded on both factors. The actual correlations between OF defecation and other variables were quite low (none exceeded .25), suggesting little breadth to this measure beyond defecation as a response in itself. Another curious thing is that male rats and mice show more OF defecation and less OF ambulation (Gray, 1979) than female rodents, a reversal of the direction of sex differences found in humans, in whom females are higher on *emotionality* and males are higher on *sensation seeking* and *psychopathy*. Gray reports other sex differences in rats that suggest that the male rat's greater emotionality is not limited to the OF situation.

There is one respect in which most animal models of emotionality fail to mirror an essential distinction in human anxiety. Human fears can be empirically classified into several categories, including fears of physical harm from various sources and social fears. It is the social fears and inhibitions that constitute the core of human neuroticism. Most animal models place the animal in a situation where there is a real danger, usually of getting shocked, or a "biologically prepared" fear such as the OF for rodents. One notable exception is the File and Hyde (1978) model, which uses the uncertainty produced by unfamiliar surroundings to measure the effect on social inhibition. Social contact with another rat is measured under four conditions ranging from a familiar environment to a maximally unfamiliar one. Previous experience in the environment and lighting conditions are varied over the four conditions to increase unfamiliarity and anxiety. During the test trials, objects are hung on the walls to measure nonsocial investigation as well as social behavior. Social contacts decrease linearly over the four degrees of increasing unfamiliarity. Antianxiety drugs and alcohol reduce the effects of unfamiliarity on social interaction (File, Hyde & Pool, 1976).

This seemingly relevant model can be contrasted with the more widely employed Geller and Seifter (1960) model for anxiety, which provides a more quantitative method of assessing anxiety as a fluctuating state that affects ongoing behavior. Animals are trained in a Skinner box on a schedule that alternates punishment and unpunished segments. Lever pressing is maintained by variable interval positive reinforcement such as food. In the punishment periods, a response results in both punishment (shock) and reward. Like the conditioned emotional response model (Estes and Skinner, 1941) it equates anxiety with conditioned-response suppression by stimuli associated with pain. The model incorporates the conflict aspect of human neurotic anxiety but assumes that the source of the conflict is irrelevant. Most human anxiety cannot be traced to situations involving pain conditioning, and most human conflict is not between fear of pain and hunger. Although this model has been extremely useful in the study of drug effects, showing that all of the widely used tranquillizers increase the rate of punishment suppressed responding, its relevance to human anxiety is questionable at the theoretical level.

Assuming that the main effect of anxiety is the activation of a "behavioral inhibition system," Gray (1982) used a variety of experimental paradigms to investigate the basic neurophysiology of anxiety. These include shuttle-box avoidance learning, the Sidman avoidance paradigm, measures of passive avoidance, and measures of insensitivity to signals of nonreward. The orienting reflex (OR) is also included among anxiety measures because it involves an interruption of ongoing behavior produced by a signal. The fact is that the OR, as assessed by the rearing response in rodents, is usually associated with subsequent activity and exploration rather than freezing. In fact, Goma and Tobeña (1985) have suggested that rearings in a specially designed rearing cage are a better measure of exploratory activity than OF activity. Human ORs are differentiated from defensive and startle reflexes (DRs and SRs) by the pattern of physiological responsivity to stimuli (Graham, 1979). ORs tend to be weakened by anxiety and DRs and SRs are potentiated by anxiety (see chapter 6). Even Gray does not claim that all interruptions of ongoing behavior are caused by signals of punishment or nonreward. Attention may be engaged by signals of potential reward as well as by signals of punishment, and the OR is a sign of a shift in attention to an external stimulus that has "biological significance."

Another problem with conflict models is that a lack of inhibition may be related to the approach motive as well as to the avoidance motive. This could link disinhibition in a conflict situation to the *impulsivity* or P dimension of personality as much as to the *anxiety* or N dimension. Gray (1981) has suggested that an important dimension of personality may run from *anxiety* at one pole to *venturesomeness* (sensation seeking) at the opposite pole. Thus, a psychopath would be characterized by an abnormal absence of anxiety and the tendency to take risks. But the absence of anxiety alone does not explain sensation seeking or psychopathic behavior (chapter 9). Sensation seeking as a trait is uncorrelated with *neuroticism* or *anxiety,* which means that an equal number of extreme sensation seekers are low and high on *anxiety,* at least the social kind of anxiety that is involved in the N dimension (Zuckerman, 1979).

Both Eysenck and Gray have suggested that aggressiveness in animals is the primary expression of the P dimension in animals, although studies show that other traits such as *impulsivity* and *sensation seeking* are involved in that dimension in humans. Aggression has been studied in animals, and intraspecies aggressiveness seems to constitute a dimension of personality (Chamove et al., 1972). Aggressiveness against other species, such as mouse killing in rats and rat killing in cats, has been used as an index of this trait. However, predatory aggression and intraspecies or "defensive" aggression seem to constitute two different traits in animals. Hunting other species by animals or humans does not require anger or even strong emotional arousal. However, a person who can kill fellow humans without strong emotional arousal is regarded as psychopathic (or patriotic if he is a soldier in war). Nonlethal intraspecies aggression is quite common in response to intrusion of strangers, competition over mates, nests, or territory, and ordinary dominance conflicts. Testing aggressiveness in contrived laboratory situations is more difficult. Presenting an animal suddenly with a strange member of the species, infliction of pain, and raising animals in isolation are methods that have been used to stimulate aggressive behavior. Attack behavior in such conditions is more characteristic of some strains of rodents than others (chapter 3) and can be made more likely by certain neurochemical changes in animals (chapter 4).

Most of the animal models discussed have certain limitations as models for human personality. To select animal models, one must consider the situations in which the response usually occurs, the typical natural behaviors of the species and their functional significances, and, ultimately, the underlying biological mechanisms. The use of animal models implies an evolutionary view of basic personality traits in humans. However, speculation about the adaptive values of these traits during the millions of years they have been evolving in our hominid ancestors is pointless unless we understand the biological mechanisms that are *currently* mediating them. One can find an adaptive value for any extreme of a trait on a post hoc basis. Unfortunately, these hypotheses cannot be tested in the laboratory; natural selection cannot be tested in the laboratory, but artificial selection can be used and that is one of the subjects of chapter 3. Situations used in behavioral breeding studies must employ appropriate animal models for any cross-species generalizations.

Summary

All sciences require some kind of classification of the basic phenomena of study. In the case of personality psychology the basic unit would be the trait, conceived of as a group of related habits. Habits consist of consistent behaviors in specific situations. Types are conceived of as extremes on dimensions of supertraits; supertraits are correlated groups of narrower traits. Unlike older concepts of types, these are now conceived of as continuous dimensions of broad and basic personality traits rather than unique constellations of traits that are discontinuous.

Although distinctions have been drawn between temperaments and dimensions of personality, such as style versus content or direction of response, such distinctions may not be valid because all traits are defined in terms of situationally delimited areas of behavior. The term *basic dimensions of personality* is suggested to refer to supertraits that have internal reliability and can be identified in terms of their constituent traits across methods, genders, and cultures. Supertraits should be identifiable in childhood but not necessarily in infancy. Basic personality traits should show consistency over time; but because the phenotype and environment interact throughout life, one would not expect perfect or even near perfect consistency over long periods of time. From a psychobiological viewpoint there are several more expectations concerning basic personality traits. They should be identifiable in species other than the human on the assumption that they have been shaped by natural selection. They should show at least moderate heritability and be related to significant biological markers. Eventually, their biological basis in the structure and physiology of the nervous system should be identifiable, though classification is a necessary first step in discovering biological bases of traits.

The system developed by Thomas and Chess for classifying temperament traits was developed too narrowly around the limited kinds of behaviors that could be observed in infants. For this reason the system does not have an adequate representation for the important dimension of *sociability*, and the important rating for the *emotionality* dimension is unreliable. The system developed by Buss and Plomin is broader, including *emotionality*, *activity*, *sociability*, and *impulsivity* in the first version. Later they decided that *impulsivity* did not qualify as a basic dimension of temperament and excluded it. However, this left no representative trait for the socialization dimension of personality (P in Eysenck's system). Eysenck's 3-superfactor model, which includes *extraversion (sociability)*, *neuroticism (emotionality)*, and *psychoticism (asocial tendencies)*, has shown remarkable stability across methods and populations. The more recent introduction of the P dimension into the basic questionnaire method has caused some perturbations in the older system. The E dimension, for instance, no longer seems to contain *sociability* plus *impulsivity; impulsivity* has now become a more basic part of the P dimension. Many questions have been asked about the Eysencks' concept of what the P dimension measures and the psychometric accuracy of the scale developed to measure it.

Strelau's neo-Pavlovian 3-factor model of temperament represents a different kind of approach to classification, based on hypothetical qualities of nervous system functioning: *strength of excitation, strength of inhibition,* and *mobility* (from excitation to inhibition or vice versa). Rusalov developed a model for temperament based on four stages of information processing and object (work) and social expressions for each stage. Both of these investigators have developed questionnaires to assess their temperament types in humans.

Since 1949 a 5-factor model of personality, based largely on personality ratings rather than questionnaire measurement, has shown remarkable durability. The five factors – *extraversion, neuroticism, agreeableness* (vs. hostility), *conscientiousness,* and *culture* (or *intellectance* or *openness to ex-*

perience) – have been found in many studies using ratings. However, unlike Eysenck's 3-factor model, little theory or research has been generated by this model.

Zuckerman et al. (1988) did factor analyses of 46 personality scales comparing 7-, 5- and 3-factor solutions, and factors were traced through the levels using factor score correlations. At the broad trait level, *activity* and *sociability* merged into the supertrait of E; *anxiety, hostility,* and *neuroticism* merged into N; and *impulsivity, lack of socialization, sensation seeking,* and *aggression* combined to form P. The three supertraits showed excellent convergent and discriminant validity in replication across gender. Some of the narrower traits could be replicated across gender, but few showed much discriminant validity.

Animal models are needed to establish biological bases of personality because they make possible a biological experimental approach that would be difficult or impossible with humans. There is a problem in establishing the equivalence of human and animal behavior because every species has its own characteristic responses. However, it is suggested that behaviors that have the same functional significance and biological correlates across species are good candidates for models.

The Pavlovian model was originally based on conditioning studies of dogs. The variables derived from these studies are taken as surrogates of constructs representing hypothetical qualities of the nervous system. Ethological studies observe natural behavior occurring in natural settings. Although instances of behavior are observed that might elude observers in laboratory settings, the approach is limited by the ethologists' stricture against intervention and experimentation. Animal colonies in more controlled field or laboratory seminatural settings allow correlational and experimental studies while preserving the animals' natural social reactions. Special kinds of laboratory apparatus mimic situations encountered by animals in natural habitats. The open-field (OF) test has been used to test either *emotionality* (defecation) or *exploration* (activity), or both. Which of these tendencies is predominant depends on characteristics of the experimental set-up as well as those of the animal. Increasing background noise or brightness of light makes the situation more arousing. In a low-arousing situation, *activity* in the OF has been proposed as an animal model for *extraversion*. The question has been asked of whether the OF might be a better model for the P dimension in view of its association with *aggressiveness, sensation seeking,* and *impulsivity*.

Factor analyses of seminatural behaviors of monkeys have yielded factors resembling E, N, and P: *play* with E, *fearful withdrawal* with N, and *aggression* with P. Factor analyses of rodent behavior have yielded activity, defecation, and urination–territory-marking factors, which some investigators have identified with E, N, and P. However, intraspecies aggression would seem to provide a more reasonable model for the P dimension, and

measures of social inhibition in unfamiliar situations or inhibition of behavior in threatening situations might provide a better model for the N
dimension. One problem with animal models of fear is that the neurotic
kind of fear in humans concerns social threat rather than threat of physical
punishment (pain). The two kinds of fear are not highly correlated. Most
animal models use physical threat based on pain conditioning, conflict
between pain threat and hunger, or the fear of extreme novelty or open
spaces. In animal colonies fear is often observed as a response to threat
from another animal, a situation more like those eliciting human fear.

Animals who are frightened tend to freeze as the initial fear reaction.
Some animal models for fear use the interruption of ongoing behavior as
an index of anxiety. However, attention may also involve momentary interruptions of behavior, as in the orienting reflex, and should not be con-
fused with fearfulness. In fact, orienting is most often followed by approach
and is positively related to activity in the open field.

Although the problems of extrapolating from animal to human behavior
are acknowledged, it is suggested that some of the animal models, particularly those that study natural social behaviors in seminatural environments, may be useful for investigating the biological bases of human
personality.

2   Consistency of personality

Overview

In chapter 1, traits were defined as "correlated habits of reaction," including cognitive and affective reactions as well as overt behavior in the term *habit*. Because *habit* implies some consistency of behavior over time and situations, varying to some degree in particulars, the idea of a trait also implies a degree of consistency. This concept of a trait also suggests an aggregation of relevant behaviors in relevant situations over a number of time samples, rather than a single kind of behavior in one specific situation at one particular instant. More than one item is usually used in a trait questionnaire, not only to increase the reliability of the measure but also to sample reports of the theoretically relevant kinds of behaviors, attitudes, and feelings. When a single self- or peer-rating trait item is used, a subjective aggregation process is assumed. When people are asked to indicate their position on a self-rating scale of dominance–submission, they must consider their general tendency to dominate or submit as indicated by various kinds of behavior (such as yielding a position in an argument or conforming to the wishes of another person), in response to various persons (but particularly peers rather than authorities, younger or lower status persons), in certain kinds of situations (particularly those in which their beliefs or wishes are in opposition to those of others), and over some extended period of time (not the last day or even the last week, if those aggregates of instances are not typical). But until recently the responses and situations assumed to be intrinsic to the trait have not been systematically sampled in the trait measurements. Tests have been developed that do vary response and/or situation in a systematic fashion (e.g., Endler, Hunt, & Rosenstein, 1962; Endler & Okada, 1975; Zuckerman, 1977), and such tests indicate that subjects' situations and responses, and their interactions with overall trait differences often contribute significant variance to test responses (Zuckerman & Mellstrom, 1977). But the concept of consistency has become a central issue in a much broader debate about the proper paradigm for personality study that goes beyond the narrow confines of the trait questionnaire.

As Cronbach (1957) pointed out, there are two disciplines of scientific psychology, the individual differences and the experimental approaches. The traditional trait approach involves evaluations of general behaviors in the natural environment over relatively long periods of time. The tradi-

44

tional experimental approach studies specific behaviors in controlled laboratory situations on only one occasion. Quite naturally, the trait approach paid little attention to the specifics of behavior and its situational determinants, and the experimental approach ignored the questions of reliability and generality of behavior across situations. Cronbach pleaded for a combined approach that would study individual differences as moderators of response in specific situations. During the 1960s there was an increase in studies in which personality measures were used to predict responses to standard laboratory situations, often with disappointing results. But the era of rapprochement, such as it was, ended with the paradigm challenge by Mischel (1968).

Mischel acknowledged the consistency of measured traits over time (classical reliability) and some fair degree of correlation between self-report trait measures and evaluation of traits by others, but he questioned whether there was much evidence for consistency of relevant behavior over situations or prediction of behavior in situations using traditional trait measures. After reviewing many studies, he concluded that such consistencies of trait-relevant behavior across situations rarely exceeded a correlation of .30. Because the existence of broad traits was assumed by lay persons as well as personality psychologists, it was concluded that consistency of behavior across situations was an illusion fostered by the similar appearances of persons and beliefs of observers. The social-learning approach of Mischel suggested a kind of uniqueness of the individual due to specific cognitive mechanisms learned in specific and sometimes unique circumstances. If social behavior is determined primarily by situations and narrow learned habits, what is the "person" in personality study? Is there a need for a discipline of personality psychology, as distinct from that of social psychology?

In the 1970s, personality psychologists chose sides, a great amount of research was done, and some interesting intermediate positions emerged. More research was done on behavior or reports of behavior at different times in natural environmental situations. In 1975 a conference was held in Sweden at which many of the antagonists presented their positions. Magnusson and Endler (1977) titled the book of conference papers: *Personality at the Crossroads*. It was apparent that a kind of person-situation interactional consensus was reached at the conference. The issue was not whether there was consistency in personality, but what kinds of behaviors or cognitions were consistent, in what kinds of persons, and was such consistency better assessed by nomothetic or idiodynamic methods? Solutions to the paradox of perceived trait consistency in spite of behavior inconsistency are described in this chapter. But first let us consider some of the conceptual and methodological distinctions that must be made between and within the classifications: traits, states, situations, and behavior.

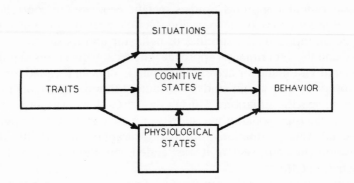

Figure 2.1. A model for the relationships among traits, states, situations, and overt behavior.

Traits, states, situations, and behavior

Figure 2.1 shows a model for the relationships among traits, states, situations, and overt behavior. As indicated by the arrows, traits influence some kinds of situations as well as the states which are influenced by both the traits and the situations. Traits are involved in the choice of situations as well as the responses to them.

Traits

Traits can be defined in two ways: (1) as systems or dispositions in persons that predispose them to perceive situations in particular ways and to react in a consistent manner across situations as perceived (Allport, 1937) and (2) as a summary of the frequency and intensity of past reactions (both covert state and overt behavioral ones) to situations (Spielberger, 1966; Zuckerman, 1976, 1977, 1979a; Zuckerman, Persky, Eckman, & Hopkins 1967). The first definition views traits as dynamic causal agents, whether their sources are biological or cognitive structures. The second definition is more operational, describing the usual objective methods of assessing traits. In this latter sense the trait is a construct, construed by psychologists (nomothetic), by the individual subjects of study (idiodynamic), or by both (as hoped by nomothetic psychologists), which is used to classify instances of past behavior-in-situations. Broad trait measures like those described by adjectives used in self-ratings are subcategories of a self-concept that helps individuals predict or anticipate their own future reactions in certain categories of situations. It may be, as suggested by situationists, that persons exaggerate their behavioral consistency in these self-characterizations, but the fact that they do make trait attributions about themselves and others, with or without the assistance of psychologists, suggests that their estimates may have some basis in their actual reactions to past situations.

States

States are a person's self-perceived affects, impulses, and physiology for a short period of time ranging from a given instant to as long as a day. Research suggests that any self-evaluations that go back before the current day tend to show more characteristics of trait than state measures. Although both traits and states are types of constructs, states are more transient, less reliable from day to day, and more reactive to immediate situations (Zuckerman, 1976). In fact, these are the characteristics that differentiate state from trait measurements, apart from the actual temporal instructions given to the subjects and the wording of the items (Zuckerman, 1983a). States can be regarded as dependent variables, but because they often reflect the immediate impact of situation on person, they are more likely to be related to subsequent behavior than traits are (Zuckerman, 1977, 1979a). However, states must be distinguished from overt behavior in situations. Overt behavior is more constrained by anticipated consequences than covert behavior. In a frustrating interaction with an authority figure, one may feel angry and physically aroused and be aware of an impulse to act aggressively, but overt behavior may not reflect any of these covert responses because of anticipated consequences.

Situations

In an experimental study, situations are imposed on the subjects. Subjects are free to interpret the situation as they wish, but instructions usually attempt to minimize the ambiguity of the situation and variety of interpretation. Personality differences are more predictive of differences in behavior when the situation and socially demanded response are less obvious. We would not expect much variation in drivers' responses to a red traffic light (except in New York City), though there might be some differences in when the brakes are applied. However, a yellow traffic light poses a more ambiguous situation. To the more impulsive driver the yellow light is a signal to press down on the accelerator, whereas to the more constrained person it is a signal to start applying the brakes.

In the natural environment, investigators choose some situations and others are imposed; some situations are relatively novel and others routine. Personality would be expected to play a role in situations that we choose but not in situations that are imposed. Personality plays a role in novel situations in which outcomes are not well known but is less likely to be a strong influence in routine situations in which expectations are common to all. Unless distinctions are made among types of situations, little generalization should be made about the role of situation relative to that of personality in determining behavior.

Predicting behavior in situations can be enhanced by constructing the trait measure to incorporate the situation itself. Although such tailoring of the trait measure to the specifics of a situation may enhance predictive validity for *that* situation, it may reduce the applicability of the instrument to other situations.

Behavior

The distinction has been made between states, which have an internal referent, and behavior, which is overt. If behavior is observed, some estimate must be made of the reliability of observers making independent judgments. Often, more than one type of behavior is considered relevant to the trait being studied. Some of the variations in results may be a function of the behaviors studied and their consistency. If only one kind of behavior is studied, how do we know that it is a representative measure of the trait we hope to assess? Behaviors are often chosen as trait expressions on the basis of a kind of "face validity". Face validity is the same as faith validity. It is not acceptable for personality tests (except by some projective testers) and should not be for behavioral definitions of traits either. One of the basic issues raised by Mischel is the generality of behaviors across situations, as opposed to the reliability of traits or states. Are there really *correlated habits of reaction* forming the basis of traits? Mischel (1968, 1981) argues that consistency of behavior is overestimated by classical trait theory.

Although it is relatively simple to study some kinds of behavior in the laboratory, studies of behavior in natural circumstances are more difficult. It is a rare experiment that assigns observers to every subject to follow them about their daily activities. Methods have been devised to obtain self-reports of activities during a day, and a few studies have used beeper devices to obtain descriptions of subjects' activities at randomly sampled points in time during the day. Can such reports be accepted as behavior? The answer depends on the methodology and the kinds of checks on compliance and memory.

Analysis of variance approach to interactionism

Linear regression models do not lend themselves to the study of interactions among independent variables. Perhaps this is why the analysis of variance (ANOVA) approach to estimating the effect of persons, responses, and situations on behavior had an initial appeal to those engaged in the great debate between situationists and personologists. The omega-squared ratio, derived from the ANOVA, can be used to estimate the proportion of variance explained by each source of variance in an ANOVA. Most of this research has involved anxiety or hostility responses to hypothetical situa-

Table 2.1. *Percentages of variance accounted for by different sources of variance in self-report measures of affect and behavior*

Source of variance	Affects				Behaviors		
	Anxiety	Dep.	Vigor	Pleasant.	Partic.	Affil.	Leadership
Persons (P)	25	27	25	13	5	18	12
Situations (S)	7	0	5	2	11	5	1
Responses (R)	6	0	2	13	0	0	1
P × S	21	29	29	15	20	9	24
P × R	8	4	5	7	19	16	10
S × R	1	1	2	4	4	2	2
Residual (P × S × R)	31	39	32	47	42	51	50

Source: Moos (1969); table 1, p. 408, first set of observations. Copyright 1969 by American Psychological Association. Adapted by author's permission.

tions (Endler & Hunt, 1966, 1968, 1969; Endler et al., 1962; Endler & Okada, 1975). More rarely, the model has been applied to either state reactions or overt behaviors in real situations.

Moos (1969) studied the responses of 16 patients who were observed and who self-reported their reactions to six hospital situations: an intake or discharge meeting, an individual therapy session, a group therapy session, a community meeting, lunch in the dining room, and free time on the ward. The self-report reactions contained four measures of affective response and three reports of self-behavior. Each of these categories contained a number of adjectives describing affect or behavior; these are listed in Table 2.1 as the response dimension in each category of response. The results show that persons accounted for considerably greater portions of the total variance than situations, for every variable except reported participation. Apparently, there were reliable differences among the patients in self-reported reactions across all situations, but little difference that was due simply to the differences among situations. However, the person by situation source of variance also accounted for a significant portion of the variance that was generally equal to that accounted for by differences among persons alone. The interactions indicate that some of the differences among persons varied as a function of the situations to which they were exposed.

The results for *observed behaviors* are listed in Table 2.2. Persons accounted for more variance than situations for all body movement variables, smiling, and smoking, but situations determined more variance for nodding yes and talking. It is not difficult to understand why communication would vary among situations that involved various numbers of persons other than the patient. The person versus situation interaction was also a major source of variation for almost every variable.

Table 2.2. *Percentages of variance accounted for by different sources of variance in observed behaviors*

Sources of variance	Hand & arm movements	Foot & leg movements	Scratch & rub	Gen. move.	Nod yes	Smile	Talk	Smoke
Persons (P)	17	27	31	17	4	35	11	42
Situations (S)	12	10	13	1	43	4	68	7
P × S	32	27	25	47	34	35	14	21
Within	39	36	32	34	19	26	7	30

Source: Moos, (1969); table 3, p. 409, first observations. Copyright 1969 by American Psychological Association. Adapted by author's permission.

Besides supporting person-situation interaction as a major source of behavior and affective states, Moos' results suggest that the person is an important part of the equation. If individual differences were not reliable across situations then only person-situation interactions or situations would contribute to the variance. However, there is evidence from earlier studies by Moos (1968) and later studies by Endler and Okada (1975) that reactions may be less differentiated by situation in patients than in normals.

The ANOVA method was applied to different kinds of anxiety responses in a self-report state test given to normal subjects just before exposure to potentially anxiety-provoking situations (Mellstrom et al., 1976; Mellstrom, Zuckerman, & Cicala, 1978). In the first experiment (Mellstrom et al., 1976) all subjects were exposed to a snake, an open high place, and a dark room on three different occasions. In the second experiment (Mellstrom et al., 1978) another group of subjects was confronted while being observed with a different set of situations: a rat, a test, and an interview. The responses consisted of three ratings from the Zuckerman (1977) Inventory of Personal Reactions, state version ("My heart is beating faster," "I feel fearful," and "I want to avoid or get out of the situation"). The results in terms of proportions of variance accounted for by the sources of variance in the experiment are shown in Table 2.3.

Persons accounted for almost the same percentage of variance in both studies (28–29%), and *persons × situations* interactions accounted for another significant portion of the variance (22–23%). The percentages of variance accounted for by these two sources of variance are very close to those reported for anxiety reactions in the Moos (1969) study previously described: *persons* = 25%; *persons × situations* = 21%. The results for the *situations* factor in the studies were less consistent. In the Mellstrom et al. (1976) study *situations* accounted for 21% of the variance, due largely to the greater fear elicited by the anticipation of the snake exposure in contrast to the other situations. But in the Mellstrom et al. (1978) study,

Table 2.3. *Percentages of total variations by sources in experimental fear situations*

	Mellstrom et al. 1976[a]	Mellstrom et al. 1978[b]
Persons (P)	28	29
Situations (S)	21	1
Responses (R)	1	6
P × S	23	22
P × R	10	12
S × R	1	1
Residual	17	31

[a]Situations: exposures to snake, heights, darkness
[b]Situations: exposures to rat, "intelligence test," interview
Source: Mellstrom et al. (1976, 1978). Copyright 1976, 1978 by American Psychological Association.

all three situations elicited an equal amount of fear, and therefore *situations* accounted for less than 1% of the variance. These results illustrate one of the problems with the ANOVA approach and why one should not make general statements about the relative importance of *persons* and *situations*. The proportions of variance may depend entirely on the range of *situations* or *persons* used in the study. If the situations are very different in the responses they elicit, then *situations* will seem to be important in behavior. Similarly, if we use a wide range of persons, the same kind of bias could occur. If, for instance, we had used a number of clinically anxious persons in the Mellstrom et al. studies, the *person* factor would have accounted for even more variance than it did. Still, the fact that the variance accounted for in anxiety reactions was similar for both *persons* and *persons* × *situations* in the patient population in the Moos (1969) study and the unselected normals in the Mellstrom et al. (1976; 1978) studies suggests that consistent individual differences in anxiety are not entirely a function of the populations used.

Consistency between self-descriptive questionnaires and ratings by others

The capacity to see ourselves as others see us is not a given, and it is not surprising to find marked discrepancies between self-descriptions and descriptions by others. Discrepancies between the private and public personality can be caused by defensiveness or lack of insight. Both a person and a peer may see a similar kind of behavior but construe it differently. In a study by Black (1953), female college students who scored highest on the Hypomania scale of the MMPI agreed with their peers that they were *energetic* and *enterprising* but disagreed with their peers in almost all other evaluations. They saw themselves as *self-confident* whereas their peers saw them as *boastful*. They saw themselves as *popular, self-controlled, peace-able, independent,* and *adaptable;* their peers saw them as *not popular, not self-controlled, not peaceable, not loyal,* and *inflexible.* They saw themselves as *unconventional,* and their peers described them as *immature.* Occasionally, there is a hint of insight in their description of themselves as *not reliable.* Their peers put it a little more negatively: *not honest.*

Considering these possibilities for inconsistency in self- and other evaluation, the degree of consistency that can be achieved with well-designed questionnaires and ratings of traits by others is impressive. Table 2.4 lists some findings using the Jackson (1967) Personality Research Form, the Jackson (1976) Personality Inventory, and the NEO Personality Inventory (Costa & McCrae, 1985). The peer-rating studies cited are those using multiple judges because correlations between self-report measures and peer ratings increase as a function of the number of judges employed and the use of only one or two judges does not yield data that reflect the potential consistency between self and observer (Rushton, Jackson, & Paunonen, 1981). The median correlations for the four categories of traits range from .45 to .48, and some correlations reach .70. Three-quarters of the correlations are between .30 and .59. Ninety-three percent of the correlations are equal to or higher than .30, 73% are over .40, 41% are higher than .50, and 18% exceed .60. Ninety-eight percent of the correlations are significant below the .05 level, 89% below the .01 level, and 75% are significant below the .001 level of confidence. Given the limitation on validity set by the reliability of the measures involved, particularly the ratings by others, the degree of consistency between trait judgment by others and well-designed trait scales is impressive. Generalizations about consistency are often made on the basis of ad hoc measures with little attention given to their internal reliability or validity.

Bem and Allen (1974) suggest that inconsistency in expressions of the trait is a major source of discrepancy between self-evaluation and evaluations by others. Self-reports were compared with ratings from mothers, fathers, and peers, and with behavioral measures obtained in certain situations. Two traits were studied: friendliness and conscientiousness. The subjects rated their own consistency "from one situation to another" on both traits, and these self-ratings were used to classify subjects into consistent and inconsistent groups for each trait.

Comparisons of correlations among the various sources of trait assessment were generally higher for those subjects who said they were consistent than for those who admitted that they were inconsistent. Mean correlations among all variables for friendliness were .57 for the consistent and .27 for the inconsistent subjects. For conscientiousness the mean correlations were

Table 2.4. *Correlations between questionnaire measured traits and ratings by others*

Scale	Author(s) (date)	Rates	Scale types							
			Extraversion	r	Neuroticism	r	P-type scales	r	Others	r
NEO	Costa & McRae (1985)	Peer[a]	Extrav.	.47	Neurot.	.42	Conscientious	.43	Openness	.57
		Spouse[b]	Extrav.	.72	Neurot.	.47	Agreeableness	.30	Openness	.60
		Spouse[c]	Extrav.	.46	Neurot.	.56			Openness	.45
JPI	Jackson (1976)	Peer[d]	Social Part	.47	Anxiety	.43	Responsibil.	.46	Value or.	.57
			Self esteem	.66	Inter. Affect.	.32	Risk taking	.52	Innovation	.37
			Energy	.47			Conformity	.38	Complex.	.37
									Interests	.43
PRF	Jackson (1967)	Peer[e]	Affiliation	.43	Deference	.57	Autonomy	.54	Achieve.	.52
			Dominance	.69	Succorance	.59	Aggression	.66	Nurtur.	.34
			Exhibition.	.71	Abasement	.17	Harm-avoid.	.60	Endurance	.52
			Play	.48			Impulsivity	.34	Sentience	.10
								Order	.63	Understa.	.50
								Cog. structure	.35	Social rec.	.47
								Change	.28		
Median r				.48		.45		.45		.45
Range r				(.43–.72)		(.17–.59)		(.30–.66)		(.34–.60)

[a]Subjects = 255–267 men and women
[b]Subjects = 139 men rated by their spouses
[c]Subjects = 142 women rated by their spouses
[d]Subjects = 51 men and women college students
[e]Subjects = 70 men and women college students

.36 for the consistents and .12 for the inconsistents. Mean correlations between Eysenck's Extraversion scale (Eysenck & Eysenck, 1964) and other sources of trait assessment was .51 for those describing themselves as consistent on friendliness compared with .31 for inconsistent subjects.

Bem and Allen maintain that only some people are consistent on some traits, particularly those traits that are salient and predictive for themselves. Both these authors and Mischel argue that an idiodynamic approach is necessary to identify the traits that are relevant for particular individuals. However, the correlations that Bem and Allen report for their consistent subjects only, are typical for all subjects using the well-designed nomethetic questionnaires listed in Table 2.4. The fault may not be the inconsistency of subjects but the adequacy of the instruments (often one-item rating scales) used for self and other evaluation and the arbitrary behavioral definitions in other methods. Another problem is that self-rated consistency may be confounded with level of the trait. When people say that they are inconsistent on a trait they are likely to endorse some of the items and not endorse others in a trait questionnaire measure. If we select only those who say they are consistent, we are likely to be selecting a group of extreme lows and highs on the trait; leaving the inconsistents in a narrow range of variability about the mean. Predictions are likely to be better for the consistents than for the inconsistents simply because they are more extreme on the trait.

In a sense, Bem and Allen are telling us nothing new: A single average score on a nomethetic trait test offers little predictability because on this trait the person is like most other persons and responses are likely to vary primarily as a function of the specifics of the situation or transient motive states. However, a profile of scores on a multitrait test indicates which traits are salient (deviant from the norm) for a given individual without the need to devise an individualized idiodynamic assessment for every subject.

Consistency of personality traits over time

Intrinsic to the idea of temperament, or inherited dispositions, is the assumption that there should be some consistency in these dispositions from infancy to childhood, adolescence, and adult life. Those who take a more dynamic stance would assume that stability in personality would not be achieved until after some critical period. Those who believe that the earliest interactions in infancy are crucial for personality development would expect to see some consistency after infancy. Those who believe in the Oedipal period as crucial would not expect consistency until after five years of age, or whenever the final defense mechanisms are formed. Those who think of adolescence as the crucial socialization period expect prediction of adult personality to begin then. Finally, those who see personality as a constant flux of specific adaptations would not expect much consistency over any part of the life span. Perhaps the most realistic expectation is that some elements of early dispositions might be evident in later life, but most would be changed by interactions with environment. The fate of an early appearing personality trait will depend on its congruency or conflict with the family environment and future environments to which the individual is exposed.

Another problem is the change in the form of the expression of traits as people mature. Gross expressions of smiling and crying may be the only clues to the dimension of emotionality in infants, but speech and an increasing behavioral repertoire change the typical expressions in different ways in different children. Some may primarily express emotions verbally, and others may remain silent and express the emotional reaction by reducing communication. The net result would be a reduction in the correlation between the indicators of emotionality in childhood and any one of the indicators in adult life.

Assessment of personality of children is generally limited to ratings based on observations of the children by researchers, teachers, and parents. Researchers only observe a narrow segment of behavioral reactions in what is generally a novel situation for the child. Teachers are most impressed by what affects classroom behavior so that a bright child may create a positive halo effect and a dull child a negative one. Parents can observe a broad segment of the behavior of their children, but their observations may be biased by their personal involvement, and they may see more consistency in traits than is really there. Later, when the children have become adults, they usually provide most of the information about themselves through interviews or self-report tests. Such methodological problems may either reduce or increase apparent consistency in traits or increase consistency for some individuals and reduce it in others. However, people do change and much of the changeableness or stability itself is a function of their own personalities (Block, 1971).

Table 2.5 presents data from the longitudinal study by Thomas and Chess (1986) showing the consistency of their dimensions of temperament as assessed for children by interview-based ratings of parents and between childhood ratings and ratings of adult temperaments based on interviews with the subjects. The childhood ratings cover the ages 1–5, and the early adult ratings were made when the subjects were 18–24 years of age.

One other study (Huttunen & Nyman, 1982), which assessed the Thomas and Chess dimensions using a questionnaire designed by Cary, is included. The authors gave the questionnaire to mothers visiting a well-baby clinic in Helsinki when the children were 6–8 months old. Five years later a translated version of the questionnaire was given to the parents of the same children. A subsample of 299 cases was selected from children with acute

Table 2.5. *Prediction of adult temperament from ratings made in infancy and early childhood*

Dimension	Prediction of 5 yr ratings from year:					Prediction of adult ratings[b] from year:				
	6–8 mo[a]	1	2	3	4	1	2	3	4	5
Activity	.24[c]	.18[c]	.20[c]	.25[c]	.37[c]	.06	.08	.02	.15	.07
Rhythmicity	.32[c]	.22[c]	.10	.15	.35[c]	−.10	.00	.11	−.05	.02
Adaptability	.30[c]	.14	.29[c]	.31[c]	.52[c]	.14	.15	.21[c]	.22[c]	.18
Approach-with.	.29[c]	−.03	.06	.03	.40[c]	−.02	−.01	.29[c]	.20[c]	.16
Threshold	.23[c]	.22[c]	.03	.24[c]	.28[c]	.15	.06	.14	.04	.04
Intensity	.15	.02	.09	.11	.33[c]	.20[c]	.01	.09	.26[c]	.03
Mood	.26[c]	.08	.12	.13	.29[c]	−.07	−.03	.17	.18[c]	.10
Distractibility	.02	.15	−.05	.34[c]	.11	.03	−.08	−.15	−.01	.01
Persistence	.21[c]	.02	.14	.24[c]	.14	−.13	−.18[c]	−.03	−.12	.02

[a] 6–8 month predictions from Huttunen & Nyman (1982); all other data from Thomas & Chess (1986)
[b] Adults 18–24 years of age
[c] $p < .05$, two-tailed test
Source: Thomas and Chess (1986), in R. R. Plomin & J. Dunn (Eds.), *The study of temperament*, table 4.2, p. 44. Copyright 1986 by Lawrence Erlbaum Associates. Adapted by permission.

behavioral problems for analysis. The table presents the consistency of the temperament scores from 6–8 months to 5 years.

Seven of the nine correlations were significant in predicting 5-year-old ratings from 6–8 months ratings (Huttunen & Nyman, 1982). In contrast, only three of the nine correlations were significant in predicting from years 1–5 in the Thomas and Chess (1986) study. The difference in results is probably a function of the superior reliability of the questionnaire used in the Huttunen and Nyman study compared with the interview method used by Thomas and Chess. Consistency correlations in the Thomas and Chess study increase in most traits as a function of proximity in time to the year–5 ratings; they were highest for year 4 where seven of the nine correlations were significant.

Prediction of adult temperaments from the same dimensions in childhood are also shown in the table. There was little prediction of adult from child temperament for years 1 and 2. Both *adaptability* and *approach-withdrawal* during 3 and 4 years of age were significantly correlated with the adult expressions of these dimensions in early adult life; during year 4, *intensity* and *mood* also predicted the corresponding adult temperaments. Surprisingly, none of the ratings from age 5 significantly predicted adult temperament.

The main purpose of the Thomas and Chess (1977) project was to see if adult adjustment could be predicted from childhood temperament and environment measures. There were three measures of adult adjustment:

Table 2.6. *Prediction of adult adjustment from easy–difficult child ratings*

Child ratings from year:	Bootstrap	Clinical diagnosis	Easy–difficult adult rating
1	.08	.03	.17
2	.09	− .03	.09
3	.21[a]	.05	.31[a]
4	.32[a]	.24[a]	.37[a]
5	.23[a]	.19[a]	.15

[a] $p < .05$
Source: Thomas & Chess (1986), in R. R. Plomin & J. Dunn (Eds.), *The study of temperament*, table 4.4, p. 46. Copyright 1986 by Lawrence Erlbaum Associates. Adapted by permission.

one was an *easy–difficult* dimension score based on both interviews and a questionnaire; a second was a "bootstrap" *adjustment* score based on post hoc analyses of variables; and the third was a score based on the presence or absence of a clinical diagnosis from the adult interview. Table 2.6 shows the correlations between the *easy–difficult* dimension from each of the first 5 years of childhood and the early adult indices of adjustment.

None of the correlations from the global temperament score assigned to subjects in the first 2 years after birth were predictive of adult adjustment. Years 3, 4, and 5 yielded significant predictors but could not predict adult adjustment independently of other variables such as maternal attitudes; but the *easy–difficult child* continuum based on these variables when the child was 3 years old predicted adult adjustment and *easy–difficult* temperament independently. The nine temperament variables could also predict adult temperament accounting for about 7–9% of the variance after the influence of other variables was removed in the interview data, but 15–18% in predicting the adult temperament data derived from the questionnaire. Of the nine temperament variables, *mood* is the one that was significantly predictive of adult temperament in both analyses, and *adaptability* was also predictive of the interview-based analysis of adult temperament. Apparently, childhood temperament is most effective in predicting adult temperament but less important as a predictor of adult adjustment. Part of the problem in this study is the interview methodology. Both in the continuity and predictive data, it is apparent that the use of objective questionnaire techniques increases the size of the relationships.

Consistency using direct observation or objective measurement

When the same observers (parents in the case of Thomas and Chess) are used over time, there is a question of how much of the perceived consistency in the children is due to the observers and how much actually reflects consistency in the children's behavior. Buss, Block, and Block (1980) measured activity with actometers worn on the wrist or forearm on three occasions when children were 3 years old and on four occasions when they were 4 years old. Teachers rated the children's activity levels at ages 3 and 4, and project examiners rated them at age 7. The correlations between the composite actometer-measured activity at a given age and the ratings were .53 and .61 for boys and .48 and .50 for girls. Judge-based consistency from age 3–4 to age 7 was .75 for boys and .51 for girls; actometer-based consistency over the same ages was .43 for boys and .44 for girls. The data may indicate that for boys, at least, the teacher ratings exaggerate the consistency of behavior. However, a study by Eaton (1983) suggests that reliability of the actometer increases as a function of how many actometers are worn. Because Buss et al. used only one actometer, the measured activity may have had less than optimal reliability.

Kagan (1971) tested infants and children in response to a number of different situations and stimuli. The results on measures such as fixation time, smiling, vocalization, and heart rate deceleration showed small, occasionally significant consistencies over time, the size and significance of the correlations depending on the specific stimuli or situations and the sex of the subjects. Even the minority of significant correlations seldom exceeded .4, and most were in the .25–.35 range. Whether we consider more global ratings or more direct assessment of behavior in infancy or early childhood the evidence of consistency in what could be early behavioral manifestations of personality dimensions is not overwhelming. Given these findings one should not be too sanguine about the possibility of predicting later childhood and adolescent behavior or personality traits from laboratory observations made in early childhood. However, there have been two longitudinal studies with successful predictions.

Kagan, Reznick, and Snidman (1988) observed the reactions of 21-month-old children to situations involving exposure to unfamiliar women and objects in an unfamiliar laboratory setting. Another group consisting of 31-month-old children was initially observed reacting to an unfamiliar child of the same sex and age and an unfamiliar woman dressed in an "unusual costume." Extreme groups of inhibited (shy, quiet, and timid) and uninhibited (sociable, talkative, and affectionately spontaneous) children were selected on the basis of behavioral indices such as latencies to play with, speak to, or interact with strangers. These groups were studied at various periods up to 7.5 years of age (at the time of the report). At this age the children were put into a laboratory play situation involving unfamiliar children. Behavioral indices were used to assess interaction with the other children.

Most of the children who were inhibited at 2 to 3 years of age were still socially inhibited at 7.5 years of age, and most of the children who were socially spontaneous at the younger age interacted quickly with strangers at the later age. However, these samples were selected from extreme reactors among the children initially tested. Little overall prediction was found in a third group of children who were unselected.

Mischel, Shoda, and Peake (1988) have shown more-impressive prediction from behavioral data in early childhood (4 years) to trait ratings in adolescence (16 years). At 4 years the children were tested on their capacity to delay gratification. Seconds of delay in waiting for a prize correlated positively with adolescent trait descriptions such as "is attentive and able to concentrate," "is planful and thinks ahead," and negatively with traits such as "tends to go to pieces under stress," and "reverts to more immature behavior when under stress." Correlations were as high as .49. Capacity to delay response in preschool also predicted the parents' ratings of social competence in their adolescent children (boys' $r = .43$; girls' $r = .34$).

The Berkeley Guidance and the Oakland Growth Studies

In the late 1920s and early 1930s two longitudinal studies of personality began in the San Francisco Bay area. Bronson (1966) reported data on the ratings of personality traits of children in the Berkeley Guidance Study (BGS) from ages 5 to 16 and prediction of adult patterns from two major dimensions found in the children (Bronson, 1967). Block reported on the prediction of adult personality ratings (Q-sorts), based on extended interviews with subjects in both the BGS and Oakland Growth Study (OGS). He also used the Q-sort, a method in which the relevance of a set of statements describing subjects are assessed by judges who sort the statements into a ranking or forced distribution from those least like the person to those most like him or her. The ratings were based on extended interviews with the subjects in both studies. Block used sets of data from these subjects when they were in junior and senior high school to predict the adult personality when the subjects were in their 30s. Correlations are provided for the individual items across the three periods.

Neither investigator did the type of factor analysis required to group items into scores on dimensions of personality like those described in previous sections. However, both investigators presented consistency data on individual items which were grouped into the three major superfactor dimensions (E, N, & P) discussed in chapter 1. These were grouped rationally on the basis of the information about the structure of the superfactors from the study by Zuckerman, Kuhlman, and Camac (1988) and other factor analytic studies and whatever information could be gleaned from the cluster analyses of Bronson. Items that did not seem to fit clearly into any of these three dimensions or the traits that comprise them were not included. The median correlations within the three groupings from both studies were used to summarize the results.

Correlations were selected from Bronson's (1966) data (Table 2.7) that show the prediction of adolescent personality (ages 14–16) from the ratings

Table 2.7. *Prediction of adolescent (age 14–16) personality traits from earlier years*

	Median correlations by groupings between ratings of adolescent traits and traits from:					
	5–7 years		8–10 years		11–13 years	
	M	F	M	F	M	F
Extraversion-sociability[a]	.41	.30	.56	.48	.53	.58
Neuroticism-emotionality[b]	.21	.12	.38	.30	.42	.35
P-Impulsive-unsocialized SS[c]	.09	.19	.17	.39	.39	.43

[a]Items: reserved-expressive, shy-socially easy, passive-domineering, reactive-phlegmatic, inner oriented-outer oriented, exhibitionistic-withdrawn, restless-inactive
[b]Items: somber-gay, explosive-calm, complaining-uncomplaining, emotionally labile-stable, anxious-relaxed, vulnerable, emotionally dependent, fearful-unafraid, tantrums
[c]Items: resistive-compliant, quarrelsome-placating, adventurous-cautious, evasive-truthful, competitive-uncompetitive, jealous
Source: Bronson (1966)

made in earlier age periods (ages 5–7, 8–10, and 11–13). The median coefficients for the traits included in each of the three supertrait groupings are shown in the table.

Block (1971) extended Bronson's analyses, predicting from junior and senior high school years to adult personality in the more extended sample. The items of the Q-sorts used at all three age periods were again grouped into the three supertrait categories. Median correlations within categories are shown in Table 2.8. Block also provides the consistency coefficients corrected for attenuation due to the unreliability of the ratings at any given period. These corrected coefficients convey an estimate of what the actual consistency would be if the judges Q-sort ratings were perfectly reliable.

Both studies showed that consistency was poor over long periods of prediction but fairly good over shorter periods of age intervals. The E dimension seemed to show more consistency over time than the N and P dimensions. N and P represent dimensions defined by psychopathology at the high extremes whereas sociability is a normal and socially desirable dimension. A transient period of anxiety or depression, produced by fortuitous external events, could elevate N-Emotionality scores for that particular time period but not produce more permanent changes. Acute exacerbations of either negative emotions or impulsive antisocial activities could produce lower consistencies in these traits than in the normal extraversion dimension.

Block (1977c) gave a questionnaire called "What I like to do" (WILTD) to junior and senior high school subjects. An overcontrol score was derived from this test and correlated with an ego-control score derived from the

Table 2.8. *Prediction of personality traits from junior high school (JHS) to senior high school (SHS) and from senior high school to adult (in their 30s)*

	Median correlations by groupings of traits[a]			
	JHS to SHS		SHS to adult	
	Males	Females	Males	Females
Extraversion-sociability[b]	.45 (.67)	.40 (.59)	.28 (.41)	.36 (.49)
Neuroticism-emotionality[c]	.41 (.60)	.38 (.63)	.26 (.36)	.18 (.30)
P-Impulsive–unsocialized SS[d]	.41 (.67)	.43 (.64)	.32 (.43)	.27 (.37)

[a]First correlation is uncorrected, correlation in parentheses is corrected for attenuation
[b]Items: talkative, introspective, expressive, warm, fantasy and daydreaming, distant, gregarious, responds to humor, satisfied with self, social poise and presence, self-dramatizing.
[c]Items: anxiety related symptoms, withdraws when frustrated, calm-relaxed, irritable, hostile, fearful-feels threatened, maladaptive under stress, feels guilty, ruminates-preoccupied, fluctuating moods, cheerful vs. gloomy, emotionally bland.
[d]Items: values autonomy, dependable and responsible, sympathetic and considerate, extrapunitive, overcontrol of impulses, rapid personal tempo, negativistic, guileful and deceitful, unconventional thinking, distrustful, uncontrolled expression of needs, enjoys sensuality, rebellious, stretches limits, self-indulgent–egocentric, eroticizes situations, projects onto others, expresses hostility directly, comfortable with uncertainty.
Source: Block (1971)

California Psychological Inventory (CPI) given to the same subjects 25 years later. The WILTD overcontrol scores correlated .48 for males and .66 for females between junior and senior high school. The WILTD score from senior high school correlated .52 for males and .53 for females with the adult CPI ego control scale. These results for objective questionnaire measures were superior to those obtained with the single Q-sort overcontrol item (.43 for males and .25 for females from high school to adult) showing the superiority of objective instruments in terms of reliability. The questionnaire results are impressive considering the length of the time interval between last testings (25 years) and the fact that the scores were from two different instruments.

Haan (1981) derived five factors from the Q-sort data in these studies, using a method of factor analysis that locates factors that are the same at all age periods.

1. *Cognitively invested.* An intellectual factor reflecting an interest in ideas; it resembles the *culture* factor in the 5-factor model (chapter 1).
2. *Emotionally under/overcontrolled.* Aggressive, rebellious, and unpredictable at one extreme and emotionally guarded and submissive at the other; it resembles the P factor.
3. *Open/closed to self:* Resembles the *openness to experience* factor suggested by Costa.

Table 2.9. *Correlations between time periods for common factors of personality*

Q-sort factors	Oakland Growth Study		Berkley Guidance Study	
	14–17	17–37	14–17	17–30
Females				
Cognitively invested	.70[b]	.54[b]	.52[b]	.42[a]
Emotionally under/overcontrolled	.58[b]	.30	.72[b]	.54[b]
Open/closed to self	.43[b]	.39[a]	.75[b]	.57[b]
Nuturant/hostile	.57[b]	.49[b]	.54[b]	.27
Under/overcontrolled, heterosex.	.64[b]	.46[b]	.54[b]	.62[b]
Self-confident	.48[b]	.44[b]	.54[b]	.36[a]
Males				
Cognitively invested	.63[b]	.58[b]	.73[b]	.40[a]
Emotionally under/overcontrolled	.52[b]	.26	.67[b]	.21
Open/closed to self	.30	−.08	.35	.36
Nuturant/hostile	.55[b]	.30	.65[b]	.24
Under/overcontrolled, heterosex.	.65[b]	.21	.62[b]	.29
Self-confident	.61[b]	.24	.66[b]	.27

[a] $p < .05$
[b] $p < .01$
Source: Haan (1981), in D. H. Eichorn et al. (Eds.), table 5.3, p. 128. Copyright 1981, Academic Press. Adapted by permission.

4. *Nuturant versus hostile:* Resembles the *agreeableness* factor in the 5-factor model.
5. *Under/overcontrolled, heterosexual:* Reflects control exerted, particularly in sex.

Table 2.9 shows the short-term prediction from early to late adolescence (14–17 years) and long-term predictions from late adolescence to middle age (17–30 or 37) in males and females from both samples. All of the short-term 3-year predictions were significant for both sexes. The long-term predictions were nearly all significant for women, but only the *cognitive investment* factor was significant for men. The authors speculate that men were less predictable because of the more dramatic shifts in their work role responsibilities between adolescence and middle-age.

The Fels Institute longitudinal program

The Fels sample (Kagan & Moss, 1962) consisted of 44 boys and 45 girls studied from "birth to maturity." The data presented in the Kagan and Moss book consist partly of ratings of traits made during four periods of childhood (0–3, 3–6, 6–10, 10–14 years of age) and predictions from each of these periods to adult life (19–29 years of age). Many of the variables

Table 2.10. *Prediction from childhood and early adolescence ratings of passivity and independence to adult ratings on dependency*

	Adult ratings									
	Dependency on love object		Dependency on parents		Dependency on friends		Withdrawal from stress[a]		Dependency and vocational choice[b]	
	Boys	Girls	Boys	Girls	Boys	Girls	Boys	Girls	Boys	Girls
Passivity										
Ages 0–3	.47[d]	.26	−.32	.17	.05	.28	−.06	.22	.00	.25
Ages 3–6	.16	.20	−.28	.05	−.01	.15	.06	.26	−.03	.24
Ages 6–10	.25	.33[c]	−.18	.29[c]	−.03	.07	.27	.48[e]	.05	.55[e]
Ages 10–14	.26	.23	.01	.47[d]	.02	−.44[d]	.36[c]	.67[d]	.22	.54[e]
Independence										
Ages 3–6	.00	−.13	.18	−.19	.00	−.07	−.05	−.29	.00	−.38[d]
Ages 6–10	−.02	−.35[d]	−.04	−.29[d]	−.08	.16	−.31[c]	−.35[d]	−.03	−.40[d]
Ages 10–14	−.25	−.41[d]	.10	−.39[d]	−.13	−.47[d]	−.25	−.57[e]	−.28	−.48[d]

[a]Adults' tendency to withdraw from tests of competence, avoidance of responsibility, postponing difficult tasks or decisions because of anticipated failure, reluctance to interact with strangers
[b]Concern with financial security and avoidance of risk in occupational choice
[c]$p < .10$, two-tailed test
[d]$p < .05$, two-tailed test
[e]$p < .01$, two-tailed test
Source: Kagan and Moss (1962), parts of tables 3–5, and 7, pp. 64–71. Copyright 1962, Wiley Press. Adapted by permission.

selected reflect the influence of psychodynamic theories popular at the time the study was designed, (e.g., dependency, aggression, anxiety over aggression or sex, repression of aggression or sex). What is particularly interesting about the results are sex differences in consistency over time and the forms and directions that dependency or aggression takes as the subjects proceed from birth to maturity. It is to the credit of Kagan and Moss that their trait measures were partly situation- and response-specific before this issue was paramount in personality assessment: for instance, differentiating between aggression to mother and aggression to peers, and between milder verbal aggression such as "criticism" and explosive tantrums and destructive expressions of anger ("behavioral disorganization"). Some of the variables were redefined at certain age levels to take account of the characteristic modes of expression at the particular level of maturation (Tables 2.10 to 2.13).

Prediction of personality in the preadolescent period (10–14 years) from variables rated in the first 3 years of life was poor. Significant predictions from the 3–6-year period tended to be gender specific, girls showing more consistency on measures of passivity-dependency and boys more consistency on aggressivity. Ratings made in the 6–10 year-old period were more highly related to adolescent ratings for both sexes.

Because personality traits begin to show stable prediction for adolescence in the years 6–10 in the children, we might expect that prediction of adult behavior would also begin to show significance from this age. The data for passivity and independence shown in Table 2.10 support this supposition. Only 1 of 10 correlations from the 0–3 year period and only 1 of 20 correlations from the 3–6 year period to the adult period were significant. In contrast, most (17 of 20 correlations) correlations from the subsequent age periods (6–10 and 10–14) were significant for the females, but only 2 of 20 were significant for males. Passivity and independence ratings of girls between the ages of 6 and 14 were predictive of their dependency as adults as manifested in dependence on love objects, parents, friends, and in vocational choices, as well as the tendency to withdraw from stress rather than confronting it. Boys were not consistent in these traits. The direction of the correlations were all in the expected positive direction except for dependency on friends. Apparently, the adult women who are dependent on spouses, lovers, or parents do not turn to friends when in need of help, whereas those women who are more emotionally independent of love objects and parents tend to rely more on friends when needing support.

Table 2.11 shows prediction from childhood to adult age of aggression, rage, and conformity, markers for the P dimension in adult analyses. As with the dependency variables, consistent prediction of adult personality was not found until the child age periods 6–10 and 10–14, with the later age period (10–14) showing the highest correlations with adult personality. As with dependency, the correlations were gender specific, but in the case of aggression they were generally significant for males and not for females. Boys who were aggressive to their mothers and showed intense rage reactions between ages 6 and 14 continued to show aggressive reactions, quick anger arousal, competitiveness, little anxiety about aggression or repression of aggression as adults. Conformity in boys from the age of 3–14 was primarily related to adult competitiveness rather than aggressiveness. Conforming boys tended to become noncompetitive adults. Compulsivity was consistent in boys during all four age periods of childhood, but was not significantly correlated with adult ratings of compulsivity or its converse, impulsivity.

Table 2.12 shows correlations of heterosexual interactions between 6 and 14 and interest in activities of the opposite sex (between 3 and 14), rather than usual sextyped activities, as predictors of sexual interests as adults. As with aggression variables, these childhood-to-early-adolescent ratings were more predictive for males than for females. For males, low heterosexual interactions during the early adolescent period were related to avoidance of premarital sexual activity, sexual anxieties, and repression of sex in adult life. The boys between 3 and 14 years of age who were interested

Table 2.11. *Prediction from childhood and adolescence ratings of aggression, rage, and conformity to adult ratings of aggression, anger arousal, competitiveness, anxiety over aggression, and repression of aggression*

| | Adult ratings | | | | | | | | | |
| | Aggressive reaction | | Anger arousal | | Competitiveness | | Aggression anxiety | | Repression of aggression | |
	Boys	Girls	Boys	Girls	Boys	Girls	Boys	Girls	Boys	Girls
Agg.-mother										
Ages 0–3	.19	.11	−.02	.19	.00	.08	.02	−.34	.22	−.12
Ages 3–6	.25	.00	.39[b]	.10	.37[b]	−.57[a]	−.12	−.02	−.05	−.04
Ages 6–10	.32[a]	.09	.37[b]	.23	.36[b]	−.09	−.44[b]	−.42[a]	−.41[b]	−.30
Ages 10–14	.47[b]	.13	.77[c]	.24	.28	−.07	−.42[b]	−.36[b]	−.56[c]	−.02
Rage[d]										
Ages 0–3	.28	−.21	.35	.04	.13	.00	−.22	−.06	−.45[b]	−.09
Ages 3–6	.12	.05	.30[a]	−.06	.11	.11	−.12	−.02	−.17	−.02
Ages 6–10	.37[b]	.03	.42[b]	.12	.34[b]	.15	−.39[b]	−.18	−.38[b]	−.13
Ages 10–14	.51[c]	.09	.52[c]	.08	.59[b]	−.39[a]	−.34[a]	−.14	−.54[c]	−.07
Conformity										
Ages 0–3	−.29	.01	−.12	.05	−.34	−.23	.08	−.02	−.10	−.10
Ages 3–6	−.11	.05	−.10	.05	−.40[b]	.00	.25	.16	.06	.06
Ages 6–10	−.26	−.11	−.09	−.04	−.48[c]	.09	.44[c]	.35[a]	.31[a]	.22
Ages 10–14	−.24	.02	−.26	−.08	−.54[c]	.15	.25	.11	.20	−.02

[a] $p < .10$, two-tailed test
[b] $p < .05$, two-tailed test
[c] $p < .01$, two-tailed test
[d] Behavioral disorganization (tantrums, rage, destructiveness)
Source: Kagan and Moss (1962), parts of tables 2–5, pps. 96–109. Copyright 1962, Wiley Press. Adapted by permission.

in activities that were traditionally associated with girls continued to show these gender atypical interests as adults. They also tended to show little interest in premarital sex and much sexual anxiety and repression of sex.

Table 2.13 shows the correlations between measures of anxiety versus spontaneity in novel or social situations. Anxiety elicited by strangers or novel situations during the first 6 years of life predicted adult anxiety for boys but not for girls. In the later periods of childhood (6–10) and early adolescent period (10–14) measures of social anxiety correlated with adult anxiety over social interactions in both males and females.

The Kagan and Moss data show two important aspects of personality consistency. Personality assessed in the preschool years (0–6) is generally not consistent with either early adolescent or adult personality. In this respect, the findings are consistent with those of Thomas and Chess (1977), who found low levels of prediction from the first 5 years to adult temper-

Table 2.12. *Prediction from childhood and early adolescence ratings of heterosexual interaction and opposite-sex activities and interests to adult ratings of sexuality, repression of sex, and opposite-sex activities and interests*

	Adult ratings							
	Avoidance of premarital sexuality		Sexual anxiety		Repression of sex		Opposite-sex interests, activities	
	Boys	Girls	Boys	Girls	Boys	Girls	Boys	Girls
Heterosexual interaction								
Ages 6–10	.06	−.27	.15	−.34	−.01	−.18	$.35^a$	−.04
Ages 10–14	$−.47^b$	−.06	$−.39^a$	.15	$−.40^a$	−.04	−.05	−.32
Opposite sex interests								
Ages 3–6	$.49^b$	−.14	$.41^b$	−.23	.18	−.09	$.54^c$	.10
Ages 6–10	$.65^c$	.13	$.61^c$	.11	$.30^a$	−.07	$.63^c$	$.44^c$
Ages 10–14	$.35^a$	.22	.18	−.01	.02	.07	$.57^c$	.10

$^a p < .10$, two-tailed test
$^b p < .05$, two-tailed test
$^c p < .01$, two-tailed test
Source: Kagan & Moss (1962), parts of tables 2–4, pps. 159, 168. Copyright 1962, Wiley Press. Adapted by permission.

ament and adjustment, and Bronson (1966), who found low levels of prediction from ages 5 to 7 to adolescence. Because adult personality involves social interactions with peers more than with parents, it is not surprising that behavior during the school years is more predictive of adolescent and adult behavior than the early life with the parents.

Although the early period of life encompasses what many psychodynamic theorists view as the critical periods of familial interaction in which personality dispositions are formed, the fact remains that the personality traits that emerge in this period do not foretell later trait expressions in adolescence or adult life. Important things seem to happen to children in what Freudians call the "latency" period, which shape the emerging personality into the forms that are discernible in later life.

Some of the crucial interactions between early personality and environment can be inferred from the sex differences in consistency of traits in the Kagan and Moss study. Society tends to positively reinforce gender-appropriate behavior and punish (or negatively reinforce) gender-inappropriate behavior. Although the definitions of gender-appropriateness vary with cultures and times, some of these expectations may be based on biologically influenced sex differences. Aggression is an example of a

Table 2.13. *Prediction from childhood and early adolescence ratings of anxiety and spontaneity in novel and social situations, expectations of rejection and withdrawal, to adult ratings of social interaction anxiety*

	Adult ratings social interaction anxiety	
	Boys	Girls
Anxiety reactions to Fels Instit. visitor		
Ages 0–3	.29	− .33
Ages 3–6	.30[a]	.25
Anxiety in novel situation		
Ages 0–3	.07	− .08
Ages 3–6	.53[b]	.02
Spontaneity in social interaction		
Ages 0–3	− .45[b]	.35
Ages 3–6	− .27	.09
Ages 6–10	− .41[b]	− .30[a]
Ages 10–14	− .50[b]	− .56[c]
Expectation of rejection		
Ages 6–10	.18	.09
Ages 10–14	.41[a]	.48[b]
Withdrawal from social interactions		
Ages 10–14	.65[c]	.54[b]

[a]$p < .10$, two-tailed test
[b]$p < .05$, two-tailed test
[c]$p < .01$, two-tailed test
Source: Kagan and Moss (1962), part of table 7, p. 171. Copyright 1962, Wiley Press. Adapted by permission.

trait that is more likely to be accepted as natural in boys than in girls. The converse would be true for passivity and dependency, which are regarded by many parents as more normal in girls than in boys. Thus, there would be more pressure on boys than girls to become less passive and more independent. Because the outcome of the conflict between the early disposition and parental and societal pressures would vary, consistency in these traits would be attenuated. The passive or dependent disposition would tend to be positively reinforced in girls, and the disposition would be likely to persist into adult life. From these assumptions, one would predict more consistency for aggressive tendencies in males and more consistency in passive and dependent traits in females, which is what Kagan and Moss found. However, the hypothesis would not have predicted that interest in the activities appropriate to the opposite sex would persist into adult life for either males or females. Given the homophobic attitudes of the society, one would expect less consistency than was actually found, particularly in males. One would also not expect adult anxiety in males to be as predictable from early ages as it was, given that fearfulness is less likely to be accepted in young males than in females.

Thomas and Chess (1986) have suggested a similar explanation of the fate of children with "difficult" temperaments. They found that if parents were more tolerant of difficult children, the outcome in adult adjustment was more likely to be benign than if there was a constant conflict between parents and children and if the parents forcibly tried to change the child's temperament. In the latter case, the difficult temperament was more likely to end as an adult behavior disorder.

Prediction of adult impulsivity from childhood hyperactivity

Ratings of aggressiveness, motor restlessness, and concentration difficulties were made by teachers for Swedish school boys at age 13 and used as predictors of adult impulsivity at ages 26–27 by Klinteberg, Magnusson, and Schalling (1989). Adult impulsivity was assessed by an Impulsivity questionnaire scale. All of the behavior ratings made by teachers at age 13 correlated with impulsivity at ages 26–27 (r's = .33–.37), but partial correlations showed that the ratings of hyperactivity (motor restlessness and concentration difficulties) influenced the relationship more than aggression ratings.

Summary of personality consistency into adulthood

Personality is generally consistent for short periods of a few years, from childhood to early adolescence (Bronson, 1966; Kagan & Moss, 1962) and from early adolescence to late adolescence (Block, 1971), but less consistent from adolescence to adult life: There is consistency, particularly for traits relating to sociability, but the degree of consistency is less than would be expected by those with a biological viewpoint who underestimate the influence of environment in interaction with the genotype. What is more remarkable than the size of the typical correlation, is the generalization across diverse kinds of interactions as adults. The fact that ratings of traits in childhood or adolescence can predict the altered forms of the trait expression in different kinds of interactions in adults is a refutation of the radical situationist view of personality.

Personality consistency in adult life

Although the studies of consistency from childhood to adolescent and adult years primarily used ratings by observers, the studies of consistency over the adult years have generally used self-report questionnaires and ratings;

the exception is the use of spouse ratings in the Baltimore Longitudinal Study of Aging (McCrae and Costa, 1982).

Costa and McCrae (1977) found that 10-year retest correlations ranged from .70 to .84 for extraversion and from .58 to .69 for anxiety on scores derived from the 16 PF test. Costa, McCrae, and Arenberg (1980) and Douglas and Arenberg (1978) presented stability and consistency data on scales from the Guilford–Zimmerman Temperament Survey given to adult subjects in intervals of 6 to 12 years. The mean reliability coefficients were .77 for a 6-year interval and .73 for a 12-year interval. These high correlations were the same in the young adult (17–44 years), middle adult (45–59 years) and old adult (60–85 years) age ranges, suggesting no decline in the consistency of personality through the adult years. Longitudinal data did show a decline in *general activity* and *masculinity* in older men; cross-sectional data supported the decline in scores on these variables though they did not accelerate markedly until ages 60 to 80. There were no age changes or declines in measures of *sociability* and *emotional stability*.

In the longest follow-up study of adult subjects, Finn (1986) retested men after an interval of 30 years. Two cohorts were studied: (A) college students, ages 17–25 at first testing; (B) business and professional men, ages 43–53 at the initial test. The test used was the MMPI, scored for 15 factor scales. The mean 30-year retest correlation for all variables was .38 for group A (college students) and .53 for group B (middle-aged men). The reliabilities for *social extraversion* were .49 for group A and .56 for group B; for *neuroticism* the coefficients were .45 for group A and .56 for group B; and for *psychoticism* the retest correlations were .26 for group A and .56 for group B. Two higher order factor scores were *constraint* (r's .40 for group A and .66 for group B) and *negative* versus *positive affectivity* (r's .55 for group A and .57 for group B). The older age group showed more stability, in terms of higher reliability coefficients. Both age groups showed low stability for *depression* and *neurasthenic somatization* and high stability for *delinquency* and *religious fundamentalism*.

Although most of the consistency coefficients are not as high as in the study by Costa et al. (1980), the Costa et al. study covered a period of the adult life span of 6–12 years whereas Finn's data cover a 30-year period. The data support the notion that personality reaches maximal stability in middle age and is relatively constant from then until old age. Some trait scales, such as *depression,* may be less stable than others because they tend to assess symptoms that are transient and related to current life circumstances; they may assess something between a trait and a state.

Schuerger, Zarrella, and Hotz (1989) analyzed test-retest reliabilities from 106 groups in 89 studies. The initial age of the subjects, length of test-retest interval, the homogeneity and number of items in the test all affected the test-retest stability, but the most powerful effect was the interval between test and retest. Reliabilities fall off rapidly as a function of intervals up to 3 years, but beyond that, decline is more gradual. As in previously described studies, the reliabilities for extraversion type scales tend to be higher than those for anxiety or neuroticism scales for all age intervals.

Consistency of states and behavior over time and situations

Much of the controversy about the stability and consistency of personality has centered around the reliability of states or overt behavior rather than that of traits. It has been argued that the perceived consistencies in traits are illusory and not based on real consistencies in behavior across situations and time. Mischel (1968) has pointed out that studies of behavior across situations have rarely yielded correlations between behaviors in two situations greater than .30. The classical and often cited study is that by Hartshorne and May (1928), in which a group of children were exposed to a number of situations in which cheating, lying, stealing, and faking were possible, and in which a child's actual behavior could be detected. Because of the very low intercorrelations between single tests of different techniques (almost all positive but none exceeding .3), Hartshorne and May concluded that: "honesty or dishonesty is not a unified character trait in children of the ages studied, but a series of specific responses to specific situations" (p. 243). However, other data in this volume suggest the existence of at least narrow traits. Many of the comparisons between two responses involved variations in time, settings, and type of response called for. Each variation produces a different kind of unreliability, and the effect is cumulative. Average temporal reliabilities, based on the same behavioral test repeated after some period of time, were .57 to .68 for three categories of tests.

When two tests that were given on the same day, based on the same testing technique but employing different materials, were correlated, the median correlation was .46 and the range was from .24 to .84 (see their table CLXVIII). This latter comparison is the equivalent of alternate-form reliability used with paper-and-pencil tests. When one test situation was correlated with another test situation involving different responses, the median correlation was .20. But when these correlations were corrected for attenuation using the reliability estimates from the alternate form method, the median of corrected correlations was .41. Although correcting for attenuation can be misleading when the goal of analysis is practical prediction, such correction can be done when the aim is to make broad theoretical statements concerning the consistency of behavior (as in Block, 1971).

Burton (1963) further analyzed the Hartshorne and May study by aggregating scores within six categories of tests and subjecting them to factor analysis. One major factor involved the tests that were made in the classroom and two others contained only single test loadings. A Guttman Simplex analysis indicated that one factor could account for the matrix with errors arising from the less reliable tests.

Thus, the Hartshorne and May prototype study, though showing some specificity of the behavioral trait of honesty, also showed that when measures were aggregated within classes of behavioral tests, there was a moderate degree of consistency among the behaviors in various situations. An analogy can be made with the classical item-test statistics. Single interitem correlations are usually low, but when items with low degrees of relationship are combined in a scale, the total score has reliability far higher than any single item. A behavioral instance is like a single item in a scale in making generalizations about a trait. The correlations of any two behavioral events thought to reflect a common trait would not be expected to be high. However, the real test of consistency lies in the comparisons of aggregated behavioral events, not just two such events. The studies next discussed have pursued this strategy of *aggregation*.

Zuckerman et al. (1967) suggested that traits might be defined by the mean and variance of an individual's states. Some evidence for this was provided in an unpublished study by these authors (described in Zuckerman, 1976, pp. 148–150). Student nurses from the same class who lived together in a dorm and followed the same class schedule took the Multiple Affect Adjective Check List (MAACL, Zuckerman & Lubin, 1965, 1985) on 77 consecutive evenings, describing their affect states during the current day. Figure 2.2 shows the mean levels of the *anxiety* and *depression* scales for each of the 77 days. Almost every peak in the chart represents the evening after an exam; and in the case of final exams, a rising trend in negative affect can be seen on the days leading up to the exam. The low points on the scales are the weekends. What the chart illustrates is the strong influence of actual events and situations on state affect. Given this strong influence of situation, is there any evidence for significant individual differences in levels of affect states over time?

There was little correlation between affects on any 2 days (around .2–.3), but an average of anxiety state measures on the first 7 days correlated substantially with the anxiety measures on each of 11 subsequent days, regardless of whether these were weekdays (mean $r = .51$), weekend days (mean $r = .60$), or examination days (mean $r = .57$). A single day's state is predictable from an adequate aggregation of previous days' states even though it is weakly or not at all predictable from a state on a previous day.

Patrick, Zuckerman, and Masterson (1974) extended this analysis to a variety of motive states by using the Gough and Heilbrun (1965) Adjective Check List (ACL). Ordinarily, the ACL is used as a trait test, but it is easily adapted as a state test by changing the instructions from an "in general" self-description to "today." The trait version consists of 15 Murray

72　　*Psychobiology of personality*

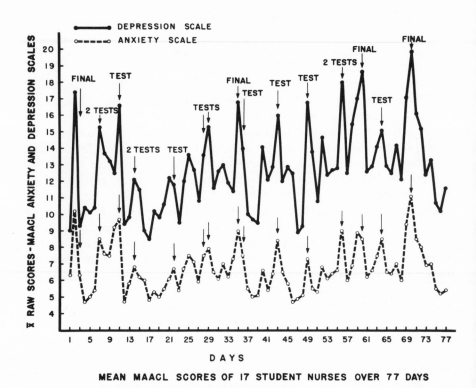

MEAN MAACL SCORES OF 17 STUDENT NURSES OVER 77 DAYS

Figure 2.2. Mean raw scores on the Multiple Affect Adjective Check List (MAACL); raw scores for *anxiety* and *depression* state scales for 17 student nurses on 77 successive days. From "General and situation-specific traits and states: New approaches to assessment of anxiety and other constructs" by M. Zuckerman, 1976, in *Emotions and anxiety: New concepts, methods and applications* (p. 148), M. Zuckerman & C. D. Spielberger (Eds.), Hillsdale, NJ: Erlbaum. Copyright 1976 by Lawrence Erlbaum Associates. Reprinted by permission.

(1938) need-type scales, 5 scales measuring adjustment or neuroticism, and 4 response set scales. The same scales were used for the state version. Thirty-seven undergraduates took the state version during 11 class sessions one week apart. On the first and last classes of the semester they also took the regular trait version of the test.

The mean correlations of all pairs of the 11 states was .38. The mean correlation between the state test given on the second week of the term and that given in the next to last week (separated by 11 weeks) was .27. The mean correlation between the state tests given on two class examination days (3 weeks apart) was .42. Tests were done to see how quickly the mean of all 11 states could be predicted from averaging successive state scores. The first state test correlated .53 (average for all variables) with the mean of states, the average of states 1 and 2 correlated .75, and the average of states 1, 2, and 3 correlated .84 with the mean of states.

Table 2.14. *Correlations among need-achievement (nAch) states in four nAch arousal conditions and mean of four neutral conditions*

	SAA	S-F	CA	EC
Social ability arousal (SAA)	—			
Success-failure (S-F)	.06	—		
Conventional nAch arousal sit. (CA)	$.26^a$	$.34^a$	—	
Extrinsic competition (EC)	.18	$.64^b$	$.53^b$	—
ACL mean of states on neutral occasions	.23	$.61^b$	$.52^b$	$.65^b$

[a] $p < .05$, two-tailed test
[b] $p < .01$, two-tailed test
Source: Patrick and Zuckerman (1979), table 1, p. 462. Copyright 1977, Academic Press. Reprinted by permission.

Mathematically, the rate at which the averaging approached the mean for any given variable depended on the communality among state tests. The higher the average correlation among states, the fewer states were necessary to estimate the mean of states. Typically, a sampling of 3 consecutive states could provide a very good estimate of the ultimate mean of the 11 states for individuals. Unfavorable self-concept and other neurotic-type scales showed the more rapid acceleration of prediction coefficients whereas favorable and good adjustment adjectives showed the slowest acceleration as a function of sampling size increases.

It could be argued that all ACL tests were given in the same classroom situation and therefore the study did not really assess the degree of state arousal in different situations. Patrick and Zuckerman (1977) therefore studied one ACL scale, *need Achievement* (nAch), on four neutral class occasions and during four sessions in which an attempt was made to arouse nAch by using four different manipulations: (1) *social ability,* while expecting feedback from a bogus test of "sensitivity to the needs of others"; (2) *success-failure,* while expecting feedback on predicted grade-point averages from a bogus test on which a failure experience had been contrived; (3) *conventional nAch,* while waiting to take a test related to "intelligence and leadership"; and (4) *extrinsic competition,* before taking a test for which there was to be a $10 prize for the best score.

State scores on nAch were significantly higher during the arousal situations than during the neutral ones. Females were significantly lower in nAch than males across arousal and neutral conditions but showed greater nAch increase during the *social ability* testing condition. Table 2.14 shows the correlations among nAch states in each of these conditions and the mean of the state scores on the four neutral occasions.

All of the correlations among nAch states assessed during three of the four arousal conditions and the mean of states on the four neutral occasions

Table 2.15. *Median and ranges of correlations among different types of state anxiety measures within situations and across situations*

	Within situations	Across situations
Mellstrom et al. 1976[a]		
Self-report	.77 (.61–.85)	.38 (.24–.76)
Observer ratings	.60 (.50–.62)	.22 (.22–.42)
Performance		.21 (−.10–.55)
Mellstrom et al. 1978[b]		
Self-report	.52 (.39–.75)	.38 (.22–.45)
Observer ratings	.70 (.53–.70)	.24 (.16–.27)

[a]Situations: exposure to snake, heights, darkness
[b]Situations: exposure to rat, testing, interview situations. Only one performance measure in one situation used
Source: Mellstrom et al. (1976, 1978); Zuckerman (1979)

were significant, and five of the six correlations were above .50. NAch in the other arousal condition, *social ability,* only correlated significantly with nAch in the conventional achievement situation. The results provide evidence for a high degree of consistency in nAch state arousal across three of the situations and the ability to predict such arousal from the mean level on neutral days.

The experiments by Mellstrom et al. (1976, 1978) provide assessments of cross-situational consistency of anxiety states, measured by self-report, observers ratings, and performance measures in fear-provoking situations. The 1976 study compared responses of subjects before and during exposure to a snake, heights, and darkness; the 1978 study used situations of exposure to a rat, testing, and interview. Table 2.15 shows the median and range of correlations among anxiety measures of a particular class (self-report state, observers ratings, and performances) in the three situations in each of the experiments, and the cross-situational correlations of particular measures from one situation to another. Correlations among self-report state measures in situations, and observer rating measures in situations were high; correlations between self-report and observer ratings were high in the 1976 study but low in the 1978 study because of methodological problems with the ratings.

Cross-situational correlations for particular methods were more modest. In both experiments, anxiety assessed by self-report methods typically correlated .38 across conditions; observer ratings correlated .22–.24, and performance measures correlated only about .21. These findings tend to support the idea that behavioral measures correlate lowly across particular pairs of situations, and state measures correlate only a little higher. How-

Table 2.16. *Mean reliability coefficients for major classes of daily self-reports*

	Day 1 vs. day 2	Last vs. next to last day	All odd vs. all even days
Emotions[a]	.36	.34	.88
Impulses[b]	.19	.27	.76
Behavior[c]	.06	.28	.74
Situations[d]	.00	.09	.55

[a]Happy, kindly, calm, adequate, unified, energetic.
[b]Pleasure seeking, nuturance, exuberance, stimulus seeking, problem solving, affiliation, achievement.
[c]Nuturance, exhuberance, pleasure, affiliation, problem solving, stimulus seeking, achievement.
[d]Entertainment, love and affection, freedom, positive evaluation, affiliation, adequacy, pleasant physical stimulus, relief, aesthetic stimulus.
Source: Epstein (1979)

ever, aggregation over additional samples of situations can raise these consistencies to respectable levels of reliability (Epstein, 1979).

Epstein (1979) hypothesized that "stability can be established over a wide range of variables so long as the behavior in question is averaged over a sufficient number of occurrences" (p. 1105). He believes that this principle of *aggregation* is equally applicable to self-reports, ratings by others, and objective behaviors. The corollary to the hypothesis is that reliable relationships will be found between trait measures and objective behavior if aggregates of behavioral instances are used instead of single samples of behavior.

Epstein had a group of 28 undergraduates keep daily records for one month of their most pleasant and most unpleasant experiences for each day. Subjects recorded their reactions to these experiences using check lists assessing emotions, impulses to action, and actual behavioral responses. The narratives of the the events were also classified into situational categories. Table 2.16 compares the typical (mean) reliabilities for each major category of response from one day to another, with the aggregated odd–even day correlations (subjects' means of 12 odd days versus means of 12 even days). The day-to-day correlations were low, as expected, but aggregations of days produced very high reliabilities for emotions and impulses and for behaviors and moderate reliabilities situations. The situational reliabilities were also lowered by a low interjudge agreement on classification. It is interesting that even moderate situational reliabilities are achieved by aggregation. This suggests that situations are not arbitrary but reflect to some degree the choices made as a function of personality. Figure 2.3 shows how the reliability coeffi-

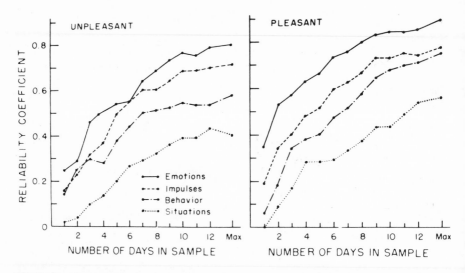

Figure 2.3. Between-subjects reliability coefficients as a function of the number of days in the odd–even samples. From "Traits are alive and well" by S. Epstein, 1977, in *Personality at the crossroads: Current issues in interactional psychology* (p. 88), D. Magnusson & N. S. Endler (Eds.), Hillsdale, NJ: Erlbaum. Copyright 1977 by L. Erlbaum Associates. Reprinted by permission.

cients rise to the maximal values as a function of the number of days in each aggregated sample.

Epstein (1979) also reported a similar study done with observers' daily ratings of subjects over a month, with similar results to self-report data: Mean reliabilities of aggregated data range from .60 to .79 for the various major categories of response. One of the variables, relevant to the trait of *sociability,* was the number of times that subjects initiated contacts with others. This variable started with an unusually high 1-day reliability (.67), and with a 6-day aggregation the coefficient rose to .90.

Aggregation does not always increase the reliability of a measure to such high levels. Moscowitz (1982) used observations of children in classes for 5 days a week over an 8-week period. Ratings were made of behaviors grouped under the general categories of dominance (displace, command, suggest, and threat) and dependency (proximity, touch, seek help, seek recognition, and seek supervision). Comparing 1-week's data produced a coefficient of generalizability of .34 for dominance, which increased to .76 for 8 weeks of observation. However, dependency had a coefficient of .07 for 1 week and increased only to .38 for 8 weeks.

Behavioral observations were used in another study by Epstein (1979) with tallies of behavioral instances kept by subjects on such things as telephone calls made and received, observations such as heart rate made in the classroom by the subjects, and observations such as lateness, errors, erasures on daily mood scales, and pencils forgotten made by the instructor. The selection of variables seemed to be more practical than rational. Behaviors were selected that occurred with some frequency and could be easily and objectively recorded, rather than representing an attempt to measure prototypical behaviors for particular traits. The median 1-day reliability for the behavioral variables was .43 and that for the 12-day aggregated samples was .90. In another study of behavioral observations, Epstein reported mean correlations of .44 for a 1-day sample, .79 for a 7-day sample, and .88 for a 14-day sample. Social contacts, recorded heart rates, and somatic (perhaps psychosomatic) symptoms all showed high reliabilities even from one day to another, and all were over .90 for the 14-day aggregate. What is remarkable is that these behavioral variables reached higher reliabilities than reported negative emotions.

Mischel and Peake (1982) questioned the relevance of Epstein's findings on the issue of trait consistency across situations. They referred to the high reliabilities for aggregates of single behaviors as temporal rather than cross-situational consistency, but it is not clear how they distinguish between the two kinds of consistency. A person does not encounter the same situations from one day to the next even if they are in the same setting, such as a classroom or a dormitory room. Number of social contacts is not a situation-specific response, and yet it achieves reliabilities of over .60, even on the basis of 1-day comparisons.

Mischel and Peake refer to the correlations among various kinds of behavior as the crux of the cross-situational question. Only 7 of 105 of these correlations in Epstein's data were significant, and these were with closely related behaviors such as reports of stomachaches and headaches, or calls made with calls received. But these behaviors were selected on a pragmatic basis rather than as attempts to measure particular traits. The authors did their own study in which they selected behaviors that were assumed to assess the trait of *conscientiousness*. Seventy-eight percent of the correlations among behaviors were positive, and 20% were significant. Although they concede that some of the aggregated variables correlated highly in a trait-consistent manner (e.g., class attendance with appointment attendance, $r = .67$, and assignment punctuality, $r = .53$), they chose to emphasize the low mean correlation of .13 among all 19 categories of behavior.

The arbitrary and sweeping conclusions about trait consistency that Mischel and Peake draw from a mean tendency among their selected behavioral variables are questionable. Suppose one developed a trait questionnaire from rationally derived items and proceeded to generalize about the intrinsic internal consistency of the trait without further selection of items using the initial data or factor analyses to see if more than one factor might be measured by the items. Essentially, this is what some investigators are doing with behavioral data.

Houts, Cook, and Shadish (1986) reanalyzed some of the Mischel and Peake data, grouping the measures into rationally selected categories such as attendance, punctuality, neatness, and self-directed studying. They also applied z' conversions before averaging and report mean correlations corrected for attenuation. The results show values that lead to different or less extreme conclusions than those reached by the original authors. Punctuality, for instance, yields a cross-situational coefficient of .55 instead of .17. It might be argued that by dividing the behaviors into subareas, Houts et al. are simply demonstrating the limitation on trait generalities. As will be seen in a later section, narrowly defined test measured traits are often more predictive of behavior than more broadly defined traits. However, this is an intermediate position that recognizes that there are cross-situational consistencies in behavior even if the response generalization is narrower than has been asserted. Probably most investigators would agree that the generality of behavioral traits has been defined too broadly. All of which brings us to the final question: How well can we predict states or behavior using broad or narrow trait measures?

Predictions of states and behavior from conventional trait measures

Although traits might be better defined from samples of states and behavior across situations and time, most personality assessors do not have the time or resources to do such longitudinal studies of subjects in their natural environments or in the laboratory. It is clear that conventional trait measures cannot be expected to highly predict single-state or behavioral responses because of the intrinsic unreliability of such responses and the variations in situations affecting the responses. But the more basic question is whether trait measures can predict states or behavioral responses aggregated over situations and time. A second question is whether trait measures that are narrowly designed to describe situations are more effective at predicting those situations than broader trait measures in which items are general statements with less attention to situational context.

In the Zuckerman (1976) study, the MAACL General Anxiety scale significantly predicted aggregates of 7–11 days and the mean of 77 days of state anxiety scores ($r = .51$ to .68). Patrick et al. (1974), using the Gough-Heilbrun Adjective Check List as a trait and a state measure, found that the mean prediction from traits to the subsequent means of daily state measures was .41, which rose to .55 when corrected for attenuation. The mean correlations of the trait measures with nonaggregated, 1-day state measures was only .27.

General versus specific traits

Mellstrom et al. (1976, 1978) aggregated trait measures to test the predictive validity of various types of trait measures for self-report, observer, and performance indices of anxiety in six different controlled situations. Three kinds of trait measures were used: (1) broad *neuroticism* or *anxiety*, using scales like the Taylor (1953) Manifest Anxiety Scale, the Spielberger, Gorsuch, and Lushene (1970) State-Trait Anxiety Inventory, and the Eysenck and Eysenck (1964) Neuroticism scale from the EPI; (2) broad omnibus anxiety scales in which anxiety or fear report is summed over many situations, like the Geer (1965) Fear Survey Schedule and the Zuckerman (1977) Inventory of Personal Reactions; (3) specific anxiety scales appropriate to the situation being measured were derived from the last two mentioned scales plus special questionnaires devised for each situation in the first study. Table 2.17 shows the correlations between aggregated *omnibus, neuroticism,* and *specific-anxiety* trait scales and the three classes of response variables in each situation. In the first experiment, the first two response measures (*A-state* and *fear thermometer*) are both self-report measures; in the second experiment the three self-report measures were combined.

In general, the predictive validity correlations were higher and more significant for the specific-fear measures than for the broad omnibus or neuroticism measures. However, this was not the case for all situations. The superiority of specific-fear trait measures was most pronounced in the snake, rat, and height situations, which pose physical danger threat; but in the darkness, test, and interview situations (ambiguous or social threats), there was little difference among the three types of trait measures in their predictive validities. Spielberger (1966) has pointed out that conventional anxiety or neuroticism trait scales assess social anxiety rather than fear of physical harm, and these results would indicate that such scales may have a broad applicability to this type of anxiety. Although these studies did not measure aggregation of response measures across situations, such aggregation might have raised the correlations *if* we had aggregated measures within the two classes of fear situations: physical and social.

Aggregation of response measures does not guarantee that traits will be predictive of the averaged response tendency. In the study by Patrick and Zuckerman (1977), three widely used measures of need achievement – the Thematic Apperception Test (TAT), scored using the McClelland et al. (1953) criteria, the nAch measure from Gough and Heilbrun's (1965) ACL,

Table 2.17. *Prediction of responses in fear situations using three types of anxiety trait measures*

Situation	r-Measure	Types of predictors		
		Omnibus	Neuroticism	Specific-fear
Snake	A-state	$.42^b$	$.25^a$	$.61^b$
	Fear thermometer	$.38^b$	.13	$.62^b$
	Observers ratings	$.42^b$	.15	$.62^b$
	Behavioral index	$.23^a$	.04	$.64^b$
Heights	A-state	$.25^a$	$.36^b$	$.29^b$
	Fear thermometer	$.25^a$	$.27^a$	$.48^b$
	Observers ratings	.16	.12	$.37^b$
	Behavioral index	$.29^b$	.15	$.44^b$
Darkness	A-state	$.38^b$	$.37^b$	$.35^b$
	Fear thermometer	$.41^b$	$.25^b$	$.49^b$
	Observers ratings	$.28^a$	.08	$.30^b$
	Behavioral index	.09	.07	.06
Rat	Self-report	.25	$.34^b$	$.52^b$
	Observers ratings	$.27^a$	.18	$.41^b$
	Behavioral index	.02	.02	$.34^b$
Test	Self-report	$.54^b$	$.51^b$	$.50^b$
	Observers ratings	.16	$-.07$	.23
	Behavioral index	.07	.15	.08
Interview	Self-report	$.49^b$	$.51^b$	$.66^b$
	Observers ratings	.19	$.26^a$	$.38^b$
Median correlations–all		.26	.17	.40

$^a p < .05$
$^b p < .01$
Source: Mellstrom et al. (1976), for situations Snake, Heights, and Darkness; Mellstrom et al. (1978), for situations Rat, Test, and Interview

and the nAch measure from the Edwards (1957) Personal Preference Schedule – could not predict the mean of the nAch states' four nAch arousal conditions, and only the ACL measure was able to predict the nAch state in any one of the four conditions. Interestingly, there was no correlation among the four ostensible measures of the same trait. A lack of coherence in trait measures is a bad sign for validity, and aggregation of trait measures cannot help when they do not correlate among themselves.

Epstein (1979) reported the correlations among various trait scales and 14-day aggregated samples of emotional states and observable events. Subjects had taken a general trait form that asked them to estimate how frequently they experienced each of the emotional states and engaged in the behaviors listed in the daily report form. In the terms in which broad, general, and narrow, specific traits were previously discussed, these would be regarded as specific trait scales. The mean of trait versus state correlations for 15 state scales was .47, and almost all of the trait-state correlations were significant. The mean trait correlations with 12 objective behavioral events was .53. Epstein also included a number of trait measures including the Eysenck *extraversion* and *neuroticism* scales from the EPI. Extraversion correlated significantly with 5 of 15 aggregated emotional states and neuroticism with 10 of them. Because neuroticism is supposed to measure emotionality, its better showing in predicting emotional states is understandable. The states that extraversion correlated with were outgoing versus seclusive, spontaneous versus inhibited, powerful versus helpless, optimistic versus pessimistic, and happy versus sad. All of these describe behavioral styles and positive affect, which are part of the construct of extraversion. In contrast, neuroticism correlated with the negative poles of most of the bipolar emotional states. Of the behaviors selected, extraversion might have been expected on an a priori basis to correlate with calls made and received and social contacts. The other behaviors would have to be regarded as irrelevant for the construct. Actually, E only correlated with numbers of social contacts made ($r = .52$). Neuroticism correlated significantly with heart-rate range, headaches, and stomachaches. Mischel and Peake (1982) criticized the paucity of correlations between trait and aggregated behavior measures, but given the lack of relevance of most of the behavioral measures to the two major traits assessed in the study, the number of significant correlations is less important than the fact that the ones found were precisely the ones that would be predicted.

Mischel (1984) has suggested that we must look for prototypical behaviors that are temporally stable but cross-situationally discriminative. The variable of *social contacts* should be considered such prototypical behavior because it is consistent across time but is also situationally discriminative. Even the most extraverted person shows some selection of whom they seek to talk to and socialize with. Finding prototypical behaviors for the neuroticism or anxiety trait is more difficult because this trait is best defined by the frequency of states of anxiety, which usually cannot be objectively observed. State tests given on a daily basis are probably the best way to assess this trait over time. Apart from frequent psychophysiological monitoring, complaints of psychophysiological symptoms such as headaches and stomachaches may be the most prototypical kinds of "behavioral" events that can be aggregated over time, but self-reported symptoms are really no more behavioral than affect states.

Personality and time in situations

In experimental study of personality the situation is an independent variable, but in real-life, situations are both independent and dependent variables. People select their friends and many of the situations they enter, and these in turn influence their own behavior. Diener, Larsen, and Emmons (1984) sampled subjects' activities and moods twice a day for a period

Table 2.18. *Correlations between personality trait scales and time in situations*

| Situations | Scales from Personality Research Form (Jackson 1974) | | | | | | Eysenck PI |
	Achieve.	Affiliation	Autonomy	Cog. structure	Order	Play	Extraversion
Social	−.07	−.13	.02	−.29	−.39^b	.16	.19
Novel	−.53^a	−.38^b	−.05	−.26	−.58^b	.14	.06
Work	.30^a	.09	.24	.36^a	.13	−.01	.06
Recreate-social	−.03	−.04	.07	−.34^a	−.38^a	.17	.41^b

$^a p < .05$, two-tailed
$^b p < .01$, two-tailed
Source: Diener et al. (1984), adapted from table 2, p. 585. Copyright 1984, American Psychological Association. Adapted by author's permission.

of six consecutive weeks. The subject wore an alarm wristwatch that was set to a randomly generated schedule of signal times, and reports were made concurrent with the signal. Trait measures from the Jackson (1967) Personality Research Form were correlated with the percentages of time in situations. The results are shown in Table 2.18. Time spent in social situations as opposed to time spent alone correlated negatively with need for order. Time spent in novel situations as opposed to typical situations correlated negatively with needs for achievement, affiliation, and order. Time spent in work as opposed to recreation correlated positively with needs for achievement and cognitive structure. Time in recreation with others (recreate social) as opposed to solitary recreation correlated negatively with need for cognitive structure and positively ($r = .41$) with the extraversion scale of the Eysenck Personality Inventory.

Negative affect in situations showed no significant pattern of correlation with the personality variables. *Autonomy* correlated negatively with positive affect in the social, typical, and work situations. *Extraversion* correlated positively with positive affect in the social, typical, and recreation situations.

In a later study Emmons, Diener, and Larsen (1986) distinguished between situations that were chosen and those that were imposed on the subjects. *Extraversion, sociability, affiliation,* and *impulsivity* trait scales correlated positively with time spent in *chosen* social situations and negatively with time spent in *imposed* social situations. If the distinctions between chosen and ignored were not employed, no correlations would have been found between social activity and any of these variables. *Extraversion* correlated significantly ($r = .49$) with percentage of time in chosen social recreational activities but did not correlate at all with time in imposed social recreational activities; *sociability* and *impulsivity* showed the same

Table 2.19. *Mean correlations between category judgment and frequency of molecular behavioral features*

	Aggregate of 10 prototypic features	Most prototypic single feature
Aggression	.52	.53
Withdrawal	.40	.43
Prosocial	.35	.48

Source: Mischel (1984), table 4, p. 362. Copyright 1984, American Psychological Association. Adapted by author's permission.

pattern of results, and *impulsivity* correlated negatively and significantly with time spent in imposed social recreational activities. *Endurance* and *achievement* correlated positively (*r*'s: End = .52; Ach = .46) with percentage of time in chosen work situations but did not correlate significantly with time spent in imposed work situations. In contrast, *extraversion* correlated negatively (*r* = −.40) with time spent in chosen work situations and positively, but nonsignificantly (*r* = .34), with time spent in imposed work situations. The findings were rather clear: Personality largely influenced time spent in chosen situations and was either unrelated or negatively related to time in imposed situations. *Extraversion,* for example, correlated positively with time spent in chosen social and social-recreational situations and negatively with time spent in chosen work situations. Extraverts like to party when they feel like it and at parties of their own choosing, but they do not spend much time at obligational social activities or self-initiated work activities. This study indicates the need to make distinctions among types of situations in order to provide fair tests of the ability of trait measures to predict behavior.

Mischel (1984) has recently emphasized the need to relate traits, as judged by the observer, to molecular behavioral acts that are judged to be prototypical for the trait. Molecular acts recorded by observers were rated for prototypicality for the traits of aggression, withdrawal, and prosociality. Independent observers made global ratings of the children on these traits. Table 2.19 shows the correlations between the rated global traits and prototypical behavioral instances in aggregation and for the single, most prototypic instance. The single most prototypic act correlated more highly than the aggregates for the three traits.

Mischel has shown how behavior in the delay-of-gratification situation varies with all kinds of cognitive manipulations of the situation, but his own recent data (Mischel et al., 1988) show that behavior in this laboratory situation predicts traits years later. The answer to this paradox may be that, in spite of the specifics of situations, the habitual interpretations of situations are partly a function of the dispositions of persons.

Summary

Traits do not "determine behavior." According to the view taken here, they are personal and general constructs that are used to summarize individual consistencies in behavior. States may influence behavior, but the way in which they do so is not necessarily a direct one because the state includes a combination of aroused affects, cognitions, impulses, and appraisals of possible outcomes. States are more related to immediately subsequent behavior than traits (Zuckerman, 1979a), but states must be assessed just prior to the behavioral event, which is not usually practical. Individual differences are only weakly suggested if we examine consistency in states or overt behaviors at two different times or in two different situations. Reliable evidence of individual differences and the importance of the person in situations are only apparent when we average or aggregate states or behaviors over time.

The need for aggregation to demonstrate trait lawfulness or predictability is not unique to personality psychology. Psychologists who study operant behavior do not attempt to predict single bar presses but examine cumulative curves, which are aggregations of responses. Psychophysiologists who analyze the cortical responses to stimuli do not look at the raw EEG following a stimulation, which looks like hash; they sum that segment of the EEG along with many others in a computer, which averages the output signals for each post-stimulus point in time. What emerges is a clear and replicable function called the "average evoked potential" (see chapter 6). One can obtain a measure of heart rate using only two heart beats, and two measures from three heart beats, using the interresponse intervals. But no one would claim that an individual's heart rate is inherently unstable or that individuals do not show reliable differences in heart rates on the basis of the relation between two measures of heart rate from only three consecutive beats. Even physicists must sometimes resort to aggregating when working with microparticles because of the largely unpredictable action of a single particle.

Mischel (1984) claims that aggregation is simply treating lawful variation due to situations or person-in-situation interactions as error. There is nothing wrong with this approach. The vast majority of experimental and social psychologists treat individual variation as error in their focus on the stimulus or situation variance. If one wants to focus on the person or the situation, one to the exclusion of the other, one treats the other source of variance as error and attempts to reduce it to a minimum. However, if one wants to study the person–situation interaction, one must use an appropriate experimental design. Studies of the actual influences of persons, situations, and their interactions on states or behaviors usually show that the person–situation interaction is important, accounting for a proportion of the variance equivalent to that of persons (about 25% each in studies of real situations). The effects of situations on behavior are more variable from study to study and from one response measure to another because they seem to depend on how much contrast there is in the few situations selected for comparison. There is usually enough variance in persons to produce a significant effect.

Although the situation is imposed in an experiment, in real life some situations are selected by people and others are avoided. Personality is one important determinant of where individuals choose to spend their time and what they do in those situations, as shown in the studies by Diener et al. (1984) and Emmons et al. (1986).

Some investigators, such as Thomas and Chess and Kagan and Moss, have attempted to identify what they call "temperamental traits" in the first years of life and to use these to predict similar traits and adjustment in adult life. In most cases, observations of children before school age (6 years) have not predicted adult personality or adjustment with any moderate degree of significance. After 6–7 years of age we begin to see better prediction of adolescent and adult personality, particularly for the super-trait of *sociability*. Consistency of personality during short periods of childhood and from junior high school to senior high school is good, but prediction from high school to later adult life is poor. The Kagan and Moss study showed an interaction of gender and environment in determining consistency of some traits. Females showed more consistency for passivity and dependency, and males showed more for aggression, nonconformity, and competitiveness traits from childhood to adult life. Some of the problems in long-term prediction are due to the unreliability of the rating methods used. Questionnaires used during these periods show much more consistency in personality traits. Questionnaires also show much higher consistency of personality over long periods (20–30 years) of adult life. Apparently, personality stabilizes between adolescence and young adult life and shows good consistency thereafter, with little change in consistency of traits.

Two major sources of information about traits are self-descriptive measures and ratings made by others. Such characterizations range from very narrow situation-specific ones to very general trait descriptions. When well-designed and reliable questionnaires are contrasted with reliable ratings by several observers or peers, or one who knows the subject very well (a spouse, for instance), the typical self–other correlations fall between .3 and .6 (median about .45) and 93% of the correlations exceeed the .30 barrier suggested by Mischel for trait versus behavior correlations. In the cases of both self and other evaluations we are comparing two subjective aggregations of past behaviors and subjective reactions. Conceivably, such correlations could be made higher by more attention to the bases for the judgments and better descriptions of prototypical behaviors to define the trait for the observers. But there are limits to how much consistency can be achieved. Sometimes correlations of .6 or higher can be achieved and in these cases we are predicting for most of the people most of the time.

Certainly, as Bem and Allen (1974) suggest, "some of the people" are simply more variable in their expressions of a trait and therefore harder to describe or predict. But these are likely to be the persons who are not extreme on the particular trait and whose behavior is determined more by situations than by dispositions. Other traits may be more predictable for them. It has been suggested that we adopt an idiodynamic approach and assess what traits or idiosyncratic cognitions are relevant for individuals rather than applying the same trait constructs to all individuals (Kelly, 1955). But idiodynamic approaches, though beloved by clinicians, have proven to be a scientific dead end. If we hope to develop generalized laws of behavior, the same concepts and measurements must be applied to all persons.

Aggregation of either states or behavior can rapidly increase the reliabilities of state measures, and reasonably reliable estimates of the mean of a great number of states can sometimes be achieved by averaging only a few states. Predicting states or behaviors from trait tests depends on the reliability of both types of tests (state and traits). Although single trait tests are generally reliable, it does not hurt to combine one or more relative trait tests to predict to aggregated state or behavior measures. It is essential to aggregate the state and behavior measures because a single state or behavioral index is generally unreliable. Some specific trait measures, narrowly designed around specific situations, achieve higher prediction levels than broader trait measures. However, in the case of social anxiety situations, general measures are just as predictive as narrow specific trait measures. In this case, the general trait measure should be used in preference to the specific one because it is more generalizable to other situations.

Table 2.20 summarizes the consistency findings for one of the major traits found in all analyses of personality dimensions: *extraversion*. The table shows the findings divided into trait and state reliability, consistency between self and other observations, and consistency between trait measures and aggregated behaviors and states.

Overall, the consistency picture for E-Sociability is good. The trait measure is reasonably stable over long periods of peoples' lives, and the states aggregate to high levels of reliability over time. Self and other reports are fairly consistent with each other. The trait measure does correlate with appropriate behavioral indices, particularly proportion of time spent in social recreational situations.

The picture for the N and P dimensions would probably not be too different except that one must rely more on self-report states of dysphoric feelings than on overt behavior for N. Prototypical and frequently occurring behavioral examples of P might also be difficult to obtain in a normal

Table 2.20. *Summary of findings on the consistency (reliability and validity) of the trait of extraversion-sociability*

Authors (year)	Trait measure	Assessment interval	Correlations
Reliability:			
Traits over time			
Block (1971)	Median ratings on E variables	Junior h.s. to senior h.s.	M = .45 (.67)[a] F = .40 (.59)
		Senior h.s. to adult	M = .28 (.41) F = .36 (.49)
Kagan & Moss (1962)	Ratings: social interaction	10–14 yrs to adult	M = .65, F = .64
Costa et al. (1980)	Sociability Questionnaire	Adult: 6-yr interval	.81
		Adult: 12-yr interval	.74
Kelly, E.L. (1955)	Sociability Questionnaire	Adult: 20 yrs (25–45)	.47
Finn (1986)	Social introversion Q. (MMPI)	Adult: 30 yrs (21–51)	.49
		Adult: 30 yrs (45–75)	.56
States over time (aggregates[b])			
Epstein (1979)	Daily self-report scales:	Affiliation behavior	.77
		Affiliation impulse	.68
		Affiliation situations	.55
	Observed behavior:	Initiated contact with others	.90
Validity			
Self vs. other trait assessment			
McCrea & Costa (1982)	Spouse vs. self ratings	Extraversion	Males = .51–.68 Females = .50–.52
Various (Table 2.4)	Peer vs. self ratings	Extraversion-type scales	.48 (.43–.72)
Questionnaire measures vs. behavior			
Epstein (1979)	Social contacts vs. extraversion scale		.52
Diener et al. (1984)	% time in social recreational situations vs. extraversion		.41
Emmons et al. (1986)	% time in chosen social situations vs. extraversion		.40
	% time in chosen work situations vs. extraversion		− .40
	% time in chosen social recreational situations		.49
Questionnaire measures vs. emotional states			
Diener et al. (1984)	Positive affect in social situations vs. extraversion		.32
Emmons et al. (1986)	Positive affect in chosen recreational social situations vs. extraversion		.31
Zuckerman et al. (1978)	Trait vs. mean 11 daily state measures of affiliation		.35 (.57)[a]

[a] Corrected for unreliability
[b] 12-Day aggregates—odd-even day reliability

population but could be more easily observed in an institutionalized delinquent group. For instance, Farley and Farley (1972) found that incarcerated delinquents who scored high on the General Sensation Seeking Scale (Zuckerman, 1971b, Zuckerman et al., 1964) engaged in fighting, made escape attempts, and were punished for disobedience with greater frequency than low sensation seekers.

The current phase of the controversy over the consistency of personality has lasted about 20 years now. There is certainly enough data to give us a good idea of the sources of inconsistency and the best methods for assessing the consistencies. As Epstein (1979) says, "traits are alive and well." The next task is to begin the long-delayed inquiry into the sources of some broad traits of personality. The subsequent chapters of this book attempt to describe what is known about the biological bases of these traits.

3   Behavioral genetics and personality traits

Overview

Psychology is not the only science that makes use of hypothetical constructs such as traits. Until the 1950s the gene was a hypothetical construct in the science of genetics. In 1953 James Watson and Francis Crick proposed that deoxyribonucleic acid (DNA) is the basis of the gene and constructed a molecular structure that could account for its biological properties. Since that momentous discovery, the molecular mechanisms of heredity have been extensively investigated, and experimental work in manipulating genes, genetic engineering, has begun. Recombinant DNA techniques have made the mapping of the genetic code in the DNA of humans a feasible project. Although there is a wide gap in complexity between molecular genetics and behavioral genetics, the understanding of genetic mechanisms will eventually narrow that difference.

Genes are chemical templates that control the production and regulation of proteins, which form the structures of cells, act as neurotransmitters and hormones, and form enzymes that determine the chemical reactions in the cells. The genes that regulate the proteins involved in the structure and function of the nervous system must be important in the cognitive and behavioral functions that emerge from that system.

Most persons concede a genetic influence on physical characteristics such as height, in which parent-child and sibling resemblance is evident, or the precise physical similarity of identical twins. But there is more resistance to accepting the inheritance of behavioral characteristics and disorders. Part of the "negative halo" effect that hangs over behavioral genetics stems from the abuse of Darwinian evolutionary and genetic theory by racists and other people who seek to justify the usurpation of power in terms of inherent superiority. The misinterpretation and misuse of scientific knowledge for spurious goals is not limited to genetics. Science that serves racism or religious or political ideology is usually bad science, as was that of the German Third Reich and the Lysenko period of Soviet genetics. Scientists have a responsibility to challenge unwarranted generalizations from their findings and theories as well as a responsibility to defend freedom of inquiry (Zuckerman, 1990). Scientific questions must be settled by scientific methods not by debate in the public forum.

One cannot discuss heritability without discussing environment as well. Recently, behavior geneticists such as Plomin (1986) have become more

89

interested in the important environmental influences that play a role in personality traits. The results from this science will make us rethink the entire question of which environmental influences are important in personality. Even extreme environmentalists would do well to read these studies because they provide surprising information on the type of environment that is influential. This information is important apart from the quantitative question of the relative effects of heredity and environment. This chapter discusses genetic and environmental influences on personality traits as assessed by questionnaires and behavior ratings in humans and various behavioral methods in animals. Later chapters deal with the genetic influences on more basic physiological phenomena such as biochemical processes and cortical electrical potentials. The genetic influences in behavior disorders are discussed in chapters 8 and 9.

Concepts of heredity

Major sources of misunderstanding about heredity stem from misconceptions. We do not inherit behavior, habits, personality traits, intelligence, or even height. These are *phenotypes,* which are influenced by but are not direct expressions of *genotypes,* the actual structures in the DNA molecules. Genes code for the construction of sequences of amino acids. These sequences form polypeptides or enzymes and other proteins. Any behavioral or trait characteristic depends on a number of such biological actions. Variations in these actions can contribute to variations in the phenotypical expression. Almost any complex behavior is likely to involve many biological actions, each of which is determined by many genes. A gene is likely to influence many different kinds of behaviors (*pleiotropy*). Conversely, any behavior is likely to be influenced by many different genes. For these reasons, it is necessary to employ the methods of quantitative genetics to assess genetic influences on the phenotype.

Genes interact with environment from conception onward. A person has genes that are "programmed" for large bone growth and strong production of growth hormone, but a lack of protein and calcium in pre- or postnatal environments will stunt the growth regardless of genetic coding. Genes assemble the building materials but the materials must be available for assembly.

Genes affect behavior in a probabilistic fashion; they are not deterministic in themselves. Let us take alcoholism as an example. Both separated twin (Pederson et al., 1984) and adoption (Goodwin, 1979) studies suggest that alcoholism can be inherited: A subject may become alcoholic even if there has been no shared family environment with an alcoholic. Certain strains of mice (C57BLs) drink much more alcohol than other strains (DBA/2s & BALBs) (Rodgers, 1966) and show more tolerance for alcohol (Kakihana et al., 1966), which also suggests that there is much more than human social influences involved in alcoholism. However, people do not become alcoholics if there is no alcohol in their environment, whatever their genome. Unfortunately for potential alcoholics, most human societies discovered and used alcohol early in their history. But different cultural-ethnic groups developed different drinking patterns (Bales, 1946), and ethnicity is an important determinant of risk for alcoholism. Genes may determine susceptibility to alcohol by affecting an enzyme that is involved in the metabolism of alcohol. Persons who cannot tolerate even small quantities of alcohol without physical discomfort are unlikely to become alcoholic, but those who tolerate large quantities of alcohol, because of an efficient metabolic mechanism, are at increased risk for alcoholism (Rodgers, 1966). Genes may also increase or decrease vulnerability by their effect on broad personality dispositions. Alcoholic males tend to have impulsive, extraverted, sensation-seeking personalities before they become alcoholic. In many social settings this kind of person almost inevitably engages in heavy social drinking. If the other genetically affected vulnerabilities are in line, the heavy drinking pattern can easily slip into the alcoholic pattern.

The influence of genes on behavior is complex and is always intertwined with the physiology and environmental possibilities of the organism. It is the task of biometric genetics to analyze the genetic influence by means of appropriate statistical models, which give population probabilities for genetic influence. To say that a trait has a 50% heritability does not tell us what determined the level of that trait in a particular individual. Siblings share half of their segregating genes on the average, but the genetic similarity for any particular sibling pair depends on how many chromosomes from their father and mother they have in common. Behavior genetics is not different from most of psychology in using statistics to generalize about the behavior of populations from samples of limited size. Large samples and replications of findings, as well as the fit of the findings to models, are what inspire confidence in the methods and the results they yield.

Modes of inheritance

Genes are coded pieces of the DNA located on chromosomes. Chromosomes occur in pairs, one of which is from the mother and the other from the father. Most human cells have 23 pairs of chromosomes, 46 in all, but in sex cells (sperm and eggs) there are 23 chromosomes. These 23 chromosomes represent various combinations of one parent's chromosomes, which create a great deal of genetic variability. During conception the sets of 23 chromosomes from each parent combine to form a new set of 46, which contain the genes of the new organism. *Alleles* are alternative forms of genes located at the same places, or *loci,* on the matching chromosomes.

Mendel's experiments on the pea plant in the middle of the nineteenth century inspired a formulation of the hereditary mechanism of *dominance.*

The prevailing theories of the time assumed that the "germ stuff" of the parents somehow blended after conception to produce a mixture of the parents' traits. Mendel correctly assumed that there are two elements of heredity, one from each parent, which do not blend but remain independent but linked after conception. Mendel happened to experiment with a plant whose characteristics, such as the form of the seed and the length of the stem are determined by pairs of alleles at a single locus. When the two strains were crossed, all of first generation showed the characteristics of one of the parent strains. However, in the next generation the traits of the other strain appeared in nearly one of every four plants. This lawful ratio of 3 to 1 (dominant to recessive) proved that the hereditary component of the strain that did not appear in the first generation was not blended but was simply "dominated" by the other component in determining the phenotypic expression. When two of the *recessive* genes combined, as happens in one of four cases if we assume random combination, the trait governed by that recessive gene was characteristic of the offspring.

In humans, single-gene dominant-recessive heredity is most often associated with certain disorders such as phenylketonuria (PKU), in which an enzyme that is necessary for the conversion of phenylalanine to tyrosine is absent or inactive, resulting in high levels of phenylalanine in the blood. The result is that the developing nervous system is deprived of nutrients, which causes mental deficiency. If the condition is discovered early enough, the child can be put on a low phenylalanine diet, which prevents mental deficiency. The interesting point of this discovery is that *heredity is not destiny;* proper adjustment of the environment (in this case nutrition) can prevent the phenotypic expression that might otherwise occur. The gene does not directly "cause" the mental deficiency; the behavioral effect is a byproduct of the brain damage caused by an enzyme deficiency, caused by an unfortunate combination of recessive genes.

Mental retardation is one of the clinical symptoms of about one quarter of the known 466 autosomal recessive disorders (Plomin, DeFries, & McClearn, 1980). However, another type of mental deficiency represents the lower range of the normal variation in the distribution of intelligence. This so-called familial mental deficiency represents, in large part, an averaging of the effects of many genes from both parents. Single-gene effects are not likely to be responsible for most complex behavioral traits that show a normal distribution in the population, though dominance effects may be involved in many genes affecting the biological determinants of some of these traits. One of the tasks of quantitative behavior genetics is to distinguish the roles of dominance and additive effects in the polygenetic determination of a trait.

In additive genetic inheritance, it is the sum of alleles at a single locus or of many alleles at many loci that determines the trait. Dominance also can involve more than one locus, and when many genes are involved, the distribution of phenotypes resembles a normal distribution that is indistinguishable from the distribution produced by additive inheritance. In some plants, crossing a pure (homozygous) tall strain with a pure short strain immediately produces plants of intermediate height rather than the uniformly tall strain in the first generation and the dichotomous distribution in the second generation in Mendel's experiments with peaplants. In the case of additive inheritance the average offspring show a trait that is the average of the trait shown by the two parents, but in the Mendelian type of inheritance the typical offspring tend to match either one parent or the other in the trait. In additive inheritance the child of two tall parents is more likely to be tall, the child of two short parents is more likely to be short, and the child of one tall and one short parent is likely to be of intermediate height.

Dominance concerns the interaction of two alleles at a single locus on a homologous chromosome. However, interaction can occur between two alleles at different loci. This is called *epistasis*. Additive and dominance effects are summed across loci, but the interaction of alleles at different loci may result in effects that are more complex than the sum of the alleles. Epistasis can give complex configural results so that there is no family resemblance between siblings or between parents and children on the trait. Only in identical twins, in which the full complement of genes is the same, do we see similar epistasis effects. Lykken (1982) believes that epistasis has been underestimated as a genetic influence. He has developed a new term, *emergenesis*, to describe these unusual, specific, and complex traits or behaviors, which are duplicated only in identical twins.

Siblings usually differ widely in traits such as voice quality and the pattern of evoked cortical potentials (see chapter 6), whereas identical twins are remarkably alike in such traits. The strange coincidences of habits and mannerisms reported for separated identical twins are also evidence of the effects of emergenesis.

Quantitative genetics: assessment of family relationships

Quantitative genetics in humans rests on comparisons of biological and adoptive family relationships in which genetic and environmental influences are naturally varied. Table 3.1 shows the sources of similarities and differences among relations differing in genes and shared environments. In addition to the hereditary mechanisms already discussed, a further distinction must be made between two types of environment. Relations in intact families share a common family environment (Ecf) to the extent that parents treat children similarly and interactions are of a sort that foster positive modeling among family members. Age differences can produce nonshared effects, even within the family, so the best comparisons are between twins because the age is the same. What is called common family

Table 3.1. *Sources of similarities and differences among family members*

Relationship	Sources of similarities			Sources of differences			
	Ga	Gna	Ecf	Ga	Gna	Ens	Error
ITs-apart	1.0	1.0	—	—	—	1.0	1.0
ITs-together	1.0	1.0	1.0	—	—	1.0	1.0
FTs & sibs-apart	0.5	0.25	—	0.5	0.75	1.0	1.0
FTs & sibs-together	0.5	0.25	1.0	0.5	0.75	1.0	1.0
Biol. parent-child	0.5	—	1.0	0.5	1.0	1.0	1.0
Adopted sibs, parents, & children	—	—	1.0	1.0	1.0	1.0	1.0

Note: Ga, additive genetic; Gna, nonadditive genetic (includes dominance and epistasis); Ecf, common family environment; Ens, nonshared environment; Error, error of measurement of phenotype, e.g., test unreliability; IT, identical twins; FT, fraternal twins. Proportions in table indicate the maximal influences in a population that could be due to the particular source of similarity or difference.

environment here is called *shared environment* by other investigators because children in one family usually share other aspects of environment such as schools, teachers, and friends. *Nonshared environment* is all of the environment that is different for persons. Biologically related children who are separated after birth and raised in different families live in nonshared environments. Nonshared environments produce only differences among persons unless something produces correlated environments like selective placement of adoptees.

Another source of differences for all of the relationships listed is the error involved in assessing a trait. If trait measurement changes in an unpredictable fashion, it limits the extent of measured similarity. In the usual way of calculating heritabilities, the error of measurement, which is usually about 15–25% of the total variance, is counted as part of the environmental variance. This tends to exaggerate the part of the variance that is said to be due to environment and underestimates the proportion of variance due to heredity.

Identical twins who are separated and adopted soon after birth and reared in different family environments constitute the pure cases for heredity. If there has been no contact between the twins during their formative years and if the initial placement was not selective in respect to dependent trait variables, similarities between such twins are due only to genetic influences; environment can produce only differences between them. Both twins have the same set of genes produced by the fertilization of a single ovum by a single sperm (monozygotic) and therefore share genetic influences of all types, additive and nonadditive, the latter including both dominance and epistasis kinds. In this case, the correlation between the two twins should be a direct expression of the proportion of the reliable variance in the trait due to their common genetic influence. If separated identical twins correlate .50 on some trait, we can say that 50% of the variance in that trait is due to the *broad heredity* influences (*broad* referring to all three types of genetic mechanisms in common). Most behavior geneticists would then obtain the environmental influence by subtraction from 1.0, ignoring the fact that the remainder also includes the error of measurement. Corrections of genetic and environmental variances for unreliability are almost never done for reasons that are not clear.

Many more studies of identical twins raised in the same family than of separated twins have been done because they are so much more accessible and there are so many more of them. However, as shown in Table 3.1, these twins share common family environments, in addition to having the same genetic structure. To assess the influence of shared environments, the identicals are often compared with fraternal twin pairs who also share common environments, but who share only 50% of their additive genes on the average (indicated by 0.5 under Ga). Because fraternal twins are produced by fertilization of two ova by two sperms (dizygotic), they bear no more genetic relationship than any other siblings; however, being born at the same time, they may share more common environment than ordinary siblings. Although they share half of their additive genes, the shared non-additive genes are considerably less, and in the case of epistasis there is probably little shared genetic influence.

If the genetic determination of a trait is solely of the additive type, then either fraternal twins or siblings should show a correlation of the trait that is about half the size of the correlation of identical twins on the same trait. If the correlation of identical twins reared together is .60, then the correlation of fraternal twins should be .30 under the assumptions of additive type inheritance and similar degree of shared environment. A frequently used index devised by Falconer (1981) simply doubles the difference between the correlations of identical and fraternal twins to estimate the heritability $[h = 2 \times (\text{Ir} - \text{Fr})]$. Other comparisons, such as that of Jinks and Fulker (1970), compare the variance between and within sets of twins to compute heritabilities. The advantage of the analysis of variance methods is that they provide direct tests of models of heritability. Correlational models provide only some rough indications of the fit of the data to the models of heredity. If the heritability is not solely of an additive type, the correlation between fraternal twins is lower than half the correlation between identicals; and if epistasis were of major importance, the correlation between fraternal twins would be close to zero. In these cases, formulas for heritability such as Falconer's, that depend on the two-to-one ratio, exaggerate the heritability of the trait.

The main purpose of comparisons of fraternal and identical twins reared together is to control the factor of shared environment. Many workers insist that identicals are treated more alike and share more of a common environment than fraternals because of their greater similarity. One way to evaluate the influence of shared environment is to compare the extent of correlation of identicals raised apart with identicals raised together, fraternals raised apart with fraternals raised together, or siblings raised apart with those raised in the same environment.

Children receive half of their genes from each parent, so if additive genes were all that is involved in a trait, one would expect that the correlation between a child and one parent would be the same as that between siblings. But a parent and a child do not share nonadditive genes; and even though we assume they have a shared environment, they generally do not share the parents' past family environments or their parents' contemporary extrafamily environment, such as friends and work associates. However, most personality theories assume that parents influence their children through their role modeling and direct training and reinforcement, which should foster imitation of parental traits.

Adopted children provide the pure case for environment. The only factors producing similarity between adopted children and their adopting parents, and between adopted siblings from different biological parents, is shared environment. Comparisons of adoptive parent–child or sibling relationships with separated biological relationships provide a test of pure shared environmental influences versus nearly pure additive genetic influences; "nearly pure" because the biological mother also provided the prenatal environment.

Studies of personality genetics: human adults

Identical and fraternal twins reared together in the biological family of origin.

Most biometric genetic studies require large numbers of relatives to produce reliable results of sufficient power to test differences in correlation and models of inheritance that require at least several categories of relationships. For this reason, the data selected for this section give priority to the larger biometric studies in which there are at least 100 twins of each type. Nine such studies of adult identical and fraternal twins reared together are listed in Table 3.2. These studies used questionnaire scales relevant to at least one of the three supertraits: E-*sociability*, N-*emotionality*, and P-*impulsive unsocialized sensation seeking.* The studies are listed in rough order of the age ranges of subjects used in order to examine possible changes in heritabilities as a function of adult age. However, because no elderly-twin studies could be found, this question cannot be fully addressed.

The data show some age decline, particularly for the identical twins' correlations on E-Sy trait measures. However, in all three trait dimensions

Table 3.2. *Correlations among adult identical (I) twins and fraternal (F) twins on personality scales assessing the three major dimensions of personality*

Study	Subjects (sex/ages)	In's	Fn's	E-Sy I	E-Sy F	N-Emo I	N-Emo F	P-ImpUSS I	P-ImpUSS F
Loehlin & Nichols (1976)[a]	18	490	317	.61	.25	.54	.22	.54	.32
Tellegen et al. (1988)[b]	M 21	217	114	.54	.06	.54	.41	.58	.25
Rose (1988)[c]	M&F 14–34	228	182	.60	.42	.41	.22	.70	.41
Floderus-Myrhed et al. (1980)[d]	M 17–49	2279	3670	.47	.20	.46	.21	—	—
Floderus-Myrhed et al. (1980)	F 17–49	2720	4143	.54	.21	.54	.25	—	—
Rose et al. (1988)[e]	M 24–49	1027	2304	.46	.15	.33	.12	—	—
Rose et al. (1988)	F 24–49	1293	2520	.49	.14	.43	.18	—	—
Eaves & Young (1981)[f]	M 31	303	172	.55	.19	.47	.07	.47	.28
Rushton et al. (1986)[g]	M 30	296	179	—	—	—	—	.52	.20
Fulker et al. (1980)[h]	M 31	466	378	—	—	—	—	.60	.21
Pederson et al. (1988)[i]	M 59	151	204	.54	.06	.41	.24	—	—
Median correlations				.54	.19	.46	.22	.56	.27
Falconer (1981) heritability = 2 (Ir-Fr)				.70		.48		.59	

[a]Subjects were twins in their senior year of high school contacted after taking National Merit Scholarship Examination. Scores are based on factors derived from items of the California Psychological Inventory by Eaves and Young (1981).
[b]Factor scores from the Tellegen Multidimensional Personality Questionnaire: Positive *emotionality* (E) combines *well-being, social potency, achievement* and *social closeness* scales; negative *emotionality* (N) uses *stress reaction, alienation,* and *aggression* scales; *constraint* (P−) combines *control, harm avoidance* (SS reversed), and *traditionalism*.
[c]Subjects were college students; E, N, & P are factor content scores derived from the MMPI.
[d]12,812 twins from Swedish population. Study uses a short form of the Eysenck Personality Inventory E and N scales (no P scale).
[e]14,288 twins from Finnish population. Study uses same form of EPI as Swedish study.
[f]Used Eysenck Personality Questionnaire containing E, N, and P scales. Subjects from University of London, Institute of Psychiatry Twin Register (IPTR).
[g]Subjects from IPTR. Study uses scales of *altruism, empathy,* and *nurturance* (traits negatively associated with P), and *aggressiveness* and *assertiveness* (which should be positively associated with P). Median correlations from the five scales are reported under the P heading. For ITs r's ranged from .40 to .54; for FTs r's went from .04 to .25.
[h]Subjects from IPTR. Study uses the *sensation seeking* scale (form V) listed under P.
[i]Older cohort of Swedish twins. Used short form of EPI as in Floderus-Myrhed.

there is a remarkably narrow range of correlations between identical twins: 22 of the 24 (92%) correlations range between .41 and .61. There is more variation in the fraternal twin correlations; the equivalent 92% range is .01 to .28. The median identical twin correlations for E-Sy, N-Emo, and P-ImpUSS are .54, .46, and .56, respectively. The median fraternal twin correlations for the corresponding three dimensions are .19, .22, and .27. For the N and P-ImpUSS dimensions, the median fraternal twin correlations are just about half of the identical twin correlations, suggesting a fair fit to the additive genetic variance model. The application of the Falconer index to these median correlations yields heritabilities of 48% and 59% for N and P dimensions, respectively. The Falconer index would yield a heritability of 70% of the E-Sy dimension, but this is exaggerated because of the low fraternal twin correlation relative to the expected one-half of the identicals. Because the heritability should not exceed the correlation between identical twins, this value must be exaggerated by the low fraternal twin correlations. In such a case, the identical twin correlation should be used in preference to the result obtained from the correlation difference. Following this rule, the identical twin heritability of .54 for E would be close to the heritabilities for the other two traits (.48 for N, and .59 for P). From these data alone, one would conclude that the heritabilities of the three main supertraits were all in the narrow range of 48 to 59% without correction for unreliabilities of the measures. The correlations alone would suggest the appropriateness of the additive genetic model for N and P, but not for E, in which nonadditive genetic mechanisms may be lowering the fraternal twin correlations. As will be seen, more sophisticated model testing analyses also support the conclusion that E may differ from N and P in the greater influence of nonadditive genetic mechanisms in the former.

The Jinks and Fulker(1970) model uses the between and within variance of twins or other relations to test the fit of the data to specified models, and it derives measures of heritability and environment from the data, based on the maximum data available. Eaves and Young (1981) claim superiority for this model to correlational ones because the model provides tests of assumptions and alternate hypotheses; each observation counts and no parts of the data are preferred arbitrarily to others; and parameter estimates are more precise and standard errors of estimates can be obtained. In Table 3.3, the Falconer index of heritability is compared with the estimates from Jinks and Fulker's model, as calculated by Eaves and Young (1981).

Analyses of the EPQ E and N from the correlations for twins using the Falconer index in the Eaves and Young (1981) study would yield high heritabilities of 72 and 80% for E and N, respectively, values out of line with the identical twin correlations of .55 and .47. Again, the very low fraternal twin correlations are producing the exaggerated h^2 values. In contrast, the Jinks and Fulker ANOVA method produces reasonable heritabilities of 49% for E and 41% for N, which are only slightly below the identical twin correlations. The identical and fraternal twin correlations for the P scale are .47 and .28, yielding a Falconer h^2 index of 38%. The Jinks and Fulker method yields an h^2 of 47%, precisely matching the identical twin correlation of .47.

Eaves and Young applied the Jinks and Fulker method to the data from the large twin study by Floderus-Myrhed et al. (1980). As in the previous analyses, the fraternal twin correlations in many of the age-sex cohorts are

Table 3.3. *Comparisons of heritability estimates from Falconer (Fa) correlational and the Jinks and Fulker (J & F) model-fitting methods*

	Extraversion				Neuroticism			
	Correl.[b]		Heritabilities (h^2)		Correl.[a]		Heritabilities (h^2)	
Cohort	I r	F r	Fa	J & F	I r	F r	Fa	J & F
Eaves & Young (1981)								
Males, age 40–49	.46	.21	.50	.45	.40	.16	.48	.38
Males, age 30–39	.37	.19	.36	.38	.39	.19	.40	.39
Males, age 20–29	.51	.18	.66	.51	.53	.24	.58	.53
Females, age 40–49	.51	.14	.74	.50	.42	.18	.48	.40
Females, age 30–39	.50	.16	.68	.49	.51	.24	.54	.51
Females, age 20–29	.58	.27	.62	.57	.62	.29	.66	.61
Eaves & Young (1981)[c]	.55	.19	.72	.49	.47	.07	.80	.41
Rushton et al. (1986)	*P type Scales*							
Altruism	.53	.25	.56	.51				
Empathy	.54	.20	.68	.51				
Nurturance	.49	.14	.70	.43				
Aggressiveness	.40	.04	.72	.39				
Assertiveness	.52	.20	.64	.53				
Eaves & Eysenck (1977)								
EPQ psychoticism	.47	.28	.38	.46				
Fulker et al. (1980)								
Sensation seeking scale	.60	.21	.78	.58				

[a]Data from Floderus-Myrhed, Pederson, and Rasmuson (1980)
[b]I: identical twins; F: fraternal twins
[c]Data on E from Eaves & Eysenck (1975); data on N from Eaves & Eysenck (1976)

considerably lower than the expected half of the identical twin coefficient, producing high heritabilities by the Falconer formula but lower heritabilities by the Jinks and Fulker method. As an example, look at the group of females in Table 3.3, ages 40–49, for which the identical and fraternal twin correlations for *extraversion* are .51 and .14, respectively. The Falconer (1981) formula produces a heritability of 74% whereas the Jinks and Fulker method results in heritability of 50%, the same as the correlation for identical twins of .50 and most of the estimates from the other groups of about 50% heritability for E. For *neuroticism,* there is little disagreement between the two methods because most of the fraternal twin correlations are close to the expected additive variance proportion of one-half of the identical twin value.

Rushton, Fulker, Neale, Nias, and Eysenck (1986) examined the twin correlations on a group of scales, four of which are theoretically related to the P dimension: altruism, empathy, nurturance, and aggressiveness.

Assertiveness might be more properly regarded as an E subtrait. The median correlations for all five scales were included in Table 3.2. Table 3.3 shows the values for the individual scales and the heritabilities calculated from the two methods. All five scales show higher heritabilities using the Falconer method. In the case of *altruism,* the difference (.56 versus .51) is not great, but for the other scales the differences are large, due primarily to the low fraternal twin correlations. Note that the Jinks and Fulker heritabilities are quite close to the correlations for identical twins. The same type of finding is obtained for sensation seeking (Fulker, Eysenck, & Zuckerman, 1980), which yields a very high heritability of .78 by the Falconer method, but a heritability of .58, closer to the identical twin correlation of .60, by the more sophisticated biometric method.

The conclusions from these comparisons are that derivation of heritabilities by application of the Falconer method (which seems to be the one most widely used) for correlational data can lead to exaggerated heritability values when the ratio of 2:1 for identical to fraternal twin correlations is not found. The method seems to depend on this finding, based on the assumption of purely additive genetic variance, which does not seem to hold in many cases. When the heritability obtained by this method exceeds the correlation for identical twins, it would be better to take that correlation as the best estimate of heritability within the limitation of correlational data. Using the correlation between identical twins reared together as an estimate of heritability assumes that there is no shared environmental influence affecting the correlation.

Comparisons of separated twins

One of the most frequent objections to the twin method is that comparison of identical and fraternal twins reared together does not really control shared environment because identical twins are really treated more alike by parents and other persons than fraternal twins, and therefore much of their greater psychological similarity is due to environment rather than heredity. Loehlin and Nichols (1976) developed scales to measure treatment of twins and did indeed find that identicals are treated more alike than fraternals, though consistency was more the rule than differential treatment for both types of twins. Furthermore, identicals share more experience outside of the family, having more common friends and spending more time together. However, when Loehlin and Nichols correlated these environmental differences with the differences in personality test scores, they found practically no correlations of any significance.

An even better way of examining the total influence of shared environment is the comparison of identicals and fraternals raised together with those raised in different environments. Table 3.4 presents the correlations between identicals raised apart, identicals raised together, fraternals raised

Table 3.4. *Correlations of identical (I) and fraternal (F) twins raised apart and together on physical traits*

Traits	Study	I apart	I together	F apart	F together
Ridgecount	Lykken (1982)	.98	.96	—	.46
Height	Lykken (1982)	.94	.93	—	.50
	Pederson et al. (1984)[a]	.82	.90	.62	.70
	Pederson et al. (1984)[b]	.92	.84	.72	.70
	Stunkard et al. (1986)[c]	—	.91	—	.50
	Stunkard et al. (1986)[d]	—	.88	—	.48
Weight	Lykken (1982)	.51	.83	—	.43
	Pederson et al. (1984)[a]	.74	.73	.34	.48
	Pederson et al. (1984)[b]	.82	.86	.58	.57
	Stunkard et al. (1986)[c]	—	.85	—	.46
	Stunkard et al. (1986)[d]	—	.74	—	.34

[a] Old cohort
[b] Young cohort
[c] Male soldiers; mean age, 20
[d] Follow-up of same population 25 years later; mean age, 45

apart, and fraternals brought up together on two physical variables, height and weight. If a trait were entirely determined by heredity (additive) and the measurement of the trait were perfectly reliable, one would expect a correlation of 1.0 between identicals reared apart or together and a correlation of .50 between fraternals reared apart or together. Fingerprint ridge counts, often used to establish zygosity, approach this perfect genetic model with correlations of .98 for identical reared apart, .96 for identicals reared together, and .46 for fraternals reared together (Lykken, 1982). Height would not be expected to be influenced by environment except for severe dietary deficiencies during the developmental years. But weight, being in large part a function of eating habits, might be expected to show more environmental influence. The data on height shown in Table 3.4 conforms fairly close to the heriditary model, with correlations of about .9 for identicals raised apart or together. Both Lykken (1982) and Stunkard et al. (1986) found the expected .5 correlation for fraternal twins, but Pederson et al. (1984) found somewhat higher correlations for fraternal twins, both those reared together and apart. This result may be due to the crude method for establishing zygosity in this study, which may have caused some identicals to be misclassified as fraternals. Stunkard et al. studied veterans who were followed up after a 25-year interval. As we would expect, time made little difference in the already established heights of adults.

In contrast to height, common family influences did make a difference for weight in the Lykken study, in which the correlation between identicals

Table 3.5. *Comparisons of identical and fraternal twins raised apart and together*

	Intraclass correlations				% of variance[a]		
	I A	I T	F A	F T	*h*	e-s	e-ns
Extraversion							
Shields (1962)[b]	.61	.42	—	−.17	—	—	—
Pederson et al. (1988)[c]	.30	.54	.04	.06	41[d]	7	52
Tellegen et al. (1988)[e]	.34	.63	−.07	.18	40[d]	22	38
Neuroticism							
Newman et al. (1937)[f]	.58	.56	—	.37	—	—	—
Shields (1962)	.53	.38	—	.11	—	—	—
Pederson et al. (1988)	.25	.41	.28	.24	31	10	58
Tellegen et al. (1988)	.61	.54	.29	.41	55	2	43
P-ImpUSS							
Pederson: *impulsivity*	.40	.45	.15	.09	45	0	55
Monotony avoidance	.20	.26	.14	.16	23	5	72
Tellegen: *constraint* (P−)	.57	.58	.04	.25	58	0	42

[a]I: identical twins; F: fraternal twins; A: reared apart; T: reared together; h: heredity; e-s: shared environment; e-ns: nonshared environment
[b]Identicals: A 42, T 43 pairs; fraternals: tog 25 pairs; 71% of identicals separted at birth or during first year of life
[c]Identicals: A 99, T 160 pairs; fraternals: A 229, T 212 pairs; 48% of total sample separated before age of one, 64% by 2 years, 82% by 5 years
[d]Primarily nonadditive genetic variance
[e]Identicals: A 44, T 27 pairs; fraternals: A 27, T 114 pairs; 97% of identicals separated in first year of life, 83% before 6 months
[f]N measure was the Woodworth-Mathews Personal Data Sheet;
Identicals: A 19, T 50 pairs; fraternals: T 50

raised apart was .51 and that between identicals raised together was .83. Later analyses of these data by Bouchard, Lykken, Segal and Wilcox (1986) on a larger sample of 40 identicals raised apart showed that the difference in correlations between twins reared apart and together was produced by the females and was not found in the male group. This is an interesting example of a gender-heredity interaction: Shared environmental influences in the family may affect the weight of women more than men. Bouchard et al. also found a similar interaction in the data of Shields (1962) in which the correlation of weight for separated male twins was .87 in contrast to that for female twins of .37. The data of Pederson et al. do not show more difference in weight as a function of common rearing influences, possibly because of less variation among dietary habits in Sweden.

Now let us examine the twin comparisons on personality data (Table 3.5). The study by Tellegen et al. (1988) is probably the best of these in terms of (1) the factorial purity of the scales used; (2) the zygosity determination; and (3) the application of a sophisticated biometric model in order to test the fit of the data to additive or nonadditive genetic models, to distinguish between shared and nonshared environmental variance, and to derive a heritability index that uses all of the data from the four relationships studied. The only problem with this study is the relatively small number of fraternal twins raised apart.

Comparing twins reared apart and together on extraversion scales, the studies by Shields (1962) show a somewhat greater similarity for identicals reared apart than for those raised together. However, the reverse was true for the Tellegen et al. (1988) and the Pederson, Plomin, McClearn, and Friberg (1988) studies. In both studies the extraversion scores were higher for identicals reared together than for those raised apart. Fraternal twins showed little correlation whether raised together or apart. Application of the biometrical model to E in these two studies revealed a better fit to a nonadditive genetic model than to an additive model. In both studies, heredity accounted for about 40% of the variance. Shared environment accounted for 7% of the variance in the Pederson et al. and 22% of the variance in the Tellegen et al. studies. Nonshared environment and error of measurement accounted for the remaining 38% and 52% of the variance in the two studies.

The separated identicals showed slightly higher correlations for *neuroticism* than fraternals in two of the studies, considerably higher correlations in the Shields (1962) study but lower correlations than the identical twins reared together in the Pederson et al. study. The biometric model used by Tellegen et al. shows that the data fit an additive genetic model best for the N factor score. Heritabilities calculated in the Pederson et al. and Tellegen et al. studies were 31% in the former and 55% in the latter. Pederson et al. showed 10% of the variance due to shared environment whereas Tellegen et al. showed an inconsequential 2% due to this factor. The remaining variance was due to nonshared environment and the unreliability of measures.

Pederson et al. included two scales from the KSP, *impulsivity* and *monotony avoidance,* which are representative of the P factor (Zuckerman, Kuhlman & Camac., 1982). Tellegen et al.'s *constraint* factor is the P factor reversed, consisting of scales measuring *control, harm avoidance,* and *traditionalism.* On all three measures, the correlations of identicals reared apart and together were very close, showing no effect of shared environment. Heritability estimates were 23%, 45%, and 58% for *monotony avoidance, impulsivity,* and the *constraint* factor, respectively. The latter is probably a more reliable estimate because the two KSP measures are short scales of limited content.

The finding of little shared family environment influence in broad personality traits is reexamined in the light of other kinds of data from nontwin relationships. The finding is important because most psychological theories emphasize what is learned in the family. One could suppose that differences in treatment of children are more important than shared influences, but this does not explain why such differences in family treatment of individual twins do not correlate with the personality differences (Loehlin & Nichols, 1976).

The authors of a large twin study conducted in Finland (Rose, Koskenvuo, Kaprio, Sarna, & Langinvainio, 1988) have shown that there is a relationship between the frequency of social contact between twins and their personality similarities or differences. This was not a sample of separated twins, and most lived in the same families throughout childhood and adolescence. The authors concede that this relationship does not tell us direction of causation, and it is plausible that the closeness of twins' personalities determines how much time they want to spend together after they mature. Because personality changes more during childhood than during adult life, it is likely that personalities of the twins were already formed before the periods of variable social contact. Furthermore, the amount of contact was related to extraversion with the highest E scores in twins who saw each other on a daily basis and the lowest scores in those who saw each other rarely. A subgroup who were cohabiting had even lower scores on E.

Correlations between children and parents and between siblings reared together

There is little difference in genetic similarity between the fraternal twins, ordinary siblings, or parents and children. As far as additive genetic determination goes, all of these share half of their genes (on the average). On the assumption of purely additive genetic variance there should be little or no difference between the correlation of identical twins and the child-midparent (average of the two parents on the trait) correlation. Shared environment is likely to differ less for fraternal twins than for other types of siblings because fraternal twins are of the same age and therefore more likely to be exposed to the same environmental influences at the same time in their development. Because the age gap between parents and children is even wider than between siblings, we might expect even less similarity. Sex role expectations and training could also cause similarities due to environment. One might expect children's personalities to resemble those of same-gender parents more than opposite-gender parents and same-gender siblings to be more alike than opposite-gender siblings.

Table 3.6 shows the correlations from a large-scale study by Ahern, Johnson, Wilson, McClearn, and Vandenberg (1982) between parents and their adolescent offspring and between siblings, all of whom share both genes and environment. The investigators used a variety of personality scales; the scales most obviously relevant to the tripartite organization of

Table 3.6. *Correlations between parents and adolescent offspring, between siblings, and between parents*[a]

Scales	Child-midparent	Child-father	Child-mother	Sib-sib	Brother-brother	Sister-sister	Brother-sister	Husband-wife
EPI extraversion	− .10	− .11[a]	.01	.25[b]	.23[c]	.32[c]	.29[c]	.12[a]
Comrey extraversion	.44[c]	.22[b]	.25[b]	.03	.08	.01	.08	.06
Comrey activity	.28[c]	.12	.22[b]	.03	.09	− .14	.07	.25[b]
ACL affiliation	.18[c]	.06[a]	.12[c]	.08[b]	.09[a]	.06	.15[a]	.04
ACL dominance	.16[c]	.08[b]	.08[b]	.06[a]	.08	.01	.16[a]	.04
16PF outgoing	.11	.07	.04	.01	− .19	.26[a]	.17	.04
Median r E-Sy scales	.17	.08	.10	.05	.09	.04	.16	.05
EPI neuroticism	.19[c]	.12[c]	.11[c]	.07[a]	.05	.05	.14[a]	.22[a]
Comrey neuroticism	.19[a]	.11	.12	.13[a]	.16	.07	.12	.19[a]
ACL adjustment	.18[c]	.06[a]	.12[c]	.05[a]	.09[a]	.04	.06	.06
16PF emot. stability	.21[a]	.17[a]	.04	.17[a]	.34[a]	.22	.02	.07
16PF tense	.11	.06	.07	.22[b]	.26[b]	.26[a]	.31	− .04
Median r N-Em scales	.19	.11	.11	.13	.16	.07	.12	.07
Comrey rebellious	.49[c]	.30[c]	.34[c]	.37[c]	.46[c]	.39[b]	.30[a]	.33[b]
ACL autonomy	.17[c]	.09[b]	.06[a]	.04	− .01	.04	.06	− .01
ACL aggression	.19[c]	.08[b]	.07[a]	.02	.02	.03	.02	− .08
ACL change	.14[b]	.07[a]	.08[a]	.01	− .06	.06	.00	.03
16PF tough-minded	.23[a]	.05	.19[a]	.06	− .15	.08	.22	.19
16PF superego	.13	.09	.08	.17[a]	.39[b]	.16	.17	.06
Sensation seeking	.23[b]	.11	.18[a]	.06	.00	.13	.11	.18[a]
Median r P-ImpUSS	.19	.09	.08	.06	.00	.08	.11	.06
EPQ lie scale	.83[c]	.56[c]	.62[c]	.38[c]	.31[c]	.40[c]	.53[c]	.41[c]

Note: n's for ACL: 707–860; EPI: 422–502; Comrey PS: 107–118; 16PF: 93–105; SS: 168–187
[a] $p < .05$
[b] $p < .01$
[c] $p < .001$
Source: Ahern, Johnson, Wilson, McClern, and Vandenberg (1982). Copyright 1982 by Plenum Publishing Co. Adapted by permission.

personality traits used in this book have been grouped accordingly on the basis of the findings discussed in chapter 1. Although there are exceptions on individual scales, the median correlations in each of the three major dimensions are not as high as one would expect from the twin data, assuming additive genetic variance. Although the median correlations between identical twins raised together (Table 3.2) were .54 for E, .46 for N, and .56 for P, the median child-midparent correlations from this study were .17 for E scales and .19 for both N and P scales. The child-midparent correlations are only about one-third as high as the identical twin correlations! However, it must be remembered that the offspring-midparent correlations are estimates of heritability of the narrow type (only additive genetic influences). There were no significant differences between father-son, father-daughter, mother-son, or mother-daughter correlations, suggesting that there is no effect of same-gender versus opposite-gender parent-child relationships on similarity in personality traits. However, over all personality traits, combining male and female offspring, the authors found a significant difference between the proportions of mother-child and father-child correlations. This might suggest a slightly greater influence of mothers on personality development in children, but the actual differences in typical magnitudes of correlations for the variables selected in Table 3.6 are small.

The median correlations for fraternal twins raised together (Table 3.2) were .18 for E, .22 for N, and .25 for P scales. The relationships among ordinary siblings in the Ahern et al. study were .06 for E, N, and P scales or between one-third and one-quarter the size of the fraternal twin correlations! There is little indication of an influence of sex of siblings. For extraversion scales, for instance, the median brother-sister correlation is actually higher than the brother-brother and sister-sister correlations. The average correlations over all scales in the study were very close for the three sibling combinations.

The last column in Table 3.6 shows the correlations between husbands and wives on the scales. Husbands and wives are not usually related genetically, but if there is assortative mating (selection of mates for similar traits), the correlations between siblings among their offspring would be increased. There was little evidence of assortative mating on most of the scales.

A curious thing about these data is that some particular test scales show higher relationships than others for particular traits. The EPI *extraversion* scale, for instance, yields sibling correlations that are more in line with data obtained from fraternal twins, but the child-parent correlations for this scale are close to zero, and two are even negative. In contrast, the Comrey *extraversion* scale shows significant values for child-parent relationships but none for sibling relationships. The EPI Lie scale, not ordinarily considered a personality trait, shows outstanding high familial relationships, suggesting a higher degree of intrafamilial similarity than has been reported for any personality trait to date! The anomalies in this study are not readily explainable.

Contrasts of biologically related and adopted children and parents

The correlations among parents and children and siblings who share common environments cannot be used by themselves to separate the portions of variance due to heredity and environment. However, adoption provides

Table 3.7. *Correlations between biological as contrasted with adoptive relations*

Scales	Parent-child relations				Sibling-sibling relations		
	Biological		Adoptive		Biol. sibs	Adopt. adopt	Adopt. biol.
	fa-ch	mo-ch	fa-ch	mo-ch			
Number of pairings	52	53	241	253	16	77	48
Extraversion scales							
CPI dominance	.13	.25	.04	−.04	−.18	.03	.05
CPI capacity for status	.18	.18	.20	.09	.60	.12	.01
CPI sociability	.20	.15	.18	.01	.22	.13	−.06
CPI social presence	.42	.26	.18	.06	.70	−.05	−.12
TTS active	.33	−.02	.03	.02	.06	.03	−.28
TTS dominant	.09	.14	.04	.04	.42	.08	.05
TTS sociable	.22	.13	.07	.03	.38	.21	.05
Median r extraversion scales	.20	.15	.07	.03	.38	.08	.01
Neuroticism scales							
CPI self-acceptance	.20	.42	.04	.07	−.01	.05	−.13
CPI sense well-being	−.16	.02	.13	.00	−.03	.14	.12
TTS stable	.06	.01	.06	.02	.27	.01	.02
P-ImpUSS scales							
CPI responsibility	.12	.06	.06	.05	.61	.00	.33
CPI socialization	.16	.06	−.03	−.02	−.01	.03	.10
CPI self-control	.00	−.07	.08	.03	.34	−.06	.03
TTS impulsivity	.13	.05	.07	.01	.23	.27	.10

Source: Loehlin, Willerman, and Horn (1985), parts of tables 3–6, pp. 381–382. Copyright 1985 by American Psychological Association. Adapted by author's permission.

the pure case for environment. Barring selective placement of adoptees, the resemblances between adopting parents and their adopted children, and between adopted siblings and their natural on adopted siblings, can be due only to shared environmental factors. Contrasting these adoptive relationships with biologically related individuals who share environments can tell us how much of the similarities between those persons are due to the shared environment alone.

The results on personality scales, selected and grouped by this author under the E, N, P categories from the study by Loehlin, Willerman, and Horn (1985) are presented in Table 3.7. The subjects were parents and children in families who had adopted at least one child. The children were a mixture of adolescent (14–19 years) and young adults (20–30 years) at the time of the study. On the *extraversion* scales used by the authors, the median correlations for biological parents and children were .20 and .15 for fathers and mothers, respectively. The corresponding correlations for adopted children and adopting parents were only .07 and .03. The median correlation on E scales between biologically related siblings was .38 whereas those between biologically unrelated siblings were only .08 and .01. Medians were not calculated for the N and P scales, but for most of these the correlations were very low for both biological and adoptive relationships. However, in a later study by Loehlin, Willerman, and Horn (1987), MMPI scale scores of adoptive children (mean age now 17 years) were correlated with the original scores of the adoptive parents and the biological mothers. The median correlations of eight MMPI scales of adoptive fathers and adopted children was .02, and those of adoptive mothers with adoptive children was .00. None of the individual scale correlations was significantly different from zero. In contrast, the median correlations of MMPI scales of adopted children and their biological mothers (whom they never knew) was .18, and five of the eight correlations for individual subscales were significant (*depression, psychopathic deviate, psychasthenia, schizophrenia,* and *hypomania*). The midparent MMPI correlations of adopted offspring with both adoptive parents was .03 in contrast to that of nonadoptive children with their biological parents, which was .24. The median sibling correlation for biologically unrelated children raised in the same family was .08 whereas that for biologically related siblings was .15.

Loehlin et al. (1987) provide other data on the 16 PF scales. Adoptive parents versus adopted children median correlations were .03 for fathers, .04 for mothers, and .01 for the midparent-adopted child correlations. Biological parents versus offspring correlations on the 16 PF were .11 for fathers, .16 for mothers; and for midparent-offspring correlations, they were .26 in one study and .24 in another. On the 16 PF scales, median correlations were .02 for biologically unrelated siblings and .04 for biologically related siblings, a result that is discrepant with the parent-child data.

It would appear that most of the similarity on E and N and P traits of biological parents and children or siblings can be attributed to heredity. If the adoptive correlations are interpreted as true estimates of the influence of shared environment, then it must be concluded that little or no similarity between individuals in the same families can be attributed to their common family environment. In contrast, narrow (additive) heredity accounts for 25% of the similarities of parents and children. This is lower than the estimates of 50% derived from twin studies, but the latter are estimates of broad heritability, including nonadditive effects. But either type of study leaves a substantial component due to environment; it is simply not the environments that distinguish one family from another that are most important.

A similar study by Scarr, Webber, Weinberg, and Wittig (1981) contrasts biological and adoptive relationships in biological and adopting families. Unlike the Loehlin et al. study, the biological families in this study were a different sample from the adopting families. Only E and N scales were

Table 3.8. *Correlations between biological as contrasted with adoptive relations*

Scales	Midparent-child		Siblings	
	Biological	Adoptive	Biological	Adoptive
EPI-extraversion	.19[a]	.00	.06	.07
DPQ-social closeness	.28[a]	.00	.10	.13
DPQ-social potency	.21	.10	.20	.27
DPQ-impulsivity	.14	−.02	.20	.05
EPI-neuroticism	.25[d]	.05	.28[a]	.05
APQ-social anxiety	.03	.17	.17	.36
APQ-physical anxiety	.21	.06	.24	.04
APQ-total anxiety	.14	.11	.32	.29
EPI-lie scale	.20	.06	.18	.26
Midparent median r	.20	.06	.20	.07
Single-parent median r	.15	.04	—	—

[a]Significant difference between biological and adoptive relationship
Source: Scarr, Webber, Weinberg, and Wittig (1981), table 5, p. 895, and part of table 6, p. 896. Reprinted with permission.

used in this study (Table 3.8). The midparent median correlation for all scales was .20 for the midparent biological parent-child relation and .06 for the adoptive midparent-child relationship. The correlation between the single biological parent and child was .15 and for the single adoptive child and parent the correlation was .04. Biologically related siblings correlated .20 whereas adoptive siblings correlated only .07.

Scarr et al. contrast the heritabilities (Falconer method) of about .54 calculated from twin studies with those of .26 from these sibling data and .22 from the single-parent–child data. The authors offer a number of hypotheses to explain the contradictions between twin and parent-child and nontwin sibling studies. Fraternal twins may resemble each other more than siblings because of greater prenatal and postnatal environmental similarities. The same-age factor might explain why single-parent–child correlations were lower than sibling correlations in this study, but nonadditive genetic effects could also cause lower parent-child correlations because these effects are partially shared by siblings but not by parents and offspring. Finally, the authors suggest that the main factor determining personality may be neither heredity nor shared environment but specific environmental factors affecting one individual in a family more than another. But then, how would we explain the high correlations between identical twins raised in different environments? Here the authors suggest an interesting hypothesis: "it may be, however, that individual genotypes evoke and select different responses from their environments, thereby creating genotype-environment correlations of great importance. . . . Thus, it may be that the unique genotypes of individual children determine much of the environment they experience and explain much of the variance we are able to measure in studies of personality" (p. 897). This kind of genetic-environment correlation is not dealt with in most biometric models, but it may be a major part of the answer to the discrepancy between twin data and nontwin familial data.

Genetics and development

One of the popular misconceptions of genetic determination is that all individual differences determined in major part by heredity make their appearance at birth or shortly thereafter and persist throughout life. But it takes time for physical maturation or development to occur, and one phase of development is conditional on a previous one. Behavioral traits that have a strong biological determination appear or diminish as a function of the changes in the structure and physiology of the organism. As Freud pointed out, sexual interests exist before puberty, but there is a remarkable quantitative and even qualitative change in the expressions of these interests during puberty when there is rapid growth in the gonads, or sex glands. The genes that affect the hormones such as gonadotrophic hormone must have some kind of timing and regulatory mechanisms that "switch on" at an appropriate temporal phase of development. Although some genetic defects such as phenylketonuria are apparent at birth, others such as Huntington's chorea may lie dormant until the fourth or fifth decade of life. There is even speculation that how long we live, barring accidents, is also programmed in the genes. Some traits that are crucial in early life, such as the expression of distress through crying, may show strong heritability when assessed in infancy but little heritability after other forms of communicating distress are learned or emerge from an interaction of the same genes and the environment.

The molecular genetic mechanism responsible for the timing of gene activation are not fully understood although models have been suggested (Jacob & Monod, 1961). "Operator" genes, which act as on-off switches could be the basis of changing heritabilities, which are seen in some human traits as a function of age. However, the change in the molar phenotypical expression of the genotype could be due to an increasing importance of environment for a particular trait. If environment becomes more important as the organism matures, we would expect to see drops in heritability from infancy onward. In actual fact, the general trend is in the other direction. Increasing heritabilities could have more to do with the reliability of assessment as a function of the maturational capacities at the time. It is difficult to assess intelligence in an infant prior to the age of 2 years because most of the measurements of this trait depend on attention, understanding of instructions, and verbal or gestural responses in response to complex stimuli. *Sociability* may be assessed in infancy as response to the caretaking familiar persons or to strangers, but this trait is somewhat different from *sociability* in older children and adults, which is usually assessed by responses to peers. The response to strangers may be a precursor of shyness, which involves some degree of anxiety as well as sociability. In other words, we may be assessing different traits by observing the same phenomena at different ages. Consistency of behavior over age, discussed in chapter 2, is therefore a crucial component in evaluating developmental genetic studies.

Genetics during infancy and early childhood

The most useful studies during the early periods of life are those that combine the behavior genetic and longitudinal strategies, assessing heritabilities in the same traits of the same group of children at different ages. Torgerson (1985) used the set of temperament categories developed by Thomas and Chess (1977) to assess heritabilities of temperament at 2 months, 9 months, and 6 years of age. These categories were described in chapter 1, and consistency of the measurements was treated in chapter 2. In the study by Torgerson (1985), the parents of 34 identical and 15 fraternal twins were interviewed, and transcripts of the interviews were rated at each of the three ages. The significance of heritabilities for each trait at each age was assessed by Vandenberg's (1966) method, an F-test based on dividing the variance within fraternal twin pairs by the variance within identical twin pairs. These results are presented in Table 3.9 along with the correlations for identicals and fraternals at age 6.

At 2 months of age only three of eight categories of assessed temperament showed significant heritability variance ratios: *regularity, intensity of reaction,* and *threshold.* These are the salient kinds of behavior that one might expect to be able to observe in a 2 month old. At 9 months all categories showed significant heritability F ratios, with *activity, regularity, threshold,* and *approach* versus *withdrawal* showing the highest heritabilities. At 6 years also, all the heritability ratios were significant with *activity* and *approach-withdrawal* still among the highest in heritability and approaching a value suggesting total genetic determination. *Mood* and *adaptability* had relatively low heritabilities at all ages. It is difficult to separate real changes in heritability from problems with the particular scales at the different ages even though these investigators did report satisfactory reliabilities for the scales that they used. However, it is interesting to compare the heritability values over time.

The lowest heritabilities were found at 2 months of age. Thomas and Chess had also noted unsatisfactory assessment at such an early age. The behavioral repertoire of the typical 2-month-old neonate is limited, and

Table 3.9. *Comparisons of identical and fraternal twins at two months, nine months, and six years of age on the Thomas and Chess ratings of infant temperaments*

Temperament Factor	F ratios[a]			Correlations at 6 years		
	2 months	9 months	6 years	I	F	Falconer h^{2b}
Activity	1.52	55.26[e]	11.34[e]	.93	.14	.93
Regularity	4.98[e]	12.86[e]	4.22[e]	.81	.47	.68
Approach/withdrawal	.83	6.77[e]	8.80[e]	.94	.45	.94
Adaptability	.57	2.28[c]	2.23[c]	.81	.68	.26
Intensity	2.55[c]	5.32[e]	9.56[e]	.95	.54	.82
Threshold	2.82[d]	9.90[e]	2.91[d]	.85	.23	.85
Mood	1.54	3.31[e]	3.32[d]	.37	−.06	.37
Attention span & persistence	—	4.40[e]	5.13[e]	.73	−.27	.73
Distractibility	1.40	3.94[e]	—	—	—	—

[a]*F* is variance within fraternal twins/variance within identical twins (Vandenberg, 1966).
[b]When Falconer heritability (h^2) value exceeds the correlation for identical twins, the latter correlation is used as the index of heritability.
[c]$p < .05$
[d]$p < .01$
[e]$p < .001$
Source: Torgerson (1985). In J. Strelau et al. (Eds.) *The biological basis of personality and behavior*, tables 1–3, pp. 230–231. Copyright 1985 by Hemisphere Publishing Corp. Adapted by permission.

behavior that might be used is often transient and state-dependent. Comparing the 9 month and the 6 year assessments, it can be seen that *activity, regularity,* and *threshold* yield higher heritabilities at 9 months; *activity; approach-withdrawal,* and *intensity of reaction* showed the higher F ratios at 6 years; and *adaptability, mood,* and *attention-span–persistence* did not differ much in heritability, the former two being low at both ages. Because the 6-year-old has more mobility and expressiveness than the 9-month-old, it is not surprising that *approach-withdrawal* and *intensity* show better heritabilities at the 6-year age.

The variance ratios presented do not tell us whether heritabilities are due to high identical twin correlations, low fraternal twin ones, or a combination. The author does present the correlations for the 6-year-old group, and these are presented in the last two columns of the table. With the exception of the identical twin correlation for *mood* and *attention-span,* all of the correlations for identicals are over .80, indicating an extraordinary degree of genetic determination relative to the data for adult traits described in the previous section. Almost all of the fraternal twin correlations are .5 or lower, yielding Falconer indices of heritability close to 1.0 for four of variables: *activity, approach-withdrawal, threshold,* and *attention-*

span–persistence. Although these estimates are probably overestimates, they indicate an extremely strong determination of traits and justify their description as "temperaments." The greatest possibility for confounding might be that the source of the data is the parents interviews, and the parents might simply attribute more similarity to the behavior of identicals than to fraternals. However, according to Thomas and Chess (1977, p. 134) Torgersen reported that at the 2- and 9-month periods the great majority of mothers did not have any definite opinion on whether their twins were identicals or fraternals. If this is true, it is difficult to see how the mothers' observations could have been confounded by this factor in producing the high heritability ratios at 9 months.

Matheny (1980) used part of the Bayley Scales of Infant Development, the Infant Behavior Record (IBR), to study the genetic influences in twin behavior from 3 to 24 months. Two of the factors found in these ratings of infant behavior during the examination are relevant for our personality dimensions. The factor called *test-affect-extraversion* measures the degree to which infants were positive, outgoing, and involved in the social give-and-take of the test situation. It is actually a mixture of ratings of *emotionality* and *sociability* during the examination because positive emotionality is associated with sociable responses whereas fearfulness and tension tend to correlate with lack of cooperativeness with the examiner. This association of emotionality and sociability during infancy is interesting in view of the tendency of the relationship to persist despite the fact that the two factors can be separated in adult measures. It is also interesting in light of Tellegen's (1985) theory that positive affect is an essential part of extraversion. The second relevant factor in the Matheny (1980) analysis was one of activity (body motion, energy, vocalization) during the testing situation. Fearfulness also correlated negatively with this factor at 18 months but not at 24 months. Other factors found in these scales were *task orientation,* perhaps related to later intelligence, *auditory-visual awareness,* and *motor coordination,* but these will not be discussed here.

Table 3.10 shows the identical and fraternal twin correlations for the *test-affect-extraversion* and *activity* scores at 3, 6, 9, 12, 18, and 24 months of age in the same group of infants. At 3 and 9 months there was little difference between identical and fraternal twin correlations. At 6, 12, and 24 months the identical twin correlations were significantly higher than those of the fraternal twins for the *extraversion* factor. At 18 and 24 months the correlations of the *activity* factor were significantly higher for the identicals for the first time. Although the age progression is somewhat erratic, one can discern a general tendency for heritability to increase over these ages of infancy. No significant heritability is seen for either factor at 3 months, and both are clearly significant at 24 months; the correlations at that age were close to those seen in later childhood, adolescent, and adult measures.

Table 3.10. *Correlations of identical (I) and fraternal (F) twins on affect-extraversion and activity factors from ratings made at 3 to 24 months of age*

Age (Mos.)	nI	nF	Affect-extraversion		Activity		Profile similarity	
			I	F	I	F	I	F
3	76	51	.18	.26	.30	.33	.40^a	.18
6	91	54	.55^a	.10	.24	.11	.46^a	.25
9	72	35	.35	.33	.25	.22	.35^a	.20
12	94	36	.43^a	.07	.33	.28	.39^a	.25
18	79	43	.49	.37	.43^a	.14	.38^a	.19
24	80	50	.53^a	.03	.58^a	.14	.39^a	.24

^{a}Identical r > fraternal r, p < .05, one-tailed
Source: Matheny (1980), from table 7, p. 1164. Copyright 1980 Society for Research in Child Development. Adapted by permission.

Matheny also correlated an index of profile similarity for all of the factor scores. The correlations of these scores are listed in the last column of Table 3.10. At every age the profiles of the factor scores were significantly more similar for identical than for fraternal twins, and there was no significant change in the magnitudes of the correlations over age. This interesting finding suggests support for Lykken's (1982) idea that a significant part of inherited personality is the unique configuration of traits produced by epistasis. This specific and unique behavioral similarity of identical twins is detectable at the earliest ages. However, the fact that the fraternal twin correlations are close to half the identical twin correlations, rather than zero, suggests that uniqueness may be produced by additive genetic variance rather than epistasis.

Goldsmith and Gottesman (1981) studied a large sample of twins at ages 8 months, 4 years, and 7 years. Ratings were done by psychologists during mental and motor testing and during free play. Dimensions of ratings similar to those found in the Bayley IBR scales were also found in this study. At 8 months, factors of *activity* and *person interest* were found; at 4 years *task persistence, spontaneous activity,* and *irritability* factors were extracted; and at 8 years they found four factors: *active-adjustment, fearfulness, task persistence,* and *cooperation.* Table 3.11 lists some of the correlations of factor scores and individual scales grouped under *activity* and *emotionality-cooperativeness* at each age used.

Measures of activity level showed little change in heritability over the three age ranges. Although the differences between identical and fraternal twin correlations were significant only for the 8-month and 7-year ages, it can be seen that there is little change in the magnitudes of identical twin correlations although fraternal twin correlations tend to be

Table 3.11. *Correlations of identical (I) and fraternal (F) twin ratings for activity, person interest, and emotionality*

Age Groups[a]	8 months		4 years		7 years	
	I	F	I	F	I	F
Activity						
Activity level	.41[b]	.23	.44	.34	.41[b]	.10
Activity vs. passivity	.57[b]	.35	.41	.37	.55[b]	.22
Impulsiveness	—	—	.29	.22	.25	.09
Spontaneous conversation	—	—	.41	.28	.37[b]	.17
Person interest						
Interest in persons	.28	.20	—	—	—	—
Degree of social contact with mother	.22	.30	—	—	—	—
Acceptance/cooperation of examiner	.40	.28	.41[b]	.23	.14	.08
Emotionality						
Irritability, hostility	—	—	.40[b]	.06	−.09	.16
Emotional reactivity	—	—	.29	.17	—	—
Fearful/inhibited	—	—	—	—	.36[b]	.21
Concern over mother separation	—	—	—	—	.45[b]	.07
Self-confidence	—	—	—	—	.33[b]	.03
Friendly vs. shy	—	—	—	—	.44[b]	.14

[a] n's: 8-month identicals 111–117, fraternals 187–223; 4-year identicals 109–111, fraternals 206–211; 7-year identicals 87–121, fraternals 169–217
[b] r identicals > r fraternals, $p < .05$, one-tailed
Source: Goldsmith and Gottesman (1981), selected data from table 4, p. 97. Copyright 1981, Society for Research in Child Development. Adapted by permission.

higher in the 4-year-old group. *Cooperativeness* and *person-interest* variables were primarily assessed during infancy (8 months), at which time there was no evidence of significant heritability. The variable measuring acceptance of the examiner versus cooperation with examiner showed some evidence of heritability at 8 months (but not significant) and 4 years, but the correlations dropped and heritabilities were insignificant at 7 years. Perhaps this variable is less continuous and the variables of emotional reactions to the examiner, mostly measured at 7 years, are the ones that pick up the *sociability* and *acceptance* traits. *Fearfulness-inhibition, concern over separation, self-confidence* and *friendly versus shy with examiner* all show significant heritabilities at 7 years of age. *Irritability-hostility,* which shows significant heritability at 4 years, does not at 7 years. The authors also examined sex differences in twin correlations and found no consistent trend for male twins to correlate more or less highly than female twins except where the variance on the measure was greater for one or the other. As with the sibling data reported previously, opposite-sex fraternal twins show no tendency toward lower correlations than same-sex fraternals and are actually higher on a few

Table 3.12. *Correlations of identical (I) and fraternal (F) twins in middle childhood on temperament ratings by parents*

	Activity		Sociability		Emotionality		ImpUSS	
	I	F	I	F	I	F	I	F
Buss and Plomin (1984)[a]	.62	−.13	.53	−.03	.63	.12	—	—
Matheny and Dolan (1980)[b]	.66	.19	.56	.06	.45	−.11	.60	.25
Buss et al. (1973)[c]: Imp, boys	—	—	—	—	—	—	.90	.17
Imp, girls	—	—	—	—	—	—	.85	.75
Plomin (1974)[d]: Imp, boys	—	—	—	—	—	—	.65	−.07
Imp, girls	—	—	—	—	—	—	.49	.17

[a]Based on 228 identical and 172 fraternal twins, mean age, 5.1 years
[b]Based on 68 identical and 37 fraternal twins, 7–10 years of age.
[c]Based on 78 identical and 50 fraternal twins, average age 4 years, 7 months; Imp. is impulsivity.
[d]Based on 60 identical and 51 fraternal twins, average age 3 years, 6 months; Imp. is impulsivity.

measures of activity. As in the previously discussed developmental studies, heritabilities tend to increase rather than decrease from early infancy (first year of life) to childhood, except for *activity*.

Genetic studies of early to middle childhood

Most studies of twins during early to middle childhood use parental ratings. The results of several such studies are presented in Table 3.12. Buss and Plomin (1984, table 9.2, p. 122) combined the data from a number of studies using their EAS rating scales. Earlier studies by these authors on *impulsivity* are also included as a measure of the third dimension of personality. Matheny and Dolan (1980) used ratings of children by mothers and factored their scales into six categories, five of which resemble those described by the 5-factor model of personality (see chapter I). More detailed data from this study are presented in the next table. The *compliant morality* and *tough-minded* factor scores are included as representatives of the third dimension of personality (P).

Both the Buss and Plomin (1984) and the Matheny & Dolan (1980) studies show high identical twin correlations (.62, .66) relative to very low fraternal twin correlations (−.13, .19) for *activity* ratings. Either nonadditive genetic variance or extreme parental bias in seeing greater behavioral similarities in identical twins could explain these data. Similar results are seen for *sociability, emotionality,* and *impulsivity* ratings, with the exception of the girls in the Buss, Plomin, and Willerman (1973) study, in which the fraternal twins show extremely high correla-

Table 3.13. *Correlations of identical and fraternal twins on behavioral factor scores*

Factors[a]	Identicals ($n = 68$)	Fraternals ($n = 37$)
I Compliant morality	.60[b]	.25
II Applied cognitive	.67[b]	.18
III Sociability	.56[b]	.06
IV Emotionality	.45[b]	−.11
V Tough-minded	.39	.15
VI Activity-distractibility	.66[b]	.19
Profile correlation over 6 factors	.61[b]	.13

[a]Rating scales defining factors as follows: I conscientious: dependable, self-disciplined, takes others' views, vs. daring, slow-to-discipline; II imaginative: artistic interests, witty, excitable; III sociability: socially bold, outgoing vs. loner; IV emotionality: tense, emotional, quick-tempered; V tough-minded: hardhearted, impatient; VI activity-distractibility: overly active, inattentive.
[b]r identicals > r fraternals, $p < .05$
Source: Matheny and Dolan (1980), table 3, p. 320. Copyright 1980 by Academic Press. Reprinted by permission.

tions on *impulsivity*. It is curious that the fraternal twin correlations are almost all so much lower than those found for questionnaire data from adult twins. In contrast, the identical twin correlations are comparable with those found in adults.

Table 3.13 shows the details of the correlations on scales making up the six factors in the Matheny and Dolan study. What they call *compliant morality* is similar to the factor called *conscientiousness* in the 5-factor model; factor 2, called *applied cognitive* resembles the *Culture* or *openness to experience* factor; factor 3, *socially bold* is *extraversion* or *surgency;* factor 4, *emotionality,* is *emotional stability* or *neuroticism;* factor 5, *tough-minded,* resembles *agreeableness* versus *hostility;* factor 6, *activity,* is not part of the 5-factor model except as subsumed under *extraversion*. High identical twin correlations (over .60) are seen for ratings of *conscientiousness, imaginativeness, socially bold, quick-tempered* and *inattentive*. As with the data presented in Table 3.12, the fraternal twin correlations are lower than half of the identical twin ones in most cases and some are even negative.

Matheny and Dolan compared the profile correlations for their six primary factors in identical and fraternal twins. These profile correlations express the similarity of the pattern of the factor scores rather than their absolute levels. The correlations were .61 for identical twins and .13 for fraternal twins. The high correlation of identicals on patterns of reaction, which tend toward uniqueness, suggest once again the operation of epistasis; and in this case, the low correlation for fraternal

Table 3.14. *Parent-offspring correlations for EAS measures for 137 families*

	Correlation between midrater estimates of children's EAS and			
	mothers' self-rating of EAS	fathers' self-rating of EAS	fathers' ratings of mothers' EAS	mothers' ratings of fathers' EAS
Emotionality: distress	.34	.00	.25	−.03
Emotionality: fear	.38	.19	.41	.23
Emotionality: anger	.25	.18	.16	.18
Activity: tempo	.06	.12	.08	.04
Activity: vigor	.14	.12	.10	.10
Sociability	.26	.11	.23	.16
Median r of 6 traits	.26	.12	.20	.13

Source: Buss and Plomin (1984), table 9.3, p. 124. Copyright 1984 Lawrence Erlbaum Associates. Reprinted by permission.

twins suggests a nonadditive component like epistasis, influencing the profile similarities.

The results for parent-child correlations should resemble those for fraternal twin correlations on the assumption of additive variance. Table 3.14 from Buss and Plomin (1984) shows the correlations of mothers' and fathers' self-ratings and ratings of their spouses with their midrater estimates of the children's personality traits. The mother-child correlations, based on both the mothers' self-ratings and the fathers' ratings of the mothers, are higher than the fraternal twin correlations; but both sets of father-child correlations are low, like the fraternal twin correlations. It should be recalled that in the Ahearn et al. (1982) study a significantly greater number of mother-child than father-child correlations were significant. The greater resemblance of mother and child, particularly on *emotionality* and *sociability* factors, could indicate a sex-linked inheritance of these traits, a greater shared environmental influence on children by the mother, or the possibility that some of the personality traits, particularly *emotionality,* may be influenced by prenatal factors. Influences on the offspring of prenatal stress of the pregnant mother have been shown in rats. But apart from stress affecting the mother during pregnancy, the general hormonal makeup of the mother may play a greater role than that of the father because of a direct biochemical influence on the developing endocrine systems of the offspring during pregnancy.

Table 3.15. *Resemblance of identical and fraternal twin pairs in various personality, ability, and interest domains*

Trait domain	Typical correlations		
	Identical	Fraternal	h^2 (Falconer)
General ability	.86	.62	.48
Special abilities	.74	.52	.44
Personality inventory scales	.50	.28	.44
Ideals, goals, and vocational interests clusters	.37	.20	.34
Self-concept clusters	.34	.10	.34[a]
Activities clusters	.64	.49	.30

[a]Limited to identical twin correlation
Source: Loehlin and Nichols (1976), table 7–1, p. 87. Copyright 1976, University of Texas Press. Reprinted by permission.

Differential heritability of personality traits

In all of the studies yielding heritabilities on both broad and narrower traits, the reader may have noticed a uniformity of certain results. Both the correlations between identical twins and the calculated heritabilities, using variance methods rather than correlation comparisons, are nearly all in the range .40 to .60. Few results show much influence of shared environment. Loehlin and Nichols (1976) noted a similar uniformity in their results for personality scales though there were differences between classes of scales as shown in Table 3.15. In terms of identical twin correlations alone, personality scales show lower heritability than general and special ability scales and activities inventories but higher heritability than self-concept clusters, ideals, goals, and vocational interest scales. However, Falconer heritability values show little difference among ability, personality, and self-concept scales because the fraternal twin correlations drop in about equal proportion to the identical twin correlations for these scales. Loehlin and Nichols could see no consistent differences in heritabilities of traits measured by the standard scales of the California Psychological Inventory (CPI).

In a later reanalysis of the data from the CPI, Loehlin (1982) reached a different conclusion. The standard CPI scales were not developed from factor analyses of items and therefore tend to be factorially heterogeneous. Loehlin factor-analyzed the item responses of the 850 twin pairs involved in his study and found the factors listed in Table 3.16. He then calculated heritability (H) and shared environment estimates (SE) from the identical and fraternal twin data on these factor-derived scales, shown in Table 3.16. Analyses showed that both H and C factors vary significantly across the

Table 3.16. *Identical and fraternal twin correlations for factor scores based on CPI items, and estimates of heritability (H) and shared environment (SE)*

Factor	Identical Twins		Fraternal Twins		H^a	SE^b
	Males	Females	Males	Females		
Extraversion	.61	.66	.21	.35	.67	− .03
Neuroticism	.51	.58	.22	.38	.46	.09
Persistence	.36	.39	.23	.10	.46	− .08
Intellectual interests	.49	.53	.29	.29	.45	.06
Cynical attitudes	.42	.48	.10	.40	.33	.12
Intolerance of ambiguity	.47	.51	.41	.35	.24	.25
Stereotyped masculinity	.55	.37	.40	.40	.10	.35

[a] Genetic parameter
[b] Shared environment parameter
Source: Loehlen (1982), selected data from tables V and IV, p. 426. Copyright 1982, Plenum Publishing Co. Adapted by permission.

seven measured traits. The two largest factors were *extraversion* and *neuroticism,* which showed the relatively high heritability values and low amount of shared environment typically found in other studies. *Extraversion* showed a somewhat higher heritability than *neuroticism. Intellectual interests* also showed a high H, close to that for *neuroticism. Persistence* showed a relatively high heritability but primarily in the females and not in the males. *Cynical attitudes* showed high heritability in males but not in females. *Masculinity* and *intolerance of ambiguity* scales showed low heritabilities and some effects of shared family environment in both sexes. Loehlin attributes the uniformity of findings in the literature to the fact that most personality scales are saturated with *extraversion* and *neuroticism,* which tend to be substantially heritable.

Rose (1988) found moderate to high heritabilities for broad traits like *extraversion* derived from the MMPI (see Table 3.2), but *masculinity, religious orthodoxy,* and *intellectual interests* scales showed little heritability and strong influence of shared environment (40–64%). Scales that reflect interests, values, and beliefs are more likely to be influenced by family environment than are broader personality traits.

Genetic-environment interaction and correlation

A major criticism of the genetic methods in common use is that they ignore the interaction between genotype and environment. Of course, it is even more common for those who analyze environmental effects to ignore the possible interactions with genetic factors. But it is still true that the models discussed so far tend to be *procrustean* on the nature versus nurture problem: Whatever is not heredity is attributed to environment. Behavior geneticists such as Plomin (1986) are becoming interested in the possibilities for analyses of heredity-environment interaction and correlation. Plomin has provided a thoughtful conceptualization of the problem.

Genotype-environment interaction

Genotype-environment interaction describes the situation in which the genetic and environmental influences are completely independent. A child's genotype cannot affect the socioeconomic class of the family in which she is born, but the two independent influences may interact in various ways. Plomin (1986) describes three possible relationships between genotype and environment, pictured in Figure 3.1. In (a), both environment and heredity have significant effects, but the effects combine in an additive rather than an interactive way. In (b), there is a combination of interactive and main effects so that differences due to genotype appear in one type of environment but not in another. In (c), there is a strong interactive effect so that the effect of the genotype depends entirely on the environment, and vice versa.

Torgerson's (1985) studies of twins rated on the Thomas and Chess (1977) scales of temperament revealed the kind of environmental factors that might be involved in interactions with genotypes. Birth prematurity correlated negatively with *activity* and *adaptibility* in identical twins at both 2 and 9 months of age. Complications in pregnancy were related to the mean sums of differences between identical twins. The mother's insistence on regularity in feeding, elimination, and sleep was related to greater regularity in infants at 2 and 9 months of age. Stress on physical stimulation by the mother was correlated with greater activity and intensity of reaction in 2- and 9-month-old infants. Mothers' stress on psychical stimulation was related to the tendency to approach or withdraw from novel stimuli at 2 and 9 months of age. Although it is possible that the effect of mothers' training and stimulation could represent a genotype-environment correlation (described next) rather than an interaction, it would seem unlikely that the infant's manifestation of the genotypical tendencies would influence the mothers' training as early as 2 months of age. Torgersen did not actually investigate interaction, but it would be interesting to see the effects of such maternal practices on adopted children whose biological parents were active or inactive, or high or low sensation seekers.

Genotype-environment correlation

Genotype-environment correlation describes the degree to which children are exposed to environments or select environments on the basis of their genetic propensities. Correlation represents the possibility for two-way

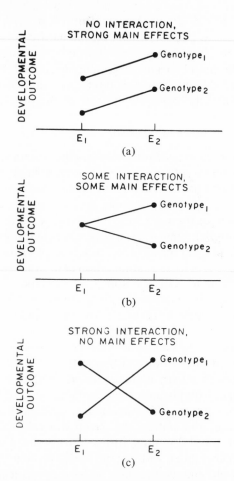

Figure 3.1. Hypothetical genotype-environment interactions. E_1 and E_2 represent two types of environment. (From *Development, genetics and psychology* fig. 3.1, p. 93, by R. Plomin, 1986. Hillsdale, NJ: Erlbaum. Copyright 1986 by L. Erlbaum Associates. Reprinted by permission.)

interactions between genotype and environment. The variance due to this kind of correlation is neither solely genetic or environmental but is both. Direction of causality cannot be assumed. Plomin (1986) describes three kinds of genotype-environment correlations.

1. *Passive* genotype-environment correlations occur when parents tend to have the same genetic dispositions as their children and therefore provide the kind of environment that reinforces the disposition. For example, antisocial parents may model and reinforce antisocial behavior in their children.

2. *Reactive* genotype-environment correlations refer to reactions of parents or others to the genetically influenced behavior of persons. Socially desirable traits such as scholastic or athletic talents and positive sociable behaviors tend to be positively reinforced, and aggressive reactions and unsociable responses tend to be negatively reinforced. However, the sensitivity to such reinforcement and training may depend on the genotype. Children of criminals have an increased risk for criminality, even if they are reared in a law-abiding household, but there is no increased risk of criminality in a child who is not genetically predisposed but is raised by an adoptive father with a criminal record (Mednick, Gabrielli, & Hutchings, 1987).

Lytton (1977) examined interactions between parents and children in an attempt to separate passive from reactive influences of parents on children. He found that parents did tend to treat identical twins more alike than fraternal twins, but this difference in treatment was mostly in their reactions to the children's behaviors. Interactions that were initiated by the parents showed little difference between identicals and fraternals. In other words, the greater similarity of parental treatment of identicals is due to the greater similarity in the behaviors of identical twins compared with fraternal pairs. The parents' actions are largely *reactive* to the child rather than being of the parent-initiated type that is associated with passive genotype-environment correlation.

3. *Active* genotype-environment correlation refers to the tendency of persons to select environments and friends that reinforce or complement their own genetic dispositions. Because increasing maturity brings more opportunity to choose among the many possible environments a society offers, this may be one of the most important types of interactions. After infancy, children can select friends and relatives to interact with who reinforce their inherited tendencies. Antisocial children seek children with similar tendencies for companionship. Although their behavior is often attributed to "bad influences" of their antisocial friends, the question that must be asked is why they sought the company of these friends. Sensation-seeking children seek environmental opportunities for exciting and stimulating activities. Sensation-seeking adults tend to marry equivalent level sensation seekers, an exception to the usual lack of assortative mating among other personality traits (Farley & Mueller, 1978). Sociable children seek other sociable children and gravitate to environmental locations in which social interactions are likely. Emotionally labile or neurotic children may tend to avoid provocative persons or situations that increase their anxiety levels.

Scarr and McCartney (1983) use these three classes to describe the major processes in development. They suggest that the three kinds of influence vary with developmental stages. During infancy the effects are likely to be of the *passive* type because the infant has little influence on parents or environment except by emotionally evocative reactions. During childhood the *evocative* type of process becomes more common as parents and others react to the personality of the child. Finally, as the child becomes the more independent adolescent there is more shifting from the passive to the *active* types of effects as persons select their own environments and friends. Considering the consistent findings of a lack of importance of shared family influences in most personality traits, the genotype-environment correlation of greatest potential significance may be the second and third types rather than the first. Yet, most dynamic theories (except for family-systems approaches) stress the passive type of influence of parents on children, and few investigators even acknowledge the potentialities for genotype-environment correlation.

Genotype-environment correlation of the evocative and active types involves a two-way interaction between the phenotypical behavior and the environment. The reaction that the phenotype evokes may positively or negatively reinforce the behavior. Socially approved behavior and expressions of positive emotions usually evoke similar reactions in others, which positively reinforce the behavioral tendency. If persons with a particular disposition actively seek friends with a similar disposition, there is more reinforcement of their own behavioral dispositions. Socially disapproved behavior and expressions of negative emotions do not always elicit positive reinforcement and may frequently result in negative reinforcement. Thus, the environment should work against the genetically disposed phenotype. However, in a cognitive sense, negative reinforcement may reinforce a cognition that is supportive of the disposition. For instance, an antisocial person may elicit considerable punishment, which repeatedly confirms his conviction that people are basically hostile and that you must "get them before they get you," or you must "always look out for number one." People who are prone to negative emotional states may elicit either avoidance or hostility in others, thereby confirming their views that people are basically unfriendly, or that they are worthless, or that the world is a threatening and frightening place. Interactions with the environment may tend to confirm, or reinforce, cognitions that maintain negative behaviors.

Genetics of animal behavior

Comparative studies of nonhuman animals enable researchers to use a broader variety of experimental methods and to control environments to a much higher degree and for longer periods of time than in research with humans. In behavior genetics this means that selective breeding can be used to alter the gene pool of organisms, and behavior in controlled environments can be used as the basis of selection for breeding. Thus, the behavior geneticist can mimic the processes of natural selection; the scientist, rather than "nature," controls the selection of traits for breeding. However, these methods require fast-breeding animals of an easily manipulable size. Probably the most popular organism for selective breeding is the fruit fly *Drosophila,* for which the interval from egg to adult is only two weeks and so they are easily reared. However, the behavioral differences between a fly and a human are vast, and only the most obtuse environmentalist would insist that they are due solely to environment or diet. A compromise is the relatively fast-breeding rodent. Although not nearly as like humans in social behavior or DNA as primates such as gorillas and chimpanzees, mice and rats do share some of the common mammalian behavioral features such as dominance, social interaction, maternal care, fear, aggression, and explorativeness.

Animal studies have contrasted strains and in some cases have attempted to selectively breed behavioral traits, starting with hybrid strains. The open-field test and variants of it have been widely used for assessing *exploratory* and *emotional* behavior with these methods, though variations in the methods may have contributed to discrepancies in the results (Walsh & Cummins, 1976). Investigators have found reasonably consistent differences in mouse strains (McClearn, 1959; Thompson, 1953) in both activity and defecation responses to the open field, and these responses have been successfully used in selective-breeding studies in mice (DeFries, Gervais, & Thomas, 1978; McClearn, 1959; Reading, 1966; Thompson, 1953; van Abeelen, 1976) and rats (Broadhurst, 1975). Such studies have shown that activity and defecation are phenomenally and genetically correlated responses: Breeding for high scores on one of the responses produces animals who are low on the other response. Although selection studies have succeeded in breeding lines of animals with no overlaps in the distributions of scores on the measure used for selection, actual heritabilities calculated from the data (DeFries & Hegman, 1970) are in about the same range as the narrow heritabilities in humans from parent-child studies.

On the bases of some consistencies among strains in open-field behavior and behavior in other situations, investigators have assumed enough generality of response to call activity in the open field *exploration* and defecation in the open field *emotionality.* However, some investigators such as Simmel (1984; Simmel & Bagwell, 1983) have criticized these trait definitions and shown that other kinds of operational definitions of the trait can yield other kinds of strain differences. This influence of the environmental situation on strain difference is apparent in other areas such as the genetics of aggression.

Strains that are aggressive in one situation may be the losers in other situations. When the male C57BL mouse encounters a BALB (B-albino) mouse for a limited period in a novel environment it is likely to be the more aggressive one (Ginsburg & Allee, 1942) and win contests for food (Frederickson, 1951); but if the animals are confined in a small living box for a more extended period of time, the BALB emerges as the survivor in most cases (Frederickson & Birnbaum, 1954). The BALB is less active than the C57BL in the open-field and seminatural environments during day time but is actually more active than the C57BL in nocturnal activity and activity in home cages (Lassalle & LePape, 1978). In fact, the albino strain may have a general aversion to open and well-lighted places (McReynolds, Weir, & DeFries, 1967; Whitford & Zipf, 1975). The C57BL seems to inherit an advantage for operating in daytime conditions in open spaces. Under these conditions it is active and nonemotional. When encountering a BALB in these conditions, it has the fighting edge. This advantage is missing in living areas over extended periods of time. In these conditions the BALB becomes the superior fighter, perhaps because of its stronger emotionality, which may tend to prolong the aggressive encounter. Although these genotype-environment interactions confound the idea of inheritance of a general trait like *aggressiveness,* more systematic study may reveal better ways of defining traits through animal models.

It is tempting to see supertraits that characterize some species. The C57 strain (males) is active in open spaces, low in emotionality, aggressive, high in social grooming, and sexually proficient (Vale & Ray, 1972). In contrast, the A/J strain is inactive, emotional in novel situations, nonaggressive, low in social grooming, and sexually inept (at least with females of another species). Can the C57BL mouse serve as a model for human extraversion or sensation seeking? If this were so, we might learn much about the biological bases of human traits by examining the biological differences of strains (Zuckerman, 1984a). However, the generality of these species characterizations is based mostly on piecemeal studies of a single dependent variable in a restricted situation. We have seen how such differences disappear or even reverse when environmental conditions are altered. We need more studies of strain interactions over extended periods of time in normal seminaturalistic settings in which social interactions can be observed.

The sociobiological approach to human behavior is speculative, and the historical processes of evolution that shaped a species cannot be reliably reconstructed. However, laboratory studies of natural selection can illustrate why traits such as male aggressiveness and dominance may have enhanced genetic fitness and increased the likelihood of the genetic survival of a strain or individual in the natural environment. Intrastrain aggressiveness can be selectively bred in mice (Lagerspetz & Lagerspetz, 1971; van Oortmerssen & Bakker, 1981). Experiments in which males of different strains are housed together with a single female mouse show that the more aggressive mouse usually succeeds in impregnating the female, thereby insuring the continuity of his genes. Mating behavior itself may also contribute to fitness. But different strains have different advantages. The C57BLs are fast and uninhibited in copulation, but they have a long recovery time between ejaculations. The particular advantage of one pattern over another depends on the environmental circumstances. In one case, speed may confer the greater advantage and in another environment persistence may pay.

The models chosen for behavior genetic study in the laboratory all have a degree of inappropriateness to natural behavior. Fights between mice in the wild are probably less frequent and vicious because space is less limited and a loser has room to establish his territory away from the dominant mouse. Different strains usually live in different areas. The inappropriateness for human social genetics is obvious. Pair bonding in humans has separated dominance and aggressiveness from reproductive fitness. In fact, the human's control of physical aggression and our ability to separate sexual behavior from reproduction confounds the usual concepts of biological selection. Most of our personality traits are maladaptive at both extremes and have probably not exerted an evolutionary trend for many thousands of years. Selection probably stabilized in the distant past, and with each generation there is simply a reassortment of the polygenetic combinations that form our basic personality traits.

Summary

Once hypothetical, genes are now known to be chemical codings on the DNA molecule, which controls the development and maintainance or structure and physiology of the organism. The science of behavior genetics studies genetic and environmental influences on behavior through biometric studies of humans, showing degrees of genetic and environmental relationships, and through studies of animals bred in pure strains. A method used with animals is selective breeding based on behavioral traits.

Genes may affect behavior through very narrow control of a single enzyme, the lack or excess of which may be crucial in a particular behavioral outcome. Phenylketonuria (PKU) is an example of an enzyme controlled by a single gene, in which the absence of the gene and the enzyme it controls can retard brain development and therefore indirectly cause a broad intellectual deficit. In mice, single genes can cause neurological movement and seizure disorders, though some of them may also be involved in broad biological traits such as arousability or reactivity.

Most complex behavioral traits are probably influenced by many genes (polygenic inheritance). But the mechanisms of gene combination may be additive, dominant-recessive (Mendelian), epistatic (configural combination), or some mixture of the three. Various biometric methods are used to assess the relative importance of heredity and environment in a particular trait. Some of the models allow estimation of the additive component of heredity (narrow h) only, and others permit estimation of broad heredity (additive + nonadditive types). Identical twins enable us to study broad heredity because they have identical genes of all types. Identical twins reared separately offer a pure case in which similarity is due entirely to genetic influences of all types. Comparing adopted children with other adopted siblings and adopting parents provides a measure of similarity based on purely environmental influence. Other kinds of relationship are intermediate in their genetic or environmental influences.

Biometric studies of personality traits in humans suggest the following general conclusions:

1. The three supertraits (E, N, and P) and most of their primary trait components show a broad heritability of about 40–60%. This conclusion is based on data from twin studies. Narrow heritabilities calculated from sibling and parent-child data yield lower heritabilities of 20–40% for *extraversion* and even less for N and P. The discrepancy between twin and nontwin studies may mean that most traits represent some mixture of additive and nonadditive variance. To the extent that variance is nonadditive, the correlations between fraternal twins and siblings may be reduced considerably below the expected half of the identical twin correlation.

2. There is little or no influence of a shared family environment in most personality traits. This conclusion, which goes against much of what has been written about the importance of family environmental influences, is reached on the basis of a lack of difference in correlations of identical twins reared together and apart, and the minimal correlation (.07) that is typical between traits of adopted siblings or of adopted children and adopting parents. The data suggest that only a third of the similarities between parents and their biological children can be attributed to environmental influences; the rest comes from the parental genes.

3. Although shared environment cannot explain much of the similarity between persons in the same families, a substantial part of the reliable variance can be attributed to nonshared environmental influences. Such influences may include sibling interactions, differential parental treatment of their children *not evoked by actual differences in behavior of the children,* and specific peer and authority influences outside of the family. Although personality differences within a family are often attributed to differential parental treatment, the data suggest that most of the differential treatment is due to a genotype-environment correlation.

4. Although many workers believe that genetic influences must be maximal at birth and decline in importance as the child matures, the data support the idea that genetic influences in many traits become stronger as the child develops. Modern molecular genetics suggests that genes switch on or off at different stages of development, thus exerting different influences at these stages. Adaptive behavior for an infant is not necessarily adaptive for an older child and is certainly not adaptive for an adult. In the first months of life, behavior is rather unstable, and little significant

genetic influence can be detected. However, by 9 months of age, many of the broad temperamental traits such as *activity, regularity, thresholds,* and *approach-avoidance* show strong genetic influences; by 24 months the emotional tone of social responses is genetically influenced, and by 6 years of age the genetic influences are apparent in most broad personality traits including *activity, sociability, emotionality,* and *impulsivity.*

5. Although there tends to be a great deal of similarity, or limitation of range, in the heritabilities of various personality traits, the attitudes, values, beliefs, and traits such as masculinity-femininity, which are more dependent on learned interests, show lower heritabilities and more effects of shared environment than those found for the three supertraits, E, N, and P, and the narrower traits associated with them such as *sensation seeking* and *impulsivity.*

6. Although most simple additive models assume no interaction between heredity and environment, such interactions are probable and may explain many of the inconsistencies in the data. One-way interactions, in which the environment and phenotype are independent but the influence of the genotype on the phenotype depends on the environment, have not been often found in humans, largely because they have not been looked for in most studies. Animal studies showing disappearances or reversals of strain differences when variations in environments or behaviors are studied, suggest that such interactions may be of primary importance in understanding what is really inherited.

In humans there is currently more evidence for genotype-environment correlations in which the parent rewards behavior because of the common genetically determined disposition, in which the environmental reactions are produced by the genetically influenced behavior pattern, and in which persons choose from among environmental possibilities as a function of their genotype. Investigators of ostensible environmental influences have largely ignored the possibilities for two-way genotype-environment interactions in interpreting the data.

Both human and animal studies have shown the significant influence of genetics in the complex patterns of behavior involved in traits. Because genes work through particular biological mechanisms, a knowledge of what we inherit at the biological level closest to the genotype may enable us to change behavior by biological or behavioral methods. Heredity is not destiny unless we ignore it or refuse to understand it. The next chapter attempts to describe genetically shaped differences in the structures and physiologies of nervous systems that may be relevant to personality differences.

4   Neuropsychology

Overview

Twenty years ago there would have been little if any substance to discuss in a chapter on the neural bases of personality. Even now, despite the explosion of behavioral brain science research during the last 20 years, much of what will be said is speculative, resting on crude clinical neuropsychology and extrapolated from the more precise but still inconclusive experimental work with nonhuman species. As in previous chapters the human findings, based largely on studies of psychosurgery and brain-damaged patients, are presented first, followed by the experimental animal studies. Finally, some attempt is made to integrate the two bodies of literature in terms of biological personality models.

The triune brain

MacLean's (1970, 1976, 1982) seminal concept of the *triune brain* provides a good starting point for visualizing the overall design of the brain. MacLean suggests that the brain has evolved in three organizational stages: the reptilian, paleomammalian, and neomammalian brains. Each brain is conceived of as having its own type of intelligence, memory, motor, and motivational functions. Although all three brain organizations are still present in the human and are extensively interconnected and interdependent, MacLean (1976) says that each is capable of functioning somewhat independently of the others in special circumstances. Issacson (1982), however, cautions that we should not make the mistake of regarding any of the brain *nuclei* or regions as entities rather than as parts of unified structures or systems.

Figure 4.1 shows the reptillian brain. The organization is centered on what has been called the "striatal complex." Although the brain of a lizard is much simpler than that of a mammal, the behavior of these animals is quite complex and includes many behaviors that are also seen in mammals, such as territoriality, fighting, dominance, greeting, grooming, courtship, mating, flocking, and migration. What distinguishes the behavior of reptiles and mammals is the mediation by fixed action patterns ("instinct") in the reptile, contrasted with the greater plasticity of mammalian behavior. In reptiles, behavior is more closely tied to innate releasors and is less modifiable than in mammals.

130

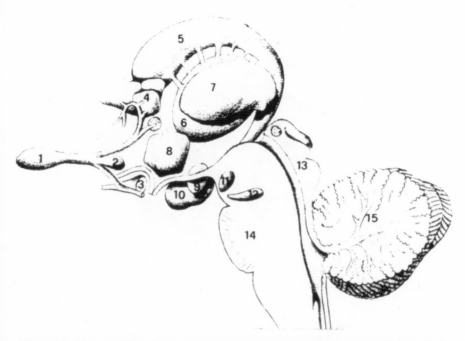

Figure 4.1. The "reptillian" brain. 1, olfactory bulb; 2, olfactory tubercule; 3, optic chiasma; 4, septal nuclei; 5, caudate; 6, putamen and globus palladus; 7, thalamus; 8, hypothalamus; 9, mamillary body; 10, amygdala; 11, intereduncular nucleus; 12, substantial nigra; 13, quadrigeminal bodies (tectum mesencephali); 14, pons; 15, cerebellum. (From *Psychobiology of aggression and violence*, p. 34, by L. Valzelli, 1981. New York: Raven Press. Copyright 1981 by Raven Press. Reprinted by permission.)

Figure 4.2 shows the paleomammalian brain, which closely corresponds to what is called the *limbic system*. There is some overlap between the reptillian and paleomammalian brains. MacLean regards the latter as the evolved executive part of the reptillian complex, perhaps accounting for the greater flexibility and modifiability of behavior in mammals. Issacson (1982) again cautions that each of the limbic structures, such as the hypothalamus, is a complex set of substructures with their own connections to other brain systems. He says that it is incorrect to speak of a "limbic system" when there are only "limbic systems." Many of these limbic systems are involved in emotional, motivational, appetitive, aversive, exploratory behaviors, and the learning and memory functions that are connected with these behaviors; therefore, they may constitute the most basic psychobiological levels of personality traits.

The neomammalian brain is represented by the cerebral cortex, which covers the reptillian and paleomammalian brain structures (Figure 4.3). Its development is greater in the more recently evolved mammals including the primate apes and humans. In humans, it is essential for language and

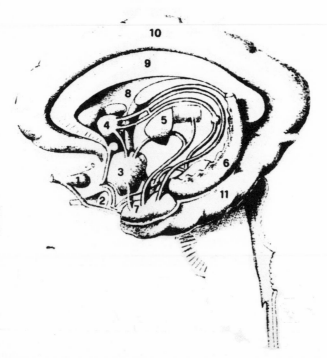

Figure 4.2. The "paleomammalian" [limbic] brain. 1, olfactory tubercle; 2, optic chiasma; 3, hypothalamus; 4, septal nuclei; 5, thalamic nuclei; 6, hippocampus; 7, amygdala; 8, septum; 9, corpus callosum; 10, cingulate gyrus; 11, hippocampal gyrus (temporal lobe). (From *Psychobiology of aggression and violence*, p. 35, by L. Valzelli, 1981. New York: Raven Press. Copyright 1981 by Raven Press. Reprinted by permission.)

speech, which form the basis for society and culture. The cortex receives and processes sensory information and integrates information from separate sensory modalities in terms of memory of past experience. A large part of the cortex consists of association areas, which are not essential for sensory reception but are important for interpretation of such information. What we regard as self-awareness in humans may exist in some rudimentary fashion in other mammals and perhaps even in reptiles, but it is language that sharpens human self-perceptions and facilitates the long-term retention of experience in memory. The development of the neocortex in humans enables us to extend our consciousness further back into the past and forward into the future to anticipate consequences.

Systems such as Freud's Id-Ego-Superego system are easy to reify. Although MacLean's three brains are based on actual neurology, the inference of three separate organizations also invites reification. Bailey (1987) has used a construct of "phylogenetic regression", or the temporary dominance of one of the two lower brains over the neomammalian brain, to explain examples of psychopathic, sadistic human behaviors. However,

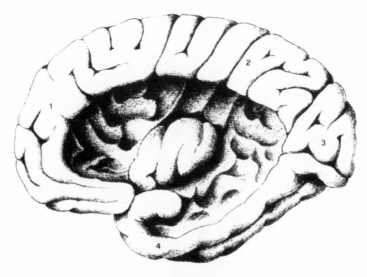

Figure 4.3. The "neomammalian brain". 1, frontal lobe; 2, parietal lobe; 3, occipital lobe; 4, temporal lobe. (From *Psychobiology of aggression and violence*, p. 37, by L. Valzelli, 1981. New York: Raven Press. Copyright 1981 by Raven Press. Reprinted by permission.)

such behavior is not typical of the reptillian brain, which MacLean suggests is involved in the tendency to follow fixed action patterns and rituals (like religious ceremonies and the pledge of allegiance). The point of presenting the concept of the triune brain is to suggest that normal personality traits are probably related to all systems. This is in contrast with social approaches to personality that seem to assume that only the neocortical parts of the brain are relevant to personality.

Personality theories and neuropsychology

H. J. Eysenck

Few of the many theories of personality have anything to say specifically about neuropsychology. Hans Eysenck was the first major modern theorist to address the biological bases of personality. On the basis of his earlier theory of extraversion, Eysenck (1957) proposed that brain damage in general and the lobotomy and cingulectomy operations produce an increase in extraversion, which he attributed to the increased strength of central neuronal inhibitory, relative to excitatory, mechanisms. In this earlier theory extraverts were said to be characterized more by central nervous system inhibition and introverts by excitation. The stronger tendencies toward reactive inhibition, satiation, and habituation in the extraverts was said to result in poor conditionability, and consequently poor socialization, and

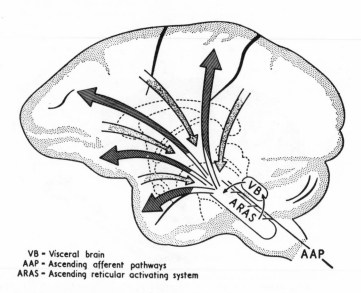

VB = Visceral brain
AAP = Ascending afferent pathways
ARAS = Ascending reticular activating system

Figure 4.4. Eysenck's schematic of interactions among ascending reticulocortical activating system, visceral (limbic) brain, and cortex. (From *The biological basis of personality*, p. 231, by H. J. Eysenck, 1967. Springfield, IL: Charles C. Thomas. Copyright 1981 by Charles C. Thomas. Reprinted by permission.)

in traits of changeability and lack of persistence. There was no clear neuropsychological hypothesis about how damage to the cortex caused increased neuronal inhibition.

In Eysenck's earlier biological theory (Eysenck, 1967), which is essentially unchanged in its latest formulation (Eysenck & Eysenck, 1985), extraversion is said to be determined by the general level of cortical arousal as regulated by the ascending reticulocortical activating system (ARAS in Figure 4.4), first described by Lindsley, Bowden, and Magoun (1949) and Moruzzi and Magoun (1949). This feedback loop is regulated by incoming stimulation and cortical activity itself. Depending on the load on the brain, the cortex may open channels for incoming stimulation or close them through descending pathways to the RAS. Introverts and extraverts differ in the sensitivity of their arousal mechanisms and the thresholds at which cortical mechanisms inhibit arousal. The net result is that introverts are generally in a higher state of arousal than extraverts and are more easily aroused by lower intensities of stimulation.

The limbic system, or visceral brain (VB in Figure 4.4), including the hippocampus, amygdala, cingulum, septum, and hypothalamus, is involved in emotional reactivity and is therefore postulated as the neuroanatomical basis for the dimension of neuroticism or emotionality. The two arousal systems are not independent because activity in the VB stimulates the ARAS through collaterals. In other words, the cortex can be aroused either through sensory stimulation, including that from the musculature and internal organs, external stimuli, or from emotional arousal that is engendered in the VB from reactions in higher centers. Figure 4.4 suggests that the VB can arouse the cortex only through collaterals to the ARAS. Developments since the 1950s suggest that there are more-direct pathways between the VB and the cortex (Routtenberg, 1968) such as the dorsal ascending noradrenergic bundle (discussed in the next chapter). Another challenge to the nonspecific arousal role attributed to the ARAS comes from studies of single-unit activity in freely moving cats, in which activity of particular neurons is closely related to specific movements of the eyes, ears, face, head, body, and limbs (Siegel, 1979, 1983). Apparently, the ARAS is more a specific than a general arousal system, though the activity of the various components may be correlated during states of high tension, arousal, or activity. Specificity of response is a challenge to general arousal theories, which are addressed again in chapter 6.

Eysenck's theory has been criticized as too broad on the neurophysiological side (Blakemore, 1967). The theory makes little or no distinction between left and right cortex, or among the various lobes of the cortex. Similarly, there is little distinction among the various systems of the limbic brain, all being characterized as serving emotionality.

J. A. Gray

Gray brings the expertise of a comparative neuropsychologist to the field of personality. Unlike Eysenck, who developed his personality measures on humans and then made some extrapolations to animal behavior, Gray worked exclusively with animals, mostly rats, and then attempted to extrapolate his findings to humans. This approach has led to more specificity in the neuropsychological and psychopharmacological models. Gray has accepted Eysenck's primary dimensions of personality at the human level and attempted to map hypothesized neuropsychological dimensions within this three-dimensional framework. Like Eysenck's theory (1957–1967), Gray's theory has undergone some important changes over the years. Even before Eysenck (1967), Gray (1964) identified the Pavlovian concept of *strength of the nervous system* and extraversion with the reticulocortical activating system. Later, Gray (1971) identified three limbic pathways that are associated with generalized tendencies for *approach, stop (inhibition),* and *fight-flight* as shown in Figure 4.5. In his current model, Gray (1987) has separated the approach system from this model and described a somewhat different pathway (the ascending dopaminergic system).

Initially, Gray (1971) suggested that the activity in the septohippocampal system (Figure 4.6) was the biological basis of introversion-extraversion, high activity in the system being identified with introversion. Later (Gray, 1973), he postulated that the septohippocampal system was the biological

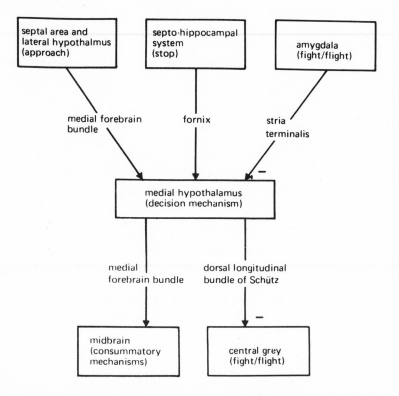

Figure 4.5. Gray's three systems [approach, stop (passive avoidance) and fight-flight] and their neurological bases. From *The psychology of fear and stress*, fig. 13.8, p. 213, by J. A. Gray, 1971. Copyright J. A. Gray; reprinted with permission.

basis of an *anxiety* dimension of personality, which ran from stable ex-traversion to neurotic introversion (Fig. 4.7). The main functions of the system are (1) to inhibit all ongoing behavior in response to novel stimuli or signals associated with punishment or nonreward; (2) to increase sym-pathetic system arousal; (3) to focus attention on the significant stimuli. Orthogonal to this primary dimension is an *impulsivity* dimension, which goes from stable neuroticism to neurotic extraversion. At that time, the septal-lateral hypothalamic and medial forebrain bundle, together with a midbrain consummatory mechanism were suggested as the biological basis for the *impulsivity* dimension. It corresponded roughly to the reward system discovered by Olds and colleagues in brain self-stimulation studies (Gray has never put much faith in this paradigm as a method of studying reward or identifying its biological substrate). The third system, corresponding to the P dimension in Eysenck's scheme, *fight-flight* has a biological substrate in the amygdala, medial hypothalamus, central grey pathway. It was based on a series of lesioning experiments (Deutsch & Deutsch, 1966) and on de

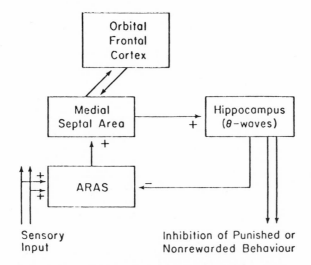

Figure 4.6. Schematized septohippocampal system; inputs from orbital frontal cortex and arousal produced by sensory input into the ARAS stimulate the medial septal area, which produces theta waves in the hippocampus. Output of the hippocampus inhibits punished or nonrewarded behavior. (From "Causal theories of personality and how to test them," by J. A. Gray, 1973, in *Multivariate analysis and psychological theory*, p. 424, J. R. Royce, Ed. New York: Academic Press. Copyright 1973 by Academic Press. Reprinted by permission.)

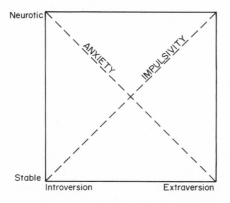

Figure 4.7. Gray's hypothesized "anxiety" dimension of personality, running from stable *extraversion* (E) to *neurotic* (N) *introversion* (I).

Molina and Hunsperger's (1962) experiments on cats, which showed defensive aggression and escape attempts in response to stimulation of this pathway.

More recently, Gray (1987) has realigned his biologically based dimensions with Eysenck's three-factor system (Figure 4.8). Now the *anxiety* dimension is bipolar, with *anxiety* at one end and *psychopathy* (high P,

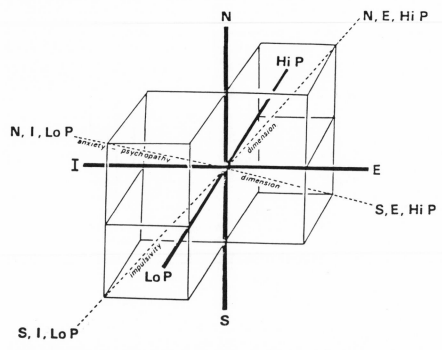

Figure 4.8. Gray's three-dimensional conceptualization of *anxiety-psychopathy* and *impulsivity* dimensions (dashed lines) within coordinates of Eysenck's three dimensions (thick solid lines) of *extraverion* (E)-*intraversion* (I), *neuroticism* (N)-*stability* (S), and *psychoticism* (P). (From "The neuropsychology of emotion and personality," by J. A. Gray, 1987, in *Cognitive neurochemistry*, p. 186, S. M. Stahl, S. D. Iverson, and E. C. Goodman, Eds. Oxford: Oxford University Press. Reprinted by permission.)

absent or weak emotionality, and extraversion) at the other. *Impulsivity,* or approach behavior, comprises a dimension running from *stable introversion* to *neurotic* or unstable *extraversion* combined with high P. This approach system is now identified with a dopaminergic system which ascends from the substantia nigra and nucleus A10 in the ventral tegmental area to innervate various regions of the basal ganglia, neocortex, and limbic system. This system is discussed in chapter 5.

The orbital frontal cortex receives input from the medial septal area, involved in the septohippocampal inhibitory system and also provides input into the system. In his most recent formulation, Gray (in press) does not mention the orbital frontal input but, instead, stresses the input to the hippocampal formation from the entorhinal cortex in the temporal lobe, shown in Figure 4.9. The sensory information received by the hippocampal formation comes through the entorhinal cortex, which receives projections from the amygdala, limbic cortex, and all areas of the neocortex. The figure shows the pathway through the perforant path to the dentate gyrus,

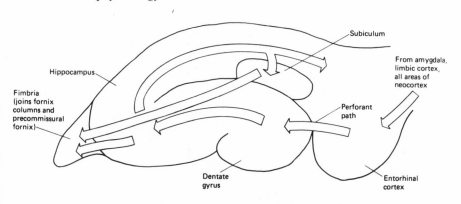

Figure 4.9. Connections of components of hippocampal formation. (From *Physiology of behavior*, 3rd ed., p. 578, by N. R. Carlson, 1986. Newton, MA: Allyn & Bacon. Copyright, 1986 by Allyn & Bacon. Reprinted by permission.)

which leads to the hippocampus. Efferent pathways go through the subiculum, which projects to the posterior cingulate cortex and the fornix columns. Gray (1987) provides a schematic diagram (Fig. 4.10) of the loops that compose the septohippocampal system and the associated Papez (1937) circuit.

Information from the prefrontal cortex (PFC) and the neocortical association areas, where incoming sensory information has already been elaborated, is said (Gray, 1987) to enter the hippocampal formation (HF) from the entorhinal cortex (EC). Presumably, concepts embedded in language would affect the input from the left temporal lobe, though this is not made explicit in Gray's model. The subicular (SUB) area acts as a comparator of incoming information with past information, receiving input directly from the entorhinal area and also after the information has passed around the entire hippocampal circuit [septal areas (SA) to mammillary bodies (MB) to anteroventral thalamus (AVT)]. Only a part of the information from the world is selected for processing in the comparator. The hippocampal formation plays a major role in selecting items that have strong biological significance (i.e., are connected with stimuli associated with primary reinforcement). In routine circumstances, the comparator may serve simple cognitive functions, like working memory; but in stressful conditions, the monoaminergic (noradrenergic and serotonergic) tracts (discussed in chapter 5) engage the comparator function, directing it particularly toward threatening stimuli. Presumably, in a chronically anxious or neurotic person the system is frequently in the stress mode.

As in Eysenck's concept of the feedback loop between the visceral brain and the ARAS, Gray states that the septohippocampal system arousal increases cortical arousal through the ARAS (Figure 4.4). In Gray's analysis, the cortical arousal function mediated by the ARAS is activated by

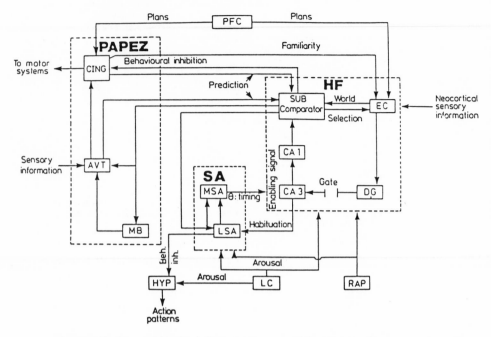

Figure 4.10. The neurology of the behavioral inhibition system. The three major building blocks are shown in heavy print and outlined by dashed boxes: the hippocampal formation (HF), made up of the entorhinal cortex (EC), the dentate gyrus (DG), areas CA 3 and CA 1 of the hippocampus proper; the subicular area (SUB); the septal area (SA), containing the medial septal area (MSA), and the lateral septal area (LSA); and the Papez circuit, which receives projections from and returns them to the subicular area via the mammillary bodies (MB), anteroventral thalamus (AVT), and cingulate cortex (CING). Other structures shown are the hypothalamus (HYP), the locus coeruleus (LC), the raphe nuclei (RAP), and the prefrontal cortex (PFC). Arrows show direction of projection; the projection from SUB to MSA lacks anatomical confirmation. Words in lower case show postulated functions; beh. inh. is behavioral inhibition. (From "The neuropsychology of emotion and personality," by J. A. Gray, 1987, in *Cognitive neurochemistry*, p. 177, S. M. Stahl, S. D. Iverson, and E. C. Goodman, Eds. Oxford: Oxford University Press. Copyright 1987 by Oxford University Press. Reprinted by permission.)

the sum of activity in the approach and behavioral inhibition systems whereas extraversion-introversion represents the balance of activities in these systems (Gray 1973; Gray, 1987).

Studies in human neuropsychology

Neuropsychology of the human is fraught with methodological problems. Most of our knowledge is based on studies of brain-damaged persons, in whom the boundaries of the damage are imprecise, or psychiatric patients with functional disorders who have undergone brain-lesioning operations in the hope of remedying their conditions. A few studies are based on stimulation of particular brain areas in wakeful patients able to report sensations, images, feelings, and cognitions. Special experimental and test methods have been developed to study right versus left hemisphere function or functions putatively related to one lobe of the cortex as opposed to others, but the relation of these to actual activation of brain areas is complex and can be altered by variations in experimental procedures. New methods of imaging the brain's activity, such as Position Emission Tomography (PET) scans, are promising, but data from them are still fragmentary (see chapter 6).

There are no baseline measures of functions for most brain-damaged patients. The baseline functioning of psychiatric patients who have been subjected to neurosurgery is abnormal, and it is difficult to ascertain whether the changes in function are due to the brain lesion or to nonspecific factors that are secondary to the actual site of the lesion. Similarly, much of the emotional disturbance of brain-damaged patients may be reactions to their recognition of loss of intellectual function rather than direct effects of the damage to a particular area of the brain that regulates emotional function. With these limitations in mind, let us examine the implications of these results for the neurobiology of personality.

The cerebral hemispheres

The cerebrum is composed of right and left hemispheres. Figure 4.11 shows an external lateral view of the left side of the human brain with the lobes of the left cerebral hemisphere identified: frontal, parietal, occipital, and temporal. The central sulcus divides the frontal lobe from the parietal lobe, and the lateral fissure divides the frontal and parietal lobes from the underlying temporal lobe.

The effects of damage to the cerebral hemispheres on personality seem to depend both on the extent and on the location of the damage. Lishman (1968) investigated the effect of penetrating head wounds in 670 cases rated for extent of "psychiatric disability," defined in a broad way to include emotional, behavioral, social, somatic, neurotic, and psychotic dysfunctions. When the patients were classed according to total brain tissue destroyed, the percentage of patients with severe psychiatric disability was clearly related to the amount of brain affected: 13% of those with least damage, 39% of those with moderate amount of damage, and 72% of those with the greatest degree of brain damage showed the more severe psychiatric disability. A similar relationship was seen for depth of penetration of the injury, with the most severe disabilities found in persons with wounds penetrating to the ventricles. In the latter cases, subcortical limbic structures would be likely to be damaged.

Although such data establish a clear relationship between degree of brain

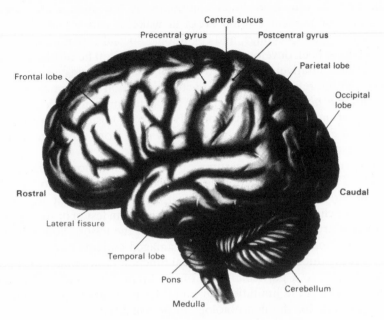

Figure 4.11. A lateral exterior view of the left side of the human brain. (From *Physiology of Behavior*, 3rd ed., p. 98, by N. R. Carlson, 1986. Newton, MA: Allyn and Bacon. Copyright 1986 by Allyn and Bacon. Reprinted by permission.)

damage and broad personality dysfunction, they do not show how much of the change in personality is related to loss of cognitive and sensory-motor function, often involved in the more severe degrees of brain damage. Also, the more extensive the damage, the more likely subcortical structures are involved. But even if subcortical areas are not involved, regulation of subcortical structures depends to some degree on intactness of cortical areas. Disinhibition of emotions or behaviors can disrupt the balance between social regulation and inhibition of impulses toward personal gratifications. Such inhibition seems to be more localized in some lobes of the cerebrum than in others, but the more extensive the damage, the more likely that more lobes of the cerebrum are involved.

Lateralization

In the nineteenth century, neurologists became aware that the two cerebral hemispheres had somewhat different functions in humans. Broca (1864) proposed that the capacity for speech was generally limited to the left hemisphere, and Jackson (1868) suggested the idea of a "leading" (dominant) hemisphere, which for most persons is the left hemisphere. He further postulated that the right hemisphere mediated automatic behavior and the left hemisphere voluntary behavior. Later studies showed that the right hemisphere had its own "silent" functions, including visual-spatial perception and a global-holistic mode of analysis, in comparison with the more analytic approach characteristic of left hemisphere function. In the normal brain, the hemispheres are connected through the corpus callosum, and the functions are integrated, though individual differences in hemisphere dominance may make some individuals relatively more proficient, faster, or more prone to use one intellectual style as opposed to another. The dichotomy between the "two modes of consciousness" mediated by hemispheric specialization has been elaborated by Ornstein (1972) as the basis for many classical dichotomies between the rational and intellectual and the more intuitive and mystical.

Perhaps the most significant fact of lateralization for personality is that language functions are generally in the left hemisphere. Freud (1915, 1957) spoke of two types of thinking, the primary and secondary process. He saw primary process as usually appearing in visual imagery and as existing in infants before the development of language but as coexisting with secondary-process thinking in adult fantasy and dream expressions. Primary process, he thought, is timeless, irrational, and preoccupied with immediate gratification whereas secondary process is mediated through language and consensually accepted meanings and is concerned with reality and problem solving. Naturally, we are more aware of our secondary process, but primary process is not necessarily unconscious. Primary process is more immediately reflective of basic emotions. We might equate secondary process with left-brain function and primary process with right-brain functioning and therefore expect to find emotionality more directly expressed in right-hemisphere function. The right brain can experience feelings and sensations, but only the left brain can translate these experiences into language.

Hemispheric dominance

Dominance can be assessed by hand or foot preferences, eye movements during thinking, and information processing effectiveness when material is transmitted to left or right visual or auditory fields. These methods do not yield highly related criteria of dominance, so the results of any study must be regarded as specific to the method used to establish dominance until otherwise demonstrated.

Given individual differences in dominance and the fact that the right hemisphere seems to be more involved with emotional analysis and expression, one might expect to find that individuals who are high in traits of *emotionality (neuroticism)* would show evidence of right-hemisphere dominance. Using a picture-recognition task, supposedly related to right-hemisphere function, Thompson and Mueller (1984a) found no relationship of the dominance measure to *extraversion* or *neuroticism* scales. Tucker,

Antes, Stenslie, and Barnhardt (1978) found that individuals high on the trait of *anxiety* show a right-ear attentional bias and a low incidence of left lateral eye movements, suggesting "a high level of left hemispheric activation without hemispheric-specific task demands." (p. 382) These latter results are opposite to theory that would predict right-hemisphere dominance in emotionally overreactive subjects.

Right- versus left-hemisphere brain damage

Table 4.1 summarizes studies relating brain damage at particular brain loci to personality traits and psychopathology. Three studies of brain-damaged individuals provide information on the role of the two hemispheres in personality. Flor-Henry (1969) found that in epileptic patients who manifested signs of psychosis, the form of the psychosis was related to the damaged hemisphere. Manic-depressive symptoms were more frequent in persons with right-hemisphere damage, and confusional and schizophrenic symptoms more frequently accompanied left-hemisphere damage. The results are consistent with the greater role of the right hemisphere in emotions because manic-depressive disorder is a severe mood disorder whereas schizophrenia is usually regarded as a cognitive disorder, consistent with the role of the left hemisphere in symbolic activity.

Black (1975) compared MMPI scores of groups of right- and left-hemisphere damaged veterans injured by missiles or shrapnel. The cases of left-hemisphere damage showed significant elevations on *depression, hypochondriasis,* and *schizophrenia* scales and were also significantly higher than the right-hemisphere cases on MMPI F (general response deviancy sometimes caused by misunderstanding of the items), *paranoia,* and *social introversion* scales. The mean profile of the right-hemisphere cases was within normal limits. In sharp contrast to these results are those of Woodward, Bisbee, and Bennett (1984) who found essentially normal MMPI profiles in a group of veterans with left-hemisphere damage and significantly elevated peaks on *hypomania, schizophrenia, depression, hysteria,* and *psychopathic deviate* scales in a group with right-hemisphere damage. Woodward et al. attributed the discrepancy between their data and Black's to the fact that Black's subjects were tested in the acute phase of reaction to left-hemisphere impairment, which tends initially to be profound and is associated with "catastrophic anxiety" and depression reactions in many patients. The Woodward et al. patients were tested much later, after their conditions developed. Right-hemisphere patients are more likely to seem initially unimpaired because the cognitive deficits are more subtle and perhaps because of a dampening of emotional reaction produced by the injury. Later they tend to show "irresponsible and childlike behavior."

It is interesting that the peak scale in the MMPI profiles of the Woodward

Table 4.1. *Summary of human neuropsychological studies*

Study	Subjects	Results[a]
Right vs. left hemisphere		
Flor-Henry (1969)	Epileptics with psychoses	R hem: manic-depressive symptoms L hem: schizophrenic symptoms
Black (1975)	Brain damaged veterans	R hem: MMPI normal L hem: MMPI + F, D, Hs, Sc, Pa, Si
Woodward et al. (1984)	Brain damaged veterans	R hem: MMPI + Ma, Sc, Hy, Pd L hem: MMPI normal
Frontal lobes		
Mettler (1952)	Psychotics, mainly schiz.; topectomies: frontal tissue	− Anxiety, complaint scales; + impulsivity. (Porteus maze) but 0–1 yr later
Hetherington et al. (1972)	Chronically depressed patients Prefrontal lobotomy	− Anxiety, depression, neurotic symptoms + "Outspokenness," hostility
Kelly et al. (1972)	Chronic anxiety, depression, O-C, prefrontal lobotomy	− Anxiety, N scales; O on E scales; − EEG, − Heart rate, blood pressure, blood flow
Levinson & Meyer (1965)	Depressive & anxiety patients, orbital frontal undercutting	− Anxiety, N scales; + E scale changes normalized scores
Miller (1985), Miller & Milner (1985)	Epileptics, operated for relief of focal epilepsy	Frontotemporals + > other lesions on impulsivity (guessing on cognitive tasks)
Hacaen (1964)	Frontal tumor patients	+ Irritability & euphoria, mild depression, little anxiety
McAllister & Price (1987)	Veterans, frontal lobe damage showing psychiatric symptoms	+ 60% had disinhibited behavior with affective lability; 35% mood problem
Grafman et al. (1986)	Veterans with brain wounds	R orbitofrontals + hostility, anxiety, P scale; L dorsofrontals + anger, hostility
Temporal lobes		
Falconer (1973)	Temporal lobe epileptics Temporal lobe extirpation	47% psychopathic, 25% show outbursts of "explosive aggression" Reduction in aggression
Hill et al. (1957)	Temporal lobe extirpation	Increase in sexual drive
McIntyre et al. (1976)	Temporal lobe epileptics	R temporals + > normals, L temporals − < normals on impulsivity (decision time, Matching Figures Test)
Lansdell (1968)	Temporal lobe epileptics after unilateral operation	R temporals + > L temporals MMPI N reduction in N scores
Limbic system		
Meyer et al. (1972)	Chronic subjects, mainly schizophrenic, depressive, alcoholic Cingulotomy	Depressives, anxiety benefited most, alcoholics, schizophrenics least − MMPI anxiety, depression, hostility
Mitchell-Heggs et al. (1976)	Chronic patients, O-C, anxiety, depression Cingulotomy + orbitofrontal	− Anxiety, N scales; 0 on E scale − Heart rate & blood pressure

Table 4.1 (*continued*)

Study	Subjects	Results[a]
Limbic system (*continued*)		
Laitenan & Vilki (1973)	Chronic patients, schizophrenic, anxiety Cingulotomy	$-$N scale; 0 on E scale
Choppy et al. (1973)	Psychiatric patients, diagnoses?	L thalamus $-$ MMPI D, Si scales
	Unilateral thalamotomy	R thalamus 0 on MMPI D, Si
Heimberger et al. (1972)	Aggressive, severe epileptics Amygdalectomy	$-$ Aggression
Mark et al. (1972)	Fearful/aggressive epileptics Amygdalotomy	$-$ Aggressive & impulse dyscontrol
Siegfried & Ben-Shmuel (1972)	Psychiatric patients, diagnoses?	Amygdalotomy; $-$ aggression
	Amygdalotomy vs. lobotomy	Prefrontal lobotomy: 0 aggression

[a]R = right; L = left; Hem = hemisphere, MMPI = Minnesota Multiphasic Personality Inventory; + = increases on variable(s) listed; $-$ = decreases on variables listed; o = no change on variables listed.

et al. right-hemisphere group was *hypomania* because Flor-Henry (1969) found manic-depressive psychosis predominating in right-hemisphere epileptics who showed psychotic symptoms. Manic-depressive reactions are characterized by impulsivity, overactivity, transient psychopathic and irresponsible behaviors, and euphoria or anger in the manic phases and profound retarded depression in the depressed phases. These results suggest that awareness of negative emotions and control of impulses are more functions of the right hemisphere than of the left.

Frontal lobes

Lobotomies

The roles of the various lobes in sensory reception and initiation of motor behavior have been fairly well defined, but the relation of the lobes to emotions and personality is still somewhat of a mystery. Figure 4.12 shows the concept underlying the prefrontal lobotomy operation, which suggests that the prefrontal lobe influences affective-ideational experience by integrating and directing somatic and sensory motor experience from particular sensory association areas to an area of convergence in the anterior temporal region and through connections with deeper lying limbic centers.

The first frontal lobotomies were performed by Egas Moniz in Lisbon

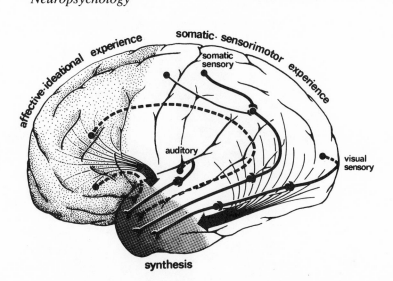

synthesis

Figure 4.12. Conceptualization of the influence of the frontal lobes on the synthesis of experience and affective ideational processes in the anterior temporal region. (From "The continuing evolution of the limbic system concept," by K. E. Livingston and A. Escobar, 1972, in *Psychosurgery*, p. 31, E. Hitchcock, L. Laitenen, & K. Vaernet, Eds. Springfield, IL: Charles C. Thomas. Copyright 1972 by Charles C. Thomas. Reprinted by permission.)

in 1936, and the technique of prefrontal lobotomy was popularized in the United States by Freeman and Watts in the 1940s. The early procedure consisted of cutting the pathways between the frontal lobes and the deeper structures of the brain. Figure 4.13 shows some of the incisions used. Based on personal follow-up studies, Freeman (1972) reported greater success in schizophrenics with the transorbital lobotomy (3B in the figure) than with the standard prefrontal lobotomy (2B).

Thousands of patients were lobotomized throughout the world by surgeons who had little basic knowledge of the role of the frontal lobes and their connections with the limbic systems. Operations involving lesioning of connections in other areas of the brain were developed. The neurosurgeons' reports provide a remarkable contrast between accounts of the precise surgical techniques and the imprecise or totally absent methods of evaluation (Hitchcock, Lattinen, & Vaernet, 1972; Laitinen & Livingston, 1973). Control groups were virtually nonexistent and, with the exception of an occasional use of the MMPI, observations of change were based on the crudest kind of clinical observations, with no tests of reliabilities of ratings or single-blind controls.

Studies of changes in psychiatric patients after topectomies, prefrontal lobotomies, and oribital-frontal undercutting (Hetherington, Haden, & Craig, 1972; Kelly, Walter, Mitchell-Heggs, & Sargant, 1972; Levinson & Meyer, 1965; Mettler, 1952) are summarized in Table 4.1. Mettler's was the only study using a control group of untreated patients. The questionable

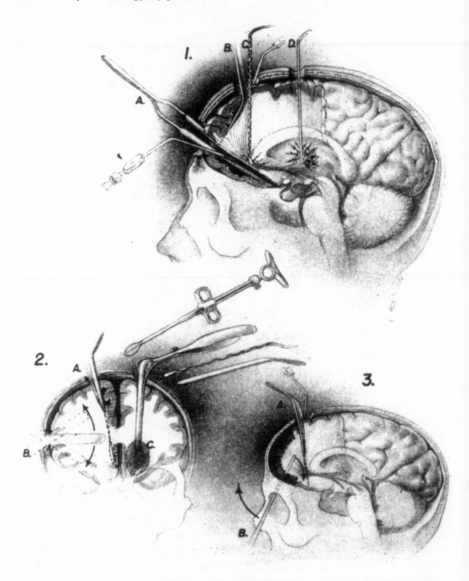

Figure 4.13. Types of incisions used in brain surgery. 1A, orbital undercutting (Scoville); 1B, undercutting of the superior convexity (Scoville); 1C, inferior quadrant leukotomy (Grantham, electrical); 1D, thalamotomies; 2A, undercutting of rostral cingulate gyrus (Scoville); 2B, standard closed lobotomy (Freeman and Watts); 2C, instruments used in inferior quadrant leutcotomy; 3A, standard open lobotomy (Poppen); 3B, transorbital lobotomy (Freeman); 3, cross hatch and dotted lines indicate areas of topectomy (Pool). (From "Introduction," by W. B. Scoville, 1972, in *Psychosurgery*, p. xxi, E. Hitchcock, L. Laitenen, and K. Vaernet, Eds. Springfield, IL: Charles C. Thomas. Copyright 1972 by Charles C. Thomas. Reprinted by permission.)

assumption seemed to be that the chronic patients used in most of the studies had stabilized and that any enduring changes subsequent to treatment must have been due to the treatment. But it has been shown repeatedly that novel treatments and the increased social attention accompanying them often have salutary effects even on chronic patients.

All studies showed that the prefrontal operations resulted in decreases of symptoms of anxiety and/or scores on *anxiety* and *neuroticism* scales. Kelly et al. also showed significant decreases in physiological measures of arousal. The Mettler study showed no corresponding changes in anxiety in the control group until one year post operation when the differences between groups was no longer significant. Unfortunately, the operated groups started with higher levels of anxiety and mental symptoms, and this lack of equivalence makes the first-year change comparisons equivocal. Kelly et al. found that anxiety and depressive disorders showed greater improvement after the operation than obsessionals, schizophrenics, and personality disorders; but the former groups generally had a better prognosis than the latter. However, an 18-month follow-up study showed that the changes on the anxiety scale and some of the physiological measures remained significant in the operated patients.

The operation also produced some disinhibition and increase in sociability in patients, as reflected in increased assertiveness and hostility (Hetherington et al., 1972) and scores on Eysenck's *extraversion* scale (Levinson & Meyers, 1965). Miller (1985; Miller & Milner, 1985) studied epileptics treated with neurosurgery for relief of focal epileptic symptoms. He found that patients with lesions made in right frontal and temporal lobes did more impulsive guessing in a recognition task than groups with lesions of the left frontal or temporal lobes, even though they were punished by loss of money for inaccurate guesses. The results suggest that damage to the frontal lobes, particularly if combined with damage to temporal lobes, results in an increased tendency to take risks or to an impulsive cognitive style.

Table 4.1 also includes studies of groups with "natural" brain damage to the frontal lobes (Grafman, Vance, Weingartner, Salazar, & Amin, 1986; Hacaen, 1964; McAllister & Price, 1987). Anxiety was not a symptom in most of these cases. Only 2% of Hacaen's frontal tumor patients showed anxiety, and only 5% demonstrated depression, even though these symptoms are common in functional patients referred for psychiatric disturbances. The most common symptoms (60% of the patients) associated with frontal lobe damage was disinhibited behavior with affective lability (McAllister & Price, 1987). Grafman et al. (1986) found hemispheric differences interacting with lobe loci of brain wounds. Patients with right orbitofrontal damage reported a great deal of anger and aggressive impulses at initial evaluation after the operation, which later simmered down to hostility and anxiety. In contrast, patients with left orbitofrontal lesions showed little mood change. Both right and bilateral orbitofrontal patients had higher scores on Eysenck's *psychoticism* (P) scale than groups with lesions in other areas. It should be remembered from chapter 1 that the P scale is an excellent marker for a dimension of personality measuring antisocial, impulsive, and sensation-seeking tendencies. These results suggest an involvement of the right orbitofrontal area in the inhibition of such tendencies. Behavioral signs of sexual disinhibition were also noted in these patients.

The results of both neurosurgery and studies of brain-damaged patients show three types of effects of frontal lobe damage or disruptions of frontal-limbic system connections: (1) reduction of anxiety, (2) the appearance of impulsive disinhibited behaviors, and (3) the release of angry and aggressive feelings in some patients. Laterality plays an important role because many changes are limited to damage of right-hemisphere frontal areas. Within the frontal lobes, the orbitofrontal area, which is one of the main sites of entry from cortex to the limbic systems (like the septohippocampal system), seems crucially involved in both the reduction of anxiety and the disinhibition of behavior.

Clinicians have noted either apathy or inappropriate euphoria and hostility in many patients after prefrontal lobotomy. The latter results could be produced by a disregulation of limbic centers for rage and euphoria from the inhibiting effects of centers in the frontal lobes involved in the negative emotions of anxiety and depression. Apathy could be produced by a general lowering of arousal levels. Apart from the autonomic arousal reduction found in the study by Kelly et al. (1972), Homskaya (1973) reported lowered electroencephalogram (EEG) arousal in patients after lobotomy, as evidenced by an increase in the percentage of alpha wave activity relative to other types. The beneficial effect of lobotomy may depend on the preoperative level of arousal; the operation would be contraindicated for patients already low in arousal and involvement in the environment. But for patients who are high in anxiety and arousal, drugs and/or behavioral therapy or even time alone would probably achieve the same effect as lobotomy, without producing irreversible neural damage.

All of the evidence from the first cases operated on by Moniz to the peak of the operation's popularity in the late 1940s tends to show that those who benefitted most from it were anxiety, obsessive, and affective disorders, and younger patients who had been hospitalized for a shorter period of time. These are the patients who had the best prognosis to begin with. As a treatment for chronic schizophrenia it was generally a failure, not producing rates of recovery in excess of those found in less radical treatments. No wonder that the operation began to decline as soon as antipsychotic and antidepressive drugs appeared. In the meantime, the operation seems to have substituted an organic psychosis for a schizophrenic one in many patients. If controlled longitudinal studies on a smaller scale had been done at the start, the tens of thousands of lobotomies throughout the world would not have taken place. The lack of adequate theory and careful research can be fatal in medicine when enthusiastic advocates like Freeman popularize a drastic treatment. Lobotomy has been described as one of those "great and desperate cures" that have often cropped up in the history of medicine when physicians are confronted with a serious dysfunction that they do not understand (Valenstein, 1986).

Temporal lobes

The temporal lobe surrounds the amygdala and other structures implicated in aggression and rage and therefore has been hypothesized to be involved in the regulation of related behaviors. Aggression and psychosis have been reported in high percentages of patients with temporal lobe epilepsy (Falconer, 1973). Falconer says that 40% have been institutionalized in mental hospitals or prisons, and 47% were viewed as psychopaths. Falconer reported pathology in the temporal lobe neurons and connected limbic structures, particularly what he calls "mesial temporal sclerosis." About a quarter of the patients operated on had suffered from unpredictable outbursts of aggression in response to minor frustrations prior to the operation. Of the patients whose extirpated tissues showed mesial temporal sclerosis, about half recovered from their aggression, as revealed in long-term follow-up studies of the majority of patients for more than 10 years. But only a fifth of the patients with other types of lesions or no evidence of neuronal damage recovered from aggressive fits. As usual, the lack of a control group makes this clinical evidence questionable. Aggression and psychopathy are traits that decline normally with age, perhaps as a function of the decline in testosterone in males, and reported changes may not be due to the operations.

Changes in sexuality were another result of the operation in the same series of patients. Hill, Pond, Mitchell, and Falconer (1957) stated: "In general the change experienced was of increased sexual drive and potency" (p. 23). In some patients these changes consisted of changing the objects of sexual desire whereas in others they were in the sheer force of the drive.

McIntyre, Pritchard, and Lombroso (1976) reported a more controlled study of temporal lobe epileptics using a control group of normal persons and some objective behavioral measures that were possibly valid for traits relevant to dysfunction of the temporal lobes. The study also examined right and left temporal lobe dysfunctions separately. On the Kagan Matching Figures Test, a putative measure of *impulsivity,* the patients with left temporal lobe foci tended to take longer in making discriminations (reflective style) whereas patients with right temporal lobe foci tended to respond more quickly than controls (impulsive style).

Lansdell (1968) presented results on patients with unilateral temporal lobe epilepsy on the MMPI given before and after surgical removal of

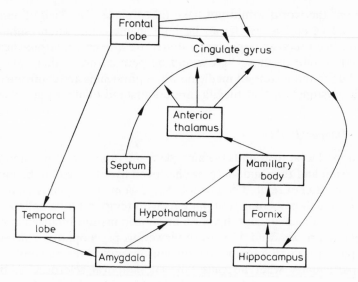

Figure 4.14. Diagrammatic representation of the Papez circuit. (From "A survey of the effects of brain lesions upon personality," by G. E. Powell, 1981, in *A model for personality*, p. 71, H. J. Eysenck, Ed. Heidelberg: Springer-Verlag. Copyright, 1981 by Springer-Verlag. Reprinted by permission.)

temporal lobe foci for seizures. Configural MMPI scores reflecting profile indications of neuroticism showed higher scores for this trait in the preoperative right temporal lobe foci group than in the left temporal lobe foci group. The operation tended to reduce *neuroticism* scores, and the extent of change correlated significantly with the amount of tissue removed for one of the two measures. The extent of surgery depended on the preoperative estimate of the extent of the foci, and this may explain the correlation of both *neuroticism* measures with the preoperation test. This correlation was largely a function of the correlation in the right temporal cases.

Subcortical lesions

The frontal and temporal lobes are interconnected with pathways in the limbic system, of which the Papez (1937) circuit is thought to provide a major part of the neuroanatomical basis for many of the emotions. As seen in Figure 4.14, the cingulate gyrus is a primary area of interaction between the frontal lobe of the cerebral cortex and the limbic system via the hippocampus. Another pathway leads from the cortex of the temporal lobe to the amygdala. In Figure 4.2 we can see that the cingulate gyrus forms the highest level of development of the limbic system and is regarded as the cortex of the limbic system or the "emotional cortex" (Isaacson, 1982).

The structure forms the upper arch of the limbic vault and lies directly above the corpus callosum, the fibers that connect the cerebral hemispheres. At its posterior end it broadens into a transitional area called the *precuneatus,* which curves around the splenium of the corpus callosum and merges with the hippocampal gyrus. Meyer, McElhaney, Martin, and McGraw (1972) have described the stereotactic cingulotomy operation (also see 2A in Figure 4.13) and the effects of electrical stimulation of the cingulum. About a third of the reactions to stimulation were affective: 17% intense fear, 9% agitation, and 12% pleasurable. The operation was reportedly most successful with cases of anxiety, depression, and obsessive-compulsive symptoms and least successful with alcoholics and schizophrenics. Operated patients were also judged to show reductions of anxiety, depression, and hostility, as judged by comparisons of pre- and post-Rorschach and MMPI measures, though the actual data were not presented in their report.

Mitchell-Heggs, Kelly, and Richardson (1976) and Laitenan and Vilki (1973) reported the effects of cingulotomies on questionnaire measures and observer ratings of anxiety, depression, and neuroticism, and they also used Eysenck's questionnaire measure of extraversion. In both studies, anxiety and neuroticism were reduced after the operation, but extraversion showed no significant change. In the study by Mitchell-Heggs et al., heart rate and blood pressure during basal and stress periods were also reduced by cingulum lesioning.

Little objective data are available for operations on human limbic structures such as the hypothalamus, amygdala, and thalamus, though all of these have received some attention from the neurosurgeons, such as Andy and Jurko (1972) who did thalamotomies (1D in Figure 4.13) for aggressive and hyperresponsive syndromes. Choppy, Zimbacca, and LeBeau (1973) found significant reductions on the depression and the social introversion (Si) scales of the MMPI and on a scale measuring the trait of self-criticism (in patients with left thalamus lesions but not in patients with right thalamus lesions). It should be pointed out that the Si scale in the MMPI is as much a measure of neuroticism as it is of introversion, so the changes in the scale could be a function of the general reduction in neuroticism rather than introversion per se.

Patients who were episodically aggressive and uncontrolled and who were treated by unilateral or bilateral amygdala destruction were reported to show marked reduction of hostile and aggressive behavior in several studies (Heimburger, Whitlock, & Kalsbech, 1972; Mark, Sweet, & Ervin, 1972; Siegfried & Ben-Shmuel, 1972). The changes were said to persist for years after the operations. Similar reductions of aggressiveness were not seen after lobotomies on the same types of patients (Siegfried & Ben-Shmuel, 1972).

Sano, Sekino, and Mayanagi (1972) made stereotaxic lesions in an area of the posteromedial hypothalamus of patients with violent, aggressive, or restless behaviors. Most of these patients also suffered from epileptic seizures. We are told that all patients were so violent or restless that their families had to keep constant watch over them, and the police had sometimes to be called. Follow-up of 43 adult patients for more than 2 years found that 30% never again showed violent, aggressive, or restless behavior, becoming "calm and placid"; another 65% became generally calm and "tractable" with only occasional irritability and no need for constant observation and care, for a remarkable improvement total of 95%!

These clinical studies suggest that amygdalotomy and posteromedial hypothalamotomy have specific ameliorating effects on aggressive behavior and uncontrollable rage reactions, but lack of controls and reliable observation methodologies require a great deal of faith in the clinical judgments and objectivity of the investigators.

Summary of human brain lesion studies

Despite the uneven quality of these studies, certain consistencies are apparent. Comparisons of right and left hemisphere brain damage results yielded somewhat contradictory results on the two studies using the MMPI for reasons already discussed. However, there is some evidence that right hemisphere damage is likely to produce manic affective disturbances, and left hemisphere damage is more likely to produce cognitive symptoms, or anxiety in the initial phases of adjustment to the cognitive problems. Other evidence of a dependence of laterality of the lesion is apparent in studies of particular brain areas. Right frontal and temporal lobe damage is more likely to produce increased impulsivity than left lobe damage. Even in limbic structures there are some laterality differences. Lesioning of the left thalamus seems to produce depression and neurotic introversion not seen in right thalamic operations.

Almost all frontal lobotomy and cingulotomy studies show decreases on scales for anxiety, depression, and neuroticism, and these operations were most successful in patients with chronic anxiety, depression, and obsessive-compulsive symptoms. Apart from reduction of felt anxiety, physiological studies showed decreases in autonomic and cortical arousal. Reduction in cortical arousal might account for the apathy sometimes noted in lobotomized patients. Increases in extraversion are less commonly found and those that are found might be due to the *impulsivity* component of the E scales used at the time of the studies. Behavioral tests also suggest that there is an increase in impulsivity and a decrease in reflectiveness in patients whose frontal-limbic connections have been severed. Patients with disease- or wound-damaged frontal lobes seem to exhibit more irritability, euphoria, and emotional lability than depression or anxiety. Many frontals show disinhibited behavior. The data suggest an increase in the P dimension of personality rather than the E dimension.

Temporal lobe operations were done primarily on epileptics or others showing psychiatric symptoms, usually of an explosive aggressive nature. The operations seem to have been largely successful in reducing aggression, and anxiety as well. Similarly, amygdalotomy reduced aggression. Because patients were often selected for problems of aggression associated with temporal lobe epilepsy, the lack of control groups in most studies is a serious problem because the site of the operation may not have been crucial in the reduction of aggressive outbursts. However, one study (Siegfried & Ben-Shmuel, 1972) compared the effectiveness of amygdalotomy and prefrontal lobotomy and found a clear superiority of the former in reducing aggression. Not enough data are available on thalotomy or hypothalamic lesions to say much about them.

Relevance of human neuropsychology findings for Eysenck's and Gray's theories

Eysenck's theory predicts that nonspecific brain damage would increase *extraversion* by reducing arousal in the cerebral cortex. Although there is evidence that frontal brain damage does reduce cortical arousal, as measured by the EEG, there is little or no change in *extraversion*. Instead, there are reductions in *neuroticism* and *anxiety* and increases in *hostility, impulsivity,* and traits relevant to the P dimension. Autonomic arousal is also reduced by reducing input to the visceral brain by lobotomy or orbital-frontal undercutting. This is not inconsistent with Eysenck's localization of emotionality in the limbic brain. But Eysenck's theory has been criticized for being too unspecific, and this charge is underlined by findings that there are loci in the brain, such as the orbitofrontal, that specifically mediate the personality-neuropsychology connections. General arousal may be less relevant than arousal of these areas.

In contrast to Eysenck's theory, Gray's model is specific about the neuropsychology of personality. Most of the evidence for Gray's model comes from neuropsychological experiments on rats (discussed in the next section). However, some of the human neuropsychology is relevant to Gray's theory as well. Gray has suggested two major inputs to the septohippocampal system and Papez circuit that comprise the biological basis of the anxiety trait, one from the orbitofrontal cortex and the other from the cingulate gyrus through the entorhinal cortex in the temporal lobe. Both orbitofrontal undercutting and cingulotomies of humans point to an involvement of these areas in *neuroticism* and *anxiety* but not in *extraversion*. However, temporal lobe destruction seems to have more effect on *impulsivity* and *aggression* than on *anxiety*. The *aggression* reduction effects of amydalectomies supports Gray's suggestion that this structure is the source of the fight-or-flight trait, or the P dimension in humans.

The evidence from these human clinical studies cannot be conclusive for either theory because of the imprecise nature of the brain damage and the poor methodology and lack of controls in most of the studies. Another problem is that the patients were already abnormal in some of these personality dimensions when operated on. Patients selected for prefrontal lobotomies were already extreme on dimensions of *anxiety* and *depression* as well as severe psychopathologies such as schizophrenia. Many of the patients selected for amygdalectomies and temporal lobe destruction were characterized by aggressive outbursts and epilepsy. Focus on the primary symptoms of interest may have resulted in overlooking other emotions and behaviors of relevance for an understanding of the behavioral involvements of these brain structures. A general reduction in emotionality could explain many of the results. The *impulsivity* and *disinhibition* seen in many cases could have resulted from either a reduction in anxiety or a primary loss of behavioral inhibition of the type characterizing the P dimension.

Studies of animal neuropsychology

Frontal lobes

Much of our information about brain behavior relationships must, of necessity, come from studies of nonhuman species. Yet for all the reasons mentioned in chapter 1, animal models of human personality traits must be regarded cautiously. Passingham (1970) reviewed the studies of lesioning of the frontal lobes in primates as a comparative test of Gray's (1970) earlier theory relating the orbitofrontal-septohippocampal system to *extraversion*. Looking first at studies in which an attempt has been made to examine broad behavioral categories in animals relevant to those in humans (*activity, impulsivity, carefreeness, dominance, sociability*), there is little evidence of consistent findings across species. In fact, findings differ for different species, as noted by Passingham. Frontal lesions that increase locomotor activity in rhesus monkeys, in accordance with the theory, do not affect activity in cats, dogs, or even squirrel monkeys. Somewhat better results are obtained using experimental tasks more closely resembling those used with humans as experimental measures of the traits. Frontal lesions in nonhuman primates tended to produce increased response to novelty, more variability and errors in visual discrimination (like vigilance in humans), and poorer conditioning. All of these are said to be characteristic of increased extraversion or impulsivity in humans. However, it is not clear how much of the changed behavior ascribed to changes in personality might be due to changes in cognitive abilities.

Septal and hippocampal functions

Gray's theory regards the reciprocal relations between septal and hippo-campal systems as mediating a system that monitors the environment and responds with inhibition of ongoing behavior and increase in general arousal in response to signals of novelty, punishment, or nonreward. From this postulate one can deduce some of the predicted effects from lesioning these two structures in the system. In essence, the reduction of inhibition in response to threat should produce an animal that is totally unafraid and more active in novel environments or in response to novel stimuli, an animal that is less dissuaded from responding by the threat of punishment and which does not extinguish response quickly in reaction to nonreinforce-ment. At the human level, Gray regards the person who is extremely low on this dimension as a potential psychopath.

In what must be one of the most exhaustive (and exhausting) reviews of comparative literature, Gray and McNaughton (1983) asked: What are the similarities and differences in the effects of total septal and hippocampal lesions on particular behavioral paradigms? Reviewing over 600 studies, the authors undertook the gargantuan task of grouping and interpreting results. Although box-score comparisons are not the final answer in the science of behavior, the search for the ultimate experimental paradigm or the definitive experiment seems as elusive as the holy grail. It is too easy to select the results from the literature that fit one's theory and either ignore the others or ascribe them to poor methodology. Given the nature of the variability of behavior and its sensitivity to what often seem to be minor variations in the experimental procedures, it is essential to get an overview of the literature.

In the final table (29) of the article, the authors distill the results into four major categories: (1) behavioral paradigms in which both septal and hippocampal lesions produce impairment in the large majority of studies; (2) paradigms in which both types of lesions produce improvements in functioning; (3) paradigms in which the results are different depending on the locus of the lesion; (4) paradigms in which there is simply no effect produced by either type of lesion. Looking first at the results common to both types of lesions (1 and 2), we see an improvement on bar-press avoidance, two-way active avoidance, motor reactions to discrete stimuli and shock, and general motor activity (excluding the running wheel). What all of these seem to have in common is an improvement on tasks that depend on active solutions or the readiness to move rather than freeze or remain immobile. Both types of lesions produce impairment on most types of passive-avoidance tasks, exploration (apart from open-field ambulation), spatial tasks (maze learning, alternation, and reversal), extinction after reward omission or delay (increased resistance to extinction), and succes-sive discrimination tasks. What some (but not all) of these seem to have in common is the capacity to inhibit behavior or to "stop and think" whether or not it is adaptive to do so. Conversely, measures of active avoidance show improvement after septal or hippocampal lesions. Motor activity and reactivity are also generally increased by these lesions. Thus, the literature tends to support Gray's concept of the septohippocampal system as part of a "behavioral inhibition" mechanism. One group of findings does not fit the hypothesis linking the septum and hippocampus to anxiety: Neither type of lesion produces consistent changes in classical conditioning of fear response.

Different effects of septal and hippocampal lesions are found for a variety of behaviors. Rewarded responses increase after septal lesions but are not affected by hippocampal damage. Intraspecies aggression is increased by septal but reduced by hippocampal lesions. The contradictory results with septal lesions may be due to a greater role of the septum than of the hippocampus in emotionality. Defecation in the open field or shuttle box during avoidance training is reduced in septal lesioned rats but not in hippocampal lesioned ones. Open-field ambulation is increased in hippo-campal lesioned rats, but the results are variable in septal lesioned rats. However, it cannot be claimed that the hippocampal lesions increase ex-plorativeness because, in other types of tasks that are ostensible measures of exploration or variety seeking, such as spontaneous alternation, habit-uation, and rearing, both types of lesions reduce such behavior. Septal lesions clearly increase social interactions among rodents, but there are not enough studies of hippocampal lesions to assess this factor. The results suggest a possible differential involvement of the septum and hippocampus in emotional behavior. The septum may be more involved in fear arousal, and the hippocampus may be more involved in the inhibitory mechanisms secondary to fear arousal. Judging from the effects of lesioning, both limbic structures are normally involved in approach tendencies, curiosity about the environment, and sensitivity to changes in the environment, as well as emotionality.

The amygdala

Over 50 years ago Kluver and Bucy (1939) described a dramatic syndrome resulting from total destruction of the temporal lobes in rhesus monkeys. In removing the temporal lobes the investigators actually removed parts of the limbic system including the rhiencephalic cortex, the amygdala, and portions of the hippocampus. It is now known that some of the syndrome can be produced by removal of the amygdala alone. The syndrome included some marked changes in temperament: a decrease in belligerence and a reduction of fear toward fear-inducing objects, a tendency to investigate orally and even eat or drink usually inedible objects including feces and urine, and increased and unusual sexual behaviors. Part of the syndrome seemed to be based on a kind of visual aphasia in which object recognition is lost. Another aspect of the disorder seems to be a general reduction of emotionality, including anger and fear, and positive emotions such as those involved in social responses and sexuality.

Gray (1987) has described the amygdala as a neurological substrate for the fight-flight reaction whose final common pathway lies in the central grey region. The septohippocampal (stop) system is involved in an antagonistic relation to the action system in the amygdala. Gray states that it has been impossible to separate loci responsible for aggression from those responsible for flight and that the choice of mechanism seems to depend on the environmental context. For this reason he speaks of it as a unitary mechanism. This poses some problem for personality theorists who see more habitual use of flight (physical or cognitive) in *neuroticism* (N) and fight in *aggression* (P). The two kinds of behaviors would seem closely correlated with separate emotions of fear and anger. Wilson, Barrett, and Gray (in press) developed a questionnaire to measure active avoidance, passive avoidance, extinction, fight, and flight as behavioral traits in humans. Flight did not correlate with fight as would be predicted from the model. Instead, flight and passive avoidance were positively correlated supporting the idea that both are expressions of trait *anxiety*.

The amygdala complex contains several nuclei. Reviews of the comparative literature by Chozick (1986) and Isaacson (1982) suggest that different divisions are more closely associated with aggression (fight) and fear. Valzelli (1981) regards the basolateral amygdala as a site for the suppression of predatory, defensive, territorial, and maternal-protective aggression and the centromedial amygdala as the locus of a trigger for competitive and aggressive types of aggression. Ursin and Kaada (1960), using the intracranial stimulation technique with cats, found a dissociation of flight, fear, and aggressive responses in terms of their loci of stimulation in the amygdala. A mapping of the stimulation loci in the amygdala shows separation, but the areas defined do not correspond to the established divisions of the amygdala. Actually, they found a sequence of reactions from the same site as stimulation intensity was increased. First, and the most common response from about two-thirds of the sites, was "attention" or an orienting response characterized by the cessation of all activity and a searching of the environment with the eyes and head. EEG recordings also revealed an accompanying increase in cortical arousal. Although Gray attributes this type of response to the septohippocampal system, Ursin and Kaada found it elicited by stimulation of the basolateral division of the amygdaloid complex. Higher voltages caused "fear" or "anger" responses to appear at the same sites that produced orienting at lower intensities of stimulation; but the two emotional responses (fear and anger) were almost never produced by stimulation at the same site. The autonomic signs of fear such as pupil dilation and rapid searching movements were succeeded by flight.

In this study, fear and flight appear as sequential responses to stimulation at the same site (in contrast to Gray's theory in which they are mediated by different mechanisms). "Anger" responses, *at other sites,* were those characteristic of defensive aggression such as growling and hissing. Although the sites localized in the study do not group in the standard divisions of the amygdala, the study does provide definite evidence for separate localizations of fight and flight (anger and fear) in the amgydala. It also finds orienting and general emotional reactions stimulated by amygdaloid sites.

Davis (1986) has suggested that the amygdala is the major locus for fear and anxiety. His hypothesis stems from study of the fear potentiated startle response: a test of conditioned fear in which the amplitude of the conditioned acoustic startle reflex is increased in the presence of a cue previously paired with shock. The fear potentiated startle is decreased by drugs that reduce anxiety and increased by drugs that produce anxiety in humans. Stimulation and lesioning studies in animals show the pivotal role of the central nucleus of the amygdala in the fear response. Davis, Hitchcock, and Rosen (1987) have pointed out that the central nucleus of the amygdala projects to a variety of brain regions, mediating various aspects of the fear response via the stria terminalis and the ventral amygdalofugal pathway. Figure 4.15 shows the target areas that mediate behavioral, autonomic, and facial expressive forms of fear.

Amygdalectomies in monkeys markedly affect their social dominance behaviors. When a dominant monkey is amydalectomized, he rapidly drops to the bottom of a social hierarchy (Rosvold, Mirsky, & Pribram, 1954). A series of studies summarized by Kling and Stelkis (1976) suggests that the amydala, together with the posterior medial orbital cortex and temporal pole cortex may furnish "a neural substrate for affiliative behavior in nonhuman primates." Vervet monkeys subjected to bilateral amygdalectomies showed social indifference when returned to the wild and unlike control monkeys did not rejoin their groups. In laboratory settings they did not show social grooming behavior and were attacked by other monkeys. Lesioned females lost sexual interest, even when in estrus, and showed no maternal behavior toward juveniles. It is not clear to what extent the loss of sociability of amygdalectomized animals is a function of their hypoemotionality and their other deficits in discriminating emotional significance of objects or other animals.

Jonason and Enloe (1971) contrasted the effects of amygdaloid and septal lesions on social and emotional behavior of pairs of rats in the open field. Septal lesions produced marked increases, and amygdaloid lesions produced marked decreases in social contact. The amygdaloid lesioned rats were hyperactive in the open field and spent their time exploring the field but, except for occasional brief contacts, tended to ignore their partners. The increased contact of the septal lesioned rats appeared to represent an

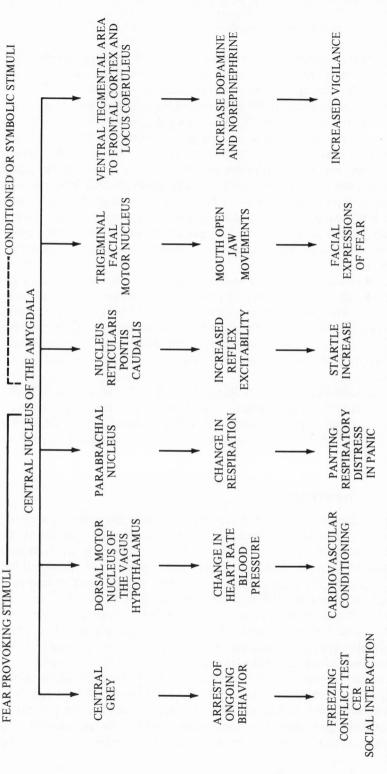

Figure 4.15. Connections of the central nucleus of the amygdala to a variety of target areas that are probably involved in the pattern of behaviors typically associated with fear. (From "Anxiety and the amygdala: Pharmacological and anatomical analysis of the fear-potentiated startle paradigm," by M. Davis, J. M. Hitchcock, and J. B. Rosen, 1987, in *The Psychology of learning and motivation*, vol. 21, p. 293. New York: Academic Press. Copyright 1981 by Academic Press. Reprinted by permission.)

initial reaction to extreme fear in the open field and a way of reducing fear in a strange environment. The amygdaloid lesioned rats, however, appeared socially indifferent rather than frightened by the situation.

Aggleton and Mishkin (1986) have described the amygdala as the "sensory gateway to the emotions," emphasizing the role of the amygdala as a crucial relay between cortical sensory systems and subcortical structures involved in various aspects of emotional response. LeDoux (1987) points out that there are direct pathways between the thalamus and amygdala that would allow emotional reactions to stimuli before they have reached the cortex or hippocampus for more elaborate processing. Thus, although both the hippocampus and amygdala may serve as "comparators" (to use Gray's term), the amygdala could trigger emotional reactions at a more basic level. Such responses might be modified by later input from higher brain centers.

Aggleton and Mishkin (1986) and LeDoux (1987) suggest that the amygdala is involved in the assigning of emotional significance to stimuli from various sensory modalities. Although Aggleton and Mishkin are not certain whether this role of the amygdala in general emotionality includes positive emotions, the loss of these could explain the deficits in affiliative behavior. Different nuclei within the amygdala may mediate fear and anger-aggression. The evidence certainly suggests a role for the amygdala in the trait of emotionality as commonly understood in humans to include the negative emotions: fear, anger, and depression. Pathways between the amygdala and dopamine pathways to the striatum, which are strong sources of reward, suggest an involvement of the amygdala in positive emotions as well as negative ones.

The hypothalamus

The hypothalamus is a small but vital structure that sits at the base of the brain under the thalamus (Figure 4.2). For years it was regarded as the center for emotions in the brain, though we now know it is involved with other limbic structures in the generation and regulation of emotional behavior. A glance at Figure 4.2 shows its central position and its interconnections with all of the limbic structures discussed to this point. It controls the peripheral autonomic nervous system, which is discussed in subsequent chapters, particularly in relation to psychophysiological approaches (chapter 6). It also exerts a neurochemical control over the pituitary gland, which in turn regulates the endocrine systems (chapter 5). Along with other limbic structures it organizes behavior that is essential to survival, including feeding, sexual behavior, fighting, fleeing, and the emotional reactions connected with these behaviors. It is also one of the sites for the intrinsic reward and punishment systems discovered by the intracranial self-stimulation method. Thus, along with the other limbic structures, the hypothalamus plays an essential role in the understanding of the biological substrate for personality.

Lesions of the hypothalamus can interfere or even abolish activities involved in survival. Destruction of the lateral hypothalamus in rats can eliminate eating and drinking behaviors (Anard & Brobeck, 1951). However, it is not the capacity for the behaviors themselves that is abolished by lesions, because tempting the animals with more palatable foods can restore eating behavior (Teitelbaum & Epstein, 1962). The loss seems to be motivational, due to destruction of the nigrostriatal bundle, a dopaminergic pathway that passes through the lateral hypothalamus on its way to the caudate nucleus, an integrative motor area.

Intracranial self-stimulation studies show the lateral hypothalamus to be an area that sustains strong and prolonged responding for stimulation from electrodes placed in it. Rolls (1980) found that the same sites in the lateral hypothalamus that yielded high rates of self-stimulation were responsive to taste stimuli in hungry monkeys. This area of the hypothalamus constitutes part of the pathway (medial forebrain bundle) for a reward mechanism.

Lesions of the ventromedial nucleus of the hypothalamus produce overeating, obesity, and "savage" aggressiveness in rats, cats, and monkeys (Colpaert, 1975; Isaacson, 1982). Lesions of this nucleus result in deficits in active and passive avoidance learning. In this respect, it is interesting that intracranial stimulation studies identify the ventromedial hypothalamic nucleus as a punishment area that produces aversive effects when stimulated.

In describing the hypothalamus, Isaacson (1982) states that "the hypothalamus is indeed a 'head ganglion' of those systems that are directed toward maintaining a favorable internal environment both through the regulation of the internal organs and through the behavior of the entire organism. But the hypothalamus does not act as if it were a motor command center. Rather it acts to bias and modulate other systems. In turn, activities and conditions in the periphery influence the activity of the hypothalamus. . . . A possible way for the modulation to occur is through the modification of reflex circuits by the hypothalamus." (p. 108).

Reward and punishment systems in the brain

The discovery of reward or "pleasure" areas in the brain by Olds and Milner (1954) was serendipitous. Olds and Milner were investigating "arousal systems" in the brain, in accordance with the prevalent theory that all behavior was learned in order to reduce some kind of generalized arousal or "drive." The idea of pleasurable high-drive states was not widely accepted because high drive was considered an aversive condition whose reduction constituted the basis of all reward. Because one of the electrodes was slightly off target, probably landing in the lateral hypothalamus, a rat who was stimulated kept coming back to the corner of the enclosure where the stimulation occurred. Olds and Milner decided to study the curious response by giving animals a chance to stimulate their own brains using an operant apparatus consisting of a lever, which when depressed by a rat would send small amounts of current through electrodes fixed in the animal's brains. The wires were insulated except at the tip so that the current could be delivered precisely to a particular area of the brain. With such stimulation in certain brain areas, animals responded with thousands of responses per hour, disregarding "natural" rewards such as food and water. One curious difference from response to natural rewards was that the animals never seemed to satiate. The closest human analogy would be drug addicts. It is interesting that certain addictive drugs seem to affect the reward centers discovered by the intracranial self-stimulation (ICSS) method (Bozarth, 1987). A historical perspective of ICSS by M. E. Olds and Fobes (1981) provides an excellent summary of the research and controversies in the field.

At the time of the discovery of the reward system in the brain, Delgado, Roberts, and Miller (1954) found areas in which the behavioral effects of stimulation were clearly aversive. "Fearlike" reactions were elicited by stimulation of the lateral thalamus, the inferotemporal part of the hippocampus, and the tectal area in the neighborhood of the spinothalamic path. Such stimulation could serve as an unconditioned reinforcer, leading to avoidance of any stimulus or activity associated with it. Olds and Olds (1963) found areas yielding high rates of escape and little approach response, which included the tegmentum just above the medial lemiscus, in periventricular areas and other parts of extreme dorsal tegmentum, parts of the thalamus, and the hippocampal fornix system. Some areas yielded mixed responses to both approach (turning on) and escape (turning off). One salient point in their data was the paucity of avoidance in the hypothalamus and the lack of approach response elicited in the thalamus. The anterior medial forebrain bundle, which connects many of the reward sites, yields very high rates of self-stimulation. Self-stimulation from electrodes planted in this area has been elicited in many species: rats, cats, dogs, dolphins, monkeys, and humans.

Studies by Olds and Olds (1969), Huang and Routtenberg (1971), and Shizgal, Bielajew, and Kiss (1980) showed that the axons responsible for the rewarding effects of medial forebrain bundle stimulation are descending, not ascending, originating in the forebrain and terminating in the midbrain. This one-way traffic for reward-related neurons suggests that the higher brain structures have a more executive function in the reward effect. Routenberg and Sloan (1972) discovered that some self-stimulation is supported in medial and sulcal areas of the prefrontal cortex. Stimulation from the medial precentral cortex affects the latero-dorsal tegmental neurons

(Highfield & Grant, 1989). Yeomans (1982) has suggested that either the diagonal band or the preoptic area may be the origin of the reward system that descends down the medial forebrain bundle.

The lateral hypothalamus is another primary center for ICSS, and the highest rates are produced by stimulation of the lateral posterior hypothalamus. The lateral septal area proved to be part of the reward system in rats, recalling Heath's (1986) initial findings on humans who reported pleasure from stimulation of this area. Other areas of ICSS reward include the dorsal frontal cortex, portions of the amygdala and hippocampus, the diagonal band of Broca, the nucleus accumbens, the medial and lateral preoptic areas, the substantia nigra, and the ventral tegmental areas, the latter yielding high rates of stimulation. In areas other than the lateral hypothalamus and medial forebrain bundle, where animals' demand for stimulation is virtually insatiable, animals may work to turn on stimulation and to turn it off if it is left on long enough (Bower & Miller, 1958; Roberts, 1958). This effect is more like natural reward in that satiation produces aversive states.

The punishment system includes the midbrain central grey, the periventricular and ventromedial nuclei of the hypothalamus, and medial lemniscus in the midbrain. Stellar, Brooks, and Mills (1979) compared the effects of stimulation of the reward site in the medial forebrain bundle and lateral hypothalamus with stimulation of the punishment site in the medial hypothalamus. Rats with lateral hypothalamic placements were quick to turn on stimulation and slow to turn it off, particularly at the lower intensities of stimulation. Rats with medial hypothalamic placements rarely turned on stimulation; and when it was turned on by the experimenters, they were quick to turn it off. Stimulation also affected approach or avoidance responses to environmental stimuli with innate reward or punishment potentialities, including light tactile probing, sugar water, female vaginal odors (all usually eliciting approach behavior), and repulsive odor and footshock (usually eliciting avoidance behaviors). Stimulation of lateral hypothalamic placements (reward) tended to increase approach to external reward stimuli and reduce responses to aversive stimuli; stimulation of the medial hypothalamus (punishment) produced converse effects with an increase in avoidance response to aversive stimuli and reduction of response to rewarding stimulation. Bilateral lesions of the lateral hypothalamus suppressed approach and increased withdrawal.

On the basis of this work, Stellar et al. (1979) hypothesized that the lateral hypothalamus is part of the biological substrate for approach behavior, and the medial hypothalamus participates in withdrawal behaviors. They further suggest that the two systems are mutually inhibiting so that activation of one results in inhibition of the other.

The work of Rolls (1980, 1986) and his colleagues indicates the roles that central reward and punishment areas may play in learning. In monkeys, they found hypothalamic neurons that responded to the taste of real foods but that also came to respond to visual stimuli associated with food when the monkeys were hungry. Similarly, other neurons in the hypothalamus responded to stimuli associated with punishment. This work is relevant to Gray's theory, which suggests limbic loci for systems affecting responses to *signals* associated with reward or punishment rather than to reward or punishment themselves. At the single neuron level, the neurons that mediate stimulus significance are segregated by sensory channels, but the great preponderance of those related to reward in the lateral hypothalamus support a general role for this nucleus in the biological reward system.

There are a number of objections to the ICSS model for exploring brain influences in motivation. For one, responses in areas such as the medial forebrain bundle are insatiable as long as stimulation reward is contingent on bar presses; but when stimulation is withdrawn, the extinction is quite rapid in contrast to the gradual extinction of naturally rewarded responses. Another objection is that stimulation of a part of the brain may affect ascending, descending, or lateral pathways to other areas where the actual effect may be taking place so that it is difficult to localize the source of the stimulation effect. Finally, it is difficult to trace the pathways involved in the systems by isolated lesioning or stimulation of any particular nuclei. This is why investigators soon turned to psychopharmacological studies of brain stimulation (discussed in chapter 5). Neurochemical lesions affect specific pathways rather than individual nuclei and can be made rather specific by selection of the site of administration and the use of blockers to protect other systems from the effects of the neurotoxin.

In response to the objection to the difference between ICSS and natural reward, Olds and Fobes (1981) said that for studies in which the animal is provided with the opportunity for brain stimulation or food and water over long periods of time, there are rest periods and evidence of satiation with self-stimulation just as there are for food and water. Rolls (1980, 1986) noted that self-stimulation can be obtained from the same electrodes that record neural activity, elicited in response to natural reward stimuli. Activity in these neurons is related to a variety of reward-related stimuli; and in regard to food, the activity in the neurons varies with the incentive value of the food and the extent of food deprivation. One of the failures of research is that an anatomically cohesive reward system has not been established. Self-stimulation can be obtained at many sites, and more than one system or one neurotransmitter may be involved (Olds & Fobes, 1981). The question is approached through studies in psychopharmacology in the next chapter.

Trying to deduce the behavioral functions of particular brain structures from lesioning studies can be tricky. If a person's legs were removed, and we observed that he became less active as a consequence, we would not conclude that the source of an activity trait is localized in the legs. Even when lesioning of central nervous system structures has a direct effect on some behavioral function, we cannot conclude that these nuclei are the source of the behavioral function. The lesion may have interrupted some pathway, originating in other nuclei, that interfered with some part of the functions involved in the behavior. The lesion may affect general arousal, activity, or some sensory or cognitive function involved in the behavior rather than the specific behavior itself. This chapter has focused on certain behavioral and emotional aspects of animal behavior that may be relevant to human personality. Apart from the problems of making the leap between animal and human traits (chapter 1), the neglect of sensory and cognitive functions may obscure the meaning of any relationships found between structure and function in the animal realm.

Similarities in human and animal neuropsychology

As discussed in chapter 1, there is no easy way to align animal behavior with personality traits in humans. Eventually, the knowledge of common biological correlates of similar traits in humans and animals will put the validity of animal models on a better basis, but for now we must proceed mainly by comparing the functional significance of behaviors in the animal and human species and our theories relating function to biology.

At the phenomenal level, the trait of *extraversion* in humans is mostly synonymous with *sociability* (chapter 1). Unfortunately, few animal models provide measures of social interaction, with the exception of studies of aggression and sexuality. *Sociability* is best studied by observing behavior in established colonies. Furthermore, the human type of social reaction is best studied in primates. This is why the studies by Kling (Kling & Stelkis, 1976; Kling, Stelkis, & Deutsch, 1979), which used monkeys in laboratory and naturalistic settings, are important. His conclusions are also supported by a study of rats in a laboratory setting (Jonason & Enloe, 1971). The amygdala seems to be involved in all of the characteristic social interactions of animals, including dominance, grooming, play, and sexual behavior. But the amygdala is also important in intraspecies aggression; human as well as animal neuropsychological studies support this conclusion. Competitive aggression may be correlated with sociability in primates, particularly in males. The more aggressive monkeys also tend to dominate others, mate more frequently, and receive social attention in the form of grooming. But other studies by Davis show that the amygdala is centrally involved in fear conditioning, so anxiety must also be recognized as being influenced by amygdaloid nuclei. Perhaps the best way to summarize amygdaloid function is in terms of *general emotionality*. Lesioned animals are emotionally apathetic, fearless, and nonaggressive and seem to lack recognition of the emotional significance of animate and inanimate objects.

Gray has suggested that the reward areas of the brain, dopaminergic pathways running through the medial forebrain bundle and the lateral hypothalamus, play an important role in the trait of *extraversion*. This is a departure from Eysenck's theory of extraversion, which placed primary emphasis on the arousal levels of the recticulocortical activating system. Evidence relating to these two biological models are presented in later chapters in regard to dopamine (chapter 5) and cortical psychophysiology (chapter 6).

The septum is also involved in social behavior but seems to play more of an inhibitory role that is disinhibited by lesions. In humans, depressant drugs such as alcohol, which first affect cortical centers, seem to have a similar kind of disinhibitory effect on social behavior. However, the neuropsychological studies of humans suggest that undercutting the orbitofrontal cortex, thus severing its connections with the amygdala, does not markedly affect sociability but does reduce anxiety and increase impulsivity. It may be the role of the orbitofrontal and temporal cortices in emotionality and inhibition that involves them in sociability in primates.

There is much support for Gray's (1982) model for the septohippocampal system, the cingulate gyrus, and the Papez circuit, together with his earlier (Gray, 1973) idea of an involvement of the orbitofrontal cortex in anxiety. Of course, Gray built this model on these data from neuropsychological animal studies. However, there is at least one crucial set of data lacking: namely, classical fear conditioning. The data substantiate a role for the septohippocampal system in instrumental behavior, particularly passive-avoidance learning and extinction. Most of the behavior affected by septum or hippocampal lesioning appears to involve learning when not to respond. By inference, the role of these structures has been interpreted by Gray as inhibition in response to signals of punishment or nonreward and *anxiety*. But looked at another way, the system could be interpreted as mediating behavioral inhibition versus impulsivity. This would suggest that the septohippocampal mechanism is more closely related to the P dimension of personality than the anxiety dimension. A challenging theory from the work of Davis suggests that the amygdala, rather than the septohippocampal mechanism is the source of an *anxiety* and general *emotionality* trait.

In contrast, Gray has proposed that the amygdala is the site for aggressiveness (fight) or active avoidance (flight), and he concludes that these are the mechanisms that underlie the P dimension in humans. However, studies show that the fight and flight reactions are mediated by different neurons in the amygdala. Flight is usually a result of continued stimulation of neurons, in which intense orienting (behavioral inhibition and focused attention) is the initial reaction, and signs of high autonomic arousal are the second reaction. This seems to fit the human data better because habitual flight (or neurotic avoidance) is related to the trait of fear, not simply to the circumstances.

Animal models for the trait of *sensation seeking* have been discussed by this author (Zuckerman, 1979b, 1984a, 1984b). Because sensation seeking at the human level is defined by the need for novel sensations and experiences and the willingness to take risks for the sake of such experience (Zuckerman, 1979b), the open-field test (OFT) was initially regarded as a possible animal model for the trait. However, the usual forms of the OFT are initially frightening to rodents and therefore confound the traits of emotionality and explorativeness. Besides, nothing is very novel in the open field after the first few exposures, and continued activity may represent the general activity drive rather than curiosity. The tendency to alternate paths in a maze or the tendencies to explore different chambers in a smaller closed-in space might be better models for sensation seeking. The tendency to approach and interact with strangers might be even closer to the type of sensation seeking called *disinhibition*. The model selected affects our judgment of possible sites for the motive. Septal and hippocampal lesioned rats are active in the open field but do not show much curiosity in the alternation behavior or rearing in a novel environment. Amygdal lesioned rats are the ones that show a deficit in social interaction, sexual behavior, and play, all attributes of the human sensation seeker. However, human sensation seeking represents a dedication to hedonism, and sensation seekers are attracted to drugs that produce euphoric states. The ICCS studies might provide a model for the strength of the hedonistic motive; and therefore, sites of self-stimulation, such as the lateral hypothalamus, might be part of the biological substrate of the human trait. Neither lesion nor stimulation studies can answer the question of the adequacy of the animal models unless we can find congruent biological findings in humans, and the access to the limbic system in humans is limited. However, the convergence of psychopharmacology, applied to humans in biological psychiatry, and psychopharmacological studies of animals may take us further toward the goal of establishing similarity among species.

Summary

Even social personality theorists would acknowledge that everything we call *personality* depends on an intact, functioning brain. Indeed, studies of brain-damaged humans show that general psychiatric disturbance is proportional to the amount of brain destruction. But beyond this crude psychophysical equivalence, is there more we can describe in the way of neurological localization of specific aspects of personality or traits?

MacLean's triune brain describes three evolutionary stages of brain development, including reptillian, paleomammalian, and neomammalian, centered around the striatal complex, limbic system, and cerebral cortex, respectively. Certainly, all three brain systems are involved in various aspects of personality. Research on humans has centered largely on the neomammalian brain, or cerebral cortex, partly because of its greater accessibility. But a vast amount of comparative research on other brain systems has shown that they must also be involved in human personality. The reason is that systems in the limbic brain and striatal complex mediate emotional responses and intrinsic reinforcement mechanisms, which theorists such as Eysenck and Gray consider to be the foundation of basic personality traits such as anxiety, impulsivity, extraversion, and emotionality. These theories also suggest that the interconnections among the three brain complexes are essential to these traits. Eysenck, for instance, emphasizes the ascending reticular activating system, originating in the brain stem, and inputs to it from the limbic brain, in modulating the arousal of the cerebral cortex and the trait of *extraversion*. Gray described the inputs to the septohippocampal system from the orbitofrontal cortex and the entorhinal cortex in the activation of the system that mediates anxiety.

Lobotomy studies in humans and animals do suggest that the connections between prefrontal cortex and the limbic brain play an important role in the traits of *anxiety* and *neuroticism* (general emotionality) because damage to these connections reduces these traits in psychiatric patients. The temporal lobes and their connection with the amygdala seem to be important in the inhibition and expression of aggressive and sexual impulses. Specific amygdaloid nuclei are involved in fear expressions and flight, and others are involved in anger and aggression. Recent evidence supports the concept of the amygdala as a center for basic emotionality, including positive social emotions as well as fear and anger. This notion is at variance with Gray's more restrictive model of the amygdala as the center for a combination fight-flight mechanism or the psychoticism (aggressive-asocial) dimension of personality.

Gray has characterized the pathways of the intralimbic system between septum and hippocampus and between this system and the entire Papez circuit as the ones involved in the basic trait of anxiety. This model is based on a host of evidence showing the role of these structures in the inhibitory responses to signals of punishment and novel stimuli. However, the absence of a link with classical fear conditioning raises some questions about this localization of the anxiety trait and raises the possibility that the inhibitory control of behavior by selected inputs to the hippocampus may be more salient than its role in anxiety arousal and expression. A lack of behavioral inhibition (disinhibition) is a central feature of the major dimension of personality called "psychoticism" by Eysenck and "impulsive unsocialized sensation seeking" by Zuckerman.

Extraversion is theoretically related to a sensitivity to reward and thus could be based on an intrinsic reward mechanism in the brain that originates in the anterior medial forebrain and involves the lateral hypothalamus, nucleus accumbens, ventral tegmental area, and the descending medial forebrain bundle. However, variations in sensitivity of these mechanisms could also be involved in human traits such as *impulsivity* and *sensation seeking*.

Discontinuities between human and animal research and the general paucity of human brain research, particularly on limbic systems, preclude definitive statements now on the neuropsychology of personality traits. Too much depends on the relevance of particular animal models for the human traits.

Even using animals as subjects in studying structure-function relationships by lesioning entire structures, such as the septum or amygdala, or even particular nuclei within these structures, has problems because such lesions may interrupt pathways originating in other structures. This approach alone could only end in some new form of phrenology, based on "bumps" in the brain instead of the skull. However, the discovery that functional pathways in the brain are served by particular neurotransmitters has provided a new approach to identifying the circuitry involved in behavioral adaptations. The next chapter describes the application of the relatively new science of psychopharmacology in areas relevant to personality.

5 Psychopharmacology

Overview

The science of psychopharmacology is just over 30 years old at this writing. The term *psychopharmacology* refers to the action of drugs on mind and behavior and reflects its inception with the advent of the psychotropic drugs in the 1950s. The broader field dealt with in this chapter is called *neuropsychopharmacology* because it includes the actions of these drugs at the cellular level, but the same breadth of coverage is generally assumed for the term *psychopharmacology.*

Biochemical basis of neurotransmission

Transmission of a neural impulse from one neuron to another is accomplished across gaps between them called *synaptic clefts.* Activation across the synaptic cleft is effected by the release of chemicals called *neurotransmitters,* which are contained in small sacs, or *vesicles,* in the cytoplasm of the terminal button of the presynaptic neuron. When the axon of a cell fires, the vesicles at the membrane rupture and spill their contents into the synaptic cleft (Figure 5.1). There are many kinds of neurotransmitters each chemically adapted to "fit" molecules on adjacent neurons called *postsynaptic receptors.* Activated by the neurotransmitter, the receptor opens the gate of a neurotransmitter-dependent ion channel, allowing certain ions to pass through the membrane. The receptors in some neurons do not directly open the ion-channel gates but cause it to open by producing "second-messengers" (*cyclic nucleotides*), which can activate enzymes. The change of ion balance between the inside and outside of the membrane results in a temporary depolarization of the membrane and an *action potential,* which travels down the axon from one end to the other in an "all or none" fashion (i.e., the action potential either occurs or does not occur, and after it starts, it is transmitted in full strength). Some neurotransmitters may have a hyperpolarization rather than a hypopolarization (or depolarization) effect, inhibiting rather than exciting the postsynaptic neuron, as do the amino acid transmitter gamma-aminobutyric acid (GABA), glycene, and the endogeneous opiates (endorphins and enkephalins).

Every neurotransmitter system involves a complex feedback system that regulates production of the transmitter substances, release and activation processes, and disposal of excess released substance by reuptake and stor-

172

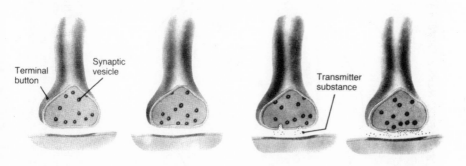

Figure 5.1. Release of neurotransmitters into the synaptic space. (From *Physiology of behavior*, 3rd ed., p. 54, by N. R. Carlson, 1986. Newton, MA: Allyn and Bacon. Copyright 1986 by Allyn and Bacon. Reprinted with permission.)

age, or catabolic breakdown. Continued activity of a system without processes that stimulate production would result in neurotransmitter depletion; and the presence of excess transmitter substance in the synaptic cleft or presynaptic neuron would be equally disruptive. The homeostatic equilibrium of the neuron is continuously restored by internal regulation. Activity is regulated by processes in the postsynaptic as well as the presynaptic neuron. For example, receptors may multiply to compensate for reduced activity in the system and the receptors that are active may show increased sensitivity to the neurotransmitter.

Neuronal dynamics in the noradrenergic system

To illustrate, let us examine the dynamics of one of the monoamine systems (discussed in greater detail in subsequent sections). Figure 5.2 is a diagram of a synapse in the noradrenergic system. The production of the neurotransmitter norepinephrine (NE) begins with the amino acid tyrosine (found in certain food-stuffs), which is taken into the cell body. Tyrosine is converted to dihydroxyphenylalanine (DOPA or L-DOPA) by an enzyme called tyrosine hydroxylase. Another enzyme, DOPA decarboxylase, converts DOPA to dopamine (DA), which is taken into the the storage vesicles that contain the enzyme dopamine β-hydroxylase (DBH). Finally, DBH converts dopamine into norepinephrine. Inactivation of any of the enzymes involved in the process results in depletion of norepinephrine.

When the action potential reaches the presynaptic nerve terminal, norepinephrine is released into the synaptic cleft. Some of the norepinephrine binds to the alpha or beta adrenergic receptors on the postsynaptic nerve terminal. The receptor binding may either induce electrical changes, as discussed, or activate biochemical processes (second messengers). Cyclic

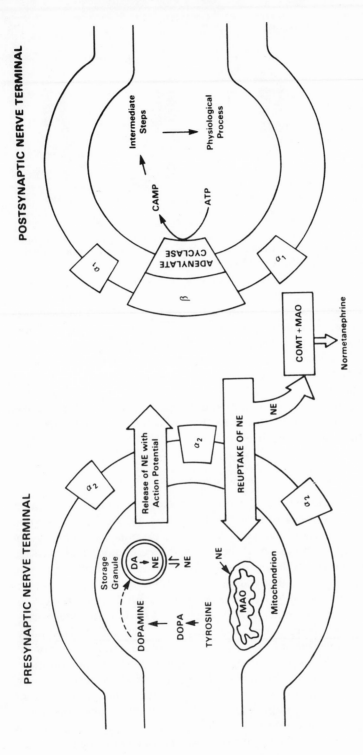

Figure 5.2. Illustration of a noradrenergic synapse. DA, dopamine; NE, norepinephrine; dihydroxyphenylalanine (dopa) is a precursor of the transmitters DA and NE. The enzymes monoamine oxidase (MAO) and catechol-O-methyltransferase (COMT) are involved in the degradation of NE; 3-methoxy-4-hydroxyphenylglycol (MHPG) and vanillymandelic acid (VMA) are metabolites in the breakdown of NE. Alpha₁, Alpha₂, and beta are receptor sites on the cell membrane. Adenosine triphosphate (ATP) is an energy source for the cell and a precursor to the "second messenger," cyclic adenosine monophosphate (cAMP). (From "Antidepressants and biochemical theories of depression," by E. T. McNeal and P. Cimbolic, 1986, *Psychological Bulletin* 99, p. 363. Copyright by American Psychological Association. Reprinted by permission.)

adenosine monophosphate (cAMP) is a second messenger that can initiate a complex cascade of events ranging from electrical changes to additional biochemical reactions.

Catabolism begins in the synaptic cleft, where some of the norepinephrine is eventually converted by the enzymes catechol-O-methyltransferase (COMT) and monoamine oxidase (MAO) to 3-methoxy-4-hydroxyphenylglycol (MHPG), some of which is further metabolized to vanillymandelic acid (VMA). These metabolites of norepinephrine, obtained in cerebrospinal fluid (CSF), blood, and urine, can provide some indication of brain activity of the noradrenergic system in living humans (in whom the brain itself is not directly accessible for assays). However, urinary MHPG does not seem to reflect brain norepinephrine activity very much (an estimated 20% of urinary MHPG comes from the brain). Plasma MHPG appears to be a better index of brain norepinephrine activity; 30–65% is estimated to originate in the brain. It is possible to measure norepinephrine directly in CSF, and this may be the closest one can get to a measure of brain norepinephrine activity in living humans. Lake and Ziegler (1985) have deduced that the "vast majority of norepinephrine in the CSF is of central origin." (p. 21). There is slow but free exchange of CSF and plasma MHPG, but CSF levels are about three times that found in plasma.

Most of the norepinephrine in the presynaptic cleft is taken up into the presynaptic terminal. MAO is also present in the neuron and may there metabolize the norepinephrine to MHPG, which also finds its way through the CSF, blood, and urine to disposal. But most norepinephrine is recycled for further participation in the neurotransmission process. Alpha$_2$ adrenergic receptors respond to norepinephrine in the synaptic cleft by slowing the synthesis and release of norepinephrine in the presynaptic neuron. This negative feedback system controls norepinephrine availability within narrow limits. If it is insensitive or blocked, it produces a state of hyperexcitability in the norepinephrine neurons; but if it is too sensitive or stimulated, it could result in an absence of norepinephrine tone. Because the transmitter substance is always being produced and some of the already produced transmitter is retaken into the presynaptic neuron, there could be danger of accumulating too much of the substance. This danger would be particularly salient if low levels of any of the enzymes involved in catabolic deamination, such as MAO, allowed an excess of the norepinephrine to be restored.

Recent theory has raised the possibility that failures of this feedback mechanism might account for certain abnormal deficits or excesses of mood and behavior such as, for instance, in manic-depressive psychosis or panic anxiety. As discussed subsequently, many personality traits seem to be related to a lack of modulation of neurotransmitter systems. The enzymes regulating the production and degradation of neurotransmitters may be as important in determining personality dispositions as the levels of the transmitters themselves.

Interaction of psychotropic drugs with neurotransmitters and enzymes

Drugs used to treat patients with psychiatric and neurological disorders, or by scientists to explore neuropsychopharmacology, can activate or suppress neurotransmission in various ways. For example, the drug L-DOPA is the precursor for dopamine and therefore stimulates the dopamine system, particularly in Parkinsonism patients, who suffer from a severe depletion of dopamine. Amphetamine and cocaine, popular drugs of abuse, are powerful stimulants because they potentiate the release of catecholamines (NE and DA) and slow their reuptake, thus temporarily increasing the levels of catecholamines in the synaptic cleft. Reserpine makes the catecholamine vesicles leaky with the result that the transmitter norepinephrine is exposed to degradation by MAO, and the catecholamine supply is depleted. MAO-inhibitors (a class of antidepressant drugs) may increase the level of available norepinephrine or dopamine by removing one of the sources of their catabolism. Other drugs act directly on the receptors; the antipsychotic drugs, for instance, block dopamine receptors, and their effectiveness in suppressing some types of schizophrenic symptoms constitutes one of the main supports of a dopamine dysfunction theory of schizophrenia. Apomorphine stimulates these receptors. Knowledge of the specific actions of drugs on the neurotransmitter systems provides valuable information about the workings of these systems and their roles in normal and abnormal behavior.

Monoamine systems

The monoamine systems are grouped together because of the similarities of their molecular structures. These systems receive particular attention in this chapter because of evidence of their involvement in human behavior disorders and in basic emotional and motivational systems in other species. Other systems described here may also be important in personality, but evidence of their relationships to personality is sparse, primarily because there are no convenient measures (metabolites) for the transmitters in humans.

The catecholamines, including norepinephrine, dopamine, and epinephrine, even more similar in structure to each other than to the indoleamine serotonin; all seem to mediate various behavioral and emotional arousal processes. Norepinephrine and dopamine comprise the principal catecholamines in the brain. Although epinephrine is found in the brain, it is of minor importance there compared to its influence, along with norepinephrine, in the peripheral autonomic nervous system.

Dopamine not only is a precursor of norepinephrine but also is a neurotransmitter. The process of biosynthesis and degradation in the dopamine

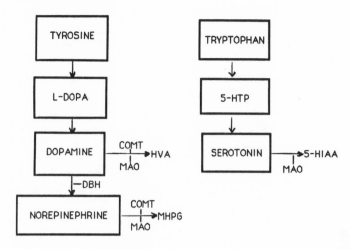

Figure 5.3. Biosynthesis and breakdown of the monoamines dopamine, norepinephrine, and serotonin.

presynaptic neuron is similar to that for norepinephrine (Figure 5.3). The final breakdown product of the dopamine catabolism is homovanillic acid (HVA). HVA is found in CSF, blood, and urine, but as with norepinephrine, the peripheral measures probably reflect some peripheral dopaminergic activity.

The biosynthesis and breakdown processes of serotonin (5-hydroxytryptamine or 5-HT) is also shown in Figure 5.3. Tryptophan, an essential amino acid supplied in the diet, is converted by the enzymes tryptophan hydroxylase and 5-HTP decarboxylase to serotonin (5-HT). Serotonin is broken down by MAO and eventually converted to 5-hydroxyindoleacetic acid (5-HIAA), the principal metabolite, which can be assayed in CSF and urine, providing a method for estimating brain serotonin levels.

A schematic of the monoamine pathways in rat brain is shown in Figure 5.4 (the norepinephrine, dopamine, and serotonin systems are shown in Figures 5.5, 5.6, and 5.7, respectively). The catecholamine pathways are perhaps the most highly divergent systems in the brain; they innervate virtually the entire neuroaxis. The monoamine cell bodies are found in clusters in the brain stem and are devoted to one particular transmitter system such as the locus coeruleus for norepinephrine, the substantia nigra for dopamine, and the raphe nuclei for serotonin.

There are two main ascending pathways of the noradrenergic system (Figure 5.5) The *central tegmental tract* begins in nuclei in the medulla (A1 and A2 in the figure), in the pons (A5), and in an area (A7) ventral to the locus coeruleus. The axons of most of these neurons end in the hypothalamus (1) and limbic system. The second system, *the dorsal tegmental*

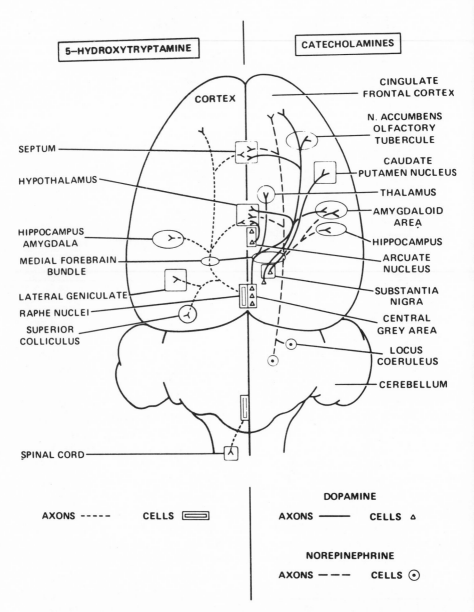

Figure 5.4. Schematic representation of serotonin (5-hydroxytryptamine), dopamine, and norepinephrine pathways in the rat brain. (From "Indoleamines and other neuroregulators," by G. E. Elliot, A. M. Edelman, and P. A. Berger, 1977, in *Psychopharmacology*, p. 38, J. D. Barchas, P. A. Berger, R. D. Ciaranello, and G. R. Elliot, Eds. New York: Oxford University Press. Copyright 1977 by Oxford University Press. Reprinted with permission.)

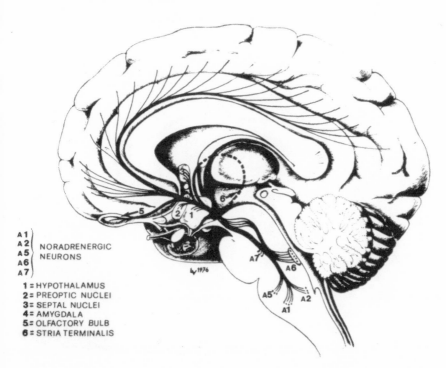

A1 ⎫
A2 ⎪ NORADRENERGIC
A5 ⎬ NEURONS
A6 ⎪
A7 ⎭

1 = HYPOTHALAMUS
2 = PREOPTIC NUCLEI
3 = SEPTAL NUCLEI
4 = AMYGDALA
5 = OLFACTORY BULB
6 = STRIA TERMINALIS

Figure 5.5. Noradrenergic system of the human brain, lateral view. (From *Psychobiology of aggression and violence*, p. 46, by L. Valzelli, 1981. New York: Raven Press. Copyright 1981 by Raven Press. Reprinted by permission.)

bundle, begins in the locus coeruleus (A6), and its axons extend to the cerebellum, thalamus, limbic system, hippocampus, and virtually the entire forebrain, including the entire neocortex. A notable exception is that the striatum receives no norepinephrine innervation. Not shown are the descending tracts to the medulla and spinal cord.

The *nigrostriatal system* (Figure 5.6) originates in the substantia nigra (A9) and projects to the neostriatum, including the putamen (1) and caudate nucleus (2). The *mesolimbic system* begins in the ventral tegmental area (A10) and projects to the nucleus accumbens (4) and limbic areas, including the amygdala (3), septum, and olfactory tubercle (5), as well as several forebrain areas including lateral and medial prefrontal cortex. The nucleus accumbens area will be shown to be more intimately involved with the process of reinforcement.

The serotonergic system (Figure 5.7), originating in the raphe nuclei, sends axons to many of the same limbic and neocortical structures innervated by the catecholamine (NE and DA) systems, such as the medial forebrain bundle, the amygdala (5), hippocampus (2), hypothalamus (4),

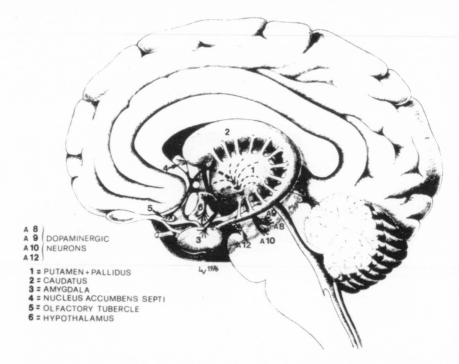

A 8
A 9 } DOPAMINERGIC
A 10 } NEURONS
A 12

1 = PUTAMEN + PALLIDUS
2 = CAUDATUS
3 = AMYGDALA
4 = NUCLEUS ACCUMBENS SEPTI
5 = OLFACTORY TUBERCLE
6 = HYPOTHALAMUS

Figure 5.6. Dopaminergic system of the human brain, lateral view. (From *Psychobiology of aggression and violence*, p. 47, by L. Valzelli, 1981. New York: Raven Press. Copyright 1981 by Raven Press. Reprinted by permission.)

thalamus (3), septum (7), striatum, and all areas of the neocortex. The pathway originating in the medial raphe (MR) seems to innervate more of the limbic system whereas the dorsal raphe (DR) projects to the neostriatum, cerebral and cerebellar cortices, and thalamus (3). This parallel distribution of catecholaminergic and serotonergic systems may underlie the complementary functions of these systems in behavior. Like the noradrenergic system, the serotonergic system also projects down to the spinal cord (9).

Benzodiazepine/GABA receptor complex

The antianxiety benzodiazepine drugs have been found to act on receptors in the brain. These receptors are parts of a larger receptor complex for the neuroregulator gamma-aminobutyric acid (GABA). GABA has high concentrations throughout the brain and spinal cord and is generally inhibitory on neurons in other systems. GABA is estimated to be present in 30% of all synapses and provides the link between benzodiazepine action

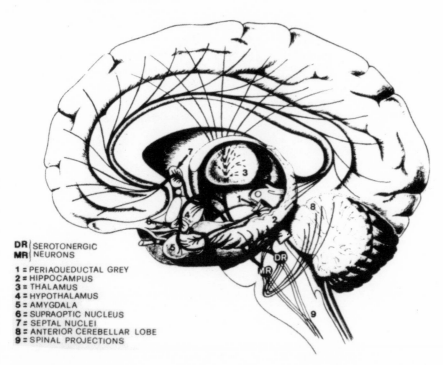

DR | SEROTONERGIC
MR | NEURONS

1 = PERIAQUEDUCTAL GREY
2 = HIPPOCAMPUS
3 = THALAMUS
4 = HYPOTHALAMUS
5 = AMYGDALA
6 = SUPRAOPTIC NUCLEUS
7 = SEPTAL NUCLEI
8 = ANTERIOR CEREBELLAR LOBE
9 = SPINAL PROJECTIONS

Figure 5.7. Serotonergic system of the human brain, lateral view. (From *Psychobiology of aggression and violence*, p. 45, by L. Valzelli, 1981. New York: Raven Press. Copyright 1981 by Raven Press. Reprinted by permission.)

and the inhibition of nuclei, thought to play a central role in anxiety, such as the locus coeruleus. Benzodiazepines augment the reactions of GABA, and GABA increases benzodiazepine receptor binding. In fact, benzodiazepines produce little inhibition without the presence of GABA.

The presence of benzodiazepine receptors in the brain suggested that there might be an endogenous "tranquilizer" fitting these receptors. Research by Braestrup, Nielson, and Olsen (1980) isolated a beta-carboline derivative with a very high affinity for the receptor, but this turned out to be an *inverse agonist,* that is, its effects are opposite to those of the benzodiapines. Given to monkeys it produced behavioral symptoms of anxiety and autonomic arousal (Ninan, Insel, Cohen, Skolnick, & Paul, 1982), and treatment with benzodiazepine reduced these effects.

Endogenous opiates

Just as the investigation of benzodiazepine action in the brain led to the discovery of a special set of receptors, the study of the effects of opiates led first to the discovery of natural opiatelike substances in the brain called

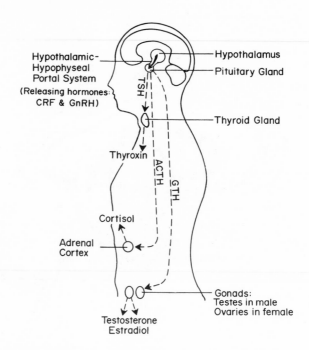

Figure 5.8. Hypothalamic-pituitary-hormone systems.

endorphins (for endogenous morphinelike). These neuropeptides come in many varieties and function as hormones in the circulatory system and as neurotransmitters or neuromodulators in the nervous system. Some of their functions may be similar to the effects of the exogenous opiates: that is, reduction of pain and anxiety or a type of intrinsic reward or pleasure related to relaxation or lowered arousal (Stein, 1978).

Hormones

Unlike neurotransmitters, which affect adjacent neurons, hormones are chemical substances that affect distant cells, usually traveling through the bloodstream. Figure 5.8 shows the neurochemical pathways of some of these hormones. Centers in the hypothalamus release hormones that stimulate the pituitary gland, situated at the base of the brain. The pituitary releases tropic hormones, each of which has a target gland. The target gland then releases its hormone, which has specific physiological effects. Circulating levels of the peripheral hormones are detected in a brain center and regulate tropic hormone production in a negative-feedback, homeostatic manner: Low levels of the circulating hormone trigger increased release of tropic hormones, and high levels of circulating hormones result in reduced release of tropic hormones. Most data on the relationship of hormones to personality are for cortisol and the gonadal hormones. Other hormones must also be important, but there are not enough data to say much about them.

Cortisol

Cortisol is released from the adrenal cortex during physical and psychological stress and normal metabolic processes. This pathway of stress response starts in the hypothalamus, which secretes corticotropin-releasing factor (CRF). CRF stimulates the anterior pituitary gland to release adrenocorticotropic hormone (ACTH). CRF release is inhibited by NE. ACTH travels through the blood stream to the adrenal cortex where it results in the release of corticosteroid hormones including cortisol. Seyle (1956) regarded adrenocortical response as an essential part of the "alarm reaction" phase of response to stress. Cortisol is specifically involved in carbohydrate metabolism by regulating the release of glycogen from the liver into the bloodstream. Cortisol also influences fat metabolism, striated muscle strength, cardiovascular response, particularly blood pressure, and lymphoid tissue (antiinflammatory effect). Cortisol is found in the CSF and urine as well as in the blood plasma. Traskman et al. (1983) reported a sizable correlation between urinary and CSF cortisol, but Ballenger et al. (1983) found no significant correlations among CSF, plasma, and urinary cortisol measurements.

Gonadal hormones

The gonadal hormones, androgens and estrogens, have a primary function in development of primary and secondary sexual characteristics in males and females and a subsequent influence on sexual arousal and function. However, both animal and human research suggests that at certain stages of development, gonadal hormones influence a variety of behaviors and traits, including those on which men and women generally differ, including aggression and dominance.

Theories of monoamine system functions

Table 5.1 compares some of the models of the effects of the three monoamines on emotions and general behavior. All theorists seem to agree that serotonin serves an inhibitory function, but they stress different kinds of inhibition. Gray (1982), Crow (1977), and Stein (1974, 1978) suggest that serotonin is inhibitory, particularly in response to conditioned signals of punishment or fear. Panksepp (1982) and Zuckerman (1984b) suggest that serotonin is involved in inhibition of all emotional systems, positive as well as negative. Soubrié (1986) emphasizes the inhibition of action and ap-

Table 5.1. *Theories of monoaminergic functions*

Author	Serotonin	Norepinephrine	Dopamine
Gray	Anxiety: high levels = inhibition of behavior; low levels = disinhibition of aggression	Anxiety: sensitization by novel stimuli & stimuli associated with punishment. Negative affect	Approach: stimuli associated with reward Positive affect
Redmond		Anxiety; low levels = novelty detection, alarm system	
Mason		Focuses attention on significant environmental stimuli, screens out irrelevant stimuli	Orienting, interest in environment
Crow & Stein	General inhibition of behavior; sensitivity to punishment or signals of punishment	Reward: guides response selection in line with previously rewarded responses	Energize & activates behavior directed to primary biological rewards
Panksepp	General inhibition of all emotive systems	General arousal of all emotive systems	Foraging, exploration, intrinsic reward; hope, desire, joy (in humans)
Soubrié	General inhibition of behavior in conflict situations. Low levels = impulsivity, aggression self or other directed (humans)		
Cloninger	Harm avoidance: behavioral inhibition, caution, indecision, anxiety	Reward sensitivity, dependence, emotional warmth, social attachment, sociability. Low levels = nonconformity, social detachment	Novelty seeking

proach tendencies in conflict situations in which signals are associated with *both* reward and punishment. Zuckerman has stressed the antagonism between behavioral patterns related to catecholamine and to serotonin systems, with the latter inhibiting social and aggressive activity as well as emotions. Soubrié has suggested that low levels of serotonergic activity are associated with *impulsivity* and *aggression,* and Zuckerman has proposed that the balance between serotonergic and catecholaminergic systems may be involved in these traits as well as *sociability* and *activity.* My model has been criticized for a lack of specificity (commentaries following Zuckerman, 1984a). An attempt to deal with this in a revised model is in the last chapter of this book.

There is less agreement on the behavioral functions of the locus coeruleus norepinephrine system. Gray (1982, 1987) and Redmond (1977, 1985) conceive of the basic involvement of this system in anxiety or fear; however, both concede that it has cognitive functions at lower levels of activity, including detection and attention paid to novel stimuli. However, Gray suggests a bias toward stimuli associated with punishment or nonreward, and Redmond describes the function as an alarm system. Mason (1984) argues against any role of the norepinephrine system in anxiety, suggesting that norepinephrine only mediates attention to novel stimuli and is associated with anxiety only when stimuli have been associated with fearful situations. This is in contrast to Gray, who regards all novel stimuli as unconditioned stimuli for anxiety. Zuckerman (1982) has argued against this view, pointing out that animals, including humans, tend to orient to, approach, and investigate novel stimuli. Mason and Iverson (1977) and more recently, Selden, Robbins, and Everitt (1990) proposed a more general cognitive function for the locus coeruleus norepinephrine system. They suggest that the system serves to focus attention on significant environmental stimuli and to filter out irrelevant stimuli. This view is not incompatible with the Gray and Redmond view of the attention function of the system at lower levels of activity. The disagreement seems to be in the relative stress laid on the cognitive and emotional functions of the system.

Although the reward function suggested for norepinephrine by Crow and Stein was previously adopted by Zuckerman (1979b) and still seems to persist in Cloninger's model, it has been difficult to maintain the hypothesis in view of conflicting evidence from selective lesioning effects on both brain stimulation and natural reward. However, it is still possible that NE may act to amplify the reward effects in the primarily dopamine affected loci, as well as punishment effects in other systems. This kind of signal amplification is consistent with the general arousal and the focusing of attention on external stimuli suggested by the theories of Mason and Aston-Jones. It is also compatible with the view of Panksepp that norepinephrine serves a general arousal function for all emotional systems, those associated with positive affect as well as those mediating negative affects such as fear, pain, and rage. An optimal level theory (Zuckerman, 1984a) suggests that catecholamines may serve "go" system functions at intermediate optimal levels but may have similar dysphoric and inhibitory effects at very low or very high levels of activity. Unlike other theorists, Zuckerman has stressed the important regulatory functions of enzymes such as MAO and DBH on the norepinephrine and other monoamine systems.

There is some general agreement on the role of dopamine in mediating approach behavior toward stimuli associated with primary rewards. Gray (1987) and Panksepp (1982) have suggested an association with tendencies to approach, forage, and explore the environment or to experience positive affect states in the human. However, both Cloninger (1987a) and Zuckerman (1984a) have proposed a role for dopamine in novelty seeking and sensation seeking. In other words, even stimuli that are novel but have not been associated with primary rewards may activate the approach mechanism mediated by dopamine. Mason stresses the cognitive function or amplification of attention to all stimuli of potential interest in the environment but also acknowledges a special role for dopamine in incentive motivation.

Dopamine seems to mediate a general behavioral approach system that might be identified with *extraversion* or *sensation seeking,* but it could also involve *impulsivity* or other P type tendencies. Many of the drugs that are abused seem to potentiate activity in dopamine systems, indicating the powerful reward or positive affect function tied to dopamine. Dopamine would seem to serve both to instigate approach behavior and to mediate reward. Norepinephrine may amplify these effects, but it is not essential for them.

It is clear that we must consider the interactions among the monoamines to understand their functions. Furthermore, the regulating influences of enzymes in each monoamine system must be considered, as well as the state of receptors mediating feedback mechanisms. Activity of any system is determined by a multitude of inhibitory and excitatory factors. It is unlikely that a simple one-to-one relationship exists between any single neurotransmitter system and a particular personality trait. What might be expected, however, is that there is a focal system for a narrow trait that is moderated by other systems.

Animal research on monoamines and hormones

Theories of a monoamine basis of personality have been derived from comparative studies. The vast amount of research using nonhuman species that has relevance for a comparative approach to personality precludes a comprehensive review here. Readers should go to general reviews such as those by Gray (1982), Panksepp (1982), Soubrié (1986), Zuckerman (1984a), or to specific reviews such as those on aggression (Bell & Hepper, 1987; Daruna, 1978; Valzelli, 1981) or sexual behavior (Gessa & Tagliomonte, 1974, 1975; Meyerson, Palis, & Sietnicks, 1979). In terms of the three major dimensions of personality, the most interesting response areas are sociability and activity (the major components of *extraversion*), emotional behavior and expressions of fear (relevant to the *neuroticism* dimension), and aggression and sexuality. Various aspects of human sexuality are related to the three supertraits (Eysenck, 1976) and to the P trait of *sensation seeking* (Zuckerman, 1979b). Recent evidence suggests that aggression and hostility may constitute a distinguishable major factor of personality in a 5-factor analysis of questionnaire data (Zuckerman, Kuhlman, & Thornquist, in press).

Aggression

Monoamines

The complexity of comparative findings on behavior in any area are illustrated by the work on aggression as reviewed by Bell and Hepper (1987). Conclusions can differ drastically, depending on the type of animal model used, the type of aggression studied, the species of the animal, the drug dosage employed, and the specificity of drug effects. Bell and Hepper (1987) discuss the findings on three major types of aggression: (1) *predatory aggression,* which involves killing members of another species; (2) *isolation-induced aggression,* in which some species, particularly mice, when reared in isolation from members of their species demonstrate intense aggression when paired with others of their species; (3) *irritable aggression,* which occurs in the presence of any attackable member of the species, or with a punishing stimulus. Although irritable aggression often occurs spontaneously among group-housed animals, it can be elicited by fatigue, pain, or frustration. Unlike predatory aggression, it is usually accompanied by emotional display (anger). Because (1) is not, strictly speaking, aggression and (2) is limited to certain species, irritable aggression would seem to be the most appropriate model for human aggression.

Amphetamine, a catecholamine stimulant, increases aggression in some dose ranges in many but not all species (Bell & Hepper, 1987). Ellison (1979) found that rats with slow-release amphetamine pellets planted in their skin showed excessive and violent behavior toward other rats in a colony in the final stage of their "addiction" (with high dose levels), a finding similar to those of human addicts and volunteer subjects given amphetamine over a protracted period. Ellison (1977) found that chemical lesioning of noradrenergic pathways produced rats that were seclusive and submissive in social interactions. However, other studies have found that such lesioning increased aggression in mice, rats, and group-housed cats. Chemical lesions of the dorsal ascending noradrenergic bundle (DANB) increased aggressive behavior in rats encountering others of their species in an open-field situation (Crow, Deakin, File, Longden, and Wendlant, 1978). Infusion studies (Geyer & Segal, 1974) showed that low doses of dopamine increased irritative aggression whereas infused NE reduced aggression in rats. Haloperidol, a dopamine antagonist used in the treatment of schizophrenics, inhibits aggression in ants and mice and reduces "sham rage" reactions in decorticate cats (brain stem transection). These last results suggest that the locus coeruleus noradrenergic system normally plays a role in the inhibition of aggressive behavior and that dopamine increases such behavior.

Soubrié (1986) maintains that the evidence is fairly conclusive regarding serotonin and aggression. Decreased serotonin levels increase shock and drug-induced aggression in male rats and filicidal (pup-killing) behavior in female rats. Thus, serotonin acts in an antagonistic way to dopamine in regard to aggressive behavior; depletion of serotonin disinhibits aggressive behavior. Human data to be presented later also support these effects of lowered serotonin levels, except that both impulsive homicide and suicide are related to low serotonin levels. It may be that the combination of high dopamine and low serotonergic levels leads to *either* outward-directed or inward-directed aggression in primates, in which the direction of aggression may depend more on individual differences. An alternative hypothesis is that dopamine simply increases general impulsivity whereas serotonin acts to inhibit or delay emotional responses. Panksepp's (1982) theory suggests this kind of role for NE and serotonin, though a more specific "foraging" role is suggested for dopamine.

Pituitary-adrenocortical hormones

Leshner (1983), summarizing the literature, notes that large increases in corticosterone levels increase aggressiveness whereas hypophysectomy (removal of anterior pituitary) and adrenalectomy reduce aggressiveness. Dexamethasone, which blocks cortisol production, also reduces aggressiveness. Although these data would suggest a direct influence of corticosteroids on aggression, other data show that corticosterone increases submissive behavior as well as aggressive behavior. Leshner suggests that corticosterone merely increases general arousal which, depending on the situation, may make either fight or flight (submission) more likely. There is also some evidence of a curvilinear relationship between cortisol and aggression. Rodgers (1979) reported that though low and intermediate doses of cortisol increased shock-induced fighting, high doses effectively suppressed it.

Gonadal hormones

It has long been assumed that testosterone influences aggressiveness, partly because of the assumption that males are more aggressive and dominant in all species. Although this assumption seems to hold true for humans (Kagan, 1978; Maccoby & Jacklin, 1974), chimpanzees (Goodall, 1986), baboons, and a number of other apes and monkeys (Floody, 1983), it is not true for gibbons, some other primates, wolves, rabbits, and hamsters, and the evidence is mixed for laboratory mice and rats (Floody, 1983). However, removal of the male gonads reduces the incidence and intensity of social aggression in fish, lizards, rodents, dogs, cats, deer, sheep, and possibly man (Brain, 1983). Restoration of testosterone in castrates restores aggressive behavior in fish, lizards, birds, rodents, nonhuman primates, and humans (Brain, 1983). However, we must specify the type of aggression in relation to hormonal influence. Whereas intermale aggression depends strongly on androgens, predatory aggression does not (Moyer, 1976); and shock-induced aggression is intermediate in androgen relatedness (Conner, Constantino, & Scheuch, 1983). Chapter 3 presented studies showing strain differences in aggressiveness in mice and the successful breeding of highly aggressive and nonaggressive mice. Maxson, Shrenker, and Vigue (1983) discuss the possible basis for these differences in inherited differences in testosterone. The general conclusion is that some of the differences between aggressive and nonaggressive strains are due to genotype and hormone interaction and that neonatal or adult androgens may activate the genes influencing aggression in males and females. If strain differences exist, then individual differences in human aggressiveness may also be based on this type of genotype-hormone interaction.

Estrogen tends to suppress social aggression in several species, but paradoxically, it also restores fighting in castrated animals. Brain (1983) suggests that this is one line of evidence for the *aromatization hypothesis,* which suggests that androgens have their major motivational effects after conversion to estrogenic metabolites. The hypothesis is further supported by the fact that the aromatizable (convertible to estrogens) androgens are all effective in maintaining fighting in males whereas, with one exception, the nonaromatizable androgens are not.

If estrogen in males is involved in aggression, is the primary estrogen in females also something that stimulates aggressiveness? Floody (1983), reviewing studies relating female aggressiveness to the estrus cycle, concluded that in most species female aggressiveness is lowest during the estrus period when estrogen levels peak. However, levels of aggressive behavior and dominance in females are said to be affected more by social interactions and relationships than by cyclic hormonal changes. Such changes do not cause change in social rank. However, testosterone may have a more direct effect on female aggressiveness. Infanticide in female and male rats is increased by the chronic infusion of testosterone and eliminated in male rats by castration (Gandleman, 1983).

The level of testosterone in males is also affected by their immediate experience in competitive-aggressive encounters (Bernstein, Gordon, & Rose, 1983). Social defeats in fighting to establish dominance among monkeys produces drastically lowered testosterone levels. Victory can raise testosterone levels, particularly in the male who assumes the alpha (most dominant) position. These studies illustrate the difficulties in assuming cause and effect relationships from purely correlative studies.

Sexual behavior

Monoamines

Increasing dopamine levels in male rats increased mounting, intromission, and ejaculation responses to a receptive female, and decreasing dopamine levels tended to reduce these components of sexual behavior (Gessa & Tagliamonte, 1975). Brackett, Iuvone, and Edwards (1986) chemically lesioned four midbrain regions (in male rats) that are believed to play a role in sexual behavior. Lesions in the A9 region of the midbrain in the compact zone of the substantia nigra produced a significant depletion in neostriatal caudate dopamine but did not affect norepinephrine in the hypothalamus or cingulate cortex. The extent of dopamine depletion correlated highly with increases in mounting latency, reduction in mount rate, ejaculation latency, and frequency of mount. However, dopamine has opposite effects in the female rat to those seen in the male, decreasing the sexual presenting (lordosis) response of the female.

Serotonin inhibits sexual behavior in both male and female rats. Norepinephrine seems to play little role in sexual activity; but in females norepinephrine turnover is high in the preestrus stage when sexual receptivity is present, and lesions to the dorsal noradrenergic bundle decrease lordosis reactions in the female. Meyerson et al. (1979) have pointed out that gonadal hormones may act on the monoamines to increase appropriate sexual activity or reduce inhibitory influences over such activity.

Hormones

Beach (1947) suggested that gonadal hormones have control over sexual behavior in lower species but that their influence is increasingly moderated by complex learning factors and social experience in mammals and primates. This evolution is particularly clear in the case of control of female receptivity by estrogen. The human is the only species in which female sexual receptivity occurs at postovulatory periods when estrogen levels are low. Also, postmenopausal or ovarectomized women do not lose their sex drive. Similarly, castration virtually eliminates sexual behavior in male rats; but in castrated postpubertal human males there is diminution of drive but usually not complete elimination of sexual arousal and behavior. However, in rats and human male castrates, injection of testosterone markedly increases sexual arousal and reactivates sexual behavior. Marked strain differences exist in sexual behavior, and these differences are correlated with strain differences in testosterone (McGill, 1978). Castration eventually eliminates mounting and ejaculation in all strains, but there are differences in how long it takes and the degree to which function can be restored by testosterone injection. These results suggest that something other than adult levels of testosterone is involved in the inherited component of sexuality.

The behavioral-gonadal relationship is a two-way street, as illustrated by the study of Michael and Zumpe (1978). Monkeys were singly housed with groups of six females that were kept in continual estrus by estrogen injections. Male monkeys initially showed high levels of sexual behavior (mounting and ejaculation), but both sexual behavior and testosterone levels gradually fell as the males became habituated to the "harem" situation and the same six females. However, the introduction of six new receptive females activated sexual behavior and increased testosterone levels, suggesting a role for novelty of sexual stimulation in increasing gonadal as well as behavioral arousal.

Sociability

Monoamines

A study (Redmond, Murphy, & Baulu, 1979) of the relation between MAO and behavior in monkeys living in a colony in a natural environment showed that low-MAO monkeys were more active, made more social contacts, and engaged in more play activities than high-MAO monkeys. The male low-MAO monkey also engaged in more aggressive and sexual activities than the high-MAO monkeys, who were less active, less sociable, and less dominant.

Ellison (1977) studied the effects of chemical lesions of either dopamine or norepinephrine systems in rats. Behavior was studied in the seminatural colony described in chapter 1. Norepinephrine-lesioned rats spent more time in their burrows and less time in a behavioral arena in which spontaneous social interactions could occur, whereas serotonin-lesioned rats spent less time in burrows and more time in the behavioral arena. In contrast to Ellison's results, Crow et al. (1978) found that specific chemical lesions of the dorsal ascending noradrenergic bundle did not affect time spent in social interactions in familiar or novel environments. The dissimilarity of findings may have something to do with the fact that Crow et al. made their chemical lesions more specifically than Ellison or with the differences between the colony situation and the experimental one.

Ellison (1979) also studied the effects of implanted, slow-release amphetamine on colony behavior of the rat. Amphetamine effects are probably mediated more through dopamine than NE. Amphetamine produced initial increases in exploratory activity but not greater social activity in the rat. Later stages produced first seclusiveness (withdrawal into burrows) and then intensely aggressive interactions with singled-out "victims." File and Velucci (1978) showed that ACTH reduces dyadic social interactions in both familiar and unfamiliar environments. Obviously, there may be an interaction between levels of arousal and social interaction. Eysenck's (1963) theory suggests that drugs like amphetamine that cause arousal promote introversive behavior whereas drugs that dampen cortical arousal elicit more extraverted behavior.

Emotionality and anxiety

Monoamines

Gray has postulated that two of the major monoamine systems, the noradrenergic and serotonergic systems mediate the emotion of anxiety as well as other, more cognitive, functions. More specifically, the noradrenergic system involved in anxiety is said to be the dorsal ascending noradrenergic bundle (DANB), originating in the locus coeruleus, and the serotonergic systems are those originating in the median and dorsal raphe nuclei. Because the role of the DANB in anxiety was originally deduced by examining the effects of antianxiety drugs on behavior, Gray has examined the literature on the effects of DANB and locus coeruleus chemical lesioning to see if the results are consistent with those found for anxiolytic drugs and septal and hippocampal lesioning.

Passive-avoidance learning, presumably depending on arousal of anxiety-produced inhibition, was not impaired in most studies. Gray claims that the technique used in most of these studies (step-down avoidance) was insensitive to hippocampal lesions and therefore not conclusive for a test of his theory. The results of a more appropriate test of DANB function (Tsaltas, Gray, and Fillinz, 1984) were said to provide no support for the reinforcement hypothesis (Stein, 1978, early theory), mixed support for the attentional hypothesis (Mason), and weak support for the anxiety hypothesis (Gray, Redmond) of DANB function. The support for the anxiety hypothesis is based on reduced suppression and more rapid extinction of conditioned suppression responses in DANB-lesioned rats, but these results were found only for conditioned stimuli associated with low-intensity and not for conditioned stimuli associated with high-intensity shock. As is the case with so many experimental tests of models, the positive results are constrained by specific parameters of the experiment that are made relevant to the theories only by post hoc rationales.

Because anxiety is expected to produce an increase of emotionality, measured by defecation, and a decrease in activity in the open-field test, lesions of the DANB should reduce the former and increase the latter.

They do not do so. In File and Hyde's (1978) test of social interaction in an unfamiliar environment, in which social interaction was increased by antianxiety drugs, DANB lesions produced no difference (Crow et al., 1978). Gray interprets rearing in the open field and alternation behavior in mazes as orienting-investigative behavior that is directly related to anxiety. Increases of rearing in the open field are produced by the stimulant amphetamine (Goma & Tobeña, 1985).

In distraction experiments, which Gray suggests pose a test between Mason's (1981) attention hypothesis and Gray's (1982) anxiety hypothesis (the former predicting increased susceptibility and the latter decreased susceptibility to distraction as a function of DANB or LC lesions), Gray claims the results do not support either theory. Although the results always lean toward the attention-theory prediction when significant, the difference depends on the type of stimulus used as a distractor.

Selden et al. (in press) found that DANB lesions impaired fear conditioning when the stimuli were out of context but actually enhanced fear response when the cues were in the context of the original learning situation (preference for a safe environment over the one in which they were shocked). This evidence is interpreted as supporting a selective attention theory of locus coeruleus DANB function rather than an anxiety function.

Areas of at least partial success for the Gray model are two-way active avoidance (enhanced by DANB lesions), the partial reinforcement extinction effect (reduced by the lesions), and successive discrimination (impaired by increased responding in the presence of the negative stimulus and by DANB lesions). However, considering the many effects demonstrated for septohippocampal lesions and/or antianxiety drugs but not for DANB lesions, the experimental literature surveyed by Gray himself does not offer unambiguous support for the role of the DANB and locus coeruleus in an anxiety mechanism.

Redmond's (1977, 1985, 1987) evidence for the DANB and locus coeruleus as primary sources for an "alarm system" related to the human affect of anxiety in the high range of norepinephrine activity is supported by research on primates, primarily monkeys but also humans, including the following findings:

1. Antianxiety drugs such as benzodiazepines and opiates reduce locus coeruleus activity and norepinephrine release.
2. Alpha$_2$ receptor antagonists, which increase locus coeruleus activity and norepinephrine release, induce anxiety in monkeys and humans as reflected in facial expression in the former or verbal report in humans.
3. Electrical stimulation of the locus coeruleus produces facial expressions and reactions in monkeys that are ordinarily seen in response to threats

from environment, and locus coeruleus lesions and drugs that decrease locus coeruleus function attenuated such reactions to a threatening stimulus.

4. Threatening stimuli from the environment, such as threatening facial expressions, produce increased locus coeruleus activity in monkeys, and locus coeruleus lesions abolish these responses to threat.

5. Symptoms produced by opiate withdrawal result in increases in locus coeruleus activity in rats and increases in MHPG in monkey brain and CSF MHPG in humans.

Although the work by Redmond and his colleagues suggests that the locus coeruleus responds to threat, the Aston-Jones and Bloom (1981) data showed that certain kinds of nonnoxious stimuli might stimulate these neurons and thereby activate a cortical arousal pathway. To clarify the nature of stimulation necessary to stimulate the locus coeruleus, Grant, Aston-Jones, and Redmond (1988) stimulated awake monkeys and recorded from the locus coeruleus during the presentation of a variety of stimuli. The neurons did not respond to initial presentations of tones of moderate intensity but did respond to novel tones of higher intensity. However, the neurons also responded to less intense stimuli that were unexpected and probably threatening, such as raps on the chamber walls or the sound of the chamber door opening. Thus, there is evidence that the response of the locus coeruleus is somewhat biased toward aversive or ambiguous stimuli and consistent with Redmond's characterization of the response as an "alarm reaction."

Soubrié (1986) has provided the most recent extensive review of the animal and human research on the function of serotonergic systems. As discussed previously, human clinical studies suggest that anxiety is associated more with reduced than with increased serotonergic function. The clinical correlates of low serotonin or its metabolite 5-HIAA include depression, suicide, and violent, impulsive aggression, hardly behaviors associated with tranquil mood. Animals chemically depleted of serotonin show exaggerated startle responses and fearfulness in novel situations (also see Ellison, 1977) suggestive of enhanced rather than reduced anxiety. Although Gray interprets these phenomena as motor disinhibition, there is ample evidence in humans that there is also dysphoria (depression and anxiety) associated with these types of behaviors. Much of the research on animals parallels some of the findings based on septal or hippocampal lesioning and the antianxiety drugs. Lesions of the raphe nuclei decrease passive avoidance, reduce the usual inhibition of feeding behavior and social contacts in unfamiliar or novel situations, and increase activity in familiar situations. Serotonergic lesions reduce the capacity of animals to withhold response in situations in which they must do so to obtain rewards.

If we look at the pattern of results in research on animal and humans, low serotonin would seem to be characteristic of persons high on P (impulsive, poor control) and N (emotional) rather than persons low on N as would be suggested by Gray's model. At the least the data suggest an interaction between serotonergic and noradrenergic systems, with facilitative behavioral effects in some situations and antagonistic effects in others.

Human monoamine studies

Before discussing the relationships among measures of neurotransmitters and their enzymes and metabolites, it is necessary to examine the reliabilities of biochemical measures and their interrelationships. In a discussion of the state-trait question in chapter 2, it was pointed out that state measures cannot be expected to correlate with trait measures unless the state tests are aggregated over time and situations. Because most correlative studies of biochemical and psychological variables are one-time samplings, it is essential that both types of measures be stable.

Three questions concerning measures of monoamine function in living humans must be answered before they can be regarded as indicators of brain monoamine activity: (1) What is the reliability of such measures over time? (2) How do measures of neurotransmitters, their metabolites, and enzymes that are obtained from CSF, blood, and urine correlate? (3) How are these measures affected by age, body size, diurnal variation, smoking, exercise, diet, and other factors that might mediate or attenuate their relationships with personality traits.

Reliability of monoamine metabolites and enzymes

Monoamine oxidase measurements

Platelet monoamine oxidase (MAO) levels are reliable and stable measures of individual differences. Samples taken 1 to 2 weeks apart correlated .94, and those taken 8 to 10 weeks apart correlated .86 (Murphy et al., 1976). Variations in level do occur in individuals, but they are small compared with between-subject differences. Unlike other biochemical indices, MAO does not show marked changes with clinical states such as depression and mania. However, MAO does change over longer periods of time, showing an increase with age in human brain, platelets, and plasma (Robinson, Davis, Nies, Revarics, & Sylvester, 1971). Sex differences are found in platelet MAO, with females showing higher levels than males (Murphy et al., 1976; Robinson et al., 1971).

Urinary MHPG

Urinary MHPG (3-hour samples) showed some increase in levels in normal males exposed to stress, but there was little change in patients or normal females (Buchsbaum, Muscettola, & Goodwin, 1981). However, in the same study the reliabilities from one time of day to another (r's > .90) and from one day to another (r's = .63, .75) were high. Buchsbaum et al. calculated the reliability of 24-hour samples collected by Hollister, Davis, Overall, and Anderson (1978) and found a coefficient of .81 in two samples taken with an intervening period of 4 to 24 weeks. In both studies there were diurnal changes in level; MHPG rose from morning to afternoon. There is a weak but significant relationship between age and urinary MHPG (Potter, Muscettola, & Goodwin, 1983), MHPG increasing with age. Males have higher levels of urinary MHPG than females in both depressed patient and normal control groups (Potter, Ross, & Zavadil, 1985). Experimentally induced changes in activity increase urinary MHPG in depressed patients but not in normal volunteers (Potter et al., 1983).

Plasma MHPG

Siever et al. (1986) assayed plasma MHPG and NE twice with at least a 2-day interval. In a group of combined patients and controls, plasma MHPG showed good reliability (r = .74), and plasma NE poorer consistency (r = .47). However, when normals were considered separately, the reliability of plasma NE (r = .61) was fair and that for MHPG was poor (r = .45). Halbreich et al. (1987) found higher reliability for normals (r = .83) for plasma MHPG sampled continuously over 3-hour periods one day apart. They also found significant positive relationships with age in normals and depressed patients and sex differences.

CSF NE, MHPG, HVA, and 5-HIAA

Studies of retest reliability in CSF measures from lumbar punctures (LPs) are rare for obvious reasons. Linnoila et al. (1983) studied the reliability of NE, MHPG, HVA, and 5-HIAA across two LPs between 1 and 6 months apart in schizophrenic subjects. Mean levels of NE and the monoamine metabolites did not change between the two LPs. Reliability correlations for averaged concentrations were NE, .60; MHPG, .72; HVA, .81; 5-HIAA, .53. Considering the time interval and the unstable subjects used, the correlations for HVA and MHPG are remarkably high. However, the finding that CSF NE is elevated and CSF DBH is depressed in patients in a manic state relative to controls and patients in a depressed state (Post et al., 1984) suggests that these measures are influenced by the clinical state of the subject and might be influenced by changes in mood or activity even in normals.

Table 5.2. *Correlations between CSF norepinephrine (NE), monoamine metabolites (MHPG, 5-HIAA, HVA) and enzymes (DBH, MAO) in CSF, plasma, and urine*

	CSF MHPG	CSF DBH	Plasma MHPG	Plasma DBH	Urinary MHPG	CSF HVA	CSF 5-HIAA	Platelet MAO
CSF NE	.48[b]	.23	.53[b]	.49[a]	−.18	.07	.04	−.08
CSF MHPG		.49[a]	.74[b]	.13	.12	.46[b]	.33[a]	.13
CSF DBH			.38	.71[b]	.14	.16	.27	.12
Plasma MHPG				−.10	.50[b]	.02	.00	.26
Plasma DBH					−.40	.03	.13	−.05
Urinary MHPG						−.28	−.24	.33[a]
CSF HVA							.79[b]	−.34[a]
CSF 5-HIAA								−.31[a]

Note: MHPG and DBH correlations among CSF, plasma, and urinary sources are in italics.
[a] $p < .05$
[b] $p < .01$
Source: Ballenger, Post, Jimerson, Lake, Murphy, Zuckerman, and Cronin (1983), table 1, p. 619. Copyright 1983, Pergamon Press. Reprinted by permission.

Monoamines and their metabolites and enzymes in CSF plasma, and urine

Table 5.2 shows the correlations among a number of monoamine-relevant measures from CSF, plasma, and urine in a group of normals studied at the National Institute of Mental Health (Ballenger et al., 1983). CSF and plasma measures of norepinephrine, its metabolite MHPG, and its process enzyme DBH tended to be moderately to highly correlated in CSF and plasma. The urinary measure of MHPG, however, was only correlated with the plasma measure. These results make physiological sense because CSF and blood are both one step removed from the brain and are metabolic routes of disposal. Urinary substances are derived only from the blood and therefore might be expected to correlate with plasma but not with CSF measures.

Platelet MAO correlated negatively with the dopamine and serotonin metabolites (HVA and 5-HIAA) and positively with the norepinephrine metabolite (MHPG). However, in a study by Oxenstierna et al. (1986), using many more subjects, platelet MAO did not correlate at all with dopamine, serotonin, or norepinephrine metabolites (HVA, 5-HIAA, MHPG) in CSF.

The human brain contains two types of MAO, A and B, whereas platelets contain only the B type. Human brain is believed to contain a predominance of the B type (70–75%). The MAO A type is primarily involved in the breakdown of norepinephrine and serotonin, and dopamine is the preferred substrate for the B type in the brain; but MAO B type is localized in serotonin-rich areas of brain and may also contribute significantly to the metabolism of serotonin (Robinson & Kurtz, 1987). Much of the research has assumed a relationship between the B type of MAO found in platelets and brain MAO of both types. Oreland, Wiberg, and Fowler (1981), for instance, suggest that platelet MAO activity is determined by the same set of genes that regulate levels of central serotonin turnover and offer evidence that platelet MAO correlates positively with CSF serotonin. However, studies by Winblad, Gottfries, Oreland, and Wiberg (1979) and Young, Laws, Sharbrough, and Weinshilboum (1986) failed to find correlations between platelet MAO type B and brain MAO of either the A or B types. The Winblad et al. study used brain tissue obtained from autopsy whereas the Young et al. study obtained live brain tissue mostly from the temporal cortex of patients operated on for epilepsy. It could be argued that the areas sampled in this study were not the areas of the brain where MAO might be related to peripheral MAO. However, Adolfsson, Gottfries, Oreland, Roos, and Winblad (1978) found fairly high correlations between MAO in nine human brain areas. There was also some weaker evidence of low significant correlations among MAO and serotonin and 5-HIAA across parts of the brain. Although larger scale studies are needed, the current situation offers no secure generalization from platelet MAO to brain MAO, and the literature relating platelet MAO to personality and psychopathology must rest on its own empirical merits rather than as data on the relationships between brain enzymes and behavior.

Until recently NE systems in brain and the peripheral autonomic system have been regarded as independent, though the role of brain NE in the regulation of autonomic arousal would suggest some relationship between the two. Reviewing the evidence in primates, Maas and Leckman (1983) believe that the data are consistent with the idea that "central and peripheral adrenergic neurons function as an interactive unit" (p. 40). Correlations between CSF and plasma NE of .73 (Lake et al., 1981) and .87 (Raskin, Peskind, Halter, & Jimerson, 1984) certainly support this assumption. Also supporting the assumption is the correlation ($r = .77$) between plasma MHPG and plasma NE (Table 5.3) (Siever et al., 1986). Plasma MHPG and NE also correlated with urinary MHPG and VMA in this study, and the two urinary metabolites were correlated.

All of these studies suggest functional relationships between NE and its metabolites in CSF and blood and therefore suggest potential usefulness for investigating the role of brain mechanisms in personality. However, urinary NE measures, though correlating with plasma measures, do not correlate with CSF measures, suggesting a limit to their usefulness as indicators of brain NE activity. Plasma MHPG would probably be the best measure to use because CSF measures cannot be done except in special research settings, and they are not practical for experimentation.

Table 5.3. *Correlations between plasma MHPG and NE and urinary MHPG and VMA*

	Plasma NE	Urinary MHPG	Urinary VMA	Urinary MHPG + VMA
Plasma MHPG	.77[c]	.50[a]	.49	.57[b]
Plasma NE		.56[a]	.50[a]	.58[b]
Urinary MHPG			.51[a]	.86[b]
Urinary VMA				.87[b]

[a] $p < .10$
[b] $p < .05$
[c] $p < .01$
Source: Siever, Uhde, Jimerson, Lake, Kopkin, and Murphy (1986), part of table 4, p. 65. Copyright 1986, Elsevier Science Publishers. Reprinted by permission.

Genetics of neurotransmitter metabolites and enzymes

Table 5.4 presents correlational data from twin, sibling, and parent-offspring studies of platelet MAO, CSF, and serum or plasma DBH, COMT activity in red blood cells, CSF and plasma MHPG, and CSF HVA and 5-HIAA. All of the data on CSF-derived metabolites are from the recent study by Oxenstierna et al. (1986) in Sweden. The numbers of twins and siblings in most of the samples are small, so the heritabilities calculated from twin data are not trustworthy. However, the correlational findings suggest practically complete genetic determination for DBH, MAO, and COMT. The correlations for identical twins approach unity for DBH and COMT and are only slightly lower for MAO. The findings for fraternal twins are more variable than for identicals. Some of the variance might depend on the substrates used for MAO determination, serum versus plasma determination of DBH, variations in procedures, or differences in the subject samples. However, when we consider the typical (median) values for fraternal twins, siblings, and parent-child pairs, the MAO correlations are slightly under, and the DBH correlations are slightly over, the .50 correlation expected in the case of complete polygenetic inheritance.

The CSF NE metabolite MHPG showed evidence of strong heritability in the twin data in the study by Oxenstierna et al. (1986), but the sibling correlation was much lower, a finding similar to those for psychological traits (chapter 3). In the same study, CSF HVA and 5-HIAA showed less heritability, particularly HVA for which the correlations of identical and fraternal twins were practically the same. In Linnoila et al. (1983), discussed in a previous section, the reliability of the 5-HIAA determination was low ($r = .53$).

Because platelet MAO shows consistent evidence of high heritability, more inquiry has been made into the specific type of hereditary mechanism

Table 5.4. *Twin (IT, FT), sibling, and parent-child correlations of platelet MAO, plasma DBH, CSF and plasma MHPG and CSF HVA and HIAA*

Author(s)	IT	FT	Sibs	Pa-Ch	h^2	MAO substrate
Monoamine oxidase (MAO)						
Murphy (1976)[a]	.88	.45	.28	—	.86	Benzylamine
Nies et al. (1974)[b]	.76	.39	—	—	.74	Benzylamine
Pawley et al. (1979)[c]	—	—	.55	.54	—	Benzylamine
Oxenstierna et al. (1986)[d]	.81	.32	.56	—	.81	Tryptamine
Winter et al. (1978)[e]	.92	.70	—	—	.44	Tryptamine
	.88	.52	—	—	.72	Tyramine
	.86	.47	—	—	.78	Phenyethlamine
COMT						
Winter et al. (1978)[e]	.95	.65	—	—	.60	
Dopamine-β-Hydroxylase						Source
Oxenstierna (1986)[d]	.98	.66	.55	—	.64	serum
	.83	.32	.47	—	.83	CSF
Winter et al. (1978)[e]	.92	.35	—	—	.92	serum
Ross et al. (1973)[f]	.96	.75	—	—	.42	
Weinshilboum & Raymond[g]	—	—	.54	—	—	serum
Sakellariou et al. (1987)[h]	—	—	.66	.45	—	plasma
MHPG						
Oxenstierna (1986)[d]	.76	.44	.17	—	.74	CSF
Jimerson et al. (1981)[i]	.70	—	—	—	—	plasma
HVA						
Oxenstierna et al. (1986)[d]	.58	.52	.40	—	.12	CSF
5-HIAA						
Oxenstierna et al. (1986)[d]	.53	.32	.40	—	.42	CSF

Note: Heritability estimated from Falconer formula: 2 X (ITr − FTr), but when h^2 exceeds ITr, ITr is used as the estimate of heritability.
[a]ITn = 9, FTn = 10
[b]ITn = 9, FTn = 11
[c]Sibs n = 75, Parent-child (pa-ch) n = 45
[d]ITn = 15, FTn = 15, sibs n = 15
[e]ITn = 21, FTn = 20 for MAO; ITn = 24, FTn = 24 for COMT; ITn = 23, FTn = 24 for DBH
[f]ITn = 10, FTn = 28
[g]sibs n = 94
[h]sibs n = 18
[i]ITn = 13

involved. Rice, McGuffin, and Shaskin (1982) concluded from analysis of a large American sample that MAO could be determined by a single major gene locus with two alleles. Cloninger, von Knorring, and Oreland (1985) reanalyzed the Rice et al. data along with their own Swedish sample and concluded that five components rather than three best describe the distribution in both samples. The results fitted a model with a minimum of three alleles at a single major locus or one with at least two polymorphic loci.

Monoamine oxidase, behavior, and personality

This review of the findings that relate biochemistry to personality includes studies of the relationships between a particular chemical and some dimension of behavior or personality, whether the sample is from a normal or abnormal population. This inclusion of data from abnormal groups is necessary because so much of the work on human psychopharmacology has been done on psychiatric populations. Population comparisons among abnormal or between abnormal and normal samples are reserved for the chapters 8 and 9 on psychopathology.

Sostek, Sostek, Murphy, Martin, and Born (1981) took umbilical cord blood samples at birth and tested the newborns with a neonatal behavioral assessment scale within the first 3 days of life. The range of platelet MAO in the newborns approximated that seen in adult humans. Infants with low MAO or low plasma amine oxidase (AO) levels were characterized by higher states of arousal, more activity, and less "consolability" when upset than high MAO or AO babies. High MAO babies slept a lot whereas lows were more likely to be crying or actively awake when observed. Low AO groups were rated as less "cuddly" than high AO groups. The low MAO group was rated "more optimal" on seven of the nine motor items on the behavioral scale, including general tonus, motor maturity, cuddliness, defensive movements, startle, and hand-mouth facility, and on two signs of autonomic lability (lability of skin color and lability of states). The low plasma AO group was more optimal on several measures of orienting response to visual and auditory stimuli. Although the significance of these early behavioral signs in terms of later personality development is problematical, one could say that the behavior of low MAO infants suggested an emotionally labile or unstable extravert in adult terms.

Extraversion-sociability

Platelet MAO correlated positively with introversion or negatively with extraversion scales in studies by Ballenger et al. (1983), Demisch Georgi, Patzke, Demisch, & Bochnik (1982), and Gattaz and Beckman (1981) in America and Germany, but not in Swedish studies by Perris et al. (1983), Schalling, Edman and Åsberg (1983), Schalling, Åsberg, Edman, & Oreland (1987) or von Knorring, Oreland, and Winblad (1984). In a study by Klinteberg, Schalling, Edman, Oreland, & Åsberg (1987), MAO and E were significantly correlated in males but not in females. Findings on the relationship of E and MAO are inconsistent.

Neuroticism-anxiety

Coursey, Buschbaum, & Murphy (1979) found that normal males with low MAO levels showed more general psychopathology on the MMPI than those with high levels, and Ballenger et al. (1983) found positive correlations between depression scales and MAO. However, other studies (von Knorring et al., 1984; Mathew, Ho, Kralik, & Taylor, 1980, Murphy et al., 1977; Perris, Jacobssen, Oreland, Perris, & Ross, 1980; Perris, Eiseman, von Knorring, Oreland, & Perris, 1984; Schalling et al., 1983, 1987, 1988; Yu, Bowen, Davis, & Boulton, 1983) could not find significant relationships between MAO and questionnaire measures of trait anxiety, depression, or neuroticism. Klinteberg et al. (1987) found a significant relationship between MAO and some anxiety scales in men, but none in women. Kralik, Ho, Mathew, Taylor, and Weinman (1982) injected epinephrine into anxious patients and controls. Anxiety and plasma norepinephrine and norepinephrine showed increases, but MAO levels remained stable. However, Mathew, Ho, Taylor, and Semchuk (1981) treated anxiety-disorder patients with relaxation for 4 weeks, producing significant decreases in both anxiety and MAO. However, it must be generally concluded that there is little relationship between MAO and the N-*anxiety* dimension of personality in normal subjects.

P-ImpUSS

Schalling et al. (1983) found low but significant negative correlations between MAO and two scales measuring impulsivity in one study, but the correlations for one of the scales was not significant in another sample. Similarly, they found that the *monotony avoidance* scale (a Swedish version of the *sensation-seeking* scale) correlated negatively with MAO in one of two normal samples. Perris et al. (1980, 1984) reported significant negative correlations between monotony avoidance and MAO in depressed patients but primarily the female patients. Perris et al. (1984) also found a negative correlation between MAO and an aggression factor derived from a questionnaire. Klinteberg et al. (1987) reported negative correlations between two types of aggression scores and MAO in males but not in females.

Using more behavioral criteria for P tendencies, Coursey et al. (1979) found that low MAO males in a normal population reported more convictions for criminal offenses and more alcohol, tobacco, and illegal drug use than high MAO subjects. Shekim et al. (1984, 1986) found that low MAO children, both normals and hyperactives, made more errors and quicker decisions on the Matching Familiar Figures test of behavioral impulsivity.

Table 5.5. *Correlations: platelet MAO vs. sensation seeking scales*

Authors	Subjects	n's	r's total, gen. scales[a]	Significantly correlated subscales[b]
Murphy et al. (1977)	F students	65	.17	none
	M students	30	$-.45^d$	Dis
Schooler et al. (1978)	F students	47	$-.43^d$	TAS, ES
	M students	46	$-.52^d$	TAS, ES, BS
Ballenger et al. (1983)	M & F adult	36	$-.17$	none
Schalling et al. (1987)	M students	40	$-.25$	Dis
Arqúe et al. (1988)	M & F adult	13	$-.66^d$	TAS, ES, Dis
	M & F pts.	44	$-.25^c$	ES, Dis
Ward et al. (1987)	M students	57	$-.24^c$	Dis
	F students	30	$-.15$	
Shekim et al. (1989)	M adults	58	$-.23^c$	ES, TAS

[a]Gen. = general scale from form IV, total = sum of 4 subscales, form V
[b]TAS = *thrill and adventure seeking*, ES = *experience seeking*, Dis = *disinhibition*, BS = *boredom susceptibility*
[c]$p < .05$
[d]$p < .01$ } Studies from Ballenger et al. (1983) on used one-tailed tests

Sensation seeking

The most consistent pattern of correlation between MAO and a personality trait is with *sensation seeking*. Table 5.5 shows the correlations obtained in 11 samples from 7 studies. The correlations were negative in all but one of the 11 samples and were significant in 7 of the 11 groups. Although the median correlation is only $-.25$, there is no question that there is a relationship between sensation seeking and platelet MAO. Various differences among the studies could account for attenuation of the correlation. The Swedish studies (Schalling et al. 1987; von Knorring, Oreland, & Winblad 1985) used translations of the SSS. A large study of army recruits in northern Sweden, (von Knorring, Oreland, & Winblad, 1984; von Knorring and Oreland, 1985) used an abbreviated SS scale that was missing all of the items in the *disinhibition* subscale, the one most consistently related to MAO in the other studies and contained only half of the items in the *experience seeking* subscale.

Despite the low, albeit significant, linear correlation with MAO in this army group, the reduced SSS proved to be the most discriminating personality scale in differentiating the extreme groups constituting the upper and lower 10% of the distribution on MAO (von Knorring et al., 1984). The only scales on which high and low MAO groups differed were the total SSS, the *boredom susceptibility* (BS) subscale of the SSS, and the *monotony avoidance* and *impulsivity* scales of the Karolinska inventory.

Table 5.6. *Correlations: platelet MAO vs. monotony avoidance**

Authors	Subjects	n	r
Schalling et al. (1987)	M students	40	−.30[a]
Schalling et al. (1988)	M adults	58	−.16
Fowler et al. (1980)	M & F adults	59	−.17
Perris et al. (1980)	M & F dep. pts.	24	−.55[b]
Perris et al. (1984)	M dep. pts.	60	−.05
	F dep. pts.	83	−.26[b]
Klinteberg et al. (1987)	M students	29	−.31[a]
	F students	32	−.16

*Note: A *sensation seeking* scale developed by Schalling et al. (1983)
[a]$p < .05$
[b]$p < .01$ } one-tailed tests

Extraversion and *guilt* scales and an estimate of adequacy of psychological functioning from an interview were not discriminating. The total SSS was the only personality measure that was significant in a discriminant function analysis, and the *boredom susceptibility* subscale of the SSS was the most powerful predictor of MAO levels in a stepwise multiple regression.

Studies in Sweden have also used the *monotony avoidance* scale (MA), which correlates .50 with the general SS scale and most highly with the *boredom susceptibility* subscale of the SSS ($r = .51$) (Schalling et al., 1983). Table 5.6 shows the correlations between this scale and platelet MAO in eight groups from six studies. All the corelations were negative, and four of the eight were significant. The median correlation is −.215.

Although there is some evidence of differences in MAO related to E or N factors, the results on these variables are inconsistent from one study to the next. But the constituents of the P dimension of personality, *impulsivity, antisocial* tendencies, and *sensation seeking,* seem fairly consistently (if not strongly) related to MAO. Behavioral reports of drug and alcohol (Coursey et al., 1979; von Knorring et al., 1985) and convictions for criminal offenses in the low MAO group, as well as findings of low MAO among chronic alcoholics (Major & Murphy, 1978), alcohol and drug abusers (von Knorring, Oreland, & von Knorring, 1987), and marijuana users (Stillman, Wyatt, Murphy, & Rausher, 1978) support the idea that low levels of MAO are related to the P factor. Donnelly, Murphy, Waldman, Buchsbaum, and Coursey (1979) attempted to develop an MMPI MAO scale consisting of items that most effectively discriminated high- and low-MAO groups. The most discriminating item for males was "During one period when I was a youngster, I engaged in petty thievery." Low-MAO males answered "true." Schalling et al. (1983) also contrasted items on an *impulsivity* scale in terms of relation to MAO. One of their discriminating items was "I have never been in trouble with the law." Low-MAO men answered "false." There appears to be a relationship between psychopathy and low MAO in men.

Although the magnitudes of correlation between MAO and P factor traits are low, the fact that there is definite evidence of a relationship is interesting in suggesting an involvement of the monoamine systems regulated by MAO in personality. Given the uncertain relationship of platelet MAO to brain MAO, and the various influences such as sex differences that might affect MAO, the finding of significant relationships with behavioral and questionnaire measured traits is not something to be dismissed lightly, even though differences in personality can be found only at the extremes of the MAO distribution. The MAO personality relationships simply point up the probable involvement of the monoamine systems in personality, suggesting more direct studies of the monoamine-personality relationships.

Personality traits and monoamines

Most of the studies relating personality traits to measures of the monoamines, their metabolites, and enzymes in cerebrospinal fluid (CSF), plasma, and urine are recent and exploratory. Results are often weak, even when significant, and numbers of subjects are usually far from optimal; therefore replication is needed to distinguish chance findings from significant relationships. Correlations that are significant in patients may not be significant in normals and vice versa. However, at this stage in formulating and testing meaningful models, there is a need for a survey of the relationships between the two domains of phenomena even though they tell us little about cause and effect. A few experimental studies have been done, and these will be discussed in the next section.

The study by Ballenger et al. (1983) (also see Zuckerman, Ballenger, Jimerson, Murphy, & Post, 1983) represents one of the few broad psychopharmacological studies of normals. The subjects were 43 male and female paid volunteers who were tested, interviewed, and had lumbar punctures (LPs) done for CSF assays, blood drawn for serum, plasma, and platelet determinations, and urine collections for three consecutive days at the National Institute of Mental Health (NIMH) Clinical Center. All subjects were put on low monamine diets for at least 2 weeks prior to assays, and the LPs were done after 9 hours of bedrest and fasting. Normals had been carefully screened for current or past psychopathology using a semistructured interview. Such screening, of course, may restrict the range of traits such as anxiety and psychopathic tendencies, but a secondary purpose of the study was to gather normative data for comparisons with groups manifesting various clinical disorders.

Table 5.7 shows the correlations obtained among personality, affect trait,

Table 5.7. *Partial correlations between CSF NE, CSF and plasma DBH, monoamine metabolites (MHPG, HVA, 5-HIAA) and measures of personality and affect (trait and state)*

Personality[a]		Monoamines, metabolites, and enzymes							
		CSF NE	CSF MHPG	Plasma MHPG	Urinary MHPG	CSF DBH	Plasma DBH	CSF 5-HIAA	CSF HVA
EPQ	E	.00	.21	−.25	.12	.25	.33	.05	.16
	N	−.15	−.20	−.44[b]	−.07	−.13	−.26	.06	.18
	P	−.23	−.23	−.26	−.04	−.06	.00	−.27	−.20
MMPI	D	−.10	−.18	−.51[c]	.05	−.11	.07	.10	.15
	Pt	−.25	−.30	−.57[c]	−.26	−.05	−.21	.36[c]	.27
	Hs	−.08	−.41	−.62[d]	−.07	−.11	.02	.11	.08
	ES	.01	−.11	.05	.02	−.05	−.33	−.36[b]	−.51[d]
MAACL-T	A	−.17	−.10	−.36	−.11	−.48[c]	−.42[c]	.03	.14
	D	−.11	.15	−.37	−.25	−.16	.04	−.03	.08
	H	−.25	.08	.08	−.08	−.23	−.15	−.04	−.01
MAACL-S	A	.19	.42[c]	.08	−.25	.45[b]	.51[b]	.14	.19
	D	.13	.26	−.24	−.19	.04	.35	.03	.23
	H	.29[b]	.23	.23	−.24	.19	.42	−.07	.02
SSS-Gen		−.49[d]	.09	.24	−.06	−.12	−.60[c]	.07	.06
B-D Assault		−.01	.27	.64[d]	.27	.07	−.06	−.04	−.13

Note: Correlations corrected for influence of height, weight, and age.
[a]EPQ = Eysenck Personality Questionnaire, E = *extraversion*, N = *neuroticism*, P = *psychoticism*, MMPI = Minnesota Multiphasic Personality Inventory, D = *depression*, Pt = *psychasthenia*, Hs = *hypochondriasis*, ES = *ego strength*, MAACL = Multiple Affect Adjective Check List, T = trait form, S = state form, A = anxiety, D = depression, H = hostility, SSS Gen = Sensation Seeking Scale, General scale, B-D Assault = Buss Durkee Hostility Scale, Assault (physical aggression) subscale
[b]$p < .10$
[c]$p < .05$
[d]$p < .01$
Source: Ballenger, Post, Jimerson, Lake, Murphy, Zuckerman, and Cronin (1983), from parts of table 1, p. 619, and table 3, p. 621. Copyright 1983, Pergamon Press. Reprinted by permission.

and state variables and CSF norepinephrine, the norepinephrine metabolite MHPG in CSF, plasma, and urine; the norepinephrine enzyme DBH in CSF and plasma; and the serotonin and dopamine metabolites 5-HIAA and HVA from CSF. Only one correlate was found for CSF norepinephrine: the Sensation Seeking General Scale. This negative correlation was highly significant ($p < .01$) and was also significant in males and females analyzed separately. CSF MHPG correlated significantly with state anxiety assessed just prior to the LP procedure but did not correlate with measures of trait anxiety. In contrast, plasma MHPG correlated significantly and negatively with the EPQ *neuroticism* (N) scale, *depression* (D), *psychasthenia* (Pt), and *hypochondriasis* (Hs) from the MMPI and had a very high positive correlation with the Buss-Durkee Assault Scale, a measure of self-reported physical aggression. In other words, persons with relatively high levels of plasma MHPG tended to be low on trait anxiety and general neuroticism and high on aggressiveness. Urinary MHPG was not significantly correlated with any of the personality or affect measures.

Both CSF DBH and plasma DBH correlated negatively with trait anxiety but positively with state anxiety as measured by the MAACL. In other words, persons with high levels of DBH, in either CSF or plasma, tended to be low on trait anxiety but high on state anxiety on the morning of the LP. Trait and state anxiety in this sample were essentially uncorrelated. Plasma DBH also correlated negatively and highly with sensation seeking.

The serotonin metabolite 5-HIAA in CSF correlated positively with *psychasthenia* (Pt) and negatively with *ego strength* (ES) measures from the MMPI. The dopamine metabolite HVA in CSF showed the same tendencies though the positive correlation with Pt was not significant. In this and subsequent studies, similar patterns of correlation for CSF 5-HIAA and HVA are found, reflecting the high correlation between the two measures themselves.

Schalling, Åsberg, and Edman (1984) studied the relationships of three monoamine metabolites obtained from CSF (MHPG, HVA, and 5-HIAA) to personality variables from the Karolinska Scales of Personality (KSP). Two groups of patients, depressed (D) and nondepressed (ND), and a group of normal volunteers (N) were studied. Table 5.8 shows their results.

Perhaps the most interesting finding is the negative correlation between the P scale and the serotonin metabolite 5-HIAA in the normals and the ND patients. Looking back to the 5-HIAA versus P correlation in the normals in the Ballenger et al. study (Table 5.7), we find a nonsignificant tendency in the same direction with a $-.27$ correlation. This illustrates one of the problems with replication attempts using statistics based on low *n*. The serotonin metabolite also had negative correlations with the *impulsivity,* and *monotony avoidance* (sensation seeking) scales of the KSP and a positive correlation with the *socialization* scale, but these correlations were significant only in the nondepressed patient group. In the normal group, 5-HIAA correlated positively with the *psychasthenia* and *inhibition of Aggression* (assertiveness) scales, but these correlations were not significant in the patient groups. Instead, in the ND patients, 5-HIAA correlated positively with measures of *verbal aggression* and *irritability*. The correlation between 5-HIAA and *psychasthenia* in normals replicates the one found between these variables by Ballenger et al. (Table 5.7).

HVA showed a similar pattern of relationships of personality traits to 5-HIAA, correlating negatively with P and positively with *psychasthenia* in normals; and negatively to *impulsivity* and *monotony avoidance* and positively to *hostility* in ND patients. The NE metabolite MHPG correlated negatively with P but only in the ND patient group. It showed a weak positive association with inhibition of assertiveness in the normals.

Table 5.8. *Correlations between CSF monoamine metabolites (5-HIAA, HVA, MHPG) and personality scales in normals, depressed patients (DPt) and nondepressed patients (NDPt)*

Pers. tests[a]	5-HIAA			HVA			MHPG		
	Normal	DPt	NDPt	Normal	DPt	NDPt	Normal	DPt	NDPt
EPQ									
E	−.16	−.06	−.10	−.11	−.09	−.23	.24	.11	−.07
N	.19	−.08	−.05	.15	.00	.18	−.06	−.13	−.13
P	−.43^d	−.18	−.32^c	−.42^c	−.13	.14	.25	.00	−.47^b
KSP									
Imp.	−.07	−.12	−.29	−.12	−.06	−.24^b	−.07	.08	−.20
Monot. Av.	−.10	−.26^c	−.28^c	−.23	−.29^c	−.26^b	.12	−.20	−.15
Socializ.	.13	.06	.32^c	.06	.10	.17	.02	−.06	.19
Psy. Anx.	.15	.13	.08	.17	.22^b	.15	−.14	.02	−.12
Psychas.	.26^b	.09	.17	.36^b	.11	−.02	−.08	.14	.16
Inhib. Agg.	.38^c	.08	−.07	.23	.14	.14	.26^b	.05	−.15
Guilt	.31^c	−.09	.05	.35	.04	.08	−.17	−.05	.03
Verbal Agg.	−.12	.09	.32^c	−.12	.09	.30^c	−.16	.08	.05
Irritability	.05	.11	.26^b	.19	−.06	.34^c	−.11	−.08	−.08

[a]EPQ = Eysenck Personality Questionnaire: E = extraversion, N = neuroticism, P = psychoticism; KSP = Karolinska Personality Inventory: Imp. = impulsivity, Monot. Av. = monotony avoidance, Socializ. = socialization, Psy. Anx. = psychic anxiety, Psychas. = psychasthenia, Inhib. Agg. = inhibition of aggression, Verbal Agg. = verbal agression
[b]$p < .10$
[c]$p < .05$
[d]$p < .01$
Source: Schalling, Åsberg, and Edman (1984 unpublished). Adapted by permission.

Schalling et al. (1990, unpublished) recently communicated some preliminary results on the personality correlates of the three monoamine metabolites in a small sample of 30 "healthy young men." In contrast to the previous findings on normals, this group showed negative relationships between CSF 5-HIAA (serotonin metabolite) and E, rather than P and, as previously found, positive correlations of 5-HIAA with anxiety, guilt, and inhibition of aggression scales. HVA, the dopamine metabolite, showed similar, but even stronger, positive correlations with introversion and anxiety. Men with low MHPG, the norepinephrine metabolite, tended to score high on P and social dominance and low on guilt scales compared with men with intermediate or high MHPG levels. These investigators are currently expanding their samples on the groups in the as yet unpublished study whose results are described in Table 5.8, so it is hoped that their correlational findings will soon be clearer.

A study of CSF monoamine metabolites in normals and depressed patients was also done by Redmond et al. (1986). Personality was assessed

Table 5.9. *Correlations between CSF monoamine metabolites (MHPG, 5-HIAA, HVA) and personality ratings of normals (Norm) and depressed patients (DPt)*

Rating	Source of Rating[a]	MHPG Norm	MHPG DPt	5-HIAA Norm	5-HIAA DPt	HVA Norm	HVA DPt
Depressed mood	Subject/self-rating	−.01	.09	.07	−.03	.04	−.12
Anxiety	Phys/interview	−.06	.26[d]	.28	−.01	.33[b]	.02
	Phys/videotape	−.12	.23[c]	.17	.05	−.01	.01
	Subject/self-rating	−.02	.17	.03	−.03	−.05	−.08
Agitation	Phys/videotape	−.02	.19	−.04	−.05	−.23[b]	−.02
Hostility	Phys/videotape	.18	.13	.11	.02	.23[b]	.16
Somatization	Phys & subject	−.29	.40[d]	−.03	.00	−.18	−.14
Distressed appearance	Phys/observ & video	.10	.27[d]	.22	.06	.22[b]	−.03
Sleep disturbance	Phys/subject/nurse	−.35[b]	.35[d]	.02	.16	.11	.03

[a]Phys = physician
[b]$p < .10$
[c]$p < .05$
[d]$p < .01$
Source: Redmond, Katz, Maas, Swann, Casper, and Davis (1986), parts of table 10, p. 944. Copyright 1986 by American Medical Assoc. Adapted by permission.

from observations of behavioral variables concerned largely with anxiety, depression, and hostility. Table 5.9 shows the correlations between the three monoamine metabolites and the personality variables in normals (N) and patients (P) suffering from major affective disorders in depressive episodes. The serotonin metabolite 5-HIAA did not correlate significantly with any of these variables in either group. In a small group of manic patients, not shown in this table, 5-HIAA correlated positively and significantly with measures of anxiety, depression, hostility, and somatization. The dopamine metabolite HVA yielded only borderline significant correlations in the normals, in which it correlated positively with physicians' ratings of anxiety, hostility, and distress.

Almost all of the significant correlations between personality and MHPG were found in the patient group, in which MHPG correlated positively with two sets of anxiety ratings and physician's ratings of somatization, distressed appearance, and sleep disturbance. In regard to sleep disturbance, it is interesting that the correlation in normals was also significant but in the opposite direction.

Other correlative findings

Other studies were examined for possible replication of the isolated findings from these three studies. In the Ballenger et al. (1983) study, the *sensation seeking* trait was correlated negatively and significantly with plasma DBH and CSF norepinephrine. The negative relationship with DBH was also found in studies by Umberkoman-Wiita, Vogel, and Wiita (1981) and Kulcsár, Kutor, and Arato (1984) but not in studies by Calhoon (1988, & unpublished manuscript), all using normal subjects. A study of depressed patients (Perris et al., 1980) found a low but significant positive correlation between plasma DBH and the KSP *monotony avoidance* scale. The Hungarian investigators (Kulczar et al.) suggested that the lack of DBH in the high sensation seeker might lead to a depletion of norepinephrine and a build up of excessive dopamine in the norepinephrine neurons. Their hypothesis is consistent with the negative correlation between CSF norepinephrine and *sensation seeking* in Ballenger et al. (1983).

Serum DBH appears to have little relation to the N dimension. In a large sample of surgical and psychiatric patients, Friedman, Stolk, Harris, and Cooper (1984) found no association between serum DBH and the Zung Depression or Taylor Manifest Anxiety scales. Furthermore, in anxiety outpatients treated with benzodiazepines, DBH change did not reflect changes in *anxiety* or *depression*.

There has as yet been no replication of the negative relationship between CSF norepinephrine and *sensation seeking* found in the Ballenger et al. (1983) study. An earlier study (Buchsbaum, Muscettola, & Goodwin, 1981), using small numbers of normals and depressed patients, found positive correlations between urinary MHPG and certain *sensation seeking* scales in the normals and not in the patients. Roy, DeJong, and Linnoila (1989) reported significant positive correlations between extraversion and CSF *and* plasma levels of MHPG in a small group of male pathological gamblers. More consistent with the direction of the CSF norepinephrine–sensation seeking relationship were negative correlations between plasma MHPG and *sensation seeking* scales in normals in the study by Arqué et al. (1988). However, the Ballenger et al. study also included MHPG measures from urine and plasma, and neither correlated with *sensation seeking*. The finding of a positive correlation between plasma MHPG and aggression on a self-report scale in the Ballenger et al. study assumes some significance in view of a positive correlation found between CSF MHPG and ratings of aggression based on case histories in a sample of personality disorders (Brown, Goodwin, Ballenger, Goyer, & Major 1979).

Redmond's (1977, 1985, 1987) and Gray's (1982) theories suggest positive relationships between measures of anxiety and depression and activity in the norepinephrine system originating in the locus coeruleus. Gray's theory also involves the serotonergic system in the anxiety dimension of personality. Although norepinephrine or MHPG in CSF or plasma is relevant to these theories, even more crucial is evidence on brain norepinephrine or MHPG, given the uncertain relationship between CSF and brain levels. In one of the few studies comparing human brain levels of neurotransmitters with behavioral characteristics (rated before death, of course), Bridge, Kleinman, Soldo, and Karoum (1987) found that MHPG in the hypothalamus correlated positively with ratings of depression, but norepinephrine correlated negatively with depression ratings as did dopamine and its metabolite HVA. The opposite results for MHPG and norepinephrine could indicate a depletion of intraneuronal NE after a period of high activity in these neurons. Such a pattern is consistent with responses to prolonged stress in rats.

In the Ballenger et al. study (1983), plasma MHPG correlated negatively with measures of trait anxiety in normals, and CSF MHPG showed non-significant negative relationships in the same direction. Redmond et al. (1986) showed largely nonsignificant relationships between CSF MHPG and ratings of anxiety, depression, and hostility in normals but positive and significant correlations in depressed patients. Similarly, Roy, Pickar, Linnoila, and Potter (1985) reported a positive correlation between CSF NE and anxiety in a group of depressed patients. Roy, Jimerson, and Pickar (1986) found a positive correlation between plasma MHPG and the Hamilton *depression* scale in patients with a major depressive episode. However, Siever et al. (1986) found negative correlations between ratings of agitation and plasma and urinary MHPG in depressed patients.

Zuckerman (1984b) suggested that the level of catecholamine activity may be curvilinearly related to measures of dysphoric emotion, with anxiety and depression found at extremes of low and high activity. The finding of inverse correlations between *anxiety* and NE or its metabolites in normals and positive correlations in patients might indicate some support for this theory, though the results in patients are not entirely consistent.

The serotonin metabolite 5-HIAA in CSF correlated low but positively and significantly with measures.of *psychasthenia,* anxiety, and inhibition of aggression in normals in the studies by Ballenger et al. (1983) and Schalling et al. (1984, 1990). No evidence of correlation with anxiety ratings in either patients or normals was found in the study by Redmond et al. (1986), though a small subgroup of manic patients did show high positive correlations between 5-HIAA and depression and anxiety ratings. In patients with the severe melancholic type of depression, Roy et al. (1985) found positive correlations between CSF 5-HIAA and ratings of depression and anxiety. In contrast to the previous findings in patients, Niklasson, Ågren, and Hallgren (1983) reported low but borderline significant negative correlations between ratings of worrying and somatic anxiety and CSF 5-HIAA in patients with major affective disorder. Madsen and McGuire (1984) reported positive correlations between whole blood levels of serotonin and type A characteristics (fast tempo, impatience) in normal males. These blood-derived measures of serotonin are much less likely than CSF serotonin to reflect brain levels of the transmitter.

The finding of Schalling et al. (1984) of a negative relationship between the P scale from the EPQ and 5-HIAA in CSF in normals and nondepressed patients has not yet been replicated. However, the results are consistent with a growing literature relating low levels of serotonin to violent suicide attempts or aggression (van Praag, 1986). Brown et al. (1979) found a very high negative correlation ($r = -.78$) betweer. a history of aggressive behavior and CSF 5-HIAA levels in a group of personality disorders. The Schalling et al. findings are also consistent with the theory of Soubrié (1986) suggesting that lowered serotonin levels in the brain increase *impulsivity* and the tendency to make responses that have a potential for punishing consequences, and they reduce tolerance for delay of gratification.

Given the high correlations between CSF 5-HIAA and HVA, it is not surprising that the results relating the dopamine metabolite to psychological variables are similar to those for 5-HIAA. For instance, in the study by Schalling et al (1984), HVA (like 5-HIAA) correlated positively with *psychasthenia* and negatively with the EPQ P scale in normal subjects. HVA also correlated negatively with the *monotony avoidance* scale in both groups of patients, as did 5-HIAA. However, HVA results did not link HVA to the P scale despite the negative correlations between P and 5-HIAA. Similar results showing negative associations of HVA and HIAA to anxiety and depression (Bridge et al., 1987; Niklasson et al., 1983) in patients have been reported. Because the linkage of the two metabolites in CSF is not likely to reflect the true relationship in the brain, one or both measures may reflect something other than brain activity of the particular system.

Theoretically, dopamine has been implicated in reward and activities in pursuit of reward. Thus, one might expect some relationship of dopamine or its metabolite HVA to *extraversion* or *sensation seeking,* but none has been found in studies by Ballenger et al. (1983) or Schalling et al. (1984). A study by King et al. (1986) found a substantial correlation between the EPI E scale and CSF dopamine in depressed patients, and Lindström (1985) reported a positive correlation between HVA and nurses' ratings of social interest in a group of drug-free schizophrenics. HVA also correlated negatively with ratings of lassitude and slowness of movements in the same subjects. Thus far, the only link between dopamine and *sociability* has been found in these two patient groups.

Experimental studies

There are two general approaches to the experimental study of the relations between neurochemistry and psychological functions: use some drug that alters the neurochemistry and observe the effect on behavior or subjective states and the target neurotransmitter, or expose the subjects to a stress or stress reduction treatment and observe the effect on the neurochemistry and the psychological variables. In the first group of studies to be discussed, the neurotransmitter is the independent variable.

Direct alteration of central norepinephrine

Studies of the noradrenergic system have recently used two drugs that have specific effects on alpha$_2$ receptors of the noradrenergic system. These receptors have a negative feed-back effect on norepinephrine activity. *Yohimbine* is a drug that has an antagonistic effect (blocks) and *clonidine* has an agonistic effect (facilitates function) on these receptors. Thus yohimbine increases norepinephrine release and norepinephrine neuronal activity whereas clonidine suppresses both activity and release. If norepinephrine activity is linked to state anxiety then yohimbine should increase anxiety and clonidine should reduce or block it.

Baseline levels of plasma MHPG in anxiety patients (Charney, Heninger, & Brier, 1984) and depressed patients (Siever & Uhde, 1983) do not differ from normal controls. Yohimbine produced anxiety, somatic symptoms, and elevated blood pressure and pulse rate in anxiety disorder patients but little or no anxiety in normal controls, despite the fact that yohimbine increased MHPG equally in both groups. The increase in MHPG was significantly correlated with the increase in anxiety in the patients but not in the controls.

Naloxone is a drug that blocks opiate receptors located on the noradrenergic neurons. The absence of this source of inhibition combined with the blocking of the alpha$_2$ receptor negative feedback could amplify the effects of the combined drugs. Charney and Heninger (1986) found that the combination of yohimbine and naloxone produced stronger anxiety effects in normals than either drug given alone, though the increase in MHPG was not greater than after yohimbine was given alone.

Siever and Uhde (1983) gave the alpha$_2$-andrenergic agonist clonidine to depressed patients and normal controls. Clonidine significantly reduced anxiety in the patients but not in the controls. The patients with the highest MHPG values prior to the clonidine treatment had the greatest anxiety reduction after being given the drug.

These studies suggest a relationship between anxiety and activity of the noradrenergic system, as assessed by MHPG, in anxious and depressed patients *but not in controls.* However, the effects of drugs that increase or reduce anxiety do not necessarily act through the central noradrenergic system, even in the patients. Other drugs such as caffeine and lactate, which have no effect on noradrenergic activity (MHPG) can also induce anxiety and autonomic system arousal in patients and sometimes in normals, too (Gorman, Fyer, Liebowitz, & Klein, 1987). The common factor in all drugs producing anxiety in patients is their capacity to increase peripheral arousal (tachycardia and hyperventilation). Patients have a special sensitivity to such arousal and are more likely than normals to interpret what they feel as anxiety.

Stress-produced increases of norepinephrine

A few studies of stress have used plasma or urinary MHPG, but most have used urinary measures of norepinephrine or epinephrine. Painful or high-intensity stimulation (Buchsbaum et al., 1981), stressful movies or performance demands (Takahashi, Nakahara, and Sakuri, 1974), dangerous natural stress situations like night landings on an aircraft carrier at sea (Rubin, Miller, Clark, Roland, & Ranson, 1970) increase levels of urinary MHPG. However, normals show more of this natural norepinephrine stress reaction than depressed patients (Buchsbaum et al., 1981; Takahashi et al., 1974). Sweeny, Maas, and Heninger (1978) reported that enhanced activity produced a correlation between MHPG increase and anxiety increase in depressed patients but not in normal controls.

Only a small portion of urinary MHPG comes from the brain so the effect of stress on it may largely reflect peripheral autonomic arousal. Urinary norepinephrine and epinephrine are derived entirely from peripheral mechanisms in the adrenal medulla and sympathetic nerves. Urinary catecholamines increase after stressful work in natural or laboratory situations (Carlson, Levi, & Orö, 1967; Forsman, 1982; Frankenhauser, 1979), parachute jumping, traveling in crowded conditions (Frankenhauser, 1979), and after viewing some types of films (Levi, 1967, 1969). Levi found that increases in urinary catecholamines were produced by sexual and comedy films as well as by stressful films provoking negative affects. Apparently peripheral catecholamine activity is not emotionally specific.

Effects of amphetamine

Amphetamine and cocaine are thought to produce their effects, such as energization and euphoria, by increasing release of brain catecholamines (dopamine and norepinephrine) and blocking their reuptake. The acute effects of the drugs are to increase activity in the systems affected, as measured by MHPG for the NE system. The benzodiazepines, used to reduce anxiety, have opposite effects on the norepinephrine system. However, almost all subjects respond more positively to amphetamine than to the tranquilizer diazepam (Carrol, Zuckerman, & Vogel, 1982; de Wit, Uhlenhuth, Hedeker, McCraken, & Johanson, 1986), including those with anxiety disorders and normals (de Wit et al.), and high as well as low *sensation seekers* (Carrol et al.). Diazepam (valium) lowers self-ratings of anxiety, but it also lowers general arousal and vigor and increases confusion (de Wit et al., 1986). To persons who are not anxious, the dearousal produced by diazepam, particularly at high doses, can be unpleasant. Amphetamine in low doses does not affect anxiety but increases euphoria, positive mood, feelings of friendliness, alertness, vigor, and mental activity and efficiency (Carrol et al., 1982; de Wit et al., 1986; Jacobs & Silverstone, 1986; Johanson & Uhlenhuth, 1980; Rapaport et al., 1980). Amphetamine increases or maintains arousal, relative to placebo or tranquilizer effects, as measured by pulse rate and systolic blood pressure (Carrol et al., 1982; Jacobs & Silverstone, 1986) and skin conductance fluctuations and plasma cortisol (Jacobs & Silverstone, 1986). Subjective feelings of mental alertness and efficiency are corroborated by increased performance, relative to placebo groups, on learning and visual motor coordination (Carrol et al., 1982), and vigilance, memory, and reaction time tests (Rapaport et al., 1980).

The dependence of the amphetamine-produced euphoria on release of catecholamines was shown in a study by Jönsson, Änggård, and Gunne (1971). The euphoric effect was blocked by pretreatment with a drug that inhibits the catecholamine precursor tyrosine hydroxylase, resulting in a depletion of catecholamines. The authors, noting that a drug (pimozide) that blocks dopamine receptors also reduces euphoric effects whereas noradrengergic blocking drugs do not do so, suggest that the mood-enhancing effect of amphetamine depends on dopamine systems in the brain and not on noradrengergic systems.

Not all of the effects of amphetamine are positive. Jacobs and Silverstone (1986) regard the effects as an experimental model for mania, and they found increased irritability and restlessness in subjects given amphetamine. Rapaport et al. (1980) reported a normalizing effect on hyperactive boys, but adult men were observed to be more "fidgety." However, performance was improved in both hyperactive and normal boys and men.

The amphetamine- and cocaine-induced psychoses are familiar to clinicians who deal with a drug-abusing population. Chronic users of these drugs may be brought to the hospital with symptoms of paranoid psychosis with delusions of persecution and hostility. Their admission is sometimes precipitated by violent aggressive acts. The amphetamine-induced psychosis has been studied in the laboratory by Griffith, Cavanaugh, Held, and Oates (1972), who gave small, frequent doses of amphetamine to volunteers with a drug history, thereby gradually building up plasma levels of amphetamine over a 5-day period. Six of the nine subjects developed an amphetamine psychosis. Initially, the subjects were mildly euphoric, but all became depressed after a certain dose. They lost interest in their surroundings, gave up former activities, became taciturn, reserved, and negativistic; and many confined themselves to their rooms. Signs of suspiciousness were followed by open expressions of delusions of persecution and ideas of reference. The process, which was rapidly accelerated in this study, ordinarily takes place over more extended periods in users who gradually develop a tolerance and increase their dosage or frequency of dose.

There is a dramatic difference in the positive behavioral and mood changes produced by acute doses of amphetamine and the negative, symptom-producing effects of larger doses. The former may mimic hypomania, as suggested by Jacobs and Silverstone (1986), and the latter more closely resembles paranoid psychosis. Acute doses lead to positive mood states and purposeful activity and (in normal adults) to sociability and talkativeness (Heishman & Stitzer (1988); frequent and high dosages lead first to anxiety and depression and then to panic, limited and stereotyped activity, social withdrawal, or hostile and aggressive interactions. Are these changes due to a curvilinear relation between catecholamine system activity and mood and behavior as was suggested by Zuckerman (1984b), or is the change due to a depletion of dopamine because of damage to the system (Ellison, 1979)? The answers to these questions may help us to understand the implications of the sensitivity and activity of catecholamine systems for normal dimensions of personality such as *extraversion* (sociability and activity) and *socialization* or P-ImpUSS.

L-DOPA

DOPA is the immediate precursor of dopamine in the catecholamine neurons. Another way to increase activity in the systems is to administer L-DOPA. Murphy (1977) says that 15% of neurological and psychiatric patients given L-DOPA exhibited some form of "behavioral toxicity." A high proportion of bipolar depressed patients given L-DOPA reacted with brief hypomanic episodes, suggesting a special sensitivity to the drug.

Sacks (1983) described his treatment of a group of postencephalitic Parkinsonism cases with L-DOPA. The volume contains brief case studies of 20 patients. Parkinsonism results from the degeneration of the dopaminergic pathway (A9) from the substantia nigra to the neostriatrum (caudate nucleus and putamen). Deficits are seen in initiating or stopping movements, tremors, rigidity of limbs, and a masklike appearance often reflecting frozen emotions as well as motor deficits. But Parkinsonism is more than a motor deficit. Often the patient is fully capable of movement and exhibits this capability under emotional stress or provocation but otherwise remains in a kind of catatonia or depression, characterized by lack of energy, initiative, vitality, and social interest.

During World War I a worldwide epidemic of encephalitis left many survivors with a slow developing Parkinsonian condition. Most Parkinsonism develops in older patients, but these patients were "frozen" in young adult life. The discovery of L-DOPA in the 1960s offered the opportunity to treat these patients, who had changed little in the years since their disease developed in the 1920s. Sacks began to give L-DOPA to a ward of these patients, with some surprising results. Almost all of these patients showed an "awakening," not only in the sense of a greater capability for normal, fluid movement but a return of motivation, positive emotions, sociability, and intensified interest in their environments.

But sooner or later most of the patients ran into trouble, perhaps because the dopamine was now acting on supersensitive receptors. From a normal exhuberance, patients slipped into hypomanic excitement, restlessness, heightened eroticism, and grandiosity. Like patients with bipolar mood disorders, they would then "crash" into deep depression. Besides implicating dysregulation of the dopamine systems in manic-depressive disorder, the reactions of these patients also suggest an involvement of dopamine, in the normal range of activity, in the trait of *extraversion* and some aspects of the P-ImpUSS dimension, particularly *impulsivity*.

5 Hydroxytryptophan (5HTP)

5 HTP is the immediate precursor of serotonin (5HT) in the brain, so an infusion of 5HTP might be expected to increase serotonergic activity. der Boer and Westenberg (1990) gave 5HTP to panic disorder patients and controls and assessed symptoms of anxiety and depression before, during, and after infusions. No increases in anxiety were found in either group, and some patients even felt relief, despite the production of physical side effects.

Human hormone studies

Cortisol

High levels of plasma, urinary, and CSF cortisol have been reported in severe types of depression (Traskman et al., 1980), but lower levels are found in bipolar disorders in the manic state, indicating a possible state correlation between cortisol and mood. Cortisol levels may show temporary elevations in normals after stress such as open heart surgery (Naber & Bullinger, 1985) but these reactions subside in all patients except those experiencing major depressive episodes after surgery. Low levels of urinary cortisol have been found in habitually psychopathic, violent offenders (Virkkunen, 1985), suggesting a negative relationship between the P dimension and cortisol. In the study by Ballenger et al. (1983) CSF cortisol correlated negatively with four markers for the P dimension: the EPQ P scale, the *sensation seeking disinhibition* subscale, the MMPI *hypomania* scale, and the variety of heterosexual partners reported in the questionnaire. Urinary cortisol correlated positively with the depression scale on the trait form of the MAACL. Longitudinal studies of the relation between plasma cortisol and depression ratings by nurses in patients with affective disorders revealed significant positive correlations in 10 of the 17 cases (i.e., on days when depression was high, cortisol also tended to be elevated) (Rubinow, Post, Gold, Ballenger, & Wolff, 1984).

A factor analysis of the major psychological and biochemical variables

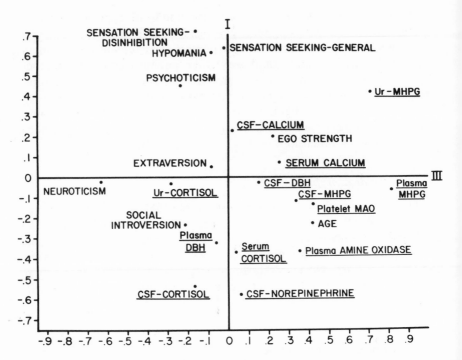

Figure 5.9. Factor dimensions of P-ImpUSS (I) and *neuroticism* (III) with plots of biochemical and personality variables. (From "The neurobiology of some dimensions of personality" by M. Zuckerman, 1984, in *International Review of Neurobiology*, vol. 25, p. 424, J. R. Smythies and R. J. Bradley, Eds. New York: Academic Press. Copyright by Academic Press. Reprinted by permission.)

in the Ballenger et al. (1983) study (Figure 5.9) revealed a dimension identifiable as P-ImpUSS with loadings of *sensation seeking, hypomania,* and EPQ P scales at the positive pole, and CSF NE and cortisol, plasma DBH, serum cortisol, and plasma amine oxidase at the negative pole. The other dimension shown in this figure is *neuroticism,* defined by the EPQ N scale at one pole and plasma and urinary MHPG at the other.

Cortisol levels, therefore, appear to be high in severe depression and stress-induced dysphoric states and low in impulsive, unsocialized sensation seekers and some psychopaths. It is clear that levels of cortisol are responsive to stress, and the findings of a negative relationship with the P dimension might simply indicate that high P volunteers are less stressed by the immediate anticipation of a lumbar puncture (Ballenger et al., 1983), particularly because CSF cortisol did correlate with a state measure of anxiety on the morning of the lumbar puncture. The results might also indicate a more generalized lack of stress response along the hypothalamic-pituitary-adrenal cortex pathway in high P-ImpUSS subjects. Experimental stress studies could test this hypothesis. Although cortisol elevation is found in response to stress, cortisol does not necessarily produce anxiety. Born, Hitzler, Pietrowsky, Pauschinger, and Fehm (1988) injected hydrocortisone into normal volunteer, thus increasing cortisol activity. High cortisol levels produced increased concentration and reduced fatigue but did not affect anxiety, depression, anger, or sociable feelings.

Gonadal hormones

The causal pathway is not always clear in hormone-behavior relationships. As an example, although testosterone influences aggression and sexual arousal, stress can lower testosterone, and sexual stimulation and arousal can raise levels of the circulating hormone (Hellhammer, Hubert, & Schwimeyer, 1985; Pirke, Kockott, & Dittman, 1974). Although there is diurnal variation in androgen and estrogen values, these values are stable and reliable over periods of 2 to 10 days if blood is drawn at the same time in the morning on each day sampled (Daitzman, Zuckerman, Sammelwitz, & Ganjam, 1978; Kreuz & Rose, 1972).

There are little data on the heritability of gonadal hormone function. Turner, Ford, West, and Meikle (1986) found a correlation of .69 for plasma testosterone in identical twins, contrasted with .50 for fraternal twins, yielding a heritability of only .38. However, Fox, Gifford, Valenstein, and Murawski (1970) found correlations of .86 for identicals and .55 for fraternal twins ($h^2 = .62$) on 17-ketosteroids, a metabolite of circulating androgens. Plasma levels of testosterone may reflect a mixture of trait and state effects whereas 24-hour urine assays may be a better trait index.

Gonadal hormones begin to influence the developing organism before birth. When a female fetus is exposed to excessive levels of androgen, anomalies in development of sexual organs may be apparent at birth. But even if these anomalies are surgically corrected, differences in personality and interests become apparent as the child develops (Ehrhardt, Epstein, & Money, 1968). Compared with other girls of their age and with their female siblings, these girls are more likely to show differences in play patterns, preferring "rough-and-tumble" play to "dolls" and "house." There is no effect on the eventual form of sexual preference, most such girls showing a heterosexual interest pattern.

Similar reversals of sex-stereotyped interest patterns have been found in boys who were exposed to excessive levels of estrogen while in the fetal stage of development. There has been some speculation about the prenatal hormonal influence in transsexual cases, in which the desire of boys to dress in female clothing and engage in opposite-sex interests appears quite early in life.

The maturation of the gonads determines the age of puberty, at which time secondary sexual characteristics and other physical changes occur as well as changes in social and sexual interests. Hormonal changes can cause indirect as well as direct changes in personality. For instance, a boy or girl who reaches puberty at a later age than their peers may become isolated and alienated because their interest patterns fail to change in the direction of heterosexual interests. Their lack of physical development may make the transition more difficult because they appear less attractive to the opposite sex. Lack of popularity may undermine self-esteem and self-confidence. Many of these changes are temporary, but in some persons they are more persisting.

Personality

Daitzman et al. (1978) first reported correlations between gonadal hormones in men and the *disinhibition* subscale of the *sensation seeking* scale (SSS). A second study by Daitzman and Zuckerman (1980), using more specific gonadal hormone assays, confirmed the results from the first study. Male subjects scoring high on the *disinhibition* subscale of the SSS had higher levels of plasma testosterone, 17-β-estradiol, and estrone than low-scoring disinhibiters. No difference was found for progesterone. The low disinhibiters had normal levels of testosterone for their age whereas the high disinhibiters had unusually high levels.

This study included a variety of personality questionnaires and a sex experience inventory. Correlations were computed among the four hormones and the various scales. Only testosterone and estradiol showed a significant pattern of correlation with psychological variables. Both testosterone and estradiol correlated positively with a variety of heterosexual experience and number of heterosexual partners. Both hormones correlated negatively with *socialization* and *self-control* scales (the negative pole of the P-ImpUSS dimension).

The correlations among all psychological and hormonal variables were factor analyzed (Figure 5.10). Factor I is defined by *sociability, self-acceptance,* and *dominance* scales at the positive pole and by social *introversion, depression, psychasthenia,* and *neuroticism* at the negative pole. The factor was therefore named *stable extraversion versus neurotic introversion.* Testosterone loaded positively on the factor; it correlated positively with stable extraversion in males.

Factor II was defined by the MMPI F, *psychopathic deviate,* and *hypomania* scales, permissive attitudes toward homosexuality and heterosexuality, and external locus of control at the positive pole, and *socialization, self-control,* desire to make a good impression, achievement, tolerance, well being and intellectual efficiency at the negative pole. The factor was called *social deviancy versus social conformity,* though now we would simply identify it with P-ImpUSS. Estradiol loaded positively on this dimension, that is to say, it correlated positively with social deviancy in males.

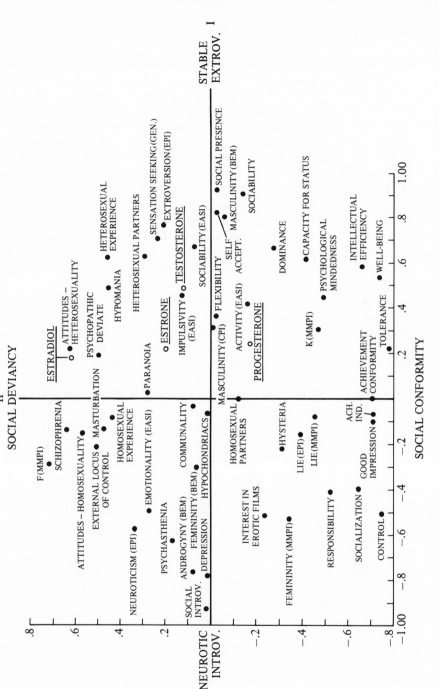

Figure 5.10. Two-factor plot of personality, attitude, and experience scales and gonadal hormone measures: I. stable extraversion versus neurotic introversion; II. social deviancy (P-ImpUSS). (From "Personality, disinhibitory sensation seeking and gonadal hormones," by R. J. Daitzman and M. Zuckerman, 1980, *Personality and Individual Differences*, 1, p. 106. Oxford: Pergamon Press. Copyright 1980 by Pegamon Press. Reprinted by permission.)

Estrone and progesterone were not associated appreciably with either factor dimension.

Although the results showing a positive relationship between testosterone and heterosexual experience, low *socialization,* and high *disinhibitory sensation seeking* were expected, the even stronger relationship of testosterone to *sociability* was not predicted. However, confirmation of this association was provided by a study of Swedish delinquents (Mattson, Schalling, Olweus, Low, & Svensson, 1980; Schalling, 1987) in which testosterone was found to correlate positively with the E scale of the EPQ or *sociability,* but no correlation was found with the N or P scales of the EPQ or an *impulsivity* scale. All correlations were higher in a subgroup of the delinquent boys who had reached the final stage of puberty, as assessed by pubic hair development. In this subgroup the *monotony avoidance* (sensation seeking) scale also correlated significantly with testosterone.

Other studies (Baucom, Beach, & Callahan, 1985; Dabbs and Ruback, 1987, unpublished; Udry & Talbert, 1988) are consistent in showing a relationship of testosterone in males to normal sociability and interest in sex as expressed in reported experience or self-description. In females, testosterone appears to be related to self-reported sociability and sexiness but also to lack of inhibition, impulsivity, and a lack of conformity to the stereotyped female sex role. The latter finding is reinforced by a study (Purifoy & Koopermans, 1979) in which androgen levels were compared among women in various occupations. Testosterone levels were higher in women in professional, managerial, and technical jobs compared with clerical workers and housewives. The latter are, of course, stereotyped occupational roles for women. There is little evidence to suggest an association of testosterone with aggression, though there is evidence of such a link in the studies of prison and delinquent male populations.

Hostility and aggression

Persky, Smith, and Basu (1971) reported a positive correlation between plasma testosterone levels and production rate and a hostility inventory in young, normal men, though they could not find the relationship in older men. Subsequent attempts to replicate the correlation in college students (Meyer-Bahlburg, Boon, Sharna, & Edwards, 1974) and prisoners could not do so (Kreuz & Rose, 1972; Ehrenkranz, Bliss, & Sheard, 1974). In the study by Schalling (1987), verbal and general aggression inventories were positively correlated with testosterone, as was a subscale expressing a preference for physical sports. Although the results linking aggression to self-report inventories are limited, there is evidence from behavioral-observational criteria of a relationship between testosterone and aggression in prison populations. In the Mattson et al. (1980) study, delinquent boys who had committed violent crimes or crimes involving armed robbery were higher in testosterone than those committing less violent crimes. Kreuz and Rose (1972) found no relationship of testosterone to fighting in prison, but prisoners with convictions for more violent crimes committed early in adolescence had higher testosterone levels than those without such a history. Ehrenkranz et al. (1974) compared three groups of prisoners, classified on the basis of observations and interviews conducted over a period of several years. Both aggressive and socially dominant groups had higher testosterone levels than the prisoner control group but did not differ from each other.

Dabbs, Ruback, Frady, Hopper, and Sgoritas (1988) compared saliva testosterone levels among groups of female prisoners. Those who had committed unprovoked violent crimes had significantly higher testosterone levels than those whose violent crimes were defensive and those incarcerated for theft. There was no relationship between testosterone levels and disciplinary infractions in prison.

Rada, Laws, and Kellner (1976) classified imprisoned rapists according to the degree of violence used in their crimes. The most violent rapists, who had inflicted physical injuries on their victims during the rape, had higher testosterone levels than all other groups of rapists as well as groups of child molesters and controls.

In summary, levels of testosterone in normal young men seem to be related to sensation seeking, sexual motivation, sociability, and a typical pattern of male interests and attitudes but not to *impulsivity* or *aggression*. Testosterone is related to histories of violent crimes in both male and female prisoners, but not to behavior in prison. There is also evidence of a relation between testosterone and social dominance in delinquents and prisoners, but in these groups there is also a link with physical aggression of an extreme or chronic type.

Sexual behavior

Although castration in the postpubertal male does not invariably cause impotence, it usually produces a marked reduction in sexual arousal, activity, interest, and fantasy (Bremer, 1959; Sturüp, 1968). Administration of antiandrogen drugs to males (usually chronic sex offenders) has similar results (Bancroft, Tennent, Loucas, & Cass, 1974). Surgical removal of the ovaries in adult women has no inevitable or marked effect on sex drive or interest in sex. This is probably because testosterone in women, produced largely in the adrenal cortex, mediates sexual arousal just as it does in men. Women with reduced adrenocortical function do show marked reduction in sexual drive and interest. The administration of testosterone to women suffering from cancer often produces marked elevations in sexual desire whereas the administration of estrogenic hormones has little effect.

However, estrogen does play a primary role in vascularization of the vagina tissue, and its absence may make intercourse difficult or painful because of a lack of lubrication.

The research reported previously linked testosterone in young, mostly unmarried males and females to extent of heterosexual experience and to traits of warmth and sociability that would be important in obtaining early heterosexual experience. Persky et al. (1978, 1982) studied the relationship of sex hormone levels to sexual behavior and attitudes in normal married couples in a longitudinal study of sexual receptivity, behavior, and satisfaction over three menstrual cycles. Women's estradiol levels were not related to measures of reported sexual arousal or frequency of intercourse, but their testosterone levels were positively related to reported sexual gratification (Persky, Charney, et al., 1978). Adding a group of older women to the sample, Persky et al. (1982) found that mean androgen levels for all women were significantly correlated with sexual responsivity during intercourse, frequency of intercourse, and reported sexual gratification.

Scores of male initiation of sex were highly correlated with female responsivity scores as were wives' initiation with husbands' responsivity scores (Persky, Lief, Strauss, Miller, & O'Brien, 1978). High testosterone males were more likely to have partners that were responsive to their sexual initiatives and were more likely than lows to respond to their wives' sexual initiatives. As in most research of this sort, the issue of what is cause and what is effect is not answerable. Although there has been some research showing improvement in sexual function by administration of testosterone, there is none showing the effect of improved sexual relationships on testosterone levels.

Summary

Many of the theories of monoamine function attempt to make the bridge between human traits and what we can learn about the biological mechanisms from animal models. Much of the divergence in theories of monoamine function stems from the different emphases placed on behavioral, emotional, cognitive-attentional, and motivational-hedonic (reward-punishment) mechanisms as underlying basic human personality differences. Most theories have assigned a general inhibitory role to serotonin, though some speak of behavioral inhibition and others of inhibition of emotional systems. Some theories ascribe a central role to serotonin in anxiety states and trait. Almost all theories implicate dopaminergic systems in approach, exploration, "foraging," sensation seeking, positive affect, attention to the environment, or "sensitivity to signals of reward." There is less agreement on the role of the dorsal ascending noradrenergic system originating in the locus coeruleus. Two theories identify it with anxiety, one with general arousal of all emotional systems, two with sensitivity to reward, and one suggests a complementary interaction with dopamine systems and a curvilinear reaction of both with mood, activity, sociability, and sensation seeking (Zuckerman, 1984b).

Although there are vast areas of uncertainty in the brain neurochemical, behavioral, and personality relationships, some convergence is discernible. In humans and other species, dopamine pathways seem to serve a vital function related to positive motivation and approach behavior characteristic of extraversion in humans. Although there is as yet little evidence linking dopamine or its metabolite HVA with extraversion in humans, there is strong evidence linking dopamine with the reward effects produced by brain stimulation in animals. Can this evidence be extrapolated to a positive affect dimension such as *extraversion* (sociability, dominance, activity) in humans? It is a reasonable hypothesis waiting for better methods for assessing dopamine activity in the brain.

Testosterone in males has been linked to disinhibition (sensation seeking), sociability, dominance, and heterosexual interests and experience. The hormone also seems to be related to strong aggressive tendencies that go beyond normal competitive aggressiveness. A general behavior inhibitory role for serotonin seems indicated in both animal and human clinical studies, with low levels of the neurotransmitter related to impulsive and aggressive behavior (P dimension). Low levels of the enzymes DBH and MAO also seem to be involved in the lack of inhibition characterizing sensation seeking, impulsive, and sometimes antisocial types of behavior. Low levels of MAO are also related to sociability in both humans and monkeys. These enzymes are reliable over time and show very high heritability. Their modulation of monoamine systems may play an essential role in two dimensions of personality.

The relation between the N-*emotionality* dimension and noradrenergic activity is less clear. Although some weak correlational and stronger experimental evidence suggest a positive relationship between noradrenergic activity and anxiety in patients, there is little evidence supporting such a relationship in normals, and even some evidence of a negative relationship between the norepinephrine metabolite MHPG and *neuroticism-anxiety* trait in normals. It may be that anxiety must be analyzed into its components: Autonomic arousal may be produced by high but not moderate levels of noradrenergic activity, and serotonin may mediate the behavioral inhibition characteristics of the anxiety state. Autonomic arousal per se is not necessarily associated with the feeling of anxiety. The human cognitive components of anxiety may depend more on cholinergic or GABAnergic pathways between frontal cortex and the limbic system and benzodiazepine agonists and inverse agonists, yet to be identified.

6   Psychophysiology

Overview

The previous chapters on neuropsychology and psychopharmacology presented research on nonhuman species as well as humans because the usual methods of studying the nervous system, such as brain lesioning and stimulation, are not applicable to humans. Psychophysiology involves the recording of bioelectric potentials from the surface of the body and can be used to study humans. Because there is a large body of research on humans, this chapter does not present much research on other species, except for studies with comparative behavioral relevance.

Another advantage of most psychophysiological methods is that they allow continuous recording of physiological activity so that the effects of transient and continuous psychological stimulation can be studied. The term *psychophysiology* implies a primacy of psychological processes; in most studies, some kind of psychological stimulation is the independent variable, and physiological processes are the dependent variables. However, this is not always the case. Studies of the effect of drug-induced physiological arousal on mood and performance treat the physiological change as the independent variable. In the study of personality, physiological processes can be regarded as either dependent or independent variables. A theory may regard level of physiological arousal as a determinant of behavior or personality, or merely as an epiphenomenon of the behavioral or cognitive activity that define the trait. Much of the research is correlative and therefore cannot distinguish which variable is dependent.

Theories

The role of arousal of the autonomic nervous system in producing emotions has been a source of theoretical controversy from the time of William James to the present. Do emotional cognitions trigger autonomic reactions or do particular patterns of physiological arousal lead to the identification of emotional states? The relevance of psychophysiology to personality may depend on the answers to these questions because some theories suggest that primary traits are based on differences in the physiology of essentially emotional systems (e.g., Gray, 1987a), and others propose that personality is based on individual ways of interpreting environmental events (e.g., Mischel, 1981) and expectancies regarding the self in relation to

226

these events (e.g., Bandura, 1986). The viewpoint that claims that particular patterns of physiological arousal identify particular emotions (Ax, 1953; James, 1894) allows for the possibility that differences in emotional traits might be based on differences in tonic activity or reactivity of physiological systems. The theories that suggest that arousal of physiological systems determines the intensity of emotions but not their qualitative differences (Cannon, 1927; Lazarus, 1968; Mandler, 1975; Schachter & Singer, 1962) are more compatible with cognitive theories of emotion because identification of an emotion depends on appraisal and interpretation of the stimulus context. Both types of theories suggest that an emotion may be elicited by some type of external stimulus. The disagreement concerns the level of information processing necessary to provoke a particular emotion and the role of physiological information. Peripheral autonomic system theories are compatible with the idea that conditioned stimuli elicit physiological responses that in turn produce awareness of their emotion by humans. Cognitive theories suggest that a higher level of information processing precedes and is essential to the identification of a particular emotional feeling.

Lang's (1985) model is a combination of the two types of theory. He proposes that emotions are associative networks containing correlated "propositions" that involve semantic, imagery, physiological, and motor program information. The psychophysiology of past emotions is represented in memory and is thus cognitive as well as physiological. For instance, a person who has experienced panic attacks may interpret any sudden increase in heart rate as a panic attack, and the interpretation may include a fearful-feeling state and a strong need to escape, and thus tachycardia may trigger the whole network of cognitive and motor mechanisms associated with such attacks (see chapter 8). The anxiety network can also be activated by an anxious thought.

Specificity versus generality of physiological arousal

The term *arousal* as used by Duffy (1951, 1972) meant a generalized arousal of cortical activity (EEG) and peripheral autonomic activity, including cardiovascular (heart rate, blood pressure), respiratory, electrodermal (palmar sweating, skin conductance), and muscle tension (electromyographic). The problem with such a generalized construct is that these cortical and autonomic indicators are not usually highly correlated during basal or stress conditions.

Although stress can activate all systems to some degree in most persons, the relative degree of activation of particular systems in individuals is not highly correlated. There is often an *individual response specificity;* individuals may respond reliably to stress in some systems but show little or less response in other systems (Engel, 1972). There are even dissociations of

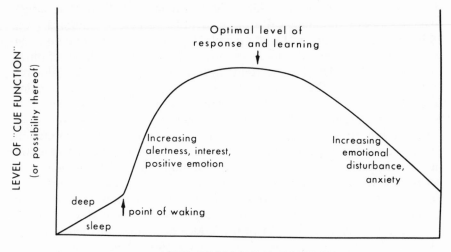

Fig. 6.1. The relationship between arousal and cue function. (From "Drives and the C. N. S. (conceptual nervous system)," by D. O. Hebb, 1955, *Psychological Review*, 62, pp. 243–254. Copyright 1955 by American Psychological Association.)

direction of activation in various physiological response systems in response to certain types of stimuli or situations. For example, in prolonged sensory deprivation, we often see decreases in cortical and cardiovascular arousal but increases in electrodermal measured arousal (Zuckerman, 1969a). In a given system there may also be *stimulus-response specificity.* Heart rate may accelerate in response to stimuli signaling a need for action or attention to internal programs and decelerate in response to situations or stimuli requiring focal attention and "sensory intake" (Lacey, 1959). For these reasons, the term *arousal* should not be used without a referent such as *cortical, autonomic,* or more specifically *cardiovascular* or *electrodermal* (Zuckerman, 1987a).

Optimal level of arousal

The relationships between affect or performance and physiological arousal are not necessarily linear. Hebb (1955) suggested that both positive affect and efficiency of performance generally occur at an optimal, intermediate level of arousal, whereas unpleasant feeling states and inefficient learning or performance are more characteristic at very low or high states of arousal (Figure 6.1). Hebb's theory is a descendant of earlier models proposing inverted-U shaped relationships between stimulus intensity and affect (Wundt, 1893) and between muscle tension and learning efficiency.

Personality theories based on physiological arousal

Optimal levels of stimulation and arousal constructs are central to Eysenck's (1967) theory of introversion-extraversion and Zuckerman's theory of sensation seeking (Zuckerman, 1969b, 1984a). Eysenck's theory is concerned with an optimal level of cortical arousal as regulated by the reticulocortical activating system. Introverts are said to function and feel better than extraverts at lower levels of stimulation and arousal whereas extraverts function and feel better at higher levels of stimulation and arousal. Thus, introverts and extraverts have different "optimal levels of stimulation." The extravert is said to be characterized by underarousal in nonstimulating conditions and thus must become more active and seek more stimulation to reach a higher level of arousal. The introvert is usually closer to an optimal level even in low-stimulation conditions and therefore does not need to seek stimuli or activity to increase arousal. Stimulation and arousal are not linearly related, particularly at high intensities of stimulation, due to transmarginal inhibition. Introverts are more sensitive to low intensities of stimulation and therefore are generally more aroused than extraverts. They may also be more aroused by moderate intensities of stimulation. But at high levels of stimulation extraverts react more strongly than introverts because introverts are more susceptible to protective inhibition.

According to Eysenck's (1967) theory, *neuroticism* is based on reactivity of the limbic system or visceral brain, which regulates the autonomic nervous system. Persons high on the *neuroticism* dimension are said to have low thresholds for activation of this system. Thus, the same degree of stress should produce more autonomic response in neurotic than in stable types.

Sensation seeking trait was directly based on an optimal level of stimulation and arousal theory (Zuckerman, 1969; Zuckerman, Kolin, Price, & Zoob, 1964). Like Eysenck's model for *extraversion, sensation seeking* was originally thought to be based on an optimal level of arousal for the reticulocortical system, but the theory was later changed to an "optimal level of catecholamine system activity" (Zuckerman, 1984). However, because the noradrenergic system seems to serve general cortical arousal functions, some of the predictions may be the same as those based on the earlier theory.

The predictions from an optimal level of arousal theory are not clearcut. Sensation-seeking behavior could be due to (1) a low tonic level of arousal leading to the seeking of exciting, novel, or intense stimuli to raise the general level of cortical arousal; (2) a low level of reactivity to stimuli requiring novel or intense stimuli to increase phasic arousal; (3) a high level of reactivity to stimuli leading to the setting of the expected level at some higher optimal level than in low sensation seekers; (4) a fast rate of habituation leading to rapid lowering of arousal in response to repetitious stimuli and a consequent need for novel stimuli to avoid boredom. Novelty and intensity of stimuli are the two dimensions that are varied in psycho-physiological studies of sensation seeking because they are the dimensions that increase the arousal-producing potential of stimuli (Zuckerman, 1990). The meanings of stimuli may also be factors in arousal.

Gray (1964b) proposed that the Pavlovian trait *strength of the nervous system* might be related to individual differences in arousability of the cortex by the ascending reticular activating system. At low levels of stim-ulation "weak nervous systems" are more sensitive to stimulation than strong ones, but at high intensities the strong nervous system is more reactive because of its higher thresholds for inhibition. Strelau (1983) made this concept of individual differences in "reactivity" central to his theory of temperament. Strelau's theory, however, makes no distinction between cortical and autonomic arousal. Resistance to emotional interference with performance seems to be as much a part of the construct of reactivity as inhibition produced by simple intensity of stimulation. In essence, reactivity is a combination of the physiological models for extraversion and neurot-icism, and the psychological trait measure correlates with both.

Despite the problems with the concepts of generalized arousal and arous-ability, they continue to play an important role in many theories of per-sonality (Strelau, 1987). These theories have been criticized (e.g., Niess, 1988; Zuckerman, 1987a) and defended (Anderson, 1990; Eysenck, 1987), but they have stimulated a great deal of psychophysiological research.

Measurements of brain activity and reactivity

Most of the personality theories discussed in the overview have suggested the importance of cortical arousal or arousability in personality. For this reason, measures of brain activity derived from the electroencephalogram (EEG) have been important in the study of personality. Hebb's arousal continuum refers to cortical arousal best indexed by the EEG.

Spectrum analysis

The raw EEG record shows characteristic changes in frequency, amplitude, and regularity, or synchronization, of wave forms in various states of arousal, as shown in Figure 6.2. The relatively large, slow, and irregular delta waves of less the 4 hertz (Hz) appear in deep sleep stages. Large amplitude theta of 4 to 8 Hz is found primarily in drowsy states between sleep and waking. Alpha waves have a more synchronized rhythm of 8 to 13 Hz, occurring primarily in the occipital region during relaxed but wakeful states. The frequency of waves in the alpha range is also an index of relative

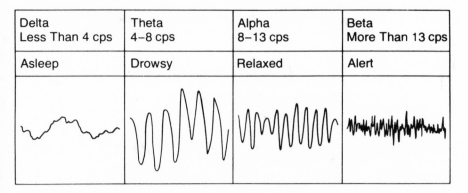

Delta Less Than 4 cps	Theta 4–8 cps	Alpha 8–13 cps	Beta More Than 13 cps
Asleep	Drowsy	Relaxed	Alert

Figure 6.2. Brain waves classified by frequency. (From *A primer of psychophysiology*, p. 104, by J. Hassett, 1978. San Francisco, CA: W. H. Freeman & Co. Copyright 1978 by W. H. Freeman & Co. Reprinted by permission.) CPS = cycles per second, or "hertz".

arousal. Beta waves, a low-voltage fast, desynchronized activity of more than 13 Hz, are found during states of hyperalertness, concentration, mental effort, and emotionality.

During any period of recording one may find some mixture of these wave forms. The characteristics of the forms may show individual differences. For instance, the amplitude of alpha or its typical frequency (between 8 and 13 Hz) can differ reliably from person to person. However, for most subjects who are not asleep (low-voltage activity appears in stage 1 sleep), amplitude varies inversely and frequency of waves varies directly with relative arousal.

Early EEG researchers used tedious visual inspection methods. Researchers who want to use quantitative indices of cortical arousal now have several options, made possible by the use of high-speed computers. They can use filters to analyze the spectrum into the component wave forms and analyze the percentage of recording time in each frequency band. Some studies have analyzed the alpha range activity alone, on the assumption that any disruption of alpha indicates states of higher arousal. However, slower theta wave activity may appear in place of alpha, particularly if the subject is not being stimulated. Studies that use alpha alone usually measure both alpha amplitude and frequency. A *power spectrum analysis* (Figure 6.3) of twins in a study by Lykken (1982) gives a graphic distribution of the relative power at various frequencies and thus represents an overall summary of types of activity in a given period.

Many EEG studies use only one or two recording sites. However, differences in activity at many different brain sites can be assessed simultaneously and analyzed by computer, enabling investigators to localize the sources of brain activity in a topographic map of the cortex.

A. MZ TWINS

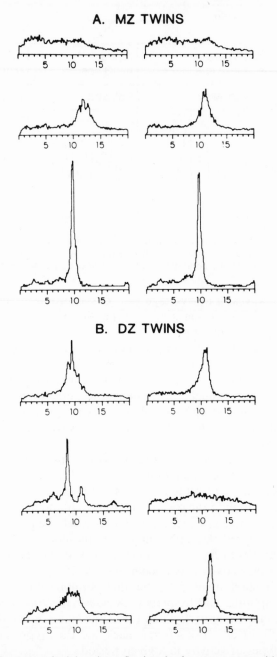

B. DZ TWINS

Figure 6.3. EEG spectra of adult twins reflecting the frequency composition from 0 to 20 Hz of a 3-minute sample recorded from the occipital midline with respect to linked ear lobes while the subject rested with eyes closed. Monozygotic (MZ) twins typically give spectra that are very similar, as shown here, whereas dizygotic (DZ) twins produce spectra that are no more similar than those of unrelated persons. (From "Research with twins: The concept of emergenesis," by D. T. Lykken, 1982, *Psychophysiology*, 19, p. 366. Copyright 1982 by the Society for Psychophysiological Research. Reprinted by permission.)

Genetic analyses

The question of the heritability of brain activity has been addressed in several twin studies using spectrum analysis. Vogel (1970), reporting on the results of previous twin studies (Vogel, 1958), concluded that "the variability of the EEG under normal conditions is exclusively determined by heredity" (p. 93). However, studies by Claridge, Canter, and Hume (1973) and Young, Lader, and Fenton (1971) comparing identical and fraternal twins reared together showed moderate heritabilities of EEG spectrum activity ranging from 50 to 70%.

Lykken's (1982) study included 25 identicals separated at birth and reared apart, and 89 identicals and 53 fraternals raised together. The overall spectrum similarity, illustrated in Figure 6.4, shows that the spectrum differences tend to be minimal between most identicals whereas fraternals show a distribution of difference ratios that are the same as those for the normal population. The results were the same in two separate studies conducted in 1974 and 1980.

Table 6.1 shows the correlations of identicals reared apart, presumably reflecting the purely genetic factor, and identicals and fraternals reared together on EEG activity in the different spectrum bands. There is little difference between identicals raised separately and those reared together, indicating the lack of any influence of shared environment. If we use the correlations of the identicals raised apart as an index of the pure genetic factor or the difference in correlation between identicals and fraternals raised together, the conclusion is that 80–82% of the activity in spectrum parameters is genetically determined. Considering that most of the remaining variance may be due to unreliability rather than environment, it is possible that Vogel (1970) did not exaggerate in his claim that the variability in the EEG under normal conditions is determined entirely by heredity.

Biochemistry of EEG measured arousal

Kemali et al. (1985) assessed CSF norepinephrine (NE) levels in a group of schizophrenics and recorded EEG on the same day. Levels of CSF NE were negatively correlated with relative alpha activity and postively correlated with relative beta activity in the EEG for frontal cortex leads. The results suggest an influence of the dorsal ascending noradrenergic bundle on cortical arousal, a conclusion already established on the basis of locus coeruleus stimulation and recording studies in animals discussed in chapter 5.

Extraversion, neuroticism, and EEG measured arousal

At any given time, cortical arousal is a transient state for any individual. All persons are likely to go through the full range of the arousal continuum

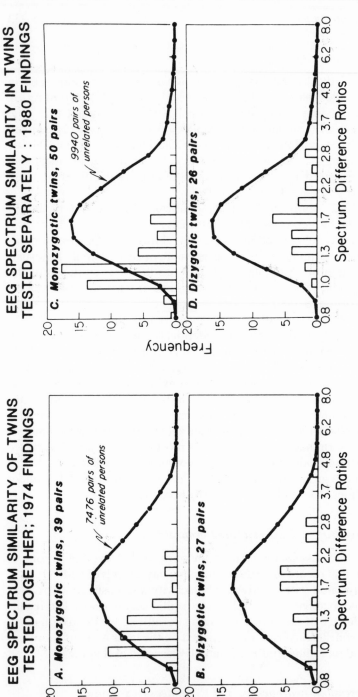

Figure 6.4. Distributions of the spectrum difference ratios (SDRs) for samples of monozygotic (MZ) and dizygotic (DZ) twins. When the SDRs equal 1.0 or less the pairs of spectra are as similar as repeated spectra from the same individuals. In the 1971 study, the readings were made from the occiput. In the 1980 study, with new subjects, the EEG was recorded from the vertex. (From "Research with twins: The concept of emergenesis," by D. T. Lykken, 1982, *Psychophysiology*, 19, p. 367. Copyright 1982 by the Society for Psychophysiological Research. Reprinted by permission.)

Table 6.1. *Intraclass correlations of five spectrum parameters in three samples of adult twins, identicals reared apart (ITa), identicals reared together (ITt), and fraternal twins reared together (FTt)*

		ITa	ITt	FTt
Spectrum parameters	*n*'s	25	89	53
Delta		.90	.84	.30
Theta		.76	.80	.43
Beta		.61	.72	.50
Mean of above		.80	.81	.40
Phi[a]		.89	.81	.13

[a]Phi is the median frequency of the alpha activity
Source: "Research with twins: The concept of emergenesis," by D. T. Lykken, 1982, *Psychophysiology*, 19, p. 366. Champaign, IL: Society for Psychophysical Research. Copyright 1982, The Society for Psychophysiological Research. Reprinted by permission.

during the course of a day, from deep sleep to the high levels induced by either cognitive effort or emotional arousal. Theories of personality based on arousal suggest either (A) there is a biological trait of cortical arousal so that one group (say, introverts) is more aroused than another (extraverts) under all conditions of stimulation, or (B) one group is more aroused than another only under specific conditions of stimulation (low, intermediate, or high). The first type of interpretation (A) suggests only main effects of the personality variable upon arousal and would predict that EEG differences are found under all conditions of stimulation. The second type of model (B) predicts that interaction effects are more likely than main effects of the personality variables, and that conditions in which personality differences are revealed must be carefully specified from the theory of the trait.

On first examination it would seem that Eysenck's (1967) theory is of the first type because he predicts greater cortical arousal and arousability for introverts than for extraverts. On closer examination, his equation of the strong and weak nervous system types with extraverts and introverts, and the optimal level of stimulation theory, would lead to an interactive hypothesis. In low to moderate stimulation conditions, the more-sensitive introvert should be more aroused than the less-sensitive extravert. But under highly stimulating conditions, the extravert should show more arousal because of the introvert's susceptibility to transmarginal inhibition.

Gale (1973, 1981, 1983; Gale & Edwards, 1983, 1986) reviewed the literature relating extraversion to EEG measures of arousal several times. He has attempted to resolve the discrepant findings with a post hoc hypothesis: Moderately arousing conditions, in contrast to low arousing and high arousing conditions, are most likely to reveal differences in arousal between introverts and extraverts. This idea is based on the assumption that in low arousing conditions extraverts engage in self-stimulating activities in contrast to introverts who simply relax. According to Gale, a low arousing condition is one in which the subjects are asked to lie still with their eyes closed or to listen to tones; a moderately arousing condition is one in which they are asked to open and close their eyes; and a high arousing condition is one in which they are required to perform difficult mental calculations.

Investigators are indebted to Gale for his thorough reviews and methodological critique as well as to O'Gorman (1984) for his review evaluating the literature and Gale's interpretations of the findings. Both reviews have rated all of the studies in terms of degree of arousal induced by the procedures, the adequacy of the methods and experimental designs, and whether or not the outcome of the research does or does not support Eysenck's theory. The most recent review (Gale and Edwards, 1986) included 33 studies, of which Eysenck's theory was said to be supported in 18, 15 were said either to show no differences between introverts and extraverts or to show differences in the opposite direction to the theoretical prediction (6 studies).

O'Gorman (1984) reviewed 39 studies of which 19 were judged to have results supporting Eysenck's theory, 10 yielded nonsignificant results, and 10 gave results contrary to the theory. According to this review, only about half of the studies supported the general theory stating that introverts are more cortically aroused than extraverts. Although a metaanalysis might show some preponderance of results in favor of the hypothesis, the effect would not be a large one. One must also consider possible studies that were never published because they did not support the hypothesis, given the bias against publishing nonsignificant findings.

Averaging effects is no answer. As Gale and Edwards (1986) have pointed out, one well-designed and well-executed study outweighs any number of results from poorly designed experiments using poor methodology. One must therefore look more closely at individual studies to see which deserve more credence. Both authors rated the studies for adequacy of methodology. Gale's evaluations were based on his own global judgment. O'Gorman used an eight-item checklist based on Gale's (1973, 1981) criticisms of previous work. The two sets of evaluations made on the same studies only correlated .47. Neither measurement correlated with outcomes of the experiments in terms of supporting or refuting the hypothesis. In terms of the aspects of methodology, O'Gorman found that the EEG methodology did not relate to outcome, but the adequacy of psychometric methodology did. Studies using a known measure of extraversion, such as the EPI or EPQ, were more likely to show results in accord with Eysenck's theory. Thus, O'Gorman has identified one source of negative findings. If one is going to test someone's personality theory, it is sensible to use the tl eorist's own methods for assessment. It is difficult to understand why researchers ignore this obvious requirement.

Given the disagreements between Gale and O'Gorman on methodological adquacy of the studies, I looked more closely at studies in which *both* rated the methodological adequacy as good (3–5 on a 5-point scale for Gale *and* 10–14 (the top rating) on an 18-point checklist for O'Gorman). These studies are described in Table 6.2.

Of these eight studies, Gale rated six as supporting the Eysenck hypothesis whereas O'Gorman regarded the outcome in only three studies as supportive of the hypothesis. They both agreed that the results in the study by Broadhurst and Glass (1969) were contrary to the hypothesis.

The first three studies listed (Deaken & Exley, 1979; Gale, Coles, & Blaydon, 1969; and Savage, 1964) are those that both reviewers agreed support the hypothesis. Note that two of them used either all female subjects (Savage) or a preponderance of females (Gale et al.) whereas the third (Deakin and Exley) had an equal number of men and women and was the only one of the eight to look for sex differences. Females were more highly aroused than males on the EEG measure. Three different versions of Eysenck's scales (MPI, EPI, and PEN) were used to define the personality dimensions. In the studies by Savage and Gale et al., all subjects were tested while lying on a couch with eyes closed, but Gale recorded during alternating periods of eyes opening and closing on command. In both studies, differences in arousal between introverts and extraverts were found in a low-stimulation eyes-closed condition. All studies found evidence of higher arousal in introverts than in extraverts but not always using the same EEG index of arousal. In the Savage study they found an interaction of extraversion and neuroticism, but no relation between EEG indices and neuroticism or psychoticism, was found in the Deakin and Exley study. Gale felt there was support for Eysenck's hypothesis in the outcomes of the next three studies (Pawlik & Cattell, 1965; Rösler, 1975; Winter, Broadhurst, & Glass, 1972), but O'Gorman did not. Both Gale and O'Gorman must have rated the Pawlik and Cattell study highly on the basis of the EEG methodology, but the psychometric methods and procedures are dubious to this writer. Cattell's objective measures of personality rather than Eysenck's tests were used, and the results were based on a factor analysis with far too few subjects, yielding a factor dubiously labeled "extraversion" with minimal loadings from any EEG variables.

What distinguishes the experiments in Table 6.2 with positive results from those with questionable, negative, or reverse outcomes? It is not methodology because all studies in the table were judged adequate in this respect. It is not the psychometric aspects because all of these studies except the one by Pawlik and Cattell used one of Eysenck's tests, either the MPI, EPI, or PEN. All three experiments with unambiguous positive outcomes

Table 6.2. Studies regarded as relatively more methodologically sound in reviews by Gale and O'Gorman

Authors	n's, sex[a]	Test[b]	EEG criteria	Conditions of EEG testing	Arousal[c]	
Both agree results support hypothesis, extraverts less aroused						
Savage (1964)	20F, 0M	MPI	alpha amplitude	lying on couch, eyes closed	1	1
Gale et al. (1969)	19F, 5M	EPI	theta, alpha, beta	lying, eyes closed and open	2	2
Deaken & Exley (1979)	48F, 49M	PEN	alpha amplitude	seated, group, eyes closed	2	3
Gale says supports hypothesis, O'Gorman says does not						
Pawlik & Cattell (1965)	26F, 39M	O-A	alpha indices	seated, eyes closed/open, tasks	1	—
Winter et al. (1972)	7F, 24M	EPI	alpha indices	seated, eyes closed/open, task	3	—
Rosler (1975)	0F, 32M	EPI	alpha, beta, theta	7 conditions, resting to task	4	—
Both agree results do not support hypothesis						
Gale et al. (1971)	0F, 60M	EPI	10 EEG f ranges	lying, eyes closed, tones	1	1
Both agree results in opposite direction to hypothesis (extraverts more aroused)						
Broadhurst & Glass (1969)	8F, 43M	MPI	alpha indices	rest, task	3	5

[a]M = males, F = females
[b]MPI = Maudsley Personality Inventory; EPI = Eysenck Personality Inventory; PEN = *psychoticism, extraversion, neuroticism* (early version of EPQ); O-A = Cattell's Objective-Analytic test battery
[c]Ratings of arousal believed to be induced by procedures. The first numerical rating is by Gale on a 1 to 3 scale, the second is by O'Gorman on a 1 to 5 scale. O'Gorman did not rate studies that used more than one condition.
Source: Gale (1983) and O'Gorman (1984)

used one of these tests, so it is not the particular form of the Eysenck tests used. It is not the kind of recording condition because differences in accord with the hypothesis have been found under all levels from least arousing to most arousing. There is some indication that studies using a predominance of females or at least an equal number of females and males yield more positive results than those using only males or a predominance of males. *Neuroticism* has been found to interact with *extraversion* in three studies, and in one study they showed independent effects. However, the direction of N effects is also inconsistent, some showing higher and some lower arousal for high N subjects. If these are the best studies from a methodological viewpoint, one must conclude that there is little support for the cortical arousal hypothesis of extraversion.

Using the larger subset of studies, O'Gorman (1984) tested Gale's hypothesis suggesting a curvilinear relationship between arousal level and outcome and could find no evidence for the hypothesis in this metaanalysis. Relationships between both Gale's and O'Gorman's ratings of methodology did not correlate significantly with rated outcomes of studies.

O'Gorman and Malisse (1984) designed a study to test Gale's hypothesized interaction between arousal conditions and E, also attempting to satisfy Gale's criteria for methodological purity as closely as possible. Although Gale (1984) regarded this as an "excellent study," he criticized the tasks used as ad hoc. O'Gorman and Malisse used six tasks, two designed to produce low, two to produce medium, and two to create high levels of arousal. Measures of alpha activity before and after each of the conditions were assessed.

Extraverts had higher amplitude alpha activity (less arousal) than introverts, but when N was used as a covariate the effect of E was no longer significant for the prestimulus values. Apparently the effect of N was a magnification of E differences; and when it was removed, differences between extraverts and introverts were not found.

The extraverts showed marked increase in arousal during the third task, requiring the opening and closing of eyes. This is the task that Gale said should reveal the greatest difference between introverts and extraverts, but in this study extraverts were more, rather than less, aroused during this procedure whereas they tended to be less aroused than introverts on all other tasks. Mean levels of alpha activity over all conditions showed significant positive correlations between both pre- and poststimulus alpha levels and extraversion. The data tend to suggest a general relationship between extraversion and low cortical arousal, but the effect seems to depend on an interaction with *neuroticism*. Gorman and Malisse suggest that the arousal dimension is most closely related to the dimension running from introverted *neuroticism* to stable *extraversion*.

Thompson and Mueller (1984b) compared introverts and extraverts on EEG and autonomic reactivity before and during sleep. They predicted that introverts would show more disturbed sleep than extraverts, as indicated by more stage changes, more body movement, and more stage 1 sleep compared with deeper sleep stages. None of these predictions was supported by the data. If arousal differences between introverts and extraverts exist, they may depend on some minimal level of arousal during waking.

Impulsivity, sensation seeking, and EEG measures of arousal

In his review of the literature, O'Gorman identified the validity of test instruments as a source of differences in outcomes of EEG studies of the personality-arousal hypothesis. Although various forms of Eysenck's E measure have been used to test the hypothesis, most studies had not looked into the question of whether a broad E trait or narrower traits such as *sociability, impulsivity,* or *sensation seeking* are related to cortical arousal.

O'Gorman and Lloyd (1987) used the EPQ *extraversion* scale, consisting mainly of sociability items, and the S. B. J. Eysenck and H. J. Eysenck (1977) *impulsivity* scale. The latter measure is scorable for broad *impulsivity* (total score), narrow *impulsivity* (reacting quickly without thinking), risk taking, and nonplanning. EEGs were recorded during a baseline period with eyes closed and an eyes open and closed condition thought by Gale to be optimal for yielding differences on E. E and broad impulsivity did not affect alpha activity. There were significant effects for the narrow impulsivity dimension plus an interaction of sex, personality, and frequency band. The narrow impulsives were less aroused, particularly among the females. In the eyes open and closed condition, high impulsives of both sexes showed more power in alpha (less arousal) than lows. This study suggests that *impulsiveness* of the narrow type rather than *sociability* may have been the aspect of E actually related to arousal in older studies, in which both contributed to an overall E score. However, narrow impulsivity is related to both P and N and sometimes to E as well. O'Gorman and Lloyd also looked at the P dimension and found that it was not independently related to cortical arousal but did increase the relationship between narrow impulsivity and alpha.

Goldring and Richards (1985) examined the relationship between cortical arousal and E, N, P, and *sensation seeking* (SS). Univariate correlations between these traits and alpha frequency or ratio measures of tonic arousal were not significant. However, P correlated with low reactivity in the alpha and slow EEG bands, and *sensation seeking* correlated with smaller evoked potentials to a single intensity of a visual stimulus. A factor analysis of measures was interpreted as supporting the view that P and SS correlate with a dimension of low cortical arousal-arousability. However, most of this relationship seemed to be accounted for by the P rather than the SS variable. Cox (1977) found no differences due to *sensation seeking* or *socialization* for EEG frequencies in the theta, alpha, and beta bands.

Anxiety and EEG measures of arousal

We have seen that the N dimension has been related to cortical arousal in some of the studies discussed; usually, but not always, N has been associated with increased arousal or an interaction with E in producing arousal. Trait anxiety is strongly associated with N and therefore might also be expected to affect EEG activity. As Eysenck (1967) pointed out, the limbic system sources of emotional responsivity activate the cortex through collaterals to the ARAS, and (as discussed in chapter 5), the noradrenergic system also stimulates cortical activity directly. Trait and state anxiety must be distinguished because one or the other may be related alone to EEG arousal. The direction of the relationship between cortical arousal and subjective state anxiety is open to question. If people become anxious because they are cortically aroused, then reducing cortical arousal will also reduce anxiety. Biofeedback experiments may provide some answers here.

Valle and DeGood (1977) studied the relationship between trait and state anxiety and enhancement or suppression of alpha activity in a biofeedback experiment. Subjects with low trait and state anxiety scores were better than high anxiety subjects at suppressing alpha but did not differ from highs in enhancing alpha. But pre- to postsession changes in state anxiety were not related to direction or success of alpha control.

Plotkin and Rice (1981) gave alpha training to subjects who were high or low on trait anxiety. Although biofeedback training reduced state and trait anxiety, the magnitude of anxiety reductions were unrelated to direction or magnitude of changes in alpha activity during training. The subjects' feelings of competence at controlling their internal states were more related to change in anxiety than their actual success in altering cortical arousal.

Hoffman and Goldstein (1981) investigated the effect of "primal therapy" (a kind of emotional release therapy) on EEG activity, comparing a group who reached high emotional intensities during therapy sessions with a low emotional response group. The group who had intense release of emotions during the sessions showed reduced arousal, particularly in the right hemisphere.

The research discussed in this section suggests some relation of anxiety or emotionality to cortical arousal, but the precise nature of the relationship is unclear. Anxiety may either enhance or reduce alpha activity, perhaps through an indirect effect of attention to external stimuli or attention turned inward toward the subjective state. Changing the emotional state through environmental manipulation may affect cortical arousal, but changing cortical arousal through biofeedback does not have predictable or direct effects on the emotional state. But perhaps "cortical arousal," like the general "arousal" construct, is too broadly defined to be useful in the study of personality. If this is true, then perhaps "cortical arousability," as measured by cortical evoked potentials, may be a more useful concept because the stimuli can be more precisely defined than the situations used in cortical arousal studies.

Averaged evoked potentials (EPs)

Measuring cortical response to a discrete stimulus is difficult using the raw EEG record. What is typically seen is a temporary blocking of alpha activity and a period of irregular, fast, low-voltage activity before alpha returns. The duration of the interruption has been used as a measure of the orienting reflex (OR); it is associated with engagement of attention by the stimulus. If the same stimulus is presented a number of times and the EEG is digitized at a fixed rate, time-locked to stimulus delivery and averaged across repeated trials, the trial-to-trial "noise" is averaged out and the resultant wave form shows a clearer and more regular picture of the characteristic response to the particular stimulus. The wave form over a 500 millisecond (msec) period is called the "averaged cortical EP" or the "visual evoked potential" if elicited by light stimulation (brief flashes) or is called the "auditory" or "somesthetic" EP depending on the particular type of eliciting stimulus. Figure 6.5 shows an example of a visual EP with particular peaks of positivity (P) and negativity (N) identified. A positive peak (P1), for instance, typically occurs at 100 msec after a light flash, though individual latencies may range from 70 to 140 msec and depend on recording sites. Latency and amplitude of a peak may also vary with the stimulus intensity as shown. A peak of negativity typically occurs at 150 msec. Amplitudes of particular peaks can be measured from baseline or as a difference score such as N1-P1.

Buchsbaum and Silverman (1968) developed a function using the EP that measures the relationship between stimulus intensity and EP magnitudes for individual subjects. This function, described as *augmenting-reducing*, has assumed a major importance in research on personality and psychopathology (Buchsbaum, Haier, & Johnson, 1983; Zuckerman, Buchsbaum, & Murphy, 1980). Visual, auditory, or somatosensory EPs are typically recorded at a vertex location for the active electrode, and EPs are averaged for four or five intensities of stimulation. The EP amplitude-stimulus intensity slope is calculated for the P1-N1 component of the wave form using one of several methods. The slope measure for any subject expresses the extent to which the stimulus intensity-cortical response function follows a positive linear pattern (augmenting) or shows a negative pattern with reducing of amplitude of response as stimulus 'intensities increase. If reduction occurs, it typically occurs at the highest

Group EP Curves-Visual ISI 17"

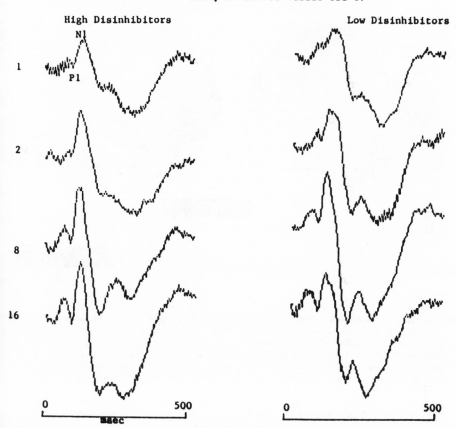

Figure 6.5. Illustrations of visual evoked potentials at different stimulus intensities. P1 and N1 peaks are indicated. These EPs are actually averaged at each point in time over a group of individuals (high and low scorers on the *disinhibition* subscale of the SSS) but illustrate typical individual EP patterns for each intensity of light flash. (From "Sensation seeking and stimulus intensity as modulators of cortical, cardiovascular, and electrodermal response: A cross-modality study," by M. Zuckerman, R. F. Simons, and P. G. Como, 1988, *Personality and Individual Differences*, 9, p. 367. Elmsford, N.Y.: Pergamon Press. Copyright 1988 by Pergamon Press. Reprinted by permission.)

intensities of stimulation. Persons with near zero slopes are often placed with reducers in analyses of data. Although the augmenting-reducing distinction is stated as a type dichotomy, it is usually measured as a continuous dimension.

In the method of *electroencephalographic tomography,* EPs are recorded from different scalp sites, and the recordings are computer analyzed to give the relative amplitudes of response in digital or pictorial form on a lateral picture of the brain. This technique provides a more differentiated

Augmenter   Reducer

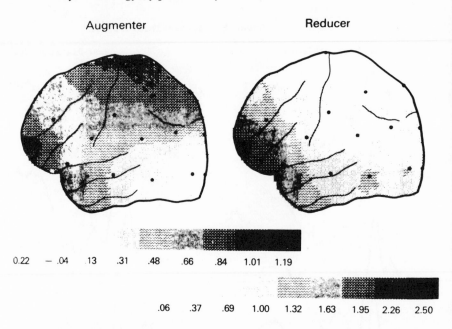

0.22   − .04   .13   .31   .48   .66   .84   1.01   1.19

.06   .37   .69   1.00   1.32   1.63   1.95   2.26   2.50

Figure 6.6. Topographic map of augmenter and reducer subjects chosen on the basis of vertex (Cz) recorded amplitude-intensity slopes. Lighter areas represent low or negative slopes (reducing) and darker areas represent high slopes (augmenting). Numbers on scale in microvolts/log foot lambert show the midpoints of the range for each shade of gray. Note central and superior parietal location of amplitude-intensity slope differences between augmenters and reducers. Occipital area, which actually has larger amplitude, does not show especially high slope values in either subject. (From "Augmenting and reducing: Individual differences in evoked potentials," by M. S. Buchsbaum, R. J. Haier, and J. Johnson, 1983, in *Physiological correlates of human behavior*, vol. 3, p. 130, A. Gale and J. A. Edwards, Eds. London: Academic Press. Copyright 1983 by Academic Press. Reprinted by permission.)

analysis of cortical response to specific stimulation. It has confirmed that the best site for eliciting augmenter-reducer differences is the vertex site (Buchsbaum et al., 1983), as shown in Figure 6.6.

Genetic analyses of evoked potentials

The evoked potential to any given stimulus is a complex wave form that is partly determined by the characteristics of the stimulus, the recording site, and the individual characteristics of each person's cortex. The wave forms for most identical twins tend to be remarkably alike, as shown in Figure 6.7 from the study by Buchsbaum (1974).

Lewis, Dustman, and Beck (1972) correlated the wave forms within pairs of twins and age-matched unrelated individuals. The latter constitute an important control because part of the similarity in wave form is a function of a general stimulus effect common to all subjects. The correlations for

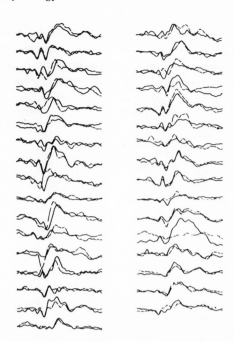

Figure 6.7. Averaged visual evoked potentials of pairs of identical twins, with one twin shown as a solid line and the other twin as a dotted line. (From "Average evoked response and stimulus intensity in identical and fraternal twins," by M. S. Buchsbaum, 1974, *Physiological Psychology*, 2, p. 367. Copyright 1974 by American Psychological Association. Reprinted by permission.)

identicals were significantly higher than those for fraternal twins and the unrelated pairs for both visual and auditory EPs, and for early and late EP wave components. The differences between the fraternal twins and the unrelated subjects were significant only for the auditory EPs. The same direction of differences was seen for the somatosensory EPs, but in this case the differences in group correlations were not significant, suggesting less genetic control of somatosensory than of visual or auditory EPs.

Rust (1975a) compared identical and fraternal twins on auditory EPs in response to a 95-decibel (dB) tone. Heritabilities were assessed using the methods of Jinks and Fulker (1970). Heritabilities of latency measures ranged from 58 to 81% and those of amplitude measures from 82 to 89%. As the author points out, generalization from the study is limited because only one stimulus was used, and a rather intense one at that.

Buchsbaum (1974) studied the heritability of the visual EP within his paradigm of *augmenting-reducing* described earlier in the methods section. Table 6.3 shows his calculated heritabilities for mean amplitudes and amplitude-intensity slope measures of augmenting-reducing for different peaks. In almost all cases the correlations for identicals were higher than

Table 6.3. *Correlations of identical twins (IT) and fraternal twins (FT) on mean amplitudes and amplitude-intensity slopes (augmenting-reducing) for different P-N components, mean deviations from baseline in different time bands and for different points in post-stimulus time*

	Mean amplitude			Amplitude–intensity slope		
	rIT	rFT	h^a	rIT	rFT	h^a
Visual inspection						
P100–N140	.59	.36	.35	.51	−.04	.52[b]
N140–P200	.57	.10	.52[b]	.56	−.10	.60[b]
Mean deviation (msec)						
76–112	.39	−.04	.41[b]	.51	.00	.51[b]
116–152	.57	.17	.46[b]	.60	.28	.44[b]
168–248	.38	−.03	.39[b]	.51	.06	.47[b]
Point-by-point						
68	.19	.44	−.44	.22	.02	.20
84	.34	.17	.20	.56	.04	.54[b]
100 (P100)	.51	.10	.45[b]	.71	.09	.68[b]
116	.54	.48	.11	.59	.39	.32
140 (N140)	.43	.57	−.32	.69	.27	.57[b]
172	.49	.20	.36	.30	.05	.26
204 (P200)	.43	.14	.33	.72	.36	.56[b]
228	.59	.21	.48[b]	.76	.14	.72[b]

[a]Heritability formula was calculated: $h = (r\text{IT} - r\text{FT})/(1. - r\text{FT})$
[b]Indicates IT–FT correlation difference significant, $p < .05$, one-tailed
Source: "Average evoked response and stimulus intensity in identical and fraternal twins" by M. S. Buchsbaum, 1974, *Physiological Psychology*, 2, p. 368. Copyright 1974, Physiological Psychology. Reprinted by permission.

those for fraternal twins, and the correlation for fraternal twins were close to zero, suggesting epistasis or a configural polygenetic mechanism for spectrum measures (Lykken, 1982). Estimates of heritability based on visual inspection and mean deviation methods, using the identical twin correlations as a maximum estimate, suggest heritabilities of about 50%, considerably lower than those obtained from frequency spectrum analyses. The point by point comparisons identify the highest and most significant heritabilities for mean amplitude measures at P100 and P228. For the amplitude-intensity slope, measures of the highest heritabilities were found for P100, N140, P200, and P228. Comparing intensities of stimulation for heritability showed that the brightest light intensity had the highest heritability.

Perhaps Rust's use of a high auditory intensity was a serendipitous methodology accounting for his higher heritabilities than those in the Buchsbaum study. With the exception of his results, it would seem that though EPs show significant heritability, they do not show as near complete genetic determination as do EEG spectrum measures. Arousal may be more genetic than arousability. This is not surprising because response measures may depend on stimulus and subject-state factors, such as voluntary attentiveness, that are less important in the basal recording conditions.

Biochemical correlates of augmenting-reducing of the EP

Negative correlations between platelet MAO levels and augmenting of visual EPs have been found in patient groups (Buchsbaum, Landau, Murphy, & Goodwin, 1973) and in students showing evidence of milder affective disorders (Haier, Buchsbaum, Murphy, Gottesman, & Coursey, 1980) but not in more normal students in the latter study. Von Knorring and Perris (1981) contrasted augmenters and reducers defined by the EP method on various enzyme and neurotransmitter metabolites. Visual EP augmenters in psychiatric patient and chronic pain patient groups were characterized by lower levels of CSF 5-HIAA (the serotonin metabolite), HVA (the dopamine metabolite), and endorphins (endogenous opiatelike substances) than reducers. CSF MOPEG, an NE metabolite, was not related to the cortical arousability measure. Von Knorring, Perris, and Ross (1980) have also found that visual EP augmenters have lower levels of serum DBH than reducers. The results are interesting in regard to the trait of *sensation seeking* (SS) because SS has been found to be negatively related to MAO and DBH (chapter 5). Sensation seekers also tend to be augmenters, suggesting a biochemical link between the trait and cortical reactivity.

The correlational results linking serotonin (through its metabolite 5-HIAA) to reducing of the EP were reinforced by experimental findings by von Knorring and Johansson (1980). These investigators gave zimelidine (a selective inhibitor of serotonin uptake) and imipramine (which affects both noradrenergic and serotonergic systems) to normals and examined the effects on the visual EP. Zimelidine, but not imipramine, reduced the amplitude-intensity slope of the P1–N1 component of the EP. Increasing availability of serotonin at the synapse increased EP reduction.

Extraversion, neuroticism, psychoticism and the cortical evoked potential (EP)

Stelmack (1981, 1990) has written brief reviews of the relation between *extraversion* and cortical EPs. The results are complicated, varying as interactive functions of subjects' ages, personality, and the characteristics of the stimuli used to evoke the cortical responses. Ashton, Golding, Marsh, and Thompson (1985) compared EPQ scores with a later component of the somatosensory EP (N1P2). P, E, and N scores were not significantly correlated with either latency or amplitude EP measures, though the correlations tended to be negative for P and E. Mauhauser, Ehmer, and Eckel

(1981) correlated EPI scores and an anxiety measure from the Fear Survey Schedule (Wolpe & Lang, 1964) with somatosensory EPs at N1, P1, and N2. Although E did not correlate with EP measures, N and anxiety scores correlated positively with peak latencies.

Hendrickson (1973) found significant negative correlations between E and amplitude of the auditory EP to 1,000-Hz, 60-dB tones, but Rust (1975b) could not replicate these results in either of two studies using 55-, 75-, and 95-dB tones. The correlations between E, N, P, and state anxiety scores and seven EP measures were almost all close to zero.

Stelmack, Achorn, and Michaud (1977) reported more positive findings relating auditory EPs to *extraversion*. Introverts had greater amplitudes of EPs than extraverts for low-frequency tones (500 Hz), but there were no differences for the high-frequency tones (8,000 Hz). Stelmack (1981, 1990) hypothesized that low-frequency tones are more differentiating because they elicit more amplitude and greater subject variation in EPs. He interpreted the findings as supporting the Eysenck hypothesis of greater arousability in introverts than in extraverts. The limitation of the finding to moderate range low-frequency tones is problematical. The 1,000-Hz tones used by Hendrickson (1973) and Rust (1975a) are certainly closer to the lower of Stelmack's frequencies than the higher one, and yet Rust could not replicate the relationship between *introversion* and EP amplitude found by Hendrickson.

The P300 (P3) is thought to reflect some attentional processes more directly than earlier components. It is enhanced by novelty, surprise, or unexpectedness of the stimulus event and reflects the allocation of attentional resources to the stimulus. Whereas the P1 represents a passive reaction to the stimulus, the P3 reaction involves cortical engagement with the stimulus. Because introverts perform better than extraverts on tasks requiring vigilance, they might also be expected to show an enhanced P3 when required to discriminate among tones in a long series. Daruna, Karrer, and Rosen (1985) tested this hypothesis and found that introverts had higher amplitudes of EP response for the P3 than extraverts even when N and anxiety levels were controlled by covariance.

Stelmack and Wilson (1982) studied the relationships among E, frequency, and intensity of auditory stimuli and the brainstem EP. The earlier components of the EP are thought to be of subcortical origin. Auditory EP components with latencies of less than 3 msec probably originate in the cochlear nerve (peak I); those that have latencies between 3 and 10 msec are believed to arise from brainstem nuclei (peaks II to IV) between the cochlear nucleus and the lateral lemnisci or the pons (peak V). In the first study, introverts had longer latencies for 500-Hz tones whereas extraverts had longer latencies for higher frequency (2,000 and 4,000 Hz) tones for the peak V component. No amplitude effects were found.

Monaural clicks were used instead of tones in a second experiment.

Intensity levels ranged from 50 to 90 dB in steps of 5 dB. Significant effects due to E were found for the wave V latency: Extraverts had longer latencies than introverts at all levels of intensity except 90 dB. Stelmack interprets these findings as evidence for personality differences in the sensitivity of the auditory system, extending down the brain stem.

Campbell, Baribeau-Braün, and Braün (1981) failed to find any relationship between auditory-evoked brainstem potentials and E for any levels of stimulus intensity and concluded that the differences found for cortical EPs are not due to brain stem influences. Stelmack and Wilson (1982) claimed that Campbell did not use a sufficiently extreme extraversion group.

Szelenberger (1983) also studied the auditory brainstem EP using schizophrenics and normal male controls tested on the EPQ. Although extraversion showed some positive correlations with EP latencies, the positive correlations between the P scale and EP latencies and interpeak conduction times were particularly significant, especially for the earlier components (II and III peaks and I to II peak conduction times). Stelmack did not report on results for P. Szelenberger suggests that P is related to strong inhibition at the subcortical level. Although one might expect to find cortical inhibition in subjects scoring high on E or P, the evidence of subcortical inhibition seems paradoxical. If the findings in Stelmack's studies are reliable, they suggest a broader type of neural inhibition than the cortical one hypothesized to be associated with *extraversion*.

Augmenting-reducing of the EP and E, N, and P sensation seeking and impulsivity

Zuckerman, Murtaugh, and Siegel (1974) related scores on the *sensation seeking* scales (SSS) to augmenting of the visual EP in response to a range of stimulus intensities. The EPI was also given to the subjects in the experiment and scored for E and N. Of the four SS subscales, only *disinhibition* was significantly correlated with the slope measure of EP augmenting. E and N scales from the EPI were not correlated with EP augmenting. The high and low scorers on the *disinhibition* scale were compared on the EP amplitudes over the five intensities of stimulation, as shown in Figure 6.8. Although they did not differ in EP magnitudes at the lowest stimulus intensity, high disinhibition subjects showed a general augmenting of the EP, particularly at the highest stimulus intensity; and lows showed little augmenting over the first four intensities and a marked reduction of EP amplitude at the highest intensity. These results are in accordance with the Buchsbaum (1971) hypothesis.

This initial finding has been replicated many times, as described in a recent review (Zuckerman, 1990a). Figure 6.9 shows one result with the

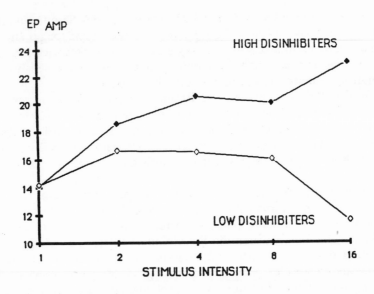

Figure 6.8. Mean visual evoked potential amplitudes (P1–N1) at five levels of light intensity for low and high scorers on the *disinhibition* subscale of the *sensation seeking* scale. (From "Sensation seeking and cortical augmenting-reducing," by M. Zuckerman, T. T. Murtaugh, and J. Siegel, 1974, *Psychophysiology*, 11, p. 539. Copyright 1974 by the Society for Psychophysiological Research. Reprinted by permission.)

auditory-evoked potential. The studies constitute fairly robust results linking *sensation seeking,* particularly of the *disinhibition* variety, to augmenting of visual (five studies) and auditory (seven studies) EPs, with failures of replication in two studies for each modality. The results are even more impressive when one considers the variety of EP methods, subject populations, and the translated scales used in Sweden and the Netherlands. The robustness of the finding in spite of procedural differences strengthens the connection and the theoretical arguments underlying it (Zuckerman, 1986). The relevance of the paradigm to Pavlov's construct of *strength of the nervous system,* which is defined by the phenomenon of transmarginal inhibition and which represents the capacity of the nervous system to respond to high intensities of stimulation, has been pointed out (Zuckerman, 1984a; Zuckerman et al., 1974). The biochemical data, discussed in a previous section, suggest that the neurotransmitter serotonin and the endorphins may influence the reduction process.

Barratt, Pritchard, Faulk, and Brandt (1987) found a relationship between *impulsivity,* particularly "cognitive impulsiveness," and augmenting of the visual EP. Impulsiveness versus lack of restraint seems to be a major component of the behavioral differences seen in augmenting and reducing cats, as next described.

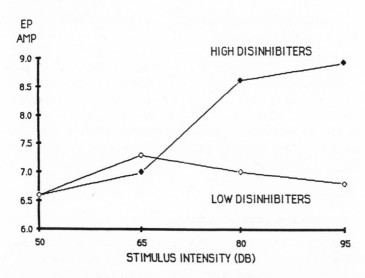

Figure 6.9. Mean auditory evoked potential amplitudes (P1–N1) at four levels of sound intensity (50–95 dB) for low and high scorers on the *disinhibition* subscale of the *sensation seeking* scale. (From "Sensation seeking and stimulus intensity as modulators of cortical, cardiovascular, and electrodermal response: A cross-modality study," by M. Zuckerman, R. F. Simons, and P. G. Como, 1988, *Personality and Individual Differences*, 9, p. 368. Elmsford, NY: Pergamon Press. Copyright 1988 by Pergamon Press, Reprinted by permission.)

EP augmenting-reducing in cats and its behavioral correlates

Further evidence of the adaptive biological significance of the augmenting-reducing paradigm comes from studies of EP augmenting and its behavioral correlates in cats. Hall, Rappaport, Hopkins, Griffin, and Silverman (1970) classified cats as augmenters or reducers on the basis of their visual EPs and compared the two groups on their reactions to the sudden presentation of novel and/or frightening stimuli. EP augmenting was positively related to ratings of exploration, activity, and aggressiveness, but its relationships with fear, rage, and excitability were nonsignificant. Reducer cats showed more withdrawal than augmenters. A study by Lukas and Siegel (1977) found more activity and exploration, as well as emotional fight-flight responses to a threatening stimulus in augmenter than in reducer cats. Saxton, Siegel, and Lukas (1987) essentially replicated earlier results showing that augmenter cats were more behaviorally active, tended to show more exploratory behavior, and approached the novel stimuli. In this study, however, the reducer cats were more emotional and tense and reacted more strongly to the threatening stimuli, tending to withdraw.

The cats in this study were then tested in two experimental paradigms: a simple fixed interval (FI) bar-pressing task for food reward and a differential reinforcement for low rate of response (DRL) bar-pressing task, in which a failure to inhibit response delayed reinforcement. Augmenters adapted more quickly to the test chamber, and reducers took longer to habituate to the novel situation. Augmenters learned the FI task more quickly and were rated as overall more proficient in the task. However, reducers were better on the DRL task because they were more able to inhibit bar pressing in periods when it was penalized by a delay of reinforcement. They took less time to learn the task and made fewer errors (i.e., pressing the bar when it was nonadaptive). These results suggest that augmenting cats, like sensation-seeking humans, may be good at tasks in which their explorativeness and general activity are adaptive but poor at tasks requiring inhibition.

Contingent negative variation

Contingent negative variation (CNV) is another kind of event-related potential discovered by Walter, Cooper, Aldridge, McCallum, & Winter (1964). In many EP experiments, slow potentials are filtered out of the EEG record. Walter et al. allowed these low-frequency drifts to appear in the record in an experiment in which a *warning stimulus* (S1) was followed by an *imperative stimulus* (S2) that was the signal for a subject to press a key. The investigators noticed a slow increase in negativity at the vertex scalp location that appeared just before the button press. Averaging of at least several stimulus presentations clarified the form of this potential. It was maximal over the frontal cortex, and though it reached maximal amplitude after 20 trials, it did not habituate over hundreds of trials. The magnitude of response was related to the speed of reaction times.

The CNV has been shown to occur in two waves, given an adequate interstimulus interval between S1 and S2: an *orienting* (O) reaction to the initial stimulus and an *expectancy* (E) or "readiness for reaction" response to the imperative signal (Loveless & Sanford, 1974; Weerts & Lang, 1973). Extraverts show a sensitivity of reaction to the stimulus-and-response demands of the situation whereas introverts fail to shift from the orienting to the response-readiness mode when the circumstances call for it (Janssen, Mattie, Plooij; van G.P.C. & Werre, 1978). O'Connor (1982, 1983) has shown that in extraverts the frontal CNV E-wave amplitudes are increased by smoking (nicotine-stimulated arousal) and by a signal-detection task whereas in introverts the E waves decreased in these conditions. The O wave, in contrast, decreased in extraverts during arousal and remained unchanged in introverts. O'Connor interpreted these results as suggesting that increased arousal reduces orienting and increases action-readiness in extraverts whereas introverts continue to scan and remain restrained. Auditory stimulation also increases the E wave and distraction reduces the O wave in extraverts (Dincheva, Piperova-Dalbokova, & Kolev 1984). The idea of differences in arousal is too simplified to account for the data. It is the relation of arousal to attention and response demands in the context of the situation rather than the absolute magnitudes of general arousal or arousability that differentiate extraverts from introverts.

Neuroticism interacts with *extraversion* in the CNV (Lolas & de Andracca, 1977; Lolas & Anguilear, 1982; Ploog-van Gorsel, 1981). The involvement of *neuroticism* or *anxiety* with the CNV depends on the type of stress and whether the stress is connected with the stimuli or not. Stress, particularly on ego-involved tasks, seems to reduce the CNV in high N subjects and reflects disruption of the attentive or learning process (Glanzman & Froelich, 1984; Rizzo et al., 1984). However, if the CNV stimulus itself is the signal for the onset of stress, and if the high N subjects have learned the association, their enhanced attention may be reflected in a high CNV amplitude (Proux & Picton, 1984).

Positron emission tomography

Positron emission tomography (PET) is a technique that enables analysis of brain responses at all levels, not just cortex, and from more localized brain areas than by EEG methods. A radioactively tagged glucose analog is injected into the subject and is taken up by the brain during the next 35 minutes. The structures of the brain that are most active during that time interval absorb the most glucose, which remains stable in those areas for several hours. The glucose emits positrons that decay into gamma rays at 180° angles. The subject's head rests in a PET scanner which contains a ring of crystals that detects the gamma rays. A computer translates the data from "slices" of the brain that cut across structures at various depths. The computer generates images of the brain or digital data showing activity in "pixel boxes" (Figure 6.10) and calculates the mean glucose metabolic rate within each box or area of the brain. Areas of the brain within one or more boxes can be identified with particular brain structures by using standard reference points. Statistical analyses can be done using the absolute glucose rate within a box or the relative rate calculated by dividing the mean rate within a box by the whole slice rate. The relative rate controls for large individual differences in brain glucose use. However, the absolute rate may be more appropriate in testing a general arousal hypothesis such as the one for extraversion.

The first study using the PET scan to study personality was reported by Haier, Sokolski, Katz, and Buchsbaum (1987). The subjects were 18 outpatients suffering from generalized anxiety disorder and 9 normal controls. Only the data from the anxiety patients are reported, and even these must be regarded as tentative pending enlargement of the sample and the study of an adequate number of normals for comparisons.

Little correlation was found between *extraversion* and glucose use in a nontask condition; but in a stressful condition (a difficult signal-detection

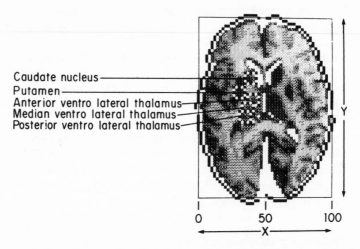

Figure 6.10. Region-of-interest box analysis from the *positon emission tomography* (PET) scan: A digitized "slice" from the brain atlas corresponding to supraventricular level. Glucose use is determined within boxes and for the whole brain areas corresponding to particular clusters of boxes as indicated. (From "The study of personality with positon emission tomography," by R. J. Haier, K. Sokolski, M. Katz, and M. S. Buchsbaum, 1987, in *Personality dimensions and arousal*, p. 255, J. Strelau and H. J. Eysenck, Eds. New York: Plenum Press. Copyright 1987 by Plenum Press. Reprinted by permission.)

task) *extraversion* correlated positively with absolute glucose use in frontal and temporal cortex and also with glucose uptake in caudate, putamen, cingulate, hippocampal, and parahippocampal areas of the right hemisphere. The laterality of the limbic relationships was quite striking. *Neuroticism* showed little correlation with either cortical or limbic system arousal. P showed negative correlations with glucose use in cortex, particularly occipital, and thalamic and cingulate areas of the limbic system.

The results with *extraversion* were surprising because Eysenck's theory predicts that introverts are more cortically aroused and arousable than extraverts. However, the subjects all had anxiety disorders, and the correlations with extraversion emerged only during performance of a stressful task. The data could indicate stronger task coping in the extraverts than in the introverts, though the correlations with limbic structures could also indicate stronger emotional arousal. The lack of relationship with *neuroticism* is surprising because Eysenck's theory predicts a stronger limbic arousability in neurotics. However, the fact that these were all anxiety neurotics might account for the negative results in terms of a limited range of *neuroticism;* all subjects must have been high N scorers.

Cerebral blood flow

Cerebral blood flow (CBF) is a means of measuring cortical arousal that takes advantage of the relationship in the normal brain between blood flow and function. One method is to have the subject inhale xenon–133 mixed with air through a face mask for 1 minute. The rate of removal of the radioactive isotope from various parts of the brain is traced by a system of 16 scintillation counters mounted in a helmet and applied to the scalp for 10 minutes. Grey-matter blood flow is computed for eight areas in each hemisphere.

CBF, extraversion, and neuroticism

Mathew, Weinman, and Barr (1984) studied the relationships between CBF, using the xenon-inhalation technique, and *extraversion* and *neuroticism* scales in a sample of 51 normal females. Measurements were made in low-arousal conditions with subjects lying with eyes closed in a semi-darkened, quiet room. One would guess that the low level of stimulation may have been partly offset by the possibly frightening procedure involving breathing treated air through a face mask. The investigators say that none of the subjects became drowsy. E correlated negatively with CBF values in all cortical areas in both hemispheres. Although the correlations were not high ($-.24$ to $-.41$), all were significant. These results are more in line with Eysenck's theory suggesting a negative relationship between general cortical arousal and *extraversion*.

Spinal motoneuronal excitability

Although almost all current theories assume that the primary relationships between personality and arousability of neurons are limited to the central nervous system (CNS), this is not necessarily so. *Extraversion* might be related to some general property of neurons that is true for those in the peripheral sensory-motor system as well as those in the CNS. This possibility is highlighted by the study of Pivik, Stelmack, and Bylama (1988). These investigators applied stimulation to the posterior tibial nerve in the leg and recorded potentials from the medial gastrocnemius-soleus muscle group. Threshold and maximum values were obtained for direct and reflex responses, and variations in reflex responses were studied yielding measures of reflex amplitude recovery. Personality groups did not differ on sensory-threshold measures, but high scorers on the *extraversion* scale of the EPQ and the *disinhibition* scale of the SSS showed reduced motorneuronal excitability relative to low scorers on these scales, as measured by the analysis of reflex recovery functions. The authors suggest that because increased dopaminergic activity is associated with decreased motorneuronal excitability, both extraverts and disinhibitors might have increased dopaminergic activity. Although the functional significance of reduced motoneuronal excitability for extraverts or sensation seekers is not surmised, the authors suggest that the emphasis on *sensation seeking* or *sensitivity* in both dimensions of personality could be mistaken. Extraverts and introverts and high and low sensation seekers may differ more in motoric expressiveness (activity?) than in sensitivity or need for stimulation.

Summary

Studies of brain activity using PET-type methods have not given conclusive findings applicable to Eysenck's hypotheses on the cortical arousal basis of *extraversion* or the limbic arousal basis of *neuroticism*. In fact, the Haier et al. (1987) and Mathew et al. (1984) studies yielded different results. However, the differences may be due to different PET methodologies, the different conditions in the experiments, or the differences in subject populations. Stelmack's studies on spinal motoneuronal reactivity, like his studies on the auditory brain stem EP, suggest that differences related to *extraversion* or *disinhibition* can be produced by more generalized neuronal characteristics rather than being limited to cortical neurons.

Peripheral autonomic measures

The distinction between activity in central and peripheral autonomic systems based on the loci of psychophysiological recording (cortical versus peripheral sites) is not entirely tenable because the brain ultimately regulates peripheral autonomic functions, and the higher cortical centers have a marked influence on autonomic functioning in an awake person. Some indices such as palmar skin conductance (SC) seem to be directly related to cortical events and general cortical arousal though they may become disassociated in some conditions such as sleep and sensory deprivation.

In a general sense, the sympathetic nervous system (SNS) and parasympathetic nervous system (PNS) branches of the autonomic nervous system (ANS) are antagonistic in function. The PNS maintains the steady state in the internal environment necessary for internal processes such as digestion and elimination, and the SNS diverts the body's resources to the brain and peripheral musculature and instigates certain preparatory defensive mechanisms such as vasoconstriction of small blood vessels close to the surface of the skin. SNS function represents a preparation for active coping and activity, but it can be instigated by cortical activity in situations in which there is no obvious environmental instigation. SNS activation normally inhibits PNS activity though there may be compensatory rebound effects in PNS activity, as when fear-stimulated SNS activation constricts the bladder and bowel sphincters and a compensatory surge of PNS activity relaxes them, producing an embarrassing incontinence. This is why defecation provides a reliable index of fearfulness in rodents. These two systems and their functions are contrasted in Table 6.4 and Figure 6.11.

Table 6.4. *Comparisons between functions of the sympathetic and the parasympathetic nervous systems*

	Sympathetic	Parasympathetic
Function	Catabolism	Anabolism
Activity	Diffuse, long-lasting	Discrete, short-acting
Anatomy		
Emerges from spinal cord	Thoracolumbar	Craniosacral
Location of ganglia	Near spinal cord	Near target organs
Postganglionic neurotransmitter	Noradrenaline[a]	Acetylcholine
Specific actions		
Pupil of eye	Dilates	Constricts
Lacrimal gland	—	Stimulates secretion
Salivary glands	Scanty secretion	Profuse secretion
Heart rate	Increase	Decrease
Contractility of heart	Increase	—
Blood vessels	Generally constricts[a]	Slight effect
Bronchial tubes of lungs	Dilates	Constricts
Sweat glands	Stimulated[a]	—
Adrenal medulla	Secretes adrenaline and noradrenaline	—
Male genitals	Ejaculation	Erection
Motility and tone of G.I. tract	Inhibits	Stimulates
Sphincters	Stimulates (contracts)	Inhibits (relaxes)

[a]The postganglionic SNS neurotransmitter is acetylcholine for most sweat glands and some blood vessels in skeletal muscles. The adrenal medulla is innervated by preganglionic cholinergic sympathetic neurons.
Source: *A primer of psychophysiology*, by J. Hassett, 1978, p. 14. New York: W. H. Freeman. Copyright 1978, W. H. Freeman and Company. Reprinted by permission.

The most common neurotransmitter for the SNS is norepinephrine (NE) and that for the PNS is acetylcholine (ACh), but there are notable exceptions. For one, the preganglionic fibers for the SNS use ACh for a neurotransmitter. For another, the SNS pathway to the sweat glands is mediated by ACh neurons, and the sweat glands are entirely under SNS control. The adrenal medulla is innervated by ACh fibers, but its secretory cells are adrenergic and release NE and epinephrine (Epi), which further increase and prolong the SNS reaction. Epi increases heart rate and constricts peripheral blood vessels, two ANS reactions.

Electrodermal activity

Activity in the sweat glands has been an important source of data for psychophysiologists because of their sensitivity to arousal from both external and internal stimuli and from general emotional arousal. Eccrine

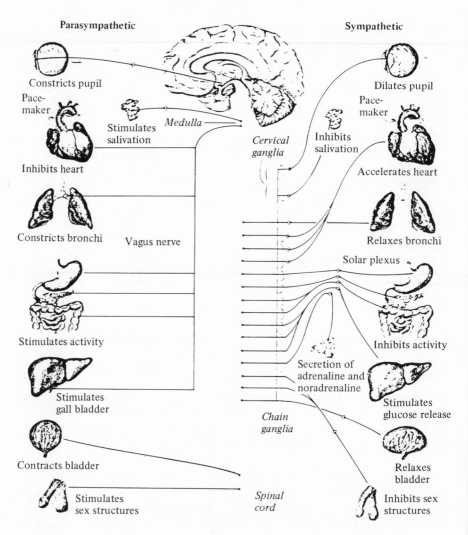

Figure 6.11. The autonomic nervous system. (From instructional transparency made for psychology courses. Newton, MA: Allyn and Bacon. Reprinted by permission.)

sweat glands are found in most areas of the body, varying in concentration from the densely populated sites of the palms of the hands and the soles of the feet to less populated sites such as the back. Although all sweat glands respond to temperature and emotional arousal, those on the palms and soles seem particularly sensitive to environmental stimuli and emotional arousal. Evolutionists have speculated that this emotional response was adaptive to ancestors of hominids who lived in trees where climbing was a vital reaction to threat from predators. Moisture facilitates grip,

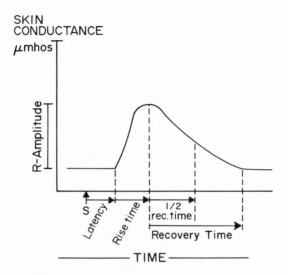

Figure 6.12. A skin conductance response

making a climber less likely to slip. Even in human history one can see the value of an emotion-sensitive palm for other activities such as holding clubs or swords. The palm is useful for measuring ANS-related reactions. The more commonly used method for assessing electrodermal activity (EDA) is to attach two electrodes filled with an electrolyte to the palmar surface of the hand or the fingers and measure the resistance to a small electrical current passed between the electrodes. Resistance is decreased as a function of the filling of the sweat ducts in the skin under the electrodes. Skin conductance (SC) is the reciprocal of skin resistance (SR).

Tonic and *phasic* indices must be distinguished in all psychophysiological methods. Tonic measures reflect relatively slow-changing events; phasic ones reflect more transient changes that rise and subside in relatively short periods of time. In EDA, skin conductance level (SCL) is a tonic measure that reflects the slow changes in resistance to an electrical current in prolonged response to a situation or internal level of activation. SCL is minimal during sleep. A skin conductance response (SCR) is a phasic reaction to a specific stimulus as pictured in Figure 6.12. The reaction occurs in two phases, a slow rise and a recovery to SCL baseline, which can be fast or slow. Measures of response include amplitude (prestimulus baseline to peak of response), frequency of response, onset latency, and recovery time (peak to post stimulus baseline). Amplitude of the SCR is directly related to stimulus intensity, and reactions are usually stronger to the first presentation of any stimulus and habitutate with repetition of the stimulus.

SCRs may appear as fluctuations in the SCL when there are no apparent changes in the external environment, as when the subject is sitting in a

Table 6.5. *Intraclass correlations and biometric modeling results from identical twins reared together (ITt) identical twins reared apart (ITa), and fraternal twins reared together and apart (FT)*

Variables[a]	n's	Correlations			Variance (%)		
		ITt	ITa	FT		Environmental	
		36	43	42	Genetic	Shared	Unshared
Slope	.72	.54	.05	70.3[a]	5.2	24.5[a]
Y-intercept	.69	.53	−.05	64.0[a]	3.8	32.2[a]
X-intercept	.47	.16	.25	21.7	18.5	59.8[a]
Trials	.42	.43	.13	40.7[a]	0.0	59.3[a]
SCR (raw)	.62	.52	.10	59.1[a]	0.0	40.9[a]
SCR max	.45	.37	.13	56.0[a]	0.0	44.0[a]
Y-int (r-c)	.64	.61	.34	59.2[a]	5.8	35.0[a]
SCR (r-c)	.66	.58	.35	54.1[a]	11.1	34.8[a]

Note: Unshared environmental variance includes variance due to both measurement error and trait instability. Slope, Y-intercept, and X-intercept are parameters of the habituation curve; trials is number of trials to two consecutive zero responses; SCR max is the subject's largest SCR; SCR (raw) is the mean of the first 4 SCRs in conductance units; SCR (r-c) is the raw SCR range, corrected by dividing by that subject's SCR max.
[a]Significantly different from zero at $p < .05$ by likelihood ratio test.
Source: "Habituation of the skin conductance response to strong stimuli: A twin study" by D. T. Lykken et al., 1988, *Psychophysiology*, 25, p. 9. Copyright 1988 by The Society for Psychophysiological Research. Reprinted by permission.

soundproof recording chamber during a baseline recording. These have been called spontaneous skin conductance responses (SSCRs) or nonspecific SCRs. The rate of SSCRs during a period of time can be regarded as another type of tonic arousal measure for that period. SSCRs can occur in response to internal stimuli in the form of cognitive activity or the release from cortical inhibition during deep sleep.

Genetics of EDA

Lykken, Iacono, Haroian, McGue, and Bouchard (1988) used an EDA paradigm consisting of a series of 17 presentations of a 105-dB tone. SCR levels were corrected for the individual ranges of response. The Y intercept, a measure of initial arousal, correlated highly with the habituation regression slope. The X intercept and trials required to extinguish the SCR response were regarded as better measures of habituation. Table 6.5 shows the correlations of the various measures in identical twins raised together and apart, fraternal twins raised together, and proportions of variance attributed to genetic and environmental sources.

Genetic variance was significant for all EDA variables except the X intercept. Unshared environment was significant for all variables, but shared environmental variance was not significant for any. However, these group data conceal a vital sex difference. When the identicals reared together and apart were analyzed by gender, the males reared apart were either not different in correlations or the separated twins showed *higher* correlations. However, the female twins reared apart showed much lower correlations than those reared together, suggesting that EDA responsivity may be more influenced by shared environment in women than in men.

The two measures showing the strongest genetic influence were the slope ($h = 70\%$) and Y intercept ($h = 64\%$) measures of initial EDA response. Trials to habituation and the X-intercept measure of habituation showed much lower heritabilities.

Tonic levels of EDA and personality

Although the EEG may be the more appropriate measure for testing theories of extraversion, peripheral autonomic SNS measures are best for testing Eysenck's (1967) idea that *neuroticism* or trait anxiety reflects a high level of tonic activity in the SNS. Reviews of the literature relating tonic EDA (SCL and SSCLs) to *neuroticism* or trait anxiety have been universally negative (Fahrenberg, 1987; Hodges, 1976; Naveteur & Baque, 1987) despite the fact that patients with anxiety disorders do show differences from normals on SNS measures (chapter 8). Eysenck and Eysenck (1985) acknowledged this general failure of prediction but suggested that differences between high and low N subjects might be found if aversive stimuli or situations were used.

Fahrenberg (1987) described two large-scale studies in which EDA (SSCRs) and other physiological measures were taken in resting basal conditions and in various stressful circumstances including mental arithmetic, interview, cold-pressor test, preparing a free speech, anticipation, and blood taking. Some of these represent physical stress and others social stress of the type that would be expected to relate most highly to N. In the study by Fahrenberg, Walshberger, Foester, Myrjok, & Müller (1983), all of the psychophysiological criteria variables increased for the total group in at least two of the four stress conditions, and four of them increased significantly in all conditions; but questionnaire scales of neuroticism and somatic complaints were unrelated to EDA or other physiological measures in any of the conditions. Such results suggest that the lack of findings on tonic measures of EDA cannot be attributed to lack of stress in experimental situations.

Smith (1983) reviewed studies of EDA in relation to *extraversion*. Although some studies have reported a higher rate of SSCRs in introverts than in extraverts, an equal number have found no differences in this measure of tonic EDA arousal. Most studies have found no differences on SCL between extraverts and introverts in baseline conditions, but some interesting interactions between SCL and conditions suggest support for the inverted-U hypothesis of the relationship between E and arousal. Low-intensity stimuli and less-arousing conditions (Fowles, Roberts, & Nagel, 1977) or placebo conditions (Smith, Wilson, & Jones, 1983) do not reveal differences between extraverts and introverts in SCL; but loud tones, difficult learning tasks (Fowles et al.), and large doses of caffeine (Smith et al.) produce higher levels of SCL in extraverts than in introverts. As with CNV results, extraverts and introverts do not differ much during baseline conditions, but extraverts tend to show more arousal in response to intensive stimulation, stress, and stimulant drugs.

Similar mixed findings have resulted in analyzing tonic SCL and *sensation seeking*. Smith, Perlstein, Davidson, and Michael (1986) and Stelmack, Plouffe, and Falkenberg (1983) found higher SCLs in high sensation seekers than in lows during visual or auditory presentations of word stimuli but not during presentations of other types of stimuli. However, most studies have found no differences in SCL during any type of stimulus conditions (Zuckerman, 1990).

Phasic EDA and personality

The reviews by Hodges (1976) and Naveteur and Baque (1987) are just as negative for attempts to relate trait or state anxiety to phasic EDA as for tonic EDA. Despite findings of differences in magnitude of the electrodermal orienting response (OR) in anxiety patients (who show a weaker initial OR but delayed habituation), O'Gorman's (1977) review found little effect of trait anxiety in normals on habituation of the SCR. Orlebeke and Feij's (1979) review also found little evidence relating trait anxiety scores to the OR amplitude in normals. Neary and Zuckerman (1976) found no influence of trait anxiety on initial SCR or habituation, but subjects high in state anxiety showed weaker initial OR's in reaction to novel auditory stimuli than those low in state anxiety just prior to the experiment.

Failures to find similar results in anxiety patients and high trait anxiety nonpatients may be due to the fact that nonpatients are not anxious on most occasions. Under sufficient stress all subjects may show equivalent increases in state anxiety. The differences between high and low trait anxiety may only appear in situations that specifically affect those high in trait anxiety.

Stimulus characteristics are important in the comparison of introverts and extraverts on the EDA OR. Stelmack's (1981, 1990) reviews of the literature suggest that auditory stimuli of low-frequency (200–500 Hz) and moderate intensity (75–90 dB) are most likely to reveal differences in OR magnitude between introverts and extraverts. Wigglesworth and Smith (1976) have shown an interaction between E and stimulus intensity on the effect of the first auditory stimulus on the SCR (Figure 6.13). At the

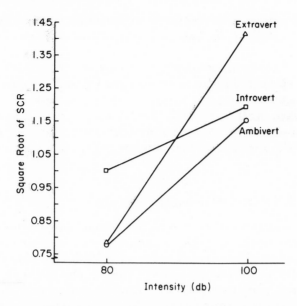

Figure 6.13. The effect of stimulus intensity on skin conductance response for extraverts, introverts, and ambiverts. (From "Habituation and dishabituation of the electrodermal orienting response in relation to extraversion and neuroticism," by M. J. Wigglesworth and B. D. Smith, 1976, *Journal of Research in Personality*, 10, pp. 437–445. Copyright 1976 by Academic Press. Reprinted by permission.)

moderate level of 80 dB, introverts showed the stronger OR; but at the higher level of 100 dB, extraverts had a stronger OR. Ambiverts reacted like extraverts to the 80-dB stimulus but like introverts in response to the 100-dB stimulus.

Neary and Zuckerman (1976) found that high sensation seekers showed stronger intial SCRs to a simple visual stimulus than lows. As soon as the stimulus was repeated, the SCR of the high sensation seekers dropped to the level of the lows; but after 10 presentations, when a new visual stimulus was presented, the difference reappeared. The authors concluded that highs differed from lows only in response to a novel stimulus. Similar results were found in a second experiment in response to auditory (70-dB tone) as well as visual stimuli. Feij, Orlebeke, Gazendam, and van Zuilen (1985) reported a low positive but significant correlation between the general SSS and the magnitude of the initial SCR in response to an 80-dB auditory stimulus. Subsequent studies by Ridgeway and Hare (1981) and Zuckerman, Simons, and Como (1988) failed to replicate the EDA-SS relationship. However, Smith et al. (1986) contrasted the SCRs of high and low sensation seekers to loaded and neutral words (spoken), scenes (slides), and videotapes. The loaded stimuli were relevant to sensation seeking themes. High sensation seekers showed stronger initial SCRs than lows in response to loaded stimuli, but the groups did not differ in response to neutral stimuli.

The research on tonic and phasic EDA suggests that differences in personality interact with differences in the situation and stimulus characteristics and meanings, but the nature of the interactions is not always predictable from the theories of the personality traits. One cannot always predict in advance how arousing a particular situation is or how much arousal potential a specific stimulus has, and many of the conclusions seem post hoc.

Cardiovascular and respiratory measures

In ancient times the heart was considered by many philosophers to be the seat of the emotions, probably because it is the internal organ whose changes are most salient during states of intense emotion. Changes in breathing patterns are also conspicuous during intense emotional states. However, the primary functions of the cardiovascular and respiratory systems are not to express emotions but to keep the various parts of the body supplied with oxygen and nutrients and to remove waste products. Homeostatic regulation of the functioning of these organs is essential to regulation of the internal milieu and adaptation to changing conditions in the environment. Sympathetic system arousal prepares the organism for coping with environmental challenges with increased brain and muscle activity. Apart from speeding heart rate, there is a general reallotment of resources favoring the peripheral parts of the body such as head, arms and legs rather than the central organs such as the intestines. Increased blood pressure and blood flow in the limbs and vasodilation of blood vessels leading to the peripheral muscles are part of this generalized pattern of emergency response. Under stress or anticipated stress, the heart pumps faster and harder, moving more blood under higher pressure. Because breathing is reflexly linked to heart action, an increase in one produces an increase in the other.

Subjective sensations of intense anxiety or fear usually involve the sensation of heart or respiratory changes, though the reverse is not always true. An increase in heart rate may be interpreted as an appropriate response to exercise or as a symptom of a cardiac malfunction rather than as the experience of an emotion such as fear. Awareness of emotional change need not depend on discriminable changes in heart or respiratory rates, and sensitization to such internal changes may be a characteristic not highly associated with the neuroticism or the readiness to experience anxiety states.

The electrocardiogram (EKG) can be recorded from electrodes placed on the surface or sides of the chest or the limbs of the body. The recordings

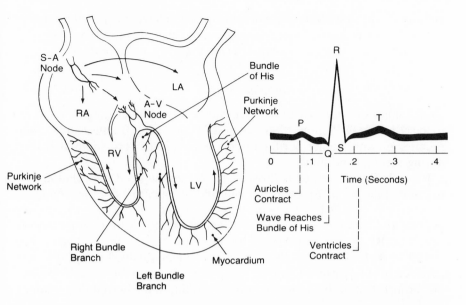

Figure 6.14. EKG wave-form and electrical events in the heart. (From *A primer of psycho-physiology*, p. 57, by J. Hassett, 1978. San Francisco, CA: W. H. Freeman & Co. Copyright 1978 by W. H. Freeman & Co. Reprinted by permission.)

show a characteristic pattern (Figure 6.14) with particular peaks representing specific electrical events in the heart during a single heart beat. Heart rate can be recorded over a specified period of time by simply counting the R spikes during that period, usually expressed as a per-minute rate. However, phasic changes in heart rate require a beat-by-beat measure of rate. The rate can be expressed either as interbeat intervals, or the intervals can be converted to rate as beats per second.

Blood pressure (BP) is the force built up in the arteries when the blood encounters resistance in the peripheral circulation. BP peaks during the contraction of the heart, or its systole, and is at a minimum during the period when the heart relaxes before the next beat, its diastole. The sphyg-momanometer is a device commonly used to measure BP. An inflatable cuff is attached around the upper arm and inflated until it cuts off the circulation of the blood. The cuff is slowly deflated until the sound of the blood can just be heard in a microphone or stethoscope pressed to the artery just below the cuff. The systolic BP is read from a pressure gauge at this time. The deflation of the cuff is continued until the blood sounds disappear completely, indicating that there is no further interference with the flow of blood, and the pressure is less than the diastolic BP.

Respiration is most commonly measured by a stretchable strain gauge strapped around the chest or abdomen or both. The inhalation and ex-halation movements are displayed on a polygraph as changing resistance measures. The amplitude and rate of respiration have been used as indices of emotional changes. Some investigators have measured oxygen consumption using a closed system covering the nose and mouth.

Genetics of cardiovascular measures

Twin studies of tonic heart rate have shown heritabilities ranging from .40 to .60 (Boomsa & Plomin, 1986; Lader & Wing, 1966). Boomsa and Plomin found somewhat higher heritabilities when subjects were stimulated than during resting conditions.

Rose, Miller, Grim, and Christian (1979) investigated the relations between systolic BP in 76 identical twins and 610 members of their families. Correlations of BPs for the twins was .72, for siblings it was .23, and for parents and children it was .26. The regression of offspring on midparent values for BP, a direct estimate of heritability assuming an additive genetic model, was .40. However, this estimate was nearly halved when BPs were adjusted for body size. Midparent-offspring regression for diastolic BP was .42; adjustment of this value for body size reduced the heritability estimate to .36.

The ranges of heritabilities for cardiovascular measures are about the same as those for personality traits. Boomsa and Plomin (1986) concluded that genetic factors do not play a role in the relationships between cardiac and personality trait measures. By inference we might conclude that neither cardiovascular nor personality measures have a genetic priority in explaining the origins of differences in anxiety proneness.

Tonic cardiovascular and respiratory measures and personality

Hodges (1976) found no more evidence for the relation of cardiovascular measures to anxiety than for electrodermal measures, though under some circumstances (e.g., Hodges & Spielberger, 1966) a trait measure that was consistent with the situation in which psychophysiological responses are assessed (e.g., fear of shock predicting HR in a shock-threat situation) may predict the physiological response. Fahrenberg's (1987) studies included heart rate, finger pulse volume, and respiratory irregularity in rest and various kinds of stress situations. Trait measures of emotionality failed to predict any of the physiological responsiveness.

The experiments by Myrtek (1984) used a personality inventory containing scales for *extraversion* and *emotional lability (neuroticism)* that correlated highly with corresponding E and N scales of Eysenck's tests, and other scales such as *aggressiveness* and *inhibitedness* that might assess the P dimension. He also included a somatic complaint scale and state affect or mood measures and behavioral (activities) self-report measures. Over 700 subjects, in seven groups of normals and two groups of cardiovascular patients were run, providing more than ample chance for replication of results. Experimental situations included rest, hyperventilation, a reaction-time task, multiple reaction, a cold-pressor, and performance stress tests. Many cardiovascular and respiratory measures were used. Before the experimenters compared personality and physiological measures, factor analysis was used to combine variables within each of the domains. The mean correlations between personality variables and physiological scores were about .08 for single scores and .10 for factor scores, and there were few significant correlations that could be replicated across samples. The general conclusion was that there is no systematic variation between personality traits and cardiovascular or respiratory measures in any of the situations from rest to stress.

In contrast to the generally negative results attempting to relate tonic levels of heart rate (HR) to personality, Kagan and his colleagues (Kagan, Reznick, Clarke, Snidman, & Garcia-Coll, 1984; Kagan et al., 1988) have found that young children characterized as "inhibited" or "shy" showed higher and less-variable HRs during various conditions than children described as "noninhibited" and characterized by spontaneous interaction with others, positive mood, and approach behavior. HRs at both 21 and 48 months were related to this personality pattern, and HR at 21 months actually predicted the behavior pattern at 48 months. Kagan has related these differences in HR to Lacey's (1967) idea of HR deceleration as indicative of an attitude of "environmental intake" and HR acceleration as related to an attitude of "environmental rejection." At the level of the trait, Kagan identifies the behavior pattern with *introversion-extraversion,* though the "shyness" component of *introversion* suggests that the dimension may run from *neurotic-introversion* to stable *extraversion.* It may also have some relevance for *disinhibition* trait.

Another study showing some predictive power for HR was reported by Vaillant and Schnurr (1988). In a longitudinal study of college men, initially screened for mental or physical health problems, pulse rate during a physical exam in college correlated with subsequent diagnostic status and general adult adjustment when the men were 30 to 47 years of age. High pulse rate was associated with poorer adjustment 15 years later. Although the correlations were not high (about .25) they were highly significant and as high as the correlations between personality ratings in college and subsequent adult adjustment.

In contrast to the generally negative results for Western personality measures, positive findings for the reactivity dimension (Strelau, 1983) in relation to electrodermal and respiratory measures have been reported by Klonowicz (1987). High "reactives" showed higher levels of EDA SSCRs, ventilation, oxygen consumption, respiratory quotients, and energy consumption than low reactives under resting conditions. Because Strelau's reactivity questionnaire measure seems to be a combination of E and N, with high reactives being low on E and high on N, it may be that Western investigators should look more carefully at combinations of E and N rather than examining each variable independently as is usually done. A contrast between neurotic *introverts* and stable *extraverts* might show greater difference in tonic levels of arousal.

Phasic heart rate and personality

The SCR to discrete stimuli were partly successful in distinguishing introverts and extraverts and high and low sensation seekers, though results seemed to depend on certain characteristics of the stimuli and their meanings. The cardiac phasic response to discrete stimuli offers a greater potential for assessing individual differences. Because of the biphasic nature of the beat-by-beat cardiac reaction to stimuli, one can distinguish between orienting, defense, and startle reflexes (Graham, 1979). Cardiac deceleration in response to stimuli is considered an orienting reflex (OR). Maximal response is usually on the first presentation of a stimulus of moderate intensity. In response to subsequent stimulus presentations the OR shows rapid habituation if the stimulus is a simple one. Defensive reflexes (DRs) are characterized by cardiac acceleration and are produced by stimuli of higher intensity. Habituation to a DR should be slow or even absent. Startle reflexes (SRs) are also characterized by HR acceleration, though of shorter latency than DRs. SRs also depend partly on the unexpectedness as well as the intensity of the stimulus. According to Graham, the OR is "input enhancing." It reflects the attention to the focal stimulus and constitutes the first phase of information processing. The defensive response is called "output enhancing" and reflects the readiness for action or motor activity. If the stimulus is aversive, for instance, the DR would reflect the incipient tendency to flee or avoid it. The SR is an interruptive pattern of generalized response characterized by flexor movements. Perhaps it is closest to the concept of anxiety because it reflects a hyperexcitability of the nervous system. Anxiety neurotics tend to startle at all kinds of unexpected or loud stimuli. The SR, in contrast to the DR, shows rapid habituation.

Orlebeke and Feij (1979) studied the HR phasic characteristics in subjects responding to a series of five tones of 60-dB intensity and 1,000-Hz frequency. Both high N and high E subjects showed more HR deceleration than low N and low E (introverts) subjects over the first five trials. The high E subjects showed less acceleration of HR in the second phase of the response. In another study, the authors selected subjects who were high or low on a Dutch translation of the *disinhibition* (Dis) subscale of the SSS. Subjects received a series of ten 80-dB, 1,000-Hz tones. Figure 6.15 contrasts the phasic HR responses of high and low disinhibitors averaged over the first three trials. The high Dis subjects showed more immediate and stronger deceleration to the stimulus than those scoring low on Dis.

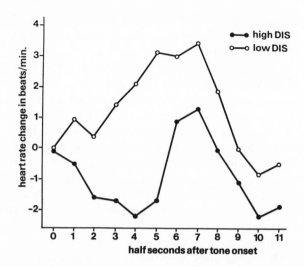

Figure 6.15. Phasic heart-rate responses (averaged for first three trials) of subjects scoring high or low on the *disinhibition* subscale of the *sensation seeking* scale. (From "The orienting reflex as a personality correlate," by J. F. Orlebeke and J. A. Feij, 1979, in *The orienting reflex in humans*, p. 579, by H. D. Kimmel, E. H. van Holst, and J. F. Orlebeke, Eds. Hillsdale, NJ: Erlbaum. Copyright 1979 by L. Erlbaum Associates. Reprinted by permission.)

The low Dis subjects showed an accelerative response beginning about 1 second after the stimulus, peaking about 3.5 seconds after the stimulus, and then declining to baseline and slightly below. The differences between the groups disappeared by the third trial as the OR habituated.

These results were essentially replicated by Ridgeway and Hare (1981) using a 60-dB stimulus tone, and Zuckerman, Simons, and Como (1988) using stimuli ranging from 55 to 90 dB. High sensation seekers, particularly of disinhibiter type, manifest a strong cardiac orienting response to auditory stimuli of low to moderate intensities whereas low sensation seekers tend to show defensive or startle reactions (cardiac acceleration) to either moderate or intense auditory stimuli. These differences are found only on the first or first few presentations of the stimulus and they quickly habituate.

Blood pressure and hypertension

Essential hypertension is a disorder for which both biological and psychological etiologies have been hypothesized. Tonic levels of systolic blood pressure (SBP) and diastolic blood pressure (DBP) are normally distributed in the population. Although transient elevations of blood pressure (BP) can be produced by physiological and environmental stressors or by activity, in some significant proportion of the population these reach tonic levels that pose serious health problems. Reliable individual differences in BP may be associated with other biological or personality traits. Elevated BP may be a function of high levels of noradrenergic activity. Lake et al. (1981) found that patients with essential hypertension had higher levels of norepinephrine (NE) in cerebrospinal fluid than normal controls though they were not higher on plasma NE. The β-adrenergic blocking drugs such as propranolol are used in the treatment of hypertension to reduce BP. Such drugs also have anxiety-reducing effects, and anxiety may accompany elevated BP in some cases of hypertension, so it is possible that chronic anxiety may be a personality factor involved in hypertension.

Experimental studies have shown that psychological stressors like ego-attack or frustration may produce elevations in BP that are more quickly reduced by the expression of aggression either verbally or physically against the instigator. Conceivably, persons who never respond to attack or frustration with open expressions of anger might be vulnerable to hypertension. However, nonpsychological factors, such as age, gender, weight, use of alcohol or other drugs, and a genetic disposition toward the disorder, must be considered either separately or in interaction with personality and gender factors (Russo & Zuckerman, 1988).

Schalling and Svenson (1984) compared groups selected from a population of 18-year-old draftees in Sweden and defined as "hypertensives," "normotensives," and "hypotensives" on the basis of BPs measured during a preinduction physical examination. These labels were not clinical diagnoses and described only the relative BP on the single occasion. Hypertensives scored higher than normotensives on several types of anxiety trait scales and on a scale measuring inhibition of aggression or assertiveness. Hypotensives were higher than normotensives on scales measuring aggression and hostility and lower than normotensives on a socialization scale, but they did not differ significantly from hypertensives on any of these scales. The results suggest a nonlinear relationship between BP and some personality traits. The normotensive group was lower than those with either high or low BPs on all of these scales except socialization, on which they were higher. The hypertensive group was characterized by the highest levels of anxiety, but the hypotensive group was intermediate rather than the lowest on this trait. The hypotensive group was characterized by high levels of aggression and hostility and antisocial tendencies, with the hypertensive group intermediate on these traits.

Interestingly, the hypertensives had significantly higher unpleasantness ratings of medical-pain situations. Because the BPs were obtained during a medical examination by a strange doctor, the BPs could represent phasic reactions to the situation rather than characteristic tonic BPs. Von Knorring et al. (1984) found a low but significant negative correlation between sensation seeking and blood pressure during a medical exam given to Swedish army inductees. Carrol et al. (1982) found that low sensation seeking volunteers for an experiment had higher BP readings than high sensation seekers when BP was taken during a medical examination by a physician, but no differences were found between groups on BP readings taken by a nurse on subsequent days.

Because BPs taken by a strange physician may be reactive rather than representing natural tonic levels, some investigators have used ambulatory monitors to record BPs in natural settings or trained subjects to record their own BPs during the day. Both SBP and DBP were reportedly higher after reported states of anger and anxiety than after happiness, and anxiety states had a greater effect on BP at work than at home (James, Yee, Harshfield, Blank, and Pickering, 1986). BP also varied with intensities of emotional states, but in two different directions for positive and negative affect. Anxiety intensity was associated positively with BP whereas degree of happiness was correlated negatively with BP. This is an example of affect-response specificity.

Schneider, Egan, Johnson, Drobney, and Julius (1986) studied students defined as borderline hypertensives on the basis of a single screening BP at a university clinic. Subjects were trained to take their own BPs and then took them three times a day at home over a period of at least one week. They were divided into two groups: one whose mean BP readings were equally as high in the home as in the clinic and another whose BP taken at home was in the normal range. The consistently high BP group (home and clinic) had higher scores than the group with normal home BPs on reported intense angry feelings and reactions to time pressures. The consistent hypertensives also scored higher on the Spielberger, Johnson, Russell, Crane, and Worden (1984) anger-in scale but did not differ from the normotensive home group on anger-out or total anger expression.

Gerardi, Blanchard, Andrasik, and McCoy (1985) found that consistent or generalized BP responders scored higher than either office or home responders on scales of hostility and trait anger, but the groups did not differ from them on anxiety or depression trait scales. In both studies anger tended to be associated with elevated BP only in groups in which the BP was consistently elevated in both home and clinic situations.

The second approach to studying the personality correlates of hypertension is the observation of persons at genetic risk for the disorder because of a family history of hypertension. Epidemiological evidence shows a substantially increased risk of hypertension among those with at least one hypertensive parent (Paffenberger, Thorne, and Wing, 1968; Paul, 1977). Adolescents or young adults with one or two hypertensive parents tend to show greater BP increases than controls without a family history of hypertension during certain types of stress situations, particularly those requiring active coping during difficult timed tasks (Hastrup, Light, & Obrist, 1982; Manuck & Proietti, 1982; Russo & Zuckerman, 1988). Findings on BP increase are less pronounced in women who are at risk by reason of a positive family history (Russo & Zuckerman, 1988). Differences are clearer for BP change scores in response to stress than for tonic baseline measures of BP.

Russo and Zuckerman (1988) compared subjects with positive and negative family histories on BP response to stress and personality traits and states. They found that males with positive family histories of hypertension showed higher SBP and DBP increases in response to performance stress than those with a negative family history. Body mass and reported alcohol use were also related to a positive family history in men, but none of these variables were related to family history in women. In the women, a factor consisting of high scores on measures of neuroticism and anger-in, and a state of dysphoria just prior to the experiment were found in the group with a family history of hypertension. One personality trait was associated with a positive family history in both men and women: trait anger. These results are consistent with previous findings on persons identified as hypertensive on the basis of their current BP levels. Potential hypertensives, even those not clinically diagnosed as such, tend to be angry people who do not seem able to express their anger but turn it inward.

Summary

The concept of arousal as the source of individual differences in temperament or personality provided a bridge between the neo-Pavlovian and Western concepts of the biological basis of personality (Gray, 1964; Eysenck, 1967; Strelau, 1987). Advocates of generalized arousal theory have been undaunted by the psychophysiological evidence of a lack of correlation in degree or even direction of activity in various physiological systems, though such findings pose serious problems for many theories. Some investigators, such as Claridge (1967, 1987), have suggested that the dissociation of arousal itself may be a characteristic of at least one personality dimension. Others, such as Eysenck (1967), proposed that arousal of particular brain systems, reticulocortical and limbic, are related to particular personality traits. The theory of cortical arousal and its relationship to optimal levels of stimulation and *extraversion* is complicated by the phenomena of sensitivity and transmarginal inhibition; whereas introverts may be more aroused by low to moderate intensities, extraverts are more aroused by high intensities of stimulation.

Level of cortical arousal, as assessed by EEG spectrum analysis, shows substantial heritability. But despite this evidence of heritable individual differences in arousal, a substantial body of research relating cortical arousal level to *extraversion* has yielded equivocal results, even when we limit our analysis to the most methodologically and conceptually sound studies. Although differences supporting the hypothesis are frequently found between introverts and extraverts, they are just as often not significant or in the opposite direction to that predicted from theory. Many studies suggest an interaction between *extraversion* and *neuroticism* in cortical arousal.

New methodologies for assessing brain activity provide some hope for clarification of the relationship between cortical arousal and the *introversion-extraversion* dimension (Haier et al., 1987). Preliminary results with positon emission tomography (PET) are inconsistent with respect to the direction of the brain arousal and *extraversion* relationship, and there is little evidence relating *neuroticism* to limbic activation as suggested by the theory. However, like the EEG studies, the results may be complicated by situational factors affecting arousal states.

Cortical arousability, as assessed by cortical reactivity to stimuli of varying intensities, shows more replicability of relationships to some personality traits. Extraverts show smaller amplitudes of evoked potentials (EPs) than introverts in some studies but not in others. The effect depends on certain characteristics of the evoking stimulus such as stimulus frequency and intensity. Buchsbaum (1971) has provided a paradigm for examining individual differences in cortical arousability to a range of stimulus intensities. Cortical "augmenting" or "reducing," using visual or auditory stimuli, has been repeatedly related to the trait of *sensation seeking,* particularly to the subtrait of *disinhibition.* Furthermore, this paradigm has provided one of the rare animal models for psychophysiology. Cats with EP augmenting or reducing traits show behavior suggestive of *sensation seeking* and *impulsivity* or constraint in humans.

Another phasic measure, the contingent negative variation, a slow EEG wave form, has also provided data on the relationship between arousability and personality. Extraverts show a readiness to shift from orienting to preparation for action (expectancy) when the situation demands it, whereas introverts seem less likely to move away from the orienting or observation phase even under response-demand conditions. There are also differences between neurotics and stables in CNV response, though these depend on the type of stress and the association between the eliciting stimuli and the stress. Whereas stress reduces CNV in high N subjects, stress-related stimuli may increase CNVs in this group.

Genetic studies of electrodermal responses show moderate heritability, particularly for measures of initial response to stimulation. Mixed findings characterize the literature of studies contrasting introverts and extraverts on tonic levels of skin conductance (SCL) in unstimulated conditions. As with cortical arousal, the differences related to personality often appear in the contrasting responses under arousal enhancing and basal conditions. Whereas introverts are either lower or the same as extraverts in SCL under basal conditions, intense stimuli or stimulant drugs seem to affect extraverts more than introverts in raising SCL. Contrasts on phasic electrodermal

responses (SCRs) have also produced interactions with stimulus characteristics. When differences are found between introverts and extraverts,
introverts are usually found to give larger SCRs at low to moderate stimulus
intensities and frequencies, but extraverts tend to give larger SCRs to high-
intensity stimuli. Differences are usually found in response to the initial
stimulus presentation when the stimulus is novel.

Like electrodermal phenomena, cardiovascular measures show only
moderate heritability, not much higher than that found for most personality
traits. Despite the saliency of heart and respiration responses to the demonstrated differences between clinically anxious patients (and others) and
the theories linking the N dimension to autonomic system activity, there
is little evidence of a relationship between these variables and N or anxiety
traits in normal adults during periods of rest or stress. However, Kagan
and his colleagues have shown a relationship of HR to a dimension of
inhibition versus *shyness,* probably running from *neurotic introversion* to
stable *extraversion.*

The phasic heart rate response to stimulation has yielded more interesting results relating to the *disinhibition sensation seeking* subscale. High
disinhibiters demonstrate a stronger HR orienting response (deceleration)
in response to novel auditory stimuli of low to moderate intensity. Low
disinhibitors, in contrast, show either a HR defensive or startle reaction
(acceleration of HR) in response to novel auditory stimuli of moderate to
high intensity, or a weaker OR in response to stimuli of low to moderate
intensity. Taken together with the previously discussed findings relating
disinhibition to augmenting of the EP, the psychophysiological findings
suggest that *disinhibition* may have a physiological basis in mechanisms for
stimulus intensity modulation.

Tonic levels of blood pressure are an exception to the general failure of
tonic levels of other cardiovascular measures to show relationships to personality. Although the relationship may not be linear, hypertensives (consistently high tonic levels of BP) typically are characterized by high levels
of anger and hostility traits, combined with a tendency to avoid expression
of anger and to deny aggressive impulses. Heritability of essential hypertension has been demonstrated. What is inherited may include some of
these personality traits and/or a tendency to react to certain types of stress
with exaggerated BP reactions.

Physiological arousal is a function of internal states and the attempts of
the organism to adjust to rapidly changing situations in the external environment. It is the sensitivity of arousal to specific circumstances that
makes it difficult to relate tonic levels of physiological activity to stable
personality traits. As long as we are awake, we are generally responding
to some situation or stimulus. The experimenter defines reclining in a chair
or bed in a sterile laboratory environment as a basal condition, but the
subject may react to such a situation with anything from boredom to panic.

Discrete, nonmeaningful stimuli such as tones provide less ambiguous elicitors of reaction, but the precise qualities of stimuli that will differentiate personality types must be determined. Perhaps the most useful paradigms are those that study the effects of a range of stimulation in every subject, such as Buchsbaum's augmenting-reducing paradigm for the cortical EP. Similar kinds of broad range assessment are needed on the personality side. Increasing evidence suggests that, to the extent that arousal or arousability are related to personality at all, they are related to narrower dimensions than *extraversion, neuroticism,* or *psychoticism,* such as narrow *impulsivity* and the disinhibitory type of *sensation seeking.* This narrowing of the psychophysiologically relevant personality traits is also apparent in regard to conditioning, discussed in the next chapter.

7   Learning

Overview

Learning is involved in nearly all behavior with the exception of simple reflexes, and even these may be modified by the simpler kinds of learning like habituation. Instinctual behavior is often regarded as rigid, stereotyped patterns of behavior that are determined by heredity and unmodifiable by experience. But even in this behavior there is room for some modification in ways of adapting to the immediate environmental circumstances. The organism may not have to learn what its food source is or how to forage, but the way to a particular source at a given time will depend on prior learning.

Learning is the nexus between variations in physiology and individual differences in social behavior. Pavlov described temperamental differences in dogs in terms of their "conditionability," and Eysenck has used this concept to explain differences between introverts and extraverts in social behavior. Many of the major psychobiological theories of personality are also learning theories. Although it is true that the biological aspect of differences in learning have been described largely in terms of a "conceptual nervous system," the models have provided the bases for hypotheses concerning the real nervous system.

This chapter focuses primarily on human research involving personality traits. Some of the learning phenomena in animals have been discussed in chapter 5 on psychopharmacology. Comparative studies have been vital in the basic study of learning, and many of our concepts have been developed from studies of other species; but space in this volume does not allow any comprehensive treatment of this vast research literature. The reader should consult Gray's (1975) book for a general discussion of comparative learning theory and research.

Types of learning

Learning is a general term covering different ways of acquiring information about the world and altering behavior in terms of that information. A somewhat less broad classification contrasts associative learning and non-associative learning. In nonassociative learning, the organism learns about a single stimulus through single or repeated exposures to that stimulus. Associative learning involves either the learning of a predictable relationship between two stimuli (classical conditioning) or the relationship between behavior and its immediate consequences (operant or instrumental conditioning).

Habituation and sensitization are simple forms of nonassociative learning found in all species from the simplest protozoa to humans. Habituation is learning not to respond to a repeated stimulus of no immediate biological significance to the organism. To learn an association to a stimulus, one must be able to attend to that stimulus in preference to competing stimuli in the environment. The novel stimulus commands attention and appraisal, described as the orienting reaction (OR) in the previous chapter. The repeated or constant stimulus loses its ability to command attention unless it becomes conditioned to stimuli of greater significance. Whereas habituation is a mechanism for narrowing the range of stimuli that require response, sensitization broadens the range of effective stimuli. Following the presentation of an intense or noxious stimulus, a sensitized organism shows strong defensive reflex reactions to a wide variety of stimuli, including those that do not normally elicit such responses or those already habituated. The anxiety neurotic or the soldier recently emerged from combat may respond to all kinds of unexpected sounds in a nonthreatening environment with exaggerated startle or protective reactions.

Associative learning in its simplest form has been described in two conditioning paradigms. The English philosophers conceived of learning as the association of ideas, and Pavlov (1927/1960), working with dogs, translated this mentalistic concept into one involving the association of stimuli. Some (unconditioned) stimuli have the innate capacity to elicit a reflexive (unconditioned) response (UCR). If such stimuli are repeatedly paired with a previously neutral stimulus, the now conditioned stimulus (CS) acquires the capacity to elicit a (conditioned) response (CR) that is part of or resembles the UCR. This type of learning is called classical conditioning. Two subtypes of classical conditioning can be differentiated. When the unconditioned stimulus (UCS) is normally rewarding, as is food or water, the conditioning is called appetitive. Conversely, if the UCS is painful or otherwise noxious, the conditioning is called defensive. Food delivered to the tongue is an appetitive UCS eliciting UCRs such as salivation or mouth movements. After a CS, such as a bell or light, is presented a number of times just prior to the UCS, the CS can elicit salivation without the presentation of the UCS. This is an example of appetitive conditioning. A reflexive leg flexion (UCR) is elicited from a dog by a shock admistered to the forepaw (UCS). Pairing of the shock with a previously neutral stimulus such as a bell or light results in the CS eliciting the leg flexion. This latter case would be called defensive conditioning.

It should be noted in these examples of classical conditioning that the

CR was *elicited* by the CS through its association with the UCS. The CR does not determine the consequences of the response. Whether or not the animal lifts its paw does not affect whether it will be shocked. But in instrumental or operant conditioning, the CR is selected from among the natural *emitted* responses of the organism by selective reinforcement. If a rat presses a bar, it will receive a food pellet, but no other response occurring in the situation is reinforced.

The CR is said to be instrumental in obtaining reinforcement or operating on the environment to produce rewarding stimulation. The term *reinforcement* is not synonymous with reward or punishment. Reinforcement is any consequence of behavior that increases the probability of the behavior being emitted again in the situation. Positive reinforcement accomplishes this by the presentation of some stimulus contingent on the response, such as food for a hungry animal. Negative reinforcement increases the frequency of the behavior by removing or delaying a presumably noxious stimulus such as shock. The former kind of learning would be called appetitive, and the latter would be termed avoidance learning. Punishment is a consequence of behavior that decreases the probability of that behavior recurring in the situation.

Extinction describes the tendency of the CR to weaken and disappear with the absence of reinforcement by pairing of CS and UCS in classical conditioning or the omission of the reinforcer after the response in instrumental conditioning.

More complex forms of learning do not fit as easily as habituation or conditioning into the distinction between nonassociative and associative learning. Animals and humans show evidence of observational learning without obvious reinforcement. Animals learn something through exploration of a novel environment that can be demonstrated later when reinforcement is made contingent on demonstrated knowledge of that environment. Humans, primates, and some other organisms can observe the performance of another and imitate it later. To some extent this type of learning may represent the simple transmission of sensory events into long-term memory storage, from which it can be withdrawn on a later occasion for use in guiding behavior. However, memory depends to a large extent on associations and learned significance of stimuli. Associations can be formed between elements of the current situation in particular ways. For instance, a witnessed behavior may be associated with an observed negative outcome or it may not.

Finally, concept learning involves not just the simple registration or association of stimuli but requires the formation of some abstract concept embodied in the relations among stimuli or stimulus elements such as shape, number, form, and color. Because language involves the manipulation of abstract symbols such as words, verbal learning is also abstract learning.

Theories of learning

Pavlovian

Pavlov's theory of temperament began with the observation of individual differences in the conditionability of dogs in his laboratory. However, these differences depended on certain characteristics of the stimuli, such as their strength and novelty, and the situation. Dogs who were active and sociable in their living environment often fell asleep in the conditioning apparatus, and dogs who were fearful and unsociable in their habitat sometimes showed the strongest conditioning because of their hyperalertness. Pavlov found that the former type of dog could be conditioned if the conditioned stimuli were varied to maintain the dog's orienting reactions or attention. There are parallels between this interaction of temperament and environment and the trait of *sensation seeking* related to preferences for novelty and strong ORs in response to novel stimuli.

Strength of the nervous system (SNS) was defined by Pavlov as the working capacity of cortical cells in terms of their ability to function and resist the effects of transmarginal inhibition produced by strong, prolonged, or recurrent stimulation (Strelau, 1983). SNS was assessed in dogs by varying the strength of the CS, the UCS, or increasing excitability of the nervous system by depriving the animal of food or by giving it varying doses of caffeine. The resistance of the CR to inhibition produced by high levels of stimulation or stimulant dosage was used as a definition of SNS. Dogs with strong systems were thought to be those in whom the CR is quickly evoked and stable (resistant to inhibition produced by high stimulation or extinction). Because Pavlov and his students presented data on individual dogs and did not use correlational methods, it is difficult to tell if the various ways of defining SNS were related or how the diagnoses made on the basis of laboratory methods were related to natural behavior outside of the laboratory.

According to Strelau (1983) the method of extinction with reinforcement, first used in Pavlov's laboratory on dogs and later adapted for humans, is still one of the most popular methods of defining SNS in the Soviet Union. In its present use on humans, a CR is established by pairing a UCS and CS. The magnitude of the CR (CR1) is measured in an unreinforced trial. Then the UCS and CS are presented again in a series, and exhaustion is promoted by frequent trials with short rest intervals, high intensity CS or UCS, and/or a great number of trials. After the reinforced series, which are calculated to promote transmarginal inhibition, the CS is presented alone, and the difference between the CR1 and CR2 is measured. The method has been used with photochemical conditioned reflexes, EEG alpha blocking, and skin conductance. According to Strelau's summary of the research literature, the methods of extinction with reinforcement have shown spotty and often unreplicable relationships with other methods of defining SNS. One of the dangers of using a laboratory-defined technique for a trait assumed to have broad behavioral significance is that erroneous theoretical generalizations may be made from what is essentially a highly specific behavioral response. Although the method shows fair retest reliabilities, correlations between identical and fraternal twins suggest little genetic contribution to scores based on this method. Strelau has based his construct of reactivity on the SNS or strength of excitatory processes but has used many other methods to define this dimension, including his own questionnaire method (described in chapter 1).

A new generation of neo-Pavlovians in the Soviet Union in the 1960s began to use the advances in neurophysiology in their theory and methods. The leaders in this movement were Teplov (see Gray, 1964a) and Nebylitsyn (1972). Nebylitsyn emphasized the interaction between frontal cortex and subcortical limbic areas including the reticular activating system and septal and hippocampal regions. He also promoted the use of EEG measurement to define properties of the nervous system. The strength of the nervous system construct was related to the property of sensitivity and separated from the idea of conditionability or speed of formation of conditioned responses. This was done on the basis of empirical studies that showed little relationship between these two properties. Nebylitsyn used the term *dynamism* to refer to the speed of formation of response to positively reinforced CSs. Strength of excitatory and inhibitory processes were regarded as independent characteristics as in the Pavlovian construct of equilibrium, or relative strength of the two. Although Eysenck stimulated interest in the concept of conditionability, Soviet investigators became more interested in the idea of reactivity to intensity of stimulation and the dynamism of excitation rather than inhibition. Eysenck also moved away from the idea of equilibrium and the dynamism of inhibition, fundamental to his earlier theories (Eysenck, 1957) to one of arousal (Eysenck, 1967). Gray (1981) has discussed some of the problems entailed by this shift of emphasis.

Eysenck

Conditioning is a construct that has a central role in Eysenck's theory of personality. Even before the construct of arousal became central to his theory, Eysenck (1957) suggested that the differences among the social behaviors of introverts, extraverts, neurotics, and stables might depend on their conditionability.

The general hypothesis was that introverts were more conditionable than extraverts, but this was qualified by the parameters of conditioning. Factors such as weak versus strong CS and UCS, which are related to conditionability and brain excitation in the Pavlovian theory, or complete versus partial reinforcement, related to inhibition, were considered to be crucial in the relationship between *extraversion* and conditioning. Introverts should condition better than extraverts in conditions in which excitation is relatively low and inhibition is maximized. Drawing on Gray's (1964b) description of the neo-Pavlovian work, Eysenck (1967) equated the *introversion-extraversion* dimension with the strength of the nervous system dimension as developed by Teplov, Nebylitsyn, and others following Pavlov. Introverts were said to have stronger excitatory brain potentials than extraverts and therefore should be more arousable by weaker stimulation (as described in the previous chapter). Extraverts are regarded as having less excitatory and stronger inhibitory brain potentials, making them less arousable by weak stimuli. From these theoretical assumptions, Eysenck predicted that under conditions of weak stimulation (low-intensity CS, UCS) and maximal inhibitory potential (partial reinforcement or short CS-UCS intervals) introverts would be superior in conditioning. Note that the model describes classical rather than instrumental conditioning, though it has been extended to other types of performance involving instrumental conditioning. Considering the phenomena of transmarginal inhibition, Eysenck predicted that when conditions were different, as when the CS or UCS were intense and partial reinforcement or long intertrial intervals allowed the dissipation of reactive inhibition, extraverts would be superior in conditioning.

The poor conditionability of extraverts is said to underlie their greater propensity to engage in antisocial or generally deviant and uninhibited behavior compared with introverts. Eysenck (1967, 1977, 1983) assumes that socialization, or the learning of the rules of society, takes place largely through classical conditioning. Conditioned cues of temptation are presumably associated with aversive UCS produced by punishment. This assumption is questionable because punishment seldom follows misbehavior soon enough to produce classical conditioning. Even instrumental conditioning may not be adequate to explain the acceptance or rejection of parental or societal mores, though it may come closer because inconsistent discipline is frequently found in the type of disorganized family setting that is conducive to criminality. Observational learning may play an even greater role in social deviancy, and cognitive mechanisms may mediate the capacity to delay gratification (Mischel, Ebbeson, & Zeiss, 1972).

However, accepting the basic assumption of the conditioned origin of "conscience" or "self-control," it follows that a deficit in conditionability produced by underarousal in extraverts would make it more difficult for them to form strong or permanent conditioned responses based on punishment *or* reward (Eysenck's theory makes no distinction between appetitive and aversive conditioning in speaking of "conditionability"). Conversely, introverts should readily learn whatever is reinforced by parental discipline, and therefore their behavior should be more moral, or constrained, by whatever values existed in the family, school, or peer environments. Data on criminality, delinquency, sexuality, substance abuse, values, and attitudes (Wilson, 1981) bear out the end result of the hypothesized etiology, though they do not validate the intervening conditioning mechanisms.

The dimension of *psychoticism* (P) was not emphasized in earlier discussions of criminality. Factor analyses that include the P scale (Zuckerman, Kuhlman, & Camac, 1988) as well as clinical and biological studies suggest that the P dimension is closely related to psychopathy or antisocial personality disorder at its extreme (Zuckerman, 1989). Eysenck's earlier conception of criminality, not well distinguished from psychopathy, suggested that criminals are high on E and N. Eysenck and Eysenck (1985) now concede that it is the *impulsivity* rather than the *sociability* dimension of E that is related to criminality. One type of *impulsivity* is involved in the P dimension. This type of narrow *impulsivity* may also account for the relation of E to general cortical arousal (O'Gorman & Lloyd, 1987). Given these facts, it is a distinct possibility that conditionability might be more closely related to the P dimension or to its narrower component of *impulsivity* than to E or N.

What of the *neuroticism* dimension? Spence (1958), working from the drive theory of Hull, suggested that *anxiety* is a trait that represents a general drive increment facilitating simple conditioning but interfering with more complex learning. Because *anxiety* trait is closely related to *neuroticism* (N), his theory identified N as a more basic determinant of conditioning than *extraversion*. This theoretical divergence led to a series of studies and debates between Spence and Eysenck that are described in a later section of this chapter.

Gray

Gray's theory unquestionably represents the most advanced and detailed application of learning theory to the explanation of individual differences in personality. Gray (1975) has written a book on a "two-process" learning theory as a foundation for his psychobiological model of personality. He examines many of the fundamental debates of learning theory and attempts to identify the basic learning systems and their neuropsychological substrates. The research is almost all from the comparative literature, over 90% of which deals with the albino rat. Although the reasons for this have already been discussed, a comparative approach that does not include data on humans may occasionally lead to inappropriate generalizations. For example, Gray claims that there is no evidence for the effect of stimulus deprivation on stimulus seeking. This may be true, based on the animal literature, but it overlooks the elegant series of experiments by Jones (1969) that show a relationship between hours of stimulus deprivation and instrumental responding of human subjects for visual or auditory stimuli with high informational (unpredictable) characteristics. Gray's neuropsychological structural models have been described in chapter 3, and his psychopharmacological ideas have been described in chapter 4. The focus in this chapter is primarily on the learning and information-processing aspects of the theory.

Gray classifies unconditioned reinforcing events in instrumental conditioning in terms of the procedures and the effect on the probability of the reinforced response. Operations that increase the probability of response include presentation of reward (approach), termination of punishment (escape), and omission of punishment (active avoidance). The terms in parentheses in these cases refer to the types of response that are instrumental in obtaining reinforcement in each condition. Procedures that decrease the probability of response include presentation of punishment (passive avoidance), termination of reward (time-out), and omission of reward (extinction). Noting that stimulation of the lateral hypothalamus can produce eating in a satiated animal and that the same area is a focus for self-stimulation of the brain (a reinforcement procedure described in chapter 4), Gray suggests that induction of the hunger drive rather than its reduction is reinforcing. With less experimental evidence, he also suggests that arousal of the sex drive is reinforcing. His general conclusion from a number of sources of data is that drive is not necessary for reinforcement, and reinforcement does not consist of drive reduction. Gray points out that, unlike instrumental conditioning, classical conditioning has no goal direction. Although both acid and food may be used as UCS to stimulate the UCR of salivation, there is no way to distinguish their aversive or appetitive properties from the response itself. Drive deprivation may, however, affect classical conditioning by altering the nature and intensity of the UCR. A dog is more prone to salivate to the CS when deprived of food.

If primary drive reduction is not necessary for reinforcement, what is the mechanism? Because humans spend little time in primary reinforced activities, it would follow that much of their behavior during the remaining time is governed by stimuli with secondary reinforcing qualities (money, attention, approval, etc.). Gray's theory emphasizes the motivation induced by secondary reinforcers or stimuli, associated with the presentation or withdrawal of primary reinforcers. Of course, the connection in humans between these kinds of reinforcers and primary reinforcement is rather tenuous, but there is no question of their operation as reinforcers. According to Gray, secondary reinforcers acquire their reinforcement and motivational properties through classical conditioning (association with a UCS).

Gray views positive reinforcement as a positive feedback mechanism, or a situation in which the consequences of an output tend to potentiate further output. At the point of satiation, the system is switched to negative feedback. At this conceptual level these feedback formulations are clearly tautalogical, but their isomorphism with known biological feedback systems makes them heuristic. For instance, hunger is regulated by blood sugar levels, which are detected in the lateral hypothalamus and instigate or make eating behavior more likely until centers in the medial hypothalamus respond to elevated blood sugar levels with an inhibition of appetite.

The reinforcing stimulus activates the feedback mechanism and acts as the UCS for other stimuli. Gray proposes a "two-process theory of learning" in which classical conditioning is responsible for the transfer of the reinforcing qualities of primary reinforcers to other stimuli, and instrumental conditioning is responsible for the guidance of behavior to maximize positive reinforcement and minimize punishment or frustration. The primary role of drive in this theory is its relation to the strength of the UCR, which in turn is related to the strength of the secondary reinforcement stimuli associated with the UCS through classical conditioning.

Gray makes an important distinction between active avoidance (escape) and passive avoidance (inhibition of response) as responses for avoiding punishment. Active avoidance in response to signals of punishment is regarded as part of a reward mechanism. The inhibition of behavior in passive avoidance is a primary mode of response of the behavioral inhibition system (BIS) to stimuli that are (CS) signals of punishment or nonreward. Although common sense suggests that freezing and escape are merely two aspects of a common fear mechanism, Gray argues from a substantial body of empirical data that the two modes of response are mediated by different mechanisms and controlled by different conditions.

Gray describes a third system associated with unconditioned fight-or-flight responses to direct punishment rather than the anticipation of punishment, or threats from animals of the same species. It is not clear why threat from a conspecific should be regarded as a UCS, though there is certainly evidence that threat expressions or behavior can elicit innate fear response. When pain is inflicted on an animal, it will fight (even to the extent of biting an electrified grid) or flee. The behavior depends on the circumstances of the moment. Many species fight when they cannot escape.

With these basic systems and mechanisms in the system, Gray provides a conceptual outline for an information-processing system that responds to the world in terms of past reinforcements. The model is shown in Figure 7.1. The suggested neurological sites of these systems are discussed in chapter 4. Signals of reward (or nonpunishment) activate a reward mechanism; and signals associated with punishment (or nonreward), as well as signals generated by novel or uncertain stimuli, are routed to the punishment mechanism. Both mechanisms stimulate the arousal mechanism (reticulocortical activating system) and compete for control of the decision mechanism. In a conflict situation in which both kinds of signals are received, the outcome in the decision mechanism depends on the relative

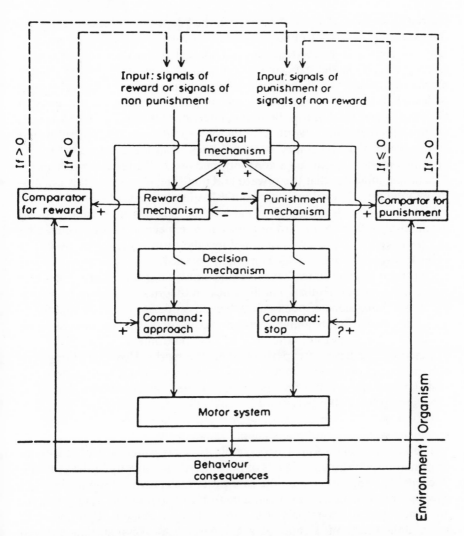

Figure 7.1. Gray and Smith model, Mark 3. Dashed lines indicate inputs that occur on trial *n* + 1 as a consequence of classical conditioning of exteroceptive, interoceptive, or proprioceptive stimuli to the consequences of behavior on trial *n* (see text). (From *Elements of a two process theory of learning*, p. 347, by J. A. Gray, 1975. New York: Academic Press. Copyright 1975 by Academic Press. Reprinted by permission.)

strengths of the associations between the signals and expectations of reward and punishment. The basic decision is made to approach or stop, and then it is transmitted to a command mechanism. The arousal mechanism strengthens the behavior in the case of approach and possibly inhibition as well. The behavior is executed by the motor system and leads to certain behavior consequences such as reinforcement. Negative feedback loops from the behavioral consequences to comparators enable comparison of the received reward or punishment with the "expected" consequences. At this point the reward or punishment mechanisms are modified by the current experience. If the consequence of approach behavior is a reward equal to or greater than the expected reward, there is an input to the reward mechanism. However, if the consequence of the previous behavior is zero or less than the expected reward, the output of the comparator goes to the punishment mechanism. Similar connections are described for the outcome of the behavior governed by the punishment system, except in that case a confirmed expectancy is routed back from the comparator to the punishment mechanism and a nonconfirmed one to the reward mechanism. The model indicates that the reward and punishment mechanisms are mutually inhibitory (based on data from self-stimulation studies).

Gray has provided us with a model that suggests how central brain mechanisms related to reward or punishment expectancies are modified by the results of behavior. As noted before, the term *expectancies* describes a mechanism not a mentalistic construct. Arousal (or general drive) in this system merely potentiates behavior and thus is not the central construct as it is in Pavlovian, Hullian, and Eysenckian theories. This theory suggests that basic dimensions of personality depend on the potential of stimuli for arousing positive or negative emotions associated with the conditioning history of the organism. The reward and punishment mechanisms are changed on the basis of experience with the world. However, Gray also recognizes innate biological differences in the structural pathways in the real nervous system that are the basis for these mechanisms. Figure 7.2 shows the relationship between Eysenck's dimensions of E and N, Gray's suggested primary dimensions of *anxiety* and *impulsivity* and susceptibilities to signals of reward and punishment, respectively.

The primary dimension of *anxiety* reflects "increasing levels of sensitivity to signals of punishment, signals of nonreward and novelty" (Gray, 1981). "Sensitivity to signals" means the ease with which previously neutral stimuli can become CS. Gray's primary dimension of *impulsivity* represents increasing sensitivity to signals of reward or nonpunishment. Eysenck's primary dimensions of E and N are regarded as secondary or derived dimensions to those of primary biological significance. E is said to reflect the relative strengths of the reward and punishment systems, and N reflects their joint strength. In contrast with Eysenck's theory, which simply predicts a general difference in conditionability between introverts and extraverts, Gray's theory predicts a superiority of introverts in aversive conditioning and a superiority of extraverts in appetitive conditioning. Because the contrast between appetitive and aversive conditioning is clearer for instrumental conditioning, this type of conditioning may be more appropriate than classical conditioning for testing the model.

Gray's (in press) more recent outline of dimensions takes the P dimension into account and places the *anxiety* dimension closer to *introversion,* with

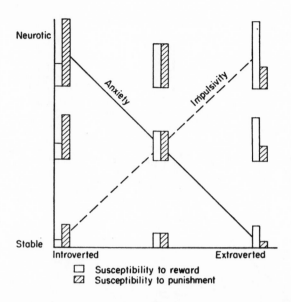

Figure 7.2. Rotation of Eysenck's dimensions of *neuroticism* and *introversion-extraversion* to dimensions of *anxiety* and *impulsivity* as proposed by Gray. Open bars indicate strength of susceptibility to reward; hatched bars indicate strength of susceptibility to signals of punishment. *Anxiety* represents the steepest rate of growth in susceptibility to signals of punishment; *impulsivity* represents the steepest rate of growth in susceptibility to signals of reward. *Introversion-extraversion* now becomes a derived dimension reflecting the balance of susceptibility to signals of punishment and reward, respectively; and *neuroticism* represents the sum of these two types of susceptibility to signals of reinforcement. (From *The psychology of fear and stress*, p. 351, by J. A. Gray, 1987b. Cambridge: Cambridge University Press. Copyright 1987 by Cambridge University Press. Reprinted by permission.)

the dimension running from high N, low E, and low P to low N, high E, and high P (see Figure 4.8). This has the effect of placing one type of psychopathy (primary) at the opposite end of the dimension from *anxiety*. Because *anxiety* is supposed to reflect an enhanced sensitivity to signals of punishment, the findings for aversive conditioning, particularly the learning of passive avoidance, should be opposite for anxiety neurotics and psychopaths, with the former showing good and the latter poor conditioning. Such studies are reviewed in chapters 8 and 9 on the clinical disorders. However, in the normal range, this realignment suggests that all three Eysenckian dimensions should be related to aversive conditioning, with the best conditioners being neurotic, introverted, non-psychopathic types and the worst conditioners (unable to learn from signals of punishment) would be stable, extraverted, psychopathic types.

The *impulsivity* dimension, related to sensitivity to signals of reward, is also related to all three of Eysenck's dimensions, running from high N, high E, and high P (impulsive) to low N, low E, and low P. Neurotic, extraverted, psychopathic types (secondary psychopaths) should be most

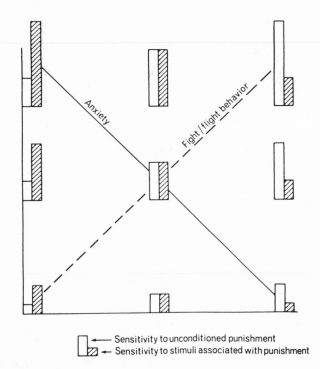

Figure 7.3. Dimensions of *fight-flight* (P) and *anxiety* and sensitivity to unconditioned punishment (open bars) and to stimuli associated with punishment (hatched bars). (From "Neural systems, emotion, and personality," by J. A. Gray, in press, in *Adaptation, learning and affect*, J. Madden, S. Matthysee, and J. Barchas, Eds. New York: Raven Press. Copyright 0000, Raven Press. Reprinted by permission.)

susceptible and impulsive in reaction to signals of reward whereas stable, introverted, nonpsychopathic types should be less susceptible and more inhibited or constrained in response to signals of reward (temptation).

The third dimension of the Gray system consists of unconditioned fight-or-flight reactions to pain or threat. It remains identified with the P dimension in Eysenck's system, with the emphasis on the *fight* or aggressive component of the human trait. As with the *anxiety* and *impulsivity* dimensions, the dimension of *aggression* is amplified by the N dimension, so that for high P persons the difference between sensitivity to stimuli associated with punishment and sensitivity to actual unconditioned punishment becomes larger, as shown in Figure 7.3. This suggestion recalls that trait *aggression* and *anger* did fall in the quadrant defined by the high N and P dimensions in the factor analysis of human traits by Zuckerman, Kuhlman, & Camac (1988), described in chapter 1.

Gray has built a biologically rooted theory carefully reasoned from comparative studies of learning and neurophysiology. There is a problem in the fact that the theory was derived almost entirely from comparative studies and therefore is not designed for operational testing in humans. The data on humans that are appropriate to this theory are not plentiful and consist mainly of personality correlates of habituation, conditioning, and reinforced instrumental learning.

Habituation and sensitization

Neurophysiological basis

The cellular mechanisms of habituation involve the inactivation of calcium ions leading to a reduced output of the neurotransmitter in the synaptic connections between sensory and motor neurons (Kandel, 1985). Kandel worked out the molecular mechanism using a relatively simple organism, a marine snail. Pribram, Reitz, McNeil, and Spivak (1979) asked if habituation in such a simple nervous system means that neuronal models or representations are formed throughout the nervous system in more complex organisms. It is clear in complex organisms that certain parts of the brain are vital to habituation. Pribram cites studies showing that resection of the amygdala or frontal cortex in rhesus monkeys removed the visceroautonomic components of the orienting reflex, though reflex visceroautonomic activity remained intact. Behavioral orienting also remained intact but failed to habituate. Resection of the hippocampus enhanced the visceroautonomic components of orienting and reduced the susceptibility of the habituated monkeys to dishabituation. Apparently, the limbic brain and neocortex are vital in habituation in more complex organisms.

Habituation and personality in humans

In Eysenck's (1957) earlier theory, there is no question that the kind of inhibitory process involved in habituation would be related to the E dimension and that extraverts should show more rapid habituation than introverts. Although the prediction is less obviously deduced from the arousal theory (Eysenck, 1967), the prediction still seems to hold for the new model (Eysenck & Eysenck, 1985). The model clearly predicts that introverts are more arousable than extraverts and therefore should show stronger initial orienting responses (ORs); the evidence for this was discussed in chapter 6. But if the habituation process is considered separately from the strength of reaction to the initial stimulus, why should extraverts habituate more quickly than introverts unless there is a difference in inhibitory as well as excitatory process? Many of the studies discussed here have not adequately controlled differences in strength of initial OR in their measures of habituation, such as trials to habituation.

As in other areas of psychophysiology, one must ask if the particular physiological measures of habituation show enough trait characteristics, such as reliability and generality, to support a role for habituation in the determination of personality traits. Data summarized by O'Gorman (1977) are not reassuring on the question of reliability. Retest reliabilities of electrodermal response habituation, though significant, are not of the magnitude we expect in more stable psychometric measures. Koriat, Averill, and Malmstrom (1973) found no reliability for uncorrected HR and SCR habituation measures and significant but very low reliability for corrected (for initial response amplitude) measures. They also found no relationship between HR and SCR measures of habituation. O'Gorman (1977) also summarizes a general lack of correlation among various response measures of habituation even within the same general psychophysiological system. Koriat et al. (1973) suggest that the lack of reliability and generality of habituation measures reduces the possibility that they could be related to personality.

Is there generalization of habituation across stimulus modalities? Lynn (1966) reported the data from a study by Rozhdestvenskaya, Nebylitsen, Borisova, and Ermolaeva-Tomina (1960) showing a high correlation ($r = .65$) between number of trials necessary to extinguish the OR produced by a visual stimulus and the same habituation measure produced by an auditory stimulus. However, both habituation measures correlated substantially with initial ORs to the two types of stimuli, so we cannot take the results as evidence of cross modality generalization of habituation per se. In another study by Nebylitsin (1963), described by Lynn (1966), extinction of the OR, defined by alpha wave blocking, was highly correlated with extinction of conditioned alpha blocking, showing the relevance of the inhibitory processes involved in habituation for the process responsible for the extinction of conditioned responses. Conditioning experiments start with habituation of the OR to the stimulus to be conditioned. After the response has been habituated, it is reinstated by the conditioned association with the UCS. Obviously, the persistence of the response during extinction is influenced by the same processes that affected its initial habituation.

Stelmack, Bourgeois, Chain, and Pickard (1979) compared habituation rates of three kinds of psychophysiological responses to two kinds of visual stimuli: simple colors and word stimuli. Neither SCR nor heart rate habituation measures correlated significantly across the two kinds of stimuli, even within the same stimulus modality. The pulse amplitude measure did show a moderate correlation across stimuli. Given these problems in generality of the habituation process, one cannot be too sanguine about the possibilities of finding relationships to broad personality traits. Much would depend on using the right kinds of stimuli and response measures.

O'Gorman (1977) provided a comprehensive review of 46 studies attempting to relate habituation of human psychophysiological measures to personality. The review also includes a review of the theoretical and methodological problems entailed in these studies. Of 20 studies attempting to define the relationship between *extraversion* and habituation, 8 found the predicted relationship, extraverts showing more rapid habituation, and 12 reported nonsignificant findings. O'Gorman claims, however, that in all but one of the 12 studies reporting nonsignificant results and none of those reporting significant results, at least one experimental condition that is known to influence response habituation may have confounded the results. But one must be wary about explaining away nonsignificant replications by post hoc criticism.

There is also another factor to consider. Most measures of habituation, such as trials-to-criterion, difference scores, and amplitude-trial slope (Lykken et al., 1988), confound the habituation score with the strength of the initial OR to the first stimulus presentation. Because a number of studies discussed in the previous chapter show introverts to have stronger initial ORs than extraverts, it is possible that differences in habituation are actually due to differences in the strength of the initial response (perhaps an index of sensitivity). Only one index, Lader and Wing's (1966) H score, directly controls the index of habituation, by using the slope of amplitude on trial number, covarying the Y intercept and thus freeing the measure of its dependence on the initial response. Of the five studies listed by O'Gorman as showing significant relationships between E and habituation, none used this measure whereas all used the trials-to-criteria measure, which is highly influenced by the initial response amplitude. Of the studies finding no relationship, three used the H score, and the others used a variety of methods.

Trait anxiety is often presumed to be an index of autonomic arousal or arousability, though the research cited in the previous chapter gives little support to this assumption. However, if the assumption were true, one would expect that high-anxiety subjects would show delayed habituation of physiological measures, which are presumed to be a more direct index of autonomic than cortical arousal. Three studies did find the expected relationship, but nine did not. All three studies with positive results used finger pulse volume responses whereas all those that did not find significant results used electrodermal measures, suggesting a response specific relationship. However, only two studies, both in the negative results group, used the H method to control the habituation measure for initial response magnitude. All three studies reporting positive results used the trials-to-criteria method and one of these also used another method.

Five studies are described as showing a significant relationship between *neuroticism* (N scale) and habituation, and six studies failed to find a relationship. However, only one of the studies with significant findings showed a relationship solely in the predicted direction; two showed findings in the opposite direction to the hypothesis, and two had findings in both directions, depending on stimulus intensity or level of *extraversion*. All of the studies were judged by O'Gorman to have methodological problems.

Two of the three studies showing slower habituation for neurotics as opposed to stables used the H method, but two of the six studies with completely nonsignificant findings also used this method.

O'Gorman's general conclusion is that *extraversion* is related to habituation of the electrodermal response, trait *anxiety* is related to habituation of the finger vasomotor response, and *neuroticism* is not related to habituation at all. As we have seen, these conclusions must be tempered by the failure of most studies to control for initial response amplitude in their measures of habituation. O'Gorman does not seem to regard this as a critical question, saying "whether or not initial level should be controlled for depends on theoretical considerations rather than purely methodological concerns" (O'Gorman, 1977, p. 276). I would agree with this, but it is precisely because the measure of initial OR represents an important theoretical construct, strength of arousability, that it must be distinguished from habituation, which is a measure of strength of inhibition.

As with the review of EEG studies of arousal in the previous chapter, we are left with inconclusive results, which seems to be an inevitable result of "box-score" tallies. On the assumption that one good study is worth any number of studies using poor methodologies and weak tests of the hypotheses, let us just examine one of the studies in the review more closely. O'Gorman criticized the study by Coles, Gale, and Kline (1971) because of the relatively long interstimulus interval (2 minutes), which he claims interferes with habituation. However, Coles et al. do show a typical habituation curve, and their reported rates of habituation resemble those in other studies.

A number of factors recommend this study as a good test of the hypothesis: (1) The investigators used the EPI, a direct measure of Eysenck's variables of E and N; (2) they used an adequate number of subjects (60) compared with most of the other studies in the review, and all subjects were of one sex (male), thus eliminating the confounding of mixed sex groups; (3) the subjects were selected from a larger number of potential subjects on the basis of sampling different levels of E and N combinations, thus insuring adequate representation of all levels of one of the critical personality variables (a middle group was used for E but not for N); (4) a simple auditory stimulus of moderate intensity (65 dB) was used; (5) in addition to standard measures of habituation such as trials-to-extinction, they used the Lader H measure that controls level of initial response in assessing the habituation slope. The results showed no significant effect of E on either trials-to-extinction or the H measure of habituation. However, the N variable was significant for both measures. High N subjects took twice as many trials as low N subjects to habituate, and the low N group had a steeper slope of habituation amplitude response, controlling for level of initial response.

Smith, Rypma, and Wilson (1981) studied the effects of caffeine and personality on dishabituation and spontaneous recovery of the electro-dermal OR. A novel stimulus presented after the OR has habituated often dishabituates the OR to the previously habituated stimulus. The OR may also show spontaneous recovery if the habituated stimulus is not presented for some period of time. Introverts showed a stronger initial OR than extraverts following a placebo, and extraverts showed greater response following caffeine. The E scale was also analyzed separately for the *impulsivity* and *sociability* components. Low impulsives gave stronger responses to the second dishabituation stimulus, and caffeine produced a greater increase in spontaneous recovery amplitude in low impulsives than in high impulsives. *Sociability* had no effect on any of these measures, and habituation rate itself was unaffected by caffeine or personality groupings. A similar lack of findings relating E or caffeine to habituation rate obtained in the study by Smith, Wilson, and Jones (1983).

Smith et al. (1981) found that overhabituation of the SCR produced no change in introverts but increased response in extraverts. During the first 60 exposures of the stimulus, introverts had stronger responses than extraverts, but after 100 trials the difference disappeared, supposedly due to the dissipation of inhibition in extraverts produced by overhabituation. Smith et al. (1983) found that response amplitudes during overhabituation did not differ in introverts and extraverts in placebo or low caffeine dosage conditions. However, extraverts showed an increasing response amplitude in relation to caffeine dosage, and introverts showed decreasing response. These data are simply an extension of the findings on initial response amplitude and tonic levels of SC during the prehabituation phase, all of which show a facilitating effect of caffeine in extraverts and an inhibitory or no effect in introverts.

Smith et al. (1986) studied the effects of attentional conditions on electrodermal responses to a high-intensity auditory stimulus (110-dB tone). Introverts gave larger SCRs than extraverts in initial response to the tone, and extraverts habituated in half the number of trials taken by introverts. Introverts also showed greater dishabituation effects following presentation of a novel stimulus and representation of the standard stimulus. In contrast to the Smith et al. (1981) study, this one did show differences in habituation as well as dishabituation. Perhaps the stronger stimulus (110 as opposed to 80 dB) produced the difference. Although not totally consistent with past findings, Smith's work seems to show a stronger inhibitory mechanism in extraverts than in introverts, as indicated by habituation (at least to a strong stimulus) and dishabituation. Extraverts have a weaker tendency to overcome previous habituation, but caffeine helps.

Neary and Zuckerman (1976) investigated the habituation of the electrodermal OR in relation to the traits of *sensation seeking* and *anxiety*. It was hypothesized that high *sensation seekers* would show more rapid habituation than lows. Using the H measure of habituation, which controlled for differences in the OR to the initial stimulus presentation, there was no difference in habituation between high and low sensation seekers or between subjects high or low on trait *anxiety* in response to either visual or auditory stimuli. It was concluded that high sensation seekers differ from lows in strength of excitation (OR) but not in strength of inhibition (habituation).

Smith, Davidson, Perlstein, Oster, and Gonzalez (1989) studied *sensation seeking* and electrodermal ORs using meaningful and arousing (sexual and aggressive) stimuli presented in auditory and visual modalities. Over three trials of exposure, the high sensation seekers habituated and the lows sensitized to the most arousing stimuli. The high sensation seekers had responded more strongly to these stimuli on initial presentation. There is an analogue of life behavior of sensation seekers in this study. They often seek intense or unusual forms of stimulation but quickly tire of them and need to move on to some novel source of excitement.

Most Western studies of habituation have used HR, SCR, or vasomotor measures of habituation. Stelmack and Michaud-Achorn (1985) studied habituation in the auditory evoked potential (EP). They found a decline within a train of four stimuli, all of which took place between the first and second stimulus presentations. Although introverts showed a larger amplitude EP to the first stimulus in the train, there was no difference between introverts and extraverts in habituation on trials two to four.

Although there are suggestive findings throughout the literature, it must be concluded that there is no consistent or firm evidence that habituation of psychophysiological responses in humans is related to personality (O'Gorman, 1983). Perhaps the problem is with the psychophysiological methodology. The same problem of reliability and generality that hindered tests of arousal hypotheses (chapter 6) applies equally to the idea of generalized habituation mechanisms. Furthermore, the habituation measures must not be confounded by amplitude of initial response, which is independently related to several personality traits. Unfortunately, most investigators have not used the type of habituation measure that can accomplish this.

Conditioning

Neurophysiological basis

Kandel (1985) extended his studies on habituation and sensitization of the gill withdrawal response in the sea snail to classical conditioning. On the basis of these studies, he suggested that the cellular mechanisms of classical conditioning are merely an amplified form of those involved in sensitization. Kandel may be correct in describing learning as an extension of sensitization at the most elementary cell assembly level, but Thompson (1986) asked a somewhat different question: Where is the "essential memory trace" in the mammalian brain? By "essential memory trace" he means "the neuronal processes of plasticity that are necessary and sufficient to store the memory in question" (p. 942). Memory trace circuits are thought to be localized in the mammalian brain, not in the sense of the involvement of a single locus but in the sense of particular pathways that involve several structures, including the cerebellum, hippocampus, amygdala, and cerebral cortex.

Thompson used the conditioned eye-blink response in the rabbit. This model is convenient for comparative research because one of the most popular conditioning paradigms related to personality in humans has been the conditioned eye-blink response. Thompson cites earlier work of Soviet scientists showing the central role of the cerebellum in conditioned leg flexion and salivation responses in dogs. The work of Thompson shows the essential role of the cerebellum in both learning and memory for adaptive behavioral responses to aversive events such as puffs of air on the cornea of the eye. In fact, one region of the cerebellum (lateral interpositus nucleus) is said to be essential for the learning and memory of the conditioned eye-blink response, even though destruction of this area does not affect the basic unconditioned reflex itself. A schematic for the circuitry of the conditioned eye-blink response is shown in Figure 7.4.

Classical conditioning of auditory or visual stimuli with punishment-produced stimuli (like shock) is the first stage in avoidance learning in two-process theories such as those of Mowrer (1939), Miller (1948), and Gray (1975). Conditioned cardiovascular responses, produced by association of shock UCS to auditory or visual CS's in baboons, are abolished by lesions of the perifornical region of the hypothalamus. The lesion has no effect on reflex cardiovascular responses or those associated with exercise. But surprisingly, such lesions also have no effect on an instrumental measure of fear-conditioned suppression of lever pressing. In pigeons, cardiovascular conditioning is dependent on an efferent pathway that includes parts of the amygdala, hypothalamus, and descending pathways to the brain stem and spinal cord. The amygdala also seems to be involved in the startle reflex.

The hippocampus has been implicated in many forms of human amnesia, but in monkeys it seems to be involved only in recent memory and not in long-term memory storage. Hippocampal activity is involved in both classical and instrumental learning tasks, but Thompson claims that it is not essential for the learning or memory of these tasks. Short-term memory, as in the delayed-response problem, is also impaired by lesions to one part of the frontal lobes. Although the evidence from animal studies does not support a major role of cerebral cortex in long-term memory, "language memory" is stored there, and cognitive processes there are quite important for much human learning.

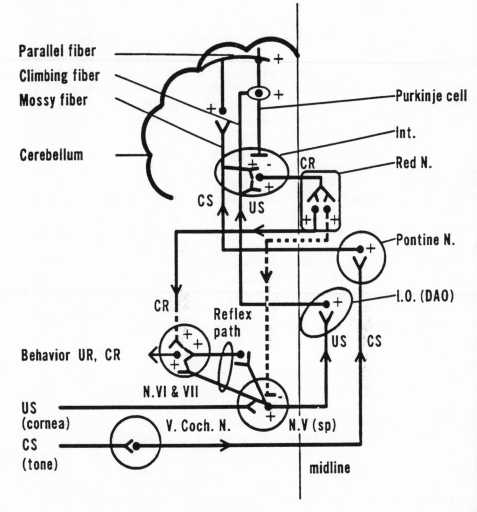

Figure 7.4. Simplified schematic of hypothetical memory trace circuit for discrete behavioral responses learned as adaptation to aversive events. The US (corneal air puff) pathway seems to consist of somatosensory projections to the dorsal accessory portion of the inferior olive (DAO) and its climbing fiber projections to the cerebellum. The tone CS pathway seems to consist of auditory projections to pontine nuclei (Pontine N) and their mossy fiber projections to the cerebellum. The efferent (eyelid closure) CR pathway from the interpositus nucleus (Int) of the cerebellum to the red nucleus (Red N) and via the descending rubral pathway is thought to act ultimately on motor neurons. The red nucleus may also exert inhibitory control over the transmission of somatic sensory information about the US to the inferior olive (IO), so that when a CR occurs (eyelid closes), the red nucleus dampens US activation of climbing fibers. Evidence to date are most consistent with storage of the memory traces in localized regions of cerebellar cortex and possibly interpositus nucleus as well. Pluses (+) indicate excitatory and minuses (−) inhibitory synaptic action. Additional abbreviations: N V (sp), spinal fifth cranial nucleus; N VI, sixth cranial nucleus; N VII, seventh cranial nucleus; V Coch N, ventral cochlear nucleus. (From "The neurobiology of learning and memory," by R. F. Thompson, 1986, *Science*, 233, p. 943. Copyright, 1986, American Association for the Advancement of Science. Reprinted by permission.)

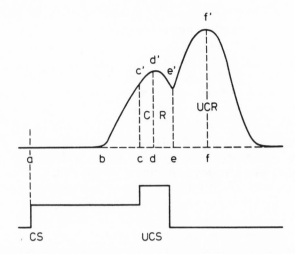

Figure 7.5. The major parameters of the conditioned and unconditioned response: a, CS onset; b, CR onset; c, UCS onset; d, point of maximum CR amplitude; e, UCR onset; f, point of maximum UCR amplitude. (From "Personality and conditioning," by A. B. Levey and I. Martin, 1981, in *A model for personality*, p. 151, H. J. Eysenck, Ed. New York: Springer-Verlag. Copyright 1981 Springer-Verlag. Reprinted by permission.)

Eyelid conditioning and personality

Eyelid conditioning has been a favorite paradigm for testing personality theories (Levey & Martin, 1981). Technically, this type of conditioning should be regarded as the classical type because the response is elicited by the UCS (usually an air puff to the cornea of the eye) and is then transferred to control by an associated CS. Figure 7.5 shows the major parameters of the CR and UCR. As in all classical conditioning, the UCS is delivered during conditioning whether or not a CR appears before it. However, in this case, the reflexive response of eye closure protects the cornea from the full impact of the air puff (point c) if it is timed right. Thus, there can be instrumental reinforcement for the CR and it could be regarded as an example of avoidance learning, though this interpretation is disputed. Even when infraorbital shock is used as the UCS (unlike tactile corneal stimulation it is not attenuated by the CR), the typical change in timing of the CR and UCR is seen: The UCR moves back and the CR moves forward during the course of conditioning until they become integrated. It is true that the eye blink is under some degree of voluntary control, and therefore subjects could deliberately attempt to avoid the puff by blinking even if instructed not to do so. However, the voluntary blink can be differentiated from the reflexive one by its early onset, sharp rise time, and long smooth closure. Frcka, Beyts, Levey, and Martin (1983b) found few instances of subjects showing these types of responses; even a small minority of subjects who claimed they used this strategy did not really show the characteristics of voluntary responses in their blinks. However, they did show more typical CRs than other subjects, suggesting that their interpretation of control was illusory and based on awareness of their high frequency of true CRs.

Some cognitive psychologists would interpret all learning as dependent on cognition, usually defined in humans in terms of an awareness of the contingencies and purposes in experiments. Frcka et al. (1983b) studied the role of awareness in conditioning using a post experimental questionnaire to assess awareness. Practically no relationships were found between awareness and the experimental conditions or conditioning performance of the subjects, giving strong support to the idea that conditioning, unmediated by cognition, is certainly possible and probably accounts for most of the variance in typical eyelid conditioning experiments. Awareness was correlated with the personality factors of P and E, as well as to three measures of *impulsiveness:* narrow *impulsivity, empathy,* and *venturesomeness (sensation seeking). Venturesomeness* was the only one of these personality traits related to awareness. The subjects reporting awareness of the purposes of the experiment or the CS-UCS contingency were significantly higher on this scale. These findings corroborate our impressions that high sensation seekers generally seem more curious than lows about experiments; the highs usually look around and ask questions whereas the lows are usually passive and uncurious.

Eyelid conditioning was first related to personality by Taylor (1951) who devised and used an *anxiety* scale called the *Taylor Manifest Anxiety Scale* (TMAS) (Taylor, 1953). Spence and Taylor (1951) interpreted anxiety as a measure of general drive state, equivalent to arousal, and seemed to also assume that persons who scored high on the scale would more likely be in a high drive state during an experiment. The distinction between trait and state *anxiety* was not salient at this time. In the content of Hullian learning theory, drive state (D) was assumed to interact with habit strength (sHr, based on previously reinforced trials) to produce reaction potential. For a situation in which there is only one conditioned response, increases in D should produce greater learning. Eyelid conditioning represents one such high-D situation. For situations in which there are competing responses, increases in D should cause greater interference from competing habits and reduced learning rates. The predictions for eyelid conditioning (better conditioning in high-anxiety trait subjects) were generally confirmed at the University of Iowa but not confirmed at some laboratories elsewhere in the country.

Spence (1964) reviewed all of these studies and identified a number of factors that could have contributed to the failures of replication. One is the smaller numbers of subjects run in the non-Iowa studies. The personality effects are small relative to the variability of individual conditioning data. However, in three of the failures of replication the nonsignificant mean differences were in the opposite direction to the hypothesis. A more likely source of differences was the conditions of the experiments. The Iowa investigators deliberately tried to increase the *emotionality* (anxiety) of subjects by selecting only subjects who had never been in psychology experiments before, instructing experimenters to be formal and impersonal, and seating the subject in a dental chair in an isolation chamber with low illumination. Sensory deprivation experiments have demonstrated that subjects put into such conditions show a high initial level of anxiety (Zuckerman, 1969a). In the non-Iowa experiments most subjects had been in previous experiments, they were seated in a well-lighted room, and they may have received more reassurance from the experimenters. Spence makes a plausible case for this being an early example of a person-situation interaction, though the alleged situational influence was not subsequently investigated in a more controlled fashion.

Eysenck approached eyelid conditioning from a somewhat different theoretical perspective. His theory (Eysenck, 1957) at that time emphasized differences between extraverts and introverts in cortical inhibition relative to excitation (equilibrium). Another Hullian concept, reactive inhibition, was invoked to suggest that on unreinforced trials extraverts would develop stronger reactive inhibition than introverts. This model required the use of partial reinforcement. All of the Iowa studies used 100% reinforcement and did not find any relationship of conditioning to E or E-type scales. Studies by Franks (1956, 1957) found negative relationships between E and eye-blink conditioning in mixed clinical and normal and university student samples. Later, Franks (1963) was unable to replicate his own results in smaller samples of patients and normals. In all, Eysenck reported 11 studies of which 6 supported the hypothesis at a significant level. The failures to replicate were attributed to the use of immigrant subjects unfamiliar with personality scales, subjects who were too young for the scale, and testing in inappropriate environments such as jails.

To determine exactly how personality interacted with specific experimenter conditions, Eysenck and Levey (1972) ran a large number of male subjects assigned to one of eight combinations of three experimental conditions: high versus low air puff (UCS) intensity, continuous versus partial reinforcement, and long versus short CS-UCS intervals. According to Eysenck's (1967) theory, conditioning in introverts should be favored by the low-intensity UCS, partial reinforcement, and short CS-UCS ISIs. Results showed that taken separately the experimental factors did work as predicted in mediating the relationship between E and conditioning, except for the partial versus continuous reinforcement effect, which was in the right direction but not significant. Figure 7.6 contrasts the acquisition curves of introverts and extraverts under the conditions theoretically favorable to introverts, and Figure 7.7 contrasts the two groups under the opposite conditions. Actually, the introverts perform about the same under both

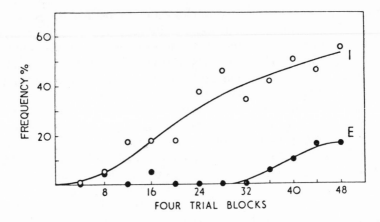

Figure 7.6. Rate of eyelid conditioning for introverts and extraverts under conditions of partial reinforcement, weak UCS, and short CS-UCS interval. (From "Conditioning, introversion-extraversion and the strength of the nervous system," by H. J. Eysenck and A. B. Levey, 1972, in *Biological bases of individual behavior*, V. D. Nebylitsyn and J. A. Gray, Eds. New York: Academic Press. Copyright 1972 by Academic Press. Reprinted by permission.)

sets of conditions, though maximal conditioning is achieved earlier under the strong stimulus conditions. Extraverts, however, show a dramatic difference in acquisition between the strong and weak conditions. In the weak condition (partial reinforcement, short CS-UCS interval, weak UCS), they hardly showed any conditioning, but in the strong condition they rose quickly to levels of conditioning that were superior to those attained by introverts.

These results suggest changes required in the nature of the theory of conditionability and social learning. It can no longer be maintained that introverts are more conditionable than extraverts in general. Only under certain conditions are introverts more conditionable; under other conditions extraverts show greater conditionability. In terms of socialization, occasional but consistent weak punishment or reward following disapproved or approved behaviors should instill parentally valued behaviors in introverted children. However, only strong and constant punishment or reward can reinforce the learning of social behaviors in extraverts. Such reinforcement should also work for introverts, but for them it would be less necessary.

Although the Eysenck and Levey study showed the interaction of *extraversion* with experimental conditions, a subsequent analysis of the data suggested a narrowing of the personality focus. The E scale of the EPI used in the study has two components: one group of items pertaining to *sociability* and another group suggesting *impulsivity*. When the scale was analyzed in terms of these subscales, it was discovered that the interaction of conditions with personality was entirely due to the *impulsivity* aspect of

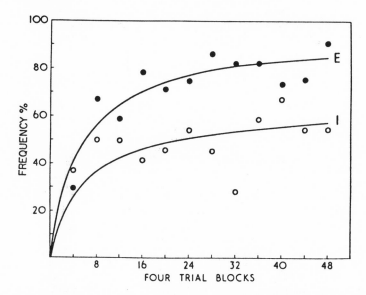

Figure 7.7. Rate of eyelid conditioning for extraverts and introverts under conditions of 100% reinforcement, strong UCS, and long CS-UCS interval. (From Eysenck and Levey, 1972, as in Figure 7.6. Reprinted by permission.)

E rather than to the *sociability* aspect. This posed no problem at the time because the E factor was conceptualized in terms of both components. Now, however, *impulsivity* in its narrow sense is conceived of as more of a P-type component. Later studies have pointed more to *impulsivity* than to a broad E factor as the source of differences in conditionability.

The role of E in the conditioned eyelid response was reexamined in a study by Jones, Eysenck, Martin, and Levey (1981) using only women as subjects (Eysenck and Levey used all male subjects) and three experimental conditions. Subjects were classified as high, medium, or low on the E scale of the PEN (an earlier form of the EPQ) (P and N scales were found to be unrelated to conditioning). E correlated negatively and significantly with 10 to 12 of the 19 measures of conditioning, showing a broad if not strong influence (most r's were in the .2 to .3 range) of personality. The highest correlations ($-.38$ to $-.52$) were with CR frequency, the usual criteria for conditioning. The differences in conditioning of introverts and extraverts were about the same as the differences produced by low- and high-intensity stimuli as shown in Figure 7.8. Note that the difference between I's and E's in the first block is the same as the difference between E1 (response of E's to the low-intensity UCS) and E3 (response of E's to high-intensity UCS) or I1 and I3. As the authors summarize: "Introverts react as if they were responding to more intense stimuli than extraverts" (Jones et al., 1981).

At this point we may ask "What ever happened to anxiety?" Anxiety,

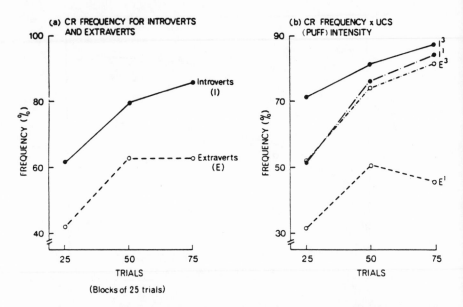

Figure 7.8. (a) CR frequency for introverts and extraverts. (b) CR frequency for personality × unconditioned stimulus (US) intensity. (From "Personality and the topography of the conditioned eyelid response," by J. Jones, H. J. Eysenck, I. Martin, and A. B. Levey, 1981, *Personality and Individual Differences*, 2, p. 70. Copyright 1981 by Pergamon Press. Reprinted by permission.)

as measured by the TMAS, correlates highly with N, but N has never been shown to relate to conditionability in the English studies, perhaps because they use nonanxiety provoking conditions and instructions in their experiments (Levey and Martin, 1981). Eysenck (1957) had claimed that the TMAS might sometimes correlate with eyelid conditioning because it also correlated with *introversion* (those high on *anxiety* are also high on N and low on E). Piers and Kirchner (1969) correlated both E and N scales from the MPI and the TMAS with eyelid conditioning performance in college students. The conditions favored a relationship with E rather than N or MAS because the CS and UCS were relatively weak, a 50% partial reinforcement schedule was used, and no attempt was made to make the situation fearful by apparatus, surroundings, or instructions.

The high conditioners scored significantly higher on the TMAS and N scales and lower on the E scale. The significant correlations between the conditioning criterion and the scales were − .223 for E, .305 for TMAS, and .341 for N. It is interesting that, despite the fact that the conditions of the experiment favored findings for E, the results showed slightly stronger effects for N and TMAS. E, N, and TMAS were all intercorrelated (E about − .40 with TMAS and N; N and TMAS + .79). When the effects of E were partialled out of the correlation between TMAS and conditioning, the partial correlation (.24) was still significant ($p < .05$). The reverse partialling was not reported, but given the smaller relationship between E and conditioning, it would probably be reduced to insignificance by removing the influence of manifest anxiety. The results argue for an important role for *anxiety* in conditioning, even in conditions favoring the involvement of *extraversion*.

Barratt (1971) studied the influence of *impulsivity* and *anxiety* in a differential eyelid conditioning paradigm, simultaneously measuring EEG to assess the role of arousal in conditioning. *Anxiety* was defined by the TMAS and *impulsivity* by the Barratt *impulsiveness* scale (BIS). The latter correlated .60 with the E scale, so it can probably be regarded as the equivalent of the *impulsivity* component of the EPI E scale that was related to conditioning in the Eysenck and Levey (1972) study. Differences between high- and low-anxiety subjects were in the predicted direction but not significant. The best conditioners were low on *impulsivity* and high on *anxiety,* and the poorest were high on *impulsivity* and low on *anxiety* (psychopathic?).

The high-impulsive, low-anxious group, who showed the poorest conditioning, showed evidence of lower arousal than other groups in their EEG records. This difference was notable in the 4-second periods immediately preceding the presentation of the CS. These results are supportive of Eysenck's theory suggesting that differences in conditionability are a function of differences in cortical arousal, though it would have been interesting to know the actual correlation between conditioning and EEG-measured arousal in this study. The results of a study by McDonald and Johnson (1975) suggest that the correlation would be positive. Subjects rated as being alert during classical conditioning showed electrodermal and vasomotor conditioning, but the drowsy subjects generally did not. Arousal was directly manipulated in the study by Franks and Trouton (1958), who administered sodium amobarbital, dexamphetamine, or placebo to groups of female students. The group receiving the stimulant dexamphetamine conditioned better, and the group getting the depressant amobarbital conditioned worse than the placebo group.

Beginning in the 1980s a Maudsley Hospital group under the leadership of Irene Martin began to investigate the role of the P factor and *impulsivity* of various types in conditioning. Changes in the EPQ and conceptualizations of the roles for various types of *impulsivity* in the Eysenckian model required a reevaluation of the critical personality determinants of eyelid conditioning. The studies by Eysenck and Levey (1972) and Barratt (1971) had suggested that it was the *impulsivity* component of E and not the *sociability* one that was responsible for the relationship with conditioning. Eysenck and Eysenck (1977) had developed various scales of *impulsivity* that were differentially related to E and P. Were P, E, or both, or some kind of broad *impulsivity* factor related to conditioning, or was some narrower type of *impulsivity* related to this kind of learning?

Frcka et al. (1983b) analyzed eyelid conditioning as a function of P and

E scores from the EPQ, gender of subjects, and UCS intensity. Females conditioned better than males, and the more intense UCS air puff resulted in better conditioning than the weaker one. For women, but not for men, E was related to conditioning. Introverted women began responding with a high rate of CRs in the first block of trials, and the difference remained throughout the acquisition period. For all subjects, a significant interaction was found between E and P. Particularly at the lower UCS intensity, the subjects either high on both E and P or low on both variables showed better conditioning than those high on one and low on the other. Like the differences for E, these appeared in the first block of trials and persisted through the acquisition. The traits of *impulsiveness* and *venturesomeness* are also analyzed as determinants of conditioning with no significant findings. There seemed to be no credible theoretical explanation for the E-P interaction. The *impulsivity* scales used in this study were not the ones used in earlier studies, so the failure to find a role for this variable required further investigation.

Beyts, Frcka, Martin, and Levey (1983) repeated the experiment just described with one important change in procedure. In the second study they used a paraorbital shock to the external canthus of the eye instead of an air puff as the UCS. This kind of UCS makes the eyelid conditioning more of a pure classical conditioning paradigm because it eliminates the instrumental avoidance aspects of eye-blink. Another matter of relevance is the finding that psychopaths are particularly unresponsive to pain-induced punishment in instrumental conditioning. Shock is generally perceived as more threatening than air puffs even when levels of shock below usual pain thresholds are used.

The P scale had an independent effect on conditioning (Figure 7.9). During the first trial block, low and high P subjects showed no difference in CR frequency; but beginning with the second block of trials, the low Ps exceeded the high Ps in conditioning. There was marked habituation to the UCS in this study, and high P subjects showed the most marked decrement, particularly in the groups receiving the higher intensity UCS. However, because the UCR frequency and amplitude analyses did not show differences due to P, the authors conclude that the lower CR frequency in high P subjects represents a general failure of conditioning rather than a failure of responsivity per se. *Impulsivity* and *venturesomeness* again showed no relationship to conditioning when subjects were classified on these variables instead of E and P.

Frcka and Martin (1987), unsatisfied with the apparent lack of relationship between the *impulsiveness* (IMP) scales used in the earlier study (Frcka et al., 1983a), reported a new analysis of the data using IMP scales derived from a factor analysis of the IMP scale items. Two new IMP factors were derived. One was defined by a relatively narrow range of content referring to the tendency to act quickly on impulse without

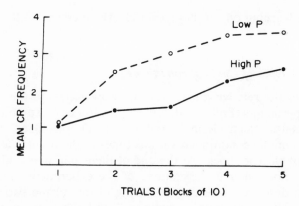

Figure 7.9. CR frequency in acquisition for high *psychoticism* (P+) and low *psychoticism* (P−) subjects. (From "The influence of psychoticism and extraversion on classical eyelid conditioning using a paraorbital shock UCS," by J. Beyts, I. M. Frcka, I. Martin, and A. B. Levey, 1983, *Personality and Individual Differences*, 4, p. 278. Copyright 1983 by Pergamon Press. Reprinted by permission.)

thinking (IMPn). The second factor was a broader one (IMPb), including mostly items that seem to have originated in current and earlier forms of the *disinhibition* and *boredom susceptibility* subscales of the *sensation seeking* scale (SSS, Zuckerman, 1979b). The third factor consisted of some of the *venturesomeness* (V) items from the standard Eysenck IMP scale, most of which originated in the SSS *thrill and adventure seeking* subscale. IMPn closely resembles the *impulsivity* subscale of the EPI E scale that was responsible for the conditioning results in the Eysenck and Levey (1972) study.

The IMPn scale was most clearly related to conditioning in this study. High IMPn subjects started to respond later than low IMPn subjects and responded with smaller amplitude CRs than low IMPn subjects. IMPb and *venturesomeness* were not related to these criteria of conditioning. Conditioning performance of high IMPn subjects was not affected by UCS intensity, but low IMPn subjects showed a higher level of response to high-intensity UCSs.

The trend of the results in this series of studies by Martin and her co-workers strongly suggests that the earlier work relating E to conditionability was a function of the narrow *impulsivity* component of the E scale in versions prior to the EPQ. In the Frcka and Martin (1987) study, the factor analytically derived IMPn scale correlated equally with E and P whereas the IMPb scale correlated more with P than E. Given the level of most of these correlations, the results for P and E cannot be easily predicted. The recent studies indicate that both P and E may be involved in eyelid conditioning. The P variable itself assumed greater independent significance in the study in which shock instead of air puff was used as the UCS. It may be that learning on the basis of a clearly aversive UCS may be the crucial factor for P.

Other types of classical conditioning

In contrast to the relative unimportance of awareness in the eyelid conditioning experiments (Frcka et al., 1983b), awareness of stimulus relations may be crucial in electrodermal conditioning. Fuhrer, Baer, and Cowan (1973) differentially conditioned various tones to the occurrence and nonoccurrence of electric shock. At the end of the experiment, subjects were interviewed about their understanding of the experiment. Subjects who were able to describe correctly the pairing of one of the two tones with shock were called "accurate verbalizers," and the other subjects were classified as "inaccurate verbalizers." The accurate verbalizers showed strong conditioning and resistance to extinction of the SCR response to the CS$^+$ relative to the CS$^-$ whereas the inaccurate verbalizers showed little or no differential conditioning. Awareness may influence conditioning through the mechanism of attention. Supporting this interpretation is the finding that the magnitude of the ORs also predicted conditionability but only for subjects who verbalized the correct CS-UCS contingency.

Fuhrer et al. (1973) failed to find any relationship between the TMAS or the E scale and any of the indices of conditionability or the index of awareness. As Fuhrer et al. point out, other investigators using loud tones or shock as UCSs for differential electrodermal conditioning have also failed to find any relationship between this type of conditionability and E or N in normal populations.

Raine and Venables (1981) attempted to test the relationship between classical conditioning and antisocial tendencies more directly by using various self-report (including the *socialization,* P, and SSS *disinhibition* scales) and teacher ratings of *socialization* of 15-year-old male schoolchildren. The UCS was a loud 105-dB tone and the CS was a moderate 65-dB tone. None of the correlations between a *socialization* factor score and conditioning were consistently significant for the entire group; but when they divided their sample into lower and higher socioeconomic groups, conditionability tended to be negatively correlated with *socialization* in the higher social class and positively correlated in the lower class group. The authors interpreted their findings within the context of a speculative theory of Eysenck (1977), which suggests that good conditionability in children who grow up in socialized homes promotes socialization, but good conditionability in children growing up in homes with antisocial attitudes and behaviors facilitates learning the antisocial patterns of the parents. However, it is a huge leap from this theory to a generalization about home environments based on social class.

Perhaps, it is significant that the few positive studies relating E to electrodermal conditioning are those using clinical samples (Halberstam, 1961;
Lykken, 1957; Vogel, 1961). A recent study by Pitman and Orr (1986)
used cases of anxiety disorders and matched normal controls. Based on
studies of "biological preparedness," they used facial expressions as CS^+;
an angry expression is assumed to be more conditionable by aversive reinforcement than a neutral expression. The UCS was a mild electric shock.
Their findings, comparing the clinical groups, are presented in the next
chapter. Of interest here is the finding of a significant positive correlation
between the Hamilton *anxiety* scale and magnitude of response to the CS^+
(angry face) and a negative correlation of the E scale with conditioned
response to the same stimulus during extinction. After the acquisition
phase, the shock electrodes were removed and the subjects were told that
no more shocks would be administered. The anxious introverted subjects
showed less extinction than the nonanxious more extraverted subjects, even
after verbal reassurance of the contingency change. The study suggests that
we must use extreme ranges of N and E, stimuli that have some "biological
preparedness," and look at resistance to extinction as a possible critical
variable if we are to relate personality to aversive classical conditioning.
High *neuroticism* may be related to a generalized punishment expectancy,
even when contingencies change.

Almost all of the classical conditioning studies in humans have used an
aversive UCS, probably because of the problems in manipulating an appetitive UCR such as the salivary response. Eysenck's and Gray's theories
make the same prediction for aversive conditioning (better conditioning
in introverts) but different predictions for appetitive conditioning (Gray
predicts better conditioning in extraverts; Eysenck still predicts better conditioning in introverts). For this reason, studies of appetititive conditioning
might provide a more crucial comparison of the theories. Kantorowitz
(1978) compared conditioning of the penile erectile response with E and
N scales in a sample of only seven subjects. Conditioned arousal was
positively related to E, and conditioned de-arousal was negatively related
to E. Even though these correlations are significant and supportive of
Gray's theory, the study still awaits replication with an adequate *n*. Given
the current climate of neopuritanism, it may be a while before this experiment is replicated, so let us now turn to the topic of instrumental conditioning, in which it is easier to provide positively reinforcing stimuli.

Instrumental (operant) conditioning

Both Eysenck's (1967) and Gray's (1973) theories apply to instrumental
(operant) as well as classical conditioning. Gray uses a two-factor learning

theory in which signals associated with reward and punishment acquire secondary reinforcing potential and "expectancy" through classical conditioning that may be modified by the outcomes of instrumental behavior. As with classical conditioning, Eysenck's theory predicts a general superiority of conditioning in introverts, except in conditions strong enough to elicit transmarginal inhibition; Gray's theory predicts a superiority of introverts or anxiety types in conditioning when punishment is the consequence but a superiority in learning by extraverts or impulsive types when reward is the consequence of a particular class of response.

Verbal conditioning

The operant conditioning paradigm is not easily adapted to study of humans because it requires a behavior with some probability of spontaneous emission of brief enough duration to be selectively reinforced. The verbal conditioning technique (Taffel, 1955) offers one possibility for using reinforcement to shape speech. The subject is shown a card with a verb in the past tense and five pronouns (I, WE, YOU, HE, THEY) inserted below the verb and is instructed to make up a sentence using one of the pronouns. The class of personal pronouns (I, WE) may be selected for reinforcement. A number of trials without reinforcement are run to determine the base rate of use of the personal pronouns. In the reinforcement series the experimenter can administer verbal positive reinforcement or punishment by saying "good" or "bad" after the reinforced pronoun. Physical punishment in the form of shock can also be used. Finally, a series of test trials without reinforcement is run to assess the change in verbal behavior from the baseline. The factor of awareness seems to be quite important in verbal conditioning (Miller, 1967), and in fact some investigators would claim that no conditioning can occur without awareness. Degree of awareness is usually assessed in a postexperimental questionnaire. The problem with this method is that one cannot determine if the subject became aware of the contingency before or after conditioning had occurred. The difference between learning with and without awareness is the difference between concept-formation learning and conditioning per se.

A series of studies by Gupta and his colleagues have addressed the theoretical issues in both Eysenck's and Gray's theories. Gupta (1973) first examined the effects of *extraversion* (E scale) and drugs on verbal conditioning reinforced with verbal reward. Both depressant drugs, phenobarbitone and chlorpromazine, reduced conditioning whereas the stimulant, dexedrine, increased conditioning relative to placebo levels. These data support Eysenck's theory that conditioning performance is a function of the level of cortical arousal (except that chlorpromazine tends to dampen limbic arousal more than cortical). Also supporting Eysenck's theory, but not Gray's, is the fact that introverts conditioned better than extraverts (and ambiverts) under placebo conditions, even though the reinforcement was reward. Dexedrine did not improve conditioning in introverts, though it did so in extraverts. This is consistent with the idea that CNS stimulants bring underaroused extraverts closer to their optimal level of arousal. Phenobarbitol, however, lowered conditioning performance about equally at all levels of *extraversion*. This would be consistent with the theory if it is assumed that introverts were already at their optimal level of arousal.

Gupta (1976) next investigated the differential effect of reward and punishment using verbal ("good") and nonverbal (a buzzer) rewards, and verbal ("bad") and nonverbal (mild electric shock) punishments. All subjects were males. Some of the subjects were run by a male and some by a female experimenter. Both rewards increased the designated verbal behavior, and both punishments reduced it. Punishment reduced the incidence of the response more for introverts than for extraverts. The effects of the verbal reward for extraverts depended on the genders of the experimenters and the subjects. Extraverted male subjects responded more to a female experimenter's "good" than to a male experimenter's use of that verbal reward. For introverts, the sex of the experimenter made no difference. The nonverbal reinforcer did not show any differences due to E. The data from subjects run by the female experimenter supported Gray's theory of a differential response to reward and punishment by introverts and extraverts. It also suggests that the impact of verbal reinforcement may sometimes depend on the characteristics of the reinforcing person.

Gupta and Nagpal (1978) examined the interaction of reinforcement and personality, looking separately at the *sociability* and *impulsivity* components of the E scale from the EPI. Gray would probably predict greater effects for the *impulsivity* dimension, in which the contrasts between response to signals of reward and punishment are maximal according to his model. This time the subjects were female instead of male. The rewards were verbal ("good") and nonverbal (buzzer), and electric shock was used as the punishment. Neither reward nor punishment or the personality variables had independent effects, but the interactions between both *impulsivity* and *sociability* and the reinforcement type were significant. Both high impulsives and high sociables conditioned better than lows on both traits in response to both types of positive reinforcement. For punishment, the findings were reversed; that is, greater response (reduction of responding from baseline) of low impulsives and sociables than highs. Thus, the results of this study provide the clearest support for Gray's hypotheses compared with those of Eysenck. Both *impulsivity* and *sociability* yielded similar results, but reward conditioning was slightly better for high impulsives than for high sociables.

Nagpal and Gupta (1979) had not included the N scale in these studies because of some earlier evidence that it was irrelevant to verbal conditioning. According to Gray's theory, it is the N factor not E that is related to general conditionability and therefore magnifies differences in relative reinforcement by reward or punishment. According to this idea, the introverted neurotic (high N, low E) should show the greatest response to punishment whereas the extraverted neurotic (high N, high E) should show the greatest response to reward. The subjects were all females selected for extreme scores on both E and N of the EPI. Reinforcements were the same as in the previous study. Confirming Gray's theory, the neurotic extravert group showed better conditioning than all other groups in the verbal reward condition, and the neurotic introvert group showed the greatest decrement in response due to punishment conditioning.

Gupta's final experiments returned to the interaction of drugs and *extraversion* with the addition of the reinforcement factor. Comparing the results of a study using phenobarbitone (Gupta, 1984) with the results of another study using amphetamine (Gupta & Gupta, 1984), the researchers found that the drugs do not have markedly different effects on extraverts and introverts except for specific dosage effects. Both drugs reduced reward conditionability in extraverts but did not affect the conditioning of introverts reinforced by reward. Both drugs, at different doses, increased the response of extraverts (low dose) to punishment and decreased that of introverts (high dose). Although they implicate arousal in the interaction of reinforcement and personality, the differential effects of dosage in introverts and extraverts are not immediately deducible from Eysenck's theory. Of course, the fact that both drugs tend to reduce differences between extraverts and introverts by eliminating some of the differences in arousal is one possibility. The high dose of the depressant drug reduced response to punishment in both groups; but in relation to the much larger response of introverts under undrugged (placebo) conditions, the difference is more significant for them. Given the high basal arousal of the introvert, it would take more dosage to effect a significant antipain or antianxiety effect. But why should a low dose effect an increase in arousal in the extravert? It is known that many depressant drugs have disinhibitory effects at lower doses, causing some increase in arousal, which is reversed at higher doses of the drug. This is why people speak of "getting high" in reference to alcohol or other depressant drugs. Perhaps extraverts, impulsives, and sensation seekers are more vulnerable to this disinhibitory effect than persons low on these traits.

The consistent results in nondrug experiments and the placebo conditions are supportive of Gray's theory of differential reinforcement sensitivity. But the interaction of drugs and personality is more predictable from Eysenck's theory centering around the optimal level of arousal construct. However, as discussed in chapter 5, drugs act on particular neurotransmitter systems associated with central reward and punishment; so the interactions with personality may have more to do with these effects than with their effects on nonspecific arousal systems.

Other types of learning

Trial and error learning

Gorenstein and Newman (1980) have devised a theory purporting to link human "disinhibitory psychopathology," including antisocial personality and alcoholic disorders, and the trait of *extraversion* with a septohippocampal disorder that manifests itself as a failure to inhibit punished responses or as a deficit in passive avoidance. The theory is quite similar to that of Gray (1973, 1982, 1987), who has defined *anxiety* as the clinical expression of an overactive septohippocampal mechanism (but involving other systems), with primary *psychopathy* as the other end of the continuum. Gray defines this dimension of *anxiety* within Eysenck's coordinates as a dimension running from the *neurotic-introversion* pole to the *stable-extraversion* pole. Gorenstein and Newman simply identify the dimension with *extraversion*. Gray's dimension does contrast introverts and extraverts, but in terms of *neuroticism* as well. Fowles (1980) has also suggested that a weak behavioral inhibition system is involved in *psychopathy*. All of these investigators identify the learning deficit as one of passive avoidance or, in general terms, the "failure to learn from experience" [of punishment].

Newman, Widom, and Nathan (1985) have tested the theory using a trial-and-error task with positive reinforcement or punishment. They have studied both the antisocial personality in clinical populations and *extraversion* in normal populations. Here we deal with their work on *extraversion* and other traits in normal, or at least nonincarcerated populations, reserving discussion of their work with diagnosed antisocials for Chapter 9.

The task used by the investigators (Newman et al., 1985) involved learning to respond to certain numbers in two-digit combinations and not respond to others. In a *passive avoidance with loss of reward (PALR)* condition, correct responses are rewarded with tokens redeemable for money or other reinforcers, and incorrect responses are punished with loss of money. No rewards are won or lost for not making a response. In a *passive avoidance with no reward (PANR)*, the subjects are given a sum of tokens at the outset. They get no rewards but can lose tokens either by making a response to the incorrect stimulus (error of commission or a failure of passive avoidance) or by not making a response to the correct stimulus (error of omission).

Extraverts in a situation in which a response may elicit either punishment or reward are more likely to make passive avoidance response errors than introverts; that is, extraverts respond when they should not do so and therefore get punished (Newman et al., 1985; Patterson, Kosson, & Newman, 1987). Furthermore, after they receive punishment, extraverts fail to hesitate longer on the next trial, as introverts do (Patterson et al. 1987).

This means that they have less chance to reflect on and register the association between the stimulus and the punishment. For this reason they do not learn from the experience of punishment as well as introverts. However, Patterson et al. (1987) point out some advantages of this strategy of ignoring the possibility of punishment in the pursuit of reward. Extraverts are more likely to be persistent, optimistic, and undeterred by failure. Introverts, in contrast, may be more likely to develop "learned helplessness" after minimal experiences of failure or nonreinforcement. Neurotic extraverts are particularly prone to make passive avoidance errors and to display a generalized unreflective tendency. This would fit Eysenck's theory that neurotic extraverts are prone to criminality and other antisocial behavior and Gray's theory that *neuroticism* amplifies the difference in reactions to signals of reward and punishment in both introverts and extraverts. Emotional arousal assumes the form of anxiety and inhibition in the neurotic introverts and the impulsive approach response in the extravert. But both theorists have also recognized the important role of the P dimension in antisocial behavior. Although they used the EPQ, which contains the P scales, Newman and his colleagues have not provided any analyses of their results in terms of P or its interactions with E and N. The prisoners in the Newman and Kosson (1986) study were given the EPQ and a number of other questionnaires measuring various forms of *anxiety, impulsivity,* and *sensation seeking.* The only scales differentiating prisoners who were rated as more psychopathic and a nonpsychopathic group of prisoners were the P scale, (but not the E or N scales from the EPQ), Gough's socialization scale, and the *monotony avoidance (sensation seeking)* scale of the Karolinska Personality Inventory. It is clear that psychopathy in the clinical sense is more associated with P than with E. Therefore, more work on reinforcement should be done using the P scale to establish a connection between the syndrome of psychopathy and the dimension most closely and directly related to it.

Concept learning with reinforcement

Many theories of personality revolve around "personal constructs" (G. A. Kelly, 1955), "personifications" (Sullivan, 1953), or concepts of self and others (Rogers, 1959). Humans tend to respond to generalized concepts, even to nonpersonal stimuli. The learning of constructs is not only part of being a thinking human, but the particular way humans cognitively organize the social and impersonal environments identifies the society they come from and the unique persons they are. Concept formation is highly involved with frontal lobe function of the cortex. Damage to this area interferes with performance on the Wisconson Concept Formation Test.

The effects of reinforcement on concept formation has been used in the study of schizophrenics' sensitivity to verbal punishment, but the method has not been widely used in the study of personality. Ball and Zuckerman

(1990) studied the effects of reward and punishment on learning concepts before and after a nonreversal shift in the concept designated as correct.

Subjects were tested on the SSS, EPQ, and a new experimental scale called the *generalized reward and punishment expectancy scale* (GRAPES) was used. GRAPES is an unpublished 20-item questionnaire yielding scores for expectations regarding personal outcomes from various life events; it was included to assess its construct validity as a predictor of sensitivity to reward or punishment. GRAPES has two scores: generalized reward expectancy (RE) and punishment expectancy (PE).

Our experiment differed from studies by Newman and his associates in that a more complex type of learning (concept formation) was required, and reward and punishment were completely separated in the conditions. Newman's results in regard to E were found for a condition in which both reward and punishment were used for the same subjects.

In our experiment, differences between extraverts and introverts were found for response latencies in the postshift task. Probably the increased arousal of the postshift in contrast to the preshift task contributed to the result. Extraverts were slowed relatively more by frustrative nonreward, and introverts showed stronger inhibition after punishment. Extraverts had a stronger generalized reward expectancy than introverts as shown by the correlation between the E and the GRAPES RE scales. When reward is not forthcoming, extraverts may be more aroused because there is a greater discrepancy between expectation and outcome than for introverts.

In the case of neurotics, the slowed reaction time following punishment was specific to the verbal reinforcement and was not seen in a monetary reinforcement condition. Neurotics generally suffer from social anxiety related to a fear of criticism or loss of positive regard, which may make verbal reinforcement relatively more potent for them than for more secure stables. Nagpal and Gupta (1979) found that an introverted neurotic group showed a strong decrement in response to direct verbal punishment. In contrast, Patterson et al. (1987), using monetary reinforcement and computer-generated feedback, could not find an effect of N on passive avoidance learning, though neurotic introverts did show a failure of response to correct cues. Neurotics in our study seemed to be particularly susceptible to disruption by the frustration induced by the unexpected shift in reinforcement contingencies. Although they were superior to stables in learning the preshift task, the high N subjects were more frustrated and took longer to adapt to the changed contingencies. Perhaps level of arousal was optimal for the high N group prior to shift, but the failure experience raised the arousal level to a point at which it was disruptive of learning.

Classroom learning and reinforcement

Personality theory is rarely tested in learning situations outside of the laboratory. An exception is the study by McCord and Wakefield (1981).

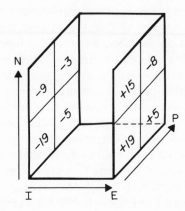

Figure 7.10. Classroom learning as a function of reward and punishment and positions in three dimensions of personality, *extraversion-introversion* (E−I), *neuroticism* (N), and *psychoticism* (P). Expected number of points gained (+) or lost (−) from teacher most consistently using reward (as compared to teacher at midpoint). Prediction made from regression equation. *Extraverts* gain more from reward than introverts, high P subjects gain or lose little from either type of teacher. Figure constructed from data in McCord & Wakefield (1981).

These authors used Gray's theory to predict results in classroom learning. Five teachers were observed during their arithmetic classes. The number of times the teachers used verbal rewards or punishments were recorded, and the teachers were ranked according to the ratio of reward to punishment. They ranged from one teacher whose reward to punishment ratio was about 10:1 to another teacher who used reward and punishment in equal proportion. The 9–10-year-old students in all five classes were administered the Junior EPQ and were given arithmetic achievement tasks before and after an 8-week session. In classes where reward was most predominant, E was directly correlated with arithmetic achievement over the period relative to a preinstruction baseline; but in classes where reward was less broadly used and punishment was relatively more frequent, the correlations with E were negative, indicating superior achievement by introverts. Multiple regression analysis showed that the interactions between the degree of classroom reward and P were as large as those between reward and E. Although N also made a significant contribution in prediction of arithmetic achievement, it was smaller than those for E and P. Using the results of the multiple regression, predictions were made for the number of points gained or lost by children in relative arithmetic scores in contrast to the course taught by the most consistently rewarding teacher and the teacher at the median for classroom reward. These results are plotted as a function of E, N, and P in Figure 7.10.

Extraverts showed a greater increment in learning in the class where more reward was used, and the introverts responded more to the class where reward was mixed with some punishment. P seemed to reduce all effects of E, perhaps reflecting a greater insensitivity to both reward and punishment. The effects of N seem secondary to those of E and P, generally reducing the effect of reward, particularly for high E subjects. The greatest contrasts in effects of reward as contrasted with punishment can be seen in the contrast between introverts and extraverts who are all low on P and N. P seems to attenuate these results more than N.

There is no certainty that other aspects of the teachers or their instructional techniques interacted with personality to produce differences in learning. Ideally, one would have the same teachers using different reward and punishment techniques in different classes to separate the effects of reinforcement from those due to the teachers per se. As far as these results go, they seem to support the Gray hypothesis of a greater susceptibility to reward in extraverts than in introverts, with both P and N showing some attenuation effect on this difference. But these attenuation effects are not deducible from the theory. If anything, P and N should amplify differences between extraverts and introverts in response to signals of reward and punishment.

Imitation

It has been suggested that most social learning takes place by observation without obvious reinforcement (Bandura, 1977, 1986). Once the expectations are encoded, their subsequent performance may be affected or further shaped by reinforcement. Few studies have been done on the interaction of personality traits with conditions in observational learning or imitation experiments, largely because social learning theorists do not see much value in the concept of generalized traits and feel they have minimal predictive value for behavior in real situations. In the classic "Bobo doll" experiment, Bandura (1965) reported that the observed consequences (reward or punishment) of aggressive behavior influence children's behavior whether or not the behavior is spontaneously imitated on a subsequent occasion. However, the sex differences of results in this study were much greater than the observed consequences. Boys were more prone than girls to learn and imitate the aggressive behavior of the model. Seeing the model punished for aggression reduced imitation in girls but had no significant effect on boys. In fact, boys who saw the model punished imitated the model more than girls who saw the model rewarded. Bandura interprets these sex differences in terms of sex-role training and "prior history of reinforcement of imitative behavior." Regardless of whether the sex differences are attributed to biosocial predispositions or purely social reinforcement, the data show that the persisting group differences in behavior are more powerful than the immediate environmental manipulations. It would not be unreasonable to expect that a good measure of general aggressiveness would predict the likelihood of imitating aggression for individuals in a natural or experimental setting.

Bauer, Schlottmann, Bates, and Masters (1983) investigated the effects of state and trait anxiety on imitation of prestigious and nonprestigious models. The response modeled was running a pencil maze, and the models both exhibited a deliberate slow approach to the problem. All subjects' times in the maze were slower in imitation of the restrained technique of the more prestigious model than in imitation of the same behavior in the less prestigious model, but the differences were larger for high trait anxious subjects than for lows. The result was predicted because anxious individuals tend to be more dependent, suggestible, and less self-confident and therefore are considered more likely to be affected by the prestige status of the model. This study indicates the potential, largely unexplored, research possibilities in the area of trait interaction with imitation learning. The question of who we choose to imitate is crucial to the idea of genotype-phenotype correlation as discussed in chapter 3.

Summary

Evolution of learning begins with simple nonassociative learning such as habituation and sensitization, which is present in the simplest animal forms, and proceeds to classical and instrumental conditioning, concept formation, and verbal learning. More complex animals differ from less complex forms in their capacity to maintain previous learning in memory, utilize it on future appropriate occasions, and generalize learning experiences in terms of probability of reinforcement and higher order classifications facilitated by language in humans. However, humans demonstrate all types of learning, from the simplest to the most complex; therefore, studies of the neurophysiological mechanisms of learning in simple organisms promise to be of some relevance for the biological understanding of learning in humans.

Pavlovian theory suggests that learning (classical conditioning) depends on certain properties of the nervous system that vary consistently among individuals, including strength of excitatory process (reactivity), strength of inhibitory process, and balance between the two processes and their mobility from one state to the other, in terms of environmental demands. Eysenck described the trait of "conditionability," differentiating introverts and extraverts in particular conditions. These differences affect the learning of inhibition of behavior, involved in the process of socialization.

Gray has based a model on modern neuropsychological data and theory, which describes individual differences in learning according to differences in the physiology of brain systems that mediate reinforcement and punishment and responses to the stimuli associated with these. He proposes a two-process theory of learning in which stimuli acquire secondary reinforcing properties by association with primary reinforcers (classical conditioning) and guide subsequent behavior by the process of instrumental conditioning. Applying this theory to Eysenck's dimensions, Gray concludes that the E dimension represents the relative strength or sensitivity of reward and punishment analyzing systems, rather than a general conditionability factor, as suggested by Eysenck. Extraverts are thought to be relatively more conditionable to stimuli that are associated with reward whereas introverts are said to be more sensitive and to learn more from cues that are associated with punishment. The N dimension is thought to amplify the magnitude of both responses to cues of reward and those for punishment. The P dimension is related to unconditioned responses to punishment and a fight-or-flight mechanism.

Habituation of the orienting reflex in humans as assessed by psychophysiological measures, has shown uncertain evidence of reliability across time, response measures, or stimulus modalities using the same measure. Furthermore, habituation rate is usually influenced by the strength of the initial response to the stimulus, and many measures of habituation do not control this factor. A review of studies by O'Gorman concluded that E is related to habituation, and N is not. An argument can be made for the opposite conclusion if we consider only studies using the appropriate controls for initial response amplitude and incorporating other important requisites.

Eyelid conditioning also poses a number of methodological problems, including the role of awareness. However, studies suggest that although awareness is related to personality measures, it is not related to conditioning per se. Experiments in Iowa, done in the Spence–Hullian framework, showed a primary involvement of the trait of *anxiety* in eyelid conditioning; those done in England, based on Eysenck's theory, suggested a primary role for the E dimension in conditionability, but subsequent research seems to have narrowed the relevant trait even more to a type of *impulsivity*. The broader P factor has also been found to play a role in conditionability, either by itself or in interaction with E. Studies using EEG to assess cortical arousal during conditioning and other studies that manipulated arousal with stimulant and depressant drugs found that conditioning is directly related to degree of arousal and suggest that arousal may mediate the relationship between personality and conditionability.

A series of experiments by Gupta and his colleagues using the verbal instrumental conditioning paradigm has provided generally consistent support for Gray's theory, suggesting that introverts should learn more from punishment and extraverts more from reward. In fact, they have shown that the major lines of conditioning effects follow Gray's conceptualization, with neurotic extraverts or impulsives conditioning best when reinforced by reward and neurotic introverts showing more effect with punishment.

Newman and his associates have also conducted a fruitful series of experiments relating *extraversion* to instrumental conditioning. For situations in which both reward and punishment are possible, extraverts differed from introverts in their greater tendency to make passive avoidance errors, that is, responding when they should not do so and thereby incurring punishment. Furthermore, when they are punished, extraverts fail to show inhibition or slowing of response on the next trial. This tendency to be reflective or unreflective immediately following punishment is related to success or failure in learning to avoid punishment. Neurotic extraverts show a generalized unreflective tendency even more than stable extraverts. Newman's results are supportive of both Eysenck's and Gray's theories, though more so of Gray's in that they show a deficit in extraverts specific to passive avoidance learning rather than conditioning in general.

Ball and Zuckerman (1990) extended the reward and punishment model to concept formation. The results on N were particularly interesting, implicating the effects of emotional arousal in learning. Although the high N subjects were good at learning a concept in nonfrustrating conditions, they showed a stronger emotional response and a difficulty in learning when the correct solution changed so that they encountered sudden and unexpected nonreward or punishment. When an incorrect response had the consequence of loss of reward, the extraverts responded more slowly; but when the incorrect response led to punishment, the introverts responded more slowly on the subsequent trial. The type of reinforcement was also a factor in the reaction of neurotics. After punishment or loss of reward in the form of verbal reinforcement, neurotics were slower to respond than stables; but this difference was not found with monetary reinforcement. Such results suggest that we must consider some distinctive human characteristics when adopting reinforcement models derived from animal models in which clearcut primary reinforcers are used. Punishment may not be the equivalent of loss of reward, and verbal incentives may be more significant than low monetary incentives, particularly for neurotics.

The argument that social patterns of response are primarily learned by observation and subsequently reinforced after spontaneous imitation is compelling. However, this does not account for large individual differences among children or adults who are exposed to the same models, witness the same outcomes, and yet behave differently. The differences between children raised in the same families are a case in point (Plomin & Daniels, 1987). Social learning theory does not explain why, given the range of models available, some children imitate one model and others imitate another. Children learn a great deal from their peers, but they choose to associate with certain peers rather than others. Imitational learning would seem to offer a useful way to study the interaction of personality and environment, but this approach has been neglected, perhaps due to the antipathy of social learning theorists to the trait approach. Bandura (1977) states that the interaction between the person and the environment is two-way, but his definition of the "person" may shift from one situation to the next. The study of learning and reinforcement processes is of equal significance to psychobiological and social approaches to personality. All adaptive behavior must be learned; but what we choose to learn, how easily we learn it, and how we respond to the reactions of the social world to our demonstrations of what we have learned, all depend to some extent on our biological makeup.

8   Anxiety disorders

Overview

Since the ancient Greek humoral theory, our concepts of normal and abnormal personalities have been influenced by medical models, which differ in some respects from the psychological trait model in definition of abnormalcy. A clinical disorder can be a transient condition produced in part by internal factors. An analogous contrast is between affective and motivational states and traits (Spielberger, 1972; Zuckerman, 1976). A distinction can be made between generalized anxiety disorder (GAD), in which a person is anxious much of the time and in many situations, and panic disorder (PD), in which attacks of intense anxiety occur for short periods, but the person may be free from anxiety at other periods. The symptoms of other disorders may appear only under particular environmental provocation. A simple phobia, for instance, may reveal itself by intense anxiety only in the presence of the phobic object. It is only the aggregation of the incidents and the resultant patterns of avoidance that define some disorders.

The *Diagnostic and Statistical Manual* (DSM III-R, 1987) of the American Psychiatric Association differentiates episodic clinical disorders (axis I) and longstanding personality disorders (axis II). The distinction is one of time (how long the person has demonstrated these traits), intensity (how severe is the expression of the trait), and adaptability (how well the person has been able to function in spite of the handicap). Personality disorders are distinguished from variations in normal personality traits by their inflexibility, maladaptibility, and production of functional impairment and distress.

The symptoms of the clinical disorder may be distinctive, with features that are not found at all or are found to a minimal degree in the normal population, such as cancer or the disorganized type of thought in schizophrenia. If minor forms of the symptom are found in the normal population (e.g., atypical cells or mild peculiarities of thinking), the distribution is not likely to be normal because most persons show none, and smaller numbers show some. In bipolar scales like *compulsivity* versus *impulsivity,* in which abnormal manifestations represent extremes at both ends of the continuum, one may find a continuous and bell-shaped normal distribution. But when one assesses traits that are abnormal at one pole only, like Eysenck's P

320

scale, one usually finds a reverse J-shaped or highly skewed distribution (Eysenck, Eysenck, & Barrett, 1985).

Most clinical diagnoses are based on syndromes, which are clusters of symptoms occurring together, rather than single symptoms. The question of distribution of the disorders is obviously affected by the number of symptoms involved. When we combine several traits in certain specifications, we rapidly approach smaller groupings of persons. The rationale of the usual medical model is that empirically observed groupings of symptoms are comprehensible in terms of an underlying organic condition that produces the covariation of symptoms. One of the objections to the medical model, as applied in psychiatry, is that it assumes an organic rather than a social explanation for mental illness. This presumption has been disowned by the originators of the current American Diagnostic System for Mental Disorders (DSM III), who argue that, before we can do any good research on the origins of these disorders, whether social or organic, we must define them reliably enough to be sure that investigators of a disorder are studying the same disorder. The DSM III takes pains to avoid language that carries the implication of type of etiology if the cause of the disorder is unknown.

Freud (1895/1937) discussed the application of the medical model to his newly defined "neuroses" in terms of (a) predisposition, (b) specific cause, (c) contributory cause, and (d) releasing cause. The *predisposition* are those factors that are a necessary background to the more immediate causes and are necessary for the disorder to appear but cannot in themselves cause the disorder. These would be understood as the genetic disposition, and Freud's definition is the same as the postulated role of genetic factors in the "diathesis-stress" model (Meehl, 1962). Given the presence of the predisposition, the *specific cause* is also necessary for the disorder to occur. In contrast, *contributory causes* are not always present, necessary, or able to produce the behavior alone, but they potentiate the predisposition and the specific causes. The *releasing cause* is simply the last cause immediately preceding the clinical condition, and it may be either a specific or a contributory cause. Much of the debate over the biological or social causes of behavior disorders would benefit from consideration of these distinctions. We must ask if any single biological or social cause is sufficient in itself to produce the particular disorder. In some or, perhaps, most disorders, it may be that there are no specific causes, only contributory causes.

Modern biological psychiatry has played an essential role in the development of a psychobiological approach to personality. If we can find psychiatric disorders that share some phenomenology with personality traits, then information about their genetics, associated brain structures, biochemistry, psychophysiology, and learning characteristics can make significant contributions to an understanding of the psychobiology of personality in the normal range.

This chapter and the next will deal with two major classes of disorders because of their putative relationship with two of the major dimensions of personality, N and P. As Zuckerman, Kuhlman, and Camac (1988) found, the N dimension is primarily defined by negative emotionality (anxiety and hostility). Freud grouped a number of disorders under the neurosis designation, including what are now called (DSM III-R) anxiety, somatoform, dissociative, and dysthymic disorders, on the assumption that all represented either the direct expression of anxiety or defensive modes of coping with anxiety such as conversion, repression, and displacement. The DSM III, in contrast to earlier DSMs, does not use the major category of neurosis or the term itself (except in parentheses) because it implies the Freudian idea that symptoms are defenses. The category of anxiety disorder is reserved for those disorders in which anxiety is clearly manifest in the symptomatic picture of the disorder and includes panic disorder, agoraphobia, social phobias, simple phobias, obsessive-compulsive disorder, posttraumatic stress disorder, and generalized anxiety disorder. Psychobiological investigations of these disorders are the topics of this chapter. The issues of whether somatoform and dysphoric disorders should be included in the spectrum of anxiety disorders are considered in terms of familial association, that is, do the disorders tend to aggregate in the families of those patients with clear-cut anxiety disorders?

The next chapter deals with the disorders that may define the extreme of the P dimension. Antisocial personality disorder is the pure case, but other disinhibitory disorders are also worth examining because of the high incidence of psychopathy in populations with these problems. These include criminality and substance abuse, particularly the abuse of illegal drugs.

Definitions (DSM III-R)

Panic disorder and agoraphobia

Panic disorder is defined by episodic attacks of severe anxiety in the form of intense symptoms of autonomic arousal such as rapid heart rate, shortness of breath or smothering sensations, shaking, sweating, dizziness, and nausea. It is associated with ideas of dying, "going crazy", or doing something "uncontrolled." Because of the absence of any external stimulus or explanation for the attack, it is often not identified as an emotional or "anxiety" response by the patients themselves. Conscious anxiety arises in anticipation of the attacks themselves, particularly in public places or in circumstances in which one cannot easily escape to the home. This is why agoraphobia is frequently associated with panic disorder. Severe agoraphobics cannot leave their homes at all, and others can go out only for brief periods if accompanied by a close companion. If they do go out, they avoid situations such as crowds, lines, restaurants, and theaters from which escape might be difficult or embarrassing in the event of a panic attack. Despite the close connection between agoraphobia and panic disorder, there are cases of agoraphobia with no history of panic disorder and many cases of panic disorder that do not develop into agoraphobia (Stein & Uhde, 1988; Tyrer & Gall, 1983).

In the case of panic disorder with agoraphobia we have the purest example of "fear of fear" or, more precisely, fear of panic. Klein (1981) has claimed that separation anxiety and school phobias are found in 50% of the childhood histories of female agoraphobics, though lower rates of 22–24% have been reported by Berg, Marks, McGuire, and Lipsedge (1974) and Perugi et al. (1988).

Other phobias

Agoraphobia is the most severely restrictive type of phobia. *Social phobias* are limited to situations in which the person might be exposed to embarrassment or humiliation by other persons. Parties, public performances, and any situations involving interactions with nonintimates results in anxiety. *Simple phobias,* even more circumscribed, involve specific stimuli such as fears of blood, or of particular animals such as dogs, cats, birds, insects, snakes, or mice, or situations such as closed spaces, high places, or air travel. Although the stimulus or situation, or anticipation of encountering the situation, produces anxiety, anxiety is not ordinarily present. The person avoids the feared object or situation at all costs.

Generalized anxiety disorder

Generalized anxiety disorder (GAD) is defined as "excessive" anxiety or worry about life circumstances when there is little or no realistic basis for the worry. The worry in adults may be over children, job, or finances, and in children and adolescents it may concern academic or social performance. Unlike episodic or stimulus-bound anxiety disorders, people with GAD are anxious or worried "more days than not." Generalized anxiety may also be observed in more than half of the patients diagnosed as panic disorder (Koehler, Vartzopoulos, & Ebel, 1988).

Obsessive-compulsive disorder

Obsessive-compulsive disorder (OCD) is also associated with generalized anxiety for most persons with the disorder. Obsessions are recurrent, unwanted thoughts that interfere with daily routine and cause distress. They seem senseless and even contrary to the person's normal feelings, as in the idea of hurting a loved one. Compulsions are repetitive behaviors that seem pointless to the person but result in more anxiety if the person tries to resist acting them out. Obsessions about contamination from dirt or physical contact with others, thoughts of violence, and doubt about whether one has carried out certain actions such as turning off gas jets or locking the house are common. Related compulsions are excessive hand-washing, and recounting and checking on previous actions.

Posttraumatic stress disorder

Posttraumatic stress disorder (PTSD) was recently added to the DSM III because of the large number of cases consequent to the Vietnamese war. However, persistent reactions to major trauma have been noted after every war and civilian catastrophe. Those occurring after World War I impelled Freud (1920/1937) to reconsider his entire theory and to postulate a "death instinct." The traumatic event is persistently reexperienced in recollection, dreams, and feelings even though the person tries to avoid such thoughts and feelings and sometimes represses some of the traumatic event itself. Persistent anxiety and a feeling of detachment from others and diminished . interest in activities and job characterize the syndrome, which may persist for years.

Dysthymia

Dysthymia was formerly known as depressive neurosis and was classified along with anxiety disorders in the major category of neurosis. It is now classified, in terms of its major symptom, in the *mood* disorder category. It is primarily defined by a chronically depressed ("more days than not") mood, along with other symptoms of depression such as low self-esteem, feelings of hopelessness, difficulty in making decisions, and low energy or fatigue. These were also general symptoms of neurosis. It is seen as a less intense but more chronic form of *major depressive disorder,* though it is not clear whether it is really closer to anxiety or major mood disorders. Major depressive disorder itself does frequently occur as a secondary re-action to prolonged panic disorders (Stein and Uhde, 1988).

Somatoform disorders

Somatoform disorders were formerly included under the general category of neurosis but are now described as a distinct group characterized by physical symptoms or complaints suggesting real physical disorders for which there is no evidence of organic causes and positive evidence that the symptoms are linked to psychological factors or conflicts. In the DSM III there is no assumption of an underlying anxiety that is defended against by the symptoms.

Comments on definitions

A number of personality disorders obviously represent even more habitual forms of some of the traits described in the clinical disorders but without the debilitating symptoms. Any of these disorders describe some aspects of general neuroticism as a broad personality trait as described in chapter 1.

A continuity theory of psychopathology would predict that most clinical disorders (axis I) would show some tendencies toward the syndrome in the personality before the clinical episode. Is this true of anxiety disorders? Tyrer, Casey, and Gall (1983) compared neurotic and personality disorder diagnoses. On the basis of trait ratings from the interview, a computer program classified the patients into one of five categories: normal, sociopathic (antisocial personality), passive-dependent, anankastic (obsessive-compulsive), or schizoid. With the exception of *obsessional neurosis,* in which seven of the eight cases were diagnosed as having an obsessive-compulsive personality, anywhere from 52 to 80% of the other patients in the other neurosis categories and 60% of the total group were classified as normal, that is, having no personality disorder prior to the clinical disorder. Except for the obsessive-compulsive group, there appears to be no reliable relationship between the clinical disorder and a preexisting personality disorder.

Clearly, there is a large overlap of the various anxiety disorders and of these and depressive disorders. The overlap exists in both concurrent symptomatology and over the life histories of the disorders. Those persons who were involved in the DSM III have elected to define more specific disorders rather than group them into broader disorders on the basis of phenomenology. Many of the distinctions are obviously arbitrary, based on symptom counts, durations, and age of onset. Diagnostic conflict is avoided by establishing hierarchies; for example, if one has panic attacks, other types of anxiety symptoms are ignored in the diagnosis. However, given the limitations of the medical model, this may be the best strategy. Many medical disorders with different etiologies have overlapping syndromes. Until there is definite understanding of etiology, it would be premature to group disorders solely on the basis of their phenomenology alone. Simple dimensions such as anxiety and depression characterize most disorders, but other evidence suggests that disorders can be distinguished by other factors such as prognosis or course, their familial and genetic overlap, the biological factors, and their response to various treatments.

Genetic studies

Genetic studies of psychopathology rely primarily on three methods: twin comparisons, family incidence compared with incidence of the disorder in

326   *Psychobiology of personality*

Table 8.1. *Twin studies of anxiety disorders*

Authors	Diagnoses	Concordance for any anxiety disorder			
		ITn	FTn	IT%	FT%
Slater and Shields (1969)	Anxiety disorders	17	28	42	4
Torgersen (1983)	All anxiety disorders	32	53	34	17
	Panic disorder	5	6	60	33
	Agoraphobia	11	15	36	13
	Social phobia	1	3	100	0
	Generalized anxiety dis.	12	20	17	20
	Obsessive-compulsive	3	9	33	11
Rasmussen & Tsuang (1984)[a]	Obsessive-compulsive	51	—	57	—
Carey & Gottesman (1981)[b]	Obsessive-compulsive	15	15	33	7
	Phobic disorders	8	13	13	8
Eckhart et al. (1981)[c]	Phobic disorders	9	—	67	—

[a] Data from 10 other studies
[b] Data from Maudsley twin register in cooperation with Shields
[c] Identical twins separated at or near birth

families of controls, and adoption studies. The first method uses concordance statistics and is based on the same assumptions as those described for the parametric type of data described for traits in chapter 3. Family data are based on observed versus expected incidences of the disorder in first-degree relatives. When based on intact families, as nearly all studies are, the method cannot separate the genetic and environmental influences; the adoption studies are most valuable for this purpose because they clearly separate the two influences. Unfortunately, they have not been used, as yet, to study anxiety disorders except for a small sample of separated twins with phobias in the Minnesota study (Eckart, Heston, & Bouchard, 1981).

Twin studies

Twin studies of anxiety neuroses have been less common than of major mood disorders and schizophrenia, and those that have been done have not used large numbers of subjects, an important requisite for reliability in twin data. Twin studies of anxiety disorder are shown in Table 8.1. The study of anxiety neuroses in general by Slater and Shields (1969) shows a high degree of heritability for these disorders as judged by the identical twin: fraternal twin (IT: FT) ratio of 10 to 1. However, the 4% incidence of the disorder in FTs is quite low compared with the incidence found in family studies or even the 10–15% lifetime prevalence of these disorders in the general population (Karno et al., 1987; Robins et al., 1984). Torgerson's data show no evidence of heritability of particular types of anxiety disorders. In no case was there any concordance between an identical twin and the proband (the one with the current disorder) for the particular type of anxiety disorder (e. g., panic or agoraphobia), though, with the exception of generalized anxiety disorder, which shows no evidence of heritability, there seems to be some broad susceptibility to various anxiety disorders. However, the small n for specific diagnoses in this study would make any conclusions premature.

Carey and Gottesman (1981) presented data, collected with Shields, on twins in which one twin had an obsessive-compulsive neurosis. The concordance rates for both ITs and FTs were higher for a broad criterion of obsessive-compulsive trait, but the IT:FT ratio was higher (almost 5:1) for the narrower criterion (the clinical disorder). Rasmussen and Tsuang (1984) listed IT concordance rates for ITs from 10 studies, 7 of which reported on only 1 to 3 pairs. The concordance rate for the 51 pairs of ITs was 57%. If the rate for diagnosed obsessive-compulsive FTs is 7% as in the previous study, which is also the rate found in ordinary siblings, then the rate for ITs represents a substantial heredity for the disorder (8:1).

Carey and Gottesman (1981) also reported twin data for phobic disorders. The low rates for both ITs and FTs for this disorder indicated a low degree of heritability. Torgersen studied mood disorders including the dysthymic disorder. Although the concordance rate was not high for this kind of disorder, the ratio of about 4:1 indicates some influence. But what is more interesting is that there was little evidence of either major affective or anxiety disorders in the cotwins (Torgersen, 1979; 1983).

Nine pairs of identical twins reared apart from infancy, of which at least one member of each pair had fears or phobias, were uncovered in the Minnesota twin study (Eckart et al., 1981). The twins of each pair were interviewed separately by two psychiatrists. In six of the nine cases, the twins were concordant for the disorder, and in some cases they had the same phobias. These data strongly suggest a role for heredity in the broad class of anxiety disorders because environment could play no role in the 67% rate of concordance for these pairs.

Family prevalence studies

Family studies tell us something about the relatedness of disorders and something about the genetic patterns of disorders, to the extent that genetics determines the tendency of the disorder to run in families. Carey and Gottesman (1981) list four studies of broad anxiety neurosis among the first-degree relatives (parents, siblings, and children) of probands with the disorder. All studies were close in the incidence of anxiety disorders reported in relatives, with 15 to 18% of the relatives showing evidence of the disorder. A study by Noyes, Clancy, Crowe, Hoenk, and Slymen (1978) was clearly superior to Carey and Gottesman (1981) in methodology, using blind data collection and explicit definitions of disorders for diagnosis. They

Table 8.2. *Frequency (%) of disorders in agoraphobic, panic disorder, and control relatives*

	Relatives of (%)			
	Agoraphobic	Panic disorder	Control	p^a
n's	256	241	113	—
Anxiety disorder	27.7	25.7	13.3	.01
Panic disorder	7.0	14.9	3.5	.001
Agoraphobia	9.4	1.7	3.5	.001
Social phobia	3.5	1.7	0.9	NS
Simple phobia	2.7	1.7	1.8	NS
Generalized anxiety	3.9	5.4	3.5	NS
Obsessive-compulsive	0.8	—	—	NS
Alcohol disorders	12.9	6.6	4.4	.01
Affective disorders	4.7	4.1	7.1	NS
Other disorders	7.0	6.6	3.5	.05
All disorders	52.3	43.2	28.3	.001

[a]Probabilities refer to comparisons across all three groups and are based on chi-square tests with 2 df. NS, not significant.
Source: R. Noyes et al. (1986), *Archives of General Psychiatry*, 43, 227–32. Copyright 1986 American Medical Association, with permission.

found an 18% (age corrected) incidence of clear-cut anxiety disorder in the relatives of probands, compared with 3% in the relatives of controls. There was a slightly greater incidence of alcoholism in the "at risk" relatives than controls but no difference in the rate of depression. The incidence of disorders was twice as great in the probands' female relatives (24%) as in their male relatives (13%). The risk in siblings varied as a function of how many parents were affected. If neither parent was affected, the rate was 9%; if one parent had the disorder the rate was 24%, and if both parents were affected, the rate in the siblings was 44%. This pattern suggests additive genetic influence with both parents contributing equally to the genes of the disorder.

Noyes et al. (1986) attempted to answer some of the questions about the relationship between panic disorder and agoraphobia. All available adult relatives of agoraphobics, panic disorders, and a matched group of normals were given structured interviews and rated blindly and independently by two psychiatrists using DSM III criteria for diagnosis. Table 8.2 shows the results.

Agoraphobia was diagnosed more often in relatives of agoraphobic patients than in relatives of probands with panic disorders or controls, but nearly as many of these relatives of agoraphobics were diagnosed as having panic disorders as agoraphobia. However, the families of panic disorder patients showed a predominance of this disorder, and only a few agoraphobics were found. The family groups did not differ from each other significantly on any of the other types of anxiety disorders aggregated in this table or on affective disorders, but alcohol disorders were more frequent in the agoraphobic family group than the controls. Age-corrected morbidity risks for agoraphobia and panic disorders combined was 20% among the agoraphobic families and 19% among panic disorder families. A breakdown of the data by relationship and gender showed no difference between parents and siblings but a marked difference as a function of gender: Females were 3 times more at risk for agoraphobia than males and two times more at risk for panic disorders. The risk of primary alcoholism was higher among the male relatives of agoraphobics than among panic or control relatives. Alcoholism was also a complication that occurred more often in the agoraphobic than in the panic probands themselves.

All of the agoraphobics in the study gave a history of panic attacks, leading the authors to conclude that agoraphobia is a severe variant of panic disorder. This hypothesis is supported by their test data showing agoraphobics scoring higher than other types of phobics on the EPI N scale (but not E) and on anxiety, phobia, and interpersonal sensitivity scales.

Weissman, Heckman, Marikangas, Gammon, and Prusoff (1984) found that the children of parents with agoraphobia or panic disorder in addition to a major depression were more likely to have received treatment for either major depression or anxiety disorders than children of either generalized anxiety disorder patients or normal controls. Separation anxiety was particularly salient in the children of parents with depression and panic, with a 37% incidence compared with 6% in children of generalized anxiety disorders and 0% of the children of normals or depressive patients without anxiety disorder. Children of agoraphobics had the highest rate (11%) for social phobia.

Rosenbaum et al. (1988) studied the children (ages 2–7 years) of anxious and depressed patients in the laboratory, using standard tasks designed to assess behavioral inhibition versus spontaneity in response to novel situations and strangers. Children of parents with panic disorders, with or without agoraphobia or major depression, showed significantly more signs of behavioral inhibition than children of controls and were found to be at risk for anxiety disorders themselves (Biederman et al., 1990).

Both Carey and Gottesman (1981) and Rasmussen and Tsuang (1984) have summarized previous studies of family incidence of obsessive-compulsive disorder, but the former breakdown is more detailed. Although the findings are variable from study to study, the general incidence of this disorder is about 7% for parents and 5% for sibs for obsessional disorder itself, and 17% for parents and 12% for sibs for obsessional features or personality. The incidence for the actual disorder itself in relatives is not much higher than the 2–3% prevalence in the general American population

(Karno et al., 1987; Robins et al., 1984). The data suggest inheritance of a broad obsessive-compulsive trait rather than an inheritance of the clinical disorder.

Cloninger, Martin, Guze, & Clayton (1986) reported no family aggregation of somatoform disorders in men with the disorder and a higher than expected family incidence only in women who showed a large number of symptoms. Cloninger, Reich, and Guze (1975 a,b) found a sex-linked association between hysteria and sociopathy in the male relatives of women diagnosed as hysteric. There was a tendency toward assortative mating of hysterical women and psychopathic men, but the association between hysteria (in the female relatives) and sociopathy in the male relatives of hysterical women remained significant even when assortative mating was statistically controlled.

Bohman, Cloninger, von Knorring, and Sigvardsson (1984) found that the biological fathers of somaticizers were frequently characterized as having criminal records and records of alcohol abuse, though the particular kind of crime and alcoholism varied with the type of somatization disorder. The predominant influences seem to come from genetic rather than environmental factors. However, different genetic dispositions were apparent in men and women (Cloninger, von Knorring, Sigvardsson, & Bohman, 1986).

Testing specific genetic-environment models with the usual concordance data in clinical groups and their relatives is difficult because of the low numbers of twins and the difficulty in separating environmental and genetic factors in the family data. For this reason Kendler, Heath, Martin, and Eaves (1986) used a symptom questionnaire distributed to almost 3800 pairs of Australian twins in the general population. There were seven anxiety and six depression items. All items were worded in state ("recently. . . . ") rather than trait form to detect current symptomatology. Models incorporating various combinations of additive, dominant genetic, shared, and nonshared environmental variance were tested against the data. A simple model consisting of additive genetic and specific environmental variance provided an adequate fit for 12 and the best fit for 7 of the 13 items. Two items that showed evidence of genetic dominance referred to feelings of panic and heart and breathing symptoms suggestive of panic disorder. The proportions of variance due to the additive genetic factor ranged from .34 to .46. A genetic factor seemed to contribute equally to the phenotypic variance in males and females. Like most of the studies of the N dimension in questionnaires (chapter 3) this one indicates the lack of influence of shared environmental exposures within the family or elsewhere on symptoms and suggests that the environmental influence, which is still substantial, is based on fortuitous or specific influences outside of the home or differential parental treatment of twins.

Kendler, Heath, Martin, and Eaves (1987) applied multivariate genetic methods to analyze the relationship between anxiety and depressive symptoms. Genetic influences seemed to be relatively nonspecific, creating a vulnerability to general distress or negative affect, though there was some evidence that genes might influence the distinction between reported somatic and psychological symptoms of anxiety. The tendency of anxiety and depression to covary was attributed to environmental factors.

A third analysis by Martin, Jardine, Andrews, and Heath (1988) looked more closely at the distinction between two symptoms of panic and the N scale of the EPQ. The results confirmed those of the earlier analysis, which showed the genetic determination for panic symptoms to be primarily of the dominant type. Pauls, Bucher, Crowe, and Noyes (1980) reached a similar conclusion from analyzing relatives of panic disorder patients: Panic disorder is inherited as a autosomal dominant trait. In females, the genetic common factor that accounted for half of the variance in *neuroticism* only accounted for small proportions of the variance for panic symptoms. In males, however, the genetic variation for panic was the sum of the dominant general gene effects and the specific effects that produce the physical symptoms of panic (heart pounding and breathlessness).

Neuropsychology of anxiety disorders

Until recently, the definition of the neuroanatomical basis of anxiety was derived primarily from animal studies in which direct stimulation and lesioning of brain structures are possible (chapter 4). These studies have led to models implicating the Papez circuit (MacLean, 1949), the septohippocampal system (Gray, 1982) and the ascending noradrenergic and serotonergic pathways originating in the locus coeruleus and raphe nucleus. Recent methodological developments in position emission tomography (PET) have made it possible to study the functioning of cortical and subcortical structures in patients suffering from generalized anxiety disorder and episodic panic attacks (Reiman, 1988). This methodology has great promise for extending the study of the neuropsychological bases of anxiety to human anxiety.

Reiman et al. (1986) used PET to study cerebral blood flow (CBF) in anxiety patients, half of whom were vulnerable to lactate-induced panic attacks and half of whom were not, and in normal controls. They confirmed previous findings of an abnormal asymetry of parahippocampal blood flow in the panic-disorder–lactate-susceptible group. This group had low left-to-right volume and higher whole brain metabolic rate for oxygen than the other two groups. The parahippocampal asymmetry seemed to be due to an abnormally high right parahippocampal blood flow.

Reiman et al. (1986) suggest several hypotheses to explain their findings. First, an increase in right parahippocampal neural activity may reflect activity in terminal fields that innervate the region. Projection to the area starts in the hippocampus, subiculum, entorhinal cortex, amygdala, raphe nuclei, and locus coeruleus, most of which are areas that have already been associated with anxiety in comparative studies. Second, the abnormality could be a structural one that is confined to the parahippocampal gyrus itself. This possibility is being investigated with magnetic resonance imaging. Third, the abnormality could represent a relative or absolute increase in blood-brain barrier permeability in the right parahippocampal region. Studies have suggested that this permeability is influenced by the noradrenergic ascending system arising in the locus coeruleus. Antidepressants, which block anxiety attacks, increase brain permeability.

Supporting the role of the parahippocampal gyrus in anxiety is the finding that stimulation of that structure, as well as of the hippocampus and amygdala, produces feelings of fear in awake human subjects during surgery for epilepsy (Glor, Olivier, Quesney, Andermann, & Horowitz 1982). Reiman et al. propose a model for anxiety that strongly resembles the one proposed by Gray (1982). However, one does wonder why the parahippocampus alone should reveal an abnormality of function if it is only one link in the neural pathway that mediates anxiety. Perhaps the PET technique is simply too gross to distinguish the particular pathways in structures like the hippocampus, hypothalamus, and amygdala that are actually involved in the susceptibility to anxiety attacks.

Another approach is to study changes in blood flow patterns in the brain during induced anxiety states. Reiman et al. (1989) showed that lactate-induced panic in panic disorder patients was associated with significant increases of blood flow in temporal poles, insular cortex, lateral putamen, superior colliculus, and anterior cerebellar vermis. On the other hand, a study of anxiety induced in phobic patients by presentation of the phobic stimuli produced no differences in cerebral blood flow (Mountz et al., 1989), and Zohar et al. (1989) found decreases rather than increases in cerebral blood flow, during in vivo exposures of obsessive-compulsives to their phobic stimuli.

Buchsbaum et al. (1987) used the PET scan to examine the effects of benzodiazepines on regional glucose metabolism rates in generalized anxiety disorder. Scans were done under baseline conditions and after a stressful vigilance task conducted during the period when the tagged glucose was being taken up in the brain. Glucose metabolic rates were measured for 12 brain structures for which data on human benzodiazepine receptor binding were available. Decreases were found in right visual and frontal cortex activity under the influence of the benzodiazepine. Little change during stress was found in subcortical structures, including hippocampus, cerebellum, caudate nucleus, thalamus, putamen, corpus callosum, and pons. The changes in glucose metabolism in the various areas were highly correlated with the benzodiazepine receptor density of these areas.

The finding of greater action of benzodiazepines in the right brain is consistent with the parahippocampus right-side findings in the Reiman et al. (1986) study, though that study found no difference in total left-right ratio of total hemisphere blood flow. Buchsbaum et al. did not examine the parahippocampal reactivity, but they did measure hippocampal activity and, like Reiman et al., found no differences in this area, which is central in Gray's model for anxiety. However, Buchsbaum et al. were not comparing anxiety patients with controls but looking only for the locus of action of benzodiazepines in anxiety disorder patients under stress. Not surprisingly, benzodiazepines act most strongly in areas that are rich in benzodiazepine receptors. The findings of high glucose uptake in the occipital cortex were probably a function of the visual stimulation task used to induce stress. The frontal cortex, particularly the orbital frontal area, is generally theorized to be the origin of the anxiety response that is triggered by internal stimuli.

These two studies are pioneering efforts in the study of the functional neuroanatomy of anxiety. Major developments in PET, such as neurochemically selective PET scans, may provide a better picture of the neurotransmitter pathways involved in anxiety reactions, rather than the grosser structures that are currently being studied. A major drawback to the current method is that it can picture only what happens in the brain during a certain period of time and, thus, cannot show the sequence of reactions in the human brain following an anxiety provoking event. It is difficult to tell which neural events have a primary role in the initiation of anxiety and which are secondary. An anxiety attack is a neural avalanche, starting small and expanding, eventually involving much of the brain. Special attention should be paid to areas of putative origin, but some of these, such as the locus coeruleus, are too small to be studied with present PET scan methods.

Psychopharmacology of anxiety disorders

Platelet monoamine oxidase

In chapter 5, monoamine oxidase (MAO) was said to be inversely related to traits such as *sensation seeking, impulsivity,* and *extraversion,* but little evidence was cited for any correlation between MAO and trait or state *anxiety.* However, because stimulation of the sympathetic nervous system by injection of epinephrine has been shown to raise MAO levels (Owen, Acker, & Bourne, 1977) and both plasma epinephrine and norepinephrine correlate positively with MAO in some studies (Mathew, Ho, Kralik, Taylor, & Claghorn, 1980), MAO may be elevated in anxiety disorders.

Several studies have found elevated MAO levels in various anxiety disorders, including generalized anxiety disorder (Davidson, McLeod, Turnball, White, and Feuer, 1980; Mathew et al., 1980; Mathew, Ho, Kralik,

Weinman, & Claghorn, 1981), and agoraphobia with or without panic disorder (Gorman et al., 1985; Yu, Bowen, Davis, & Boulton, 1983), and relaxation-training reduced levels of MAO as well as questionnaire measures of anxiety (Mathew et al., 1980; Yu et al., 1983).

In contrast to these studies, Khan et al. (1986) and Norman, Acevedo, McIntyre, Judd, and Burrows (1988) found no evidence that patients with panic disorder or agoraphobia were higher on MAO than depressives or normal controls. Davidson et al. (1985) found lower levels of MAO in a group of posttraumatic stress disorder patients. However, these were veterans in whom the stress reaction was long delayed after presumably traumatic events, and the low MAO levels were found only in those who had a history of alcohol abuse. Low MAO levels are characteristic of chronic alcoholics.

Davidson, Linnoila, Raft, and Turnbull (1981) treated patients with a mixed symptomatic picture involving anxiety, depression, panic, and somatization with amitriptyline. This tricyclic antidepressant has some MAO-inhibitory effects, and it did reduce MAO as well as self-reported symptoms of anxiety and depression in these patients. The extent of MAO inhibition correlated positively with the amount of reduction in anxiety, phobic, and somatization symptoms.

Although a number of studies report high-MAO levels in patients with a primary anxiety disorder, there is no correlation between MAO and anxiety levels in these populations. Still, the reduction of MAO and anxiety by relaxation training and antidepressant drugs does suggest some kind of association between the enzymes and this class of disorders. Because it is unlikely that MAO itself is pathogenic for anxiety, it is likely that MAO may be a sign of increased catecholamine or serotonergic activity; some or all of these monoamines may play a more direct role in the intense levels of arousal during panic attacks or the more chronic, if less intense, anxiety experienced in cases of generalized anxiety disorder. The evidence of catecholamine arousal cited thus far refers to peripheral catecholamines. Is there any evidence of central adrenergic hyperarousal in these disorders, as suggested by the theories of Gray (1982) and Redmond (1987)?

Catecholamines

The somatic symptoms of anxiety disorders during a panic attack or exposure to a feared stimulus strongly suggest involvement of the peripheral sympathetic nervous system. Tachycardia, rapid breathing, sweating, dry mouth, and stomach contractions point to a dysregulation of the autonomic balance with a dominance of sympathetic system activity. Injection of epinephrine increases heart rate and systolic blood pressure but does not usually produce a panic attack (Gorman et al., 1987). Even the milder anxiety symptoms seen in some subjects suggest that sympathetic nervous system arousal is not a necessary or even sufficient condition for anxiety. Schachter and Singer (1962) have shown that the emotional reactions to infused epinephrine may be influenced by induced cognitive expectations and cues from the environment. Persons with generalized anxiety or panic disorders may have developed such expectations and therefore may be more likely to identify any autonomic arousal symptoms as signals of an anxiety or panic attack. It is also possible that these patients have low biological thresholds for the catecholaminergic reactions to stress.

Several studies have found elevated epinephrine in anxiety disorders during baseline conditions (Mathew et al., 1981; Neese, Cameron, Curtis, McCann, & Huber-Smith, 1984; Villacres, Hollinfield, Katon, Wilkinson, & Veith, 1987). Some have also found high norepinephrine levels in anxiety disorders (Mathew et al., 1981; Neese et al., 1985).

Although peripheral catecholamines do not cross the blood-brain barrier, there is a strong possibility that they are controlled by or correlated with activity in central catecholamine systems. Metabolites of these catechol- amines in cerebrospinal fluid (CSF), plasma, and urine provide some es- timate of central catecholaminergic activity, as described in chapter 5. As pointed out there, although CSF and plasma contain a substantial amount of MHPG (the norepinephrine metabolite) from the brain, neither is a pure measure of such activity because much MHPG orginates in peripheral sources.

Redmond et al. (1986) measured CSF MHPG in hospitalized depressives, manics, and normal controls. MHPG did correlate with anxiety ratings by observers and self-ratings by patients in the patient groups, but even though the depressives were the group scoring highest in anxiety, those in a manic state showed the highest levels of MHPG, with depressives considerably lower on the metabolite, though higher than controls. When the groups were divided by level of anxiety and agitation rather than by diagnosis, the group in the middle range had the highest MHPG levels, suggesting a non-linear relationship between NE activity and anxiety.

Generally, no differences have been found between anxiety patients and controls in levels of plasma MHPG in basal, nonstimulated conditions (Charney & Heninger, 1985a, 1985b, 1986a; Charney, Heninger, & Brier, 1984; Charney, Heninger, & Jatlow, 1985; Woods, Charney, McPherson, Gradman, & Heninger, 1987). Yohimbine, an alpha-$_2$ adrenergic receptor antagonist, by interfering with the negative feedback mechanism of these receptors, potentiates the activity of the NE system and produces marked increases in anxiety in panic disorder patients but does not have this effect in patients with other disorders, including generalized anxiety disorders or controls. (Charney, Woods, & Heninger, 1989). Patients with histories of frequent panic attacks had a greater increase in MHPG after yohimbine infusion than normal controls and patients with a history of infrequent attacks (Charney et al., 1984); however, this finding was not replicated in a subsequent study (Charney & Heninger, 1985a).

Alprazolam is a benzodiazepine, which reduces panic attacks as well as generalized anxiety (Ballenger et al., 1988). Charney and Heninger (1985a) found that long-term alprazolam treatment reduced baseline MHPG in agoraphobics with panic attacks and attenuated yohimbine-induced increases in MHPG, self-reported anxiety, and blood pressure (but not heart rate). Alprazolam treatment blocked yohimbine-induced panic symptoms in all but one of 14 patients.

Long-term imipramine treatment also reduced baseline MHPG levels and blood pressure but, unlike alprazolam, it did not prevent yohimbine-induced increases in MHPG or anxiety (Charney & Heninger, 1985b). The authors speculated that the effects of imipramine in panic disorder may be related to decreases in norepinephrine turnover whereas those of alprazolam may counteract the blocking of alpha$_2$ receptors by yohimbine. Other reports show the effectiveness of antidepressants such as chlomipramine in the treatment of agoraphobia, panic disorder, general anxiety, and general phobic symptoms (Ballenger, 1986; Buigues & Vallejo, 1987; Johnston, Troyer, & Whitsett, 1988).

Clonidine, an alpha$_2$ noradrenergic agonist that inhibits locus coeruleus activity, has been used in humans to block the anxiety-like withdrawal symptoms associated with opiate withdrawal, presumably by potentiating alpha$_2$ noradrenergic function. Charney and Heninger (1986b) investigated the effects of acute clonidine treatments, compared with placebo effects, in patients with agoraphobic and panic symptoms. Clonidine produced some decreases in plasma MHPG in normal control subjects but significantly larger MHPG decreases in agoraphobic panic patients. The subjective effects of clonidine were confined primarily to reports of increased drowsiness reported by both controls and patients but more so by controls. Diastolic blood pressure was reduced by clonidine in both groups but more so in the patients.

Table 8.3 shows the contrast in the findings comparing responses of patients and controls given clonidine (Charney & Heninger, 1986a) and yohimbine (Charney et al., 1984). The effects are opposite for some factors such as MHPG, blood pressure, and cortisol, but different for the subjective effects of drowsiness and anxiety. Yohimbine increases anxiety more in patients, but clonidine does not reduce anxiety; it just makes the controls more drowsy than the patients. The findings suggest that some patients with panic disorders exhibit abnormal regulation of noradrenergic function by alpha$_2$ receptors rather than simple deficiencies or excesses of the neurotransmitter. Charney and Heninger suggest that the deficit in regulation of the noradrenergic system may become apparent only when demands are made on the system by stress. To what extent does exposure to phobic

Table 8.3. *Comparison of abnormal responses to clonidine and yohimbine in patients with agoraphobia and panic disorder*

Response[a]	Charney & Heninger (1986) Clonidine	Charney, Heninger, & Breier (1984) Yohimbine
MHPG	Greater decrease	Greater increase (high panic f group only)
Blood pressure	Greater decrease (diastolic)	Greater increase (systolic)
Cortisol	Greater decrease	Greater increase
Growth Hormone	Blunted increase	Not tested
Drowsiness	Blunted increase	No difference
Anxiety	No difference	Greater increase

[a]Responses that have been shown to be significantly different from normal healthy subjects
Source: D. S. Charney and G. R. Heninger (1986), "Abnormal regulation of noradrenergic function in panic disorders: Effects of clonidine in healthy subjects and patients with agoraphobia and panic disorder," *Archives of General Psychiatry*, 43, p. 1051. Copyright 1986 by American Medical Association. Reprinted by permission.

objects or situations act as a releasor of the kinds of biochemical, psychophysiological, and psychological responses seen in response to norepinephrine dysregulators such as yohimbine?

Ko et al. (1983) exposed patients who had agoraphobia with panic to the situations that were likely to elicit their panic reactions. Exposure to these situations led to rises in both self-rated anxiety and plasma MHPG, and anxiety and MHPG levels were significantly correlated within and between subjects. Both clonidine and imipramine reduced symptoms and levels of MHPG. The anxiety and plasma MHPG reactions to exposure to the phobic situation during clonidine treatment were not elevated above nonexposure days.

Woods et al. (1987) compared agoraphobics with panic disorders to matched controls in responses to actual situations that individual patients had rated as likely to precipitate panic. Although the patients showed significantly greater reports of panic symptoms and heart-rate increases than controls, the changes in blood pressure, plasma MHPG, and cortisol did not exceed those in controls. The different effects of yohimbine and external phobic stimuli suggest that yohimbine primarily affects the noradrenergic system, and phobic stimuli affect the amount of peripheral epinephrine released by the adrenal medulla.

Neese et al. (1985) found robust increases in plasma norepinephrine and epinephrine, as well as pulse and systolic blood pressure, cortisol, and growth hormone in patients with simple phobias who were exposed to their phobic objects (snakes, spiders, etc.). The lack of difference between patients and controls in MHPG response could reflect a faster reaction of hypothalamus (effecting direct sympathetic system activation) compared with the time necessary for release of norepinephrine in other brain centers, its breakdown to MHPG, and transport of MHPG into the blood. Three of the 18 patients did not experience any panic and another 5 had reactions lasting 5 minutes or less. The average duration of the attacks was 20 minutes, which, as the authors note, may have been too short a time for MHPG to accumulate in neuronal tissue and plasma. There is also the possibility that panic attacks are qualitatively different from the kind of anxiety found in general anxiety disorders or pure situational phobics.

The induction of panic and general anxiety by yohimbine in patients with anxiety disorders would seem to support the involvement of the noradrenergic system in these disorders, but other pharmacological agents that have little or no effect on the noradrenergic system are also capable of eliciting panic and anxiety in these patients (Gorman et al., 1987). Lactate and caffeine are two such substances that come closest to meeting the criteria for a panic model set by Gorman et al. Actually, lactate-induced panic and anxiety reactions are not specific to panic disorders but are found to the same degree in patients with generalized anxiety disorders (Cowley, Dager, McClellan, Roy-Byrne, & Dunner, 1988).

Carr et al. (1986) found that lactate infusion induced more panic and anxiety in panic disorders or agoraphobics than in controls, and chronic alprazolam treatment reduced the response to normal levels in the patients. It is interesting that lactate produced small decreases in plasma MHPG and epinephrine in both patients and controls rather than increases. In contrast, lactate produced increases of plasma norepinephrine in both groups. These findings suggest that lactate induces panic through peripheral rather than central noradrenergic mechanisms. Consistent with this interpretation are greater blood pressure responses to lactate in patients than in controls (Ehlers et al., 1986).

Charney, Goodman, Price, Woods, and Rasmussen (1985) found that nearly three-fourths of a group of panic disorder or agoraphobic patients reacted with panic to a large dose of caffeine, and these anxiety effects were significantly greater than in a control group. The anxiety effects of caffeine were not accompanied by changes in plasma MHPG in either patients or controls. Caffeine did increase blood pressure, more so in patients than in controls. As with lactate, there is no evidence of mediation of the anxiety producing effects of the drug through central noradrenergic mechanisms, *if* we assume that such mechanisms are indexed by MHPG.

Serotonin

The relationship between serotonin and anxiety has been recently reviewed by Kahn, van Praag, Wetzler, Asnis, and Barr (1988). Unlike the earlier review by Soubrié (1986), Kahn et al. concluded, on the basis of both animal and human psychiatric studies, that serotonin plays a central role in anxiety and anxiety disorders. Their evidence of a connection in animal studies is the effect of serotonin depletion in release of behavior suppression produced by signals of punishment; however, they concede that the general motor inhibition produced by serotonin function makes it difficult to interpret these results. Gray (1987) also assigns a role to serotonin in anxiety, but he suggests that it is not involved in arousal, which is mediated by the dorsal ascending noradrenergic bundle. Instead, the role of serotonin is said to be in behavioral inhibition subsequent to anxiety arousal. Actually, depletion not augmentation of serotonin in animals produces exaggerated startle responses and fearfulness in the open-field (OF) test. The OF test resembles the stress in agoraphobic disorder more than the type of conflict between appetite and threat of punishment, as in the model showing disinhibition by serotonin depletion. In humans, low levels of the serotonin metabolite 5-HIAA are found to be associated with the P dimension of personality and *impulsivity* more consistently than with *anxiety* trait (chapter 5). Low levels of serotonin and its metabolite are also associated with impulsive suicide attempts and murder.

The hypothesis proposed by Kahn et al. (1988) to reconcile some of these contradictions in the direction of the serotonin-anxiety relationship is that in certain anxiety disorders, such as panic and obsessive-compulsive disorders, the postsynaptic receptors are hypersensitive and stimulation of these receptors produces anxiety. The low levels of serotonin and its metabolites are said to be functions of the hypersensitivity of receptors, which leads to a down-regulation of production and metabolism through negative feedback mechanisms. Their hypothesis is based on the following evidence: (1) serotonin agonists are effective in treatment of panic and obsessive-compulsive disorders; (2) serotonin antagonists are effective in treatment of generalized anxiety disorder; and (3) panic disorder patients treated with serotonin agonists show an initial worsening in anxiety followed by improvement. What they suggest is that the initial worsening reflects the hypersensitivity of the serotonin receptors in PD, and the subsequent improvement represents the turning down of the system by feedback regulation receptors.

Zohar, Mueller, Insel, Zohar-Kadovich, and Murphy (1987) examined the acute effects of a potent serotonergic agonist (metachlorophenylpiperazine or mCPP) on obsessive-compulsive disorders and controls. mCPP is known to decrease central serotonergic synthesis and turnover by excessive stimulation of postsynaptic receptors. It shows behavioral (decreased appetite and locomotion), neuroendocrine (increased prolactin and cortisol levels), and physiological (hyperthermia) signs of a postsynaptic serotonin receptor agonist. mCPP increased obsessive-compulsive symptoms in almost all of the patients relative to placebo and produced large increases in anxiety and depression self-rating scales. Controls showed minimal changes on these dimensions. There was no difference between patients and controls in prolactin response, temperature rise, or plasma concentrations of mCPP. Controls showed more cortisol response to mCPP than obsessive-compulsive patients. Although the serotonin agonist clearly produced more behavioral effects in patients than controls, there is no evidence that this was mediated by a supersensitivity of serotonin receptors, as indexed by the usual neuroendocrine and physiological criteria. The mCPP challenge was repeated on a subgroup of these patients after at least three and a half months of treatment with chlomipramine, an antidepressant that is a potent inhibitor of serotonin reuptake. Treatment reduced baseline ratings of obsessive-compulsive symptoms and depression (but not anxiety) and markedly reduced acute obsessive-compulsive symptoms, and anxiety and depressive responses to mCPP. The hyperthermic response to mCPP was also reduced. The authors conclude that their findings are consistent with the development of adaptive hyporesponsivity of the serotonergic system in patients treated with chlomipramine. Observations of an initial exacerbation of symptoms in the first days of treatment are consistent with the expected biphasic nature of the drug.

Charney et al. (1988) used mCCP and tryptophan as challenges to obsessive-compulsive patients and controls. Because tryptophan is a precursor in the production of serotonin, loading the organism with tryptophan would be expected to increase serotonin activity. As previously noted, mCPP seems to decrease central serotonin synthesis and turnover. The two drugs produced different behavioral effects in both groups. mCPP tended to increase anxiety and tryptophan made subjects more drowsy and less fearful or anxious. The only difference between patients and controls was the tendency of tryptophan to make the patients feel "sad." There were no significant changes in obsessive or compulsive reactions in response to mCCP, placebo, or tryptophan. Thus, the results are at variance with those of Zohar et al. (1988) described previously. However, female obsessive-compulsive patients showed significantly reduced baseline prolactin levels and prolactin reactions to mCPP compared with female controls, indicating a possible low tonic level of serotonergic activity in these patients.

Charney and Heninger (1986c) compared the responses of panic disorder patients to tryptophan during placebo and alprazalom treatment. No differences were found between controls and panic disorder patients in prolactin during either the baseline placebo period or in the temporary increase in prolactin produced by tryptophan infusion. Separate analyses of male and female patients failed to find baseline differences or tryptophan-induced increases in either sex. The authors conclude that the evidence suggests that serotonin function is normal in panic disorder and that the antipanic mechanism of alprazolam is not related to its effects on serotonin activity.

Imipramine-binding has also been taken as an index of serotonergic activity. Lewis, Noyes, Coryell, and Clancy (1985) found lower numbers of imipramine-binding sites in a group of agoraphobics with panic disorder than in a control group. However, this result was not replicated in studies by Innis, Charney, and Heninger (1987) or Schneider, Munjack, Severson, and Palmer (1986). Balon, Pohl, Yergani, Rainey, and Oxenkrug (1987) found no difference in platelet serotonin between panic disorders and controls.

The evidence is inconclusive for a role for serotonin in obsessive compulsives and negative for an abnormality of serotonergic activity in panic disorders. The effectiveness of some antidepressants and benzodiazepines in the treatment of panic disorder (Ballenger, 1986) does not seem to be adequately explained by either norepinephrine or serotonin theories.

Benzodiazepine/GABA receptor complex

In chapter 4, studies were described that showed the ability of βCCE, a benzodiazepine antagonist with affinity for benzodiazepine receptors, to produce behavioral and physiological evidence of acute anxiety in monkeys. These results suggested the possibility of a new endogenous anxiety-producing ligand that might play a central role in anxiety disorders. However, a first step was to show that βCCE, an artificially produced agent, could produce anxiety in normal humans. Few studies, amounting to little more that anecdotal reports, have been done. Dorow, Howski, Paschelke, and Amin (1983) reported that a structural analogue of βCCE produced what sounds like panic attacks in 2 out of 5 subjects over a series of 12 trials. Using another β-carboline derivative, Dorow, Duka, Holler, and Sauerbrey (1987) claim that the substance produced "apprehension" in five subjects. However, an objective scale for state *anxiety* failed to reflect an effect of the drug. Most complaints were of restlessness and mild apprehension. Reports of cold hands indicated some peripheral vasoconstriction, but no great changes in heart rate or blood pressure were noted. Interestingly, low doses produced reports of heightened alertness, and higher doses actually improved performance on a timed test of logical reasoning. Clearly these results do not indicate that β-carboline produced panic or even acute anxiety but only somewhat heightened arousal.

Guidotti et al. (1983) have isolated a natural polypeptide from rat brain, labeled diazepam-binding inhibitor (DBI), that has an affinity for benzodiazepine receptors and increases inhibition of behavior in conflict situations. Whether this or some chemically related compound is the endogenous anxiety agent remains to be seen. Similarly, there may be an endogenous benzodiazepine that acts on the receptor sites.

To date there have not been many studies of benzodiazepine receptors or their agonists in anxiety disorder patients. Weizman et al. (1987) found a 24% reduction in benzodiazepine binding sites in a group of generalized anxiety disorder patients compared with controls. After 3 weeks of treatment with diazepam, binding sites increased to a level above that of normals, and 1 week after treatment was discontinued, the maximal binding capacity of patients was similar to that of the normal controls. Reductions of about the same magnitude as those in the anxiety patients were observed in rats exposed to uncontrollable shock stress. Could the vulnerability of anxiety disorder patients have to do with the availability of these binding sites or the endogenous agonists or antagonists that might occupy the sites?

Cortisol

The discussion of the psychopharmacology of anxiety disorders has thus far focused on the monoamines, the neurotransmitters in the central nervous system, and the hormones in the peripheral autonomic nervous system (epinephrine and norepinephrine). Another pathway for stress, described in chapter 5, is the hypothalamic-pituitary adrenocortical (HYPAC) system. Stress results in the release of corticotropin-releasing hormone (CRH) from the hypothalamus. CRH is released into the portal system of the pituitary gland where it causes synthesis and release of adrenocorticotropic hormone (ACTH). ACTH travels through the blood to the adrenal cortex where a number of corticosteroids are released, including cortisol, the most frequently used index of HYPAC activity in current psychiatric research.

A primary role of HYPAC deregulation in major depressive disorders has been supported by research results (Stokes & Sikes, 1987). Earlier work had also suggested a major role for this system in anxiety disorders (Persky, 1975), though the inadequacies of the older methods of assaying cortisol and the lack of control for the diurnal nature of cortisol release may have produced inconsistent results. CRH was isolated only in 1981, so the role of this higher level hormone in psychiatric disorders is still unknown. Gold, Pigott, Kling, Kalogeras, and Chrousos (1988) suggest an etiological role for CRH in panic disorders, citing some recent evidence that patients with panic disorder show an attenuated ACTH response to CRH, together with high levels of cortisol. The blunted ACTH response would be the negative-feedback effect of large amounts of circulating cortisol on the pituitary gland. However, as the authors concede, hypercorticalism in all types of panic disorder is not a demonstrated fact.

Cameron and Neese (1988) and Kathol, Noyes, Lopez, and Reich (1988) have reviewed the literature on hormonal function in anxiety disorders. Kathol et al. point out that psychological stressors are less effective stimulators of the HYPAC system than physical stressors. Although psychological stressors can cause small changes in acute ACTH and cortisol production, which may not be reflected in urinary free cortisol levels over more extended periods of time, chronic stress leads to attenuation of the HYPAC response. Although the evidence for elevated catecholamines in anxiety disorders is strong, that for corticosteroids is mixed, with some studies finding normal levels and others reporting elevated levels (Cameron & Neese, 1988).

Although some axiogenic agents such as caffeine, lactate, yohimbine, and mCCP, stimulate increases in plasma cortisol (Charney et al., 1985; Charney, Woods, Goodman, & Heninger, 1987; Liebowitz et al., 1985) neither baseline or reactive levels of cortisol differentiate anxiety disorders and controls (Charney et al, 1985; Charney et al., 1987; Liebowitz et al., 1985; Woods et al., 1987). However, in the study by Kathol et al. (1988), an elevation of urinary cortisol was found in panic disorders who had concomitant depression, agoraphobia, or both.

Cortisol elevation has been found in major depressive disorders. The question of whether the HYPAC axis is also abnormal in anxiety disorders has also been studied by using the dexamethasone suppression test (DST). The DST is based on the capacity of dexamethasone to suppress cortisol release for more than 24 hours in most nondepressed persons. The drug is administered on one night, and plasma cortisol levels are sampled on the following day. Nonsuppression of cortisol release is found in only 4–7% of normals, 8–14% of patients with panic or other anxiety disorders (Arana & Baldesserini, 1987; Kathol et al., 1988), and 43% in adult cases with major depression but rising to 67% for those with psychosis and 78% for manic-depressives (Arana & Baldesserini, 1987). Although anxiety disorders show rates slightly higher than normals, this could easily be accounted for by depression in some of these disorders. The results suggest that deregulation of the HYPAC system of any duration is a characteristic of major depressive disorders but not of anxiety disorders, except when the anxiety disorder is accompanied by major depressive disorder.

Psychophysiology of anxiety disorders

Patients' descriptions of their symptoms during anxiety attacks suggest a deregulation of the sympathetic nervous system. Anxiety disorder patients respond as if there were some dire threat requiring immediate flight or fight in situations in which they admit that there is no reason for such reactions. During such attacks most patients report heart palpitations, chest pain, breathing difficulties, and feelings of dizziness. Cardiovascular related symptoms are most prominent, and during their first panic attacks, many patients are convinced they are experiencing heart attacks. The questions to be answered by objective psychophysiological measurement in the laboratory and in life situations are: (1) do anxiety disorder patients have generally higher basal levels of sympathetic system arousal than normals or other types of patients, even in states in which their anxiety is minimal; (2) do anxiety disorder patients differ from normals or other types of patients in the magnitude of their physiological responses to stressful situations; and (3) are anxiety disorder patients hyperresponsive to particular situations or stimuli that are specifically related to their fears or are they simply overresponsive to all kinds of stimuli including meaningless sounds?

Basal levels of physiological activity

EEG

Early studies, using frequency analyzers, often showed less alpha and more beta waves, signs of cortical arousal, in anxiety disorders (Zahn, 1986). The older studies typically used only a single EEG active site or two active sites across the brain. The technique of topographic EEG recording uses multiple sites and feeds the data into a computer, which gives a picture of activity in the cortical areas that underly the electrodes. Buchsbaum et al. (1985) did EEG topographic mapping of the brain in general anxiety disorders and normals. Patients with generalized anxiety disorder had relatively less alpha and delta activity than normals, particularly in the lower-posterior left temporal lead (electrodes were applied only to the left hemisphere). The temporal lobe locus is interesting in view of reports of atypical panic episodes in some patients with temporal EEG abnormalities (Edlung, Swann, & Clothier, 1987) and reduced left temporal variability in obsessive-compulsives (Flor-Henry, Yeudall, Koles, & Howarth, 1979).

Unfortunately, in a subsequent paper, Grillon and Buchsbaum (1987) reported that they could find no baseline topographic EEG differences in what seems to be the same group of patients and controls on another occasion. They speculated that small procedural variations or the patients' familiarity with the lab in the two studies might account for the differences in results. However, other investigators also could not discriminate between various types of patients, including obsessive-compulsives, and controls using EEG topography. In cases, EEG topography was sensitive to drug effects even if it could not discriminate patients from controls in baseline states.

Heart rate

Kelly (1980) compared various patient groups and a group of normal controls on heart rate (HR) forearm blood flow, and blood pressure (BP) during basal resting conditions. Subjects were also given psychological tests. Table 8.4 shows the results for the various diagnostic groups. Judging from Kelly's description of "chronic anxiety" this group consisted of panic disorders with persistent symptoms against a background of GAD. The groups are arrayed in order of their scores on the Taylor (1953) Manifest Anxiety Scale (TMAS). All groups except phobic anxiety and schizophrenics had significantly higher scores than the controls. The scores on Eysenck's N

Table 8.4. *Cardiovascular basal measures and diagnosis*

Diagnosis	*n*	TMAS	N	E	HR	FBF	SBP	DBP
Chronic anxiety	54	36.4[a]	36.8[a]	15.4[a]	95.6[a]	4.4[a]	128.7[a]	82.8
Agitated depression	31	33.4[a]	33.8[a]	15.8[a]	92.6[a]	3.4[a]	135.5[a]	87.0[a]
Obsessional neurosis	40	31.7[a]	32.4[a]	16.9[a]	85.1[a]	2.7	125.4	82.6[a]
Personality disorder	25	31.1[a]	33.3[a]	17.4[a]	77.3	1.9	119.1	76.4
Depersonalization dis	10	30.9[a]	35.7[a]	18.8	86.7[a]	2.4	125.5	82.0
Nonagitated depr.	64	30.4[a]	30.7[a]	19.0	83.2	2.0	123.8	80.6
Hysteria	10	29.8[a]	30.2[a]	19.5[a]	84.1[a]	2.5	117.3	78.3
Phobic anxiety	44	28.1	30.4	21.2	82.3	2.1	123.1	81.8
Schizophrenia	23	24.3	29.0	17.6[a]	86.4[a]	3.1[a]	123.9	80.2
Normal control	60	14.0	19.7	25.9	73.7	2.2	120.1	76.5

Note: TMAS = Taylor Manifest Anxiety Scale, N = *neuroticism* scale from Maudsley Personality Inventory (MPI), E = *extraversion* scale from MPI, HR = heart rate, FBF = forearm blood flow, SBP = systolic blood pressure, DBP = diastolic blood pressure
[a]Significantly different from normal controls, $p < .05$
Source: D. Kelly (1980), *Anxiety and emotions*. Springfield, IL: Charles C. Thomas, printed with permission.

scale were similar in ranking of the groups. The *chronic anxiety* group was outstandingly high on both scales. *Extraversion* scales were almost in reverse order, with the normals highest and the chronic anxiety cases lowest, placing the chronic anxiety group in the extreme *introverted neurotic* quadrant, as suggested by Eysenck (1957).

All of the patient groups except personality disorders, nonagitated depressives, and phobic anxiety cases had significantly higher HRs than the controls. With two exceptions, the HRs seem to decline across the groups in relation to their TMAS and N scores. The exceptions were the personality disorders, whose normal HR was not in accord with their relatively high anxiety and N scores, and the schizophrenics, whose HR was higher than one would expect from their lower anxiety and N scores. Both the chronic anxiety and the agitated depressive groups had outstandingly high HRs. These two groups were also significantly higher than the normals on forearm blood flow and systolic blood pressure (SBP). Obsessional disorders also showed higher HRs and DBPs than controls. HR was the measure most closely related to the ordering of the groups on the self-report measures of anxiety.

Lader and Wing (1966) compared the resting pulse rate prior to stimulation of patients with a diagnosis of "anxiety state" with normal controls. The group had a basal HR of 92 bpm, significantly higher than the rate of 76 bpm of the controls. Table 8.5 describes the basal HRs obtained in 17 more recent studies. Kelly's (1980) normals, "chronic anxiety," and OCD disorders are also included because it is clear that the chronically anxious are panic disorders, and the obsessive-compulsive disorders would fit the current definition.

Table 8.5. *Basal mean heart rates of anxiety disorders and controls* (n's)

Authors	Controls	PD/Agora	OCD	Social phobia	Simple phobia	GAD
Ehlers et al. (1988)	70 (25)	75[a] (25)	—	—	—	—
Freedman et al. (1985)[b]	78 (11)	78 (12)	—	—	—	—
Liebowitz et al. (1985)	63 (18)	82[a] (40)	—	—	—	—
Taylor et al. (1986)	69 (12)	72 (12)	—	—	—	—
Roth et al. (1986)	66 (19)	80[a] (37)	—	—	—	—
Woods et al. (1987)	71 (13)	72 (18)	—	—	—	—
Kelly (1980)	74 (60)	96[a] (54)	85.1[a] (40)	—	—	—
Insel et al. (1985)	73 (17)	—	81[a] (18)	—	—	—
Cook III et al. (1988)	—	82 (11)	—	76 (14)	73 (13)	—
Ost (1987)	—	99[c] (100)	—	80 (80)	79 (190)	—
Balon et al. (1988)	—	86 (71)	—	—	—	—
Rapee (1986)	—	92[c] (20)	—	—	—	76 (13)
Vermilyea et al. (1984)	—	93 (28)	—	—	—	—
Sheer et al. (1987)[b]	—	79 (23)	—	—	—	—
Taylor et al. (1982)	—	81 (23)	—	—	—	—
Grayson et al. (1986)	—	—	80 (17)	—	—	—
Sartory (1986)	—	—	—	—	68 (36)	—
Weighted Mean	71 (175)	87 (474)	83 (75)	80 (94)	77 (239)	—
Unweighted Mean	70	83	82	78	74	76

Note: PD = panic disorder, agora = agoraphobia, OCD = obsessive compulsive disorder, GAD = generalized anxiety disorder
[a] PD and agoraphobia or OCD have significantly higher HRs than controls in the same study.
[b] Ambulatory monitoring of daily HRs in natural environments.
[c] PD and agoraphobia have significantly higher HRs than other types of phobics or GAD.

From these data it would appear that only panic disorders, agoraphobics, and obsessive-compulsive disorders have elevated basal HRs. Perhaps social or simple phobic disorders are physiologically aroused only when confronting the stimuli or situations that trigger their anxiety.

Electrodermal measures

Lader and Wing (1966) compared anxiety disorder and control patients on skin conductance level (SCL) and spontaneous skin conductance responses (SSCRs) during a 30-minute recording session, beginning with a 10-minute recording during rest, and followed by continuous recording during the presentation of 20 tones. During the rest period, the SCLs of patients increased slightly and those of controls declined. Mean SCLs of the two groups (Figure 8.1) were not significantly different initially but were different by the end of the rest period, reflecting the lowered arousal (relaxation) of the controls relative to the continued high arousal of the patients.

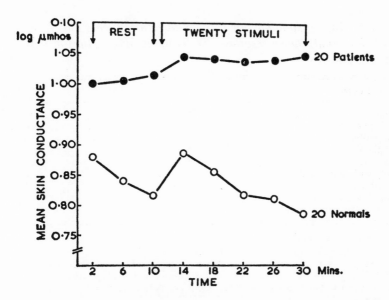

Figure 8.1. Skin conductance levels of anxiety disorder patients and normals during a pre-stimulation rest period and during presentation of 20 stimuli (tones). (From *Physiological measures, sedative drugs and morbid anxiety*, p. 83, by M. H. Lader and L. Wing, 1966. London: Oxford University Press. Copyright 1966 by Oxford University Press. Reprinted by permission.)

The SCLs of the controls were raised by the first presentation of the tones but rapidly declined during the stimulation period. In contrast, the SCLs of the patients remained elevated throughout the stimulation period and were significantly higher than SCLs of controls for most of the period. The SSCRs showed a similar tendency, but on this measure the patients were significantly higher during all phases of the experiment. The normals show habituation of arousal to the experimental situation whereas the anxiety patients react as if there were continued threat.

Lader (1975) contrasted the SSCRs of normals and various anxiety, depressive, and hysteric types of disorders (Table 8.6). Specific phobics (simple phobic disorder) showed no higher arousal than normals on this measure. Social phobics, agoraphobics, anxiety states, and patients with mixed anxiety and depression had significantly elevated levels of fluctuation in electrodermal activity. Agitated depressives showed very high activity and contrasted markedly with behaviorally retarded depressives who showed a SSCR rate even lower than that of normals. The highest rate of SSCRs was seen in chronic conversion hysterics with classical conversion symptoms. According to psychoanalytic theory these patients should be free of manifest anxiety, which is "converted" into somatic symptoms. Judging from their electrodermal and heart-rate activity (Table 8.6) they are aroused, though their scores on self-report anxiety measures do not

Table 8.6. *Rate of spontaneous skin conductance fluctuations (SSCF) and rate of skin conductance response (SCR) habituation (Hab) in various groups of patients*

Clinical groups	n	SSCF[a]	SCR Hab[b]
Normals	75	1.5	72
Specific phobics	19	2.8	68
Social phobics	18	6.2	39
Agoraphobics	19	6.0	39
Anxiety states	16	6.8	29
Anxiety with depression	18	6.9	22
Agitated depressives	17	9.2	10
Retarded depressives	13	0.5	—[c]
Chronic conversion hysterics	10	11.2	−4

[a]Rate of SSCF per minute
[b]The higher the value, the more rapid the rate of habituation
[c]So few responses were elicited that habituation rates could not be calculated.
Source: M. Lader (1975), chapter 1 in *Clinical applications of psychophysiology*, D. C. Fowles (ed.). New York: Columbia Univ. Press. Copright 1975 Columbia University Press. With permission.

reflect this fact. The discrepancy between self-report and actual physiological arousal could be regarded as an operational definition of repression.

Lader and Wing's (1966) electrodermal findings have been confirmed by Roth et al. (1986) for panic disorders and Insel, Zahm, and Murphy (1985) for obsessive-compulsives; in both studies the anxiety cases were higher on SCL and SSCRs than normal controls.

Reactivity to stress and simple stimulation

Kelly (1980) used performance stress (mental arithmetic) on the patients and normals whose basal levels on cardiovascular measures are listed in Table 8.4. Table 8.7 shows their stress levels on heart rate (HR) and blood pressure (BP) and mean increases in these measures. The normal controls had the greatest absolute increase on both measures. The chronic anxiety and the phobic anxiety groups had lower increases but did not differ significantly from the normal group on any of the change scores. Other diagnostic groups had significantly lower changes on one or more of the measures. It appears that anxiety disorders do not differ from normals in terms of their response to this type of stress, but they differ in their basal levels of arousal in a resting state. A strong physiological response to performance stress represents adaptive coping. Of course, the difference score is largely a function of the lower initial activity levels. The agitated depressives, for instance, start at a HR of 93 bpm and rise to 101 after stress; in contrast, the normals start at 74 bpm and rise to 97 under stress.

Table 8.7. *Heart rate (HR) and systolic blood pressure (SBP) increases during stress and diagnosis*

Diagnosis	n	HR	HR D	SBP	SBP D
		\multicolumn{4}{l}{Levels and increases (D)[a] during stress}			
Chronic anxiety	54	108.8	13.3	137.7	9.1
Agitated depression	31	100.9	8.3[b]	143.2	7.6[b]
Obsessional neurosis	40	100.1	15.0	133.9	8.6[b]
Personality disorder	25	92.0	14.7[b]	131.4	12.2
Nonagitated depression	64	94.9	11.8[b]	133.1	9.3[b]
Hysteria	10	96.6	12.5[b]	123.7	6.4[b]
Phobic anxiety	44	97.7	15.3	134.4	11.2
Schizophrenia	23	94.1	7.7[b]	132.6	8.7[b]
Normal control	60	97.4	23.7	137.8	17.7

[a]Difference = level during mental arithmetic stress minus level during baseline recording
[b]Significantly less than increase in HR or BP than in controls ($p < .05$)
Source: D. Kelly (1980), *Anxiety and Emotions*. Springfield, IL: Charles C. Thomas. With permission.

The specificity of the stress in its effects on particular clinical groups is nicely illustrated by a study of combat veterans with posttraumatic stress disorder (PTSD). Pallmeyer, Blanchard, and Kolb (1986) compared the psychophysiological reactions of a PTSD group with those of other veterans with or without combat experience or other psychiatric disorders. They measured HR, SBP, DBP, SCL, and frontal electromyograph (EMG) under baseline conditions, mental arithmetic stress, and recorded sounds of combat. HR, SBP, DBP, and SCL all showed significant interactions between the groups and conditions. All groups responded to the mental arithmetic stress with increases in HR but did not differ in magnitude of that increase. In fact, the PTSD and phobic groups increased less in HR than other groups in response to mental arithmetic stress. In contrast, the PTSD group was the only group to show increases in HR in response to recorded battle sounds.

Beidel, Turner, and Dancu (1985) compared socially anxious persons with nonsocially anxious subjects on HR and BP during three laboratory social situations: unstructured interaction with someone of the opposite sex, interaction with someone of the same sex, and giving an impromptu speech to a small audience. Socially anxious individuals showed more HR and BP arousal in response to the opposite sex and more BP reaction during the speech, but the groups did not differ in the same-sex interaction situation. Social anxiety was aroused primarily in response to strangers of the opposite sex or social performance demands.

Öst (1987) compared various phobic groups in HR responses to situations selected for their relevance to each of the phobic types. Social phobics were required to have a conversation with an opposite-sex stranger; claustrophobics had to stay in a small windowless room; animal phobics had to approach a cage containing a spider or snake; blood phobics watched a surgical film; and dental phobics went through a dental examination. Agoraphobics had higher HRs than all other groups, both at rest and during the exposure stress; social phobics also had higher HRs than claustrophobics and blood phobics during exposure to their phobic stimuli. Agoraphobics, social phobics, and dental phobics all had mean increases of about 14 bpm compared with only 6 or 7 bpm for blood phobics and claustrophobics and 11 bpm for animal phobics. The significant differences among changes in HR were not due to group differences in the initial resting HRs. Oddly, the agoraphobics had the lowest self-ratings for anxiety state during the test and the claustrophobics, who had the next-to-lowest HR response, had the highest self-rating for anxiety. This finding shows a dissociation between subjective anxiety and actual HR reactions. The problem with the Öst et al. study is that each group was exposed to only one condition. Differences among groups could have reflected differences in the anxiety arousal potential of the specific condition rather than the subjects exposed to that condition.

Woods et al. (1987) exposed agoraphobic patients to their most feared setting. Matched normal controls were exposed to the same settings for the same periods of time. A portable ECG was used to monitor HR before, during, and after exposures to the natural situations. At baseline and just prior to exposure there were no differences between patients and controls in HR, but patients were higher on SBP during baseline. Fifteen of 18 patients experienced a panic attack. During exposure, the HRs of patients experiencing an attack rose 23 bpm from baseline compared with a rise of only 12 bpm in controls, bringing the patients' HR to a mean stress value of 95 bpm during their attacks. One patient rose to 173 bpm during her attack. SBP rose equally in both patients and controls; the change difference was not significant.

Roth et al. (1986) recorded ambulatory HRs in agoraphobics and controls during a walk through a large shopping mall. Most of the patients could not complete the walk because of anxiety. HRs in patients were higher than in controls before, during, and after the walk, but the groups did not differ in absolute change scores.

Wolpe and Rowan (1988) have proposed a conditioning theory of panic disorder that attempts to explain the initial panic attack as produced by hyperventilation. Their model is outlined in Figure 8.2. They claim that the first panic attack occurs in a person experiencing prolonged or severe anxiety due to stressful life circumstances. During a mild anxiety attack the patient may hyperventilate, producing strong panic symptoms such as palpitations, dyspnea, faintness, and trembling. After panic attacks occur they become classically conditioned to external stimuli in the manner noted by other theories.

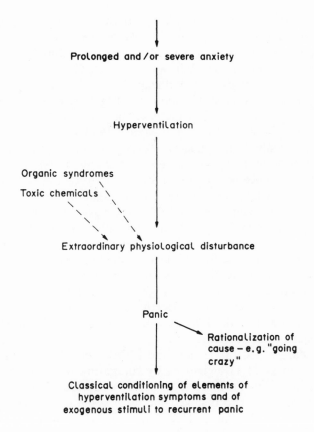

Figure 8.2. A classical conditioning model for the development of a panic disorder. (From "Panic disorder: A product of classical conditioning," by J. Wolpe and V. C. Rowan, 1988, *Behavior Research and Therapy*, 26, p. 446. Copyright 1988 by Pergamon Press. Reprinted by permission.)

If this theory is correct, we might expect that persons with panic disorder can be differentiated from persons with generalized anxiety in terms of the greater response of panic disorders to hyperventilation. Rapee (1986) found that panic disorders responded with more subjective symptoms and greater distress than generalized anxiety disorders to voluntary hyperventilation. Although panic disorders had higher resting HRs than generalized anxiety disorders, there was no difference in the magnitude of their HR response to hyperventilation. Interestingly, the panic disorders showed a greater tendency than the generalized anxiety disorders to hyperventilate during rest, thus producing higher pCO_2 levels. The results support Wolpe's theory suggesting a prominent role for hyperventilation in panic attacks.

The results raise questions about the actual magnitude of HR responses during panic attacks. Do panic disorders patients exaggerate these reactions? Ambulatory EKG recording has permitted investigators to study physiological changes during panic attacks occurring outside of the laboratory. Cameron, Lee, Curtis, and McCann (1987) found that HRs were elevated during some attacks but not in others. However, another study (Freedman, Ianni, Ettedgui, & Puthezhath, 1985) found increases in HR during 7 of 8 panic attacks, with a range of HR increase between 16 and 38 bpm during the attacks. HR increases began prior to the attack itself. Margraff, Taylor, Ehlers, Roth, and Agras (1987) found that HR increases did occur during situational panic attacks (in the usual types of precipitating situations outside of the home) but not in spontaneous panic attacks in the home. This difference in severity of attacks between the two settings suggests one reason why panic disorder often ends in agoraphobia.

Elevated HR does not precipitate the feeling of panic; rather it is probably the suddenly increasing HR and other physiological reactions in the absence of a reasonable cause that makes some individuals panic. Such reactions can occur in reaction to imagined stressors. Patients who panicked in response to a placebo infusion were compared with the majority who did not (Balon, Ortiz, Pohl, & Yeragani, 1988). Panickers did not differ from nonpanickers in baseline HRs (they were somewhat higher) or BPs, but they responded to the infusions of dextrose with significantly higher HRs and SBPs than nonpanickers.

Ehlers, Margraf, Roth, Taylor, and Birbaumer (1988) investigated the role of awareness of HR changes by comparing the reactions of panic disorders and controls to false feedback of an increasing HR. In contrast to controls, patients who believed the feedback was accurate showed increases in subjective anxiety, HR, SBP, and DBP during the condition. Patients were generally higher than controls on anxiety and HR during both true feedback and false feedback conditions, but the groups did not differ in change on these variables during the true feedback condition. Although the patients showed more anxiety than controls during feedback, suggesting an accelerating HR, none of them actually panicked. The results suggest that the fear of panic itself, as cued by HR and possibly other autonomic changes, is only part of the problem in these disorders.

Orienting and habituation

Lader and Wing (1966) compared the initial SCR and habituation of SCL and SCR during 20 presentations of a loud (100 dB) tone in a mixed group of anxiety disorders (about half PDs) and controls. The initial SCRs of the patients to the tones were less than those of controls, but the responses of controls showed more rapid habituation with repetitions of the tones so that by the last trials the patients were showing greater SCRs than the controls (Figure 8.3). When the slope of the habituation function was used to divide subjects into "habituators" and "nonhabituators", they found

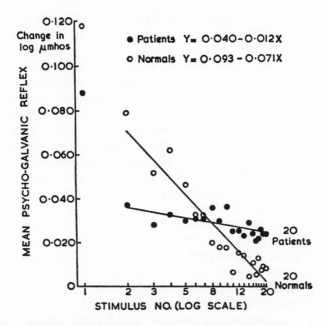

Figure 8.3. Initial response and habituation of skin conductance responses of anxiety disorder patients and normals in response to 20 presentations of a tone. Regression lines of mean SCRs on log stimulus number are shown for both groups. (From *Physiological measures, sedative drugs and morbid anxiety*, p. 105, by M. H. Lader and L. Wing, 1966. London: Oxford University Press. Copyright 1966 by Oxford University Press. Reprinted by permission.)

that all 20 of the normals but only 6 of the 20 patients were habituators. Lader(1975) contrasted the rates of habituation of the SCR in normals and a number of diagnostic groups (see Table 8.6). Specific phobics did not differ from normals, but social phobics, agoraphobics, anxiety states, agitated depressives, and chronic conversion hysterics all showed slower habituation than these first two groups. Other investigators (Chattopadhyay, Cook, Toone, & Lader, 1980; Orr & Pitman, 1987; Roth et al., 1986) failed to find differences in SCR habituation between anxiety disorders and controls. However, in the Chattopadhyay et al. study, subjects with high state anxiety showed slower habituation than calmer subjects.

Conditioning

Conditioning has been central to Eysenck's (1967) model of anxiety neurosis. The combination of an unstable limbic arousal system and a highly aroused and therefore conditionable cortex is said to lead to a readiness to develop phobias, obsessions, compulsions, and other neurotic symptoms in persons who are introverted and high on the *neuroticism* dimension. The conditioning theory of neurosis postulates that anxiety is a conditioned response associated with external stimuli through classical conditioning (Watson and Rayner, 1920; Mowrer, 1939), and avoidance reactions are reinforced (instrumental conditioning) through the reduction of anxiety by an avoidance response (Mowrer, 1939, 1950). Eysenck accepted this explanation but specified that biological factors account for individual differences in vulnerability to such conditioning. Later, Eysenck (1979) attempted to solve the "neurotic paradox," the question of why conditioned anxiety reactions (CRs) do not extinguish in some persons despite repeated exposures of the CS without the UCS. In fact, the association between the CS and CR may become stronger over time instead of extinguishing; this phenomenon is labeled *incubation*.

Eysenck accounts for the paradox in the following manner. First, he accepts the construct of "biological preparedness" (Seligman, 1970, 1971), which suggests that certain types of stimuli or situations such as animals, heights, open places, and so on, are more likely to become conditioned stimuli for a fear response than others because of their role as threats during the evolution of the human species. Second, he assumes that fear conditioning is an example of Pavlovian type B conditioning, in which the UCS elicits the complete UCR rather than a portion of it, and therefore the total UCR can be elicited by the CS. This makes it possible for stimuli produced by the CR itself to act as reinforcers for the CS-CR connection. In the case of anxiety, the result is that the internal stimuli produced by a conditioned fear response, particularly the strong autonomic reactions of a panic attack, can reinforce the connection between external CS and the CR without the need for a UCS. Continued reinforcement of this type can produce the incubation effect. The other factor maintaining incubation and preventing extinction is the short duration of exposure to the CS, thus preventing extinction. Longer durations of exposure ("flooding") could extinguish the connection between the CS and CR. What Eysenck's theory does not fully explain is the nature of the original UCS that elicited the UCR. Most adult social phobias and agoraphobias do not originate in traumatic or painful situations but "incubate" from a situation of chronic insecurity and mild anxiety.

Franks (1956) used a combination of diagnoses and scores on a scale of *extraversion* to divide patients into two groups: dysthymics and "hysterics." Actually, the hysteric group included some psychopaths. An eyelid conditioning procedure like those described in the previous chapter was used. Dysthymics gave more CRs than both normals and hysterics during acquisition and extinction trials. Normals fell between dysthymics and hysterics in CRs during both phases but did not differ significantly from hysterics. On the basis of higher correlations with the E scale than with anxiety or N scales, Franks claimed that the differences between groups in conditioning was produced by their differences on E rather than N.

Pitman and Orr (1986) attempted to test Eysenck's (1979) more recent model of conditioning in anxiety neurosis by using a differential, aversive, electrodermal conditioning paradigm. Angry and neutral faces on slides were used as discriminative CS^+ and CS^- stimuli. Angry expressions were assumed to represent biologically prepared stimuli, more easily conditionable particularly in anxious subjects. They compared the SCRs of patients with anxiety disorders and normal controls on magnitudes of SCR CRs during habituation, acquisition, and extinction phases of the conditioning procedure. The lack of difference on habituation of the CS was mentioned in an earlier section. Anxious and normal groups did not differ during acquisition; both groups showed more conditioned discrimination when the CS^+ was the angry face than when it was the neutral face. Differences between groups emerged in the extinction phase; patients showed larger responses to the CS^+ when it was the angry face than when it was the neutral face whereas the controls showed no further evidence of conditioned discrimination. During extinction trials, the shock electrodes were removed and the subjects were assured there would be no more shocks; so it is unlikely that the failure of extinction in the anxious patients was due to the conscious expectation of further shock. The results tend to support Eysenck's theory predicting greater resistance to extinction in anxious subjects, particularly in response to biologically prepared stimuli. No "incubation" or enhancement of the response to the CS^+ was seen in patients during extinction, but this would not be expected in view of the weak intensity of the UCS shock. As in the study by Franks, CRs during extinction correlated more with E than with N; but in this study, CRs correlated as highly with a scale of manifest trait *anxiety* as with E.

Summary

Most psychologists like to conceptualize psychopathology as the extreme on a continuum ranging from some normal trait manifestations to the abnormal phenomena characterizing a diagnosis. The medical model, however, is based on the idea of discrete syndromes defining various disorders with distinct etiologies, prognoses, and treatments. The DSM III enables one to distinguish between transient clinical disorders (axis I) and longer existing personality disorders (axis II). The dimensional psychological view would lead one to expect anxiety-relevant personality disorders in the background of all or most axis I anxiety disorders. However, in at least half the cases this is not true; anxiety disorders frequently occur in persons with no preexisting personality disorder. If this association is lacking, how much can we learn about normal personality traits from a study of the clinical disorders that are thought to represent their extreme manifestations? Clearly, we must proceed cautiously in generalizing from one to the other. There may be some kind of a threshold effect with clinical disorders. A physiological system that may produce few obvious phenomena up to a set point may produce abnormal manifestations beyond that point. Body temperature, for instance, may vary within a narrow range with little obvious effect; but beyond certain limits, mechanisms such as shivering or sweating are triggered in an attempt to return temperature to the healthy range.

Genetic studies of anxiety disorders indicate the likelihood of a heritable broad disposition toward disorders plus some specific genetic factors in panic or obsessive-compulsive disorders. Dysthymic disorder does not seem to belong in the anxiety disorder spectrum despite its past association with the other "neuroses." Somatoform disorders show more genetic linkage with psychopathic (antisocial) personality disorder and alcoholism (particularly in male relatives of female patients) than with anxiety disorder. Although there is a substantial environmental influence in anxiety disorders, the influence seems to be of a specific type rather than the shared familial influence, a similar result to that found for the *neuroticism* dimension in normal personality (chapter 3).

Although studies of normals have not found much association between the *neuroticism* dimension of personality and the enzyme MAO, the effectiveness of MAO-inhibiting drugs in treating certain anxiety disorders, such as panic and obsessive-compulsive disorders, suggests that MAO may be elevated in these disorders. A number of studies have found differences in MAO between anxiety and control groups before treatment, though this is not an entirely consistent finding. There is also the possibility that higher MAO may be associated with the depression that often accompanies anxiety. Another possibility is that MAO may simply be associated with increased serotonergic or catecholaminergic activity rather than being directly related to anxiety.

The peripheral catecholamines, epinephrine and norepinephrine, are often found to be elevated in panic disorders even when patients are not experiencing panic. But MHPG, the principal metabolite of norepinephrine in the brain, is not elevated in CSF or plasma in anxiety disorders. Yohimbine, an alpha$_2$ noradrenergic receptor antagonist, increases anxiety and MHPG specifically in patients with panic disorders. Clonidine, a drug that inhibits noradrenergic activity at its source in the locus coeruleus, reduces anxiety and MHPG specifically in agoraphobics with panic disorders. However, other drugs such as caffeine and lactate, which also produce increased anxiety and even panic in panic disorders, do not affect the activity of the noradrenergic system as indexed by MHPG. The common effect of most drugs that do produce anxiety in patients with the disorder is stimulation of peripheral catecholamines and/or discriminable symptoms such as palpitations (increased heart rate) and dizziness (possibly due to elevated BP). This suggests that if there is a biological vulnerability in anxiety disorders, it is one of the peripheral autonomic system. However, central mechanisms that are not fully understood or measurable at present may control the variations in the peripheral mechanisms. Inherited instability of the dorsal ascending noradrenergic system may be a contributory cause, but it is not a specific cause of anxiety.

Although several theories have suggested a major role for serotonin in anxiety disorders, baseline and serotonergic potentiation studies are inconclusive. A new theory suggests that anxiety is related to hypersensitive serotonergic receptors that down-regulate the production and metabolism of the neurotransmitter. Reported increases in obsessive and anxiety symptoms in patients produced by a drug (mCPP) that stimulates the serotonergic postsynaptic receptors have not been confirmed in subsequent studies. At present, neither noradrenergic or serotonergic theories seem capable of explaining the symptoms of anxiety disorders or their amelioration by benzodiazepine or antidepressant drugs. It is possible that these neurotransmitters may interact among themselves or with other systems to produce or reduce anxiety symptoms.

The discovery of benzodiazepine-binding sites in the brain led to the theory that the number and distribution of these sites, the availability of an endogenous benzodiazepine-like substance, or the activity of a receptor antagonist that might produce anxiety, could explain the differences between anxiety disorder patients and normals. Two benzodiazepine receptor antagonists have been found, one endogenous and the other produced in the laboratory, but behavioral results are equivocal thus far. An endogenous benzodiazepine has not yet been found.

Although chronic stress can elevate cortisol levels, the evidence suggests that excessive cortisol production is more characteristic of major depression than of anxiety disorder. Neither baseline or stress-produced levels of cortisol or reactions to the inhibition of cortisol production using the dexamethasone suppression test indicate that cortisol deregulation is a primary characteristic of anxiety disorders.

Psychophysiological studies of normals (chapter 6) have not shown a relation between the trait of *neuroticism* or *anxiety* and physiological arousal or arousability in response to the usual kinds of laboratory stressors. In contrast, psychophysiological studies of anxiety disorders, with the exception of simple phobic disorders, have usually revealed a heightened basal arousal in heart rate and skin conductance in these disorders. These differences are most pronounced in cases of "chronic anxiety," panic disorders, agoraphobia, and obsessive-compulsive disorders. Physiological reactivity to stress does not distinguish these disorders from normals. However, in simple phobias and posttraumatic stress disorder, the particular stimuli associated with their anxiety can elicit greater physiological response than in normals. What distinguishes these disorders from normals is the situation that elicits arousal and not arousal itself.

Panic reactions do produce very high levels of activation, not usually seen in normals in situations where there is little physical exertion or obvious sources of emotional stress. What produces the extreme discomfort of panic is the fact that most panic disorders start from a higher level of basal arousal and progress to even higher levels during the panic attack.

The weakening of the initial orienting reflex and the slow habituation seen in anxiety neurotics seem to depend on their level of state *anxiety* in the experimental situation. Their level of state *anxiety* may depend on the characteristics of the general situation rather than on the specific stimulus. A person with a generalized anxiety disorder is more likely to be in a high state of anxiety than a nonanxious individual in any novel situation, but there may be a stronger tendency in anxiety disorders to perceive threat in ambiguous and novel situations.

The generalized tendency to respond to a wide range of situations as threatening can be explained by conditioning in a person with a highly reactive nervous system (Eysenck). A major drawback to the classical conditioning theory of neurosis is the question of why conditioned responses to commonly encountered situations and stimuli do not extinguish with repeated exposures. Laboratory studies have shown a slower extinction of conditioned responses in anxiety neurotics, using shock as an UCS. One explanation of the failure of extinction is that the avoidance tendencies developed in the anxiety disorder result in only brief exposures to the CS and that prolonged exposures are required for extinction to occur.

Another unanswered question is what is the UCS that produces the initial panic attack? Biological theorists claim that these may arise from purely physiological factors such as a deregulation of the central noradrenergic system. Most phobias do not arise from pain conditioning, though this is the favored model used in animal and human experiments. Conceivably, situations that are traumatic enough to produce a strong perceived threat to one's survival might provide the strong internal reactions that could act as UCSs for initial conditioning. Although these situations can account for some posttraumatic stress disorders, they are not that common in the background of other kinds of anxiety disorders. Observational and purely cognitive learning may play an important role in the acquisition of fears. The key to understanding pathological anxiety, as well as variations in the normal range, may be the definition of anxiety mechanisms in neuroanatomical and neurophysiological terms. But we must also understand how such inborn vulnerabilities interact with life experiences to produce disorders and extremes of personality.

9   Antisocial personality and other disinhibitory disorders

Overview

Antisocial personality disorder (APD) was first regarded as a medical disorder in the early nineteenth century (Pichot, 1978). Pinel called the disorder "mania without delusion" and Pritchard termed it "moral insanity." Both definitions suggest that, though the behavior of these patients may be psychotic, it does not include the thinking disorders that are characteristic of other psychotics such as manics, schizophrenics, and paranoids. Cleckley (1976) regarded the ability of antisocial personalities to seem normal and well-adjusted to others as a "mask of sanity" that hides a severe psychological disturbance.

This author has suggested that APD may represent the extreme of the continuous, if not normal, distribution of the P dimension of personality (see chapter 1 of this volume and Zuckerman, 1989). Most of the traits involved in this dimension represent characteristics of the psychopath, including lack of socialization and responsibility, *impulsivity, sensation seeking* in its disinhibition and boredom susceptibility forms, and *aggression*. Of course, these are personality traits, and the current (DSM III) definition of APD rests largely on behavioral criteria. The earlier psychiatric definition of APD (APA DSM II, 1968) used many general trait terms:

... individuals who are basically unsocialized and whose behaviour patterns bring them repeatedly into conflict with society. They are incapable of loyalty to individuals, groups, or social values. They are grossly selfish, callous, irresponsible, impulsive, and unable to feel guilt or to learn from experience or punishment. Frustration tolerance is low. They tend to blame others or offer a plausible rationalization for their behavior. *A mere history of repeated criminal or social offenses is not sufficient to justify this diagnosis.* (italics are this author's)

DSM III-R (1987) defines APD almost exclusively in behavioral terms.

The essential feature of this disorder is a pattern of irresponsible and antisocial behavior beginning in childhood or early adolescence and continuing into adulthood. For this diagnosis to be given, the person must be at least 18 years of age and have a history of Conduct Disorder [another DSM III diagnosis] before the age of 15.

Consonant with the striving for objectivity in the DSM III, "irresponsible and antisocial behavior" is defined in operational terms. In childhood, the significant behaviors are truancy, running away from home, initiating phys-

359

Table 9.1. *Cleckley's characteristics of the psychopath*

1. Superficial charm and good "intelligence"
2. Absence of delusions and other types of irrational thinking
3. Absence of 'nervousness' or psychoneurotic manifestations
4. Unreliability
5. Untruthfulness and insincerity
6. Lack of remorse or shame
7. Inadequately motivated antisocial behavior
8. Poor judgment and failure to learn from experience
9. Pathological egocentricity and incapacity for love
10. General poverty in major affective reactions
11. Specific loss of insight
12. Unresponsiveness in general interpersonal relations
13. Fantastic and uninviting behavior with drink and sometimes without
14. Threats of suicide rarely carried out
15. Sex life impersonal, trivial, and poorly integrated
16. Failure to follow any life plan

ical fights and using weapons, forcing sexual relations on others, physical cruelty to animals and/or people, vandalism, fire-setting, lying, and stealing with or without violent confrontation. In the older adolescent or adult, the behavioral terms are inability to hold a job and perform it well, arrests for unlawful behavior, fighting, spouse and child abuse, failure to honor financial obligations, impulsive life-style (traveling from place to place without clear goals), lying, reckless or drunken driving and recurrent speeding, child neglect, and inability to maintain a monogamous relationship for more than one year. The only DSM III sign of dealing with emotion is the lack of remorse, but even this is inferred from attempts at self-justification.

An earlier definition of the psychopath was provided by Cleckley (1976) in a list of 16 characteristics (Table 9.1).

Two of these characteristics (2 and 3) refer to the exclusion of other disorders such as neuroses and psychoses as explanations for the positive symptoms. Items 3, 6, 9, and 10 refer to a poverty or absence of strong feelings, negative or positive. Item 11 refers to the lack of any capacity for self-criticism and the projection of blame that is characteristic of the psychopath.

Hare (Hare & Cox, 1978) based his assessment procedures on the Cleckley criteria. He began with a single 7-point rating scale for psychopathy used by clinicians trained on the Cleckley criteria. Later he developed the Psychopathy Check List (PCL) consisting of 22 items derived from the Cleckley signs of psychopathy, which are rated after an extensive review of the case record and an intensive interview with an offender (Hare, 1986). The global rating and the PCL correlated highly with each other and with the diagnosis of APD based on the DSM III. Correlations of diagnoses and PCL with questionnaire scales were lower. The best combination of scales using the *psychopathic deviate* (Pd) scale from the MMPI and the

Table 9.2. *Psychopathy checklist factors*

Factor 1: Selfish, callous, and remorseless use of others
  1. Glibness/superficial charm
  3. Egocentricity/grandiose sense of self-worth
  5. Pathological lying and deception
  6. Conning/lack of sincerity
  7. Lack of remorse or guilt
  8. Lack of affect and emotional depth
  9. Callous/lack of empathy
 20. Failure to accept responsibility for own actions
 22. Drug or alcohol use not direct cause of antisocial behavior

Factor 2: Chronically unstable and antisocial lifestyle; social deviance
  4. Proneness to boredom/low frustration tolerance
 10. Parasitic lifestyle
 11. Short tempered/poor behavioral controls
 13. Early behavior problems
 14. Lack of realistic long-term plans
 15. Impulsivity
 16. Irresponsible behavior as a parent
 17. Frequent marital relationships
 18. Juvenile delinquency
 19. Poor probation or parole risk
 21. Many types of offense

Source: "Two factor conceptualization of psychopathy: Construct validity and assessment implications," by T. J. Harpur, R. D. Hare, & A. R. Hakstian, 1989, *Psychological Assessment: A Journal of Consulting and Clinical Psychology*, 1, p. 7. Copyright 1989 by American Psychological Association. Reprinted by permission of author.

socialization (So) scale from the CPI (Pd-So) yielded a kappa of .56 with DSM III APD as contrasted with the PCL versus APD kappa of .79.

Harpur, Hakstian, and Hare (1988) found two consistent and replicable factors in the PCL items. The items describing both factors are listed in Table 9.2. The first factor, selfish, callous, and remorseless use of others, describes many of the personality traits supposedly crucial to psychopathy, including the absence of feelings of love or guilt, a general lack of empathy or insight, and egocentricity combined with exploitation of others. The second factor, chronically unstable and antisocial lifestyle and social deviance is closer to the DSM III criteria for APD, describing a long, persistent history of antisocial behavior and irresponsibility in social roles. Two personality traits are mentioned in factor 2: *boredom susceptibility* and *impulsivity*.

Harpur, Hare, and Haksitan (1989) have recently summarized their various findings using the 2-factor scoring of the PCL. Some of their results are listed in (Table 9.3). As one might expect, diagnosis of APD is somewhat better predicted from factor 2 (F2) than factor 1 (F1). What is surprising is that most of the personality measures of psychopathy from the MMPI, CPI, and *sensation seeking* scale (SSS) also correlate more highly

Table 9.3. *Correlates of the PCL: diagnosis, personality scales, behavior ratings, institutional behavior*

Variable	n	rsF1	rsF2	rsPCL Total
Diagnosis: APD	319	.42^c	.55^c	.56^c
MMPI: Pd	138	.11	.31^c	.25^b
Ma	138	.16	.32^c	.27^b
Pd + Ma	138	.18^b	.41^c	.35^c
Pd + So	117	.08	.49^c	.33^c
CPI So	223	−.06	−.44^c	−.31^c
STAI trait anxiety	111	−.20^a	.18	.01
Fenz-Epstein A scale	159	−.17^a	.10	−.01
KSP psychic anxiety	90	−.39^c	−.14	−.30
EPQ neuroticism	222	−.17^a	.16^a	.02
extraversion	222	.08	.10	.11
psychoticism	222	.01	.22^c	.14^a
SSS V total score	207	.12	.39^c	.30^c
KSP impulsivity	90	.06	.14	.09
monotony avoidance	90	.05	.16	.11
detachment	90	.21	.25^a	.24^a
Institutional behavior	313	.33^c	.50^c	.49^c
Release violations	231	.18^b	.38^c	.33^c

$^a p < .05$
$^b p < .01$
$^c p < .001$

Source: Data from various tables in "Two factor conceptualization of psychopathy: Construct validity and assessment implications," by T. J. Harpur, R. D. Hare, & A. R. Hakstian, 1989, *Psychological Assessment: A Journal of Consulting and Clinical Psychology*, pp. 11–12. Copyright 1989 by American Psychological Association. Reprinted by permission.

with F2 than with F1. The only exceptions are the traits of *anxiety* and *neuroticism,* which tend to correlate negatively with F1 and positively with F2. However, the correlations between PCL factors 1 and 2 and *anxiety* are generally low, so *anxiety* cannot be said to be a strong defining characteristic of either type. However, the finding of two clusters of traits, one associated with low *anxiety* scores and the other with high *anxiety* scores, recalls a classical distinction between the primary psychopath and the secondary psychopath. The primary psychopath is said to show impulsive, antisocial behavior combined with lack of anxiety or guilt, and the secondary psychopath is impulsive and antisocial but also anxious and disturbed. The secondary type is also called an "acting-out" or "neurotic" psychopath. Primary types have shown more severe and frequent antisocial behavior than secondary types, and both types of psychopath have exhibited more antisocial behavior than other prisoners (Fagan and Liro, 1980).

The F2 type of psychopathy is defined by *sensation seeking* at the positive pole and *socialization* at the negative pole. The P scale from the EPQ is positively associated with the F2 trait only; the N scale has a low weak positive relationship with F2 and a low weak negative relationship with F1. The E scale correlates with neither factor. These data support the author's assumption that the P-ImpUSS dimension of personality is directly associated with psychopathy. Neither E nor N correlated with the PCL total score. This contradicts Eysenck's assertion that all three primary dimensions of personality, E, N, and P are high in psychopathy. *Sensation seeking* was found to be a core characteristic of the behavioral psychopath as defined by factor 2. All of the subscales of *sensation seeking* correlated equally with the PCL, despite earlier evidence that the *disinhibition* and *boredom susceptibility* scales are more closely related to primary psychopathy than the other two subscales (Blackburn, 1978; Emmons & Webb, 1974; Zuckerman, 1978).

Table 9.3 also includes correlations with two behavioral ratings: The first refers to antisocial behavior in the custodial institution, and the second refers to the outcome of conditional release programs given to the prisoners. Scores on both factors were significantly correlated with these measures, but scores on F2 were more highly correlated with these behavioral expressions of psychopathic intractibility. From a prognostic standpoint, the writers of the DSM III may have been correct in excluding the absence of anxiety or strong feelings from their definition of APD. However, the personality traits *narcissism* and *lack of emotion* described by F1 may be more useful in describing the APD who does not end up in prison and thrives in the community. These are the types exemplified in most of the cases described by Cleckley (1976).

Substance abuse

Because APD is diagnosed on axis II of the DSM III, it is potentially compatible with any clinical diagnosis. Actually it seems to be closely related to one particular clinical disorder (axis I), substance abuse. Of 48 patients receiving the diagnosis of APD on axis II, 63% received the diagnosis of substance abuse or dependence on axis I (Koenigsberg, Kaplan, Gilmore, & Cooper, 1985). Lewis, Rice, and Helzer (1983) found that all the men referred from a medical center and diagnosed APD were alcoholic, drug dependent, or both, compared with a third of those referred who did not have APD. Among women, the percentages were much lower, 34% among the APDs compared with 12% among non-APDs. Another study found a marked overlap among diagnoses of APD, alcoholism, and drug dependence, with over 84% of the cases diagnosed APD having secondary diagnoses of one or both substance abuse disorders, and little overlap among these three disorders and diagnoses of primary or secondary depression, mania, or schizophrenia. Lewis, Robins, and Rice (1985) also found a high rate of alcoholism and drug addiction among APDs and low rates of depression, anxiety, and schizophrenia.

Among opioid abusers, 27% could be diagnosed as APD in one center (Rousenville, Weissman, Kleber, & Webber, 1982), but 78% of men and about 60% of women narcotic abusers met the APD criteria in another (Lewis et al., 1983). The first unit was located in a community mental health center, and the second was in the federal facility at Lexington, Kentucky. The latter is more likely to get the hard-core opioid abuser.

Given the fact that a sizeable proportion of alcohol and drug abusing populations also have antisocial personalities, is there any value to making the diagnostic distinction in these populations? Comparisons of APDs with primary alcoholics in a population of alcoholics show that the APD alcoholic, though drinking no more than the primary alcoholic, is more likely to be fired, involved in auto accidents, arrested for public intoxication, and hospitalized for alcoholism (Jaffe & Schuckit, 1981). Alcoholics with APD are much more likely to abuse other drugs than alcoholics without APD (Lewis et al. 1983). Bland and Orn (1986) interviewed noninstitutionalized residents of a Canadian city concerning family violence and signs of psychiatric disorders. Violence toward spouse or children was admitted by 15.5% of those persons without diagnosis of any disorder, but of those judged to use alcohol and/or be dependent on it, the percentage of such violent individuals rose to 44%; and when alcoholism was combined with APD, an astounding 93% were identified as violent to their families! Alcoholism in the context of APD clearly has more severe behavioral consequences than primary alcoholism without APD.

Criminality

Much of the APD research is conducted on prisoners who are incarcerated for criminality. Given the nature of an overloaded criminal justice system, there is a tendency for prison populations to consist primarily of repeat or chronic offenders, except for cases of first-time crimes of extreme violence. There are many sociological causes of crime, the most obvious of which are poverty and joblessness, but there is a tendency to forget about these causes of crime when one focuses on the characteristics of the individual criminal. The tendency to stress the early onset of antisocial behavior in the DSM III definition of APD is probably due in large part to the longitudinal study reported by Robins (1978) following the life histories of children in St. Louis over periods of 20 to 30 years, which found that a diagnosis of APD was never made in the absence of antisocial behavior before the age of 18. The onset of psychopathy in boys, as judged by antisocial behavior, began before the age of 8 years in 58% of the cases and by 13 years in 84% of the cases. In the smaller sample of female psychopaths, the behaviors usually began between 14 and 18 years of age. The best predictor of the post-adolescent APD was the number of antisocial symptoms one had as a child. All other factors such as social class and parental characteristics were secondary to the child's own behavioral history as predictors of APD. In many communities, a certain amount of delinquency is almost normal during adolescence. Apparently those individuals who began "acting out" before adolescence have a higher risk of continuing as criminals after adolescence. These are the individuals now receiving the APD diagnosis.

A similar kind of study conducted in England (Farrington, Gallagher, Morley, St. Ledger, & West, 1988) compared members of a vulnerable group of boys from criminogenic backgrounds at ages 8 to 10 and followed up until age 32. The boys who did not acquire criminal records and who eventually had good marital and occupational histories were distinguished by more neurotic and fewer behavioral problems at age 8 to 10 and by being less daring, less troublesome, and easier to discipline than peers who went on to delinquent and criminal activities. Despite the same adverse environmental factors such as parental conflict and criminality, a personality factor consisting of ease of *socialization* and low *sensation seeking* prevents some boys from becoming criminal.

Hare (1983) examined the proportion of a prison population that could be classified as APD using the DSM III. Of 246 inmates of 2 prisons in Canada, 39% were diagnosed as APD by two judges and 50% were diagnosed APD by only one of the two. Most of those persons with APD diagnoses received other diagnoses, most frequently substance abuse disorder.

APDs are often seen as more dangerous and unpredictable than non-APD criminals. Certain personality characteristics of APDs seem to increase their involvement in the problems of prison life. *Sensation seeking* tends to be extreme in APDs, and thus the sensory and experiential restrictions of detention centers are more intolerable to them than to other prisoners. Farley and Farley (1972) found that incarcerated female delinquents who scored high on the *general sensation seeking* scale made more escape attempts, were punished more for disobeying supervisors, and engaged in more fighting with other prisoners than those lower on *sensation seeking*. Farley (1973) reported similar results for males. English and Jones (1972) also reported that high *sensation seekers* among narcotics addicts were more likely to "elope" from a treatment center than the lows.

Hyperactivity: a precursor of APD?

Many of the school problems of APDs have been attributed to their restlessness, boredom susceptibility, and impulsivity, making the usual school environment a "jail" for them. Conduct disorders among children are by definition a precursor of adult APD, but are *attention deficit* disorder or *hyperactive* disorder also antecedents of APD?

Satterfield (1987) reported on hyperactive and normal children, first

Table 9.4. *Pairwise twin concordance rates for juvenile delinquency and crime*

		Identical twins		Fraternal twins	
		Pairs *n*	%C	Pairs *n*	%C
Juvenile Delinquency					
6 studies 1941–1977	M & F	83	87	61	72
Adult Criminality					
6 studies 1931–1961	M & F	132	69	122	33
Scandinavian Studies					
Dalgaard & Kringlen (1976)	M	31	26	54	15
Christiansen (1977a)	M	73	34	146	18
	F	15	20	28	7
	M & F	88	32	174	16

Source: From table in chapter 6 by C. R. Cloninger and I. I. Gottesman, in *The causes of crime*, S. A. Mednick, T. E. Moffitt, and S. A. Stack, eds., 1987, p. 98. Copyright 1987 by Cambridge Univ. Press. Reprinted by permission.

studied at ages 6–12 years and a follow up of arrest data in Los Angeles when the subjects were 14 to 20 years old. The follow up showed marked differences between the hyperactives and controls on subsequent arrests. Nearly 50% of the hyperactives had been arrested one or more times for serious offenses compared with less than 10% of the controls. Rates for those with multiple serious offenses and institutionalization were 28 and 25 times higher, respectively, for the hyperactives than for the controls. Robins (1966) had also noted that a third of the children who were hyperactive and impulsive as children became criminal as adults.

Influence of genetics and environment on disinhibitory disorders

Twin studies

Table 9.4 summarizes the results of twin studies of juvenile delinquency and crime given in Cloninger and Gottesman (1987) and Christiansen (1977a, 1977b). The results of a number of studies of juvenile delinquency and crime, most of them conducted in the pre-WWII years, are combined because most of them used small samples of twins initially selected from crime registers. Determinations of zygosity are questionable for most of these studies because they were based on physical similarities rather than blood typing or finger prints. Definitions of criminal concordance were often fuzzy and susceptible to bias on the part of the investigators. For juvenile delinquency the overall pairwise concordance rates were high for both ITs (87%) and FTs (72%). The pattern indicates little influence of genetics and probably a strong influence of shared environment. For adult criminality, however, the rate of concordance for ITs (69%) is about double that for FT's (33%), most likely indicating a pattern of polygenetic inheritance influencing criminal behavior. Although most chronic adult criminals have records of teenage and earlier delinquency, most teenage delinquents do not show patterns of prepubertal delinquency and do not go on to become adult criminals (Wolfgang, Figlis, & Sellin, 1972).

Three postwar studies, conducted in Scandinavian countries on unselected populations of twins, yielded much smaller pairwise concordance rates for criminality than the earlier studies. In Finland, Tienari (1963) found a concordance rate of 22% for ITs among 23 pairs in a larger population of twins, in which at least one had a criminal record. Dalgaard and Kringlen (1976) drew their sample from the Norwegian Twin Register of about 33,000 pairs born between 1900 and 1935. Of these, 85 pairs were located in which at least one of the pair had a registered criminal offense. Zygosity determinations were done by blood typing in most cases. Using a strict definition of criminality (only standard penal code offenses such as violence, sexual assault, and crimes against property) the concordance was 26% for ITs and 15% for FTs. Using a broader definition (including traffic and military offenses) the rates were 22% for ITs and 18% for FTs. Neither IT versus FT difference was significant.

Christiansen's (1977b) study (updated by Cloninger & Gottesman, 1987) drew on all twins born in Denmark from 1890 to 1920. This was the first study to use substantial numbers of female twins. The rate of registered criminality was higher among the male twins (9.9%) than among the females (1.5%), and concordance rates were also somewhat higher among males, as shown in Table 9.3. The overall concordance for ITs was 32% as opposed to 16% for FTs. The concordance ratio (IT:FT) is 2 to 1, as it was in the earlier studies of adult criminality, but the absolute rates are almost half those in the earlier studies. Cloninger and Gottesman translated the condordance rates from Christiansen's study into correlational form, yielding correlations of .74 for ITs and .47 for FTs. Application of the Falconer formula yields a heritability of 54% for criminal behavior, which is very close to the figure obtained for various measures of traits constituting the P dimension of personality (chapter 3 and Zuckerman, 1989).

Cloninger and Gottesman (1987) divided the crimes into crimes against persons and those against property. The crimes against property yielded a higher heritability (78%) than those against persons (50%). They also found no significant genetic overlap in crimes against persons and those against property. The usual crime statistics confound these two sources. It is possible that crimes against persons represent the trait of *aggressiveness* whereas those against property are indicative of a general antisocial tendency. The latter may be more heritable.

Adoption studies

It is not difficult to see why ITs raised together should show a higher rate of concordance in criminal behavior than FTs. Even if they were not both genetically more inclined to engage in crime, the authorities might have some difficulty in sorting out which of two ITs committed a crime! ITs reared separately might provide a more definite answer on the heritability of criminal tendency. Christiansen (1977b) summarized reports on eight such cases. In four (50%) of these cases the ITs were concordant for criminal record. The case histories suggest reasons for differential outcomes, such as the benign influence of a foster parent or a spouse, though such post hoc inferences are not trustworthy.

Kapris, Koskenvuo, and Langinvanio (1984) investigated alcohol use and heavy drinking habits among Finnish twins, separated sometime before 11 years of age and raised in different homes, and twins raised in the same home. There was no evidence of genetic influences on alcohol use per se, but a definite genetic pattern was seen for heavy drinking habits. These were mostly attributable to males; few women in any of the twin groups were heavy drinkers. Pairwise concordance for ITs reared together was 75% compared with FTs' concordance of 41%. For separated ITs the concordance was 50% compared with 20% for FTs. Like the data for criminality, the results suggest about a 50% heritability for heavy drinking among males. Some shared environmental family influence is also suggested by the contrast in concordance between twins raised together with those reared in different families.

Crowe (1974) interviewed a sample of adoptees born to female offenders from prisons in Iowa and adopted less than 18 months after birth. Six of 46 biological children of offenders were diagnosed as definite antisocial personality; only one of 46 controls was diagnosed as antisocial personality and, unlike the diagnoses in the proband group, this one did not meet the research criteria for the diagnosis. Significant differences were also found between the groups on adult arrest records, incarceration, and psychiatric hospitilizations.

Cadoret and Cain (1980) followed up another group of Iowa adoptees, separated at birth from biological parents of whom one or both had a psychiatric condition. Control adoptees from biological parents without psychiatric conditions were used. For the total group, antisocial and alcoholic factors in the biological parents, adverse environments, and discontinuous mothering in the adoptive homes predicted antisocial symptoms in the adoptive children. However, the effects of an adverse environment were predictive of antisocial behavior in males only. Only antisocial or mental retardation in the biological parents predicted antisocial behavior in females. Cadoret, Troughton, O'Gorman, and Heywood (1986) examined the effects on children of alcohol and drug abuse, as well as an-

Table 9.5. *"Cross-fostering" analysis: percentage of adoptive sons who have been convicted of criminal law offenses*

		Are biological parents criminal?	
		Yes	No
Are adoptive parents criminal?	Yes	24.5% $n =$ 143	14.7% $n =$ 204
	No	20.0% $n =$ 1226	13.5% $n =$ 2492

Source: From table in chapter 3 by S. A. Mednick, T. Moffitt, W. Gabrielli, Jr., and B. Hutchings, in *Development of Antisocial and Prosocial Behavior: Research, Theories and Issues*, D. Olweus, J. Block, & M. Radke-Yarrow, eds., p. 40. Copyright 1986 by Academic Press. Reprinted by permission.

tisocial personality, in the biological parents of adoptees on adoptee behaviors. As before, an antisocial biological background predicted antisocial tendencies. Antisocial tendencies were highly correlated with drug abuse, but even among those adoptees without antisocial personalities, a biological background of alcoholism increased the chance of drug abuse. Environmental factors such as divorce and psychiatric disturbance in the adopting family also increased drug abuse in the adoptee. Possibly, the effects of environmental factors can be minimized in adoption studies because of the less variable and more benign environments in the adoptive homes due to screening by adoption agencies.

Mednick, Moffitt, Gabrielli, and Hutchings (1986) have updated the results of a study of a large cohort of Danish adoptees. Court conviction records were used as evidence of criminality in the adoptees, their biological parents, and their adoptive parents. Although the rate of criminality was much lower in adoptive than in biological parents, the population was large enough to construct the "cross-fostering" analysis shown in Table 9.5. These data enable comparison of the relative influence of the genetic factor (biological parents) and the environmental factor (adoptive parents). Of course, the analysis does not include the environmental factors outside of the home. Having a criminal biological parent significantly increased the chances of criminality in the adopted sons who never knew these parents but having an adoptive parent who was criminal did not increase the risk of criminality.

Biological siblings raised in different homes had a concordance rate for criminality (20%) that was twice as high as that for nonrelated adoptees reared in the same family (8.5%). Having a biological father who was criminal further increased the concordance of siblings raised apart (31%). There was no evidence of interaction between the biological and adoptive parent influence. Although convictions for the women in the study were low, the relation between biological mother and daughter conviction was significantly stronger than that between biological father and son conviction.

The percentage of adoptees with criminal records increased linearly with the number of convictions of biological parents, suggesting a stronger genetic factor influencing the children of the more chronically criminal parents. The sons of the most chronically criminal biological parents constituted only 1% of the population of adoptees, but they accounted for 30% of the convictions among male adoptees! Analysis by type of crime (Mednick, Gabrielli, & Hutchings, 1987) showed that the relationship between sons' and parents' convictions was significant for property offenses but not for violent offenses.

Cloninger and Gottesman (1987) did a longitudinal study of 1775 Swedish adoptees, representing the population of adoptees from Stockholm (born 1930–1949) and not adopted by relatives. Their results are shown in Figure 9.1. In this analysis the classification of "congenital" and "postnatal" refers to a number of factors besides actual criminality in biological and adopting parents (such as rearing experiences) that were found to be related to adoptees records of petty crime. In male adoptees (Cloninger, Sigvardsson, Bohman, and von Knorring, 1982), both congenital and postnatal influences had significant additive influences, but the nonadditive interaction was not significant. High postnatal factors doubled and high congenital factors quadrupled the rate of petty criminality over the group whose members were low in both types of predisposing factors. When both factors were high, the rate rose to 40%. Although this appears as though it might be an interaction, the data fit a simple additive model. All factors explained only about 24% of the total variance in criminality. When this explainable variance was partitioned, 59% was explained by genes only, 19% by environment only, 14% by gene-environment interaction, and 7% by gene-environment correlation.

Although the rates of crime were much lower in women in all four categories, they follow a similar pattern to that seen in males. Although no significant interactions were found, Cloninger and Gottesman (1987) concluded that "men and women were unlikely to become criminals unless they were at high risk as a consequence of both their biological-parent background and their post-natal environment." (p. 104).

Alcoholism and criminality

As noted previously, there is a significant overlap between the diagnoses of APD and alcohol abuse or dependence in men. However, the overlap could be due to the disinhibitory tendencies of the APD rather than a genetic linkage between the two. Cloninger and Gottesman claim that their adoption data do not support such a linkage. Criminality alone in the

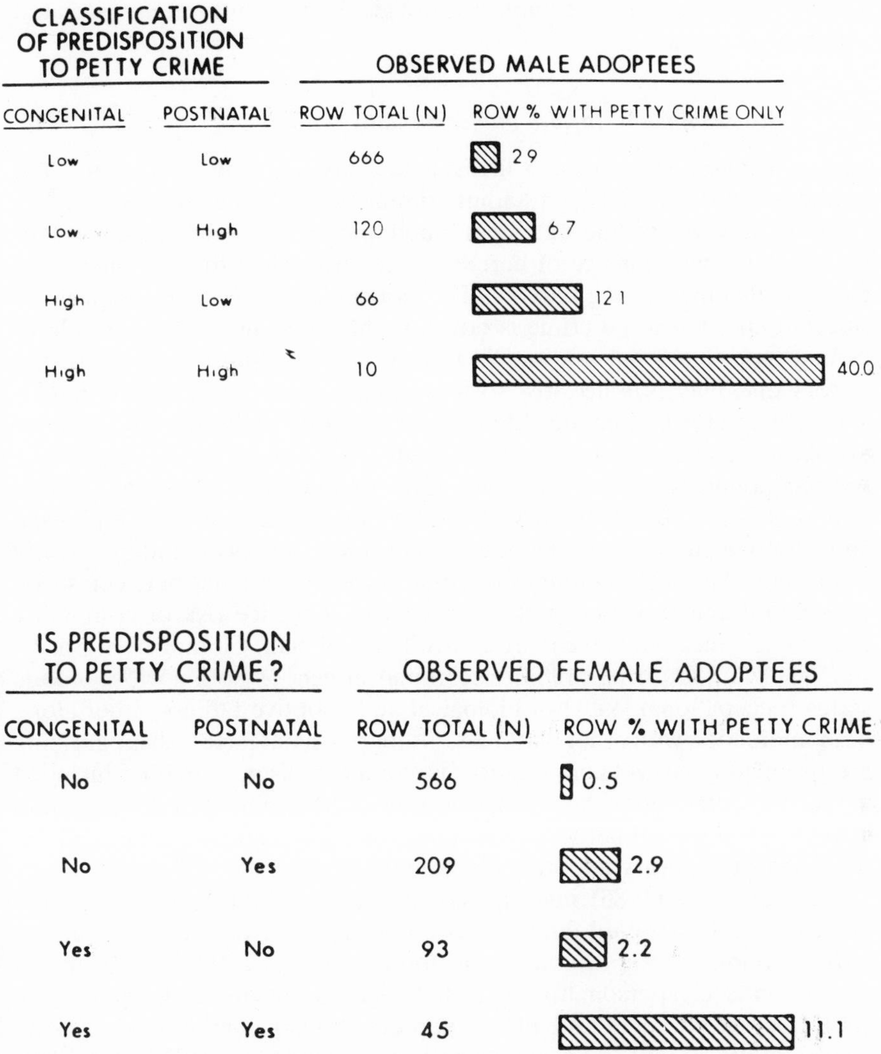

CLASSIFICATION
OF PREDISPOSITION
TO PETTY CRIME

OBSERVED MALE ADOPTEES

CONGENITAL	POSTNATAL	ROW TOTAL (N)	ROW % WITH PETTY CRIME ONLY
Low	Low	666	2.9
Low	High	120	6.7
High	Low	66	12.1
High	High	10	40.0

IS PREDISPOSITION
TO PETTY CRIME?

OBSERVED FEMALE ADOPTEES

CONGENITAL	POSTNATAL	ROW TOTAL (N)	ROW % WITH PETTY CRIME
No	No	566	0.5
No	Yes	209	2.9
Yes	No	93	2.2
Yes	Yes	45	11.1

Figure 9.1. Cross fostering of petty criminality (without alcohol abuse) in male and female adoptees. (From "Genetic and environmental factors in antisocial behavior," by C. R. Cloninger and I. I. Gottesman, 1987, in S. A. Mednick, T. E. Moffitt and S. A. Sack (Eds.), *The causes of crime: New biological approaches*, p. 105. Cambridge: Cambridge Univ. Press. Copyright 1987 by Cambridge Univ. Press. Reprinted by permission.)

biological parents increased the rate of crime but not alcoholism in the adopted-away sons. Alcoholism in the fathers increased the rate of alcoholism but not criminality in the adopted-away sons. Pure inheritance of criminality was associated with nonviolent property crimes. In cases in which crime occurred as a complication of alcoholism it was often associated with violent crimes.

Environmental factors and criminality

Although many studies have investigated environmental correlates and predictors of delinquency and adult criminality, only the adoption studies can make any worthwhile statements about the role of environment without the confounding influence of heredity that exists when the biological parents are also the rearing parents. The association between poverty or socioeconomic status and crime is obvious, though some investigators have denied its primary importance as a predictor, claiming that some of the factors that may produce low socioeconomic status, such as low intelligence, may also be genetic. Mednick et al. (1987) investigated the relationships between criminality in Danish adoptees as a function of the socioeconomic status of their biological parents and adoptive parents. Criminal risk varied inversely with socioeconomic status of both biological and adoptive parents, and the effects of both variables were independently significant. Although there may be some genetic covariance between social class and criminality, social class appears to influence risk of criminality even when genetic influences are controlled. Bohman, Cloninger, Sigvardsson, and von Knorring (1982) also found effects of both socioeconomic status (occupational skills) of biological and adoptive fathers either alone or in interaction with other variables. Other postnatal factors distinguishing groups of adoptees with criminality, and/or alcoholism, or neither included extent of contact with the biological mother (the more contact the more chance of later criminality), the extent of postnatal hospital care, and the number of temporary adoptive placements.

Cadoret et al. (1986) investigated the genetic (biological family) and environmental (adopted family) factors contributing to antisocial personality, alcoholism, and drug abuse in Iowa adoptees. Either alcohol problems or antisocial personality in the biological parents were associated with APD, alcohol abuse, or both in the adoptees, but none of the characteristics of the adoptive family were significantly associated with APD in the adoptees. However, alcohol problems in the adoptive family were associated with alcohol abuse in the adoptee, and deviant psychiatric traits and divorce or separation in the adoptive families were associated with drug abuse in the adoptee. The data suggest that substance abuse is more likely to be influenced by family environment factors than is APD.

The Cambridge-Somerville longitudinal study (McCord, 1986) of boys at risk for criminality because of residence in a deteriorating area of Massachusetts provides data that suggest why Mednick et al. (1986) failed to find any independent influence of adoptive fathers on criminality in children, and why Robins (1978) found that broken homes were of no significance in predicting criminality when social class was controlled (the influence of broken homes was also due to its correlation with having parents who were antisocial). For some reason, paternal deviance in the form of criminality has always been assumed to be the crucial factor in predicting the chances of criminality in their sons. Either the absence of a father to model and reinforce prosocial behavior or the presence of an antisocial father who models antisocial behavior have been thought to be vital environmental factors producing antisocial children. Paternal deviancy in McCord's study seemed to have only an indirect effect on criminality in sons. A comparison based on family observations of boys who later turned out to be criminal with those who did not showed that the primary predictive variables were: (1) fathers' esteem for mothers; (2) self-confidence of mothers; (3) discipline versus permissiveness of mothers; (4) aggressiveness in both parents; and (5) affection in mothers. All five of the variables involved the mothers, either separately or in interaction with the fathers; only two involved the fathers, and one of these had to do with their respect for the mothers. Because this was not a study of adoptees, it is not certain whether the influence of mothers was a function of their genetic or environmental contributions or an interaction of these. However, the results strongly suggest that mothers who are affectionate with their sons and are capable of disciplining them without punitive aggression can inoculate them against the criminogenic effects of a father who is a deviant role model. Among boys who had this type of mother, only 10% became criminal compared with 53% of those from families in which the father was deviant and had low esteem for the mother. Some of this difference could be due to genetic factors in the mother rather than the family environmental effects, but it seems reasonable that a combination of discipline and love from the mother could insulate a boy against the criminogenic effects of the father, particularly if the father does not interfere.

Robins (1978) found that the most important variable predicting adult criminality was the extent of antisocial behavior in childhood and early adolescence. When this factor was controlled, childhood social class was minimally important as a predictor of criminality in whites, though it remained a significant predictor of crime in blacks. In blacks, being middle-class reduced the risk of becoming criminal even if there was a high degree of childhood antisocial behavior. However, Robins suggests a limitation of the environmental effects of family modeling in extreme cases in which antisocial behavior makes an early appearance, possibly because of a strong genetic factor:

in neither blacks nor whites did having conforming parents reduce the risk of antisocial personality among highly antisocial children, nor did having extremely deviant parents increase the risk in very conforming children. In both blacks and whites, it was in children in the middle range of antisocial behaviour where the effect of the parents was most apparent. (p. 266)

Genetic and environmental factors in related childhood disorders

Morrison (1980) found that parents of hyperactives were more likely than parents of controls to show either antisocial personality (mostly among the fathers) or Briquet's syndrome (hysteria, mostly among the mothers). There were no differences in the incidence of affective disorders, schizophrenia, or alcoholism. Biederman, Munir, and Knee (1987), however, found that only those hyperactive boys with an associated diagnosis of *conduct* or *oppositional* disorder had relatives with significantly higher rates of antisocial disorders (46%) than the relatives of the controls (7%). Uncomplicated hyperactives' relatives had a rate of only 13% APD.

In these two family studies, as in other studies of this type, one cannot distinguish the genetic and environmental influences because one does not know if it is parental genes or treatment that influences the tendencies in the children. Anderson, Lytton, and Romney (1986) attempted to answer this question by comparing the reactions of mothers to their own 6 to 11 year boys with conduct disorders (CDs) with their reactions to a child without any disorder. Similarly, the reactions of mothers of normal children to their own child were compared with those to a CD child in the laboratory. Both types of mothers made more negative responses and addressed more requests to the CD children than to the non-CD children, and there were no differences between mothers in the two groups in the overall rate of negative responses and no interaction effect. The results show that the mothers' reactions reflected the characteristics of the children rather than of the mothers. This suggests a reactive type of genotype-environment correlation. Conduct disorder children tend to provoke negative reactions, even in strangers.

Is there a genetic link between schizophrenia and antisocial personality disorder?

Eysenck and Eysenck (1976, 1978) suggested that both schizophrenics and APDs would be found at the extreme of the P dimension of personality because of a common genetic basis for the two disorders. This conclusion was based partly on Heston's (1966) study of adopted children of schizophrenic biological mothers. Apart from the greater incidence of schizophrenic disorders in these adoptees, they also showed an increased frequency of APDs and criminal and prison records. However, Danish adoption studies of children of schizophrenic mothers do not support the genetic link between schizophrenia and APD (Kendler & Gruenberg, 1984; Kendler, Gruenberg & Strauss, 1981; Kety et al., 1975). Research on incidence of APD in the families of schizophrenics also does not show an increased rate compared with other groups (Kendler, Gruenberg, &

Tsaung, 1985); such evidence supports the view that only APD, and not schizophrenia, is relevant to the P dimension of personality and that the label *psychoticism* is not appropriate for the P dimension (chapter 1).

Sex differences and models for transmission

Although APD is more prevalent in men than in women, Cloninger, Reich, and Guze (1975b) concluded that psychopathy is more prevalent among the relatives of psychopathic women, and these women have more disturbed home experiences than psychopathic men. The parents or their surrogates who raised the female APD were more likely to have engaged in heavy drinking, have been jailed, have been neglectful or absent from home a great deal of time, and exhibited physical cruelty to the children and others. They proposed and tested a multifactorial model for transmission. The model makes four assumptions: (1) polygenetic additive factors are involved in the disorder; (2) psychopathic men and women are found in the same families; (3) the threshold for women for the disorder is higher than for men, accounting for the lower prevalence among women; and (4) the same proportion of familial (genetic and environmental) and nonfamilial (environmental) factors is involved in producing the disorder in men and women. Essentially, the model says that it takes more genetic and environmental factors to make a woman an APD.

The twin data described previously suggest a polygenetic additive model and equal heritability for men and women. Female psychopaths have a greater prevalence of psychopathic relatives than men and a higher incidence of pathogenic family environment factors. These data suggest that it does take more genetic and environmental factors to produce a female than a male psychopath. After a woman crosses that threshold she is likely to exhibit stronger general antisocial tendencies than men with the disorder, though male APDs may be more aggressive. Interestingly, incarcerated female felons score higher than male felons on the Eysenck and Eysenck (1975) P scale.

Race, crime, antisocial personality, and genetics

In the United States the rates of crime, as determined by records of convictions, are considerably higher for blacks than for white. Because blacks occupy the lowest levels of the socioeconomic scale and live in the worst neighborhoods of the inner cities, most sociological and psychological theorists have assumed that these environmental factors, together with a lack of familial cohesion, are sufficient to explain the racial difference. However, one behavior geneticist (Rushton, 1989), as part of a questionable sociobiological theory, has suggested that the racial differences in crime are of evolutionary origin or largely so. In critiques of Rushton's article

Zuckerman (1990b) and Zuckerman & Brody (1989) pointed out the inadequacies of crime statistics as an index of APD and the lack of control for differences in socioeconomic status and residence necessary even to begin to make generalizations about race. Although chronic criminality of the type that begins early and persists into adult life is associated with APD, ordinary cultural delinquency, which inflates the crime statistics, is not. In the largest survey of the prevalence of psychiatric disorder in some major American cities, no difference was found between blacks and whites in the incidence of APD, and in two of the three cities the lifetime prevalence was higher for whites (Robins et al., 1984). There may be no difference to explain as either genetic or environmental if we use the reliable diagnoses of the NIMH epidemiological study rather than crime statistics. Cloninger et al. (1975b) state that their data suggest "no genetic differences between blacks and whites for sociopathy." It must be remembered that even in the Danish adoption studies (Mednick et al., 1987), socioeconomic status of the adoptive father was a significant factor in criminality of the adopted sons. Considering the greater homogeneity of income in Denmark, compared with the United States, the U.S. socioeconomic factor must be an even stronger influence.

Neuropsychology

Psychopaths show either an inability or unwillingness to restrain their behavior within the rules of society or accepted norms of social behavior. The failure of restraint, or a strong disinhibitory tendency, could be caused by (1) failure to learn these norms; (2) failure to apply them in relevant situations; (3) lack of ability to anticipate the consequences of their actions; (4) failure to plan ahead or to integrate their actions in situations with long-term goals; and (5) failure to learn from the negative consequences of their actions. Any of these deficits might be caused by a general or specific neurological impairment. Many cases of psychopathic behavior can be traced to severe head injuries, encephalitis, or the onset of epilepsy (Elliot, 1987). However, there may be less specific etiologies in APD such as minimal brain dysfunction or differences in function that are more continuous with the normal range of function. The latter are more likely to be involved in the biological substrate for APD because the disorder is now defined as having an early origin, and the traits that are involved are continuous with normal personality traits. Persons with specific organic disorders are more likely to show episodic dyscontrol, which is usually at marked variance with their general personality. Charles Whitman, who climbed a tower in Austin, Texas, and shot 13 strangers to death, is a good example. Autopsy found a temporal lobe tumor. Elliot (1987) says that in 36% of cases of episodic dyscontrol the condition developed for the first time following a brain insult. In the remaining cases, the disorder was present in early life but commonly associated with minimal brain dysfunction. Sometimes APD is attributed to a background of emotional deprivation and neglect, but such backgrounds are also associated with physical abuse, which can leave a residual of brain damage that may be undetected unless the child is given a neurological examination. In the majority of APD cases, the dysfunction is not episodic and is congruent with a life style of antisocial behavior that does not often take the form of chronic physical aggression.

Frontal lobes

The frontal lobes of the cerebral cortex are among the primary candidates for a specific locus of APD. Luria (1980) has described the frontal lobes as an executive center assigning significance to incoming stimuli, integrating them in plans for action, and checking on the results in conformance with the plans. Dimond has said that the frontal lobes are the seat of social intelligence.

Damage to the lobes causes two types of syndromes, a pseudodepressed type characterized by apathy and indifference and a pseudopsychopathic type showing a lack of manners and restraint, and poor impulse control and judgment (Miller, 1987). The latter type is more often related to damage to the orbitomedial frontal area and its limbic connections. This is the area that regulates the septohippocampal system, described by Gray (1982) as a behavioral inhibition system, though he stresses the effects of an overactive system involved in anxiety. Gorenstein (1982) suggests that the system, involving the septum, hippocampus, and prefrontal cortex (SHF) functions to regulate goal-directed activity and act as a brake on impulsive responding. He also suggests that the frontal lobes enable a subject to shift flexibly from one concept to another as a situation requires (perhaps related to the psychopath's failure to learn from experience).

Gorenstein (1982) hypothesized that psychopaths should show the same kinds of performance on neuropsychological cognitive and perceptual tasks as patients with frontal lobe damage. Patients receiving psychiatric treatment for substance abuse and other disorders were classified as psychopathic or nonpsychopathic on the basis of the Cleckley signs and the *socialization* scale of the CPI. Although the result of the selection procedure was that all of the patients who were diagnosed psychopathic were also diagnosed APD, about a third of the controls also received a diagnosis of APD. There were also somewhat more patients with substance abuse complications in the psychopathic group. A third control group was composed of college students.

As predicted, the psychopathic patients made more perseverative errors on a concept formation test, performed more poorly on the Stroop Color-Word Interference Task, and reported more reversals on a reversible-figures test than both control groups. These kinds of deficits in performance have also been found in frontal lobe damaged patients.

Hare (1984) criticized the methods used to define the psychopathic group, the use of a nonmatched college control, and the presence of more substance abuse disorders in the psychopathic group than in the non-psychopathic group in the Gorenstein study. He repeated the study with prisoners, basing his classification of them as high, medium, and low psychopathic on ratings from interviews and case histories. The groups did not differ on any of the neuropsychological tests. Furthermore, there were no significant correlations among the putative measures of frontal lobe function. Sutker, Moan, and Allain (1983) also could not find differences between psychopathic and nonpsychopathic prisoners on these kinds of tests.

Could the social learning deficits of psychopaths be accounted for by low intelligence? Cleckley (1976) said that the psychopath has good intelligence, but his cases were largely nonincarcerated middle-class individuals. A prison sample might contain a larger proportion of less intelligent "losers." Delinquents are not necessarily less intelligent overall, but they do show a higher IQ on the performance tests of the Wechsler Intelligence Test than on the verbal tests (Miller, 1987). For many psychiatric patients the pattern is usually the reverse, that is, higher on verbal than on performance. Although this pattern might be due to the delinquent's lack of schooling or attention while in school, some investigators have interpreted the verbal-performance differential as a sign of left-hemisphere deficit.

There is a difference in the criminality of low- and high-intelligence psychopaths. The low-intelligence psychopath tends to commit more impulsive and violently aggressive crimes (Miller, 1987). However, there are notorious exceptions to this general finding. There is a subgroup of highly intelligent, sadistic psychopaths of which the late Theodore Bundy (a serial killer) was a classical example. Although the low-intelligence psychopath may be violent from a lack of empathy and poor cognitive control, the intelligent psychopath may have just enough empathy to enhance his sadistic enjoyment of the victim's sufferings (Heilbrun, 1982).

Cerebral hemisphere asymmetry

Flor-Henry (1976) advanced the hypothesis that psychopathy is associated with left-hemisphere dysfunction. This hypothesis could account for the finding of lower verbal IQ relative to performance IQ in psychopaths because verbal functions are localized in the left hemisphere. Cleckley (1976) also spoke of a peculiar "semantic dementia" in psychopaths, which results in their using words without personal meaning to themselves, a disorder that goes beyond deliberate lying. It has been this author's conviction in working with psychopathic drug abusers that they really believe the things they say at the moment they say them, but what they say is totally divorced from their past or future behavior. Intention is difficult to define, but various measures of hemispheric dominance have been used to test the hypothesis of left-hemisphere dysfunction or deviation from the usual pattern of left-hemisphere dominance in psychopaths.

Handedness is the most obvious clue to hemispheric dominance. Left-handers ("sinistres") have been suspected of sinister behavior since the age of folklore. About 90% of the population are right-handed and most are left hemisphere specialized for language. Handedness may be determined by questionnaire or giving a person certain tasks such as throwing a ball and observing which hand is used. Similarly, preferences in foot and eye use for various tasks can be determined. These three indices are not necessarily in agreement. In a study by Nachshon and Denno (1987), only 51% of the subjects consistently made right or left choices on hand, foot, and eye tests, and another 10% were consistent on hand and eye but variable on foot tests.

Gabrielli and Mednick (1980) found that a history of minor offenses (traffic and petty theft) was significantly related to both hand and foot preferences. Left preference scores rose as a function of number of offenses. Of those persons selected as left-handed by the neurologist, 65% were arrested at least once, compared with 30% of the right-handed group. Eye preference did not predict delinquency. Verbal IQ also predicted delinquency but was not related to laterality. Neurological impairment was not significantly related to delinquency or laterality. In fact, the delinquents had fewer neurological signs noted than nondelinquents.

Contrary to the Gabrielli and Mednick findings and other studies, Nachshon and Denno (1987) found that more nonoffenders than offenders showed left-hand preferences. No differences were found on foot or eye preferences. However, a breakdown by type of offense showed that though most nonoffenders showed a preponderance of right-eye preference, only 40% of the most violent offenders showed this pattern.

Another measure of laterality is the conjugate lateral eye movements (CLEMS) noted when responding to questions. When asked questions requiring verbal information for an answer, most subjects look to the right, supposedly indicating left hemisphere activation. This technique was used with right-handed patients from psychiatric and correctional institutions (Sandel & Alcorn, 1980). Personality disorders (APDs) and bipolar and schizoaffective disorders were characterized by bilaterality whereas non-paranoid schizophrenics and unipolar depressives showed right hemisphericity. No nonpatient data were provided, but it was assumed that they would be mostly left hemispheric.

Hare and McPherson (1984) suggested the hypothesis that in psychopaths, the left hemisphere is not as specialized for linguistic processing as it is in normal individuals. The investigators used the dichotic listening task in which pairs of words are presented simultaneously, one in each ear. After the divided-attention trials, the subjects are asked to recall any words heard, regardless of which ear; in the focused-attention condition they are asked to recall only the words coming into one ear. They compared four groups; prisoners classified into high, medium, and low psychopathy and a group of normals. In the divided-attention condition all groups showed a right-ear advantage, but the advantage was greater for low psychopathic prisoners and noncriminals than for medium and high psychopathic criminals. In the focused-attention condition, the psychopathic group also showed less right-ear advantage than the low psychopathic prisoners.

Hare and Connolly (1987) also studied lateralization of language function using visually presented stimuli. Criminals showed relatively less right visual field advantage than noncriminals in speed of categorization and errors, particularly in responding to abstract words. Strangely, criminals, particularly psychopathic ones, tended to perform better when stimuli were presented in their left visual field than in their right one, suggesting that they were doing much of the linguistic processing in their right hemispheres.

What bearing do these lateralization results have on the behavioral psychopathology of the psychopath? Hare and McPherson speculate that weak lateralization of the language function, perhaps based on low left hemisphere arousal, may result in dissociation between cognitive and verbal processes and behavior. These processes normally regulate and control behavior but fail to do that in the psychopath. Poor left hemisphere function, relative to right hemisphere, may also be a factor in the discrepancy between speech and intention or feeling. Speech for the psychopath is used to manipulate others rather than to express real feelings or intentions (Cleckley, 1976).

The septal syndrome

Gorenstein and Newman (1980) have suggested a parallel between "disinhibitory psychopathology" in humans and the behavior of septal lesioned rats. This comparative analysis notes that septal lesioned rats (1) respond at a higher than normal rate for positive reinforcement on a fixed interval (FI) schedule, analogous to the inability of the psychopath to delay gratification; (2) show poor performance on a schedule of differential reinforcement for low rates of responding (DRL), resembling the psychopath's inability to moderate responses over intervals of time; (3) demonstrate a deficit in passive avoidance or failure to suppress responses that have been punished, like the psychopath's repetition of antisocial behavior that has led to punishment in the past; and (4) show enhanced stimulation seeking behavior, comparable to the psychopath's antisocial *sensation seeking* behavior. As noted earlier, Gorenstein and Newman consider the septum as part of a system also composed of the hippocampus and orbitofrontal cortex. The evidence cited by these authors is interpreted by Gray in terms of a dimension of anxiety related to overactivity of the system. Do anxiety and psychopathy represent opposite ends of a continuum of frontal lobe–septal-hippocampal functioning? Modern concepts of psychopathy do not stress the absence of anxiety as a requisite for this diagnosis. The P dimension in general and *sensation seeking* trait in particular are orthogonal to the dimension of *neuroticism* or *anxiety* in humans. Perhaps *anxiety* is mediated in part by another biological system and the septohippocampal system plays a role in both the N and P dimensions.

Biochemistry

Testosterone

The higher rates of crime and prevalence of APD in men than in women have been interpreted as evidence of the influence of the gonadal hormone testosterone. However, in chapter 5 it was noted that testosterone in normal young men was related to *sensation seeking,* sexual experience, and *sociability* but not to *impulsivity* or *aggression*. Actually, in the study by Daitzman and Zuckerman (1980), estradiol in males was more highly related than testosterone to P dimension traits, but few other studies have examined the role of estrogen in males. Olweus (1987) found only weak positive correlations between testosterone in young adolescents and antisocial behavior. Testosterone was primarily related to aggressive reactions to provocation rather than unprovoked aggression of the type found in psychopaths. However, he found that testosterone was indirectly related to antisocial behavior through its association with intolerance of frustration. He suggests that *sensation seeking* may also be a mediating factor.

Although criminal populations in general do not differ from normal males in levels of testosterone, male prisoners selected for the violence of their crimes show higher levels of the hormone (Kreuz & Rose, 1972; Mattson et al., 1980; Rada et al., 1976). Ehrenkranz et al. (1974) found that both aggressive and socially dominant groups of prisoners had higher testosterone levels than other groups of prisoners. Dabbs et al. (1988) found that, though female prisoners as a group did not differ from college students in saliva testosterone, inmates whose crimes had involved unprovoked violence had higher testosterone levels than those whose crimes had involved defensive violence or nonviolent thievery.

Monoamine oxidase

Low levels of MAO have been found in psychopaths (Lidberg, Modin, Oreland, Tuck, & Gillner, 1985), alcoholics (Major & Murphy, 1978; Sullivan et al., 1979, Sullivan, Stanfield, & Dackis, 1977), and chronic marijuana users (Stillman et al., 1978). Low MAO levels have been also found in other disorders, including chronic schizophrenics and bipolar mood disorders. Although platelet MAO is fairly stable and shows a very high heritability (see chapter 5), it would be interesting to know if MAO is also related to earlier signs of disinhibitory disorder. Shekim et al. (1986) compared MAO in 6 to 12 year old boys with *attention deficit* disorder and control boys. The *attention deficit* disorders had lower MAO levels than the controls, and MAO in the combined groups was negatively related to behavioral performance measures of *impulsivity* and *attentiveness*.

Purchall, Coursey, Buchsbaum, and Murphy (1980) found a substantial correlation between parent and child MAO levels. Among the parents of the low MAO children, 19% were diagnosed as alcoholic and 14% as antisocial personalities. The corresponding figures for the parents of the high MAO children were 3% in each category. Inheritance of low MAO may be linked to inheritance of a tendency toward disinhibitory disorders.

Plasma dopamine–beta-Hydroxylase

Rogeness et al. (1984) selected boys with very low levels of plasma dopamine–beta-hydroxylase (DBH) from a children's psychiatric hospital and compared them with boys with normal levels of the enzyme. The boys with low DBH levels were most likely to be diagnosed as having *undersocialized conduct* disorder (akin to APD as an adult diagnosis) or *borderline personality* disorder, and those with higher DBH levels were more likely to be diagnosed as having *socialized conduct disorder*. The low-DBH group showed a greater frequency of symptoms involving firesetting, cruelty to animals, homicidal threats with knives or guns, and severe problems of impulse control in general. Nearly all of those in the low-DBH group, contrasted with only a few in the high-DBH group, were characterized as failing to establish any meaningful relationships, one of the characteristic signs of psychopathy.

Epinephrine and norepinephrine (peripheral)

A number of studies have found that arrested men who are high on psychopathic traits show low levels of epinephrine and norepinephrine in urine (Lidberg, Levander, Schalling, & Lidberg, 1978; Woodman, Hinton, & O'Neill, 1977). Although Dishman, Wallace, Crawford, Grant, and Hinton (1982) and Woodman and Hinton (1978) report no differences in catecholamines in familiar settings, the more psychopathic prisoners show abnormal stress responses in anticipation of stressful situations. When faced with an imminent trial, nonpsychopathic prisoners showed a normal stress response, as reflected in increases in epinephrine and norepinephrine whereas psychopathic types showed little change (Lidberg et al., 1978).

Prospective studies show that levels of peripheral catecholamine activity have predictive as well as concurrent relationships with psychopathic tendencies. Magnusson (1987) found that boys with low urinary epinephrine at age 13 had a greater risk of being registered for crimes when they were 18 to 26 years old. When they were 13, adrenaline excretion was related to both aggressiveness and motor restlessness. Boys with both high restlessness and lack of concentration (attention deficit) showed the lowest epinephrine and, unlike other groups, showed little epinephrine change in response to a stressful situation.

CSF and plasma measures of monoamine precursors and metabolites

Most of the catecholamines excreted in urine come from the peripheral nervous systems not from the brain, so it is difficult to evaluate the significance of differences in urinary epinephrine and norepinephrine in the etiology of APD. The monoamine metabolites in CSF and plasma, which have been so extensively studied in anxiety disorders, have not been widely used in the study of APD.

Little replicable evidence has been found showing abnormal levels of the norepinephrine and dopamine metabolites MHPG and HVA in persons with antisocial behavior or aggressiveness. Brown et al. (1979) reported a positive correlation between CSF levels of MHPG and aggressiveness in a group of personality disorders but could not replicate the finding in a subsequent study (Brown et al., 1982). Male pathological gamblers were reported to have higher levels of CSF and urinary MHPG than controls, but they were lower than controls on plasma MHPG (Roy et al., 1988). The differences on CSF MHPG were highest in a group of currently depressed gamblers, suggesting a state influence. CSF levels of HVA were higher in gamblers but the difference between gamblers and controls was not significant.

Both Brown et al. studies showed a significant negative correlation between a history of aggressiveness and the serotonin metabolite in CSF 5-HIAA. Low levels of CSF 5-HIAA have been found both in persons who have attempted suicide by violent means and murderers of a particular type (Lidberg, Modin, Oreland, Tuck, & Gillner, 1985). The type of murderer with low levels of the serotonin metabolites were those who killed a sexual partner ("crimes of passion") rather than those who killed a crony under the influence of alcohol or drugs. The groups did not differ from each other or from normal controls in HVA or MHPG.

The low levels of serotonin in those with violent tendencies against others or themselves might be related to a low level of activity in the system, associated with behavioral control (chapter 5), or to a lack of adequate production of serotonin from its precursors. The latter possibility is suggested by a study comparing prisoners with acute schizophrenics and controls on circulating levels of the serotonin precursor, tryptophan (Domino & Krause, 1974). After tryptophan loading, the prisoners showed a lower peak of tryptophan concentration and a more prolonged decline of tryptophan to baseline than the other two groups. Aggression was not assessed in this study.

Further evidence of a lack of tryptophan availability in disinhibitory disorders is provided in a study by Buyden-Branchey, Branchey, Noumair, and Lieber (1989). Based on work by Cloninger (1987b), they divided their alcoholic subjects into two groups: those with early onset (before age 20) and those with later onset. Earlier onset alcoholics have been shown to have a stronger genetic influence and a greater likelihood of antisocial behavior associated with drinking. Lower tryptophan ratios were found in early onset alcoholic patients, particularly those with a history of depression and crimes of violence. Taken together with other studies, the results suggest an association between a serotonin deficit and problems in control of mood and aggressive behavior resulting in violence directed toward the self or others. But in this study, violent behavior was associated with drinking, whereas in the study by Lidberg et al. (1985), the low serotonin was found in murderers in whom alcohol was not a factor in the crime.

Metabolic dysfunction: reactive hypoglycemia and cholesterol

It is usually assumed that the violent behavior associated with drinking in some alcoholics is due to direct disinhibition by alcohol of brain centers involved in behavioral control. However, another possibility has been suggested by Virkkunen (1987), who found that young, habitually violent males with APD tend to have very low cholesterol levels. Similar findings were obtained for habitually violent males diagnosed as intermittent explosive disorders. These two groups were also found to have reactive hypoglycemia during the glucose tolerance test (GTT). A third finding suggests that adults with APD that was preceded by unsocialized aggressive conduct disorder in puberty show enhanced and long-lasting insulin secretion during the GTT.

Alcohol-induced hypoglycemia, acting on a person with overreactive insulin mechanisms, may lower the threshold for violence by putting the brain into a hypoglycemic state. Some of the violent reactions may be like the seizures sometimes seen in these states. Habitually violent males who show hypoglycemic reactions to the GTT tend to report no memory of their acts, and they are described by their relatives as "quarrelsome and aggressive under the influence of alcohol." A low level of serotonin may also be involved in this vulnerability because intracellular pancreatic B-cell serotonin acts as a tonic inhibitor of insulin release. Serotonic inhibition in humans causes insulin secretion after glucose infusion. Virkkunen's studies are interesting in that they show how inherited vulnerabilities may interact with ingested substances in APDs to produce particular expressions of behavior such as violent actions against others or the self.

Psychophysiology

Unlike the paucity of biochemical data on the APD, there is a large body of research on the psychophysiology of psychopathy. Certain theories of psychopathy have suggested psychophysiological tests of hypotheses. Eysenck (1967) hypothesized that "psychopaths" (used synonymously with criminality and delinquency) are high on both N and E dimensions of personality or are neurotic extraverts. Later, with the addition of the P dimension, psychopaths were considered part of the genetic spectrum of disorders constituting the phenomenal expression of the *psychoticism* dimension. Hans and Sybil Eysenck (Eysenck & Eysenck, 1978) concluded that psychopaths were high on all three dimensions. However, they suggested that secondary psychopaths might be higher on E and N, and those high on P alone might be the primary psychopath described by Cleckley. The secondary psychopath was hypothesized to be characterized by a combination of low cortical arousal (E) and high autonomic arousal (N).

Quay (1965) postulated that psychopaths are tonically underaroused and seek thrills to increase stimulation to an optimal level and to avoid monotony and boredom, which are especially aversive to them. This formulation is identical with this author's first formulations (Zuckerman, 1969b; Zuckerman et al., 1964) of the basis of *sensation seeking,* which led to the prediction that psychopaths would score high on *sensation seeking* scales, a prediction that has been well substantiated (Zuckerman, 1979a). Quay did not differentiate between cortical and autonomic arousal, though most studies addressed to Quay's theory have used autonomic arousal measures (Doren, 1987). In the autonomic realm, one would predict opposite results from Eysenck's and Quay's theories on these measures because Eysenck would predict autonomic overarousal, and Quay would expect autonomic underarousal.

The problems with generalized arousal theory have been discussed previously (chapter 6). Quay's theory would predict lower levels of arousal or arousability on all types of autonomic measures, but in actual fact such measures show little correlation, and this kind of theory furnishes no guide for predicting why one type of measure should be more likely to show underarousal than another. As will be seen, this kind of response specificity in psychopaths greatly limits support for general arousal theories. Reviews of psychophysiology in criminals and APDs have been done by Hare (1978), Schalling (1978), Siddle (1977), Venables (1987), and Zahn (1986).

EEG studies

Crude clinical techniques were largely employed in studies of the EEG in psychopaths prior to the 1980s, so most reports were simply in terms of the percentages of "abnormal" records or descriptions of EEG "spiking" in some area such as the temporal lobes (Syndulko, 1978). Most of these studies showed a higher incidence of abnormal records in psychopaths, with the abnormality usually consisting of an excess of diffuse slow-wave activity or 14- and 6-sec positive spiking during drowsiness and light sleep. Howard, Fenton, and Fenwick (1984) found that high scores on Hare's *psychopathy* scale were associated with prominent posterior temporal slow-wave activity in prisoners. Although paroxysmal EEG features were not specifically associated with psychopathy, subjects with these EEG features were usually prisoners whose crimes involved attacks on strangers.

Blackburn (1978, 1979) compared prisoners classified as primary (sociable-nonanxious) or secondary (withdrawn-anxious) psychopaths and nonpsychopathic sociable or anxious controls. The psychopathic and non-psychopathic groups did not differ on any of the EEG indices, but primary psychopaths appeared more cortically aroused than the secondary psychopaths, as judged from their lower amounts of theta and the higher EEG alpha frequency. These results are opposite to expectations that were based on the frequent reports of less arousal in EEG records of psychopaths because the primary type would be expected to show the more extreme example of lowered arousal. However, some support for Blackburn's findings was found by Howard et al. (1984), who compared primary and secondary psychopaths as defined by Blackburn's criteria, on the contingent negative variation (CNV). Primary but not secondary psychopaths had higher voltage CNVs than controls and other types of patients. CNV amplitude correlated positively with *sociability,* one of the criteria used to distinguish primary and secondary psychopaths.

With the exception of these findings, the usual report of excess of slow-wave activity in psychopaths could be construed as support for a cortical underarousal theory. However, we cannot be certain that such characteristics did not emerge after the subjects became psychopathic or merely represents their bored and disinterested reaction to the recording procedure. Prospective studies of EEG and crime are of greater use in establishing the causal role of cortical underarousal.

Volavka (1987) described two prospective studies. The first, done in Denmark, found that the relative amount of slow alpha wave activity (8–10 Hz) predicted repeat offenses for petty thievery. The second, conducted in Sweden, also showed slow alpha activity in boys who acquired a police record of repeated thefts, and specifically ruled out head or brain injury as an explanation for the brain wave differences by excluding subjects with such injuries in their histories.

Another prospective study involved a follow up of hyperactive boys 6 to 12 years of age in America, with examination of subsequent crime records from juvenile and police records up to age 20 years (Satterfield, 1987). EEG records were taken at initial evaluation. At follow up it was found that nearly 50% of the hyperactive group had been arrested for a serious offense at least once compared with about 7% of the controls; and 25% of the hyperactives had been institutionalized for criminal acts as contrasted to 1% of the controls. The results on EEG evaluation showed that the hyperactives who did not develop into delinquent adolescents showed more abnormal EEG characteristics than those who did. Satterfield interpreted the evidence as consistent with a lower-arousal–inhibitory state in the nonoffender hyperactives. These children also responded better to treatment with stimulants. But the data also showed that arousal problems may be a more significant factor in simple hyperactivity than in hyperactivity confounded with psychopathic tendencies and, thus, were not very supportive of a cortical underarousal theory of APD.

The augmenting-reducing paradigm (Buchsbaum, 1971) has not been related directly to APD diagnosis, but augmenting of the visual EP has been found to be characteristic of disinhibitory disorder groups such as in alcoholism (Coger, Dymond, Lowenstein, & Pearson, 1976; von Knorring, 1976) and male delinquency (Silverman, Buchsbaum, and Stierlin, 1973).

Electrodermal measures

Hare (1978) combined skin conductance level (SCL) results from eight of his own experiments and found that prisoners who met his criteria for psychopathy were lower on tonic skin conductance level (SCL) than non-psychopathic prisoners. Experiments of other investigators using diverse procedures have not always found significant results, but in most cases the direction of the difference is similar to that found by Hare. Hare also noted that this initial difference in tonic SC tends to increase during certain kinds of experiments, particularly those using repetitious or monotonous procedures. Spontaneous skin conductance responses (SSCRs) during preexperimental or nonstimulation periods show similar trends to SCLs, but the differences are not as consistent (Hare, 1978; Siddle, 1977). However, Schalling, Lidberg, Levander, & Dahlin (1973) showed clear differences between psychopathic and nonpsychopathic prisoners on both SCL and SSCRs that became larger as the experiment progressed.

The amplitude of skin conductance responses (SCRs) to stimuli shows a tendency to be smaller in more psychopathic prisoners or delinquents, and these differences are more marked when responses are range corrected, in younger prisoners (Hare, 1978), and using more intense stimuli (Hare, 1978; Venables, 1987). Schmidt, Solant, and Bridger (1985) compared electrodermal activity of children with undersocialized aggressive conduct disorder (UCD) with matched control children. The UCD children showed a slightly weaker SCR than the controls to a 75 dB tone, but the difference in response to a 90 dB bell became highly significant; the response of the normal children tripled in magnitude compared with a doubling of magnitude in the UCDs.

Despite the fact that psychopaths tend to have weaker SCRs, their responses tend to take longer to recover to baseline than nonpsychopaths (Hare, 1978; Hemming, 1981). Schizophrenics show the opposite tendency, toward faster than normal recovery times. Mednick (1975) who found similar results in the sons of criminal fathers, suggested that slow recovery time interferes with avoidance conditioning, perhaps explaining the psychopath's inability to learn from aversive experience (discussed in a subsequent section).

Heart rate

Hare (1978) concluded from his studies that there was nothing different in the heart rate (HR) reactivity of psychopaths to simple stimuli, but he said nothing about tonic levels of HR. Venables (1987) cited a number of studies showing small but significant differences in tonic HRs of delinquents and nondelinquents. One study (Wadsworth, 1976) involved 5362 11-year-old boys. Pulse rate was measured during a physical exam after a waiting period considered mildly stressful. Records of delinquency were available between ages 8 and 21. Mean HR of controls was 86, delinquents 84, and for a subsample of violent sexual offenders the mean HR was 81.7. Studies of children younger than 11 have not shown much predictive relationship with delinquency.

Psychopathy and classical and instrumental conditioning and reinforcement

Quasi-conditioning paradigm

This paradigm, developed by Hare, is interesting for the study of cognitive and learning influences on the autonomic reactions of psychopaths. Hare (1978) calls it a *quasi-conditioning paradigm* because the subjects are told in advance that an aversive stimulus will be delivered, and they know exactly at what moment it will be delivered. This procedure eliminates the question of awareness of the CS-UCS contingency because the subjects are fully informed beforehand. In the first version, Hare (1965) had psychopathic and nonpsychopathic prisoners and student controls watch a sequence of numbers appearing on a revolving drum after being informed that they would receive an electric shock when 8 appeared. The psychopathic prisoners had lower basal SCL than the other two groups and showed

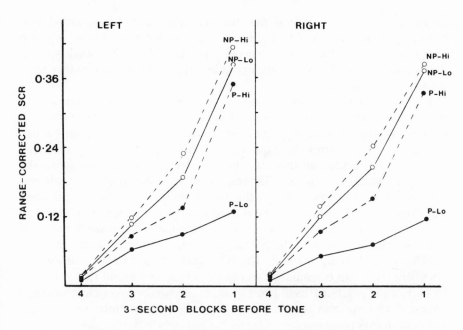

Figure 9.2. Mean range-corrected increases in SCR during the 12-sec period prior to an anticipated 120 dB tone. P-Lo = high ratings of psychopathy and low *socialization* scores; P-Hi = high ratings of psychopathy and high *socialization* scores; NP-Lo = low ratings of psychopathy and low *socialization* scores; NP-Hi = low ratings of psychopathy and high *socialization* scores. (From "Electrodermal and cardiovascular correlates of psychopathy," by R. D. Hare, 1978, in R. D. Hare and D. Schalling (Eds.) *Psychopathic behaviour: Approaches to research*, p. 123. Chichester, England: Wiley. Copyright 1978 by Wiley Press. Reprinted by permission.)

less rise in SCL in anticipation of the shock than the nonpsychopathic prisoners. In the second experiment by Hare and Craigen (1974), HR and SC were recorded while subjects received shock or administered shock to another prisoner. The psychopathic prisoners had smaller SCRs than controls both to shock received and administered to the other person, but there were no differences in HR to shock received or administered. The psychopathic group also had smaller SCRs to the CS signaling shock for self or the other person and smaller anticipatory responses just prior to the shock. On the first trial, the psychopathic prisoners showed more HR acceleration than nonpsychopaths, peaking in the first 4 sec after the CS. The blunted electrodermal response of the psychopath is interpreted by the investigators as a lack of fear response, and the acceleration of HR is interpreted as "activation of psychophysiological defense mechanisms."

Hare (1978) substituted a loud noise (120 dB fast-onset tone) for the shock used in the previous studies. Prisoners were classified as psychopathic or nonpsychopathic by raters, and the groups were further divided on the basis of scores on the Gough *socialization* (So) scale. Figure 9.2 shows the range-corrected SCL levels as the stimulus time came closer, with 1 representing the last 3 sec before the noise. Only the most psychopathic group with low scores on the So scale was differentiated from the other groups; the unsocialized psychopaths showed a less steep rise in anticipatory SCR than the other groups.

The psychopathic–low-So group that showed the least SCR response showed the greatest acceleration of HR in the 4–6 sec after the onset of the CS and prior to receiving the aversive tone. The results became much stronger on trial 2 after the experience of hearing the loud tone on trial 1. Both psychopathic groups showed the acceleration in contrast to the nonpsychopathic groups. Similar results were found in college students classified as high or low psychopathic on the So scale. Another replication was done with prisoners, and the differences were intensified by vigilance when the aversive stimulus was avoidable. However, in this study the small electrodermal responses of the psychopaths were associated with a decrease in HR rather than an increase. Tharp, Maltzman, Syndulko, and Ziskind (1980) ran a group of gamblers in the paradigm and found that the gamblers, like the psychopaths in Hare's studies, showed weaker electrodermal anticipatory responses than controls but in this study there were no differences in HR responses.

The more replicable SCL results suggest that a weak gradient of arousal increase in anticipation of aversive events may represent part of the vulnerability of the APD. However, differences in APD's responses to the unconditioned stimulus could account for weaker conditioned anticipation of the stimulus. Perhaps psychopaths have been punished so much as children that they no longer fear pain or physical harm. Failure to learn from aversive outcomes is one of the most salient aspects of the psychopath. This learning deficit could stem from an inadequate physiological response as suggested by these results. It does not seem to depend on awareness of contingencies. Of course, everyone knows that the psychopath can verbalize past mistakes, but this "insight" does not seem to affect future behavior.

Classical conditioning

Lykken (1957) compared two groups of prisoners classified as primary or secondary (neurotic) psychopaths and a group of matched normals on skin resistance response (SRR) conditioning, using shock as the UCS. Both groups of prisoners showed weaker conditioning than the normal controls, with the psychopathic group showing the weakest conditioning. Hare and Quinn (1971) studied highly psychopathic (P), nonpsychopathic, (NP), and medium psychopathic (M) groups of prisoners using a classical conditioning paradigm. Two kinds of unconditioned stimuli were used: shock and slides of nude females. Both SCRs and HRRs were used as CRs. Conditioned ORs were defined as responses occurring within 1–4 sec after the CS, and

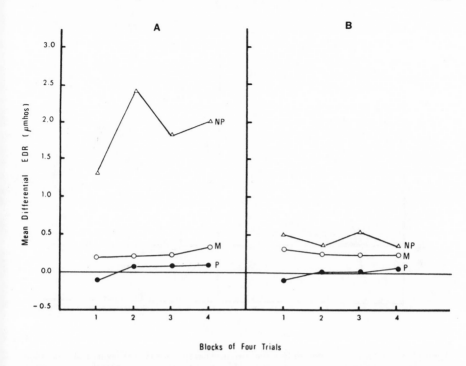

Figure 9.3. Mean differential EDR anticipation responses (ARs) elicited during conditioning with the shock UCS (A) and the slides of female nudes (B) in psychopathic (P), nonpsychopathic (NP), and mixed (M) groups of prisoners. (From "Psychopathy and autonomic conditioning," by R. D. Hare and M. J. Quinn, 1971, *Journal of Abnormal Psychology*, 77, p. 228. Copyright 1971 by American Psychological Association. Reprinted by permission of author.)

anticipatory responses were designated as those occurring between 5 and 10 sec after CS onset. Only the NP group showed evidence of electrodermal OR or anticipatory response conditioning to the shock UCS, as shown in Figures 9.3 and 9.4. Although there appeared to be somewhat greater OR conditioning of the NP group by using nude slides, the differences between groups were not significant, and they were clearly not significant for anticipatory responses. In spite of their sexy content, slides were simply too weak as UCSs. The groups did not differ in cardiac or digital vasomotor responses to either shock or picture UCSs.

Hemming (1981) selected a group of primary psychopaths in an unusual way. Using the case histories and recollections of prisoners, he selected only those criminals who came from middle-class, unbroken homes in which they were well treated, and who regarded their home life as happy. Presumably the only explanation for the criminality of such men would be genetic factors. Conditioning was done by using lights, one of which was conditioned to a (100 dB) noise. Only the conditioned discriminations

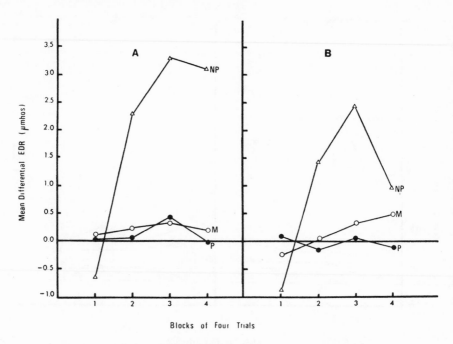

Figure 9.4. Mean conditioned differential orienting responses (ORs) elicited during conditioning with the shock UCS (A) and the slides of nudes (B) in psychopathic (P), nonpsychopathic (NP), and mixed (M) groups of prisoners. (From "Psychopathy and autonomic conditioning," by R. D. Hare and M. J. Quinn, 1971, *Journal of Abnormal Psychology*, 77, p. 229. Copyright 1971 by American Psychological Association. Reprinted by permission of author.)

during extinction were analyzed. During all three blocks of extinction the prisoners showed less conditioned discrimination than the controls.

Instrumental conditioning

Lykken (1957) designed a test of passive avoidance learning that has been used in many subsequent experiments. Subjects were given a board with four levers and required to learn a series of lever presses within 20 trials. On each of the 20 trials a choice of one of the 4 levers (always an error alternative) gave the subject an electric shock. Although the manifest task was to work one's way through the maze by making the correct sequence of choices, the hidden task was to avoid pressing the lever that was wrong and also gave a shock. The prisoner subjects were divided into primary and secondary (or neurotic) psychopaths. The control group consisted of matched normals. The primary psychopaths performed worst on the passive avoidance task, and the noncriminals performed best, whereas the secondary psychopaths fell in the middle. The groups did not differ on the manifest task.

Schmauk (1970) extended the Lykken paradigm by using social punishment (the experimenter saying "wrong"), and tangible money loss (the experimenter taking away money from the subject), as well as physical punishment (shock) for pressing the punishment lever. Following Lykken, prisoners were classified into primary and secondary psychopaths, and a third nonpsychopathic group was also used. In both the physical and social punishment conditions, the normal control group learned the latent passive avoidance task better than the primary psychopath group, but in the tangible punishment condition involving the loss of money, there were no differences among groups, and the primary psychopaths showed better passive avoidance learning than in either of the other two conditions. SCRs that were recorded during the time between choosing a lever and responding provided a measure of anticipatory arousal. The normal group showed greater arousal than the psychopathic group across all three punishment conditions, the differences being particularly marked for physical and social punishments; but the differences were less in the tangible punishment condition because the primary psychopaths showed relatively more arousal with this type of punishment than with the other two. The primary psychopaths were also more aware of the punishment contingency in this condition than in the other two.

Newman et al. (1985) devised a new experimental paradigm for investigation of the passive avoidance learning deficit in psychopaths. Delinquents in a confinement facility were classified as primary or secondary psychopathic, nonpsychopathic, and neurotic nonpsychopathic. The task involved two sets of numbers, arbitrarily designated as positive or negative stimuli. The subjects were asked to point to the correct stimuli. In the passive avoidance condition they were rewarded for responding to the correct numbers and punished by removal of money for responding to the wrong ones. They lost nothing for not responding. A second task was intended to test the role of punishment in learning inhibition. In this task, subjects were rewarded for not making an incorrect response but not punished for making an error. In the first task the primary psychopathic group made more passive avoidance errors than all of the other three groups. There were no differences among groups on errors of omission, that is, failing to respond to the correct stimulus. In the second task, in which there was no punishment for passive avoidance errors or reward for not making errors, all groups were equal in passive avoidance or commission errors. The results of this study are contrary to Schmauk's (1970) finding that loss of money is a punishment that is as effective for primary psychopaths as others. Instead the results suggest a more generalized inability to learn to avoid responding for possible reward when there is also a possibility of punishment.

Newman and Kosson (1986) extended their study to adult prisoners, using Hare's psychopathy check list to divide prisoners into psychopathic

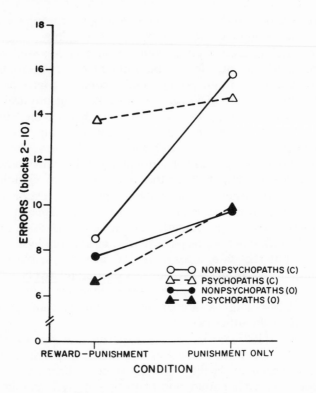

Figure 9.5. Mean number of commission (C) and omission (O) errors (covariate adjusted) as a function of group and conditions. (From "Passive avoidance learning in psychopathic and nonpsychopathic offenders," by J. P. Newman and D. S. Kosson, 1986, *Journal of Abnormal Psychology*, 95, p. 255. Copyright by American Psychological Association. Reprinted by permission of author.)

and nonpsychopathic groups. Most (90%) of the psychopathic group and few (4%) of the nonpsychopathic group fit the APD diagnosis by DSM-III criteria. Judged by psychometric criteria, the groups differed only on psychopathy and could not be characterized as primary and neurotic psychopaths. The psychopathic group scored higher on the P and *monotony avoidance* scales and lower on *socialization* but did not differ from the other prisoner group on any of the *neuroticism* or *anxiety* scales. Another purpose of this study was to contrast a reward-plus-punishment and a punishment-only condition. The authors hypothesized that the passive avoidance deficit in psychopaths is due to a selective ignoring of punishment possibilities when focusing on reward. According to this hypothesis the deficit should only appear when correct responses are rewarded and incorrect responses (commission errors) are punished.

The results of the study are shown in Figure 9.5. As predicted, the psychopaths made more commission (passive avoidance) errors in the reward-punishment conditions, and the two groups did not differ on this type of error in the punishment-only condition. Omission errors were equal in both groups in both conditions. The authors had expected the psychopaths to do better in the punishment-only than in the reward-punishment condition because of the elimination of the lure of the reward. Instead the nonpsychopaths did much worse, and the psychopaths did not do any better or worse. This result is attributed to the general difficulty and arousal produced by punishment only.

Newman, Patterson, and Kosson (1987) proposed that psychopaths tend to perseverate in a response set for reward even in circumstances in which punishment contingencies are strong. To test this hypothesis they set up a computer-operated game with rewards for hits and loss of money for misses. Subjects had the option of playing or not playing on every trial. The game was rigged so that the first block of trials provided 90% reward, the second block 80%, and so on, down to the last block in which no winning cards were present. The psychopathic prisoners persisted longer, playing more cards and losing more money before quitting the game, even when salient cumulative feedback was provided. However, the differences disappeared when the cumulative feedback was combined with the requirement that they pause for 5 sec before deciding whether to play the next card. Presumably this gave them a chance to contemplate the feedback information. The results also seem to implicate *impulsivity* in the response perseverative deficit of psychopaths.

The series of studies by Newman and his colleagues has clarified the nature of the learning deficit in psychopaths, though much remains to be learned. In a situation in which psychopaths expect a reward, based on prior experience, they become oblivious to cues for punishment or a change in contingencies. *Impulsivity,* the tendency to respond quickly without reflection, may also play a role in psychopathy because the information on contingencies is often understood by the psychopath.

Summary

Even though the current DSM III definition of APD defines the disorder almost exclusively in terms of a pattern of irresponsible and antisocial behavior starting in childhood (before the age of 15) and persisting into adult life, studies show that this history is correlated with traits of *sensation seeking* and lack of *socialization* but not strongly with *extraversion* or *neuroticism.* Thus, the hypothesis (chapter 1) suggesting that APD represents the extreme of the traits associated with the P dimension of personality rather than some combination of this dimension with the other two (E and N) is supported by data from actual psychopaths. APD is not synonymous with substance abuse or criminality, but there is evidence of a large overlap between these disorders. A person with APD is at high risk for abusing alcohol or drugs and engaging in criminal activity. Children classified as hyperactive or conduct disorder are also at risk for becoming adult APDs. However, many studies showing psychological, behavioral, and biological differences between groups of criminals and substance abusers classified as APD or non-APD suggest that such classication is meaningful and predictive.

Both twin and adoption studies show a significant role for genetic determination in APD or recidivist criminality but not necessarily for delinquency. The genetic link between schizophrenia and APD postulated by Eysenck is not genenerally supported by the evidence. Although the role of foster parents in inoculating a boy against the effects of a biological disposition is not demonstrable, other environmental factors such as socioeconomic class and peer influences do seem important. Substance abuse seems more influenced by family environmental factors than is APD. Still, there is suggestive evidence that good rearing practices by a healthy mother can have some inoculative effect against the criminogenic effects (genetic or environmental) of a deviant father. A genetic model proposing polygenetic determination with the same determinants in both sexes but a higher threshold for influence in women seems to account best for the data. The polygenetic determination could be a function of the combined genetic determination of the traits that make up the P-ImpUSS dimension of personality.

The hypothesis of a bilateral frontal lobe dysfunction in APD was based on the occurrence of pseudopsychopathic behavior in some neurological patients with frontal lobe damage and the reported deficits of APDs on certain psychological tests in which frontal lobe patients show deficits. However, when better criteria were used to define APD, these neuropsychological deficits were not found. Although not suffering from lower overall intelligence, APDs do show a deficit in verbal, relative to performance, tests of intelligence, suggesting a possible left hemisphere dysfunction. Evidence on differences in the incidence of left-handedness also support this hypothesis though there are contradictory findings. Some have suggested that left hemisphere dysfunction is specifically related to linguistic processing, which is not as specialized for left hemisphere function in APDs as in others. Both auditory and visually presented verbal stimuli support this hypothesis. However, the link between this finding and the APD's tendency to use language in a manipulative insincere manner is obscure.

Another neuropsychological model for APD is based on the type of deficits shown in septal-lesioned rats. According to this hypothesis, the disinhibitory psychopathology in humans is similar to the behavior of lesioned rats in impulsive inability to delay or inhibit responding for reward in the face of possible punishment. This deficit in passive avoidance is one of the most typical features of learning deficit in the APD. Enhanced stimulation seeking is also part of the "septal syndrome," and sensation seeking of the disinhibitory type is a major trait in human psychopathy. This localization of the origins of APD is compatible with Gray's idea of a bipolar influence of the septohippocampal system in personality; too active a system is supposedly associated with anxiety and too weak a system with psychopathy. This would presuppose that the absence of anxiety is an essential feature of APD, and that trait *anxiety* is inversely related to the P traits. In actual fact, neither of these assumptions is strongly supported in the human literature.

Although testosterone is essential to male aggressiveness, in other species it is not clearly related to trait *aggression* in humans. Among criminals, only those who have a history of extremely violent crimes show testosterone levels above normal. Testosterone is related to social dominance in prisoners just as it is in normal males. Testosterone may also be involved in the *sensation seeking (disinhibition)* aspect of psychopathic behavior as it clearly is in normal males.

Low levels of the enzymes MAO and DBH have been found in child and adult groups with disinhibitory disorders. As in normal personality, the presence of these markers in APDs points to a deregulation or weakness in some of the monoamine systems. Low levels of urinary epinephrine and catecholamine response to stress are found among APD types and are predictive of delinquency when assessed early in adolescence. Work on metabolites of brain catecholamines in CSF and plasma has revealed consistent correlation between impulsive and violent behavior and only one of these, 5-HIAA, the metabolite of serotonin. Persons with a history of emotionally uncontrolled violence toward themselves or others show low levels of the metabolite and brain serotonin. Recent work also suggests that a serotonin deficiency may originate in the production of serotonin from trypotophan. These findings are also consistent with the negative relationship between P and 5-HIAA in normals (chapter 5) and the disinhibitory effects of serotonin system lesioning in animals. One of these effects is on passive avoidance learning. Other evidence has suggested the possibility of a hypoglycemic metabolic effect in APD, related to an overreactive insulin mechanism.

Autonomic underarousal has also been suggested as an explanation for poor passive avoidance learning when the UCS is pain, though Eysenck's theory would suggest a combination of cortical underarousal and autonomic overarousal related to N. The findings on cortical arousal have been mixed. Clinical studies do suggest a high incidence of slow wave activity in the APD, but some laboratory studies actually suggest that the primary psychopath is characterized by higher arousal than the secondary psychopath. A few prospective studies have shown that low cortical arousal has some predictive value for later delinquency. However, this sign may be more characteristic of those conduct disorders who are also hyperactive as children.

Studies of tonic autonomic system underarousal reveal some weak but consistent differences, with APD groups showing lower tonic skin conductance and heart rate levels than non-APD types. More interesting differences are found in a quasi-conditioning paradigm in which an attenuated gradient of SCL change is found in APDs in anticipation of painful shock or noise. However, this difference is response specific because psychopaths tend to show a stronger rather than a weaker HRR (acceleration) in anticipation of the UCS in some studies.

In actual conditioning studies there is evidence that psychopaths show weaker electrodermal orienting and anticipatory response conditioning when shock is the UCS. Similar differences in response to positive UCSs have not been demonstrated, though this may be simply because the stimuli employed were too weak. Differences have also been demonstrated in extinction of conditioned discrimination with prisoners showing more rapid extinction than controls.

In instrumental conditioning, the human literature is consistent in showing a deficit in passive avoidance learning in situations in which there are both reward and punishment possibilities. Given the possibility of reward, the psychopath has a difficult time learning to avoid the punishment contingencies and persists longer when the contingencies shift in the direction of likely punishment.

Although the picture is far from clear, it is beginning to appear that the APD is based on a genetically influenced deficit in certain enzymes and inhibitory neurotransmitters (serotonin) that are involved in the normal modulation of behavior, such as learning when to inhibit responses that are inappropriate or dangerous. There is also a failure of autonomic response that could exert an inhibiting influence on behavior. Underarousal of central catecholamine systems may also play a role in the antisocial types of *sensation-seeking* behavior typical of psychopaths.

10   Measures and models, problems and progress

What is found in biology is *mechanisms,* mechanisms built with chemical components and that are modified by other, later mechanisms added to the earlier ones.
While Occam's razor is a useful tool in the physical sciences, it can be a very
dangerous implement in biology. It is thus very rash to use simplicity and elegance
as a guide in biological research. . . . To produce a really good biological theory
one must try to see through the clutter produced by evolution to the basic mechanisms lying beneath them, realizing that they are likely to be overlaid by other,
secondary mechanisms. What seems to physicists to be a hopelessly complicated
process may have been what nature found simplest, because nature could only
build on what was there. (Crick, 1988)

Psychological measures

Classification is a necessary first step in the understanding of personality
or any science. Analyses of self, peer ratings, and questionnaires agree on
two of the broad personality factors: *sociability (extraversion)* and *emotionality.* Beyond these two traits, "personality in the third dimension"
(Zuckerman, 1989) seems to consist of a broad factor of impulsive, unsocialized sensation seeking versus socialization and responsibility. The
currently popular 5-factor model also includes *agreeableness* (vs. *hostility*),
conscientiousness (vs. *impulsivity* and *irresponsibility*), and *cultured* (vs.
unreflective and simple).

Recent factor analyses by Zuckerman, Kuhlman, Thornquist and Kiers
(in press) show five reliable factors, similar in men and women: *sociability, neuroticism-anxiety, aggressiveness-hostility, impulsive-unsocialized-
sensation seeking,* and *activity.* The first four of these factors seem to correspond to the popular "big five" (Digman & Inouye, 1986; McCrae &
Costa, 1985a). The investigators deliberately left out potential markers for
the culture factor for reasons described in chapter 1. Their fifth factor,
activity, is regarded as one of the basic temperaments by Buss and Plomin
(1984) but is described as a component of *extraversion* by McCrae and
Costa (1985a).

Each of the broader factors can be subdivided into narrow traits, and
these in turn can be divided into even narrower traits until we get down
to situation-specific habits. Narrower traits are often more closely related
to psychophysiological and some biochemical variables and generally have
more predictive value for behavior. Narrow *impulsivity,* a subtrait of the

broader E or P factors, seems to be more closely related to arousal and conditioning phenomena than the broader traits. *Disinhibition,* a subtrait of *sensation seeking* trait, which is in turn a subtrait of the P dimension, is more specifically related to biological dimensions such as gonadal hormones and augmenting of the evoked potential than the broader traits are.

The Western approaches to personality stress naturalistic study of social behavior. In contrast, Pavlovian approaches began with animal models in laboratory situations in which dogs, and later humans, were typed on the basis of hypothetical characteristics of the nervous system inferred from conditioning, psychophysical, or psychophysiological experiments. Only recently have neo-Pavlovians such as Strelau (1983) and Rusalov (1989) developed questionnaires to assess the life-behavioral aspects of the systems. Although analyses of their questionnaires show some similarities to the E and N dimensions found in Western analyses, other dimensions are concerned primarily with energy and capacity for work (possibly related to the *activity* dimension in some Western analyses). There is little sampling in their inventories of items that might deal with the factors involved in the P dimension of personality. It is almost as if the concepts of *impulsivity, irresponsibility,* and *sensation seeking* are regarded as something outside of the realm of normal personality. Still, the development of such questionnaires is an important step in formulating a general paradigm for the study of personality and in fostering communication among investigators of personality in East and West.

Although questionnaires depend on cooperativeness and verbal capacity in subjects, they have the advantage of being able to ask subjects about their behavior, preferences, attitudes, and reactions in a variety of situations in which direct observation would be expensive, difficult, or impossible. Validity studies have shown fair prediction of aggregated behaviors from self-report trait scales in a variety of situations when relevant or prototypical behaviors are used.

Temperamental assessments of young infants have not been very successful in predicting later behavior. Too many of these assessments are specific to a given stage of development with little predictive validity for later stages or show little consistency from one situation to another. However, traits such as *approach-withdrawal* in reaction to novel situations show situation generality, consistency over time, predictive value for later development, and psychobiological significance (Kagan et al., 1984). Both *approach-withdrawal* and *activity* show nearly total genetic determination at 6 years of age (Torgerson, 1985). After infancy, early prototypes of adult traits may be assessed by using observations of psychologists, parents, or teachers. Judgments based on behavior observed in many situations are more likely to reflect consistent individual differences than narrow behavior observed only in one situation. Whether observers should use prototypical behavior or a general aggregation in making ratings is an empirical question. Certainly, an aggregation of observations in situations that are conceptually unrelated is not the way to proceed. The same psychometric considerations that are employed in test development must be used in developing sets of ratings.

Comparative methods

A psychobiological model of personality for humans must use data obtained from other species because precise biological experimentation with humans, involving brain lesioning and stimulation, is not possible. However, the adequacy of generalization from comparative studies depends on the adequacy of the animal models. Many models of anxiety do not involve social reactions, and most depend entirely on fear of physical pain, not a common source of ordinary human anxiety. Human personality is mostly defined by responses in social situations, but most animal models define *approach* or *inhibition* in nonsocial situations. Some compromise between the purely observational approach of the ethologist and the experimental approach in tightly controlled conditions is required. Observations of animals in seminatural colony environments may provide the best kind of information for models of personality. However, even in more controlled situations, such as the open field and controlled exposures to other animals, dimensions of behavior roughly comparable to human dimensions can be obtained. If such behavior has similar functional significance and biological correlates as relevant behavior in humans, it may furnish a model for investigation of the relevant brain processes.

Consistency

A frequent criticism of trait approaches to personality is a supposed lack of consistency of human behavior over time and across situations. The explanation of the latter is the powerful influence of specific attributes of situations on behavior compared with consistent characteristics of persons. If consistency of human behavior across situations does not exist, there would be no point in determining the biological bases for the nonexistent traits. For that matter there would be no point in trying to develop a science of personality if there were no consistent structure of traits. A general theory of social behavior would do nicely.

Unfortunately, traits do tend to be reified and regarded as causal agents rather than as organizations of behavior that require explanation themselves. To the extent that we can uncover the biological mechanisms underlying them and their experiential antecedents we can "explain" traits. This author regards traits as hypothetical constructs used to describe correlated habits of reaction, either overt or cognitive. Traits do not cause behavior; they are generalizations based on past behavioral and cognitive events. Affective traits such as *anxiety,* for instance, can be regarded as states or traits. Although we can use a single retrospective measure to assess the trait, the trait could be defined as the summary or aggregation of past states (Zuckerman, 1976). The idea of "state" does not imply consistency or temporal reliability, but the concept of a trait does require correlation among lower order traits or habits of reaction comprising it. If there were an average of zero for correlations among states, aggregation could not provide evidence of a trait. It is these consistencies, albeit they are low, that justify aggregation. Such aggregations do show reliability and good predictive value for future states or reactions similarly aggregated.

The question of the relative importance of situation and person has proven to be one of those issues that periodically emerge in personality psychology, engender a great deal of heat and research, and end in little significance. In the case of the situation versus person debate, almost all investigators have agreed that situation and person interact in accounting for behavior, and no generalization about the relative importance of either can be made (Magnusson & Endler, 1977). The tragedy of these debates is that they have delayed the development of a mature science of personality. We have spent half a century searching for a paradigm for the study of personality with little time left over for the substantive problems of personality.

The dichotomy between person and situation is based on the assumption of their independence. Although this may be true in the laboratory, where situations are imposed on persons, in real life a person chooses among a range of possible situations and associates. Is this person using drugs only because he is in a place where others are doing this? A yes answer would be rather naive in stressing only the proximal cause of behavior. What brought him to there to begin with? Personality traits are related to the choice of situations and people. A sociable person seeks environments containing other sociable people. A sensation seeker looks for novel, unusual, and stimulating situations. A neurotic searches for familiar and safe situations and people. In life there is generally a correlation of person and situation as well as an interaction.

Traits seems to have some predictive validity over the life history, with certain limitations. It is difficult to predict much about adults from observations made prior to age 6. Until this age most of the long-term social interactions of children are limited to parents or other caretakers. Prediction is considerably improved after they begin school. This should not be surprising. We are attempting to predict adult behavior, but most social interactions of adults are with peers, not parents. Prediction is considerably improved in the preadolescent-to-adolescent period, and reliabilities of personality measures remain high and stable for long periods over the adult life span. Prediction from childhood is also limited by the gender-related significance of traits. There is not much social pressure for change when traits are gender-role congruent, so such traits tend to be consistent compared with traits that are not consistent with gender-role. The social processes involved in such conflict or change are not difficult to surmise, but not much longitudinal research has been done on this topic. What are the limits of environmental models and social reinforcement? Genetic research suggests that the family environment is not as crucial in personality development as theories suggest.

Genetics and environment

This brings us to the next question, addressed in detail in chapter 3. To what extent is personality determined by genetics and to what extent by environmental factors? Although some workers would regard this as a meaningless question, the demonstration of genetic influence is an important foundation for psychobiological analysis, and some elegant methods have been designed to answer it. Subsidiary questions concern the type of genetic mechanisms involved and the type of environment that is important in shaping personality. Behavior genetic studies of broad human traits have provided some answers that are extremely provocative to many conventional personality theories based exclusively on social learning. The human genetic data come from separated twin and adoption studies and biometrical studies of very large populations of identical and fraternal twins reared together. For most personality traits, broad heredity accounts for 40 to 60% of the similarities and differences between individuals, with the typical figure around 50%. Environment and error of measurement account for the rest. The surprising finding is that shared environments, including common family influences, play little role in most broad personality traits, though the separated twin studies do suggest some role of shared environment in the trait of *sociability,* accounting for between 10 and 20% of the variance. However, studies of unrelated person (adoptees) growing up in the same families show no effect of shared environment on most broad personality traits. An interpretation of this discrepancy might be that shared environment is only a significant influence in *sociability* when there is some genetic similarity between parents and children to begin with.

Although most personality traits seem to fall into the 40 to 60% genetically determined range and show little effect of shared environment, the exceptions are interesting. In two studies, conventional measures of masculinity-femininity showed little genetic influence, particularly in men, and a high degree of shared environmental influence. There is evidence of an influence of prenatal androgen and estrogen provided by the mother. However, the twin studies suggest that the ultimate influences tend to be a function of shared social environment in the great majority of cases. The finding that masculinity or femininity of interests owes more to social learning than to genetically influenced biological factors supports the position of the feminists that gender-roles must be considered separate from biological sexuality, as well as the influence of culture, on definitions of masculinity and femininity (Mead, 1949).

The more important types of environmental influence on personality, accounting for up to 50% of the variance on most personality traits, are those environments that are not shared by members of the same families. Different friends and fortuitous experiences not shared by members of the same family may affect personality more than the consistent treatment or degree of emotional warmth provided by parents to all children in the family. One could argue that children in the same family are not treated alike and that such differences in treatment are what influence personality development. Children might be very sensitive in detecting such differences in attitude and treatment and may even exaggerate them. There are two problems with this argument. One is that differences in reported treatment are not much related to differences in personality either in twins reared together or those reared apart. The second is that even if such differences were found to be related to personality in children reared together, they might reflect the parental response to genetic differences in temperament of siblings rather than determing those behavioral differences. The parent-child resemblance that does exist is mostly due to shared genes rather than shared environments. Social learning is quite important, but the crucial models of personality may be peers or nonparental role models. But because children have some choice of friends among their peers, genetic influences may affect their choices, producing a genotype-environment correlation that would be hard to disentangle using conventional biometric methods.

Certainly, polygenetic influences are the rule for complex personality traits since simple Mendelian patterns are not evident. However, the differences between results for identical twins and fraternal twins or siblings, or between parents and children, suggest that epistasis and other forms of nonadditive genetic influences may play a significant role in some traits, particularly *sociability*. To the extent that this is true, a part of genetic influence is hidden in all relations but those of identical twins in which the precise patterning of genes is the same. The differences between siblings, for instance, are less likely to be due to differential parental treatment of them than to differences in the genetic "cards" they were dealt.

The idea that all genetic differences are manifest at birth is a misconception. Genes turn on and off according to a timetable during development. Genetically determined traits that are manifest during infancy may have little continuity or relevance for later developing traits. The first genetically determined and developmentally significant traits appear to be *activity* and *approach-withdrawal* (in response to animate or inanimate novel stimuli). *Activity* in newborns is significantly related to the biological marker monoamine oxidase, which is also significantly related to *sociability* and *sensation seeking* in adults. *Activity* shows genetic differences at about 9 months, and the strong genetic influence increases with age and remains significant throughout childhood. *Approach-withdrawal* also emerges as a genetically significant source of individual differences at around 9 months and becomes part of the narrower traits of *shyness, impulsivity,* and *sensation seeking* and (later) the broader traits of E and N. Although mood also begins to show some genetic influence at 9 months, the influence is weaker at that age compared with *activity* and *approach-withdrawal.* During these early years it is closely tied to social response; children who are sociable tend to show positive moods, and shy children show more negative emotionality. However, between 4 and 7 years, *fearfulness, irritability,* and *anger* become manifest as genetically influenced traits, and they eventually become a part of the broad trait of *emotionality* or *neuroticism.* The genetic bases of personality can be discerned in infancy and early childhood, but their relationship to later personality traits may not be obvious because their forms and expressions in adult personality may be quite different.

A psychobiological model for personality

As Crick says, it would be foolish to attempt to formulate an oversimplistic psychobiological model for personality for the sake of elegance. Complex models in biology are likely to be wrong in their details, but overly simple models are almost sure to be wrong because of their simplicity. We see in the human brain the outcome of countless small evolutionary survival mechanisms built on earlier mechanisms. What started as reflexive approach and withdrawal mechanisms in simple organisms have evolved into a complicated organization of interdependent biobehavioral mechanisms. To avoid the mistakes of phrenology, we must respect the complexity of the nervous systems in the human.

There is no compelling reason to believe that the organization of the nervous system is isomorphic with the structure of personality traits (chapter 1) or that each neurotransmitter or brain structure is relevant to only one specific trait. A neurophysiological system may participate in many behavioral functions, some of which may be relevant to one trait and others to other traits. The hippocampus, for instance, is involved in arousal, orienting and attention, emotion, behavioral inhibition, memory, and spatial learning. It could conceivably play a role in at least two and possibly all three of the major personality traits. Furthermore, the biological systems themselves interact in agonistic and antagonistic ways so that though we may speak of the factorial independence of personality traits, there is usually a functional interdependence of the biological systems underlying them.

Another problem with the idea of simple isomorphism, or at least its demonstration, is that the relationships among functions based on particular systems and the activity in these systems may not be linear. Catecholamine system activity, for instance, may be curvilinearly associated with many functions such as *activity* and *sociability* (Zuckerman, 1984a). Thus, we could prematurely discount the involvement of a biological system in a personality trait because of the failure to find a linear relationship between the system and the trait or because the direction of the relationship is different in normal and abnormal populations. The real problem might be that we do not have enough range and sample size to detect curvilinear relationships, or that we cannot use high enough doses of neurotransmitter agonists on humans.

A final limitation, mentioned in previous chapters, is the imperfect methodology used to gather much of the human data. Although the models are based on biological functions in the brain, studies in humans are mostly correlational and based on imperfect indicators of brain system activity such as the presence of neurotransmitters and their metabolites and of enzymes assayed from the cerebrospinal fluid, blood, and urine. Human neuropsychology is based largely on clinical studies of brain damaged or operated patients or indirect measures of brain function. Although the use of other species as subjects allows more precise experimentation on brain functions, extrapolation from such studies depends on comparative assumptions of similarity of function and the adequacy of particular animal models for human behavior. There are some recent breakthroughs in methodology, such as the PET scan, that may be helpful in bridging the gaps between personality, psychopathology, and brain function in humans and behavior and brain function in other species. Convergence among findings using these methods of studying brain functions in humans and the experimental neurobiological studies of other species should help in refining the models. Unfortunately, data from the new imaging methods for studying brain function in humans are still limited and fragmentary and will be so for some time due to the enormous expense of the methods and their early stage of development.

Given all of these limitations, it may be premature to formulate a general psychobiological model for personality. Such a model is bound to be inaccurate in many major respects. However, it is a characteristic of the human brain (mind) to seek cognitive closure with whatever information is available at a given time. Science is a system set up to challenge theories or models, ultimately reformulating or scrapping them for better ones (Popper, 1979). Even incomplete or inaccurate models are preferable to none; without models, efforts tend to be dissipated in blind, piecemeal, inductive research with no focus or direction.

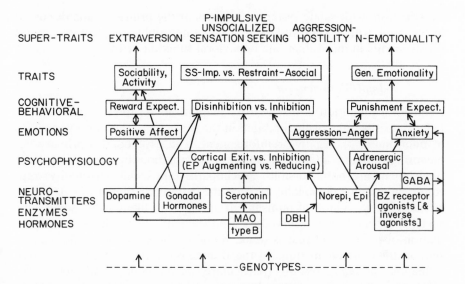

Figure 10.1. A psychobiological model for personality. Dopamine refers particularly to the A10 dopaminergic pathway from the ventral tegmental area to the nucleus accumbens via the medial forebrain bundle and the A9 pathway from the substantia nigra to the caudate-putamen. Low levels of type B monoamine oxidase (MAO) may deregulate these systems. High levels of gonadal hormones, particularly testosterone, may furnish a basis for both *sociability* and *disinhibition*. High levels of serotonin in conjunction with high levels of both type A and B MAO may provide the basis for strong inhibition; low levels of serotonin together with high activity of dopaminergic systems may be involved in *disinhibition, impulsivity*, and *aggression* or *hostility*. Regions of the septal area are particularly involved in inhibition-disinhibition of behavior. Norepinephrine (Norepi), particularly in the dorsal ascending noradrenergic pathways from the locus coeruleus v, are also involved in the adrenergic arousal found in both anxiety and anger. Low levels of norepinephrine, perhaps related to low levels of the enzyme dopamine-beta-hydroxlase (DBH), may be involved in the traits of *disinhibition* and *impulsivity*. Stimulation from the central nucleus of the amygdala to the ventral tegmental areas and the locus coeruleus may increase activity in dopaminergic and noradrenergic systems. At low levels this catecholamine system activity may be rewarding and facilitating but at high levels may be associated with anxiety, distractibility, inhibition, and adrenergic arousal. When adrenergic arousal is combined with high activity of benzo-diazepine receptor inverse agonists and low levels of GABA inhibition, the result may be anxiety. Specific combinations of these biological traits may underlie the disposition of trait anxiety and emotionality in general.

The model to be presented here owes much to the one developed by Jeffrey Gray (1982, 1987a). However, some basic revisions have been made in the structural and psychopharmacological formulations of Gray in an attempt to reconcile findings from animal and human studies. The broad outlines of the model are shown in Figure 10.1. Following the structure of this book, we move from the genotype to the level of neuropsychological structures or pathways, to the biochemical level, to the psychophysiological, to the behavioral-cognitive, and finally to the trait level. Rather than attempting to redefine the trait level to bring it into isomorphism with single systems, the lines of the primary traits discussed in this book will be kept, indicating when a neurophysiological system has involvements in more than one behavioral function or trait.

P-ImpUSS dimension

Behavioral inhibition is essential to adaptation. At times, approach behavior must be selectively inhibited in the presence of cues or anticipation of punishment or negative reinforcement. The psychopath's primary behavioral problem is a failure of inhibition in situations in which reward and punishment are both possible. Psychopaths (antisocial personality) represent an extreme personality type on the P-ImpUSS dimension. They are not insensitive to cues of punishment and are not likely to do some antisocial act while being observed by a policeman; it is the long-term anticipation of punishment that is weak. Some of these characteristics can be seen in the component traits of the P dimension: *impulsivity* and lack of reflection, *sensation seeking* (particularly *disinhibition*), and lack of *socialization*. A basic learning problem in psychopaths is their failure to learn passive avoidance, or when *not* to respond.

At a lower level of analysis, the cortical modulation of intense stimulation, as shown in the augmenting-reducing paradigm, seems to represent a direct neural expression of the behavioral disinhibition-inhibition propensity. Just as the person with a high physiological tolerance for alcohol is at greater risk for becoming alcoholic, the individual with a greater tolerance for cortical stimulation or excitation is in danger of becoming a disinhibited type of sensation seeker. The high sensation seeker is activated by high levels of stimulation whereas the low tends to "tune out" as inhibitory cortical mechanisms are triggered. There are adaptive advantages and disadvantages to both extremes. An augmenter-disinhibiter seems to have a "strong" nervous system that can continue to function well in overstimulating stressful conditions such as battle. A reducer tends to lose cortical arousal and attention in such situations and therefore suffers a loss of efficiency. However, the positive feedback system of the augmenter can constitute a vulnerability. The tendency to seek more intense levels of stimulation can lead to antisocial expressions in the psychopath. But the most extreme form of sensation seeking can be seen in the manic disorder. Hypomanics are caricatures of impulsive sensation seekers. Bipolar disorder was not included in chapter 9 because of the complication of the associated depression, but the hypomanic shares many psychological and biological characteristics with sensation seekers, including the EP augmenting tendency and low levels of platelet MAO (Zuckerman, 1985).

At the more basic biochemical level of the traits involved in the P dimension (Zuckerman, 1989), we find deficits in hormones, neurotransmitters, and enzymes that play essential roles in behavioral inhibition, including deficits of cortisol, serotonin, norepinephrine, and monoamine-oxidase (MAO) and dopamine-beta-hydroxylase (DBH). Interestingly, low levels of the serotonin metabolite (5-HIAA) and the enzymes MAO and DBH have also been found to be characteristic of the visual EP augmenter (von Knorring & Perris, 1981). At this time it is not known if the neurotransmitters or neuroregulators directly inhibit cortical arousability because the human data are entirely correlational. Low levels of MAO, are consistent correlates of *sensation seeking* and are low in disinhibitory disorders. Low MAO may be a sign of lack of serotonergic activity or excessive dopaminergic activity. Low DBH, a somewhat less consistent correlate of sensation-seeking, results in low noradrenergic activity in the limbic areas serving arousal and inhibition.

Gray has proposed that behavioral inhibition, together with adrenergic arousal and increased alertness, constitute the principal signs of an anxiety state. Behavioral inhibition is primarily related to serotonin, and arousal and alertness are related to norepinephrine. But lack of behavioral inhibition (disinhibition) is also a principal marker for antisocial personality disorder. Similarly, children with attention and hyperactivity disorders are at risk for child conduct disorder or APD. Arousal produced by epinephrine from the adrenal medulla and peripheral norepinephrine are involved in anxiety, but deficits in reactivity of these systems are also found in antisocial disorders and are predictive of later criminality and aggression.

Behavioral inhibition is not always a characteristic of anxiety except in response to immediate signals of punishment. Any salient stimulation, even stimuli associated with reward, produces a momentary inhibition. The inhibition of competing activity functions to maximize information input by minimizing distraction. Orienting is a sign of stimulus significance and interest and has no intrinsic relationship with either anxiety or positive affect. Anxiety is a drive that may energize as well as inhibit behavior; many anxious individuals engage in much agitated if inefficient activity. Arousal can also be related to disinhibition. The catecholamine stimulants amphetamine and cocaine can both increase arousal and disinhibit extremely antisocial behavior. These drugs increase activity in both norepinephrine and dopamine; the former transmitter should increase arousal and alertness, and the latter is associated with sexual, aggressive, and extraverted behavior. The combination of low serotonin (lack of behavioral control) and high norepinephrine (high arousal) can result in extremely antisocial behavior.

At the neuropsychological level, Gray has identified the prefrontal and cingulate cortices and septohippocampal system as serving inhibitory functions, stopping ongoing behavior in response to novel stimuli or stimuli associated with punishment and increasing attention to these stimuli. He believes these and other involved brain areas constitute a "behavioral inhibition system," which is the major basis of the trait of *anxiety*. Certainly this system must be involved in response to anxiety, but it may not be essential to that state or trait. This author would stress the inhibitory functions of the system and its more basic function in the P-ImpUSS (disinhibition) dimension of personality.

The animal models on which Gray bases his model involve passive avoidance learning and approach-avoidance conflict behavior. These models could be regarded as equally appropriate models for APD. Current definition of antisocial disorder does not regard low or absent anxiety as an essential, nor do factor analytic studies of antisocial traits show it to be so. It is the repeated failure to restrain antisocial behaviors that is vital to the definition. In other species, serotonin tends to inhibit sexual and aggressive behavior, and in humans a deficit in serotonin has been linked to impulsive aggression directed at the self (suicide) or others (murder). Sex and aggression are two characteristic areas of disinhibition in the psychopath, and even nonpsychopathic sensation seekers may engage in these activities as sources of strong stimulation. It is true that *low* serotonin activity is linked with states of strong negative emotions, including anger and depression, in humans, but this is opposite in direction to the hypothesis that *high* levels of serotonergic activity are related to anxiety. Depleted levels of serotonin in rats, rather than high levels, are associated with the fear-potentiated startle response and fearfulness in the open field, two models for anxiety. Serotonin may be a factor in inhibition of emotional as well as behavioral responses. Thus far, the serotonin metabolite 5-HIAA in CSF has been found to be negatively correlated with P in normals and patients but is generally unrelated to E or N.

Gonadal hormones, particularly testosterone, have been associated with sexuality, social dominance, and aggression in animals. These findings have sometimes been extended to humans without appropriate comparative studies. High levels of testosterone in prisoners have been related to histories of particularly vicious kinds of aggression, but in prisoners and normal males testosterone appears to be related to social dominance, sensation seeking (disinhibition), and heterosexual experience. Testosterone seems to be related to both the E and P dimensions, but there is also some evidence that there is less of it in anxious, introverted types of men. We must be wary of causal attributions because stress may lower testosterone levels and successful competition and sexual stimulation may raise levels in males. The testosterone-personality relationship is two-way.

Platelet MAO has been related to behavioral and personality traits in humans and monkeys. In both species, low levels of MAO are found in sociable, disinhibited males. Low-MAO human males engage in antisocial behavior and substance abuse. MAO seems to be an important factor in both the E and P dimensions. Although there is little evidence from normals relating the enzyme to the N dimension, there is some evidence of a positive relationship with anxiety in patients. The high heritability for the enzyme, and its behavioral correlates in the first days of life suggest its importance in the psychobiology of personality. The reason for its importance in at least two dimensions of personality is not clear. Some investigators suggest that MAO is a positive indicator of serotonergic activity. Others have pointed out its regulatory influence in all three monoamine systems, though the type B MAO from blood platelets in humans is more involved in regulation of the dopaminergic than other monoamine systems in the brain. Low levels of MAO would not necessarily decrease or increase activity in any of these systems, though it would deregulate them. If one of the monoamine systems were already active, and if there were little MAO in the neuron to break down the monoamine, and if there were a hyporesponsivity of presynaptic receptors that regulate production, then increased production would result in an increasing level of activity in the system. The neuronal model suggests a positive feedback system similar to the behavioral one seen in the manic disorder, in which stimulation arouses the patients to seek even more stimulation. Giving MAO-inhibiting drugs to a bipolar patient in a depressive phase often triggers the manic phase characterized by behavioral disinhibition, euphoric mood, increased activity, high levels of norepinephrine in the CSF, and possibly an increase in dopamine in areas of the brain involved specifically in activity and reward. All of these effects could be due to a deregulation of the catecholamine systems. If this state of overreactivity persists, catecholamines could be depleted with consequent behavioral changes, such as a plunge from the heights of mania to the depths of depression. The effects of deregulated catecholamine systems are portrayed in Figure 10.2.

According to the model, catecholamine systems play a role in mood, activity, social interaction, and certain clinical disorders. More specifically, striate dopamine activity may influence level of physical activity, and dopamine in nucleus accumbens and forebrain projections may influence positive feelings. Social activity would also be a function of the activity of particular dopaminergic pathways. Noradrenergic arousal may be more important in arousal of negative affect such as depression and anxiety, but norepinephrine and dopamine may have synergistic effects in manic states characterized by euphoria or hostility. Normal variations in these traits associated with personality would vary in the B to C range and would be based on tonic levels of catecholamine activity or reactivity. States associated with extreme variations in brain catecholamine system activity range from major depression produced by norepinephrine depletion to anxiety and panic produced by an excess of activity in this system. Similarly, a deficit in dopamine would produce anhedonia and social withdrawal, also characteristic of depression; a slight excess would produce euphoria, hyperactivity, and hypersociability; but at some excess doses or chronically high levels of activity (sometimes produced by stimulant drugs), the optimal effects would shift to limited stereotypical activity, social withdrawal, and

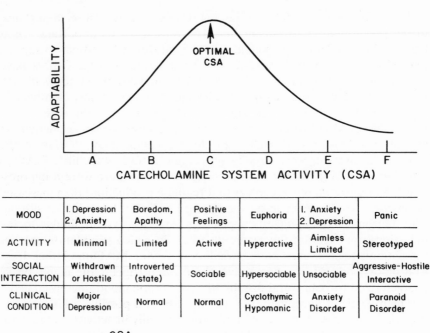

MOOD	1. Depression 2. Anxiety	Boredom, Apathy	Positive Feelings	Euphoria	1. Anxiety 2. Depression	Panic
ACTIVITY	Minimal	Limited	Active	Hyperactive	Aimless Limited	Stereotyped
SOCIAL INTERACTION	Withdrawn or Hostile	Introverted (state)	Sociable	Hypersociable	Unsociable	Aggressive-Hostile Interactive
CLINICAL CONDITION	Major Depression	Normal	Normal	Cyclothymic Hypomanic	Anxiety Disorder	Paranoid Disorder

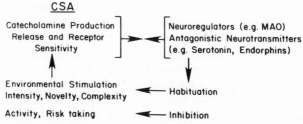

Figure 10.2. A model for the relationship of mood, activity, social interaction, and clinical conditions to catecholamine system activity (CSA). (From "Sensation seeking: A comparative approach to a human trait," by M. Zuckerman, 1984, *Behavioral and Brain Sciences*, 7, p. 431. Copyright 1984 by Cambridge University Press. Reprinted by permission.)

hostility and aggression fueled by paranoia. Such curvilinear effects of catecholamine activity have been demonstrated repeatedly in the human and animal literature. For instance, locomotor activity of rats is increased up to some dosage of d-amphetamine, and then shows a decline with increasing dosage. Their social behavior shows a similar change with increasing dosage of the stimulant drug. Such curvilinear relationships would explain some of the differences in direction of relationships between catecholamine metabolites and mood or behavior in normals and patients, because the two populations might occupy two different ranges in the level of catecholamine activity, one on the ascending and the other on the descending portion of the curve.

N-emotionality

The central characteristic of this dimension of personality is a frequent experiencing of negative affective states, including anxiety, depression, and hostility. Anxiety and depression seem to be more characteristic affects in the high-N low-P combination whereas anger and hostility are found in the high-N high-P quadrant (Zuckerman, Kuhlman, & Camac 1988). Does this mean that the emotionality dimension is specific to intensity and frequency of negative affect alone, or is the dimension a more general one referring to intensity of all emotional responses, positive as well as negative? Gray's model suggests the latter because high levels of N produce an amplification of all emotional responses, whether in response to signals of reward or punishment. More recently Gray has suggested otherwise, citing Tellegen's (1985) theory that N is related specifically to the frequent experiencing of negative affect, whereas E (*sociability*) is independently related to the experiencing of positive affect.

The difference between a theory postulating an intensity dimension of affect contrasted with a bipolar positive versus negative affect dimension, and a theory suggesting separate dimensions of positive and negative affect, is relevant to the debate about the biological bases of emotion. One theory (Schachter, 1975) proposes that degree of emotionality is a function of adrenergic arousal whereas the identification of positive and negative emotions depends on the situational or cognitive context of the arousal. This idea would be very compatible with the idea of a trait of *general emotionality*. The other theory, which goes back to William James (1884), maintains that each emotion is based on a specific pattern of peripheral physiological and behavioral responses, and it is our awareness of these changes that produces the specific emotional quality. Cannon (1927) refuted the theory experimentally and suggested that emotional reactions are organized in the hypothalamus. However, the latter theory allowed for the possibility that various parts of the hypothalamus might account for the various qualities of emotion. The debate has never been satisfactorily resolved. Unique and nearly reflexive patterns of facial muscular response suggests there is a specific but central physiological basis for individual emotions (Izard, 1977), but catecholamine arousal patterns suggest a lack of biochemical differentiation between positive and negative emotions (Levi, 1967). One of the problems is that, with the exception of strong sexual arousal, intense and physiologically arousing affects or emotions tend to be negative ones. Positive emotions such as love (not sex) are generally weak in terms of physiological responsivity. There is a basic confounding of intensity (arousal) and negativity (anxiety and anger) of emotions.

The Gray–Redmond (Gray, 1982; Redmond, 1977) hypothesis emphasizes the central role of the dorsal ascending noradrenergic bundle (DANB) from the locus coeruleus (LC) to the septohippocampal system in the generation of anxiety. This hypothesis is partly based on the role of the benzodiazepines and other antianxiety agents on the LC and the DANB. To these systems Gray adds the inhibitory effects of the ascending serotonergic system originating in the raphe nucleus. More recently, the anxiety-producing properties of yohimbine, a noradrenergic agonist, and the anxiety-reducing effect of clonidine, a noradrenergic antagonist, at the LC source, have been cited as evidence for this model. However, the evidence is limited by the failure of these drugs to produce or reduce anxiety in normals. This suggests that rather than the drugs acting directly on an anxiety mechanism, the anxiety that they produce in anxiety disorders is secondary to their production of autonomic arousal and its action as conditioned stimuli for the subjective sense of anxiety in patients. Other substances such as lactate and caffeine, which also produce autonomic arousal, are equally capable of producing panic attacks in panic disorder patients even though these drugs have no stimulant effect on the LC-noradrenergic system. Apparently the tachycardia and hyperventilation produced by the substances suggest the onset of a panic attack to patients who have experienced such attacks and thereby bring on the actual panic.

File (1988) has raised the possibility that perturbation in the noradrenergic system is more involved in panic disorder (PD), and the GABA/benzodiazepine system is more involved in general anxiety disorder (GAD). However, baseline levels of MHPG in anxiety patients and normals do not differ. Although panic disorder patients respond with more anxiety and arousal to stimulants of the noradrenergic system, other types of patients, including GADs, do not differ from controls. Perhaps PD is a less relevant model of psychopathology than GAD for the N dimension of personality. Although there is a polygenetic inheritance of vulnerability to all anxiety disorders, there seems to be a more specific dominant inheritance for panic disorder symptoms. The episodic deregulation of the autonomic nervous system in PD may be due to a small number of genes regulating some autonomic control factor. The general worries and anxiety of the GAD are more like what is seen in other neuroses.

The serotonin hypothesis of anxiety was based on reported effects of serotonin antagonists on anxiety disorders. However, both baseline and serotonergic potentiation studies are inconclusive. File (1988) says that studies in her lab and others labs have not found significant anxiolytic actions of serotonin drugs. As noted previously, there is considerable evidence relating depleted serotonin to the P dimension and possibly the N dimension as well, but in the reversed direction to the older serotonin hypothesis. Perhaps serotonin controls emotional as well as behavioral responsivity.

If norepinephrine and serotonin are only indirectly involved in anxiety trait, then we must consider the direct actions of antianxiety drugs. The benzodiazepines (BZs) act directly on BZ receptors in the nervous system.

The BZs work by potentiating the effects of GABA, an inhibitory neurotransmitter widely distributed in all major divisions of the brain and spinal cord. In many regions of the brain these neurons constitute between 20 and 40% of all neurons. However, the effects of the BZs on anxiety are desirable precisely because they have the capacity to reduce feelings of anxiety without causing a general sedation like that produced by barbiturates and alcohol. It is therefore likely that the potentiation effects of GABA that affect anxiety are specific to their action on selected parts of the brain, perhaps the locus coeruleus, as suggested by Gray (1982). GABA itself (low levels or lack of responsivity) could be the crucial basis for trait and state *anxiety,* but the widespread distribution of GABA argues against its trait specificity

Another basis for the N trait could be the concentration of BZ receptors themselves. Decreased concentrations in an anxious strain of mice suggests that these receptors might be deficient in humans who are vulnerable to anxiety disorders. Other possibilities concern endogenous BZ inverse agonists such as βCCE or DBI, which could produce anxiety, or an endogenous BZ agonist that might be lacking in anxious patients. The inverse agonist might be the agent that could "tag" emotional arousal as "anxiety." A combination of high adrenergic arousability and high levels of the tag agent might be required to produce high N trait or a vulnerability to generalized anxiety disorder.

The endogenous opiates (endorphins) may also play a role in attenuating anxiety or other kinds of emotional arousal. This would be a natural extension of their pain-reduction function. The central nucleus of the amygdala has a particularly high density of opiate receptors, and the basolateral nucleus, which projects to the central nucleus, has a high concentration of BZ receptors. The amygdala has been suggested as a primary source of emotional reaction to sensory stimuli (to be discussed). Perhaps, the identification of anxiety as affect could happen in these nuclei, and individual differences in emotional reactivity could be in some part a function of specific concentration of BZ and endorphin receptors in these nuclei.

If we are looking for a particular neurological structure that plays a crucial role in a trait of *emotionality,* the amygdala seems a promising candidate, for all of the reasons given in chapter 4. Although aggression is regulated by some amydaloid nuclei, others seem to be intimately involved in fear. As Aggleton and Mishkin (1986) and LeDoux (1987) propose, the amygdala is ideally situated to assign emotional significance to stimuli from all sensory modalities and send outputs to all of the major centers (Figure 10.3) mediating both reward (positive emotion) and punishment (negative emotion). LeDoux (1987), however, points out that there are direct pathways between the thalamus and amygdala that would allow emotional reactions to stimuli before they have reached the cortex or hippocampus for more elaborate (cognitive) processing (Figure 10.4).

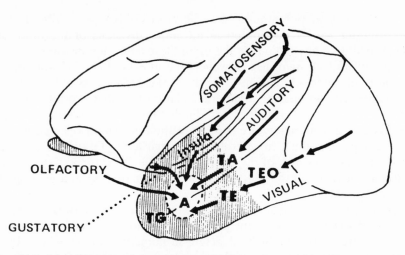

Figure 10.3. Schematization of the sensory pathways to the amygdala. The shaded areas designate the various sensory pathways' final cortical stations, which are the sources of direct amygdaloid afferents. Abbreviations: A = amygdala; TA = superior temporal cortex; TE = anterior portion of the inferior temporal cortex; TEO = posterior portion of the inferior temporal cortex; TG = temporal polar cortex. (From "The amygdala: Sensory gateway to the emotions," by J. P. Aggleton and M. Mishkin, 1986, in R. Plutchik and H. Kellerman (Eds.), *Emotion: Theory, research and experience*, vol. 3, p. 286. New York: Academic Press. Copyright by Academic Press. Reprinted by permission.)

Amygdala neurons respond preferentially to novel stimuli compared with familiar stimuli and to emotionally significant stimuli compared with neutral stimuli. Some neurons respond preferentially to stimuli with positive and some to stimuli with negative affective significance. Thus, the amygdala seems to serve at least part of the comparator function that Gray has assigned to the septohippocampal system.

Theorists have emphasized specific emotions that are disrupted by amygdaloid lesions. Davis (1986) focuses on the role of the amygdala in the fear-potentiated startle response as a model for anxiety. Gray (1982) suggests that the amygdala is a site for a fight-or-flight mechanism and the primary basis for the P dimension of personality. Kling and Stelkis (1986) have emphasized the loss of social behavior and emotions after lesioning the amygdala, suggesting that together with the temporal cortex it provides the basis for affiliative behavior (E-sociability). But as Aggleton and Mishkin (1986) point out, the amygdalectomy interferes with all kinds of emotional responses and produces an animal that is fearless, passive, unsocial, and withdrawn. Emotional responses can still be elicited by direct stimulation of emotional centers in these primates, and split-brain studies (Downer, 1961) have shown that the emotional stimuli directed to the intact hemisphere elicit emotional responses whereas those directed to the operated side do not. The function of the amygdala seems to be to integrate

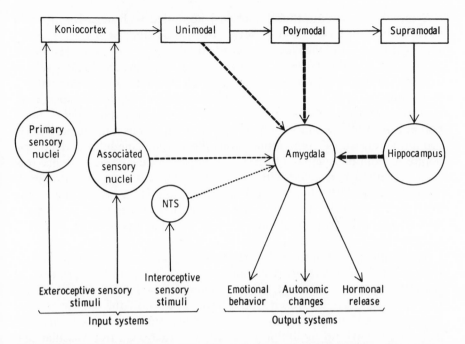

Figure 10.4. Sensory projections to amygdala and emotional evaluation. Amygdala receives inputs from various exteroceptive and interoceptive sensory modalities (*dashed lines*). Density of *dashed input lines* to amygdala signifies extent to which sensory signal is processed before reaching the amygdala. Inputs arriving from various cortical association fields have been transformed more than inputs arriving directly from thalamus or nucleus tractus solitarii (NTS). Different inputs may mediate unique aspects of emotional processing, each capable of initiating changes in emotional behavior and autonomic and humoral (hormonal) activity. (From "Emotion," by J. E. LeDoux, 1987, in *Handbook of physiology: The nervous system,* V, p. 437, F. Plum, Ed. Bethesda, MD: American Physiological Society. Copyright 1987 by American Physiological Society. Reprinted by permission.)

stimuli from all of the senses and to respond to them in terms of their emotional significance.

At the extreme of amygdaloid hyperfunction one would expect to find both fearful and angry emotional traits. Labile or intense positive emotional response are less often identified as neurotic, though we do sometimes see them in the histrionic or borderline personality disorders or the euphoria of the cyclothymic or hypomanic disorders. Why is the N dimension so closely identified with negative emotionality rather than with unstable positive emotionality? Generally, negative emotions are more intense in terms of their association with high levels of autonomic arousal. Only the peak of sexual arousal approaching or during orgasm rivals the intensity of physiological arousal of a panic attack or the fury of intense anger. Lower levels of sexual stimulation elicit more parasympathetic than sympathetic system arousal (Zuckerman, 1983b).

Sympathetic system arousal is closely identified with negative affect in the anxiety disorders. The more severe or chronic kinds of anxiety disorder show evidence of higher levels of sympathetic arousal (SCL or HR) than normals in nonstimulation conditions. However, elevated tonic levels of arousal are not usually seen in high N subjects from normal populations or in those anxiety disorders in which the anxiety response is specific to narrow stimulus conditions such as animal phobias or fear of heights. Sympathetic arousal is produced in part by adrenergic arousal in the periphery, primarily release of epinephrine from the adrenal medulla and norepinephrine from the sympathetic nerve endings. There is some evidence that such activity is correlated with, if not a function of, central adrenergic arousal, particularly that of the noradrenergic system originating in the locus coeruleus. The amygdala has connections with the LC so that the arousal effects of amygdaloid activity may be mediated by the LC-DANB system.

The problem of identifying the pathways of anxiety in the central nervous system is one of separating distal and proximal causes of the various, and sometimes poorly correlated, response phenomena defining the construct. Davis, Hitchcock, and Rosen (1987) have shown how the various projections from the amygdala may control various specific effects of anxiety, including behavioral inhibition in a conflict situation, cardiovascular and respiratory arousal, increased startle reflex, the typical facial fear expression, and the increased vigilance controlled by norepinephrine from the LC and dopamine from the ventral tegmental area. If one looked at only one of these responses, one might conclude that the crucial brain area for anxiety was the LC or the central grey, or whatever. But one must move further back along the pathways to find the distal sources of the generalized response. That would bring us closer to cortical areas such as the temporal lobes and orbitofrontal cortex, both of which project to the amygdala. Both the orbitofrontal cortex and the hippocampus have reciprocal connections with the amygdala, so the two systems may well interact in the reactions to signals associated with punishment. The frontal cortex and hippocampus may be more involved in the generalized expectancy process, drawing on memories of past events, whereas the amygdala may respond more to the simpler conditioned aspects of the signals. LeDoux (1987) points out that amygdala lesions consistently interfere with performance in tests of classically conditioned fear or anxiety, and lesions of the septohippocampal system have equivocal effects. The frontal cortical septohippocampal system may elaborate on emotional significance of stimuli and therefore modify emotional reactions regulated by the amygdala, but this system may be more devoted to the regulation of approach-avoidance or disinhibition-inhibition of behavior in terms of past experiences. Reciprocally, amygdala activity may modify the approach-avoidance mechanism in terms of conditioned emotional responses.

Reiman et al. (1989), using positron emission tomography (PET) on panic disorders and controls before and after lactate infusion have shown that the PD patients who do panic show significant increases in regional blood flow in the bilateral temperopolar cortex as well as deeper limbic structures. Although nearly all of the sensory and associational cortex may play some role in analyzing stimuli, a special pathway involved in fearful stimuli may lie in the temporal lobe input and its projection to the amygdala.

E-sociability

The first expression of the E dimension in earliest infancy may be in activity level. Extraverts tend to be more active persons than introverts, not necessarily in gross motor movement but in terms of number of activities undertaken, a particular emphasis on social activities, and a greater tendency to shift from one activity to another. Another salient feature of *extraversion* is the active pursuit of reward, again largely through other people but generally with an optimistic attitude toward the outcome. Extraverts are not necessarily indifferent or insensitive to the possibility of punishment as are psychopaths and some sensation seekers.

Ball and Zuckerman (1990) developed a scale designed to assess generalized reward and punishment expectancies (GRAPES). *Extraversion* correlated positively with *reward expectancy* but not at all with *punishment expectancy* (Table 10.1). N correlated positively with *punishment expectancy* and less so and negatively with *reward expectancy*. The results do not fit Gray's model very well if we can equate generalized expectancies of reward and punishment to sensitivities to stimuli associated with reward and punishment. That model would predict that E, related to the balance between reward and punishment sensitivities, would correlate positively with *reward expectancy* and negatively with *punishment expectancy*. It would also predict that N would correlate positively with *reward* as well as *punishment expectancy*. Because P is thought to be related to the tendency to respond to unconditioned punishment (pain) or termination of reward (frustration) with either aggression or flight, not much can be predicted about its role in generalized expectancies. But as described in chapter 9, high P antisocial types seem somewhat indifferent to prospects of pain, and pain is a poor motivator of learned inhibition for them. P did not correlate with either type of generalized expectancy in the questionnaire. *Sensation seeking* tended to correlate negatively with *punishment expectancy*.

The studies of Newman et al. (1985) have also shown an insensitivity of extraverts to punishment but only when punishment is combined with possible reward. It is as if extraverts are so strongly reward oriented that they cannot attend to the possibilities of punishment when both possibilities

Table 10.1. *Correlations between GRAPES reward and punishment expectancy and SSS total, EPQ, and SAT scales*

			n	Original correlations		SS partialled out	
				Reward	Punishment	Reward	Punishment
SSS Total			139	$.24^b$	$-.41^d$	—	—
EPQ E	All	Ss	125	$.50^d$	$-.27^c$	$.45^c$	$-.04$
	Hi	SS	64	$.51^d$	$-.02$		
	Low	SS	61	$.40^c$	$-.12$		
EPQ N	All	Ss	125	$-.26^b$	$.36^d$	$-.25^b$	$.36^d$
	Hi	SS	64	$-.27^a$	$.34^b$		
	Low	SS	61	$-.23^a$	$.40^c$		
EPQ P	All	Ss	125	$-.01$	$-.20^a$	$-.19^a$	$-.02$
	Hi	SS	64	$-.27^a$	$-.04$		
	Low	SS	61	$.01$	$.12$		
EPQ L	All	Ss	125	$-.08$	$.07$	$.03$	$-.13$
	Hi	SS	64	$.19$	$-.15$		
	Low	SS	61	$-.07$	$-.12$		
SAT (V+Q)	All	Ss	137	$.11$	$-.23$	$.06$	$-.15$
	Hi	SS	65	$.09$	$-.14$		
	Low	SS	72	$.05$	$-.27^c$		
GRAPES Reward expectancy			125	—	$-.27^c$	—	$-.20^a$

$^a p < .05$
$^b p < .01$
$^c p < .001$
$^d p < .0001$

are present. Of course, the same is true for the psychopath who is also extraverted (primary type). In the case of the extraverted psychopath heightened sensitivity to reward may be a less important factor than the insensitivity to punishment.

The combination of high activity levels and strong reward expectancy in the psychopath suggest that whatever mediates these two tendencies at the biological level may be an important part of the makeup of the extravert and introvert. Moderate doses of amphetamine increase the desire to socialize and the time spent in social talking in an experimental situation (Heishman & Stitzer, 1988). These results are contrary to Eysenck's theory, which suggests that stimulants should increase arousal and therefore make people more introverted. Secobarbitol had the same social stimulant effect in this study, consistent with Eysenck's theory of the extraverting effects of depressant drugs, but the effect was more short lived than that of amphetamine.

Three systems mediated by the neurotransmitter dopamine are implicated in both activity and reward sensitivity (see Figure 5.6). These three cell groups with long fibers and diffuse forebrain projections are A8 caudate

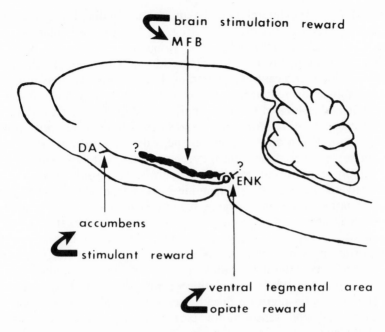

brain stimulation reward
MFB

DA

?

?

ENK

accumbens

stimulant reward

ventral tegmental area
opiate reward

Figure 10.5. Proposed brain reward circuitry (Bozarth). Nucleus accumbens is the target of psychomotor stimulant reward, and ventral tegmentum initiates reward action of opiates. The ventral tegmental action of opiates probably involves enkephalingergic system (ENK) whose anatomical location is not yet identified. Brain stimulation reward activates descending mylenated fibers within the medial forebrain bundle (MFB), which transsynaptically activate the ascending dopamine (DA) system. (From "Ventral tegmental reward system," by M. A. Bozarth, 1987, in *Brain reward systems and abuse*, p. 13, J. Engel et al., Eds. New York: Raven Press. Copyright 1987 by Raven Press. Reprinted by permission.)

nucleus (CN), A9 substantia nigra (SN), pars compacta, and A10 ventral tegmental (VT) area. The SN connections are regarded as involved in the initiation of motor activity and the VT area as concerned with the reward mechanism. However, as Stellar and Stellar (1985) point out, both the SN and CN also support electrical brain self-stimulation, and there are extensive interconnections between SN and VT systems. At the behavioral level there is certainly an association between activity and reward because reward stimuli tend to increase activity and much activity is goal-directed in search of reward (foraging), including the reward of novel stimulation (sensation seeking).

The brain self-stimulation and drug-infusion experiments using rats have been useful in identifying the particular areas of the brain and the neurotransmitters involved in biological reward processes (Bozarth, 1987). Figure 10.5 shows a model proposed by Bozarth. Although self-stimulation may be obtained from electrodes planted in many parts of the brain, including prefrontal cortex and septum, the highest rates of response are obtained from the lateral hypothalamus and medial forebrain bundle (MFB). Analyses of the effects of drugs on brain self-stimulation and of responses for direct brain infusion of drugs have shown that brain self-stimulation is both driven and reinforced by dopamine release in the nucleus accumbens and ventral tegmentum. The use of the term *reinforcement* is not simply an overextension of a behavioral referent to a neurochemical one. Stein and Beluzzi (1987) have shown that dopamine and the dopamine agonist cocaine can reinforce firing rates of single neuronal cells in vitro!

Brain stimulation does not directly activate the dopamine systems but acts on some other neurotransmitter, as yet unidentified, with descending, rapidly transmitting, myelinated neurons within the MFB. These in turn activate the ascending dopamine system from the nucleus accumbens. Amphetamine and cocaine reward is mediated by dopamine in the nucleus accumbens (Fibriger & Phillips, 1987). Opiate reward occurs in the ventral tegmental (VT) dopamine area. Intracranial self-administration of morphine is sustained in the VT but not in the periventricular gray, lateral hypothalamic area, nucleus accumbens, or the caudate (Bozarth, 1987). Stimulation of both the ventral tegmental area and the substantia nigra produced alterations of glucose metabolism in the prefrontal and sensorimotor cortex, nucleus accumbens, medialdorsal thalamus, and lateral septum, indicating that these areas are involved in the production and maintenance of behavior that is positively reinforced (Porrino, 1987).

Interestingly, both stimulant and depressant drugs act through dopamine-dependent systems, though at different loci. This offers a possible resolution of the paradox that high sensation seekers may abuse both stimulant and opiate-depressant drugs. The common need satisfied by both may be activation of dopamine systems. Extraverts may already have dopamine systems with sufficient levels of activity to sustain high levels of activity and reward pursuit without the need for drugs. However, sensation seekers who are particularly prone to use drugs may have lower levels of tonic activity in the dopaminergic systems and therefore use drugs and seek intense and novel stimulation to increase activity in this system. Some of the activity in the dopaminergic systems may be enhanced by agonistic arousal produced by the noradrenergic system originating in the locus coeruleus in response to such stimulation. The noradrenergic system may amplify all behavioral systems including those involved in approach and avoidance. Dopamine or norepinephrine metabolites are unlikely to reveal these tonic or phasic relationships of dopaminergic activity to *extraversion* and *sensation seeking*. The neurochemically selective dopamine PET scan may eventually be used to test these hypotheses.

Although dopamine is necessary for both reward-seeking activity and reinforcement, it is difficult to specify the precise nature of the dopamine-personality relationship. Extraverts and sensation seekers might seek stimulation because of a tonically overactive system, or they might seek it because of an underactive one. The compensation theory of arousal and personality (Eysenck, 1967) suggests that tonically underaroused persons seek stimuli to bring arousal up to an optimal level. Those already near their optimal levels do not seek varied intense stimulation because further stimulation would push them over their optimal level into a range in which euphoria turns to anxiety and positive sociability to withdrawal or hostile aggression.

This author has suggested that *sensation seeking* and other traits including *sociability* and *anxiety* depend on an optimal level of catecholamine system activity (Zuckerman, 1984a). In the case of reward and activity this would mean that those behavioral traits are optimal at some intermediate level of dopamine activity. Similarly, opioids are reinforcing at intermediate levels, as suggested by self-administration studies (Koob, Vaccarino, Amalric, & Bloom, 1987). Rats self-inject heroin and cocaine in inverse proportion to the dosage above their baseline dose, showing the need to maintain some optimal level of the drugs rather than increasing dosage to a maximum. The same is true for opiate self-administration in which an inverted-U shaped relationship is found between rate of responding and drug dosage (Young, Woods, Herling, & Hein, 1983). Low doses of beta-endorphins increase social contacts of rats, whereas higher doses may reduce their sociability (Van Ree, Niesink, & Resnick, 1983). These effects are like those of alcohol, of which low doses increase and high doses decrease sociability. Alcohol may actually produce its effect through actions on the opiate receptors in the brain. The concentration of beta-endorphin in the CSF of alcoholics (Genazzani et al., 1982) and sensation seekers (Johansson et al., 1979) is low. Thus, sensation seekers might be at special risk for alcoholism or opiate abuse (Zuckerman, 1987b, c) because of a low level of endorphins rather than a high level. Low levels of neurotransmitters or peptides mediating reinforcement may lead to a search for substances or activities that stimulate these systems.

Curvilinear relationships between central monoamine or neuropeptides and behavioral traits would preclude finding linear correlations between them. Demonstrating curvilinear relationships would require larger numbers of subjects than are usually used in these studies and adequate sampling from the entire range of personality. Experimental drug studies, however, strongly suggest the existence of curvilinear relationships. Conceivably, levels of brain dopamine, for instance, might be at optimal intermediate levels in extraverts but at very low or very high levels in introverts. The low levels might be characteristic of introverts who are anhedonic, whereas the high levels might be characteristic of introverts who are also highly anxious.

How do we proceed?

It would be ideal if neuropsychological systems lined up perfectly with the psychologically defined dimensions of personality described in chapter 1. If this were the case, a bottom-up approach, such as that suggested by Gray (1982, in press) would work. But for the reasons given previously, such neat isomorphism is unlikely. Gray has attempted to define new dimensions of personality involving various combinations of Eysenck's three supertraits. This author has pointed out some of the difficulties associated with this approach, particularly when we move to the human level; for instance, the fact that human anxiety neurotics and psychopaths are not really opposites but seem to represent the extremes of two separate dimensions. Furthermore, the interdependence of many of the biological systems precludes their use as dimensions to serve as criteria for psychological dimensions.

We should start from the top and work down, using the well-established psychological factors and considering how various biological systems may be involved in one or more of them. Because simple one-to-one isomorphism is unlikely, we should use the more precisely defined psychological trait dimensions as our reference axes.

Because biological systems mediate adaptive behavior patterns, it is likely that many of them will be found to be more closely related to narrower traits than the three supertraits. We have seen that traits such as *impulsivity* (of the narrow kind) and *sensation seeking* (of the disinhibition type) are more directly related to physiological factors such as augmenting of the cortical EP and biochemical factors such as gonadal hormones than are the broader traits like P. This poses no problem in a hierarchal model of traits. However, we would not want arbitrarily to realign the principal axes of personality dimensions through the points defined by these narrower traits. For one thing, that would ignore the fact that other significant biological factors are aligned more directly with the supertraits, like the relationship between the serotonin metabolite 5-HIAA and the P scale marker for the P dimension. For another, the functional significance of the correlations between physiological and personality traits are poorly understood. The relation of *disinhibition* or *impulsivity* with cortical augmenting-reducing, for instance, may be an epiphenomena of some more fundamental difference in brain functioning, or it might represent an adaptive mechanism directly related to the personality trait. In the future new biological functions that are more directly related to personality are likely to be discovered.

More important than prematurely redrawing the map of personality is the task of understanding the relationships among the psychobiological phenomena at each level. With present data, it appears that enzymes such as MAO and DBH show the strongest genetic determination. Does this mean that they are more central to the understanding of the biological basis of personality than the neurotransmitters that they regulate? This author's earlier view was that the enzymes were of little significance themselves, compared with the characteristic levels of activity in the neurotransmitter systems they regulate. Yet the most consistent findings relate the enzymes, rather than the neurotransmitters (or their metabolites), to personality. This may simply reflect the inadequacy of the current methods for assaying neurochemical brain activity from peripheral transmitters, hormones, and metabolites. But another possibility is that the regulation process involving the production and catabolism of the neurotransmitters is more essential than the fluctuating levels of the neurotransmitter activity itself. The activity in a system at any given time may reflect more of the situation and less of the person than the regulative processes that return the system to a characteristic homeostatic level.

An interesting area of potential development is the role of neurotransmitter systems in psychophysiological phenomena. How does the central adrenergic system regulate the peripheral autonomic arousal? Data certainly show effects of negative or positive stress in raising peripheral levels of catecholamines. What are the specific central neurochemical mechanisms that trigger this arousal, and what makes one person likely to show more peripheral signs of arousal than another? The answer to this question may help finally to define the psychobiology of the N dimension, which has so far eluded us.

Another field of needed immediate investigation is the effect of central neurotransmitters and enzymes on the augmenting or reducing of the cortical EP. The correlational data suggest some role of the enzymes MAO and DBH and the neurotransmitter serotonin in reducing. What would be the effect on augmenting-reducing of infusing neurotransmitters or receptor blockers directly into areas of the brain prior to cortical stimulation? Would serotonin, for instance, dampen cortical responsivity to higher intensities of stimuli?

Moving up one level, the assessment of the significance of the psychophysiological responses in behavioral traits underlying personality traits is another area in need of research. The approach to personality through emotions has been popular, but an alternative paradigm lies in the cognitive investigation of the phenomena of attention and memory. Investigators of the psychophysiology of cognitive mechanisms have largely ignored individual differences. The orienting reflex and later components of the EP are important markers for attentional processes and have been shown to be related to aspects of personality. An approach combining all three areas could tell us precisely how personality types differ in their styles of cognitive processing. As an example, this author has suggested that the sensation seeker's psychophysiology is devoted to focused attention on novel stimuli whereas the low sensation seeker has a more defensive psychophysiological style, turning to cognition in the face of novel and intense stimuli instead of allocating attentional resources to further extraction of information from the external stimulus (Zuckerman, 1990a). The former mechanism is associated with approach and the latter with withdrawal. But to investigate information processing and personality we need more than isolated studies of a particular cognitive phenomenon. Revelle, Anderson, and Humphreys (1987) have provided an exemplary model for investigating this area. Concentrating on the trait of *impulsivity,* they have shown how the trait is related to information processing according to the short- and long-term memory loads and the sustained information-transfer load. These three dimensions of cognition are related to a generalized arousal theory as an explanation of the role of impulsivity.

It is hoped that the reader understands that the concentration on the biological approach to personality in this book does not indicate an indifference to the powerful role of social learning in shaping personality. The results of behavior genetics studies, however, suggest that: (a) we must look outside of the immediate family to discover the primary sources of social learning that are ultimately important in much of personality, (b) we must understand that learning is selective and that individual differences exist in choice of learning situations and what we attend to and store in memory from experience, and (c) our capacity to recall and use what is learned. The social learning approach to personality has generally ignored individual differences. The exposure of a generally aggressive child and a shy inhibited one to a model exhibiting aggression probably does not produce the same learning and performance. So far, the approach has produced many demonstrations of the situational influences on imitation from which the generalization is made that this is the way more consistent social behavior is learned. There are signs that social learning theorists are beginning to concede the usefulness of trait constructs. As an example, we have Mischel's (Mischel et al., 1988) discovery that delay of gratification can actually predict broad patterns of behavior in adolescents years after their assessment as children.

As social-learning personality psychologists venture into the field of individual differences, they naturally favor particular cognitive traits, with little concern for how these kinds of traits fit into a broader trait approach derived from theoretical models. Incapacity to delay gratification has been regarded as a basic characteristic of *impulsivity* and *psychopathy.* How does the assessment of this narrow trait in childhood predict the broader traits and personality disorders?

Conversely, broad trait psychologists have generally neglected the cognitive styles that may characterize introverts and extraverts, high and low sensation seekers, and other broad trait extremes. They have also not been very active in testing the predictive power of traits in social learning or "game" situations. It is to be hoped that the years ahead will witness a convergence of trait and social-learning approaches to personality.

Many readers probably started reading this book with skepticism, assuming that a psychobiological approach is a contradiction in terms given the present state of knowledge in the neurosciences. These readers may finish the book confirmed in their skepticism, but it is hoped they are convinced that there is enough theory and data for a beginning. Of course, our models tend to be somewhat loosely constructed, tying together findings from personality studies, biological psychiatry, the comparative neurosciences, behavior genetics, psychophysiology, and behavioral learning studies. All of these connections among disciplines rest on a somewhat shaky foundation of assumptions, such as those about the adequacy of certain animal models.

More ideologically receptive readers may have started the book with undue faith in the establishment of a stable biological basis for personality and an accepted paradigm for the psychobiology of personality. If they have persevered through these chapters, they may be disappointed because the promise of the volume title seems less than fulfilled. They should accept the fact that biological science is not and cannot be simple at the human level. Even when the entire DNA scroll is unrolled and deciphered, the mystery of how these simple enzymes make a mind and a personality (or even a thought and a trait) will be far from solved. But complexity is no reason to abandon a field of science. Those who fear complexity and uncertainty should avoid science and study religious or political doctrine. Yesterday's scientific theories are usually confounded by today's data.

What makes one optimistic about the field is looking back several decades and appreciating the fact that most of the research described in this book comes from the last 10 years. Considering the explosion of research in the neurosciences and the cross-disciplinary interests of so many neuroscientists, psychiatrists, and personality psychologists, one can expect that progress in the psychobiology of personality will be rapid. What the next century, or even 20 years, may bring is almost beyond imagination. One can only hope that personality psychologists will not still be arguing about how many basic trait factors there are, whether behavior is consistent, or whether there is such a thing as personality. It is to be hoped that books on personality will not be devoting most of their space to century-old psychoanalytic theories with essentially untestable constructs and no real empirical basis. On the biological side, it is to be hoped that we will be talking less about hypothetical nervous systems and more about real ones.

The beauty of a psychobiological approach is that progress in understanding biological structure and function is not only possible but is inevitable. Without a foundation in biological science, psychology is doomed to an endless exchange of one set of faddish hypothetical constructs for another. The current paradigm shift from the narrow behavioral to the cognitive has filled Skinner's "empty boxes" with flow charts, but it still leaves one unsatisfied in the quest for a solid basis for psychological science. Hypothetical constructs will always play a role in psychology, as in other sciences, but psychobiology offers us the prospect of making some of the imaginal tangible. Even to a cynic like this author, that is truly an elegant magic.

References

Abeelen, J. H. F., van (1977). Rearing responses and locomotor activity in mice: Single locus control. *Behavioral Biology, 19,* 401–404.

Adolfsson, R., Gottfries, C. G., Oreland, L., Roos, B. E., & Winblad, B. (1978). Monoamine oxidase activity and serotogenic turnover in human brain. *Progress in Neuropsychopharmacology, 2,* 225–230.

Aggleton, J. P., & Mishkin, M. (1986). The amygdala: Sensory gateway to the emotions. In R. Plutchik & H. Kellerman (Eds.), *Emotion: Theory, research, and experience* (vol. 3, pp. 281–299). New York: Academic Press.

Ahern, F. M., Johnson, R. C., Wilson, J. R., McClearn, G. E., & Vandenberg, S. G. (1982). Family resemblance in personality. *Behavior Genetics, 12,* 261–280.

Allport, G. W. (1937). *Personality: A psychological interpretation.* New York: Holt.

Allport, G. W. (1961). *Pattern and growth in personality.* New York: Holt, Rinehart, & Winston.

Allport, G. W., & Odbert, H. S. (1936). Trait names: A psycholexical study. *Psychological Monographs, 47* (Whole No. 211).

Anderson, K. E., Lytton, H., & Romney, D. M. (1986). Mothers interactions with normal and conduct-disordered boys: Who affects whom? *Developmental Psychology, 22,* 604–609.

Anderson, K. J. (1990). Arousal and the Inverted-U hypothesis: A critique of Neiss's "Reconceptualizing arousal." *Psychological Bulletin, 107,* 96–100.

Andy, O. J., & Jurko, M. F. (1972). Thalotomy for hyperresponsive syndrome: Lesions in the centermedianum and intraluminar nuclei. In E. Hitchcock, L. Laitinen, & K. Vaernet (Eds.), *Psychosurgery* (pp. 127–135). Springfield, IL: Charles C. Thomas.

Annard, B. K., & Brobeck, J. R. (1951). Hypothalamic control of food intake in rats and cats. *Yale Journal of Biology and Medicine, 24,* 123–140.

Arana, G. W., & Baldesserini, R. J. (1987). Clinical use of the dexamethasone suppression test in psychiatry. In H. Y. Meltzer (Ed.), *Psychopharmacology: The third generation of progress* (pp. 607–615). New York: Raven Press.

Arqué, J. M., Unzeta, M., & Torrubia, R. (1988). Neurotransmitter systems and personality variables. *Neuropsychobiology, 19,* 149–157.

Arrindell, W. A., & van der Ende, J. (1986). Further evidence for cross-sample invariance of phobic factors: Psychiatric inpatient ratings on the Fear Survey Schedule III. *Behavior Research and Therapy, 24,* 289–297.

Ashton, C. H., Golding, J. F., Marsh, V. R., & Thompson, J. W. (1985). Somatosensory evoked potentials and personality. *Personality and Individual Differences, 6,* 141–143.

Aston-Jones, G., & Bloom, F. E. (1981). Norepinephrine-containing Locus Coeruleus neurons in behaving rats exhibit pronounced responses to non-noxious environmental stimuli. *The Journal of Neuroscience, 8,* 887–900.

Ax, A. F. (1953). The physiological differentiation between fear and anger in humans. *Psychosomatic Medicine, 14,* 433–442.

Bailey, K. G. (1987). *Human paleopsychology applications to aggression.* Hillsdale, NJ: Erlbaum.

Bales, R. F. (1946). Cultural differences in rates of alcoholism. *Quarterly Journal of Studies on Alcohol, 6,* 480–489.

429

Ball, L., Farnell, D., & Wangeman, J. (1983). Factorial invariance across sex of the form V of the Sensation Seeking Scale. *Journal of Personality and Social Psychology, 45,* 1156–1159.

Ball, S. A., & Zuckerman, M. (1990). Sensation seeking, Eysenck's personality dimensions and reinforcement sensitivity in concept formation. *Personality and Individual Differences, 11,* 343–353.

Ballenger, J. C. (1986). Pharmacotherapy of the panic disorders. *Journal of Clinical Psychiatry, 47* (6 Suppl.), 27–32.

Ballenger, J. C., Burrows, G. D., Du Pont, R. L., Lesser, I. M., Noyes, R., Pecknold, J. C., Rifkin, A., & Swinson, R. P. (1988). Alprazolam in panic disorder and agoraphobia: Results from a multicentral trial: I. Efficacy in short-term treatment. *Archives of General Psychiatry, 45,* 413–422.

Ballenger, J. C., Post, R. M., Jimerson, D. C., Lake, C. R., Murphy, D. L., Zuckerman, M., & Cronin, C. (1983). Biochemical correlates of personality traits in normals: An exploratory study. *Personality and Individual Differences, 4,* 615–625.

Balon, R., Ortiz, A., Pohl, R., & Yeragani, V. K. (1988). Heart rate and blood pressure during placebo-associated panic attacks. *Psychosomatic Medicine, 50,* 434–438.

Balon, R., Pohl, R., Yergani, V. K., Rainey, J., & Oxenkrug, G. F. (1987). Platelet serotonin levels in panic disorder. *Acta Psychiatrica Scandinavica, 75,* 315–317.

Bancroft, J., Tennent, G., Loucas, & Cass, J. (1974). The control of deviant sexual behaviour by drugs: I. Behavioral changes following estrogens and anti-androgens. *British Journal of Psychiatry, 125,* 310–315.

Bandura, A. (1965). Influence of models' reinforcement contingencies on the acquisition of imitative responses. *Journal of Personality and Social Psychology, 1,* 589–595.

Bandura, A. (1977). *Social learning theory.* Engelwood Cliffs, NJ: Prentice-Hall.

Bandura, A. (1986). *Social foundations of thought and action: A social cognitive theory.* Englewood Cliffs, NJ: Prentice-Hall.

Barratt, E. S. (1971). Psychophysiological correlates of classical differential eyelid conditioning among subjects selected on the basis of impulsivity and anxiety. *Biological Psychiatry, 3,* 339–346.

Barratt, E. S., Pritchard, W. S., Faulk, D. M., & Brandt, M. E. (1987). The relationship between impulsiveness subtraits, trait anxiety, and visual N100-augmenting-reducing: A topographic analysis. *Personality and Individual Differences, 8,* 43–51.

Baucom, D. H., Beach, P. K., & Callahan, S. (1985). Relation between testosterone concentration, sex role identity and personality among females. *Journal of Personality and Social Psychology, 48,* 1218–1226.

Bauer, G. P., Schlottmann, R. S., Bates, J. V., & Masters, M. A. (1983). Effect of state and trait anxiety and prestige of model on imitation. *Psychological Reports, 52,* 375–382.

Beach, F. A. (1947). Evolutionary changes in the physiological control of mating behavior in mammals. *Psychological Review, 54,* 297–315.

Beck, A. T. (1985). *Depression: Causes and treatment.* Philadelphia, PA: Univ. of Pennsylvania Press.

Becker, W. C. (1960). The matching of behavior rating and questionnaire personality factors. *Psychological Bulletin, 57,* 201–212.

Beidel, D. C., Turner, S. M., & Dancu, C. V. (1985). Physiological, cognitive and behavioral aspects of social anxiety. *Behavior Research and Therapy, 23,* 109–117.

Bell, R., & Hepper, P. G. (1987). Catecholamines and aggression in animals. *Behavioural Brain Research, 23,* 1–21.

Bem, D. J., & Allen, A. (1974). On predicting some of the people some of the time: The search for cross-cultural consistencies in behavior. *Psychological Review, 81,* 506–520.

Berg, I. I. M., McGuire, R., & Lipsedge, M. (1974). School phobia and agoraphobia. *Psychological Medicine, 4,* 428–434.

Bernstein, I. S., Gordon, T. P., & Rose, R. M. (1983). The interaction of hormones, behavior, and social context in nonhuman primates. In B. B. Svare (Ed.), *Hormones and aggressive behavior* (pp. 535–561). New York: Plenum Press.

Beyts, J., Frcka, I. M., Martin, I., & Levey, A. B. (1983). The influence of psychoticism and extraversion on classical eyelid conditioning using a paraorbital shock UCS. *Personality and Individual Differences, 4,* 275–283.

Biederman, J., Munir, K., & Knee, D. (1987). Conduct and oppositional disorder in clinically referred children with attention deficit disorder: A controlled family study. *Journal of the American Academy of Child and Adolescent Psychiatry, 26,* 724–727.

Biederman, J., Rosenbaum, S. V., Bolduc, E. A., Gersten, M., Meminger, S. R., Kagan, J., Snidman, N., & Reznick, J. S. (1990). Psychiatric correlates of behavioral inhibition in young children of parents with and without psychiatric disorders. *Archives of General Psychiatry, 47,* 21–26.

Birenbaum, M. (1986). On the construct validity of the sensation seeking scale in a non-English speaking culture. *Personality and Individual Differences, 7,* 431–434.

Bishop, D. V. M. (1977). The P scale and psychosis. *Journal of Abnormal Psychology, 86,* 127–134.

Black, A. W. (1975). Unilateral brain lesions and MMPI performance: A preliminary study. *Perceptual and Motor Skills, 40,* 87–93.

Black, J. D. (1953). *The interpretation of MMPI profiles of college women.* Doctoral dissertation, University of Minnesota.

Blackburn, R. (1978). Electrodermal and cardiovascular correlates of psychopathy. In R. D. Hare & D. Schalling (Eds.), *Psychopathic behaviour: Approaches to research* (pp. 157–164). New York: Wiley.

Blackburn, R. (1979). Cortical and autonomic arousal in primary and secondary psychopaths. *Psychophysiology, 16,* 143–150.

Blackemore, C. B. (1967). Personality and brain damage. In H. J. Eysenck (Ed.), *The biological basis of personality* (pp. 319–339). Springfield, IL: Charles C. Thomas.

Bland, R., & Orn, H. (1986). Family violence and psychiatric disorder. *Canadian Journal of Psychology, 31,* 129–137.

Block, J. (1971). *Lives through time.* Berkeley, CA: Bancroft.

Block, J. (1977a). The Eysencks and psychoticism. *Journal of Abnormal Psychology, 86,* 653–654.

Block, J. (1977b). P scale and psychosis: Continued concerns. *Journal of Abnormal Psychology, 86,* 431–434.

Block, J. (1977c). Advancing the psychology of personality: Paradigmatic shift or improving the quality of research. In D. Magnusson & N. S. Endler (Eds.), *Personality at the crossroads: Current issues in interactional psychology* (pp. 37–64). Hillsdale, NJ: Erlbaum.

Block, J. (1989). Critique of the act frequency approach to personality. *Journal of Personality and Social Psychology, 56,* 234–245.

Bohman, M., Cloninger, C. R., Sigvardsson, S., & von Knorring, L. (1982). Predisposition to petty criminality in Swedish adoptees: I. Genetic and environmental heterogeneity. *Archives of General Psychiatry, 39,* 1233–1241.

Bohman, M., Cloninger, R., von Knorring, A. L., & Sigvardsson, S. (1984). An adoption study of somatoform disorders: III. Cross-fostering and genetic relationship to alcoholism and criminality. *Archives of General Psychiatry, 41,* 872–878.

Bolles, R. C. (1970). Species specific defense reactions and avoidance learning. *Psychological Review, 71,* 32–48.

Boomsa, D. I., & Plomin, R. (1986). Heart rate and behavior of twins. *Merrill Palmer Quarterly, 32,* 141–151.

Born, J., Hitzler, V., Pietrowsky, R., Pauschinger, P., & Fehm, H. L. (1988). Influences of cortisol on auditory evoked potentials (AEPs) and mood in humans. *Neuropsychobiology, 20,* 145–151.

Bouchard, T. J., Lykken, D. T., Segal, N. L., & Wilcox, K. J. (1986). Development in twins reared apart: A test of the chromogenetic hypothesis. In A. Demirjian (Ed.), *Human growth: A multidimensional review*. London: Taylor and Francis.

Bower, G. H., & Miller, N. E. (1958). Rewarding and punishing effects from stimulating the same place in the rat's brain. *Journal of Comparative and Physiological Psychology, 51,* 669–674.

Bozarth, M. A. (1987). Ventral tegmental reward system. In J. Engel, L. Oreland, B. Pernov, S. Rössner, & L. A. Pellborn (Eds.), *Brain reward systems and abuse* (pp. 1–17). New York: Raven Press.

Brackett, N. L., Iuvone, P. M., & Edwards, D. A. (1986). Midbrain lesions, dopamine, and male sexual behavior. *Behavioural Brain Research, 20,* 231–240.

Braestrup, C., Nielson, M., & Olsen, C. E. (1980). Urinary and brain β-carboline–3-carboxylates as potent inhibitors of brain benzodiazepine receptors. *Proceedings of the National Academy of Science, 77,* 2288–2292.

Brain, P. F. (1983). Pituitary-gonadal influences on social aggression. In B. B. Svare (Ed.), *Hormones and aggressive behavior* (pp. 1–26). New York: Erlbaum.

Bremer, J. (1959). Asexualization: A follow-up study of 244 cases. New York: Macmillan.

Bridge, T. P., Kleinman, J. E., Soldo, B. J., & Karoum, F. (1987). Central catecholamines, cognitive impairment, and affective state in elderly schizophrenics and controls. *Biological Psychiatry, 22,* 139–147.

Broadhurst, A., & Glass, A. (1969). Relationship of personality measures to the alpha rhythm of the electroencephalogram. *British Journal of Psychiatry, 115,* 199–204.

Broadhurst, P. L. (1957). Determinants of emotionality in the rat: I. Situational factors. *British Journal of Psychology, 48,* 1–12.

Broadhurst, P. L. (1975). The Maudsley reactive and non-reactive strains of rats: A survey. *Behavior Genetics, 5,* 299–319.

Broca, P. (1864). Cited in S. P. Springer & G. Deutsch (Eds.), *Left brain, right brain* (pp. 9–11), San Francisco: CA: W. H. Freeman & Co.

Bronson, W. C. (1966). Central organizations: A study of behavior organization from childhood to adolescence. *Child Development, 37,* 125–155.

Bronson, W. C. (1967). Adult derivatives of emotional expressiveness and reactivity-control: Developmental continuities from childhood to adulthood. *Child Development, 38,* 801–817.

Brown, G., Ebert, M., Goyer, P. F., Jimerson, D., Klein, W., Bunney W., & Goodwin, F. (1982). Aggression, suicide, and serotonin. *American Journal of Psychiatry, 139,* 741–746.

Brown, G. L., Goodwin, F. K., Ballenger, J. C., Goyer, P. F., & Major, L. F. (1979). Aggression in humans correlates with cerebrospinal fluid amine metabolites. *Psychiatry Research, 1,* 131–139.

Buchsbaum, M. S. (1971). Neural events and the psychophysical law. *Science, 172,* 502.

Buchsbaum, M. S. (1974). Average evoked response and stimulus intensity in identical and fraternal twins. *Physiological Psychology, 2,* 365–370.

Buchsbaum, M. S., Haier, R. J., & Johnson, J. (1983). Augmenting and reducing: Individual differences in evoked potentials. In A. Gale & J. A. Edwards (Eds.), *Physiological correlates of human behavior* (vol. 3, pp. 120–138). London: Academic Press.

Buchsbaum, M. S., Hazlett, E., Sicotte, N., Stein, M., Wu, J., & Zetin, M. (1985). Topographic EEG changes with benzodiazepine administration in generalized anxiety disorder. *Biological Psychiatry, 20,* 832–842.

Buchsbaum, M. S., Landau, S., Murphy, D. L., & Goodwin, F. K. (1973). Average evoked response in bipolar and unipolar affective disorders: Relationship to sex, age of onset, and monoamine oxidase. *Biological Psychiatry, 7,* 199–212.

Buchsbaum, M. S., Muscettola, G., & Goodwin, F. K. (1981). Urinary MHPG, stress response, personality factors and somatosensory evoked potentials in normal subjects and patients with major affective disorders. *Neuropsychobiology, 7,* 212–224.

Buchsbaum, M. S., & Silverman, J. (1968). Stimulus intensity control and the cortical evoked response. *Psychosomatic Medicine, 30,* 12–22.

Buchsbaum, M. S., Wu, J., Haier, R., Hazlett, E., Bull, R., Katz, M., Sokolska, K. M., Lagunas-Solar, M., & Langer, D. (1987). Position emission tomography assessment of effects of benzodiazepines on regional glucose metabolic rate in patients with anxiety disorder. *Life Sciences, 40,* 2393–2400.

Buigues, J., & Vallejo, J. (1987). Therapeutic response to phenelzine in patients with panic disorder and agoraphobia with panic attacks. *Journal of Clinical Psychiatry, 48,* 55–59.

Burton, R. V. (1963). Generality of honesty reconsidered. *Psychological Review, 70,* 481–499.

Buss, A. H., & Plomin, R. (1975). *A temperament theory of personality development.* New York: Wiley.

Buss, A. H., & Plomin, R. (1984). *Temperament: Early developing personality traits.* Hillsdale, NJ.: Erlbaum.

Buss, A. H., Plomin, R., & Willerson, L. (1973). The inheritance of temperament. *Journal of Personality, 41,* 513–524.

Buss, D. M., Block, J. H., & Block, J. (1980). Preschool activity level: Personality correlates and developmental implications. *Child Development, 54,* 401–408.

Buss, D. M., & Craik, K. H. (1985). Why not measure that trait? Alternative criteria for identifying important dispositions. *Journal of Personality and Social Psychology, 48,* 934–946.

Buyden-Branchey, L., Branchey, M. H., Noumair, D., & Lieber, C. S. (1989). Age of alcoholism onset: II. Relationship to susceptibility to serotonin precursor availability. *Archives of General Psychiatry, 46,* 231–236.

Cadoret, R. J., & Cain, C. (1980). Sex differences in predictors of antisocial behavior in adoptees. *Archives of General Psychiatry, 37,* 1171–1175.

Cadoret, R. J., Troughton, E., O'Gorman, T. W., & Heywood, E. (1986). An adoption study of genetic and environmental factors in drug abuse. *Archives of General Psychiatry, 43,* 1131–1136.

Calhoon, L. L. (1988). Exploration into the biochemistry of sensation seeking. *Personality and Individual Differences, 9,* 941–949.

Calhoon, L. L. (unpublished) Sensation seeking, exercise and dopamine beta hydroxylase. New Mexico Highlands Univ., Las Vegas, NM 87701. Received August, 1990.

Cameron, O. G., Lee, M. A., Curtis, G. C., & McCann, D. S. (1987). Endocrine and physiological changes during "spontaneous" panic attacks. *Psychoneuroendocrinology, 12,* 321–331.

Cameron, O. G., & Nesse, R. M. (1988). Systematic hormonal and physiological abnormalities in anxiety disorders. *Psychoneuroendocrinology, 13,* 287–307.

Campbell, D. T., & Fiske, D. W. (1959). Convergent and discriminant validation by the multitrait-multimethod matrix. *Psychological Bulletin, 56,* 81–105.

Campbell, K. B., Baribeau-Braün, J., & Braün, C. (1981). Neuroanatomical and physiological foundations of extraversion. *Psychophysiology, 18,* 263–267.

Cannon, W. B. (1927). The James-Lange theory of emotions: A critical examination and an alternative theory. *American Journal of Psychology, 39,* 106–124.

Carey, G., & Gottesman, I. I. (1981). Twin and family studies of anxiety, phobic, and obsessive disorders. In D. F. Klein & J. Rabkin (Eds.), *Anxiety: New research and changing concepts* (pp. 117–134). New York: Raven Press.

Carlier, M. (1985). Factor analysis of Strelau's questionnaire and an attempt to validate some of the factors. In J. Strelau, F. H. Farley, & A. Gale (Eds.), *The biological foundations of personality and behavior* (pp. 145–160). Washington, DC: Hemisphere.

Carlson, L. A., Levi, L., & Orö, L. (1967). Lipid metabolism during emotional stress. In L. Levi (Ed.), *Emotion Stress: Physiological and psychological reactions: Medical, in-*

dustrial and military applications (pp. 129–136). New York: American Elsevier Publishing Company.

Carlson, N. R. (1986). *Physiology of behavior.* 3rd ed. Newton, MA: Allyn & Bacon.

Carr, D. B., Sheean, D. V., Surman, O. S., Coleman, J. H., Greenblatt, D. J., Heninger, G. R., Jones, K. J., Levine, P. H., & Watkins, D. (1986). Neuroendocrine correlates of lactate induced anxiety and their response to chronic alprazolam therapy. *American Journal of Psychiatry, 143,* 483–494.

Carrigan, P. M. (1960). Extraversion-introversion as a dimension of personality: A reappraisal. *Psychological Bulletin, 57,* 329–360.

Carrol, E. N., Zuckerman, M., & Vogel, W. H. (1982). A test of the optimal level of arousal theory of sensation seeking. *Journal of Personality and Social Psychology, 42,* 572–575.

Cattell, R. B. (1957). *Personality and motivation structure and measurement.* New York: Harcourt, Brace, & World.

Chamove, A. S., Eysenck, H. J., & Harlow, H. F. (1972). Personality in monkeys: Factor analyses of Rhesus social behavior. *Quarterly Journal of Experimental Psychology, 24,* 496–504.

Charney, D. S., Goodman, W. K., Price, L. H., Woods, S. W., Rasmussen, S. A., & Heninger, G. R. (1988). Serotonin function in obsessive-compulsive disorder: A comparison of the effects of tryptophan and m-Chlorophenyl-piperazine in patients and healthy subjects. *Archives of General Psychiatry, 45,* 177–185.

Charney, D. S., & Heninger, G. R. (1985a). Noradrenergic function and the mechanism of action of antianxiety treatment: I. The effect of long term alprazolam treatment. *Archives of General Psychiatry, 42,* 458–467.

Charney, D. S., & Heninger, G. R. (1985b). Noradrenergic function and the mechanism of action of antianxiety treatment: II. The effect of long-term imipramine treatment. *Archives of General Psychiatry, 42,* 473–481.

Charney, D. S., & Heninger, G. R. (1986a). Abnormal regulation of noradrenergic function in panic disorders. *Archives of General Psychiatry, 43,* 1042–1054.

Charney, D. S., & Heninger, G. R. (1986b). Alpha-adrenergic and opiate receptor blockade: Synergistic effects on anxiety in healthy subjects. *Archives of General Psychiatry, 43,* 1037–1041.

Charney, D. S., & Heninger, G. R. (1986c). Serotonin function in panic disorders. The effect of intravenous tryptophan in healthy subjects and patients with panic disorder before and during alprazolam treatment. *Archives of General Psychiatry, 43,* 1059–1065.

Charney, D. S., Heninger, G. R., & Breier, A. (1984). Noradrenergic function in panic anxiety. *Archives of General Psychiatry, 41,* 751–763.

Charney, D. S., Heninger, G. R., & Jatlow, P. I. (1985). Increased anxiogenic effects of caffeine in panic disorders. *Archives of General Psychiatry, 42,* 233–243.

Charney, D. S., Woods, S. W., Goodman, W. K., & Heninger, G. R. (1987). Neurobiological mechanisms of panic anxiety: Biochemical and behavioral correlates of yohimbine-induced panic attacks. *American Journal of Psychiatry, 144,* 1030–1036.

Charney, D. S., Woods, S. W., & Heninger, G. R. (1989). Noradrenergic function in generalized anxiety disorder: Effects of Yohimbine in healthy subjects and patients with generalized anxiety disorder. *Psychiatry Research, 27,* 173–182.

Chattopadhyay, P., Cook, E., Toone, B., & Lader, M. (1980). Habituation of physiological responses in anxiety. *Biological Psychiatry, 15,* 711–721.

Chess, S., & Thomas, A. (1984). *Origins and evolution of behavior disorders.* New York: Bruner-Mazel.

Choppy, M., Zimbacca, N., & Le Beau, L. (1973). Psychological changes after selective frontal surgery (especially cingulotomy) and after stereotactic surgery of the basal ganglia. In L. V. Laitman & K. E. Livingston (Eds.), *Surgical approaches in psychiatry* (pp. 174–181). Baltimore, MD: University Park Press.

Chozik, B. S. (1986). The behavioral effects of lesions of the amygdala: A review. *International Journal of Neuroscience, 29,* 205–221.

Christiansen, K. O. (1977a). A review of studies of criminality among twins. In S. A. Mednick & K. O. Christiansen (Eds.), *Biosocial bases of criminal behavior* (pp. 45–88). New York: Gardner Press.

Christiansen, K. O. (1977b). A preliminary study of criminality among twins. In S. A. Mednick & K. O. Christiansen (Eds.), *Biosocial bases of criminal behavior* (pp. 89–108). New York: Gardner Press.

Claridge, G. S. (1967). *Personality and arousal.* Oxford: Pergamon Press.

Claridge, G. S. (1987). *Psychoticism and arousal.* In J. Strelau & H. J. Eysenck (Eds.), *Personality dimensions and arousal* (pp. 133–150). New York: Plenum Press.

Claridge, G. S., Canter, S., & Hume, W. I. (1973). *Personality differences and biological variations: A study of twins.* Oxford: Pergamon Press.

Cleckley, H. (1976). *The mask of sanity* (5th ed.). St. Louis, MO: Mosby.

Cloninger, C. R. (1987a). A systematic method for clinical description and classification of personality. *Archives of General Psychiatry, 44,* 573–588.

Cloninger, C. R. (1987b). Neurogenic adaptive mechanisms in alcoholism. *Science, 236,* 410–416.

Cloninger, C. R., & Gottesman, I. I. (1987). Genetic and environmental factors in antisocial behavior. In S. A. Mednick, T. E. Moffitt, & S. A. Stack (Eds.), *The causes of crime: New biological approaches* (pp. 92–109). Cambridge: Cambridge University Press.

Cloninger, C. R., Martin, R. L., Guze, S. B., & Clayton, P. J. (1986). A prospective follow-up and family study of somatization in men and women. *American Journal of Psychiatry, 143,* 873–878.

Cloninger, C. R., Reich, T., & Guze, S. B. (1975a). The multi-factorial model of disease transmission: III. Familial relationship between sociopathy and hysteria (Briquet's Syndrome). *British Journal of Psychiatry, 127,* 11–22.

Cloninger, C. R., Reich, T., & Guze, S. B. (1975b). The multifactorial model of disease transmission: II. Sex differences in the familial transmission of sociopathy (antisocial personality). *British Journal of Psychiatry, 127,* 11–22.

Cloninger, C. R., Sigvardsson, S., Bohman, M., & von Knorring, A. L. (1982). Predisposition to petty criminality in Swedish adoptees: II. Cross fostering analysis of genetic environment interaction. *Archives of General Psychiatry, 39,* 1242–1247.

Cloninger, C. R., von Knorring, L., & Oreland, L. (1985). Parametric distribution of platelet monoamine oxidase activity. *Psychiatry Research, 15,* 133–143.

Cloninger, C. R., von Knorring, L., Sigvardsson, S., & Bohman, M. (1986). Symptom pattern and causes of somatization in men: II. Genetic and environmental independence from somatization in women. *Genetic Epidemiology, 3,* 171–185.

Coger, R. W., Dymond, A. M., Lowenstein, I., & Pearson, D. (1976). Alcoholism: Averaged visual evoked response amplitude-intensity slope and symmetry in withdrawal. *Biological Psychiatry, 11,* 435–443.

Coles, M. G. H., Gale, A., & Kline, P. (1971). Personality and habituation of the orienting reaction: Tonic and response measures of electrodermal activity. *Psychophysiology, 8,* 54–63.

Colpaert, F. C. (1975). The ventromedial hypothalamus and the control of avoidance behavior and aggression. *Behavioral Biology, 15,* 27–44.

Conner, R. L., Constantino, A. P., & Scheuch, G. C. (1983). Hormonal influences on shock-induced fighting. In B. B. Svare (Ed.), *Hormones and aggressive behavior* (pp. 119–144). New York: Plenum Press.

Cook III, E. W., Melamed, B. G., Cuthbert, B. N., McNeil, D. W., & Lang, P. J. (1988). Emotional imagery and the differential diagnosis of anxiety. *Journal of Consulting and Clinical Psychology, 56,* 734–740.

Costa, P. T., Jr., & McCrae, R. R. (1977). Age differences in personality structure revisited: Studies in validity, stability and change. *Aging and human development, 8,* 261–275.

Costa, P. T., Jr., & McCrae, R. R. (1985). *The NEO Personality Inventory Manual.* Odessa, FL: Psychological Assessment Resources.

Costa, P. T., Jr., McCrae, R. R., & Arenberg, D. (1980). Enduring dispositions in adult males. *Journal of Personality and Social Psychology, 38,* 793–800.

Coursey, R. D., Buchsbaum, M. S., & Murphy, D. L. (1979). Platelet MAO activity and evoked potentials in the identification of subjects biologically at risk for psychiatric disorders. *British Journal of Psychiatry, 134,* 372–381.

Cowley, D. S., Dager, S. R., McClellan, J., Roy-Byrne, P. P., & Dunner, D. L. (1988). Response to lactate infusion in generalized anxiety disorder. *Biological Psychiatry, 24,* 409–414.

Cox, D. N. (1977). *Psychophysiological correlates of sensation seeking and socialization during reduced stimulation.* Doctoral dissertation, University of British Columbia.

Crick, F. (1988). *What mad pursuit: A personal view of scientific discovery.* New York: Basic Books.

Cronbach, L. J. (1957). The two disciplines of scientific psychology. *American Psychologist, 12,* 671–684.

Crow, T. J. (1977). Neurotransmitter related pathways: The structure and function of central monoamine neurons. In A. N. Davison (Ed.), *Biochemical correlates of brain structure and function* (pp. 137–174). New York: Academic Press.

Crow, T. J., Deakin, J. F. W., File, S. E., Longden, A., & Wendlandt, S. (1978). The locus coeruleus noradrenergic system: Evidence against a role in attention, habituation, anxiety, and motor activity. *Brain research, 155,* 244–261.

Crowe, R. R. (1974). An adoptive study of antisocial personality. *Archives of General Psychiatry, 31,* 780–791.

Dabbs, J. M., Jr. & Ruback, R. B. (1987). Saliva testosterone and personality among male college students. Unpublished manuscript, Georgia State University, Atlanta, Georgia.

Dabbs, J. M., Jr., Ruback, R. B., Frady, R. L., Hopper, C. H., & Sgoritas, D. S. (1988). Saliva testosterone and criminal violence among women. *Personality and Individual Differences, 9,* 269–275.

Daitzman, R. J., & Zuckerman, M. (1980). Personality, disinhibitory sensation seeking, and gonadal hormones. *Personality and Individual Differences, 1,* 103–110.

Daitzman, R. J., Zuckerman, M., Sammelwitz, P. H., & Ganjam, V. (1978). Sensation seeking and gonadal hormones. *Journal of Biosocial Science, 10,* 401–408.

Dalgaard, O. S., & Kringlen, E. (1976). A Norwegian twin study of criminality. *British Journal of Criminality, 16,* 213–232.

Daruna, H. (1978). Patterns of brain monoamine activity and aggressive behavior. *Neuroscience and Biobehavioral Reviews, 2,* 101–113.

Daruna, J. H., Karrer, R., & Rosen, A. J. (1985). Introversion, attention, and the late positive component of event related potentials. *Biological Psychology, 20,* 249–259.

Darwin. (1859/1967). *On the origin of the species by means of natural selection, or the preservation of favoured races in the struggle for life* (1967 ed.). New York: Modern Library.

Davidson, J., Linnoila, M., Raft, D., & Turnbull, C. D. (1981). MAO inhibition and control of anxiety following amtriptyline therapy. *Acta Psychiatrica Scandinavica, 63,* 147–152.

Davidson, J., McLeod, M. N., Turnbull, C. D., White, H. L., & Feuer, E. J. (1980).

Platelet monoamine oxidase activity and the classification of depression. *Archives of General Psychiatry, 37,* 771–773.

Davidson, J., Swartz, M., Storck, M., Krishman, R. R., & Hammett, E. (1985). A diagnostic and family study of posttraumatic stress disorder. *American Journal of Psychiatry, 142,* 90–93.

Davis, H. (1974). What does the P scale measure? *British Journal of Psychiatry, 125,* 161–167.

Davis, M. (1986). Pharmacological and anatomical analysis of fear conditioning using the fear-potentiated startle paradigm. *Behavioral Neuroscience, 100,* 814–824.

Davis, M., Hitchcock, J. M., & Rosen, J. B. (1987). Anxiety and amygdala: Pharmacological and anatomical analysis of the fear-potentiated startle paradigm. *The psychology of learning and motivation* (Vol. 21, pp. 263–305). New York: Academic Press.

Deakin, J. F. W., & Exley, K. A. (1979). Personality and male-female influences on the EEG alpha rhythm. *Biological Psychology, 8,* 285–290.

DeFries, J. C., Gervais, M. C., & Thomas, E. A. (1978). Response to 30 generations of selection for open field activity. *Behavior Genetics, 8,* 3–13.

DeFries, J. C., & Hegmann, J. P. (1970). Genetic analysis of open-field behavior. In G. Lindzey & D. D. Thiesen (Eds.), *Contributions to behavior-genetic analysis: The mouse as a prototype* (pp. 23–56). New York: Appleton-Century-Crofts.

Delgado, J. M. R., Roberts, W. W., & Miller, N. E. (1954). Learning motivated by electrical stimulation of the brain. *American Journal of Physiology, 179,* 587–593.

Demisch, L., Georgi, K., Patzke, B., Demisch, K., & Bochnik, H. J. (1982). Correlation of platelet MAO activity with introversion: A study on a German rural population. *Psychiatry Research, 6,* 303–311.

DeMolina, A. F., & Hunsperger, R. W. (1962). Organization of the subcortical system governing defense and fight reactions in the cat. *Journal of Physiology, 160,* 200–213.

den Boer, V. A., & Westenberg, G. M. (1990). Behavioral, neuroendocrine and biochemical effects of 5-hydroxytryptophan administration in panic disorder. *Psychiatry Research, 31,* 267–278.

Deutsch, J. A., & Deutsch, D. (1966). *Physiological Psychology.* Homewood, IL: Dorsey Press.

deWit, H., Uhlenhuth, E. H., Hedeker, D., McCracken, S. G., & Johanson, C. E. (1986). Lack of preference for diazepam in anxious volunteers. *Archives of General Psychiatry, 43,* 533–541.

Diagnostic and statistical manual of mental disorders-revised. Washington, DC: American Psychiatric Association, 1987.

Diener, E., Larsen, R. J., & Emmons, R. A. (1984). Person X Situation interactions: Choice of situations and congruence response models. *Journal of Personality and Social Psychology, 47,* 580–592.

Diener, E., Larsen, R. J., Levine, S., & Emmons, R. E. (1985). Intensity and frequency: Dimensions underlying positive and negative affect. *Journal of Personality and Social Psychology, 48,* 1253–1265.

Digman, J. M. (1990). Personality structure: Emergence of the five-factor model. In M. R. Rosenzweig & L. M. Porter (Eds.), *Annual Review of Psychology* (Vol. 41, pp. 417–440). Palo Alto, CA: Annual Reviews, Inc.

Digman, J. M., & Inouye, J. (1986). Further specification of the five robust factors of personality. *Journal of Personality and Social Psychology, 50,* 116–123.

Digman, J. M., & Takemoto-Chock. (1981). Factors in the natural language of personality: Reanalysis, comparison and interpretation of six major studies. *Multivariate Behavioral Research, 16,* 149–170.

Dincheva, E., Piperova-Dalbokova, D., & Kolev, P. (1984). Contingent negative variation (CNV) and the distraction effect in extraverts and introverts. *Personality and Individual Differences, 5,* 757–761.

Dishman, D. J., Wallace, A. M., Crawford, A., Grant, J. K., & Hinton, J. W. (1982). Unusual hormonal 'stress relaxation' response in prisoners with convictions for assault with robbery. *Journal of Psychosomatic Research, 26,* 341–344.

Dollard, J., & Miller, N. E. (1950). *Personality and psychotherapy.* New York: McGraw-Hill.

Domino, E. F., & Krause, R. R. (1974). Plasma tryptophan tolerance curves in drug free normal controls, schizophrenic patients, and prisoner volunteers. *Journal of Psychiatric Research, 10,* 247–261.

Donnelly, E. F., Murphy, D. L., Waldman, I. N., Buchsbaum, M. S., & Coursey, R. D. (1979). Psychological characteristics corresponding to low vs. high platelet monoamine oxidase activity. *Biological Psychiatry, 14,* 375–383.

Doren, D. M. (1987). *Understanding and treating the psychopath.* New York: Wiley.

Dorow, R., Duka, T., Hollen, L., & Sauderbrey, N. (1987). Clinical perspectives of β-carbolines from first studies in humans. *Brain Research Bulletin, 19,* 319–326.

Douglas, K., & Arenberg, D. (1978). Age changes, cohort differences, and cultural change on the Guilford-Zimmerman Temperament Survey. *Journal of Gerontology, 33,* 737–747.

Downer, J. D. C. (1961). Changes in visual gnostic function and emotional behavior following unilateral temporal lobe damage in the "split-brain" monkey. *Nature, 191,* 50–51.

Duffy, E. (1951). The concept of energy mobilization. *Psychological Review, 58,* 30–40.

Duffy, E. (1972). Activation. In N. S. Greenfield & R. A. Sternback (Eds.), *Handbook of psychophysiology.* New York: Holt, Rinehart & Winston.

Eaton, W. O. (1983). Measuring activity level with actometers: Reliability, validity, and arm length. *Child Development, 54,* 720–726.

Eaves, L. J., & Eysenck, H. J. (1975). The nature of extraversion: A genetical analysis. *Journal of Personality and Social Psychology, 32,* 102–112.

Eaves, L. J., & Eysenck, H. J. (1976). Genotype X age interactions for neuroticism. *Behavior Genetics, 6,* 359–362.

Eaves, L. J., & Young, P. A. (1981). Genetical theory and personality differences. In R. Lynn (Ed.), *Dimensions of personality* (pp. 129–179). Oxford: Pergamon Press.

Eckert, E. D., Heston, L. L., & Bouchard, T. J. (1981) Monozygotic twins reared apart: Preliminary findings of psychiatric disturbances and traits. In L. Gedda, P. Parisi, & W. E. Nance, (Eds.), *Twin research–3: Intelligence, personality and development* (pp. 179–188). New York: Alan Liss, Inc.

Edlund, M. J., Swann, A. C., & Clothier, J. (1987). Patients with panic attacks and abnormal EEG results. *American Journal of Psychiatry, 144,* 508–509.

Edwards, A. L. (1957). *Manual for the Edwards Personal Preference Inventory.* New York: Psychological Corp.

Ehlers, A., Margraf, J., & Roth, W. T. (1986). Lactate infusions and panic attacks: Do patients respond differently? *Psychiatry Research, 17,* 295–308.

Ehlers, A., Margraf, J., Roth, W. T., Taylor, C. B., & Birbaumer, N. (1988). Anxiety induced by false heart rate feedback in patients with panic disorder. *Behavioral Research and Therapy, 26,* 1–11.

Ehrenkranz, J., Bliss, E., & Sheard, M. H. (1974). Plasma testosterone: Correlation with aggressive behavior and social dominance in man. *Psychosomatic Medicine, 36,* 469–475.

Ehrhardt, A., Epstein, K., & Money, J. (1968). Fetal androgens and female gender identity in the early treated adrenogenital symptom. *Johns Hopkins Medical Journal, 122,* 160–167.

Elliot, F. A. (1987). Neuroanatomy and neurology of aggression. *Psychiatric Annals, 17,* 385–388.

Ellison, G. D. (1977). Animal models of psychopathology: The low-norepinephrine and low-serotonin rat. *American Psychologist, 32,* 1036–1045.

Ellison, G. D. (1979). Animal models of psychopathology: Studies in naturalistic colony environments. In J. D. Keegan (Ed.), *Psychopathology in animals* (pp. 81–101). New York: Academic Press.

Emmons, R. A., Diener, E., & Larsen, R. J. (1986). Choice and avoidance of everyday situations and affect congruence: Two models of reciprocal interactionism: *Journal of Personality and Social Psychology, 51,* 815–826.

Emmons, T. D., & Webb, W. W. (1974). Subjective correlates of emotional responsivity and stimulation seeking in psychopaths, normals and acting-out neurotics. *Journal of Consulting and Clinical Psychology, 42,* 620–625.

Endler, N. S., & Hunt, J. M. (1966). Sources of behavioral variance as measured by the S-R Inventory of Anxiousness. *Psychological Bulletin, 65,* 336–346.

Endler, N. S., & Hunt, J. M. (1968). S-R inventories of hostility and comparisons of the proportions of variance from persons, responses, and situations for hostility and anxiousness. *Journal of Personality and Social Psychology, 9,* 309–315.

Endler, N. S., & Hunt, J. M. (1969). Generalizability of contributions from sources of variance in the S-R inventories of anxiousness. *Journal of Personality, 37,* 1–24.

Endler, N., Hunt, J. M., & Rosenstein, A. J. (1962). An S-R inventory of anxiousness. *Psychological Monographs, 76* (17, Whole No. 536).

Endler, N. S., & Okada, M. A. (1975). A multidimensional measure of trait anxiety: The S-R Inventory of General Trait Anxiousness. *Journal of Consulting and Clinical Psychology, 43,* 319–329.

Engel, B. T. (1972). Response specificity. In N. S. Greenfield & R. A. Sternback (Eds.), *Handbook of psychophysiology* (pp. 571–576). New York: Holt, Rinehart, & Winston.

English, G. E., & Jones, R. E. (personal communication, April 1972). Sensation seeking in hospitalized drug addicts. Atlanta, Georgia:

Epstein, S. (1977). Traits are alive and well. In D. Magnusson & N. S. Endler (Eds.), *Personality at the crossroads: Current issues in Interactional psychology.* Hillsdale, NJ: Erlbaum

Epstein, S. (1979). The stability of behavior: I. On predicting most of the people much of the time. *Personality and Social Psychology, 37,* 1097–1126.

Estes, W. K., & Skinner, B. F. (1941). Some qualitative properties of anxiety. *Journal of Experimental Psychology, 29,* 390–400.

Eysenck, H. J. (1947). *Dimensions of personality.* New York: Praeger.

Eysenck, H. J. (1952). *The scientific study of personality.* New York: Praeger.

Eysenck, H. J. (1953). *The structure of human personality.* New York: Wiley.

Eysenck, H. J. (1955). Psychiatric diagnosis as a psychological and statistical problem. *Psychological Reports, 1,* 3–17.

Eysenck, H. J. (1957). *The dynamics of anxiety and hysteria.* New York: Praeger.

Eysenck, H. J. (1959). *Manual for the Maudsley Personality Inventory.* London: University of London Press.

Eysenck, H. J. (1963). *Experiments with drugs.* New York: Pergamon Press.

Eysenck, H. J. (1967). *The biological basis of personality.* Springfield, IL: Charles C. Thomas.

Eysenck, H. J. (1976). *Sex and personality.* Austin, TX: University of Texas Press.

Eysenck, H. J. (1977). *Crime and personality* (3rd ed.). London: Routledge & Kegan Paul.

Eysenck, H. J. (1979). The conditioning model of neurosis. *Behavioral and Brain Sciences, 2,* 155–199.

Eysenck, H. J. (1981). General features of the model. In H. J. Eysenck (Ed.), *A model for personality* (pp. 1–37). New York: Springer-Verlag.

Eysenck, H. J. (1983). The social application of Pavlovian theories. *Pavlovian Journal of Biological Science, 18,* 117–125.

Eysenck, H. J. (1987). Arousal and personality: The origins of a theory. In J. Strelau & H. J. Eysenck (Eds.), *Personality dimensions and arousal* (pp. 1–13). New York: Plenum Press.

Eysenck, H. J., & Eysenck, M. W. (1985). *Personality and individual differences: A natural science approach.* New York: Plenum Press.

Eysenck, H. J., & Eysenck, S. B. G. (1964). *Eysenck Personality Inventory.* San Diego, CA: Educational and Industrial Testing Service.

Eysenck, H. J., & Eysenck, S. B. G. (1975). *Manual of the Eysenck Personality Questionnaire (Junior and Adult).* London: Hodder & Stoughton.

Eysenck, H. J., & Eysenck, S. B. G. (1976). *Psychoticism as a dimension of personality.* New York: Crane, Russak, & Co.

Eysenck, H. J., & Eysenck, S. B. G. (1978). Psychopathy, personality and genetics. In R. D. Hare & D. Schalling (Eds.), *Psychopathic behaviour: Approaches to research* (pp. 197–223). Chichester: Wiley.

Eysenck, H. J., & Levey, A. (1972). Conditioning, introversion-extraversion and the strength of the nervous system. In V. D. Nebylitsyn & J. A. Gray (Eds.), *Biological basis of individual behavior* (pp. 206–220). New York: Academic Press.

Eysenck, H. J., White, P. O., & Souief, M. I. (1969). Factors in the Cattell Personality Inventory. In H. J. Eysenck & S. B. G. Eysenck (Eds.), *Personality structure and measurement* (pp. 218–228). San Diego, CA: R. R. Knapp.

Eysenck, S. B. G. (1956). Neurosis and psychosis: An experimental analysis. *Journal of Mental Science, 102,* 517–529.

Eysenck, S. B. G., & Eysenck, H. J. (1963). On the dual nature of extraversion. *British Journal of Social and Clinical Psychology, 2,* 46–55.

Eysenck, S. B. G., & Eysenck, H. J. (1977). The place of impulsiveness in a dimensional system of personality description. *British Journal of Social and Clinical Psychology, 16,* 57–68.

Eysenck, S. B. G., Eysenck, H. J., & Barrett, P. (1985). A revised version of the psychoticism scale. *Personality and Individual Differences, 6,* 21–29.

Eysenck, S. B. G., & McGurk, B. J. (1980). Impulsiveness and venturesomeness in a detention center population. *Psychological Reports, 47,* 1299–1306.

Fagan, T. J., & Liro, F. T. (1980). The primary and secondary sociopathic personality: Differences in frequency and severity of antisocial behaviors. *Journal of Abnormal Psychology, 89,* 493–496.

Fahrenberg, J. (1987). Concepts of activation and arousal in the theory of emotionality (neuroticism): A multivariate conceptualization. In J. Strelau & H. J. Eysenck (Eds.), *Personality, dimensions and arousal* (pp. 99–120). New York: Plenum.

Fahrenberg, J., Walshburger, P., Foerster, F., Myrtek, M., & Müller, W. (1983). An evaluation of trait, state, and reaction aspects of activation processes. *Psychophysiology, 20,* 188–195.

Falconer, D. S. (1981). *Introduction to quantitative genetics* (2nd ed.). London: Longman.

Falconer, M. A. (1973). Reversibility by temporal lobe resection of the behavioral abnormalities of temporal lobe epilepsy. *New England Journal of Medicine, 289,* 451–455.

Farley, F. H. (1973). *Implications for a theory of delinquency.* Paper presented at the annual meeting of the American Psychological Association, Montreal, Canada, Sept. 1973.

Farley, F. H., & Farley, S. V. (1972). Stimulus-seeking motivation and delinquent behavior among institutionalized delinquent girls. *Journal of Consulting and Clinical Psychology, 39,* 140–147.

Farley, F. H., & Mueller, C. B. (1978). Arousal, personality, and assortative mating in marriage: Generalizability and cross-cultural factors. *Journal of Sex and Marital Therapy, 4,* 50–53.

Farrington, D. P., Gallagher, B., Morley, L., St. Ledger, R. J., & West, D. J. (1988). Are there any successful men from criminogenic backgrounds? *Psychiatry, 51,* 120–130.

Feij, J. A., Orlebeke, J. F., Gazendam, A., & van Zuilen, R. (1985). Sensation seeking: Measurement and psychophysiological correlates. In J. Strelau & A. Gale (Eds.), *Biological bases of personality and behavior* (pp. 195–210). Washington, DC: Hemisphere.

Fibriger, H. C., & Phillips, A. G. (1987). Role of catecholamine transmitters in brain reward systems: Implication for the neurobiology of affect. In J. Engel et al. (Eds.), *Brain reward systems and abuse* (pp. 61–74). New York: Plenum.

File, S. E. (1988). The psychopharmacology of anxiety. In B. Breckon (Ed.), *Emotions and emotional disorders: Reports on the first Maudsley conference on new developments in psychiatry* (pp. 19–24). London: Roche.

File, S. E., & Hyde, J. R. G. (1978). Can social interaction be used to measure anxiety? *British Journal of Pharmacology, 62,* 19–24.

File, S. E., Hyde, J., & Pool, M. (1976). Effects of ethanol and chlordiazepoxide on social interaction in rats. *British Journal of Pharmacology, 58,* 465.

File, S. E., & Velucci, S. V. (1978). Studies on the role of stress hormones and of 5-HT in anxiety using an animal model. *Journal of Pharmacy and Pharmacology, 30,* 105–110.

Finn, S. E. (1986). Stability of personality self-ratings over 30 years: Evidence for an age/cohort interaction. *Journal of Personality and Social Psychology, 50,* 813–818.

Fiske, D. W. (1949). Consistency of factorial structures for personality ratings from different sources. *Journal of Abnormal and Social Psychology, 44,* 329–344.

Floderus-Myrhed, B., Pederson, N., & Rasmuson, I. (1980). Assessment of heritability for personality, based on a short form of the Eysenck Personality Inventory: A study of 12,898 twin pairs. *Brain Genetics, 10,* 153–162.

Floody, O. R. (1983). Hormones and aggression in female mammals. In B. B. Svare (Ed.), *Hormones and aggressive behavior* (pp. 39–89). New York: Plenum.

Flor-Henry, P. (1969). Schizophrenia-like reactions and affective psychoses associated with temporal lobe epilepsy: etiological factors. *American Journal of Psychiatry, 126,* 148–152.

Flor-Henry, P. (1976). Lateralized temporal-limbic dysfunction. *Annals of the New York Academy of Sciences, 280,* 777–797.

Flor-Henry, P., Yeudall, L. T., Koles, Z. J., & Howarth, B. G. (1979). Neuropsychological and power spectral EEG investigations of the obsessive-compulsive syndrome. *Biological Psychiatry, 14,* 119–130.

Forsman, L. (1982). Consistency in catecholamine excretion in laboratory and natural settings: Correlational and variance component analysis. *Scandinavian Journal of Psychology, 23,* 99–106.

Fowler, C. J., von Knorring, L., & Oreland, L. (1980). Platelet monoamine oxidase activity in sensation seekers. *Psychiatry Research, 3,* 273–279.

Fowles, D. C. (1980). The three-arousal model: Implications of Gray's two-factor learning theory for heart rate, electrodermal activity, and psychopathy. *Psychophysiology, 17,* 87–104.

Fowles, D. C., Roberts, R., & Nagel, K. (1977). The influence of introversion-extraversion on the skin conductance response of stress and stimulus intensity. *Journal of Research in Personality, 11,* 129–146.

Fox, H. M., Gifford, S., Valenstein, A. F., & Murawski, B. J. (1970). Psychophysiological correlation of 17-ketosteroids and 17-hydroxycorticosteroids in 21 pairs of monozygotic twins. *Journal of Psychosomatic Research, 14,* 71–79.

Frankenhauser, M. (1979). Psychoendocrine approaches to the study of emotion as related to stress and coping. In H. E. Howe & R. A. Dienstbier (Eds.), *Nebraska Symposium on Motivation* (pp. 123–161). Lincoln, NE: Univ. of Nebraska Press.

Franks, C. M. (1956). Conditioning and personality: A study of normal and neurotic subjects. *Journal of Abnormal and Social Psychology, 52,* 143–150.

Franks, C. M. (1957). Personality factors and the rate of conditioning. *British Journal of Psychology, 48,* 119–126.

Franks, C. M. (1963). Ocular movements and spontaneous blink rate as functions of personality. *Perceptual and Motor Skills, 16,* 178.

Franks, C. M., & Trouton, D. (1958). Effects of amobarbital sodium and dexamphetamine sulfate on the conditioning of the eyeblink response. *Journal of Comparative and Physiological Psychology, 51,* 220–222.

Frcka, G., Beyts, J., Levey, A. B., & Martin, I. (1983a). The influence of psychoticism on classical conditioning. *Personality and Individual Differences, 4,* 189–197.

Frcka, G., Beyts, J., Levey, A. B., & Martin, I. (1983b). The role of awareness in human conditioning. *Pavlovian Journal of Biological Science, 18,* 69–76.

Frcka, G., & Martin, I. (1987). Is there- or is there not- an influence of impulsiveness on classical eyelid conditioning? *Personality and Individual Differences, 8,* 241–252.

Frederickson, E. (1951). The effects of infantile experience upon adult behavior. *Journal of Abnormal and Social Psychology, 46,* 406–409.

Frederickson, E., & Birnbaum, E. A. (1954). Competitive fighting between mice with different hereditary backgrounds. *Journal of Genetic Psychology, 85,* 271–280.

Freedman, R. R., Ianni, P., Ettedgui, E., & Puthezhath, N. (1985). Ambulatory monitoring of panic disorder. *Archives of General Psychiatry, 42,* 244–248.

Freeman, W. (1972). Frontal lobotomy in early schizophrenia: Long follow-up in 415 cases. In E. Hitchcock, L. Laitinen, & K. Vaernet (Eds.), *Psychosurgery* (pp. 311–321). Springfield, IL: Charles C. Thomas.

Freud, S. (1895/1937). A reply to criticism of the anxiety-neurosis. In J. Rickman (Ed.), *A general selection from the works of Sigmund Freud* (pp. 59–61). Garden City, NY: Doubleday.

Freud, S. (1905/1938). Three contributions to the theory of sex. In A. A. Brill (Ed.), *The basic writings of Sigmund Freud* (pp. 553–629) New York: Modern Library-Random House.

Freud, S. (1915/1957). Formulations regarding the two principles in mental functioning. In J. Strachey (Ed.), *The standard edition of the complete psychological works of Sigmund Freud.* London: Hogarth.

Freud, S. (1920/1937). Beyond the pleasure principle. In J. Rickman (Ed.), *A general selection from the works of Sigmund Freud* (pp. 189–257). Garden City, NY: Doubleday.

Friedman, M. J., Stolk, J. M., Harris, P. Q., & Cooper, P. B. (1984). Serum dopamine-β-hydroxylase activity in depression and anxiety. *Biological Psychiatry, 19,* 557–570.

Fuhrer, M. J., Baer, P. E., & Cowan, C. O. (1973). Orienting responses and personality variables as predictors of differential conditioning of electrodermal responses and awareness of stimulus relations. *Journal of Personality and Social Psychology, 27,* 287–296.

Fulker, D. J., Eysenck, S. B. G., & Zuckerman, M. (1980). The genetics of sensation seeking. *Journal of Personality Research, 14,* 261–281.

Gabrielli, W. F., & Mednick, S. A. (1980). Sinistrality and delinquency. *Journal of Abnormal Psychology, 89,* 654–661.

Gale, A. (1973). The Psychophysiology of individual differences: studies of extraversion and the EEG. In P. Kline (Ed.), *New approaches in psychological measurement* (pp. 211–256). London: Wiley.

Gale, A. (1981). EEG studies of extraversion-introversion: What's the next step? In R. Lynn (Ed.), *Dimensions of personality: Papers in honour of H. J. Eysenck* (pp. 181–207). Oxford: Pergamon.

Gale, A. (1983). Electroencephalographic studies of extraversion-introversion: A case study in the psychophysiology of individual differences. *Personality and Individual Differences, 4,* 371–380.

Gale, A. (1984). O'Gorman vs. Gale: A reply. *Biological Psychology, 19,* 129–136.

Gale, A., Coles, M., & Blaydon, J. (1969). Extraversion-introversion and the EEG. *British Journal of Psychology, 60,* 209–223.

Gale, A., & Edwards, J. A. (1983). Psychophysiology and individual differences. *Australian Journal of Psychology, 35,* 361–379.

Gale, A., & Edwards, J. A. (1986). Individual differences. In M. G. H. Coles, E. Donchin, & S. W. Porges (Eds.), *Psychophysiology: Systems, processes and applications* (pp. 431–507). New York: Guilford.

Gandelman, R. (1983). Hormones and infanticide. In B. B. Svare (Ed.), *Hormones and aggressive behavior* (pp. 105–118). New York: Plenum.

Garcia-Sevilla, L. (1984). Extraversion and neuroticism in rats. *Personality and Individual Differences, 5,* 511–532.

Gattaz, W. F., & Beckmann, H. (1981). Platelet MAO activity and personality characteristics: A study in schizophrenic patients and normal individuals. *Acta Psychiatrica Scandinavica, 63,* 479–485.

Geer, J. H. (1965): The development of a scale to measure fear. *Behavior Research and Therapy, 3,* 45–53.

Geller, I., & Seifter, J. (1960). The effects of meprobamate, barbiturates, d-amphetamine and promazine on experimentally induced conflict in the rat. *Psychopharmacologie, 3,* 374–385.

Genazzani, A. R., Nappi, G., Facchinetti, F., Mazzella, G. L., Parrini, D., Sinforiani, E., Petraglia, F., & Savoldi, F. (1982). Central deficiency of β-endorphin in alcohol addicts. *Journal of Clinical Endocrinology and Metabolism, 55,* 583–586.

Gerardi, R. J., Blanchard, E. B., Andrasik, F., & McCoy, G. C. (1985). Psychological dimensions of 'office hypertension'. *Behavior Research and Therapy, 23,* 609–612.

Gessa, G. L., & Tagliamonte, A. (1974). Role of brain monoamines in male sexual behavior. *Life Sciences, 14,* 425–436.

Gessa, G. L., & Tagliamonte, A. (1975). A role of brain serotonin and dopamine in male sexual behavior. In M. Sandler & G. L. Gessa (Eds.), *Sexual behavior: Pharmacology and biochemistry* (pp. 117–128). New York: Raven Press.

Geyer, M. A., & Segal, D. S. (1974). Shock-induced aggression: Opposite effects of intraventricular infused dopamine and norepinephrine. *Behavioral Biology, 10,* 99–104.

Ginsburg, B., & Allee, W. C. (1942). Some effects of conditioning on social dominance and subordination in inbred strains of mice. *Physiological Zoology, 15,* 485–506.

Glanzmann, P., & Froelich, W. D. (1984). Anxiety, stress and the contingent negative variation reconsidered. *Annals of the New York Academy of Sciences, 425,* 578–584.

Glor, P., Olivier, A., Quesney, L. F., Andermann, F., & Horowitz, S. (1982). The role of the limbic system in experimental phenomena of temporal lobe epilepsy. *Annals of Neurology, 12,* 129–144.

Gold, P. W., Pigott, T. A., Kling, M. A., Kalogeras, K., & Chrousos, G. P. (1988). Basic and clinical studies with corticotropin-releasing hormone. *Psychiatric Clinics of North America, 11,* 327–348.

Goldring, J. F., & Richards, M. (1985). EEG spectral analysis, visual evoked potentials and the photic-driving correlates of personality and memory. *Personality and Individual Differences, 6,* 67–76.

Goldsmith, H. H., & Gottesman, I. I. (1981). Origins of variation in behavioral style: A longitudinal study of temperament in young twins. *Child Development, 52,* 91–103.

Goma, M., & Tobeña, A. (1985). Activity measures in stress attenuated novelty tests as possible analogues for extraversion in rats: Some experimental results. *Personality and Individual Differences, 6,* 83–96.

Goodall, J. (1986). *The chimpanzees of Gombe.* Cambridge, MA: Belknap/Harvard Univ. Press.

Goodwin, D. W. (1979). Alcoholism and heredity. *Archives of General Psychiatry, 36,* 57–61.

Gorenstein, E. E. (1982). Frontal lobe functions in psychopaths. *Journal of Abnormal Psychology, 91,* 368–379.

Gorenstein, E. E., & Newman, J. P. (1980). Disinhibitory psychopathology: A new perspective and a model for research, *Psychological Review, 87,* 301–315.

Gorman, J. M., Fyer, M. R., Liebowitz, M. R. & Klein, D. F. (1987). Pharmacologic provocation of panic attacks. In H. Y. Meltzer (Ed.), *Psychopharmacology: The third generation of progress* (pp. 985–993). New York: Raven Press.

Gorman, J. M., Liebowitz, M. R., Fyer, A. J., Levitt, M., Baron, M., Davies, S., & Klein, D. F. (1985). Platelet monoamine oxidase activity in patients with panic disorders. *Biological Psychiatry, 20,* 802–857.

Gough, H. G., & Heilbrun, A. B. (1965). *The Adjective Check List Manual.* Palo Alto, CA: Consulting Psychologists Press.

Grafman, J., Vance, S. C., Weingartner, H., Salazar, A. M., & Amin, D. (1986). The effects of lateralized frontal lesions on mood regulation. *Brain, 109,* 1127–1148.

Graham, F. K. (1979). Distinguishing among orienting, defensive, and startle reflexes. In H. D. Kimmel, E. H. van Olst, & J. F. Orlebeke (Eds.), *The orienting reflex in humans* (pp. 137–167). Hillsdale, NJ: Erlbaum.

Grant, S. J., Aston-Jones, G., & Redmond, E. (1988). Responses of primate locus coeruleus neurons to simple and complex sensory stimuli. *Brain Research Bulletin, 21,* 401–410.

Gray, J. A. (1964a). *Pavlov's Typology.* New York: Macmillan.

Gray, J. A. (1964b). Strength of the nervous system and levels of arousal: A reinterpretation. In J. A. Gray (Ed.), *Pavlov's typology* (pp. 289–364). New York: Macmillan.

Gray, J. A. (1970). The psychophysiological basis of introversion-extraversion. *Behavior Research and Therapy, 8,* 249–266.

Gray, J. A. (1971). *The psychology of fear and stress.* New York: McGraw Hill.

Gray, J. A. (1973). Causal theories of personality and how to test them. In J. R. Royce (Ed.), *Multivariate analysis and psychological theory* (pp. 409–463). New York: Academic Press.

Gray, J. A. (1975). *Elements of a two process theory of learning.* New York: Academic Press.

Gray, J. A. (1979). Emotionality in male and female rodents: A reply to Archer. *British Journal of Psychology, 70,* 425–440.

Gray, J. A. (1981). A critique of Eysenck's theory of personality. In H. J. Eysenck (Ed.), *A model for personality* (pp. 246–276). New York: Springer-Verlag.

Gray, J. A. (1982). *The neuropsychology of anxiety: An enquiry into the functions of the septo-hippocampal system.* New York: Oxford University Press.

Gray, J. A. (1987a). The neuropsychology of emotion and personality. In S. M. Stahl, S. D. Iverson, & E. C. Goodman (Eds.), *Cognitive Neurochemistry* (pp. 171–190). Oxford: Oxford University Press.

Gray, J. A. (1987b). *The psychology of fear and stress,* 2nd ed. Cambridge: Cambridge University Press.

Gray, J. A. (in press). Neural systems, emotion and personality. In J. Madden, S. Matthysee, & J. Barchas (Eds.), *Adaptation, learning and affect.* New York: Raven Press.

Gray, J. A., & McNaughton, N. (1983). Comparison between the behavioural effects of septal and hippocampal lesions: A review. *Neuroscience and Biobehavioral Reviews, 7,* 119–188.

Grayson, J. B., Foa, E. B., & Steketee, G. S. (1986). Exposure in vivo of obsessive compulsives under distraction and attention-focusing conditions: Replication and extension. *Behavior Research and Therapy, 24,* 475–479.

Griffith, J. D., Cavanaugh, J., Held, J., & Oates, J. A. (1972). Dextroamphetamine: Evaluation of psychomimetic properties in man. *Archives of General Psychiatry, 26,* 97–100.

Grillon, C., & Buchsbaum, M. S. (1987). EEG topography of response to visual stimuli in generalized anxiety disorder. *Electroencephalography and clinical neurophysiology, 66,* 337–348.

Guidotti, A., Forchetti, C. M., Corda, M. G., Konkel, D., Bennett, C. D., & Costa, E. (1983). Isolation, characterization and purification to homogeneity of an endogenous polypeptide with agonistic action on benzodiazepine receptors. *Proceedings of the National Academy of Science, 80,* 3531–3535.

Guilford, J. P., & Zimmerman, W. S. (1956). Fourteen dimensional temperament factors. *Psychological Monographs, 70*(10), 1–26.

Guilford, J. P. (1975). Factors and factors of personality. *Psychological Bulletin, 82,* 802–814.

Gupta, B. S. (1973). The effects of stimulant and depressant drugs on verbal conditioning. *British Journal of Psychology, 64,* 553–557.

Gupta, B. S. (1976). Extraversion and reinforcement in verbal and operant conditioning. *British Journal of Psychology, 67,* 47–52.

Gupta, B. S., & Gupta, U. (1984). Dextroamphetamine and individual susceptibility to reinforcement in verbal and operant conditioning. *British Journal of Psychology, 75,* 201–208.

Gupta, B. S., & Nagpal, M. (1978). Impulsivity/sociability and reinforcement in verbal operant conditioning. *British Journal of Psychology, 69,* 203–206.

Gupta, U. (1984). Phenobarbitone and the relationship between extraversion and reinforcement in verbal operant conditioning. *British Journal of Psychology, 75,* 499–506.

Haan, N. (1981). Common dimensions of personality development: Early adolescence to middle life. In D. H. Eichorn et al. (Eds.), *Present and past in middle life* (pp. 117–151). New York: Academic Press.

Hacaen, H. (1964). Mental symptoms associated with tumors of the frontal lobe. In J. M. Warren & K. Akert (Eds.), *The frontal granular cortex and behaviour.* New York: McGraw Hill.

Haier, R. J., Buchsbaum, M. S., Murphy, D. L., Gottesman, I. I., & Coursey, R. D. (1980). Psychiatric vulnerability, monoamine oxidase and the average evoked potential. *Archives of General Psychiatry, 37,* 340–345.

Haier, R. J., Sokolski, K., Katz, M., & Buchsbaum, M. S. (1987). The study of personality with positron emission tomography. In J. Strelau & H. J. Eysenck (Ed.), *Personality dimensions and arousal* (pp. 251–267). New York: Plenum.

Halberstam, J. J. (1961). Some personality correlates of conditioning, generalization and extinction. *Psychosomatic Medicine, 23,* 67–76.

Halbreich, U., Sharpless, N., Asnis, G. M., Endicott, J., Goldstein, S., Vital-Horne, J., Eisenberg, J., Zander, K., Kang, B. J., Shindledecker, R., & Yeh, C. M. (1987). Afternoon continuous plasma levels of 3-methoxy-4-hydroxyphenylglycol and age. *Archives of General Psychiatry, 44,* 804–812.

Hall, R. A., Rappaport, M., Hopkins, H. K., Griffin, R. B., & Silverman, J. (1970). Evoked response and behavior in cats. *Science, 170,* 998–1000.

Hanni, I., & Usdin, E. (1977). *Animal models for psychiatry and neurology.* New York: Pergamon.

Hare, R. D. (1965). Temporal gradient of fear arousal in psychopaths. *Journal of Abnormal Psychology, 70,* 442–445.

Hare, R. D. (1978). Electrodermal and cardiovascular correlates of psychopathy. In R. D. Hare & D. Schalling (Eds.), *Psychopathic behaviour: Approaches to research* (pp. 107–143). Chichester: Wiley.

Hare, R. D. (1983). Diagnosis of antisocial personality disorder in two prison populations. *American Journal of Psychiatry, 140,* 887–890.

Hare, R. D. (1984). Performance of psychopaths on cognitive tasks related to frontal lobe function. *Journal of Abnormal Psychology, 93,* 133–140.

Hare, R. D. (1986). Twenty years of experience with the Cleckley psychopath. In W. H. Reid, D. Dorr, J. I. Walker, & I. J. W. Bonner (Eds.), *Unmasking the psychopath* (pp. 3–27). New York: W. W. Norton.

Hare, R. D., & Connolly, J. F. (1987). Perceptual asymmetries and information processing in psychopaths. In S. A. Mednick, T. E. Moffitt, & S. A. Stack (Eds.), *The causes of crime: New biological correlates* (pp. 218–238). Cambridge: Cambridge Univ. Press.

Hare, R. D., & Cox, D. N. (1978). Clinical and empirical conceptions of psychopaths and the selection of subjects for research. In R. D. Hare & D. Schalling (Eds.), *Psychopathic behaviour: Approaches to research* (pp. 1–22). Chichester: Wiley.

Hare, R. D., & Craigen, D. (1974). Psychopathy and physiological activity in a mixed-motive game situation. *Psychophysiology, 11,* 197–206.

Hare, R. D., & McPherson, L. M. (1984). Psychopathy and perceptual assymmetry during verbal dichotic listening. *Journal of Abnormal Psychology, 93,* 141–149.

Hare, R. D., & Quinn, M. J. (1971). Psychopathy and autonomic conditioning. *Journal of Abnormal Psychology, 77,* 223–235.

Harpur, T. J., Hakstian, A. R., & Hare, R. D. (1988). Factor structure of the Psychopathy Checklist. *Journal of Consulting and Clinical Psychology, 56,* 741–747.

Harpur, T. J., Hare, R. D., & Hakstian, R. (1989). Two-factor conceptualization of psychopathy: Construct validity and assessment implications. *Psychological assessment: Journal of Consulting and Clinical Psychology, 1,* 6–17.

Hartshorne, H., & May, M. A. (1928). *Studies in deceit.* New York: Macmillan.

Hassett, J. (1978). *A primer of psychophysiology.* New York: W. H. Freeman.

Hastrup, J. L., Light, K. C., & Obrist, P. A. (1982). Parental hypertension and cardiovascular response to stress in healthy young adults. *Psychophysiology, 19,* 615–622.

Heath, R. G. (1986). The neural substrate for emotion. In R. Plutchik & H. Kellerman (Eds.), *Emotion: Theory, research and experience* (pp. 3–35). New York: Academic Press.

Hebb, D. O. (1955). Drives and the C. N. S. (conceptual nervous system). *Psychological Review, 62,* 243–254.

Heilbrun, A. B. (1982). Cognitive models of criminal violence. *Journal of Consulting and Clinical Psychology, 50,* 546–557.

Heimburger, R. F., Whitlock, C. C., & Kalsbeck, J. E. (1966). Stereotaxic amygdalotomy for epilepsy with aggressive behavior. *Journal of the American Medical Association, 198,* 741–745.

Heishman, S. J., & Stitzer, M. L. (April 1988). *Effects of d-amphetamine and secobarbitol on speech and preference for socializing.* Paper presented at the meeting of the Eastern Psychological Association. Buffalo, NY.

Hellhammer, D. H., Hubert, W., & Schwimeyer, T. (1985). Changes in saliva testosterone after psychological stimulation in men. *Psychoneuroendocrinology, 10,* 77–81.

Hemming, J. H. (1981). Electrodermal indices in a selected prison sample and students. *Personality and Individual Differences, 3,* 37–46.

Hendrickson, D. E. (1973). *An examination of individual differences in cortical evoked response.* Doctoral dissertation, University of London.

Heston, L. L. (1966). Psychiatric disorders in foster home reared children of schizophrenic mothers. *British Journal of Psychiatry, 112,* 819–825.

Hetherington, R. F., Haden, P., & Craig, W. J. (1972). Neurosurgery in affective disorder. In E. Hitchcock, L. Laitinen, & K. Vaernet (Eds.), *Psychosurgery* (pp. 332–345). Springfield, IL: Charles C. Thomas.

Highfield, D., & Grant, S. J. (October 1989). Electrophysiological evidence for an excitatory amino-acid pathway from medial prefrontal cortex to lateral dorsal tegmental nucleus and rostral locus coeruleus. Society for Neuroscience Meeting, Phoenix, AR (Abstracts, p. 644).

Hill, D., Pond, D. A., Mitchell, W., & Falconer, M. A. (1957). Personality changes following temporal lobectomy for epilepsy. *Journal of Mental Science, 103,* 18–27.

Hitchcock, E., Laitinen, L., & Vaernet, K. (1972). *Psychosurgery.* Springfield, IL: Charles C. Thomas.

Hodges, W. F. (1976). The psychophysiology of anxiety. In M. Zuckerman & C. D. Spielberger (Eds.), *Emotions and anxiety: New concepts, methods and applications* (pp. 176–194). Hillsdale, NJ: Erlbaum.

Hodges, W. F., & Spielberger, C. D. (1966). The effects of threat of shock on heart rate for subjects who differ in manifest anxiety and fear of shock. *Psychophysiology, 2,* 287–294.

Hoffman, E., & Goldstein, L. (1981). Hemispheric quantitative EEG changes following emotional reactions in neurotic patients. *Acta Psychiatrica Scandinavica, 63,* 153–164.

Hogan, R. (1982). A socioanalytic theory of personality. In M. M. Page (Ed.), *Personality: Current theory and research. Nebraska Symposium on Motivation* (pp. 55–89). Lincoln, NE: Univ. of Nebraska Press.

Hollister, L. E., Davis, K. L., Overall, J. E., & Anderson, T. (1978). Excretion of MHPG in normal subjects: Implications for biological classification of affective disorders. *Archives of General Psychiatry, 35,* 1410–1415.

Homskaya, E. D. (1973). The human frontal lobes and their role in the organization of activity. *Acta Neurobiological Experimentalis, 33,* 509–522.

Horney, K. (1939). *New ways in psychoanalysis.* New York: Norton.

Houts, A. C., Cook, T. D., & Shadish, W. R., Jr. (1986). The personality-situation debate: A critical multiplist perspective. *Journal of Personality, 54,* 52–105.

Howard, R. C., Fenton, G. W., & Fenwick, P. B. (1984). The contingent negative variation, personality, and antisocial behavior. *British Journal of Psychology, 144,* 463–474.

Huang, Y. H., & Routtenberg, A. (1971). Lateral hypothalamic self-stimulation pathways in Rattus Norvegicus. *Physiology and Behavior, 7,* 419–432.

Huttunen, M. O., & Nyman, G. (1982). On the continuity, change, and clinical value of infant temperament in a prospective epidemiological study. In Ciba Foundation Symposium 89, *Temperament differences in infants and young children* (pp. 240–247). Aulander: NC Pitman.

Innis, R. B., Charney, D. S., & Heninger, G. R. (1987). Differential–3H-imipramine platelet binding in patients with panic disorder and depression. *Psychiatry Research, 21,* 33–41.

Insel, T. R., Zahn, T., & Murphy, D. L. (1985). Obsessive-compulsive disorder: An anxiety disorder? In A. H. Tuma & J. Maser (Eds.), *Anxiety and the anxiety disorders* (pp. 577–589). Hillsdale, NJ: Erlbaum.

Isaacson, R. L. (1982). *The limbic system* (2nd ed.). New York: Plenum.

Izard, C. E. (1977). *Human emotions.* New York: Plenum.

Jackson, D. N. (1967). *Personality Research Form manual.* Goshen, NY: Research Psychologists Press.

Jackson, D. N. (1976). *Manual, Jackson Personality Inventory.* Goshen, NY: Research Psychologists Press.

Jackson, J. H. (1868/1958). In J. Taylor (Ed.), *Selected writings of John Hughlings Jackson.* New York: Basic Books.

Jacob, F., & Monod, J. (1961). On the regulation of gene activity. *Cold Spring Harbor Symposia on Quantitative Biology, 26,* 193–209.

Jacobs, D., & Silverstone, T. (1986). Dextroamphetamine-induced arousal in human subjects as a model for mania. *Psychological Medicine, 16,* 323–329.

Jaffe, L., & Schuckitt, M. A. (1981). The importance of drug use histories in a series of alcoholics. *Journal of Clinical Psychiatry, 42,* 224–227.

James, G. D., Yee, L. S., Harshfield, C. A., Blank, S. G., & Pickering, T. G. (1986).

The influence of happiness, anger, and anxiety on the blood pressure of borderline hypertensives. *Psychosomatic Medicine, 48,* 502–508.

James, W. (1894). What is emotion? *Mind, 9,* 188–205.

Janssen, R. H. C., Mattie, H., van Plooij, G. P. C., & Werre, P. F. (1978). The effects of a depressant and a stimulant drug on the contingent negative variation. *Biological Psychology, 6,* 209–218.

Jimerson, D. C., Nurnberger, J. I., Jr., Post, R. M., Gershon, E. S., & Kopin, I. J. (1981) Plasma MHPG in rapid cyclers and healthy twins. *Archives of General Psychiatry, 38,* 1287–1290.

Jinks, J. L., & Fulker, D. W. (1970). Comparison of the biometrical, genetical, MAVA, and the classical approaches to the analysis of human behavior. *Psychological Bulletin, 73,* 311–349.

Johanson, C. E., & Uhlenhuth, E. H. (1980). Drug preference and mood in humans. *Psychopharmacology, 71,* 275–279.

Johansson, F., Almay, B. G. L., von Knorring, L., Terenius, L., & Åström, M. (1979). Personality traits in chronic pain patients related to endorphin levels in cerebrospinal fluid. *Psychiatry Research, 1,* 231–239.

Johnston, D. G., Troyer, I. E., & Whitsett, S. F. (1988). Chlorimipramine treatment of agoraphobic women: An eight week controlled study. *Archives of General Psychiatry, 45,* 453–459.

Jonason, K. R., & Enloe, L. J. (1971). Alterations in social behavior following septal and amygdaloid lesions in the rat. *Journal of Comparative and Physiological Psychology, 75,* 286–301.

Jones, A. (1969). Stimulus-seeking behavior. In J. P. Zubek (Ed.), *Sensory deprivation: Fifteen years of research* (pp. 167–206). New York: Appleton-Century-Crofts.

Jones, J., Eysenck, H. J., Martin, I., & Levey, A. B. (1981). Personality and the topography of the conditioned eyelid response. *Personality and Individual Differences, 2,* 61–83.

Jönsson, L. E., Änggård, E., & Gunne, L. M. (1971). Blockade of intravenous amphetamine euphoria in man. *Clinical pharmacology and therapeutics, 12,* 889–896.

Jung, C. G. (1933). *Psychological types.* New York: Harcourt Brace Jovanovich.

Kagan, J. (1971). *Change and continuity in infancy.* New York: Wiley.

Kagan, J. (1978). Sex differences in the human infant. In T. E. McGill, D. A. Dewsburg, & B. D. Sachs (Eds.), *Sex and behavior* (pp. 305–316). New York: Plenum.

Kagan, J., & Moss, H. A. (1962). *Birth to maturity.* New York: Wiley.

Kagan, J., Reznick, J. S., & Snidman, N. (1988). Biological bases of childhood shyness. *Science, 240,* 167–171.

Kagan, J., Reznick, J. S., Clarke, C., Snidman, N., & Garcia-Coll, C. (1984). Behavioral inhibition to the unfamiliar. *Child Development, 55,* 2212–2225.

Kahn, A., Lee, E., Dager, S., Hyde, T., Raisys, V., Anery, D., & Dunner, D. (1986). Platelet MAO-B activity in anxiety and depression. *Biological Psychiatry, 21,* 847–849.

Kahn, R. S., van Praag, H. M., Wetzler, S., Asnis, G. M., & Barr, G. (1988). Serotonin and anxiety revisited. *Biological Psychiatry, 15,* 189–208.

Kakihana, R., Brown, D. R., McClearn, G. E., & Tabershaw, I. R. (1966). Brain sensitivity to alcohol in inbred mouse strains. *Science, 154,* 1574–1575.

Kandel, E. R. (1985). Cellular mechanisms of learning and the biological basis of individuality. In E. R. Kandel & J. H. Schwartz (Eds.), *Principals of neural science* (pp. 816–833). New York: Elsevier.

Kantorowitz, D. A. (1978). Personality and conditioning of tumescence and detumescence. *Behavior Research and Therapy, 16,* 117–123.

Kapris, J., Koskenvuo, M., & Langinvanio, H. (1984). Finnish twins reared apart. IV. Smoking and drinking habits: A preliminary analysis of the effects of heredity and environment. *Acta Geneticae Medicae et Gemellologiae, 33,* 425–433.

Karno, M., Hough, R. L., Burnan, A., Escobar, J. L., Tembers, D. M., Santano, F., & Boyd, J. H. (1987). Lifetime prevalence of specific psychiatric disorders among Mexican American and non-Hispanic whites in Los Angeles. *Archives of General Psychiatry, 44,* 695–701.

Kartsounis, L. D., Mervyn-Smith, J., & Pickersgill, M. J. (1983). Factor analyses of the responses of British university students to the Fear Survey Schedule (FSS-III). *Personality and Individual Differences, 2,* 157–163.

Kathol, R. G., Noyes, R., Lopez, A. L., & Reich, J. H. (1988). Relationship of urinary free cortisol levels in patients with panic disorder to symptoms of depression and agoraphobia. *Psychiatry Research, 24,* 211–221.

Kelly, D. (1980). *Anxiety and emotions.* Springfield, IL: Charles C. Thomas.

Kelly, D., Walter, C. J., Mitchell-Heggs, N., & Sargant, W. (1972). Modified leucotomy assessed clinically, physiologically, and psychologically. *British Journal of Psychiatry, 120,* 19–29.

Kelly, E. L. (1955). Consistency of the adult personality. *American Psychologist, 10,* 659–681.

Kelly, G. A. (1955). *A theory of personality: The psychology of interpersonal constructs.* New York: Norton.

Kemali, D., Maj, M., Iouo, G., Marciano, F., Nolfe, G., Galderisi, S., & Salvati, A. (1985). Relationship between CSF noradrenaline levels, EEG indicators of activation, and psychosis ratings in drug-free schizophrenic patients. *Acta Psychiatrica Scandinavica, 71,* 19–24.

Kendler, K. S., & Gruenberg, A. M. (1984). An independent analysis of the Danish adoption study of schizophrenia. VI. The relationship between psychiatric disorders as defined by DSM III in the relatives and adoptees. *Archives of General Psychiatry, 41,* 555–568.

Kendler, K. S., Gruenberg, A. M., & Strauss, J. S. (1981). An independent analysis of the Copenhagen sample of the Danish adoption study of schizophrenia. *Archives of General Psychiatry, 38,* 973–987.

Kendler, K. S., Gruenberg, A. M., & Tsaung, T. (1985). Psychiatric illness in first-degree relatives of schizophrenic and surgical control patients: A family study using DSM III criteria. *Archives of General Psychiatry, 42,* 770–779.

Kendler, K. S., Heath, A. C., Martin, N. G., & Eaves, L. J. (1986). Symptoms of anxiety and depression in a volunteer twin population. *Archives of General Psychiatry, 43,* 213–221.

Kendler, K. S., Heath, A. C., Martin, N. G., & Eaves, L. J. (1987). Symptoms of anxiety and symptoms of depression: Same genes, different environments? *Archives of General Psychiatry, 44,* 451–457.

Kety, S. S., Rosenthal, D., Wender, P. H., Schulsinger, F., & Jacobsen, B. (1975). Mental illness in the biological and adoptive families of adopted individuals who have become schizophrenic: A preliminary report based on psychiatric interviews. In R. R. Fieve, D. Rosenthal, & H. Brill (Eds.), *Genetic Research in Psychiatry* (pp. 142–165). Baltimore, MD: Johns Hopkins Univ. Press.

Khan, A., Lee, E., Dager, S., Hyde, T., Raisys, V., Anery, D., & Dunner, D. (1986). Platelet MAO-B activity in anxiety and depression. *Biological Psychiatry, 21,* 847–849.

King, R. J., Mefford, I. N., Wang, C., Murchison, A., Caligari, E. J., & Berger, P. A. (1986). CSF dopamine levels correlate with extraversion in depressed patients. *Psychiatry Research, 19,* 305–310.

Klein, F. (1981). Anxiety reconceptualized. In D. Klein & J. Rabkin (Eds.), *Anxiety: New research and changing concepts* (pp. 235–265). New York: Raven Press.

Kling, A., & Stelkis, H. D. (1976). A neural substrate for affiliative behavior in non-human primates. *Brain, Behavior and Evolution, 13,* 216–238.

Kling, A., Stelkis, H. D., & Deutsch, S. (1979). Radiotelemetered activity from the amygdala during social interactions in the monkey. *Experimental Neurology, 66,* 88–96.

Klinteberg, B., Magnusson, D., & Schalling, D. (1989). Hyperactive behavior in childhood and adult impulsivity: A longitudinal study of male subjects. *Personality and Individual Differences, 10,* 43–50.

Klinteberg, B., Schalling, D., Edman, G., Oreland, L., & Åsberg, M. (1987). Personality correlates of platelet monoamine oxidase (MAO) activity in female and male subjects. *Neuropsychobiology, 18,* 89–96.

Klonowicz, T. (1987). Reactivity and the control of arousal. In J. Strelau & H. J. Eysenck (Eds.), *Personality dimensions and arousal* (pp. 183–196). New York: Plenum.

Klüver, H., & Bucy, P. C. (1939). Preliminary analysis of the temporal lobes in monkeys. *Archives of Neurology and Psychiatry, 42,* 979–1000.

Ko, G. N., Elsworth, J. D., Roth, R. H., Rifkin, B. G., Leigh, H., & Redmond, E. (1983). Panic-induced elevation of plasma MHPG in phobic-anxious patients: Effects of clonidine and imipramine. *Archives of General Psychiatry, 40,* 425–430.

Koehler, K., Vartzopoulos, D., & Ebel, H. (1988). The relationship of panic attacks to autonomically labile generalized anxiety. *Comprehensive Psychiatry, 29,* 91–97.

Koenigsberg, H. W., Kaplan, R. D., Gilmore, M. M., & Cooper, A. M. (1985). The relationship between syndrome and personality disorder in DSM III: Experience with 2,412 patients. *American Journal of Psychiatry, 142,* 207–212.

Koob, G. F., Vaccarino, F., Amalric, M., & Bloom, F. E. (1987). Positive reinforcement properties of drugs: Search for neural substrates. In J. Engel, L. Oreland, B. Pernov, S. Rössner & L. A. Pellhorn (Eds.), *Brain reward systems and abuse* (pp. 35–50). New York: Raven Press.

Koriat, A., Averill, J. R., & Malmstrom, E. J. (1973). Individual differences in habituation: Some methodological and conceptual issues. *Journal of Research in Personality, 7,* 88–101.

Kralik, P. M., Ho, B. T., Mathew, R. J., Taylor, D., & Weinman, M. L. (1982). Effects of adrenalin administration on platelet MAO of anxious and normal subjects. *Neuropsychobiology, 8,* 205–209.

Kreuz, L. E., & Rose, R. M. (1972). Assessment of aggressive behavior and plasma testosterone in a young criminal population. *Psychosomatic Medicine, 34,* 321–332.

Kuhn, T. S. (1970). *The structure of scientific revolutions.* Chicago, IL: University of Chicago Press.

Kulcsár, Z., Kutor, L., & Arató, M. (1984). Sensation seeking, its biochemical correlates, and its relation to vestibulo-ocular functions. In H. Bonarius, G. van Heck, & N. Smid (Eds.), *Personality psychology in Europe: Theoretical and empirical developments* (pp. 327–346). Lisse, The Netherlands: Swets & Zeitlinger.

Lacey, J. I. (1959). Psychophysiological approaches to the evaluation of psychotherapeutic process and outcome. In E. A. Rubenstein & M. B. Parloff (Eds.), *Research in psychotherapy.* Washington, DC: American Psychological Association.

Lacey, J. I. (1967). Somatic response patterns and stress: Some revisions of activation theory. In M. H. Appley & R. Trumbell (Eds.), *Issues in research* (pp. 14–22). New York: Appleton.

Lader, M. H. (1975). The psychophysiology of anxious and depressed patients. In D. C. Fowles (Ed.), *Clinical applications of psychophysiology* (pp. 12–41). New York: Columbia Univ. Press.

Lader, M. H., & Wing, L. (1966). *Physiological measures, sedative drugs and morbid anxiety.* London: Oxford Univ. Press.

Lagerspetz, K. M. J., & Lagerspetz, K. Y. H. (1971). Changes in the aggressiveness of mice resulting from selective breeding, learning and social isolation. *Scandinavian Journal of Psychology, 12,* 241–248.

Laitinen, L. V., & Livingston, K. E. (1973). *Surgical approaches in psychiatry.* Baltimore, MD: University Park Press.

Laitinen, L. V., & Vilkki, J. (1973). Observations on the transcallosal emotional connections. In L. V. Laitinen & K. E. Livingston (Eds.), *Surgical approaches in psychiatry* (pp. 74–80). Baltimore, MD: University Park Press.

Lake, C. R., Gullner, H. G., Polinsky, R. J., Ebert, M. H., Zieglery, M. G., & Barterr, F. C. (1981). Essential hypertension: Central and peripheral norepinephrine. *Science, 211,* 955–957.

Lake, C. R., & Ziegler, M. G. (1985). *The catecholamines in psychiatric and neurologic disorders.* Boston, MA: Butterworth.

Lang, P. J. (1985). The cognitive psychophysiology of emotion: Fear and anxiety. In A. H. Tuma & J. D. Maser (Eds.), *Anxiety and the anxiety disorders* (pp. 131–170). Hillsdale, NJ: Erlbaum.

Lansdell, H. (1968). Effect of extent of temporal lobe surgery and neuropathology on the MMPI. *Journal of Clinical Psychology, 24,* 406–412.

Lassalle, J. M., & LePape, G. (1978). Locomotor activity of two inbred strains of mice in a seminatural and a breeding cage environment. *Behavior Genetics, 8,* 371–376.

Lazarus, R. S. (1968). Emotions and adaptation: Conceptual and empirical relations. In W. J. Arnold (Ed.), *Nebraska Symposium on Motivation* (Vol. 16, pp. 175–270). Lincoln NE: University of Nebraska Press.

LeDoux, J. E. (1987). Emotion. In F. Plum (Ed.), *Handbook of Physiology.* 1: The *nervous system, Vol. 5, Higher functions of the brain* (pp. 419–460). Bethesda, MD: American Physiological Society.

Leshner, A. I. (1983). Pituitary-adrenocortical effects on intermale agonistic behavior. In B. B. Svare (Ed.), *Hormones and aggressive behavior* (pp. 27–38). New York: Plenum.

Levey, A. B., & Martin, I. (1981). Personality and conditioning. In H. J. Eysenck (Ed.), *A model for personality* (pp. 123–168). New York: Springer-Verlag.

Levi, L. (1967). Stressors, stress tolerance, emotions and performance in relation to catecholamine excretion. In L. Levi (Ed.), *Emotional stress: Physiological and psychological reactions; medical industrial and military implications* (pp. 192–200). New York: American Elsevier Publishing Co.

Levi, L. (1969). Sympatho-adrenomedullary activity, diuresis and emotional reactions during visual sexual stimulation in human females and males. *Psychosomatic Medicine, 31,* 251–268.

Levinson, F., & Meyer, V. (1965). Personality changes in relation to psychiatric states following orbital cortex undercutting. *British Journal of Psychiatry, 111,* 207–218.

Lewis, C. E., Rice, J., & Helzer, J. E. (1983). Diagnostic interactions: Alcoholism and antisocial personality. *Journal of Nervous and Mental Disease, 171,* 105–113.

Lewis, C. E., Robbins, E. N., & Rice, J. (1985). Association of alcoholism with antisocial personality in urban men. *Journal of Nervous and Mental Disease, 173,* 166–174.

Lewis, D. A., Noyes, R., Coryell, W., & Clancy, J. (1985). Triated imipramine binding to platelets is decreased in patients with agoraphobia. *Psychiatry Research, 16,* 1–9.

Lewis, E. G., Dustman, R. E., & Beck, E. C. (1972). Evoked response similarity in monozygotic, dizygotic and unrelated individuals: A comparative study. *Electroencephalography and Clinical Neurophysiology, 23,* 309–316.

Lidberg, L., Levander, S. E., Schalling, D., & Lidberg, Y. (1978). Urinary catecholamines, stress, and psychopathy: A study of arrested men awaiting trial. *Psychosomatic Medicine, 40,* 116–125.

Lidberg, L., Modin, I., Oreland, L., Tuck, J. R., & Gillner, A. (1985). Platelet monoamine oxidase activity and psychopathy. *Psychiatry Research, 16,* 339–343.

Liebowitz, M. R., Gorman, J. M., Fyer, A. J., Levitt, M., Dillon, D., Levey, G., Appleby, I. L., Anderson, S., Palij, M., Davies, S. O., & Klein, D. F. (1985). Lactate provocation of panic attacks. II. Biochemical and physiologic findings. *Archives of General Psychiatry, 42,* 709–719.

Lindsley, D. B., Bowden, J., & Magoun, H. W. (1949). Effect upon EEG of acute injury to the brain stem activating system. *Electroencephalography and Clinical Neurophysiology, 1,* 475–486.

Lindström, L. H. (1985). Low HVA in normal 5-HIAA CSF levels in drug-free schizophrenic patients compared to healthy volunteers: Correlations to symptomatology and family history. *Psychiatry Research, 14,* 265–273.

Linnoila, M., Ninan, P. T., Scheinin, M., Waters, R. M., Chang, W. H., Bartko, J., & van Kammen, D. P. (1983). Reliability of norepinephrine and major monoamine metabolic measurements in CSF of schizophrenic patients. *Archives of General Psychiatry, 40,* 1290–1294.

Lishman, W. A. (1968). Brain damage in relation to psychiatric disability after head injury. *British Journal of Psychiatry, 114,* 373–410.

Loehlin, J. C. (1982). Are personality traits differentially heritable? *Behavior Genetics, 12,* 417–428.

Loehlin, J. C., & Nichols, R. C. (1976). *Heredity, environment, and personality.* Austin, TX: University of Texas Press.

Loehlin, J. C., Willerman, L., & Horn, J. M. (1985). Personality resemblances in adoptive families when the children are late-adolescent or adult. *Journal of Personality and Social Psychology, 48,* 376–392.

Loehlin, J. C., Willerman, L., & Horn, J. M. (1987). Personality resemblance in adoptive families: A 10-year follow-up. *Journal of Personality and Social Psychology, 53,* 961–969.

Lolas, F., & Aguilera, N. (1982). Extraversion and inhibition. *Biological Psychiatry, 17,* 963–969.

Lolas, F., & de Andracca, I. (1977). Neuroticism, extraversion, and slow brain potentials. *Neuropsychobiology, 3,* 12–22.

Loveless, N., & Sanford, A. (1974). Slow potential correlates of preparatory set. *Biological Psychology, 1,* 303–304.

Lukas, J. H., & Siegel, J. (1977). Cortical mechanisms that augment or reduce evoked potentials in cats. *Science, 196,* 73–75.

Luria, A. R. (1980). *Higher cortical function in man* (2nd ed.). New York: Basic Books.

Lykken, D. T. (1957). A study of anxiety in the sociopathic personality. *Journal of Abnormal and Social Psychology, 55,* 6–10.

Lykken, D. T. (1982). Research with twins: The concept of emergenesis. *Psychophysiology, 19,* 361–373.

Lykken, D. T., Iacono, W. G., Haroian, B. K., McGue, M., & Bouchard, T. J. (1988). Habituation of the skin conductance response to strong stimuli: A twin study. *Psychophysiology, 25,* 4–15.

Lynn, R. (1966). *Attention, arousal and the orientation reaction.* New York: Pergamon.

Lytton, H. (1977). Do parents create, or respond to, differences in twins? *Developmental Psychology, 13,* 456–459.

Maas, J. W., & Leckman, J. F. (1983). Relationships between central nervous noradrenergic function and plasma and urinary MHPG and other norepinephrine metabolites. In J. W. Maas (Ed.), *MHPG: Basic mechanisms and psychopathology* (pp. 33–43). New York: Academic Press.

Maccoby, E. E., & Jacklin, C. N. (1974). *The psychology of sex differences.* Stanford, CA: Stanford Univ. Press.

MacLean, P. D. (1949). Psychosomatic disease and the visceral brain. Recent development bearing on the Papez theory of emotion. *Psychosomatic Medicine, 11,* 338–353.

MacLean, P. D. (1970). The triune brain, emotion, and scientific bias. In F. O. Schmidt

(Ed.), *The neurosciences second study program* (pp. 336–349). New York: Rockefeller Press.

MacLean, P. D. (1976). Sensory and perceptive factors in emotional functions of the triune brain. In R. G. Grenell & S. Gabay (Eds.), *Biological foundations of psychiatry* (pp. 177–198). New York: Raven Press.

MacLean, P. D. (1982). On the origin and progressive evolution of the triune brain. In E. Armstrong & D. Falk (Eds.), *Primate brain evolution: Methods and concepts* (pp. 291–316). New York: Plenum.

Madsen, D., & McGuire, M. T. (1984). Whole blood serotonin and the Type A behavior pattern. *Psychosomatic Medicine, 46,* 546–548.

Magnusson, D. (1987). Individual development in an interactional perspective. In D. Magnusson (Ed.), *Paths through life.* Hillsdale, NJ: Erlbaum.

Magnusson, D., & Endler, N. S. (1977). *Personality at the crossroads: Current issues in interactional psychology.* Hillsdale, NJ: Erlbaum.

Major, L. F., & Murphy, D. L. (1978). Platelet and plasma amine oxidase activity in alcoholic individuals. *British Journal of Psychology, 132,* 548–554.

Mandler, G. (1975). *Mind and emotions.* New York: Wiley.

Manuck, S. B., & Proietti, J. M. (1982). Parental hypertension and cardiovascular response to cognitive and isometric challenge. *Psychophysiology, 19,* 481–489.

Margraf, J., Taylor, C. B., Ehlers, A., Roth, W. T., & Agras, W. S. (1987). Panic attacks in the natural environment. *Journal of Nervous and Mental Disease, 175,* 558–565.

Mark, V. H., Sweet, W. H., & Erbin, F. R. (1972). The effect of amygdalotomy on violent behavior with temporal lobe epilepsy. In E. Hitchcock, L. Laitinen, & K. Vaernet (Eds.), *Psychosurgery* (pp. 139–155). Springfield, IL: Charles C. Thomas.

Martin, N. G., Jardine, R., Andrews, G., & Heath, A. (1988). Anxiety disorders and neuroticism: Are there genetic factors specific to panic? *Acta Psychiatrica Scandinavica, 77,* 698–706.

Mason, S. T. (1981). Noradrenaline in the brain: Progress on theories of behavioural function. *Progress in Neurobiology, 16,* 263–303.

Mason, S. T. (1984). *Catecholamines and behavior.* Cambridge, England: Cambridge Univ. Press.

Mason, S. T., & Iverson, S. D. (1977). Effects of selective forebrain noradrenaline loss of behavioral inhibition in the rat. *Journal of Comparative and Physiological Psychology, 91,* 165–173.

Matheny, A. P., Jr. (1980). Bayley's infant record: Behavioral component and twin analyses. *Child Development, 51,* 1157–1167.

Matheny, A. P., & Dolan, A. B. (1980). A twin study of personality and temperament during middle childhood. *Journal of Research in Personality, 14,* 224–234.

Mathew, R. J., Ho, B. T., Kralik, P., Weinman, M., & Claghorn, J. L. (1981). Anxiety and platelet MAO levels after relaxation training. *American Journal of Psychiatry, 138,* 371–373.

Mathew, R. J., Ho, P., Kralik, P., & Taylor, D. L. (1980). Catecholamines and monoamine oxidase activity in anxiety. *Acta Psychiatrica Scandinavica, 63,* 245–252.

Mathew, R. J., Ho, P., Kralik, P., Taylor, D., & Claghorn, J. L. (1980). MAO, DBH and COMT: The effect of anxiety. *Journal of Clinical Psychiatry, 41,* 25–28.

Mathew, R. J., Ho, B. T., Taylor, D. L., & Semchuk, K. M. (1981). Catecholamine and dopamine-β-hydroxylase in anxiety. *Journal of Psychosomatic Research, 25,* 499–504.

Mathew, R. J., Weinman, M. L., & Barr, D. L. (1984). Personality and regional cerebral blood flow. *British Journal of Psychiatry, 144,* 529–532.

Mattson, A., Schalling, D., Olweus, D., Low, H., & Svensson, J. (1980). Plasma testosterone, aggressive behavior, and personality dimensions in young male delinquents. *Journal of the American Academy of Child Psychiatry, 19,* 476–490.

454   *References*

Maushauser, C., Ehner, G., & Eckel, K. (1981). Pain, personality and individual differences in sensory evoked potentials. *Personality and Individual Differences, 2,* 335–336.

Maxson, S. C., & Shrenker, P. (1983). Genetics, hormones and aggression. In B. B. Svare (Ed.), *Hormones and aggressive behavior* (pp. 179–196). New York: Plenum.

McAllister, T. W., & Price, T. R. P. (1987). Aspects of the behavior of psychiatric inpatients with frontal lobe damage: Some implications for diagnosis and treatment. *Comprehensive Psychiatry, 28,* 14–21.

McClearn, G. E. (1959). Genetics of mouse behavior in novel situations. *Journal of Comparative and Physiological Psychology, 52,* 62–67.

McClelland, D. C., Atkinson, J. W., Clark, R. A., & Lowell, E. I. (1953). *The achievement motive.* New York: Appleton-Century-Crofts.

McCord, J. (1986). Instigation and insulation: How families affect antisocial aggression. In D. Olweus, J. Block, & M. Radke-Yarrow (Eds.), *Development of antisocial and prosocial behavior: Research, theories and issues* (pp. 343–357). New York: Academic Press.

McCord, R. R., & Wakefield, J. A. (1981). Arithmetic achievement as a function of introversion-extraversion and teacher-presented reward and punishment. *Personality and Individual Differences, 2,* 145–152.

McCrae, R. R., & Costa, P. T., Jr. (1982). Self-concept and the stability of personality: Cross-sectional comparisons of self-reports and ratings. *Journal of Personality and Social Psychology, 43,* 1282–1292.

McCrae, R. R., & Costa, P. T., Jr. (1985a). Updating Norman's "adequate taxonomy": Intelligence and personality dimensions in natural languages and in questionnaires. *Journal of Personality and Social Psychology, 49,* 710–721.

McCrae, R. R., & Costa, P. T., Jr. (1985b). Comparison of EPI and Psychoticism scales with measures of the five-factor model of personality. *Personality and Individual Differences, 6,* 587–597.

McDonald, D. G., & Johnson, L. C. (1975). Classical conditioning of autonomic responses in alert and drowsy subjects. *Biological Psychology, 3,* 101–112.

McGill, T. E. (1978). Genotype-hormone interactions. In T. E. McGill, D. A. Dewsbury, & B. D. Sachs (Eds.), *Sex and behavior.* New York: Plenum.

McIntyre, M., Pritchard, P. B., & Lombroso, C. T. (1976). Left and right temporal lobe epileptics: A controlled investigation of some psychological differences. *Epilepsia, 17,* 377–386.

McReynolds, W. E., Weir, M. W., & DeFries, V. C. (1967). Open-field behavior in mice: effects of test illumination. *Psychonomic Science, 9,* 277–278.

Mead, M. (1949). *Male and female: A study of the sexes in a changing world.* New York: William Morrow & Co.

Mednick, S. A. (1975). Autonomic nervous system recovery and psychopathy. *Scandinavian Journal of Behavioral Therapy, 4,* 55–67.

Mednick, S. A., Gabrelli, W. F., Jr., & Hutchings, B. (1987). Genetic factors in the etiology of criminal behavior. In S. A. Mednick, T. E. Moffitt, & S. A. Stack (Eds.), *The causes of crime: New biological approaches* (pp. 74–91). New York: Cambridge Univ. Press.

Mednick, S. A., Moffitt, T., Gabrielli, W. F., Jr., & Hutchings, B. (1986). Genetic factors in criminal behavior: A review. In D. Olweus, J. Block, & M. Radke-Yarrow (Eds.), *Development of antisocial and prosocial behavior* (pp. 33–50). New York: Academic Press.

Meehl, P. E. (1962). Schizotaxia, schizotypy, schizophrenia. *American Psychologist, 17,* 827–838.

Mellstrom, M., Jr., Cicala, G. A., & Zuckerman, M. (1976). General versus specific trait anxiety measures in the prediction of fear of snakes. *Journal of Consulting and Clinical Psychology, 44,* 83–91.

Mellstrom, M., Jr., Zuckerman, M., & Cicala, G. A. (1978). General versus specific traits in the assessment of anxiety. *Journal of Consulting and Clinical Psychology, 46,* 423–431.

Mettler, F. A. (1952). *Psychosurgical problems.* New York: Blakiston Co.

Meyer, G., McElhaney, M., Martin, W., & McGraw, C. P. (1972). Stereotactic cingulotomy with results of acute stimulation and serial psychological testing. In L. V. Laitinen & K. E. Livingston (Eds.), *Surgical approaches in psychiatry* (pp. 39–58). Baltimore, MD: University Park Press.

Meyer, G. J., & Shack, J. R. (1989). Structural convergence of mood and personality: Evidence for old and new directions. *Journal of Personality and Social Psychology, 57,* 691–706.

Meyer-Bahlberg, H. F. L., Boon, D. A., Sharma, M., & Edwards, J. A. (1974). Aggressiveness and testosterone measures in men. *Psychological Medicine, 36,* 269–374.

Meyerson, B. J., Palis, A., & Sietnieks, A. (1979). Hormone-monoamine interactions and sexual behavior. In C. Beyer (Ed.), *Endocrine control of sexual behavior* (pp. 389–404). New York: Raven.

Michael, R. P., & Zumpe, D. (1978). Potency in male rhesus monkeys: Effects of continuously receptive females. *Science, 200,* 451–453.

Miller, A. W. (1967). Awareness, verbal conditioning and meaning conditioning. *Psychological Reports, 21,* 681–691.

Miller, L. (1985). Cognitive risk-taking after frontal or temporal lobectomy—I. The synthesis of fragmented visual information. *Neuropsychologia, 23,* 359–369.

Miller, L. (1987). Neuropsychology of the aggressive psychopath. *Aggressive Behavior, 13,* 119–140.

Miller, L., & Milner, B. (1985). Cognitive risk-taking after frontal or temporal lobectomy—II. The synthesis of phonemic and semantic information. *Neuropsychologia, 23,* 371–379.

Miller, N. E. (1948). Studies of fear as a learnable drive: I. Fear as motivation and fear reduction as a reinforcement in the learning of new responses. *Journal of Experimental Psychology, 38,* 89–101.

Mischel, W. (1968). *Personality and Assessment.* London: Wiley.

Mischel, W. (1981). *Introduction to personality.* New York: Holt, Rinehart & Winston.

Mischel, W. (1984). Convergencies and challenges in the search for consistency. *American Psychologist, 39,* 351–364.

Mischel, W., Ebbesen, E. B., & Zeiss, A. R. (1972). Cognitive and attentional mechanisms in delay of gratification. *Journal of Personality and Social Psychology, 21,* 204–218.

Mischel, W., & Peake, P. K. (1982). Beyond déjà vu in the search for cross-situational consistency. *Psychological Review, 89,* 730–755.

Mischel, W., Shoda, Y., & Peake, P. K. (1988). The nature of adolescent competencies predicted by preschool delay of gratification. *Journal of Personality and Social Psychology, 54,* 687–696.

Mitchell-Heggs, N., Kelly, D., & Richardson, A. (1976). Sterotactic limbic leucotomy: A followup at 16 months. *British Journal of Psychiatry, 128,* 226–240.

Moos, R. H. (1968). Situational analysis of a therapeutic community milieu. *Journal of Abnormal Psychology, 73,* 49–61.

Moos, R. H. (1969). Sources of variance in responses to questionnaires and in behavior. *Journal of Abnormal Psychology, 74,* 405–412.

Morrison, J. (1980). Adult psychiatric disorders in parents of hyperactive children. *American Journal of Psychiatry, 137,* 825–827.

Moruzzi, G., & Magoun, H. W. (1949). Brain stem reticular formation and activation of the EEG. *EEG Clinical Neurophysiology, 1,* 455–473.

Moscowitz, D. S. (1982). Coherence and cross-situational generality in personality: A new analysis of old problems. *Journal of Personality and Social Psychology, 43,* 754–768.

Mountz, J. M., Modell, J. G., Wilson, M. W., Curtis, G. C., Lee, M. A., Schmaltz, S., & Kuhl, D. E. (1989). Position emission tomographic evaluation of cerebral blood flow during state anxiety in simple phobia. *Archives of General Psychiatry, 46*, 501–504.

Mowrer, O. H. (1939). A stimulus-response analysis of anxiety and its role as a reinforcing agent. *Psychological Review, 46*, 553–565.

Mowrer, O. H. (1950). Learning theory and personality dynamics. New York: Academic Press.

Moyer, K. E. (1976). *The psychology of aggression.* New York: Harper and Row.

Murphy, D. L. (1976). Clinical, genetic, hormonal and drug influences on the activity of human platelet monoamine oxidase. In *Ciba Foundation Symposium 39: Monoamine oxidase and its inhibition.* Amsterdam: Elsevier.

Murphy, D. L. (1977). The behavioral toxicity of monoamine oxidase—inhibiting antidepressants. In A. Goldin, F. Hawking, & I. J. Kodin (Eds.), *Advances in pharmacology and chemotherapy* (pp. 71–105). New York: Academic Press.

Murphy, D. L., Belmaker, R. H., Buchsbaum, M. S., Martin, N. F., Ciaranello, R., & Wyatt, R. J. (1977). Biogenic amine related enzymes and personality variations in normals. *Psychological Medicine, 7*, 149–157.

Murphy, D. L., Wright, C., Buchsbaum, M. S., Nichols, A., Costa, J. L., & Wyatt, R. J. (1976). Platelet and plasma amine oxidase activity in 680 normals: Sex and age differences and stability over time. *Biochemical Medicine, 16*, 254–265.

Murray, H. A. (1938). *Explorations in personality.* New York: Oxford Univ. Press.

Myrtek, M. (1984). *Constitutional psychophysiology.* London: Academic Press.

Naber, D., & Bullinger, M. (1985). Neuroendocrine and psychological variables relating to postoperative psychosis after open-heart surgery. *Psychoneuroendocrinology, 10*, 315–324.

Nachshon, I., & Denno, D. (1987). Violent behavior and cerebral hemisphere function. In S. A. Mednick, T. E. Moffitt, & S. A. Stack (Eds.), *The causes of crime: New biological approaches* (pp. 185–217). Cambridge, England: Cambridge Univ. Press.

Nagpal, M., & Gupta, B. S. (1979). Personality, reinforcement, and verbal operant conditioning. *British Journal of Psychology, 70*, 471–476.

Naveteur, J., & Baque, E. F. (1987). Individual differences in electrodermal activity as a function of subjects' anxiety. *Personality and Individual Differences, 8*, 615–626.

Neary, R. S., & Zuckerman, M. (1976). Sensation seeking, trait and state anxiety, and the electrodermal orienting reflex. *Psychophysiology, 13*, 205–211.

Nebylitsin, V. K. (1963). An electrographic study of the parameters, strength of the nervous system and the equilibrium of the nervous system in man, using a factor analysis. In B. M. Teplov (Ed.), *Typological characteristics of higher nervous system activity in man.* Moscow, USSR: Moscow Academy of Pedagogical Sciences.

Nebylitsyn, V. D. (1972). Fundamental properties of the nervous system. New York: Plenum.

Neese, R. M., Cameron, O. G., Curtis, G. C., McCann, D. S., & Huber-Smith, M. J. (1984). Adrenergic function in patients with panic anxiety. *Archives of General Psychiatry, 41*, 771–776.

Neese, R. M., Curtis, G. C., Thyer, B. A., McCann, D. S., Huber-Smith, M. J., & Knopf, R. F. (1985). Endocrine and cardiovascular responses during phobic anxiety. *Psychosomatic Medicine, 47*, 320–332.

Newman, H. H., Freeman, F. N., & Holzinger, K. J. (1937). *Twins: A study of heredity and environment.* Chicago, IL: Univ. of Chicago Press.

Newman, J. P., & Kosson, D. S. (1986). Passive avoidance learning in psychopathic and nonpsychopathic offenders. *Journal of Abnormal Psychology, 95*, 252–256.

Newman, J. P., Patterson, C. M., & Kosson, D. S. (1987). Response perservation in psychopaths. *Journal of Abnormal Psychology, 96*, 145–148.

Newman, J. P., Widom, C. S., & Nathan, S. (1985). Passive avoidance in syndromes of disinhibition: Psychopathy and extraversion. *Journal of Personality and Social Psychology, 48,* 1316–1327.

Nies, A., Robinson, D. S., Harris, L., & Lamborn, K. R. (1974). Comparison of monoamine oxidase substrate activities in twins, schizophrenics, depressives and controls. In E. Usdin (Ed.) *Neuropsychopharmacology of monoamines and their regulatory enzymes.* New York: Raven Press.

Niess, R. (1988). Reconceptualizing arousal: Psychobiological states in motor performance. *Psychological Bulletin, 103,* 345–366.

Niklasson, F., Ågren, H., & Hällgren, R. (1983). Purine and monoamine metabolites in cerebrospinal fluid: Parallel purigenic and monoaminergic activation in depressive illness? *Journal of Neurology, Neurosurgery, and Psychiatry, 46,* 255–260.

Ninan, P., Insel, T., Cohen, R. T., Skolnick, R., & Paul, S. M. (1982). A benzodiazepine receptor mediated model of anxiety. *Science, 218,* 1332–1334.

Norman, T. R., Acevedo, A., McIntyre, I. M., Judd, F. K., & Burrows, G. D. (1988). A kinetic analysis of platelet monoamine oxidase activity in patients with panic attack. *Journal of Affective Disorders, 15,* 127–130.

Norman, W. T. (1963). Toward an adequate taxonomy of personality attributes: Replicated factor structure. *Journal of Abnormal and Social Psychology, 66,* 574–583.

Noyes, R., Clancy, J., Crowe, R. R., Hoenk, P. R., & Slyman, D. J. (1978). The familial prevalence of anxiety neuroses. *Archives of General Psychiatry, 35,* 1057–1059.

Noyes, R., Crowe, R. R., Harris, E. L., Hamra, B. J., McChesney, C. M., & Chaudhry, D. R. (1986). Relationship between panic disorder and agoraphobia: A family study. *Archives of General Psychiatry, 43,* 227–232.

O'Connor, K. (1982). Individual differences in the effect of smoking on frontal-central distribution of the CNV: Some observations on smoker's control of attentional behavior. *Personality and Individual Differences, 3,* 271–285.

O'Connor, K. (1983). Individual differences in components of slow cortical potentials. Implications for models of information processing. *Personality and Individual Differences, 4,* 403–410.

O'Gorman, J. G. (1977). Individual differences in habituation of human physiological responses: A review of theory, method, and findings in the study of personality correlates in non-clinical populations. *Biological Psychology, 5,* 257–318.

O'Gorman, J. G. (1983). Habituation and personality. In A. Gale & J. A. Edwards (Eds.), *Physiological correlates of human behavior* (Vol. 3, pp. 45–61). New York: Academic Press.

O'Gorman, J. G. (1984). Extraversion and the EEG. I: An evaluation of Gale's hypothesis. *Biological Psychology, 19,* 95–112.

O'Gorman, J. G., & Lloyd, J. E. M. (1987). Extraversion, impulsiveness, and EEG alpha activity. *Personality and Individual Differences, 8,* 169–174.

O'Gorman, J. G., & Mallise, L. R. (1984). Extraversion and the EEG. II: A test of Gale's hypothesis. *Biological Psychology, 19,* 113–127.

Olds, J., & Milner, P. (1954). Positive reinforcement produced by electrical stimulation of septal area and other regions of rat brain. *Journal of Comparative and Physiological Psychology, 47,* 419–427.

Olds, M. E., & Fobes, J. L. (1981). The central basis of motivation: Intracranial self-stimulation studies. In M. R. Rozenzweig & F. Porter (Eds.), *Annual Review of Psychology* (pp. 523–574). Palo Alto, CA: Annual Reviews Inc.

Olds, M. E., & Olds, J. (1963). Approach-avoidance analysis of rat diencephalon. *Journal of Comparative Neurology, 120,* 259–295.

Olds, M. E., & Olds, J. (1969). Effects of lesions in medial forebrain bundle on self-stimulation behavior. *American Journal of Physiology, 217,* 1253–1264.

Olweus, D. (1987). Testosterone and adrenaline: aggressive antisocial behavior in normal adolescent males. In S. A. Mednick, T. E. Moffitt, & S. A. Stack (Eds.), *The causes* of crime: New biological approaches (pp. 263–282). Cambridge, England: Cambridge Univ. Press.

Oreland, L., Wilberg, A., & Fowler, C. J. (1981). Monoamine oxidase activity as related to monoamine oxidase activity and monoaminergic function in the brain. In B. Angrist (Ed.), Recent advances in neuropsychopharmacology (Vol. 31). Oxford: Pergamon.

Orlebeke, J. F., & Feij, J. A. (1979). The orienting reflex as a personality correlate. In E. H. van Olst & J. F. Orlebeke (Eds.), The orienting reflex in humans (pp. 567–585). Hillsdale, NJ: Erlbaum.

Ornstein, R. E. (1972). The psychology of consciousness. San Francisco: W. H. Freeman.

Orr, S. P., & Pitman, R. K. (1987). Electrodermal psychophysiology of anxiety disorder: Orienting response and spontaneous fluctuations. Biological Psychiatry, 22, 653–656.

Öst, L. G. (1987). Age of onset of different phobias. Journal of Abnormal Psychology, 96, 223–229.

Owen, F., Acker, W., & Bourne, R. C. (1977). The effect on human monoamine oxidase activity of subcutaneous injection of adrenalin. Biochemical Pharmacology, 26, 2065–2067.

Oxenstierna, G., Edman, G., Iselius, L., Oreland, L., Ross, S. B., & Sedvall, G. (1986). Concentrations of monoamine metabolites in the cerebrospinal fluid of twins and unrelated individuals: A genetic study. Journal of Psychiatric Research, 20, 19–20.

Paffenbarger, R. S., Thorne, M. C., & Wing, A. L. (1968). Chronic disease in former college students, VIII Characteristics predisposing to hypertension in later years. American Journal of Epidemiology, 88, 25–32.

Pallmeyer, T. P., Blanchard, E. B., & Kolb, L. C. (1986). The psychophysiology of combat-induced post-traumatic stress disorder in Vietnam veterans. Behavior Research and Therapy, 24, 645–652.

Panksepp, J. (1982). Toward a general psychobiological theory of emotions. The Behavioral and Brain Sciences, 5, 407–422.

Papez, J. W. (1937). A proposed mechanism of emotion. Archives of Neurology and Psychiatry, 38, 725–743.

Passingham, R. E. (1970). The neurological basis of introversion-extraversion: Gray's theory. Behavior Research and Therapy, 8, 353–366.

Patrick, A. W., & Zuckerman, M. (1977). An application of the state-trait concepts to the need for achievement. Journal of Research in Personality, 11, 459–465.

Patrick, A., Zuckerman, M., & Masterson, F. (1974). An extension of the trait-state distinction from affects to motive measures. Psychological Reports, 34, 1251–1258.

Patterson, C. M., Kosson, D., & Newman, P. A. (1987). Reaction to punishment, reflectivity and passive avoidance learning in extraverts. Journal of Personality and Social Psychology, 52, 565–575.

Paul, O. (1977). Epidemiology of hypertension. In J. Genest, E. Koew, & O. Kuchel (Eds.), Hypertension: Physiopathology and treatment. New York: McGraw Hill.

Pauls, D. L., Bucher, K. D., Crowe, R. R., & Noyes, R. (1980). A genetic study of panic disorder pedigrees. American Journal of Human Genetics, 31, 639–644.

Pavlov, I. P. (1927/1960). An investigation of the physiological activity of the cerebral cortex. Translated and edited by G. V. Anrep. New York: Dover Publications.

Pawlik, K., & Cattell, R. B. (1965). The relationship between certain personality factors and measures of cortical arousal. Neuropsychologia, 3, 129–151.

Pederson, N. L., Friberg, L., Floderus-Myrhed, B., McClearn, G. E., & Plomin, R. (1984). Swedish early separated twins: Identification and characterization. Acta Geneticae Medicae et Gemellologiae, 33, 243–250.

Pederson, N. L., Plomin, R., McClearn, G. E., & Friberg, L. (1988). Neuroticism, extraversion and related traits in adult twins reared apart and reared together. Journal of Personality and Social Psychology, 55, 950–957.

Perris, C., Eiseman, M., von Knorring, L., Oreland, L., & Perris, H. (1984). Personality traits and monoamine oxidase activity in platelets in depressed patients. *Biological Psychiatry, 12,* 201–205.

Perris, C., Jacobssen, L., Oreland, L., Perris, H., & Ross, S. B. (1980). Enzymes related to biogenic amine metabolism and personality characteristics in depressed patients. *Acta Psychiatrica Scandinavica, 61,* 477–484.

Perris, C., von Knorring, L., Perris, H., & Eisemann, M. (1983). Neurophysiological and biological correlates of personality in depressed patients. *Advances in Biological Psychiatry, 13,* 54–62.

Persky, H. (1975). Adrenocortical function and anxiety. *Psychoneuroendocrinology, 1,* 37–44.

Persky, H., Charney, N., Lief, H. I., O'Brien, C. P., Mitler, W. R., & Strauss, D. (1978). The relationship of plasma estradiol level to sexual behavior in young women. *Psychosomatic Medicine, 40,* 523–535.

Persky, H., Dreisbach, L., Miller, W. R., O'Brien, C. P., Khan, M. A., Lief, H. I., Charney, N., & Strauss, D. (1982). The relation of plasma androgen levels to sexual behaviors and attitudes of women. *Psychosomatic Medicine, 44,* 305–319.

Persky, H., Lief, H. I., Strauss, D., Miller, W. R., & O'Brien, C. P. (1978). Plasma testosterone level and sexual behavior of couples. *Archives of Sexual Behavior, 7,* 157–173.

Persky, H., Smith, K. D., & Basu, G. K. (1971). Relation of psychologic measures of aggression and hostility to testosterone production in man. *Psychosomatic Medicine, 33,* 265–277.

Perugi, G., Deltito, J., Adaligisa, S., Musetti, L., Petracca, A., Nisita, C., Maremmani, I., & Cassano, G. B. (1988). Relationships between panic disorder and separation anxiety with school phobia. *Comprehensive Psychiatry, 29,* 98–107.

Peterson, D. R. (1965). Scope and generality of verbally defined personality factors. *Psychological Review, 72,* 48–59.

Pichot, P. (1978). Psychopathic behaviour: A historical overview. In R. D. Hare & D. Schalling (Eds.), Psychopathic behaviour: *Approaches to research* (pp. 55–70). Chichester, England: Wiley.

Piers, E. V., & Kirchner, E. P. (1969). Eyelid conditioning and personality: Positive results from nonpartisans. *Journal of Abnormal Psychology, 74,* 336–339.

Pirke, K. M., Kockott, G., & Dittman, F. (1974). Psychosexual stimulation and plasma testosterone in man. *Archives of Sexual Behavior, 3,* 577–584.

Pitman, R. K. & Orr, S. P. (1986). Test of the conditioning model of neurosis: Differential aversive conditioning of angry and neutral facial expressions in anxiety disorder patients. *Journal of Abnormal Psychology, 95,* 208–213.

Pivik, R. T., Stelmack, R. M., & Bylama, F. W. (1988). Personality and individual differences in spinal motoneuronal excitability. *Psychophysiology, 25,* 16–24.

Plomin, R. (1986). *Development, genetics and psychology.* Hillsdale, NJ: Erlbaum.

Plomin, R., & Daniels, D. (1987). Why are children in the same family so different from one another? *Behavioral and Brain Sciences, 10,* 1–60.

Plomin, R., DeFries, J. C., & McClearn, G. E. (1980). *Behavioral Genetics.* San Francisco: CA: W. H. Freeman & Co.

Ploog-van Gorsel, E. (1981). EEG and cardiac correlates of neuroticism: A physiological psychophysiological comparison of neurotics and normal controls. *Biological Psychology, 13,* 141–156.

Plotkin, W. B., & Rice, K. M. (1981). Biofeedback as a placebo: Anxiety reduction facilitated by training in either suppression or enhancement of alpha brain waves. *Journal of Consulting and Clinical Psychology, 49,* 590–596.

Popper, K. R. (1979). *Objective knowledge: An evolutionary approach.* Oxford, England: Clarendon Press.

Porrino, L. J. (1987). Cerebral metabolic changes associated with activation of reward systems. In J. Engel, L. Oreland, B. Pernov, S. Rössner, & L. A. Pellhorn (Eds.), *Brain reward systems and abuse*. New York: Plenum.

Post, R. M., Jimerson, D., Ballenger, J. C., Lake, C. R., Uhde, T. W., & Goodwin, F. K. (1984). Cerebrospinal fluid norepinephrine and its metabolites in manic-depressive illness. In R. M. Post & J. C. Ballenger (Eds.), *Neurobiology of mood disorders* (pp. 539–553). Baltimore, MD: Williams & Wilkens.

Potter, W. Z., Muscettola, G., & Goodwin, F. K. (1983). Sources of variance in clinical studies of MHPG. In J. W. Maas (Ed.), *MHPG: Basic mechanisms and psychopathology* (pp. 145–165). New York: Academic Press.

Potter, W. Z., Ross, R. J., & Zavadil, P. (1985). Affective disorders and the catecholamines. In C. R. Lake & M. G. Ziegler (Eds.), *The catecholamines in psychiatric and neurological disorders* (pp. 213–233). Boston, MA: Butterworth Publishers.

Pribham, K. H., Reitz, S., McNeil, M., & Spivak, A. A. (1979). The effect of amygdalectomy on orienting and classical conditioning in monkeys. *Pavlovian Journal of Biological Science, 14,* 203–217.

Proux, G. B., & Picton, T. W. (1985). The effects of anxiety and expectancy on the CNV. *Annals of the New York Academy of Sciences, 425,* 617–622.

Purchall, L. B., Coursey, R. D., Buchsbaum, M. S., & Murphy, D. L. (1980). Parents of high risk subjects defined by levels of monoamine oxidase activity. *Schizophrenia Bulletin, 6,* 338–346.

Purifoy, P. E., & Koopermans, L. H. (1979). Androstenedione, testosterone, and free testosterone concentration in women of various occupations. *Social Biology, 26,* 179–188.

Quay, H. C. (1965). Psychopathic personality as pathological stimulation seeking. *American Journal of Psychiatry, 122,* 180–183.

Rada, R. T., Laws, D. R., & Kellner, R. (1976). Plasma testosterone levels in the rapist. *Psychosomatic Medicine, 38,* 257–258.

Raine, A., & Venables, P. H. (1981). Classical conditioning and socialization—A biosocial interaction. *Personality and Individual Differences, 2,* 273–283.

Rapaport, J. L., Buchsbaum, M. S., Weingarten, H., Zahn, T. P., Ludlow, C., & Mikkelsen, E. J. (1980). Dextroamphetamine: Its cognitive and behavioral effects in normal and hyperactive boys. *Archives of General Psychiatry, 37,* 933–943.

Rapee, R. (1986). Differential response to hyperventilation in panic disorder and generalized anxiety disorder. *Journal of Abnormal Psychology, 95,* 24–28.

Raskind, M. A., Peskind, E. R., Halter, J. B., & Jimerson, D. C. (1984). Norepinephrine and MHPG levels in CSF and plasma in Alzheimer's Disease. *Archives of General Psychiatry, 41,* 343–346.

Rasmussen, S. A., & Tsuang, M. T. (1984). The epidemiology of obsessive compulsive disorder. *Journal of Clinical Psychiatry, 45,* 450–457.

Reading, A. J. (1966). Effect of maternal environment on the behavior of inbred mice. *Journal of Comparative and Physiological Psychology, 62,* 437–440.

Redmond, D. E., Jr. (1977). Alterations in the function of nucleus locus coeruleus: A possible model for studies of anxiety. In I. Hanin & E. Usdin (Eds.), *Animal models in psychiatry and neurology* (pp. 293–305). New York: Pergamon.

Redmond, D. E., Jr. (1985). Neurochemical basis for anxiety and anxiety disorders: Evidence from drugs which decrease human fear or anxiety. In A. H. Tuma & J. D. Maser (Eds.), *Anxiety and the anxiety disorders* (pp. 533–555). Hillsdale, NJ: Erlbaum.

Redmond, D. E., Jr. (1987). Studies of locus coeruleus in monkeys and hypotheses for neuropsychopharmacology. In H. Y. Meltzer (Ed.), *Psychopharmacology: The third generation of progress* (pp. 967–975). New York: Raven Press.

Redmond, D. E., Jr., Katz, M. M., Maas, J. W., Swann, A., Casper, R., & Davis, J. M. (1986). Cerebrospinal fluid amine metabolites: Relationships with behavioral measurements in depressed, manic, and healthy controls. *Archives of General Psychiatry, 43,* 938–947.

Redmond, D. E. Jr., Murphy, D. L., & Baulu, J. (1979). Platelet monoamine oxidase activity correlates with social affiliative and agonistic behaviors in normal rhesus monkeys. *Psychosomatic Medicine, 41,* 87–100.

Reiman, E. M. (1988). The quest to establish neural substrates of anxiety. *Psychiatric Clinics of North America, 11,* 295–307.

Reiman, E. M., Raiche, M. E., Robins, E., Botler, F. K., Herscovitch, P., Fox, P., & Perlmutter, J. (1986). The application of positron emission tomography to the study of panic disorder. *American Journal of Psychiatry, 143,* 469–477.

Reiman, E. M., Raiche, M. E., Robins, E., Mintun, M. A., Fusselman, M. J., Fox, P. T., Price, J. L., & Haskman, K. A. (1989). Neuroanatomical correlates of a lactate-induced anxiety attack. *Archives of General Psychiatry, 46,* 493–500.

Revelle, W., Anderson, K. J., & Humphreys, M. S. (1987). Empirical tests and theoretical extensions of arousal-based theories of personality. In J. Strelau & H. J. Eysenck (Eds.), *Personality dimensions and arousal* (pp. 18–36). New York: Plenum.

Rice, J., McGuffin, P., & Shaskan, E. G. (1982). A commingling analysis of platelet monoamine oxidase activity. *Psychiatry Research, 7,* 325–335.

Ridgeway, D., & Hare, R. D. (1981). Sensation seeking and psychophysiological responses to auditory stimulation. *Psychophysiology, 18,* 613–618.

Rizzo, P. A., Caporali, M., Piorelli, F., Spadarao, M., Zanasi, M., Morocutti, C., & Albani, G. (1984) Pain influence on brain preparatory sets. *Annals of the New York Academy of Sciences, 425,* 676–680.

Roberts, W. W. (1958). Both rewarding and punishing effects from stimulation of posterior hypothalamus of cat with same electrode at same intensity. *Journal of Comparative and Physiological Psychology, 51,* 400–407.

Robins, L. N. (1966). *Deviant children growing up: A sociological and psychiatric study of sociopathic personality.* Baltimore, MD: Williams & Wilkins.

Robins, L. N. (1978). Aetiological implications in studies of childhood histories relating to antisocial personality. In R. D. Hare & D. Schalling (Eds.), *Psychopathic behavior: Approaches to research* (pp. 255–272). Chichester, England: Wiley.

Robins, L. N., Helzer, J. E., Weissman, M. M., Orvarechel, H., Gruenberg, E., Burke, J. D., & Reiger, D. A. (1984). Lifetime prevalence of specific psychiatric disorders in three sites. *Archives of General Psychiatry, 41,* 949–967.

Robinson, D. S., Davis, J. M., Nies, A., Revaris, C. L., & Sylvester, D. (1971). Relation of sex and aging to monoamine oxidase activity of human brain, plasma, and platelets. *Archives of General Psychiatry, 24,* 536–539.

Robinson, D. S., & Kurtz, N. M. (1987). Monoamine oxidase inhibiting drugs: Pharmacologic and therapeutic issues. In H. Y. Meltzer (Ed.), *Psychopharmacology: The third generation of progress* (pp. 1297–1304). New York: Raven Press.

Rocklin, T., & Revelle, W. (1981). The measurement of extraversion: A comparison of the Eysenck Personality Inventory and the Eysenck Personality Questionnaire. *British Journal of Social Psychology, 20,* 279–289.

Rodgers, D. A. (1966). Factors underlying differences in alcohol preference among inbred strains of mice. *Psychosomatic Medicine, 28,* 498–513.

Rodgers, R. J. (1979). Alterations in shock-induced fighting and locomotor activity following intracerebroventricular injections of hydrocortisone in the rat. *Aggressive Behavior, 5,* 31–40.

Rogeness, G. A., Hernandez, J. M., Macedo, C. A., Mitchell, E. L., Amrung, S. A., & Harris, W. R. (1984). Clinical characteristics of emotionally disturbed boys with very low activities of dopamine-β-hydroxylase. *Journal of the American Academy of Child Psychiatry, 23,* 203–208.

Rogers, C. R. (1959). A theory of therapy, personality, and interpersonal relationships, as developed in the client-centered framework. In S. Koch (Ed.), *Psychology: A study of a science:* (Vol. 3, pp. 184–256). New York: McGraw Hill.

Rolls, E. T. (1980). Activity of the hypothalamic and related neurons in the alert animal. In P. J. Morgane & J. Panksepp (Eds.), *Handbook of the hypothalamus* (pp. 439–466). New York: Dekker.

Rolls, E. T. (1986). Neural systems involved in emotions in primates. In R. Plutchik (Ed.), *Emotion: Theory, research and experience* (pp. 125–143). New York: Academic Press.

Rose, R. J. (1988). Genetic and environmental variance in content dimensions of the MMPI. *Journal of Personality and Social Psychology, 55,* 302–311.

Rose, R. J., Koskenvuo, M., Kaprio, J., Sarna, S., & Langinvaino, H. (1988). Shared genes, shared experiences and similarity of personality-Data from 14,288 adult Finnish co-twins. *Journal of Personality and Social Psychology, 54,* 161–171.

Rose, R. J., Miller, J. Z., Grim, C. E., & Christian, J. C. (1979). Aggregation of blood pressure in the families of identical twins. *American Journal of Epidemiology, 109,* 503– 511.

Rosenbaum, J. F., Biederman, J., Hirshfield, D. R., Meminger, S. R., Herman, J. B., Kagan, J., Reznick, S., & Snidman, N. (1988). Behavioral inhibition in children of parents with panic disorder and agoraphobia: A controlled study. *Archives of General Psychiatry, 45,* 463–470.

Rosenzweig, M. R., Bennett, E. L., Herbert, M., & Morimoto, H. (1978). Social grouping cannot account for cerebral or behavioral effects of enriched environments. *Brain Research, 153,* 563–576.

Rösler, F. (1975). Abhingigheit des Electroenzephalogramms von den persönlichkats Dimensionen E und N sensu Eysenck und unterschiedlich aktweerenden Situationen. *Zeitschrift für Experimentelle und Angewante Psychologie, 22,* 630–667.

Ross, S. B., Wetterberg, L., & Myrhed, M. (1973). Genetic control of plasma dopamine-beta-hydroxylase. *Life Sciences, 12* (Part I), 529–532.

Rosvold, H. E., Mirsky, A. F., & Pribram, K. H. (1954). Influence of amygdalectomy on social behavior in monkeys. *Journal of Comparative and Physiological Psychology, 47,* 173–178.

Roth, W. T., Telch, M. J., Taylor, C. B., Sachitano, J. A., Gallen, C. C., Kopell, M. L., McClenahan, K. L., Agras, S., & Pfefferbaum, A. (1986). Autonomic characteristics of agoraphobia with panic attacks. *Biological Psychiatry, 21,* 1133–1154.

Rousaville, B. J., Weissman, M. M., Kleber, H. D., & Webber, C. H. (1982). Heterogeneity of psychiatric diagnoses in treated opiate addicts. *Archives of General Psychiatry, 39,* 161–166.

Routtenberg, A. (1968). The two-arousal hypothesis: Reticular formation and limbic system. *Psychological Review, 75,* 51–81.

Routtenberg, A., & Sloan, M. (1972). Self stimulation in the frontal cortex of *Rattus norvegicus. Behavioral Biology, 7,* 567–572.

Rowe, D. C., & Plomin, R. (1977). Temperament in early childhood. *Journal of Personality Assessment, 41,* 150–156.

Rowland, G. L., & Franken, R. E. (1986). The four dimensions of sensation seeking: A confirmatory factor analysis. *Personality and Individual Differences, 7,* 237–240.

Roy, A., Adinoff, B., Roehrich, L., Lamparski, D., Custer, R., Lorenz, V., Barbaccia, M., Guidotti, A., Costa, E., & Linnoila, M. (1988). Pathological gambling: A psychobiological study. *Archives of General Psychiatry, 45,* 369–373.

Roy, A., DeJong, J., & Linnoila, A. (1989). Extraversion in pathological gamblers. *Archives of General Psychiatry, 46,* 679–681.

Roy, A., Jimerson, D. C., & Pickar, D. (1986). Plasma MHPG in depressive disorders and relationship to the dexamethasone suppression test. *American Journal of Psychiatry, 143,* 846–851.

Roy, A., Pickar, D., Linnoila, M., & Potter, W. Z. (1985). Cerebrospinal fluid monoamine and monoamine metabolite concentrations in melancholia. *Psychiatry Research, 15*, 281–292.

Royce, J. R. (1977). On the construct validity of open-field measures. *Psychological Bulletin, 84*, 1098–1106.

Rozhdestvenskaya, V. I., Nebylitsen, V. D., Borisova, M. N., & Ermolaeva-Tomina, L. B. (1960). A comparative study of a number of indices of strength of the nervous system in man. *Psychological Questions, 5*, 41–56.

Rubin, D. T., Miller, R. G., Clark, B. R., Roland, R. E., & Ranson, J. A. (1970). The stress of aircraft carrier landings. II: 3-methoxy–4-hydroxyphenylglycol excretion in naval aviators. *Psychosomatic Medicine, 32*, 589–597.

Rubinow, D. R., Post, R. M., Gold, P. W., Ballenger, J. C., & Wolff, E. A. (1984). The relationship between cortisol and clinical phenomenology of affective illness. In R. M. Post & J. C. Ballenger (Eds.), *Neurobiology of mood disorders* (pp. 271–289). Baltimore, MD: Williams & Wilkens.

Rusalov, V. M. (1989). Object-related and communicative aspects of human temperament: A new questionnaire of the structure of temperament. *Personality and Individual Differences, 10*, 817–827.

Rushton, J. P. (1989). Race differences in behaviour: A review and evolutionary analysis. *Personality and Individual Differences, 9*, 1009–1024.

Rushton, J. P., Fulker, D. W., Neale, M. C., Nias, D. K. B., & Eysenck, H. J. (1986). Altruism and aggression: The heritability of individual differences. *Journal of Personality and Social Psychology, 50*, 1192–1198.

Rushton, J. P., Jackson, D. N., & Paunonem, S. V. (1981). Personality: Nomothetic or idiographic? A response to Kenrick and Stringfield. *Psychological Review, 88*, 582–589.

Russo, K. R., & Zuckerman, M. (Oct., 1988). Psychological, physiological and physical characteristics of subjects at risk for essential hypertension. Paper presented at meeting of the Society for Psychophysiological Research, San Francisco, CA: *Psychophysiology*, 492 (abstract).

Rust, J. (1975a). Genetic effects in the cortical auditory evoked potential: A twin study. *Electroencephalography and Clinical Neurophysiology, 39*, 321–327.

Rust, J. (1975b). Cortical evoked potentials, personality and intelligence. *Journal of Comparative and Physiological Psychology, 89*, 1220–1226.

Sackett, G. P. (1972). Exploratory behavior of rhesus monkeys as a function of rearing experiences and sex. *Developmental Psychology, 6*, 260–270.

Sacks, O. (1983). *Awakenings*. New York: E. P. Dutton.

Sakellariou, G., Markianos, M., Tsichlakis, N., & Kartakis D. (1987). A family study of plasma dopamine-beta-hydroxylase in schizophrenia. *Psychiatry Research, 20*, 221–227.

Sandel, A., & Alcorn, J. D. (1980). Individual hemisphericity and maladaptive behaviors. *Journal of Abnormal Psychology, 89*, 514–517.

Sano, K., Sekino, H., & Mayanagi, Y. (1972). Results of stimulation and destruction of the posterior hypothalamus in cases with violent, aggressive, or restless behaviors. In E. Hitchcock, L. Laitinen & K. Vaernet (Eds.), *Psychosurgery* (pp. 57–75). Springfield, IL: Charles C. Thomas.

Sartory, G. (1986). Effect of phobic anxiety on the orienting response. *Behavior Research and Therapy, 24*, 251–261.

Satterfield, J. H. (1987). Childhood diagnostic and neurophysiological predictors of teenage arrest rates: An eight year prospective study. In S. A. Mednick, T. E. Moffitt, & S. A. Stack (Eds.), *The causes of crime: New biological approaches* (pp. 146–167). Cambridge, England: Cambridge Univ. Press.

Savage, R. D. (1964). Electro-cerebral activity, extraversion and neuroticism. *British Journal of Psychiatry, 110*, 98–100.

Saxton, P. M., Siegel, J., & Lukas, J. H. (1987). Visual evoked potential augmenting/reducing slopes in cats- 2. Correlations with behavior. *Personality and Individual Differences, 8,* 511–519.

Scarr, S., & McCartney, K. (1983). How people make their own environments: A theory of genotype-environment correlations. *Child Development, 54,* 424–435.

Scarr, S., Webber, P. L., Weinberg, A., & Wittig, M. A. (1981). Personality resemblance among adolescents and their parents in biologically related and adoptive families. *Journal of Personality and Social Psychology, 40,* 885–898.

Schachter, S. (1975). Cognitive and centralist-peripheralist controversies in motivation and emotion. In M. S. Gazzanigg & C. B. Blakenne (Eds.), *Handbook of psychobiology* (pp. 529–564). New York: Academic Press.

Schachter, S., & Singer, J. E. (1962). Cognitive, social, and physiological determinants of emotional state. *Psychological Review, 69,* 379–399.

Schalling, D. (1978). Psychopathy-related personality variables and the psychopathology of socialization. In R. D. Hare & D. Schalling (Eds.), *Psychopathic behaviour: Approaches to research* (pp. 85–106). Chichester, England: Wiley.

Schalling, D. (1987). Personality correlates of plasma testosterone levels in young delinquents: An example of person situation interaction? In S. Mednick, E. Moffit, & S. A. Stack (Eds.), *The causes of crime: New biological approaches* (pp. 283–291). Cambridge, England: Cambridge Univ. Press.

Schalling, D., Åsberg, M., & Edman, G. (1984, unpublished). *Personality and CSF monoamine metabolites.* Preliminary manuscript, Dept. of Psychiatry & Psychology, Karolinska Hospital and the Dept. of Psychology, Univ. of Stockholm.

Schalling, D., Åsberg, M., Edman, G., Gustavsson, P., Mårtensson, B., Nordström, P., & Bertillson, L. (1990, unpublished). Personality correlates of CSF monoamine metabolites in healthy young men. Preliminary results, Dept. of Psychiatry & Psychology, Karolinska Hospital and the Dept. of Psychology, Univ. of Stockholm.

Schalling, D., Åsberg, M., Edman, G., & Oreland, L. (1987). Markers for vulnerability to psychopathology: Temperament traits associated with platelet MAO activity. *Acta Psychiatrica Scandinavica, 76,* 172–182.

Schalling, D., Edman, G., & Åsberg, M. (1983). Impulsive cognitive style and inability to tolerate boredom. In M. Zuckerman (Ed.), *Biological bases of sensation seeking, impulsivity and anxiety* (pp. 125–147). Hillsdale, NJ: Erlbaum.

Schalling, D., Edman, G., & Oreland, L. (1988). Platelet MAO activity associated with impulsivity and aggressivity. *Personality and Individual Differences, 9,* 597–605.

Schalling, D., Lidberg, L., Levander, S. E., & Dahlin, Y. (1973). Spontaneous autonomic activity as related to psychopathy. *Biological Psychology, 1,* 83–97.

Schalling, D., & Svensson, J. (1984). Blood pressure and personality. *Personality and Individual Differences, 5,* 41–51.

Schmauk, F. J. (1970). Punishment, arousal, and avoidance learning. *Journal of Abnormal Psychology, 76,* 325–335.

Schmidt, K., Solant, M. V., & Bridger, W. H. (1985). Electrodermal activity of undersocialized aggressive children: A pilot study. *Journal of Child Psychology and Psychiatry, 26,* 653–660.

Schneider, L. S., Munjack, D., Severson, J. A., & Palmer, R. (1987). Platelet [3H] imipramine binding in generalized anxiety disorder, panic disorder, and agoraphobia with panic attacks. *Biological Psychiatry, 22,* 59–66.

Schneider, R. H., Egan, B. M., Johnson, E. H., Drobney, H., & Julius, S. (1986). Anger and anxiety in borderline hypertension. *Psychosomatic Medicine, 48,* 242–248.

Schooler, C., Zahn, T. P., Murphy, D. L., & Buchsbaum, M. S. (1978). Psychological correlates of monoamine oxidase in normals. *Journal of Nervous and Mental Disease, 166,* 177–186.

Schuerger, J. M., Zarella, K. L., & Hotz, A. S. (1989). Factors that influence the temporal stability of personality by questionnaire. *Journal of Personality and Social Psychology, 56,* 777–783.

Scott, J. P., & Fuller, J. L. (1967). *Genetics and the social behavior of the dog.* Chicago, IL: Univ. of Chicago Press.

Seldon, N. R. W., Robbins, T. W., & Everitt, B. J. (1990). Enhanced behavioral conditioning to context and impaired behavioral and neuroendocrine responses to conditional stimuli following ceruleocortical noradrenergic lesions: Support for an attentional hypothesis of central noradrenergic function. *The Journal of Neuroscience. 10,* 531–539.

Seligman, M. E. P. (1970). On the generality of the locus of learning. *Psychological Review, 77,* 406–418.

Seligman, M. E. P. (1971). Phobias and preparedness. *Behaviour Therapy, 2,* 307–320.

Selye, H. (1956). *The stress of life.* New York: McGraw-Hill.

Shear, M., Kligfield, P., Harshfield, G., Devereux, R. B., Polan, J. J., Mann, J. J., Pickering, T., & Frances, A. J. (1987). Cardiac rate and rhythm in panic patients. *American Journal of Psychiatry, 144,* 633–637.

Shekim, W. O., Bylund, D. B., Alexson, J., Glaser, R. D., Jones, S. B., Hodges, K., & Perdue, S. (1986). Platelet MAO and measures of attention and impulsivity in boys with attention deficit disorder and hyperactivity. *Psychiatry Research, 18,* 179–188.

Shekim, W. O., Bylund, D. B., Frankel, F., Alexson, J., Jones, S. B., Blue, L. D., Kirby, J., & Corcoran, C. (1989). Platelet MAO activity and personality variations in normals. *Psychiatry Research, 27,* 81–88.

Shekim, W. O., Hodges, K., Horowitz, E., Glaser, R. D., Davis, L., & Bylund, D. B. (1984). Psychoeducational and impulsivity correlates of platelet MAO in normal children. *Psychiatry Research, 11,* 99–106.

Shields, J. (1962). *Monozygotic twins brought up apart and brought up together.* London: Oxford Univ. Press.

Shizgal, P., Bielajew, C., & Kiss, I. (1980). Anodal hyperpolarization block technique provides evidence for rostro-caudal conduction of reward signals in the medial forebrain bundle. *Society for Neuroscience Abstracts, 6,* 422.

Siddle, D. A. T. (1977). Electrodermal activity and psychopathy. In S. A. Mednick & K. O. Christianssen (Eds.), *Biosocial bases of criminal behavior* (pp. 199–211). New York: Gardner Press.

Siegel, J. M. (1979). Behavioral functions of the reticular formation. *Brain Research Reviews, 1,* 69–105.

Siegel, J. M. (1983). A behavioral approach to the analysis of reticular formation unit activity. In T. E. Robinson (Ed.), *Behavioral approaches to brain research.* New York: Oxford Univ. Press.

Siegfried, J., & Ben-Shmuel, A. (1972). Neurosurgical treatment of aggressivity: Stereotaxic amygdalotomy versus leukotomy. In E. Hitchcock, L. Laitinen, & K. Vaernet (Eds.), *Psychosurgery* (pp. 214–229). Springfield, IL: Charles C. Thomas.

Siever, L. J., & Uhde, T. W. (1983). New studies and perspectives on the noradrenergic receptor system in depression: Effect of the alpha$_2$-adrenergic agonist clonidine. *Biological Psychiatry, 19,* 131–156.

Siever, L. J., Uhde, T. W., Jimerson, D. C., Lake, C. R., Kopkin, I. J., & Murphy, D. L. (1986). Indices of noradrenergic output in depression. *Psychiatry Research, 19,* 59–73.

Silverman, J., Buchsbaum, M. S., & Stierlin, H. (1973). Sex differences in perceptual differentiation and stimulus intensity control. *Journal of Personality and Social Psychology, 25,* 309–318.

Simmel, E. C. (1984). Sensation seeking: Exploration of empty spaces or novel stimuli? *Behavioral and Brain Sciences, 3,* 449–450.

Simmel, E. C., & Bagwell, M. (1983). Genetics of exploratory behavior and activity. In J. L. Fuller & E. C. Simmel (Eds.), *Behavior genetics: Principles and applications* (pp. 89–115). Hillsdale, NJ: Erlbaum.

Slater, E., & Shields, J. (1969). Genetical aspects of anxiety. *British Journal of Psychiatry,* (Special publication No. 3), 62–71.

Smith, B. D. (1983). Extraversion and electrodermal activity: Arousability and the inverted U. *Personality and Individual Differences, 4,* 411–419.

Smith, B. D., Davidson, R. A., Perlstein, W., Oster, U., & Gonzalez, F. (1989). Sensation seeking and arousal: Effects of strong stimulation on electrodermal activation and memory task performance. *Personality and Individual Differences, 10,* 671–679.

Smith, B. D., Perlstein, W. M., Davidson, R. A., & Michael, K. (1986). Sensation seeking: Differential effects of relevant novel stimulation on electrodermal activity. *Personality and Individual Differences, 4,* 445–452.

Smith, B. D., Rypma, C. B., & Wilson, R. J. (1981). Dishabituation and spontaneous recovery of the electrodermal orienting response: Effects of extraversion, impulsivity, sociability, and caffeine. *Journal of Research in Personality, 15,* 233–240.

Smith, B. D., Wilson, R. J., & Jones, B. E. (1983). Extraversion and multiple levels of caffeine-induced arousal: Effects of overhabituation and dishabituation. *Psychophysiology, 20,* 29–34.

Sostek, A. J., Sostek, A. M., Murphy, D. L., Martin, E. B., & Born, W. S. (1981). Cord blood amine oxidase activities relate to arousal and motor functioning in human newborns. *Life Sciences, 28,* 2561–2568.

Soubrié, P. (1986). Reconciling the role of central serotonin neurons in animal and human behavior. *Behavioral and Brain Sciences, 9,* 319–364.

Souief, M. I., Eysenck, H. J., & White, P. O. (1969). A joint factorial study of the Guilford, Cattell and Eysenck scales. In H. J. Eysenck & S. B. G. Eysenck (Eds.), *Personality structure and measurement* (pp. 171–193). San Diego, CA: R. R. Knapp.

Spence, K. W. (1958). A theory of emotionally based drive (D) and its relation to performance in simple learning situations. *American Psychologist, 13,* 131–141.

Spence, K. W. (1964). Anxiety (drive) level and performance in eyelid conditioning. *Psychological Bulletin, 61,* 129–139.

Spence, K. W., & Taylor, J. A. (1951). Anxiety and strength of UCS as determinants of amount of eyelid conditioning. *Journal of Experimental Psychology, 42,* 183–188.

Spielberger, C. D. (1966). Theory and research on anxiety. In C. D. Spielberger (Ed.), *Anxiety and behavior* (pp. 3–20). New York: Academic Press.

Spielberger, C. D. (1972). Anxiety as an emotional state. In C. D. Spielberger (Ed.), *Anxiety: Current trends in theory and research* (pp. 23–49). New York: Academic Press.

Spielberger, C. D., Gorsuch, R. L., & Lushene, R. E. (1970). *Manual for the State-Trait Anxiety Inventory.* Palo Alto, CA: Consulting Psychologists Press.

Spielberger, C. D., Johnson, E. H., Russell, S. F., Crane, R. J., & Worden, T. J. (1984). The experience and expression of anger. In M. A. Chesney, S. E. Goldstein, & R. H. Rosenman (Eds.), *Anger, hostility and behavioral medicine.* New York: Hemisphere.

Stein, L. (1974). Norepinephrine reward pathways: Role in self-stimulation, memory consolidation and schizophrenia. In J. K. Cole & T. B. Sonderegger (Eds.), *Nebraska symposium on motivation* (vol. 31, pp. 113–161). Lincoln, NE: Univ. of Nebraska Press.

Stein, L. (1978). Catecholamines and opioid peptides. In M. A. Lipton, D. Mascio, & K. F. Killam (Eds.), *Psychopharmacology: A generation of progress* (pp. 569–581). New York: Raven Press.

Stein, L., & Belluzzi, J. D. (1987). Reward transmitters and drugs of abuse. In J. Engel, L. Oreland, D. H. Ingvar, B. Pernow, S. Rössner, & L. A. Pellborn (Eds.), *Brain reward systems and abuse* (pp. 19–33). New York: Raven Press.

Stein, M. B., & Uhde, T. W. (1988). Panic disorder and major depression: A tale of two syndromes. *Psychiatric Clinics of North America, 11,* 441–461.

Stellar, J. R., Brooks, F. H., & Mills, L. E. (1979). Approach and withdrawal analysis of the effects of hypothalamic stimulation and lesions in rats. *Journal of Comparative and Physiological Psychology, 93,* 446–466.

Stellar, J. R., & Stellar, E. (1985). *The neurobiology of motivation and reward.* New York: Springer-Verlag.

Stelmack, R. M. (1981). The psychophysiology of extraversion and neuroticism. In H. J. Eysenck (Ed.), *A model for personality* (pp. 38–64). New York: Springer-Verlag.

Stelmack, R. M. (1990). Biological bases of extraversion: Psychophysiological evidence. *Journal of Personality, 58,* 293–311.

Stelmack, R. M., Achorn, E., & Michaud, A. (1977). Extraversion and individual differences in auditory evoked response. *Psychophysiology, 14,* 368–374.

Stelmack, R. M., Bourgeois, R. P., Chain, J. Y. C., & Pickard, C. W. (1979). Extraversion and the orienting reaction habituation rate to visual stimuli. *Journal of Research in Personality, 13,* 49–58.

Stelmack, R. M., Kruidenier, B. G., & Anthony, S. B. (1985). A factor analysis of the Eysenck Personality Questionnaire and the Strelau Temperament Inventory. *Journal of Personality and Individual Differences, 6,* 657–659.

Stelmack, R. M., & Michaud-Achorn, A. (1985). Extraversion, attention and habituation of the auditory evoked response. *Journal of Research in Personality, 19,* 416–428.

Stelmack, R. M., Plouffe, L., & Falkenberg, W. (1983). Extraversion, sensation seeking and electrodermal response: Probing a paradox. *Personality and Individual Differences, 4,* 607–614.

Stelmack, R. M., & Wilson, K. G. (1982). Extraversion and the effects of frequency and intensity of the auditory brainstem evoked response. *Personality and Individual Differences, 3,* 373–380.

Stillman, R. C., Wyatt, R. J., Murphy, D. L., & Rauscher, F. P. (1978). Low platelet monoamine oxidase activity and chronic marihuana use. *Life Sciences, 23,* 1577–1582.

Stokes, P. E., & Sikes, C. R. (1987). Hypothalamic-pituitary-adrenal axis in affective disorders. In H. Y. Meltzer (Ed.), *Psychopharmacology: The third generation of progress* (pp. 589–607). New York: Raven Press.

Strelau, J. (1983). *Temperament, personality and arousal.* London: Academic Press.

Strelau, J. (1987). Personality dimensions based on arousal theories. In J. Strelau & H. J. Eysenck (Eds.), *Personality dimensions and arousal* (pp. 269–286). New York: Plenum.

Stunkard, A. J., Foch, T. T., & Hrubec, Z. (1986). A twin study of human obesity. *Journal of the American Medical Association, 256,* 51–54.

Stürup, G. K. (1968). Treatment of sexual offenders in Herstedvester Denmark. *Acta Psychiatrica Scandinavica,* Supplement 204, 1–63.

Sullivan, H. S. (1953). *The interpersonal theory of psychiatry.* New York: Norton.

Sullivan, J. L., Cavenar, J. O., Jr., Maltbie, A. A., Lister, P., & Zung, W. W. K. (1979). Familial biochemical and clinical correlates of alcoholics with low platelet monoamine oxidase activity. *Biological Psychiatry, 14,* 385–394.

Sullivan, J. L., Stanfield, C. N., & Dackis, C. (1977). Low platelet monoamine oxidase activity in chronic alcoholics. *American Journal of Psychiatry, 134,* 1098–1103.

Suomi, S. J., & Harlow, H. F. (1976). The facts and function of fear. In M. Zuckerman & C. D. Spielberger (Eds.), *Emotions and anxiety: New concepts, methods, and applications* (pp. 3–34). Hillsdale, NJ: Erlbaum.

Sutker, P. B., Moan, C. E., & Allain, A. N. (1983). Assessment of cognitive control in psychopaths and normal prisoners. *Journal of Behavioral Assessment, 5,* 275–287.

Sweeney, D. R., Maas, J. W., & Heninger, G. R. (1978). State anxiety, physical activity, and urinary 3-methoxy-4-hydroxyphenethylene-glycol excretion. *Archives of General Psychiatry, 35,* 1418–1423.

Syndulko, K. (1978). Electrocortical investigations of sociopathy. In R. D. Hare & D. Schalling (Eds.), *Psychpathic behaviour: Approaches to research* (pp. 145–156). Chichester, England: Wiley.

Szelenberger, W. (1983). Brain stem auditory evoked potentials and personality. *Biological Psychiatry, 18,* 157–174.

Taffel, C. (1955). Anxiety and the conditioning of verbal behavior. *Journal of Abnormal and Social Psychology, 51,* 496–501.

Takahaski, R., Nakahara, T., & Sakurai, Y. (1974). In *Emotional stress and biochemical responses of manic depressive patients* (pp. 58–66). Basel, Switzerland: S. Karger.

Taylor, C. B., Kenigsberg, M. L., & Robinson, J. M. (1982). A controlled comparison of relaxation and diazepam in panic disorder. *Journal of Clinical Psychiatry, 43,* 423–425.

Taylor, C. B., Sheikh, J., Agras, W. S., Roth, W. T., Margraf, J., Ehlers, A., Maddock, R. J., & Gossard, D. (1986). Ambulatory heart rate change in patients with panic attacks. *American Journal of Psychiatry, 143,* 478–482.

Taylor, J. A. (1951). The relationship of anxiety to the conditioned eyelid response. *Journal of Experimental Psychology, 41,* 81–92.

Taylor, J. A. (1953). A personality scale of manifest anxiety. *Journal of Abnormal and Social Psychology, 48,* 285–290.

Teitelbaum, P., & Epstein, A. N. (1962). The lateral hypothalamic syndrome. Recovery of feeding and drinking after lateral hypothalamic lesions. *Psychological Review, 69,* 74–90.

Tellegen, A. (1985). Structures of mood and personality and their relevance to assessing anxiety with an emphasis on self-report. In A. H. Tuma & J. D. Maser (Eds.), *Anxiety and the anxiety disorders* (pp. 681–706). Hillsdale, NJ: Erlbaum.

Tellegen, A., Lykken, D. T., Bouchard, T. J., Wilcox, K., Segal, N., & Rich, A. (1988). Personality similarity in twins reared together and apart. *Journal of Personality and Social Psychology, 54,* 1031–1039.

Tharp, V. K., Maltzman, I., Syndulko, K., & Ziskind, E. (1980). Autonomic activity during anticipation of an aversive tone in noninstitutionalized sociopaths. *Psychophysiology, 17,* 123–128.

Thomas, A., & Chess, A. (1986). The New York Longitudinal Study: From infancy to early adult life. In R. Plomin & J. Dunn (Eds.), *The study of temperament: Changes, continuities and challenges* (pp. 39–52). Hillsdale, N:J: Erlbaum.

Thomas, A., & Chess, S. (1977). *Temperament and development.* New York: Bruner/Mazel.

Thomas, A., Chess, S., & Birch, H. G. (1968). *Temperament and behavior disorders in children.* New York: New York Univ. Press.

Thompson. (1986). The neurobiology of learning and memory. *Science, 233,* 941–947.

Thompson, W. R. (1953). The inheritance of behaviour: Behavioural differences in fifteen mouse strains. *Canadian Journal of Psychology, 7,* 145–155.

Thompson, W. B., & Mueller, J. H. (1984a). Face memory and hemispheric preference. *Brain and Cognition, 3,* 239–248.

Thompson, W. B., & Mueller, J. H. (1984b). Extraversion and sleep: A psychophysiological study of the arousal hypothesis. *Personality and Individual Differences, 5,* 345–353.

Tienari, P. (1963). *Psychiatric illness in identical twins.* Copenhagen: Munksgaard.

Torgersen, A. M. (1985). Temperamental differences in infants and 6-year-old children: A follow-up study of twins. In J. Strelau, F. H. Farley, & A. Gale (Eds.), *The biological basis of personality and behavior: Theories, measurement, techniques and development* (pp. 227–239). Washington, D. C.: Hemisphere.

Torgersen, S. (1979). The nature and origin of common phobic fears. *British Journal of Psychology, 134,* 343–351.

Torgersen, S. (1983). Genetic factors in anxiety disorders. *Archives of General Psychiatry, 40,* 1085–1089.

Traskman, L., Tybring, G., Åsberg, M., Bertilisson, L., Lantts, O., & Schalling, D. (1980). Cortisol in the CSF of depressed and suicidal patients. *Archives of General Psychiatry, 37,* 761–767.

Tsaltas, E., Gray, J. A., & Fillinz, M. (1984). Alleviation of response suppression to conditioned aversive stimuli by lesions of the dorsal noradrenergic bundle. *Behavioural Brain Research, 13,* 115–127.

Tucker, D. M., Antes, J. R., Stenslie, C. E., & Barnhardt, T. M. (1978). Anxiety and lateral cerebral function. *Journal of Abnormal Psychology, 87,* 380–383.

Tupes, E. C., & Christal, R. E. (1961). *Recurrent personality factors based on trait ratings,* US Air Force, ASD Technical Reports (No. 61–97).

Turner, C. W., Ford, M. H., West, D. W., & Meikle, A. W. (August, 1986). *Genetic influences on testosterone, hostility and type A behavior in adult male twins.* Paper presented at meeting of the Eastern Psychological Association, Washington, DC.

Tyrer, P., Casey, P., & Gall, J. (1983). Relationship between neurosis and personality disorder. *British Journal of Psychiatry, 142,* 404–408.

Udry, J. R., & Talbert, L. M. (1988). Sex hormone effects on personality at puberty. *Journal of Personality and Social Psychology, 54,* 291–295.

Umberkoman-Witta, B., Vogel, W. H., & Wiita, P. J. (1981). Some biochemical and behavioral (sensation seeking) correlates in healthy adults. *Research Communications in Psychology, Psychiatry, and Behavior, 6,* 303–316.

Ursin, H., & Kaada, B. R. (1960). Functional localization within the amygdaloid complex in the cat. *Electroencephalography and Clinical Neurophysiology, 12,* 1–20.

Vaillant, G. E., & Schnurr, P. (1988). Study of psychiatric impairment within a college sample selected for mental health. *Archives of General Psychiatry, 45,* 313–319.

Vale, J. R., & Ray, D. (1972). A diallel analysis of male mouse sex behavior. *Behavior Genetics, 2,* 199–209.

Valenstein, E. S. (1986). *Great and desperate cures: The rise and decline of psychosurgery and other radical treatments for mental illness.* New York: Basic Books.

Valle, R. S., & DeGood, D. E. (1977). Effects of state-trait anxiety on the ability to enhance and suppress EEG alpha. *Psychophysiology, 14,* 1–7.

Valzelli, L. (1981). *Psychobiology of aggression and violence.* New York: Raven Press.

van Abeelen, J. H. F., (1977). Rearing responses and locomotor activity in mice: Single locus control. *Behavioral Biology, 19,* 401–404.

Vandenberg, S. G. (1966). Contributions of twin research to psychology. In M. Manosevitz, C. Lindzey, & D. D. Thiessen (Eds.), *Behavior Genetics* (pp. 145–164). New York: Appleton-Century-Crofts.

van Oortmerssen, G. A., & Bakker, T. C. M. (1981). Artificial selection for short and long attack latencies in wild *Mus musculus domesticus. Behavior Genetics, 11,* 115–126.

van Praag, H. M. (1986). Biological suicide research: Outcome and limitations. *Biological Psychiatry, 21,* 1305–1323.

van Ree, J. M., & Niesink, R. J. M. (1983). Low doses of β-endorphin increase social contacts among rats tested in dyadic encounters. *Life Sciences, 33,* 611–614.

Venables, P. H. (1987). Autonomic nervous system factors in criminal behavior. In S. A. Mednick, T. E. Moffitt, & S. A. Stack (Eds.), *The causes of crime: New biological approaches* (pp. 110–136). Cambridge, England: Cambridge Univ. Press.

Vermilyea, J. A., Borce, R., & Barlow, D. H. (1984). Rachman and Hodson (1974) a decade later: How do desynchronous response systems relate to the treatment of agoraphobia. *Behaviour Research and Therapy, 22,* 615–621.

Villacres, E. C., Hollinfield, M., Katon, W. J., Wilkinson, C. W., & Veith, R. C. (1987). Sympathetic nervous system activity in panic disorders. *Psychiatry Research, 21,* 313–321.

Virkkunen, M. (1985). Urinary free cortisol secretion in habitually violent offenders. *Acta Psychiatrica Scandinavica, 72,* 40–44.

Virkkunen, M. (1987). Metabolic dysfunctions among habitually violent offenders: Reactive hypoglycemia and cholesterol levels. In S. A. Mednick, T. E. Moffitt, & S. A. Stack (Eds.), *The causes of crime: New biological approaches* (pp. 292–311). Cambridge, England: Cambridge Univ. Press.

Vogel, F. (1958). *Uber die Erblichkeit des normales Electroencephalogramms.* Stuttgart, Germany: Thieme.

Vogel, F. (1970). The genetic basis of the normal human electroencephalogram (EEG). *Humangenetik, 10,* 91–114.

Vogel, M. D. (1961). GSR conditioning and personality factors in alcoholics and normals. *Journal of Abnormal and Social Psychology, 63,* 417–421.

Volavka, J. (1987). Electroencephalogram among criminals. In S. A. Mednick, T. E. Moffitt, & S. A. Stack (Eds.), *The causes of crime: New biological correlates* (pp. 137–145). Cambridge, England: Cambridge Univ. Press.

von Knorring, A. L., Bohman, M., von Knorring, L., & Oreland, L. (1985). Platelet MAO activity as a biological marker in subgroups of alcoholism. *Acta Psychiatrica Scandinavica, 72,* 51–58.

von Knorring, L., (1976). Visual averaged-evoked responses in patients suffering from alcoholism. *Neuropsychobiology, 2,* 233–238.

von Knorring, L., & Johanssen, F. (1980). Changes in the augmenter-reducer tendency and in pain measures as a result of treatment with a serotonin reuptake inhibition zimelidine. *Neuropsychobiology, 6,* 313–318.

von Knorring, L., & Oreland, L. (1985). Personality traits and platelet monoamine oxidase in tobacco smokers. *Psychological Medicine, 15,* 327–334.

von Knorring, L., Oreland, L., & von Knorring A. L. (1987). Personality traits and platelet MAO activity in alcohol and drug abusing teenage boys. *Acta Psychiatrica Scandinavica, 75,* 307–314.

von Knorring, L., Oreland, L., & Winblad, B. (1984). Personality traits related to monoamine oxidase activity in platelets. *Psychiatry Research, 12,* 11–26.

von Knorring, L., & Perris, C. (1981). Biochemistry of the augmenting-reducing response in visual evoked potentials. *Neuropsychobiology, 7,* 1–8.

von Knorring, L., Perris, C., & Ross, S. B. (1980). Serum dopamine-β-hydroxlase and the augmenting-reducing response. *Biological Psychiatry, 15,* 397–406.

Wadsworth, M. E. J. (1976). Delinquency, pulse rates and early emotional deprivation. *British Journal of Criminology, 16,* 245–256.

Walsh, R. N., & Cummins, R. A. (1976). The open-field test: A critical review. *Psychological Bulletin, 83,* 482–504.

Walter, W. E., Cooper, R., Aldridge, V. J., McCallum, W. C., & Winter, A. L. (1964). Contingent negative variation: An electric sign of sensorimotor association and expectancy in the human brain. *Nature, 203,* 380–384.

Ward, P. B., Catts, S. V., Norman, T. R., Burrows, G. D., & McConoaghy, N. (1987). Low platelet monoamine oxidase and sensation seeking in males: An established relationship? *Acta Psychiatrica Scandinavica, 75,* 86–90.

Watson, D., & Tellegen, A. (1985). Toward a consensual structure of mood. *Psychological Bulletin, 98,* 219–235.

Watson, J. B., & Rayner, P. (1920). Conditioned emotional reactions. *Journal of Experimental Psychology, 3,* 1–14.

Watson, J. D., & Crick, F. H. C. (1953). Genetical implications of the structure of deoxyribonucleic acid. *Nature, 171,* 964–967.

Weerts, T., & Lang, P. (1973). The effects of eye fixation and stimulus and response location on the CNV. *Biological Psychology, 1,* 1–19.

Weinshilboum, R. M., Raymond, F. A., Elveback, L. R., & Weidman, W. H. (1973). Serum-dopamine-beta-hydroxylase activity: sibling-sibling correlation. *Science, 181,* 943–945.

Weissman, M. M., Leckman, J. F., Merikangas, K. R., Gammon, G. D., & Prusoff, B.

A. (1984). Depression and anxiety disorders in patients and children: Results from the Yale study. *Archives of General Psychiatry, 41*, 845–852.

Weizman, R., Tanne, Z., Branek, M., Karp, L., Golomb, M., Tyano, S., & Gavish, M. (1987). Peripheral benzodiazepine binding sites on platelet membranes are increased during diazepam treatment of anxious patients. *European Journal of Pharmacology, 138*, 289–292.

Whitford, F. W. J., & Zipf, S. G. (1975). Open field activity as a function of ceiling height: A genotype environment interaction. *Behavior Genetics, 5*, 275–280.

Wigglesworth, M. J., & Smith, B. D. (1976). Habituation and dishabituation of the electrodermal orienting reflex in relation to extraversion and neuroticism. *Journal of Research in Personality, 10*, 437–445.

Wilson, G. D. (1981). Personality and social behavior. In H. J. Eysenck (Ed.), *A model for personality* (pp. 210–245). New York: Springer-Verlag.

Wilson, G. D., Barrett, P. T., & Gray, J. A. (1989). Human reactions to reward and punishment: A questionnaire examination of Gray's personality theory. *British Journal of Psychology, 80*, 509–516.

Winblad, B., Gottfries, C. G., Oreland, L., & Wiberg, A. (1979). Monoamine oxidase in platelets and brains of non-psychiatric and non-neurological geriatric patients. *Medical Biology, 57*, 129–132.

Winter, H., Herschel, M., Propping, P., Friedl, W., & Vogel, F. (1978). A twin study on three enzymes (DBH, COMT, MAO) of catecholamine metabolism. *Psychopharmacology, 57*, 63–69.

Winter, K., Broadhurst, A., & Glass, A. (1972). Neuroticism, extraversion and EEG amplitude. *Journal of Experimental Research in Personality, 6*, 44–51.

Wolfgang, M. E., Figlis, R. M., & Sellin, T. (1972). *Delinquency in a birth cohort.* Chicago, IL: Univ. of Chicago Press.

Wolpe, J., & Lang, P. J. (1964). A fear survey schedule for use in behavior therapy. *Behavior Research and Therapy, 2*, 27–30.

Wolpe, J., & Rowan, V. C. (1988). Panic disorder: A product of classical conditioning. *Behavior Research and Therapy, 26*, 441–450.

Woodman, D., & Hinton, J. (1978). Catecholamine balance during stress anticipation: An abnormality in maximum security hospital patients. *Journal of Psychosomatic Research, 22*, 477–483.

Woodman, D., Hinton, J., & O'Neill, M. (1977). Abnormality of catecholamine balance relating to social deviance. *Perceptual and Motor Skills, 45*, 593–594.

Woods, S. W., Charney, D. S., McPherson, C. A., Gradman, D. S., & Heninger, G. R. (1987). Situational panic attacks: Behavioral, physiologic and biochemical characterization. *Archives of General Psychiatry, 44*, 365–375.

Woodward, J. A., Bisbee, C. T., & Bennett, J. E. (1984). MMPI correlates of relatively localized brain damage. *Journal of Clinical Psychology, 40*, 961–969.

Wundt, W. M. (1893). *Grundzuge der physiologischen Psychologie.* Leipzig, Germany: Engleman.

Yeomans, J. C. (1982). The cells and axons mediating medial forebrain bundle reward. In B. G. Hoebel & D. Novin (Eds.), *The neural basis of feeding and reward* (pp. 405–417). Brunswick, ME: Haer Institute.

Young, A. M., Woods, J. H., Herling, S., & Hein, D. W. (1983). Comparisons of the reinforcing and discriminative stimulus properties of opioids and opioid peptides. In J. E. Smith & J. D. Love (Eds.), *Opioid reward processes* (pp. 147–174). Amsterdam: Elsevier.

Young, J. R. R., Lader, M. H., & Fenton, G. W. (1971). The relationship of extraversion and neuroticism to the EEG. *British Journal of Psychiatry, 119*, 667–670.

Young, W. F., Laws, E. R., Sharbeough, F. W., & Weinshilboum, R. M. (1986). Human monoamine oxidase. *Archives of General Psychiatry, 43*, 604–609.

Yu, P. H., Bowen, R. C., Davis, B. A., & Boulton, A. (1983). Platelet monoamine oxidase activity and trace acid levels in plasma of agoraphobic patients. *Acta Psychiatrica Scandinavica, 67,* 188–194.

Zahn, T. P. (1986). Psychophysiological approaches to psychopathology. In M. G. H. Coles, E. Donchin, & S. W. Porgelo (Eds.), *Psychophysiology: Systems, processes and applications* (pp. 508–610). New York: Guilford Press.

Zohar, J., Insel, T. R., Berman, K. F., Foa, E. B., Hill, J. L., & Weinberger, D. R. (1989). Anxiety and cerebral blood flow during behavioral challenge. *Archives of General Psychiatry, 46,* 505–510.

Zohar, J., Mueller, E. A., Insel, T. R., Zohar-Kadovich, R. C., & Murphy, D. L. (1987). Serotonergic responsivity in obsessive-compulsive disorder. *Archives of General Psychiatry, 44,* 946–951.

Zuckerman, M. (1969a). Variables affecting results. In J. P. Zubek (Ed.), *Sensory deprivation: Fifteen years of research* (pp. 47–84). New York: Appleton-Century-Crofts.

Zuckerman, M. (1969b). Theoretical formulations: I. In J. P. Zubek (Ed.), *Sensory deprivation: Fifteen years of research* (pp. 407–432). New York: Appleton-Century-Crofts.

Zuckerman, M. (1971a). Physiological measures of sexual arousal in the human. *Psychological Bulletin, 75,* 297–329.

Zuckerman, M. (1971b). Dimensions of sensation seeking. *Journal of Consulting and Clinical Psychology, 36,* 45–52.

Zuckerman, M. (1976). General and situation-specific traits and states: New approaches to assessment of anxiety and other constructs. In M. Zuckerman & C. D. Spielberger (Eds.), *Emotions and anxiety: New concepts, methods, and applications* (pp. 133–174). Hillsdale, NJ: Erlbaum.

Zuckerman, M. (1977). Development of a situation-specific trait-state test for the prediction and measurement of affective responses. *Journal of Consulting and Clinical Psychology, 45,* 513–523.

Zuckerman, M. (1978). Sensation seeking and psychopathy. In R. D. Hare & D. Schalling (Eds.), *Psychopathic behaviour: Approaches to research* (pp. 165–185). New York: Wiley.

Zuckerman, M. (1979a). Traits, states, situations, and uncertainty. *Journal of Behavioral Assessment, 1,* 43–54.

Zuckerman, M. (1979b). *Sensation seeking: Beyond the optimal level of arousal.* Hillsdale, NJ: Erlbaum.

Zuckerman, M. (1982). Leaping up the phylogenetic scale in explaining anxiety: Perils and possibilities. *Behavioral and Brain Sciences,-5,* 505–506.

Zuckerman, M. (1983a). The distinction between trait and state scales is not arbitrary: Comment on Allen and Potkay's "on the arbitrary distinction between traits and states." *Journal of Personality and Social Psychology, 44,* 1083–1086.

Zuckerman, M. (1983b). Sexual arousal in the human: Love, chemistry, or conditioning? In A. Gale & J. A. Edwards (Eds.), *Physiological correlates of human behavior* (Vol. 1, pp. 299–326). New York: Academic Press.

Zuckerman, M. (1984a). Sensation seeking: A comparative approach to a human trait. *Behavioral and Brain Sciences, 7,* 413–471.

Zuckerman, M. (1984b). The neurobiology of some dimensions of personality. In J. R. Smythies & R. J. Bradley (Eds.), *International review of neurobiology* (Vol. 25, pp. 392–436). New York: Academic Press.

Zuckerman, M. (1985). Sensation seeking, mania and monoamines. *Neuropsychobiology, 13,* 121–128.

Zuckerman, M. (1986). Sensation seeking and augmenting-reducing: Evoked potentials and/or kinesthetic figural aftereffects. *Behavioral and Brain Sciences, 9,* 749–754.

Zuckerman, M. (1987a). A critical look at three arousal constructs in personality theories: Optimal level of arousal, strength of the nervous system, and sensitivities to signals of reward and punishment. In J. Strelau & H. J. Eysenck (Eds.), *Personality dimensions and arousal* (pp. 217–231). New York: Plenum.

Zuckerman, M. (1987b). Is sensation seeking a predisposing trait for alcoholism? In E. Gotheil, K. A. Druley, S. Pashkey, & S. P. Weinstein (Eds.), *Stress and addiction* (pp. 283–301). New York: Bruner-Mazel.

Zuckerman, M. (1987c). Biological connection between sensation seeking and drug abuse. In J. Engel, L. Oreland, D. H. Ingvar, B. Pernow, S. Rössner, & L. A. Pellborn (Eds.). *Brain reward systems and abuse* (pp. 165–176). New York: Raven Press.

Zuckerman, M. (1989). Personality in the third dimension: A psychobiological approach. *Personality and Individual Differences, 10,* 391–418.

Zuckerman, M. (1990a). The psychophysiology of sensation seeking. *Journal of Personality. 58,* 313–345.

Zuckerman, M. (1990b). Some dubious premises in research and theory on racial differences: Scientific, social, and ethical issues. *American Psychologist, 45,* 1297–1303.

Zuckerman, M., Ballenger, J. C., Jimerson, D. C., Murphy, D. L., & Post, R. M. (1983). A correlational test in humans of the biological models of sensation seeking, impulsivity and anxiety. In M. Zuckerman (Ed.), *Biological bases of sensation seeking, impulsivity, and anxiety* (pp. 229–248). Hillsdale, NJ: Erlbaum.

Zuckerman, M., & Brody, N. (1989). Oysters, rabbits, and people: A critique of "race differences in behaviour" by J. P. Rushton. *Personality and Individual Differences, 9,* 1025–1033.

Zuckerman, M., Buchsbaum, M. S., & Murphy, D. L. (1980). Sensation seeking and its biological correlates. *Psychological Bulletin, 88,* 187–214.

Zuckerman, M., Eysenck, S. B. G., & Eysenck, H. J. (1978). Sensation seeking in England and America: Cross-cultural, age and sex comparisons. *Journal of Consulting and Clinical Psychology, 46,* 139–149.

Zuckerman, M., Kolin, E. A., Price, L., & Zoob, I. (1964). Development of a sensation seeking scale. *Journal of Consulting Psychology, 28,* 477–482.

Zuckerman, M., Kuhlman, D. M., & Camac, C. (1988). What lies beyond E and N? Factor analyses of scales believed to measure basic dimensions of personality. *Journal of Personality and Social Psychology, 54,* 96–107.

Zuckerman, M., Kuhlman, D. M., Thornquist, M. & Kiers, H. (in press). Five (or three) robust questionnaire scale factors of personality (without culture): sociability, neuroticism-anxiety, aggression-hostility, impulsive-unsocialized-sensation seeking, and activity.

Zuckerman, M., & Lubin, B. (1965). *Manual for the Multiple Affect Adjective Check List.* San Diego, CA: Educational & Industrial Testing Service.

Zuckerman, M., & Lubin, B. (1985). *Manual for the MAACL-R: Multiple Affect Adjective Check List-Revised.* San Diego, CA: Educational and Industrial Testing Service.

Zuckerman, M., & Mellstrom, M., Jr. (1977). The contributions of persons, situations, modes of responses, and their interactions in self-reported responses to hypothetical and real anxiety-inducing situations. In D. Magnusson & N. S. Endler (Eds.), *Personality at the crossroads: Current issues in interactional psychology* (pp. 193–200). Hillsdale, NJ: Erlbaum.

Zuckerman, M., Murtaugh, T. T., & Siegel, J. (1974). Sensation seeking and cortical augmenting-reducing. *Psychophysiology, 11,* 535–542.

Zuckerman, M., Persky, H., Eckman, K. E., & Hopkins, T. R. (1967). A multitrait, multimethod approach to the traits of anxiety, depression, and hostility. *Journal of Projective Techniques and Personality Assessment, 13,* 39–48.

Zuckerman, M., Persky, H., & Link, K. E. (1969). The influence of set and diurnal factors on autonomic responses to sensory deprivation. *Psychophysiology, 5,* 612–624.

Zuckerman, M., Simons, R. F., & Como, P. G. (1988). Sensation seeking and stimulus intensity as modulators of cortical, cardiovascular, and electrodermal response: A cross-modality study. *Personality and Individual Differences, 9,* 361–372.

Index